Torah Old and New

Torah Old and New

Exegesis, Intertextuality, and Hermeneutics

BEN WITHERINGTON III

FORTRESS PRESS
MINNEAPOLIS

TORAH OLD AND NEW
Exegesis, Intertextuality, and Hermeneutics

Cover design: Lauren Osman

Print ISBN: 978-1-5064-3351-6
eBook ISBN: 978-1-5064-4649-3

The paper used in this publication meets the minimum requirements of American
National Standard for Information Sciences — Permanence of Paper for Printed
Library Materials, ANSI Z329.48-1984.

Manufactured in the U.S.A.

This observance will be for you like a sign on your hand and a reminder on your forehead that this law of the Lord is to be on your lips. For the Lord brought you out of Egypt with his mighty hand.
—Exodus 13:9 (NIV)

It came about, when Moses finished writing the words of this law in a book until they were complete, that Moses commanded the Levites who carried the ark of the covenant of the Lord, saying: "Take this book of the law and place it beside the ark of the covenant of the Lord your God, that it may remain there as a witness against you."
—Deuteronomy 31:24–26 (NASB)

The law of the Lord is perfect, refreshing the soul. The statutes of the Lord are trustworthy, making wise the simple.
—Psalm 19:7 (NIV)

For through the law I died to the law so that I might live for God.
—Galatians 2:19 (NIV)

But when the set time had fully come, God sent his Son, born of a woman, born under the law, to redeem those under the Law, that we might receive our adoption as sons.
—Galatians 4:4–5

For Christ is the end of the law for righteousness to
everyone who believes.
—Romans 10:4 (ESV)

By calling this covenant "new," he has made the first
one obsolete; and what is obsolete and outdated
will soon disappear.
—Hebrews 8:13

Ignatius of Antioch, 110 CE

Do not be deceived by strange teachings, nor with old
fables, which are unprofitable. For if we still live
according to Jewish Law, we acknowledge
that we have not received grace.
—*Letter to the Magnesians*, 8

Justin Martyr, ca. 150 CE

Is there any other matter, my friends, in which we
[Christians] are blamed [by the Jews] than this: that we
do not live according to the Law, are not circumcised in
the flesh as your forefathers were, and do not observe
Sabbaths as you do?

[*Trypho, the Jew, speaking*] This is what [we] are most at
a loss about. You [Christians], professing yourselves to
be godly and supposing yourselves better than others,
are not separated from them. You do not alter your way
of living from that of the nations in that you observe no
festivals or Sabbaths and do not have
the rite of circumcision.

We do not trust through Moses or through the Law, for
then we would be the same as you. For now I have read

that there shall be a final law, and a covenant, the
chiefest of all, which is now incumbent on all men to
observe, as many as are seeking after the inheritance of
God. For the Law promulgated on Horeb is now old
and belongs to yourselves alone, but this [new law] is
for all universally. . . .

An eternal and final law—namely Christ—has been
given to us, and the covenant is trustworthy, after
which there shall be no law, no commandment,
no ordinance.
—*Dialogue with Trypho*, 10

Irenaeus, 183–186 CE

And the apostles who were with James allowed the
gentiles to act freely, yielding us up to the Spirit of God.
But they themselves, while knowing the same God,
continued in the ancient observances. . . . Thus did the
apostles, whom the Lord made witnesses of every action
and of every doctrine—for upon all occasions do we
find Peter, and James, and John present with him—
scrupulously act according to the dispensation of the
Mosaic law, showing that it was
from one and the same God.
—*Against Heresies*, 3.12.15

Clement of Alexandria, ca. 190 CE

If . . . the Law of Moses had been sufficient to confer
eternal life, then there would have been no purpose for
the Savior himself to come and suffer for us and to live
the whole course of human life from his birth to his
cross. And it would have been to no purpose for him
[the rich, young ruler] who had done all the

commandments of the law from his youth to fall on his
knees and beg for immortality from someone else.
—*Who Is the Rich Man That Shall Be Saved?*, 8

Tertullian, ca. 200 CE

We understand that God's law was before even Moses
. . . subsequently reformed for the patriarchs [Israel's
twelve sons] and so again for the Jews at definite
periods. So we are not to give heed to Moses' Law as
though it were the primitive Law, but as a later one,
which at a definite time God set forth to the gentiles,
too, and—after repeatedly promising to do so through
the prophets—has reformed for the better. . . . Let us not
annul the power God has to reform the Law's precepts
in response to the circumstances of the time, with a
view to human salvation. To be specific, let him who
contends that the Sabbath is still to be observed as a
balm of salvation . . . teach us that in the past righteous
men kept the Sabbath or practiced circumcision and
were thus rendered friends of God. . . . Since God
originated Adam uncircumcised and inobservant of the
Sabbath, therefore his offspring, Abel, was commended
by [God] when he offered sacrifices both uncircumcised
and inobservant of the Sabbath. . . . Noah
also—uncircumcised and, yes, inobservant of the
Sabbath—God freed from the deluge. Enoch, too, that
most righteous man, while uncircumcised and
inobservant of the Sabbath, [God] translated from this
world. [Enoch] did not first taste death so that, being a
candidate for eternal life, he might in our era show us
that we may, without the burden of the Law of Moses,
please God.
—*An Answer to the Jews*, 2

Origen, 220–250 CE

We do not regulate our lives like the Jews because we are of opinion that the literal acceptance of the laws is not what conveys the meaning of the legislation. And we maintain that, "When Moses is read, the veil is upon their heart" [2 Cor 3:15]. The meaning of the law of Moses has been concealed from those who have not welcomed the way which is by Jesus Christ.

—*Against Celsus*, 5.60

Contents

Tabula Gratulorum

Just a word of thanks first and foremost to Neil Elliott at Fortress for seeing the worth of this three-volume project on intertexuality, and for his help in editing and formatting this complex material in a way that would make it reader-friendly. Second, a big thank you to my Old Testament colleagues and friends such as Bill Arnold and Tremper Longman for looking at portions of this work and giving some guidance. The errors in judgment, whatever they may be, should be laid at my doorstep. Finally, a big thanks to Moises Silva and to Zondervan for allowing me to use the NETS translation of the Septuagint (LXX) and the NIV translation especially of Old Testament (OT) passages in these volumes. The full credits can be found at the outset of *Isaiah Old and New*.[1]

Finally, I am grateful for the support of so many people who had urged me to write on these sorts of topics, and then to work my way toward finally doing a biblical theology. It is my conviction, having now written these three books, that one cannot really come to grips with a huge project like biblical theology unless one has first wrestled with the angel of intertextuality and gotten a blessing . . . and perhaps also a limp. Unless one understands the use of the Old in the New, and way the Old is viewed by the New, as well as what the Old meant in its original contexts, abandon hope of doing much of use with the subject of biblical theology. Having finished this volume, it's onward and upward as long as there is life and time to deal with that final big project.

Advent 2016

1. Ben Witherington III, *Isaiah Old and New: Exegesis, Intertextuality, and Hermeneutics* (Minneapolis: Fortress, 2017).

Abbreviations

A	Alexandrinus
Ag. Ap.	Josephus, *Against Apion*
Alleg. Interp.	Philo, *Allegorical Interpretation*
AnBib	Analecta Biblica
ANE	ancient Near East(ern)
ANET	*Ancient Near Eastern Texts Relating to the Old Testament*. Edited by James B. Pritchard. 3rd ed. Princeton: Princeton University Press, 1969.
Ant.	Josephus, *Jewish Antiquities*
ANTC	Abingdon New Testament Commentaries
AYBRL	Anchor Yale Bible Reference Library
b. Mak.	Babylonian Talmud tractate Makkot
b. Sanh.	Babylonian Talmud tractate Sanhedrin
b. Yebam.	Babylonian Talmud tractate Yebamot
B	Vaticanus
BA	La Bible d'Alexandrie
BECNT	Baker Exegetical Commentary on the New Testament
BHGNT	Baylor Handbook on the Greek New Testament
BHT	Beiträge zur historischen Theologie
Bib	*Biblica*
BNTC	Black's New Testament Commentaries

BST	Bible Speaks Today
BVNW	Beihefte zur Zeitschrift für die neutestamentliche Wissenschaft
CBQ	*Catholic Biblical Quarterly*
CD	Cairo Genizah copy of the Damascus Document
CEC	J. A. Cramer, ed. *Catena in Epistolas Catholicas*. Edited by J. A. Cramer. Oxford: Clarendon, 1840.
col.	column
Dial.	Justin, *Dialogue with Trypho*
ECC	Eerdmans Critical Commentary
Did.	Didache
ExpTim	*Expository Times*
GRBS	*Greek, Roman, and Byzantine Studies*
Hist.	Polybius, *Histories*
Hom. Gen.	John Chrysostom, *Homilae in Genesim*
Hom. Heb.	John Chrysostom, *Homilae in epistulam ad Hebraeos*
IBC	Interpretation: A Bible Commentary for Teaching and Preaching
IGUR	Luigi Moretti. *Inscriptiones Graecae Urbis Romae*. 4 vols. Rome, 1968–1990.
Inst.	Quintilian, *Institutio oratoria*
Int	*Interpretation*
ISBL	Indiana Studies in Biblical Literature
IVPNTC	InterVarsity Press New Testament Commentaries
JETS	*Journal of the Evangelical Theological Society*
JSNT	*Journal for the Study of the New Testament*
JSNTSup	Journal for the Study of the New Testament Supplement Series
JTS	*Journal of Theological Studies*
LNTS	Library of New Testament Studies
LSTS	Library of Second Temple Studies
LThPM	Louvain Theological and Pastoral Monographs
LXX	Septuagint

m.	Mishnah tractate
Mek.	Mekilta
Midr.	Midrash (followed by biblical book)
Migration	Philo, *On the Migration of Abraham*
Moses	Philo, *On the Life of Moses*
MS(S)	manuscript(s)
MSU	Mitteilungen des Septuaginta-Unternehmens
MT	Masoretic Text
NA^{28}	*Novum Testamentum Graece*, Nestle-Aland, 28th ed.
NAC	New American Commentary
Nat	Pliny the Elder, *Natural History*
NCB	New Century Bible
NCBiC	New Cambridge Bible Commentary
NewDocs	*New Documents Illustrating Early Christianity*. Edited by Greg H. R. Horsley and Stephen Llewelyn. North Ryde, NSW: The Ancient History Documentary Research Centre, Macquarie University, 1981–.
NIB	*New Interpreters Bible*. Edited by Leander E. Keck. 12 vols. Nashville: Abingdon, 1994–2004.
NIBCNT	New International Biblical Commentary on the New Testament
NICNT	New International Commentary on the New Testament
NICOT	New International Commentary on the Old Testament
NIGTC	New International Greek Testament Commentary
NIVAC	New International Version Application Commentary
Notes	*Notes on Translation*
NT	New Testament
NTS	*New Testament Studies*
Num. Rab.	Numbers Rabbah
OBT	Overtures to Biblical Theology
OG	Old Greek version of the Hebrew Bible
OT	Old Testament

OTL	Old Testament Library
OTP	*Old Testament Pseudepigrapha*. Edited by James H. Charlesworth. 2 vols. New York: Doubleday, 1983–1985. Repr. Peabody, MA: Hendrickson, 2010.
par	parallel(s)
PNTC	Pillar New Testament Commentary
Prelim. Studies	Philo, *On the Preliminary Studies*
Q	hypothetical source document for the Gospels containing the sayings of Jesus
Qed.	Qedoshim
QG	Philo, *Questions and Answers on Genesis*
RevExp	*Review and Expository*
RevQ	*Revue de Qumran*
Rewards	Philo, *On Rewards and Punishments*
Rhet. Alex.	Anaximenes of Lamsacus, *Rhetorica ad Alexandrum*
Rhet. Her.	Rhetorica ad Herennium
Sacrifices	Philo, *On the Sacrifices of Cain and Abel*
Sam.	Samaritan
Sanh.	Sanhedrin
SBLDS	Society of Biblical Literature Dissertation Series
SBLMS	Society of Biblical Literature Monograph Series
SJOT	*Scandanavian Journal of the Old Testament*
SNTSMS	Society for New Testament Studies Monograph Series
SP	Sacra Pagina
Spec. Laws	Philo, *On the Special Laws*
Syr.	Syriac
t.	Tosefta tractate
Ta'an.	Ta'anit
Tg. Onq.	Targum Onqelos
Tg. Ps-J.	Targum Pseudo-Jonathan
Theog.	Hesiod, *Theogony*

TTE	*The Theological Educator*
VTSup	Supplements to Vetus Testamentum
Vulg.	Vulgate
WBC	Word Biblical Commentary
WMANT	Wissenschaftliche Monographien zum Alten und Neuen Testament

Preface: Laying Down the Law

An Egyptian priest named Moses, who possessed a portion of the country called the Lower Egypt, being dissatisfied with the established institutions there, left it and came to Judaea with a large body of people who worshiped the Divinity. He declared and taught that the Egyptians and Africans entertained erroneous sentiments, in representing the Divinity under the likeness of wild beasts and cattle of the field; that the Greeks also were in error in making images of their gods after the human form. For God [said he] may be this one thing which encompasses us all, land and sea, which we call heaven, or the universe, or the nature of things. . . . By such doctrine, Moses persuaded a large body of right-minded persons to accompany him to the place where Jerusalem now stands.
—Strabo, *The Geography*, 16.35, 36

I am firmly convinced that the passionate will for justice and truth has done more to improve man's condition than calculating political shrewdness which in the long run only breeds general distrust. Who can doubt that Moses was a better leader of humanity than Machiavelli?
—Albert Einstein[1]

The trouble begins with the word itself. Torah in its broadest sense means instruction, which of course includes law, commandments, imperatives, and statutes. The author of Psalm 119 has a seemingly endless supply of equivalent terms to talk about laws. But that Psalm, like the Mosaic tale of the Ten Commandments, calls law "the Word of God." Indeed, the Ten Commandments themselves are originally just called "the ten words" (of God).

The trouble gets worse when we get to the LXX translation of

---

1. Albert Einstein, "Moral Decay," in *Out of My Later Years* (New York: Philosophical Library, 1950).

the term *torah*, in that it is rendered *nomos*, which has a narrower spectrum of meaning and is rightly translated most of the time as "law." Were that not enough, by the time we get to the New Testament (NT) era, "the Law" is a cipher for the first five books of the Hebrew Bible, which, not incidentally, are *not* primarily a collection of laws. In fact, the majority of the Pentateuch is narrative of one sort or another, except in the case of Leviticus.[2] But of course, Pentateuchal narrative also can be and is a form of instruction, though of a more complex sort than law. With narrative, one has to ask ethical questions like, is the reader to take this story as implying "go and do likewise," or on the contrary, as implying "go and do otherwise," or sometimes a bit of both? Or is this merely intended as commentary meant to prompt theological reflection on the ways of the God of the Bible with human beings? Or should we only think we are getting clear guidance when the voice of God speaks in such narratives? Narratives are not oracles, though they may contain them, any more than songs or psalms are oracles or late words from God, though they, too, may contain them.[3]

If we are going to explore "Torah Old and New" and by that mean the material we find in the Pentateuch, then we will necessarily be dealing primarily with two types of literature: narrative and commandments of various sorts. Yes, there is the occasional poetic piece or song to be found in the Pentateuch, for instance in the poetic prose of Genesis 1 or the Song of Moses in Deuteronomy 32, but for the most part we are dealing with prose in various forms. And while narrative has context, it doesn't come with a guidebook as to how this or that episode ought to be read. The problem with commandments, on the other hand, is often they are contextless, or almost so, and thus often we don't have clues from the context as to the meaning of the words being examined. This becomes especially an issue with lists of various commandments, such as the Ten Commandments. No wonder there has been such debate about the dictum "no killing" (Exod 20:13), which offers no context to help us understand its relationship to the killing that happens elsewhere even in the books of Torah.

This subject matter largely distinguishes this particular volume

2. John Van Seters, *The Pentateuch: A Social-Science Commentary* (London: T&T Clark, 2015), 16 "Furthermore, the Hebrew term Torah, 'Law,' is a little misleading as a description of the content of the Pentateuch, since it consists of about one half law and the other half narrative."

3. See the second volume in this series, *Psalms Old and New: Exegesis, Intertextuality, and Hermeneutics* (Minneapolis: Fortress, 2017) for the discussion of the nature and character of the Psalms.

from our previous two volumes in this series, *Isaiah Old and New* and *Psalms Old and New*, the former of which presented us with prophetic poetry by and large, and the latter of which provided us with liturgical poetry used as lyrics to songs sung in the temple and elsewhere. Like the Psalms, we are not dealing with prophecy for the most part in the Pentateuch (there are exceptions), and importantly, the use of the "law" in the NT does not focus on those exceptional parts of the first division of Tanak.[4] It is the commandments of the books of Moses, and also some narratives from those books, that come in for heavy use in the NT, as we shall see.

At this juncture, a few more preliminary remarks are in order. All of the Pentateuch was viewed as Scripture, or God's word, by the writers of the NT and by Jesus himself. There is no need to debate this point. But a distinction has to be made between how Jesus and his followers used the Pentateuch as Scripture, and how, or to what extent, they considered it binding law. The key here has to do with the whole notion of covenant. For various writers of the NT, perhaps particularly Paul, the author of Hebrews, and Luke, the followers of Jesus were not under the Mosaic covenant and therefore not bound to keep the Mosaic law, except where some part of it had been reiterated by Jesus, or Paul, or other leaders as part of the new covenant. And clearly, only a minority of the Mosaic law is reaffirmed in the NT as binding on Christians. Instead of the covenant sign circumcision, they were commanded to practice baptism (Matthew 28) as the entrance ritual into the new covenant, along with other commandments, some of which were old and some of which were new.[5]

Yes, there is law in the new covenant as there was in the old one, and it has long since been the case that we should recognize that a strong contrast between law and grace does no justice to either the OT or the NT, not even to the teachings of Paul. Law, or instruction,

---

4. TANAK is a conventional abbreviation for the Hebrew *Torah, Nevi'im* (Prophets), and *Kethuvim* (Writings), the three components of the Hebrew Bible.

5. This, of course, is a controverted issue and one which I have dealt with in considerable depth especially in my commentaries on Paul's letters, especially Ben Witherington III, *Grace in Galatia: A Commentary on St. Paul's Letter to the Galatians* (Grand Rapids: Eerdmans, 1998) and Witherington and Darlene Hyatt, *Paul's Letter to the Romans: A Socio-Rhetorical Commentary* (Grand Rapids: Eerdmans, 2004), and also in my volume *New Testament History: A Narrative Account* (Grand Rapids: Baker, 2003). In my view, there were a spectrum of views about the Mosaic law among the followers of Jesus, and they did not fall neatly along Jewish and gentile lines, by which I mean some of the Jewish followers, like Paul and the author of Hebrews, seem to have taken more radical views than some of the gentile followers as well as various Jerusalem followers of Jesus.

in either testament is teaching for devotees of God who have already been called, chosen, saved (choose what terminology you like) by a gracious and merciful God who nonetheless requires justice and righteousness of his people, as a reflection of his own character. Law in neither testament is about "getting in," but it has something to do with "staying in." The rub comes when one debates the various views of ongoing salvation and its relationship to obedience to commandments.

However, and it is a big however, none of these sorts of discussions meant that even the nonreaffirmed portions of the law, those portions seen as no longer obligations for followers of Jesus, *ceased to be Scripture* for Christians. Clearly, this was not true, as we shall see. What happens is that such materials are used christologically, or by way of typology or analogy, or homiletically, when it is applied to this or that Christian group by Paul or others. It was still the living word of God, but the primary use of the material would be theological rather than legal. We will have much more to say about all this as we go along, but here it is sufficient to say with Saint Paul that the law is holy, just, and good (Rom 7:12). It is God's word. The question is: *How does it function in the new covenant, and what does it mean in that different setting?*

One more thing of importance needs to be reiterated, especially in light of Reformation history and its continuing influence. The setting up of a paradigm of law vs. grace, or of works of the law vs. salvation by grace, has in some important ways skewed the conversation about the law and its possible roles not only in the life of the church but earlier in the life of Israel and early Judaism. A concern for, and honoring and keeping of, the law is by no means the same thing as legalism, or as works religion for that matter. As E. P. Sanders showed some time ago, *covenantal nomism* is a good description of OT religion, which involves responding to the initial and initiating grace of God by keeping the covenant with God, including obeying its laws. There is plenty of grace in the OT, and there is also law in the NT, not least in the teachings of both Jesus and Paul. While the Mosaic law is not simply the same thing as "the law of Christ" (though there is overlap), nevertheless, both the Mosaic and the new covenants indicate that the proper response to God's grace is not merely gratitude but obedience. Of course, it is true that in the case of some practitioners of Judaism and Christianity, the law came to be used in legalistic and even casuistic ways that violated the spirit, the character, and the emphasis of both OT and NT teaching on obedience.

It is also true that from a Christian theological point of view, a distinction has to be made between the intent of the Mosaic law and its effect on fallen human beings, perhaps especially on those seeking to reestablish a relationship with God. While the good and holy Mosaic law could inform a person of what they ought to do, it could not enable them to do it. That required the grace or Spirit of God. Furthermore, law functions differently when one believes the Savior has already come and provided salvation and righteousness apart from the keeping of the Mosaic law.[6] We will need to discuss these matters in some detail as we work through "the torah Old and New," but for now it is sufficient to say these things require wisdom, and hopefully, some of that will be on display in the chapters that follow. Before we get down to brass tacks, however, it is important to say a few preliminary things about evaluating narrative.

I was enjoying the 2006 World Series opening broadcast when the anonymous voice playing on top of images of previous Series games said, "tell me a fact and I will know, tell me the truth and I will believe, tell me a story and it will live in my heart forever."[7] But what is the story, or are the stories, that the Law/Pentateuch is telling us? It clearly is not telling us the story of everyone and everything. It does not provide a historical account of all of humanity. Instead, the Bible is primarily interested in telling the story of God's chosen people, from creation to sin (or fall), to various acts of redemption, and on finally to a new creation. Other peoples, such as the wives of Cain and Abel, or the Assyrians, Hittites, Philistines, Babylonians, Greeks, Romans, and others come into the story only insofar as they interact with God's people. And God's people are the Hebrews or Israelites, or as they would later be known, the Jews.

The Bible is *written by* this particular people (with perhaps the exception of one or two NT books such as 2 Peter) and *about* this particular people, even when the story takes an unexpected turn in Acts, the letters of Paul, and other later NT documents and involves an inordinate amount of gentiles in addition to the Jewish leaders of the Jesus movement. That later surprising development is at most barely

---

6. E. P. Sanders, *Paul and Palestinian Judaism,* (Philadelphia: Fortress, 1977); cf. D. A. Carson, Peter Thomas O'Brien, and Mark A Seifrid, eds., *Justification and Variegated Nomism,* 2 vols. (Grand Rapids: Baker Academic, 2001–2004).

7. See the details in my citation in Ben Witherington III, *New Testament Theology and Ethics Volume One* (Downers Grove, IL: InterVarsity, 2016), ii.

foreshadowed in the Pentateuch in an idea such as Abraham's descendants being a light to the nations.

When it comes to just the first five books of the Bible, the authors are telling us the story of the origins of creation and, most importantly, of God's people all the way back to Adam and Eve, followed by tales of their descendants Noah, Abraham, and so on. The Pentateuch does not get us beyond the point in the narrative where God's people are about to enter the promised land, Canaan. That means we are at a juncture where the liberation of God's people through the exodus and Sinai events has happened, and they are just barely beyond the wilderness wandering period.[8]

It has become commonplace in narratological studies of literature, including the Bible, to say that human beings tend to make sense of their world through the vehicle of story. Whether that broad generalization can be applied to all peoples in all ages, it is certainly true that it applies to the persons who wrote the Pentateuch, Moses and his successors and editors. But the Pentateuch was clearly felt to be, and seen to be, a story badly in need of a sequel, hence the book of Joshua and subsequent historical stories labeled Samuel, Kings, and Chronicles.

To judge from the Pentateuch alone, Hebrews made sense of their world in terms of both narrative and more didactic instruction in the form of laws, commandments, and precepts, not least because one of their most foundational stories has to do with God giving Moses commandments. It is this interweaving of law and narrative that characterizes the first five books of the Bible; and the proof that these stories, even the earliest sagas about Adam and Eve, are meant to be seen as historical stories is the use of genealogies, again and again, to link various parts of the story. The Hebrews, as we shall see, while they borrowed ideas from other ancient Near Eastern (ANE) cultures at times, were not a myth-making people, by and large; indeed, they deconstructed ANE myths, like the combat myth about creation, in order to speak about their God, whom they saw as the creator of all things, a God who was constantly involved in the history of his people.

Bearing these things in mind, we can now turn to our exploration of the stories and laws in the Pentateuch and how they are used in

---

8. See the discussion about narrative and how it functions in Ben Witherington III, *Reading and Understanding the Bible* (Oxford: Oxford University Press, 2015).

the NT.[9] For those wanting to see how the narrative material in Genesis still affects Christian thinking about evolution and whether there was a historical Adam and Eve or not, Appendix 2 provides an extended discussion of a recent important book entitled *Adam and the Genome*.[10] The final appendix, Appendix 3, deals in some depth with the complex issues of intertextuality raised by one of the most difficult passages in the NT in 1 Peter 3, the story of the "spirits in prison," which owes something not merely to Genesis 6:1–4 but to its ongoing history of interpretation in Judaism, including in 1 Enoch.

9. I have pointed out at length the danger of taking a history-of-ideas approach to the material in the Bible in order to abstract some sort of theology or ethics from it. To put the matter bluntly, even in the case of someone like Saint Paul, he is theologizing and ethicizing out of his storied world and into particular situations he is addressing involving his converts. The narrative thought-world of most of the biblical writers, including the constructors of the Pentateuch, is the matrix out of which theological and ethical ideas come to light, not in the abstract. So, when Paul thinks about sin, he thinks of the story of Adam; when he thinks about law; he thinks of Moses; when he thinks about faith, he thinks of the story of Abraham; and so on. The ideas arise in and out of the stories, and if you strip the ideas of their narrative contexts you are bound to distort and misunderstand them. This is just as true of the Pentateuch as it is of Paul. Law has to be evaluated in the context of the ongoing story. See the discussion in Ben Witherington III, *Paul's Narrative Thought World: The Tapestry of Tragedy and Triumph* (Louisville: Westminster John Knox, 1994).

10. Dennis R. Venema and Scot McKnight, *Adam and the Genome: Reading Scripture after Genetic Science* (Grand Rapids: Brazos, 2017).

1.

The "Law" by the Numbers and Its Influence in Early Judaism

"Love of God," he said slowly, searching for words, "is not always the same as love of good, I wish it were that simple. We know what is good, it is written in the Commandments. But God is not contained only in the Commandments, you know; they are only an infinitesimal part of Him. A man may abide by the Commandments and be far from God."

—Herman Hesse[1]

I have wondered at times what the Ten Commandments would have looked like if Moses had run them through the U.S. Congress.

—Ronald Reagan

According to my count, using the twenty-eighth edition of the Nestle-Aland *Novum Testamentum Graecae* (NA[28]) as a basis for comparison (see Appendix 1), there are some 236 quotations, allusions, or echoes of Genesis in the NT (with Acts being by far the largest user of the material); 239 quotations, allusions, or echoes of Exodus; 87 quotes, allusions, or echoes of Leviticus; 89 quotations, allusions, or echoes of Numbers; and 205 quotations, allusions, or echoes of Deuteronomy, making Deuteronomy the most directly and frequently quoted of the Pentateuchal books, not counting allusions or echoes. Not one of these books individually comes up for as much

---

1. Herman Hesse, *Narcissus and Goldmund* (New York: Bantam Books, 1930).

use as Isaiah or the Psalms.[2] The grand total, then, is 856 uses of the Pentateuch in the NT. Compare this to the over 600 uses of Isaiah alone in the NT, or the 300 or so uses of just the Psalms. Clearly, Genesis, Exodus, and Deuteronomy were especially important to the NT writers, but some of the most directly and frequently cited verses come from elsewhere in the Pentateuch (e.g., the love commandment in Lev 19:18). This raises the question about the use of the Pentateuch in early Judaism, the matrix out of which both Jesus and his movement came. It will be profitable to examine that subject first before we turn to the forward and backward reading of the Pentateuch in the OT and NT that is the main focus of our study.

THE EXPLOSION OF LITERATURE ON GENESIS

From the second century BCE through the first century CE, there was nothing short of an explosion of commentary on and discussion of the book of Genesis in early Judaism. Unlike later rabbinic commentary on particular discrete books of the OT, this literature mostly dwelt on important *figures* in Genesis, as can be seen just from the titles of some of these works—The Life of Adam and Eve, the Testament of Adam, the Apocalypse of Adam, 1 and 2 Enoch, The Testament of Abraham, The Apocalypse of Abraham, The Testament of the Twelve Patriarchs, The Prayer of Jacob, Joseph and Aseneth, The History of Joseph. There are, furthermore, two other fascinating works of note from the second century BCE: the Genesis Apocryphon and the book of Jubilees, which reflects a dependence on the narratives from Genesis 1 through Exodus 19. Then, too, one can mention the Pseudo-Philo work *Liber antiquitatum biblicarum*, which relies on Genesis through 1 Samuel.

In the NT era itself, we can point to the first book of the Sibylline Oracles (part of which may be older), which deals with the Genesis story about paradise (as does 2 Enoch and the Life of Adam and Eve), and the considerable interest in Genesis 6:1–4 (on which see the following chapter); and, of course, there are the various allegorical commentaries of Philo (ca. 20 BCE–50 CE) on the Pentateuch, focusing mainly on Genesis and to a lesser degree on Exodus. Flavius Josephus, in the latter part of the first century CE, was to make extensive use of

---

2. See Witherington, *Isaiah Old and New*, and *Psalms Old and New*.

Genesis in his account of *Jewish Antiquities*, his largest and most masterful work. To say that Genesis was the subject of much discussion in early Judaism, especially in its more literate circles, would be to put things too conservatively. But what prompted all this going back *ad fontes?* Why especially this focus on narrative and major characters in the Genesis narrative, a focus we also find to some degree in the teaching of Jesus (e.g., the first couple, Noah, the story of Sodom and Gomorrah) and even more in the letters of Paul (Adam, Abraham) and in Hebrews (Abraham, Melchizedek, Jacob, Joseph)? My suggestion would be that the answer has to do with the considerable turmoil of the period.

Jews had briefly gained their independence from Hellenistic rulers during the Maccabean period, and then promptly lost it again to the Herods (who at best were only partially Jewish, being of Idumean descent as well) and then to Rome, first in Judaea, and then by the time of Josephus's written works, throughout Israel. In order to understand the meaning of their current situation, they turned back to the stories of the origins of their people. They looked back to hoary antiquity for clues to their present and future. In essence, they relied on a salvation historical review, especially in its very earliest stages.

It is interesting, then, that when we find such reviews in the NT, for example in Acts 7 or in 1 Corinthians 10, the focus is not primarily on Genesis *but rather on Exodus*, on the wilderness wandering generation that set up the pattern of grumbling, of unfaithfulness, of being, as Stephen later calls it, "a stiff-necked people" about whom the prophets were later to complain, again and again. But we are getting ahead of ourselves. It will be well here to have some discussion of works of early Judaism that involved Genesis rebooted, rewritten, and rethought, for example, Jubilees and the Genesis Apocryphon.[3]

Jubilees is surely the older of these two documents, perhaps predating the Qumran community. The book is ostensibly presented as a revelation to Moses through an angelic mediator while he was on Mt. Sinai (see, e.g., Gal 3:19; Acts 7:38). The vast majority of this book is a rewriting of the primeval history (Jubilees 2–10) and the history of the patriarchs (Jubilees 11–45), delivered after the setting of the book has been introduced in the first chapter, namely, that

---

3. Here we will be interacting with the discussion of Jacques T. A. G. M. van Ruiten, "Genesis in Early Jewish Literature," in *Genesis in the New Testament*, ed. M. J. J. Menken and Steve Moyise, LNTS 466 (London: T&T Clark, 2012), 7–26.

Moses received all this while he was up on Mt. Sinai. But Jubilees is hardly just a rehashing of Genesis and a part of Exodus. It has value added, probably chiefly from the Enoch traditions (see Jubilees 4:15–26; 5:1–12; 7:20–39; 10:1–17).[4] It is possible that 4Q Visions of Amram (4Q543–4Q549) is also drawn on in Jubilees 46 as van Ruiten suggests.[5] The NT work that is most like this sort of combination approach to Genesis and Exodus read through later Jewish literature is Jude, and interestingly, the editor of 2 Peter who draws on Jude in 2 Peter 2 is apparently not happy about the use of later Jewish materials, as he eliminates the material from Enoch and the Apocalypse of Moses that is alluded to in Jude.

One question Jubilees raises is whether this sort of *relecture* of Genesis and Exodus is what prompted some early Jews to insist on a more clearly defined, if not closed canon of sacred texts. Or should we see Jubilees as a reflection of the fact that the Pentateuch is already assumed to be a rather clearly defined sacred text, so the author of Jubilees feels free to do creative additions and subtractions assuming a given stable text? In other words, is he doing midrashic interpretation of the given sacred text with the help of additional sources, not actually trying to rewrite Genesis and Exodus? Knowing what we know of the Qumran community, and how they both carefully copied OT texts but also produced creative commentaries on such texts, perhaps the author of Jubilees is doing the latter. But this leads to our discussion of the Genesis Apocryphon.

The Genesis Apocryphon was one of the earliest finds at Qumran in 1947, but it was in such deteriorating condition that it was not until 1954 that it was gently unrolled and photographs were taken of what was left of its twenty-two columns. Amazingly, the only copy we have of this work may be the autograph. It seems to have existed only at Qumran, and even there was not copied.[6] The document was written on leather, but in an ink that made the largest part of the document unreadable until infrared techniques produced further results. There is still no critical edition of the work.

The majority of the work (columns 1 through 21) is written in the first person and has Lamech, Noah, and Abram tell their own stories, but it is not simply a rehearsal of Genesis 6–13; there are

---

4. See G. W. E. Nickelsburg, *1 Enoch 1: A Commentary on the Book of 1 Enoch, Chapters 1–36, 81–108*, Hermeneia (Minneapolis: Fortress, 2001), 71–76.

5. Van Ruiten, "Genesis," 11.

6. See Sidnie White Crawford, *Rewriting Scripture in Second Temple Times* (Grand Rapids: Eerdmans, 2008).

many notable additions to those chapters. Possibly, even probably, the scroll began before Genesis 6, but the beginning of the manuscript is unfortunately missing. Suddenly, at Genesis 14, the text shifts to the third person, and involves almost a verbatim repeating of Genesis 14–15, without notable additions. This may have continued on through more chapters of Genesis, but alas, the ending of the document is also lost. Scholars are rather clear that one of the nonbiblical sources used by the author is the Lamech material in 1 Enoch 106–107.[7] Because of the similarities between the telling of the Noah story in both Jubilees and the Genesis Apocryphon, scholars have debated whether the latter might have been dependent on the former, or at least shared a common source.[8]

Scholars have long debated how much Christian redaction there has been of the basically Jewish text known as the Sibylline Oracles.[9] Sibylline Oracle 1:5–64 consists of a retelling of the story of creation, following the structure of Genesis 1–3 but paraphrasing the story in a free way. It is fascinating to compare and contrast what this work does with the story of Adam and Eve with what is done with the same story in the Slavonic Apocalypse of Enoch. The first part of Sibylline Oracle 1:5–64 consists of retelling Genesis 1:1–2.4a, whereas the second part deals with Genesis 2:4b–25 and the third part deals with life in the garden of Eden, paralleling Genesis 3. The distinctive features of the Sibylline Oracles presentation include:

1. The creation of man and woman is set apart from the rest of creation, running closely parallel to the sequence of events in Genesis, but with quite different wording;

2. Not only is the creation in general said to be good, but Eve is not created so that sin and death might fall upon Adam and humankind in general;

3. Eve is created as the equal partner of Adam;

4. While Eve is the one who persuades Adam to eat the apple, the serpent is blamed as being mainly responsible, and he is the only one who is really cursed, whereas though there is a penalty on Adam and Eve, it is mitigated by being associated with a blessing on them from God; and

5. Adam and Eve seem to have had a platonic relationship before

7. See most recently Crawford, *Rewriting Scripture*, 108–9.

8. Daniel K. Falk, *The Parabiblical Texts: Strategies for Extending Scripture among the Dead Sea Scrolls*, LSTS 63 (London: T&T Clark, 2007), 42–80.

9. On which see J. J. Collins, "Sibylline Oracles," *OTP* 1:330.

eating the forbidden fruit, but then afterwards they have a sexual relationship.

Contrast this with the Apocalypse of Enoch, which probably originated as a Greek text in the first century CE but now is available to us only in the Slavonic translation.[10] Probably the most striking portion of the document is the rewriting of Genesis 2–3, which is all integrated into an account of one tragic day, the sixth day of creation. Adam and Eve are created outside the garden and placed in it on the same day they are driven out of it! Eve is created to bring death to Adam, though 2 Enoch 30:10c says life and death are part of his nature. The first sexual relation takes place between Eve and the snake, who is said to be a demon who entered the garden, either as Satan or an emissary of Satan (2 Enoch 31:6). As van Ruiten says, the whole point of the story is to blame Eve for bringing sin and thereby death to Adam (2 Enoch 30:17). "After sin there is nothing for it but death" (2 Enoch 30:16c).[11]

Equally fascinating is the Apocalypse of Abraham, which tells the story of Abraham's conversion from idolatry. This is accomplished after Abraham has offered the sacrifice recorded in Genesis 15. He then is said to be taken up into the seventh heaven and shown God's throne, the heavens, the universe in general, and the future of his offspring until, at last, final judgment is revealed to him. This document is probably from the second century CE and could not have influenced Jesus or the NT writers, but it shows just how much speculation and rewriting of the Genesis material was going on during the whole era, from the second century BCE through the second century CE. But as we shall see, it was not just Jesus and Paul's contemporaries who were so interested in the book of Genesis. So were Jesus and his followers.

Paul, our earliest NT writer, cites Genesis more than fifteen times, but more importantly, it is the stories of Genesis "that order and make sense of his world: the creation of the cosmos, the formation of humanity, the sin of Adam, the covenant with Abraham, and the promises to the patriarchs. In fact, if we ask about narrative elements in Paul, we find that the vast majority of these come from Genesis."[12] One could even say that much of the genesis of Paul's narrative thought-world comes from Genesis, in particular from some

10. See the discussion by F. I. Andersen, "2 (Slavonic Apocalypse of) Enoch," *OTP* 1:94–97.
11. Van Ruiten, "Genesis," 15.
12. David Lincicum, "Genesis in Paul," in Menken, *Genesis in the New Testament*, 99.

form of the Old Greek version of Genesis.[13] Equally importantly, Paul engages with the text of Genesis not just by citing and talking about verses here and there but by referring to whole stories from Genesis, and he seems to assume that at least some in his audience in Galatia or Corinth or Rome know these stories so that he doesn't have to completely retell them. Perhaps Christopher Stanley is right that part of Paul's discipling of his converts involved passing on to them stories from the Pentateuch, especially Genesis and Exodus.[14]

THE SECOND LAW: DEUTERONOMY

Of most importance to the writers of the New Testament after Isaiah and the Psalms, to judge from the frequency of direct use in the NT, is the book of Deuteronomy.[15] While the current title of this book comes to us from the LXX title *deuteronomos*, meaning "second law" in the original Hebrew, the title came from the book's opening word, *devarim*, here meaning speeches, or it was called the "Book of Speeches," which certainly better comports with what we find in the document. Deuteronomy ostensibly involves three long speeches by Moses (1:1–4:43; 4:44–28:68, and 28:69–30:20), followed by a postscript that includes the reporting of the final words and death of Moses (31:1–34:12).

Of importance for our discussion is the fact that when we compare the LXX/OG and the MT of Deuteronomy, here the Greek translator seems to have taken a conservative or more literal approach to the translation than is found, for example, in the LXX translation of Genesis. "The LXX of Deuteronomy is readable for its intended Greek-speaking audience and is faithful to the Jewish religion. No overarching theological *Tendenz* can be detected in the translation. The translator was preoccupied with rendering the text from

13. The most telling evidence is where Paul has certain features in his citations that could *not* have come from the Hebrew text, or an independent translation thereof; e.g., the reference to "two" in the rendering of Gen 2:24 does not go back to the Hebrew text. See the extended discussion in Dietrich Alex Koch, *Die Schrift als Zeuge des Evangeliums: Untersuchungen zur Verwendung und zum Verstandnis der Schrift bei Paulus*, BHT 69 (Tubingen: Mohr, 1986), esp. 51–54.

14. Christopher D. Stanley, *Arguing with Scripture: The Rhetoric of Quotations in the Letters of Paul* (London: T&T Clark, 2004), esp. 76, 117, 139.

15. As we shall see, Leviticus and Numbers are much less in play in the NT, and since various of the Exodus materials are revisited in Deuteronomy, and the NT generally follows the later version of the material in that book, we will not review here the early Jewish use of Exodus, Leviticus, and Numbers.

one language to another."[16] Indeed, in the first eleven chapters of the translation, interpretative intervention or change is hard to find, and in Deuteronomy 12–26 it seems to be only of a technical nature (e.g., substituting the word *ruler* for *king* in 17:14). In Deuteronomy 27–34, the minor changes reflect the author's intention to express God's love for his dispersed people (see, e.g., the rendering of the "horror" in Deut 28:25 by "in the dispersion"; see Deut 30:4).[17]

Some thirty-one scrolls involving fragments of Deuteronomy have been found in the caves next to Qumran, and three further scrolls were found at Wadi Murabba'at, Naḥal Ḥever, and on Masada. These scrolls range widely in date from about 250 BCE (4Q46= 4QpaleoDeuts) to perhaps as late as 68 CE (XHev/Se 3 = XḤev/Se Deut) or even 70 CE (Mas1c = MasDeut). With at least twenty-nine scrolls of Deuteronomy at Qumran (the content of two scrolls from Cave 6 are debated), this seems, after the forty some scrolls of the Psalms, to be the second most copied biblical book by the sectarians.[18] Put in other terms, Deuteronomy was being copied for about three centuries by the sectarians in the Judean desert, which speaks to its ongoing importance, usually in paleo-Hebrew, and usually in a square professional script. The best-preserved copy is 4QDeutc (4Q30), which contains 120 verses from nineteen chapters of Deuteronomy that can be called proto-Masoretic since they agree with the later text in orthography, paragraph divisions, and readings.[19] The conservatism of the LXX/OG translation of Deuteronomy makes it difficult to distinguish when and where the NT writers

---

16. Timothy Lim notes that the LXX translation is far superior to the later Greek translation of Aquila, which he (following Jerome) describes as often unintelligible. See Lim, "Deuteronomy in the Judaism of the Second Temple," in *Deuteronomy in the New Testament*, ed. M. J. J. Menken and Steve Moyise, LNTS 358 (London: T&T Clark, 2008), 19n59. See, e.g., J. W. Wevers, *Notes on the Greek Text of Deuteronomy*, SCS 39 (Atlanta: Scholars Press, 1995); Wevers, *Text History of the Greek Deuteronomy*, MSU 13 (Göttingen: Vandenhoeck and Ruprecht, 1978); and Cécile Dogniez and Marguerite Harl, *Le Deuteronome*, BA (Paris: Cerf, 1992), 29–73.

17. As Wevers, *Notes on the Greek Text*, 438 notes, the LXX translator views the diaspora as a divine punishment, which of course it partially was, if we evaluate it on the basis of the way the later OT prophets viewed the Babylonian exile.

18. It is interesting that Psalms and then Deuteronomy top the list, though the intact large Isaiah scroll is of course the most famous one from that locale. Does it tell us anything about the difference between the sectarians and the followers of Jesus that the latter group relied so much more heavily on Isaiah than these two other sources, but that like the Qumranites the use of Psalms and Deuteronomy was plentiful?

19. See the work of Julie Duncan, "4QDeutc" in Eugene Ulrich, Frank Moore Cross, Sidnie White Crawford, Julie Ann Duncan, Patrick W. Skehan, Emanuel Tov, and Julio C. Trebolle Barrera, eds., *Qumran Cave 4, IX: Deuteronomy, Joshua, Judges, Kings*, DJD 14 (Oxford: Clarendon, 1995), 15–34, 199.

were following the MT rather than the LXX, though it is clear that they mostly followed the latter. But sometimes the Qumran Deuteronomy fragments preserve variants that seem to lie behind the different readings in the LXX.

Perhaps more importantly, the Deuteronomy materials found at Qumran attest to the practice of forming what one can call catenae of texts, or chains of excerpts based on some theme, idea, or catchword. For example, 4Q175, sometimes called 4QTestimonia or even the "Messianic Anthology," seems to have been copied by a scribe in the first century BCE on a single piece of papyrus that included four paragraphs with quotations from Deuteronomy 5:28–29 and 18:18–19; Numbers 24:15–17; Deuteronomy 33:8–11; and Apocryphon of Joshua (4QPsJosh), which is an interpretation of Joshua 6:26 in the LXX version. Short phrases or sentences introduce each of these four citations, but only the fourth of these citations has any commentary with it. Timothy Lim is right to conclude

> 4Q175 attests to the phenomenon among Jews and subsequently Christians in [the] late Second Temple period of excerpting texts for various purposes, whether for study, liturgical practice, or controversy. Ostensibly, the first three passages selected by the compiler of 4Q175 have a messianic theme. The passages point to the expectation of different messianic figures: a prophetic one like Moses; a royal one according to Balaam's prophecy; and a Levitical or priestly messiah.[20]

Lim might have noted that in a largely oral culture, small collections of texts like this were just memory prompts for someone studying the material, and so it is not a surprise that there wasn't commentary with these first three citations. If someone was composing commentary, it would be separate and might well include a citation of the texts from the memory prompt.

There are some four Qumran Deuteronomy texts that seem to be just biblical excerpts:

> 4Q37 = Deuteronomy 5:1–6:3; 8:5–13; 10:12–11:21; Exodus
>   12:43–13:46; Deuteronomy 32:1–9
> 4Q38 = Deuteronomy 5:28–32; 11:6–13; 32:17–18, 22–23, 25–27
> 4Q41 = Deuteronomy 8:5–10 and 5:1–6.1
> 4Q44 = Deuteronomy 32:1–43

---

20. Lim, "Deuteronomy," 13.

Notice that Deuteronomy 5 and 32 are quoted in three of the four texts, and Deuteronomy 8 and 11 in two scrolls. These excerpts seem to have been used for liturgical and devotional practices. The clue that we are on the right track in saying so is contained in mezuzot and phylacteries of that period (amulets bound on the arms and head; see Letter of Aristeas 159; Philo *Spec. Laws* 4.137; Josephus, *Ant.* 4.213; Matt 23:5). Thirty-one phylacteries were recovered from Qumran, twenty-one of which were found in Cave 4 alone. While later rabbinic tradition focused on Exodus 13:1–10, 11–16; and Deuteronomy 6:4–9; and 11:13–21 as the texts for these phylacteries, at Qumran, no fewer than eight of the Qumran phylacteries include the Decalogue. In addition to the texts used in the rabbinic traditions, Exodus 12:43–51 is added in three of the phylacteries; Exodus 13:1–16 in three others; and Deuteronomy 10–11 in yet three others. Another three phylacteries have only the texts listed above as the later rabbinic preferred texts for these amulets.

In regard to mezuzot, the regular texts included were Deuteronomy 6:9 and 11:20, the beginning of the Shema. In later rabbinic practice, the Shema involved Deuteronomy 6:4–9 and 11:13–21. Of the nine mezuzot found at Qumran, seven of which came from Cave 4, all of them contain additional passages from Exodus 20 and also Deuteronomy 6:6–18. There can be little doubt, of course, that this reflects devotional practice, and note that m. Tamid 5:1 says that the practice was to recite the Decalogue and Shema together with the daily blessing in the temple and during the Sabbath when the priestly course changed.

Deuteronomy figures not just in the material discussed above from Qumran but also in the commentaries or pesharim from that locale. One of particular importance for the study of Paul's Galatians is 4Q169, the so-called Nahum Pesher, which reads, "he will hang men alive," meaning either crucifixion or hanging by a rope. The text provides an interpretation of Deuteronomy 21:22–23, which in its original context referred to the law concerning the impaling and public shaming of a corpse. Notice the inversion of the word order in the 4Q169: "you shall hang him" and "he shall die" (cf. the Temple Scroll 64.6–13).

There is more. In the category of reading backward, it is clear enough from a manuscript like 4Q252 that Genesis was being read through the lens of Deuteronomy. Indeed, the exegesis in that scroll is full of references to Deuteronomy, including the discussion of the patriarchal period. It is no surprise either, then, that early Jewish teachers read the Adam and Eve stories in light of the Decalogue in Deuteronomy, for example, as Paul reads the commandment to Adam and Eve about avoiding the fruit of the tree as being a form of the commandment "thou shalt not covet" (Rom 7:7–13).[21] The final form of the law in Deuteronomy apparently was the norm for how the earlier books in the Pentateuch, including Genesis and Exodus, were read. To give but one further example, we turn to the famous Temple Scroll, in both copies extracted from Cave 11 at Qumran (11Q19 and 11Q20), dating to the Herodian period. 11Q19 is nothing short of a "systematic rewriting of the Biblical texts of Exodus and Deuteronomy according to a thematic order."[22] It is not too much to say that the Temple Scroll has the book of Deuteronomy as a base text and careful examination shows it is following the order of Deuteronomy 12–26.[23]

None of this comes as a surprise when one remembers the prioritizing of Deuteronomy over the other books of the Pentateuch, and indeed the using of it as a guide for how to read the earlier books. Probably this practice had a very long history, going back perhaps all the way to Josiah, as it was likely some portion of Deuteronomy that was found and reaffirmed and implemented during his reforms.

Finally, when Josephus writes his magnum opus *Jewish Antiquities,* he paraphrases a large portion of Deuteronomy for his audience in *Ant.* 4.176–331, rearranging the material so as to systematize the discussion of particular subjects one after another so the whole will seem more coherent and logical. He promises to add nothing to what Moses said, except "to classify the several subjects" (4.196–97). For him, Deuteronomy is the epitome or highest expression of the law. But he was, clearly enough, not alone in this. Many at Qumran, indeed probably many of the NT writers as well, would have said the amen to that. If even Jesus is depicted as using Deuteronomy to refute the devil during his famous temptations, it is not surprising it was a go-to source, especially when one was under duress, for early Jews of various sorts. But perhaps here is the place to say a bit more about Jesus within early Judaism and the depiction of his use of the OT, and

---

21. On which see Witherington and Hyatt, *Letter to the Romans,* on Romans 7:7–13.

22. Lim, "Deuteronomy," 21.

23. Sidnie White Crawford, *The Temple Scroll and Related Texts* (Sheffield: Sheffield Academic, 2000), 57.

especially the law. It is important to compare and contrast the above findings to what the Gospels suggest about Jesus's use of the Scripture.

JESUS WITHIN EARLY JUDAISM

Let us begin with a listing of all the direct or clear quotations from the OT found on the lips of Jesus, with brief comment on each. The purpose of the following discussion is not to offer some comprehensive discussion of Jesus's or the Gospel writers' use of Scripture at this juncture, but rather just to give us a general sense of the way Jesus's and his followers' own praxis fit into, or were distinguishable from, the way Scripture was cited or used in the larger Jewish context. To my knowledge, the material we have just discussed in the earlier part of this chapter does *not* provide evidence of historical Jewish individuals applying Scriptural texts to themselves as individuals, or in terms of their individual mission or ministry. Yes, there is evidence of applying texts to a community, like the Qumran community, but not evidence of a particular individual interpreting *himself* by Scripture—that is, until Jesus came along (unless one thinks there is clear evidence that the Teacher of Righteousness was doing this at Qumran, but the evidence is not clear on that front).

MATTHEW

Strikingly, the first quotations on the lips of Jesus come when he is doing battle with the devil in Matthew 4 and cites Deuteronomy 8:3, the "bread alone" saying, then Deuteronomy 6:16 about "not testing God," and then Deuteronomy 6:13 about worshiping only God. This is contrasted with Psalm 91:11–12, which is the sole text cited by the devil during the second temptation (in Matthew's ordering of things). Jesus is, in a word, depicted as laying down the law to the devil, and not just any form of the law but the "second law" form of it. Again, in Matthew 5:27, Jesus cites from the law, either the Deuteronomy 5:18 form of the adultery prohibition or possibly the Exodus 20:14 form. More clearly, Jesus cites Deuteronomy 24:1 about Moses's permission of divorce at Matthew 5:31. Then, at Matthew 5:33, we have a citation of the Mosaic saying about oaths, which we find in three forms in Deuteronomy 23:21 // Leviticus 19:12 // Numbers 30:2. The law of the tooth, about retribution, is cited at Matthew 5:38, which comes from Deuteronomy 19:21 // Leviticus 24:20 // Exodus 21:24. The "love neighbor" command at Matthew 5:43 clearly comes from Leviticus 19:18. The next clear citation does not occur until Matthew 10:35–36, about a family divided: it is from Micah 7:6. Then, in Matthew 11:10, Jesus speaks about John the Baptizer quoting Malachi 3:1 about the messenger who comes before and prepares the way.

When the Pharisees object to the disciples gleaning on the Sabbath, Jesus replies with Hosea 6:6, about mercy being preferred over sacrifice. In Matthew 13:14–15, there is a lengthy citation by Jesus of Isaiah 6:9–10 about the use of parables and obscure speech due to the hard hearts of God's people. In Matthew 15:4, Jesus repeats Moses's commandment about honoring parents from Deuteronomy 5:16 // Exodus 20:12, which is followed almost immediately by another saying about honor, this one from Isaiah 29:13 (LXX). In view of the fact that the first evangelist so often uses Isaiah, and perhaps particularly Isaiah in its LXX form, to explain and interpret the Christ event, many commentators have left this citation off the list of those that might possibly go back to Jesus himself.

In Matthew 18:16, there is a citation by Jesus of Deuteronomy 19:15, about the testimony of two witnesses. In Matthew 19:4–5, Jesus cites the creation account from Genesis 1:27, 5:2, and 2:24 in his discussion of marriage. Jesus's partial citation of the Ten Commandments (but not the Sabbath commandment) in Matthew 19:18–20 comes from Deuteronomy 5:16–20 // Exodus 20:12–16 // Leviticus 19:18. Jesus's retort to those priests and scribes complaining about the accolades he was receiving in Matthew 21:16 comes from Psalm 8:2. More famously, he cites the rejected stone saying from Psalm 118:22–23 at Matthew 21:42. When queried about the greatest commandment, Jesus cites Deuteronomy 6:5, about loving God with one's whole heart, followed by a further citation of Leviticus 19:18, about loving your neighbor. Matthew 22:32 has the quotation from Exodus 3:6, 15–16, about God being the God of the patriarchs. In Matthew 22:44, we have the two lords saying from Psalm 110:1 as a response about the messiah being David's son. Psalm 118:26 comes up at Matthew 23:39 as the last public quotation by Jesus prior to the crucifixion. In his private teaching to the disciples about the coming cataclysm, Jesus cites Daniel 9:27, about the abomination of desolation. Jesus also explains what will happen to the disciples once he is apprehended, citing Zechariah 13:7 about the shepherd and the scattered sheep. At his trial, Jesus responds to the high priest at Matthew 26:64 by citing Daniel 7:13 combined with Psalm 110:1. The final quotation found on Jesus's lips is the famous cry of dereliction from Psalm 22:1, partially in Aramaic, at Matthew 27:46. *The overwhelming impression one gets when one examines these citations is a strong dependency on Deuteronomy, followed by the Psalms and some prophetic texts, especially Isaiah, and then Daniel toward the end of the Gospel.*

MARK

About Mark's Gospel there is far less to say. In Mark 4 is the citation, again from Isaiah 6:9–10, which we have already seen in a fuller form in Matthew. Isaiah is again turned to in Mark 7:6–7 as a rebuttal, drawing on Isaiah 29:13, and then Exodus 21:10 // Leviticus 20:9 is cited about honoring parents. In Mark 8:18, there seems to be a combination citation from Jeremiah 5:21 and Ezekiel 12:2 about the disciples having stopped up ears and blind eyes. In the discussion about marriage and divorce in Mark 10:6–7 we have the same Genesis texts cited as in Matthew—Genesis 1:27; 5:2; 2:24—and similarly we have the same citation in Mark 10:19 of Deuteronomy 5:16–20 // Exodus 20:12–16, from the Ten Commandments, as in Matthew. The den of robbers saying in Mark 11:17 draws on Jeremiah 7:11 and possibly other texts. In Mark 12:10, the stone saying from Psalm 118:22–23 is once again found. In Mark 12:26, there is a citation of Exodus 3:6, 15–16 about the living God, and then in 12:29–30 Jesus recites the Shema as the primary command, drawing on Deuteronomy 6:4–5 and possibly Joshua 22:5. This is in turn followed by the love your neighbor command in Mark 12:31, from Leviticus 19:18. In the debate about the messiah as David's son, Mark 12:36 also cites Psalm 110:1. Mark 13:14 also has the abomination saying from Daniel 9:27. At the last supper, at Mark 14:27 we again find Zechariah 13:7 quoted. At his trial, Jesus quotes to the high priest the combination of Psalm 110:1 and Daniel 7:13 (Mark 14:62), as we found in Matthew. Mark 15:34, as in the case of Matthew, provides us with the last citation on Jesus's lips from the cross, of Psalm 22:1. While the vast majority of these citations are also found in Matthew, it is interesting that only Mark has the citation from the Shema, again drawing on Deuteronomy.

LUKE

Luke famously rearranges the order of the temptations, so that in Luke 4, while the first temptation is still the bread temptation involving the citation by Jesus of Deuteronomy 8:3, the second one is the worship temptation with the citing of Deuteronomy 6:13, and then finally the citation of Deuteronomy 6:16 about worshiping God. Scholars have speculated as to why this reordering of things has happened (is it because of the going up to Jerusalem motif in this Gospel that the temptations end with the pinnacle saying?), but it may be worth noting that Jesus cites the latter two texts from Deuteronomy in canonical order in the Lukan version of the story.

In Luke alone we have Jesus reading from the Scriptures in his hometown synagogue in Luke 4:18–19. The text in question is Isaiah 61:1–2, which announces programmatically what will happen during the ministry of Jesus. If Theophilus is a gentile convert to the faith, we might well expect less direct citations of Scripture by the narrator and by Jesus in this longest of all canonical Gospels, and this is in fact what we find. The next citation, very briefly, is Jesus's quote about John in Luke 7:27 from Malachi 3:1, without a mention of where the citation comes from. Then in Luke 8:10 we have the citation, found also in longer form in Mark and even longer form in Matthew, from Isaiah 6, in this case just verse 9.

The next clear citation does not come until Luke 12:53, where we have a lengthy citation about a family divided from Micah 7:6, but without a citation formula or attribution. Not until the passion narrative do we have another clear citation on Jesus's lips, at Luke 19:46, the combination citation about the den of thieves from Isaiah 56:7 and Jeremiah 7:11. There is then a truncated form of the stone citation at Luke 20:17 from Psalm 118:22, but it is at least clearly identified as from Scripture. Luke 20:27 gives us the saying about God being the God of the patriarchs from Exodus 3:6, 15 and, again, a short form of the two lords saying from Psalm 110:1 at Luke 20:42–43.

Uniquely, at Luke 22:37 Jesus quotes Isaiah 53:12 of himself: "and he was counted among the lawless." On the way to the cross, Jesus cites Hosea 10:8 about what will be said by God's people when God's judgment falls upon them, again a unique citation. From the cross, also uniquely in this Gospel, Jesus quotes Psalm 31:5 about the giving up of his spirit to God, here as his very last utterance, so very different from what we find in both Matthew and Mark, where Psalm 22:1 is cited. Strikingly, and uniquely, at the end of this Gospel in Luke 24, Jesus appears and concludes that the disciples need a short course in the messianic reading of the Law, the Prophets, and the Psalms, and proceeds to offer that Bible study in short form. In light of the slight use of citations in the Gospel itself, this would seem to be a signal to Theophilus that further, detailed pondering of the Scriptures would be crucial for his further understanding of Jesus and his movement.

JOHN

Finally, turning to the Gospel of John, while Jesus perhaps alludes to a den of robbers saying at John 2:16, amazingly, the first real citation on the lips of Jesus does not come until John 6:31. As a comment on Jesus and the feeding of the five thousand, John cites Exodus 16:4 // Psalm 78:24: "he gave them bread from heaven to eat." This is followed by a rebuttal by Jesus saying "they will be taught by God" in John 6:45, quoting Isaiah 54:13. It should be noted that the feeding of the five thousand story is the only Galilean miracle story (along with the walking on water which accompanies that story) in all four Gospels. My point is that here the use of Scripture seems more like what we find in the Synoptics. There are no more clear citations of Scripture by Jesus until John 10:34, from Psalm 82:6: "I said you are gods." After that there are no further quotes on Jesus's lips until John 13:18, a saying from Psalm 41:9 applied to Judas, "the one who eats my bread has raised his heel against me." There are no clear citations in the farewell discourses in John 14–17, and while there are a plethora of citations by the Fourth Evangelist to help explain the passion narrative, there are none from Jesus himself, unless one counts the "I am thirsty" citation in John 19:28, of which commentators have long debated the source. Probably this is a paraphrase from Psalm 69:21. Jesus cites no Scriptures in John 20–21. Besides the clear independence of this portrait of Jesus in the Fourth Gospel, one notes that what contributes to that impression is Jesus citing Scriptures in this Gospel that none of the Synoptics mention he used. Apart from the allusion to the den of robbers saying found also in the Synoptics, all the citations on Jesus's lips in this Gospel are unique to this Gospel. Notice that the Psalms and Isaiah are prominent, with Deuteronomy nowhere to be found.

What should we make of this evidence? Yes, Jesus was a person who spoke on his own authority, and even punctuated his own sayings with an introductory "Amen" from time to time. And yes, it is true that to get the whole picture one has to consider allusions and echoes in addition to citations to see how Jesus may have used Scripture. The overall impression is that Jesus relied heavily on the Law, particularly Genesis and Deuteronomy, but also Exodus and Leviticus, in his debates with his fellow Jews. The only book from the Writings that he cites is the Psalms, and that with some regularity. Of the prophets he relied on Isaiah, from the major prophets, and Daniel, but also on Micah and Hosea. Malachi comes in only to provide commentary on John's ministry, not Jesus's. If we take all this at face value, how does this match up with the use of the Scriptures, especially the Pentateuch, in early Judaism?[24] There are some similarities in the messianic readings we find at Qumran and on Jesus's lips, but this mainly has to do with readings of the Psalms, not the Law.

Granted, some of these clear citations may be the result of the redactional work of this or that evangelist, for example, the citation of a LXX version of a saying from Isaiah, which, as an Aramaic speaker, Jesus was unlikely to have used; but on the whole, the picture seems rather clear and probably authentic. The earliest forms of the Gospel tradition in Mark and Matthew have more scriptural citations by Jesus. The later forms of the tradition in Luke and John have *fewer*, perhaps, at least in the case of Luke, if not also of John, because the dominant audience is gentile (noting all the parenthetical explanations of Jewish matters in John, and Luke's deleting of all Aramaic sayings of Jesus from his Markan source).

At this juncture, it will be useful to interact with Steve Moyise's helpful study entitled *Jesus and Scripture: Studying the New Testament Use of the Old Testament*.[25] As Moyise says at the outset of his study, in the Gospels Jesus is depicted as quoting from about sixty different scriptural verses, and there are twice that many allusions and echoes as well to various scriptural texts. For example, the parable of the vineyard in Mark 12:1–12 owes more than a little to Isaiah 5. Moyise quickly, and rightly, counters the notion that Jesus was mainly depicted as a prophet quoting other earlier prophets; in fact, by Moyise's count, there are some twenty-six references to texts from

---

24. That is, if we assume Jesus actually used most of these Scriptures, even if some of them come to us as redactional elements from the evangelists.

25. Steve Moyise, *Jesus and Scripture: Studying the New Testament Use of the Old Testament* (Grand Rapids: Baker Academic, 2011).

the Law (eleven from Deuteronomy, eight from Exodus, three each from Leviticus and Genesis, and only one from Numbers), sixteen from the Writings (exclusively from the Psalms, except if one counts Daniel as one of the Writings, as is done in the Hebrew Bible), and finally fifteen from the prophets (seven from Isaiah, two from Hosea, and one each from Jeremiah, Daniel, Jonah, Micah, Zechariah, and Malachi). Moyise notes the similarity to the situation at Qumran, where the most cited books are Psalms, Isaiah, and Deuteronomy.[26]

Moyise says there are twenty-five OT quotes in Mark, of which twenty-two are found on the lips of Jesus, drawn from the Law (ten), Prophets (seven), and the psalms (five). They mostly conform to the LXX form of these sayings, and Moyise thinks this reflects not Mark's translating of these verses but a reliance on an earlier translation of the Aramaic sayings of Jesus, including his sayings that involved an OT quote.[27] In Mark 7, Jesus is portrayed as one who upholds at least some of the OT law and is not happy when later Jewish traditions are brought in which compromise the fulfilling of the commandments. So, the corban principle prevents children from properly taking care of, and so honoring, their parents. However, in the same chapter, Jesus is portrayed as saying that nothing that enters the mouth is defiling, but rather it is what comes out of the human heart that defiles (see v. 18). Mark clearly enough thinks this means that Jesus has declared all foods clean or at least cleansed. But there are similar issues in Mark 2:1–3:6, the so-called controversy stories, where time and again someone seems to think Jesus is breaking the Sabbath prohibition on work by healing people, perhaps especially by healing people in a nonemergency situation. Is it a telltale sign when Jesus reaffirms some of the Ten Commandments but apparently not the Sabbath commandment in Mark 10:19? It is Moyise's view that Mark must think that Jesus was not guilty of breaking the Sabbath command.[28] This is not necessarily the case. Mark seems to indicate in Mark 14:22–25 that Jesus was inaugurating a new covenant, not merely reaffirming an old one; and the new covenant did not involve food laws, or Sabbath-keeping, any more than it involved practicing circumcision.

Even less convincing is Moyise's rationale for his analysis:

26. Moyise, *Jesus and Scripture*, 4.
27. Moyise, *Jesus and Scripture*, 13.
28. Moyise, *Jesus and Scripture*, 15.

If we remember that the discussion began over the issue of Pharisaic hand-washing rituals (Mark 7:1–5) it could be argued that Mark's conclusion—"cleansing all foods"—has nothing to do with the Law's distinction between clean and unclean food. It simply asserts that food does not become defiled by breaking the detailed hand-washing rituals of the Pharisees. The status of food that the law regards as unclean is simply not in view. Indeed, although Jesus is accused of eating with tax collectors and sinners (Mark 2:16) he is never accused of eating anything unclean, which concurs with Peter's protestation in Acts 10:14 that never in his life—thus including his time with Jesus—has he ever eaten anything unclean. Therefore . . . most scholars think that Jesus kept the Jewish food laws and at no time spoke against them.[29]

It is interesting that Eli Lizorkin-Eyzenberg, who is very much interested in defending the Torah-true character of Jesus, rejects Moyise's analysis. He suggests,

Some rightly seeking to reclaim the intensely Jewish character of Mark's gospel have mistakenly suggested that vs. 19 (*Thus He* declared all goods clean) is an editorial addition to the original text, made by Gentile Christians disinterested in Jewish issues. I suggest, however, that this line is in fact an integral part of Mark's very Jewish argument! The law of bodily discharge is a case in point. Defending Torah against the Pharisees, Jesus upholds a long-standing Galilean Jewish tradition, declaring that foods cannot make an Israelite unclean, because in Torah it works the other way around![30]

That is, unscrupulous Jews can make food unclean, but not vice versa.

Neither of these explanations really pass muster from a Markan point of view. One has to account for the rising tide of hostility against Jesus himself from Pharisees. A serious disagreement is surely what prompted this. Notice, for example, that we are already told in Mark 3:6 that the Pharisees, in league with the Herodians, were plotting how to do Jesus in. The animus against Jesus did not just come from some Sadducees in Jerusalem because of his action in the temple.

A fair reading of this material and its implications involves the following: (1) Jesus did say that nothing that enters a person's mouth, namely food of whatever sort, makes them unclean. This then is not about the law of discharges from the bowels found in Leviticus 15.

29. Moyise, *Jesus and Scripture*, 16.
30. http://tinyurl.com/ycryrysf (emphasis original).

Indeed, nothing in the discussion with the Pharisees here suggests discharges was the focus of the debate; (2) Mark clearly believes that the implication of the aphorism of Jesus, whether understood at the time or not, was that in Jesus's view, all foods were clean (v. 18; we have no basis for arguing that Mark, bless his heart, must have been mistaken). On any showing, Jesus was in various respects a radical Jew, radical not only in his interpretation of work and the Sabbath but in regard to the issues of clean and unclean. If he was "lord over the Sabbath" (Mark 2) and its interpretation, we should not be surprised if he saw himself as lord over the purity laws as well. What both of the above interpretations fail to come to grips with is the eschatological context and flavor of Jesus's teachings. As Jesus already said in Mark 2, you don't put new wine in old wineskins. Jesus is inaugurating a new covenant based on the in-breaking of the divine saving activity or dominion of God. He is in the process of bringing about a new covenant relationship with God, not merely taking a new approach to the Mosaic covenant. What brings about confusion is the fact that some of the commandments found in the Mosaic covenant are reaffirmed by Jesus as part of the new eschatological covenant. (3) As with so many things, the disciples did not fully understand the teaching of Jesus on various Jewish laws until well after Pentecost, Peter being a case in point. While Acts 10:4 may mean that Peter himself had not previously eaten unclean food (and notice that nothing in the Gospels suggests the disciples ate with tax collectors and sinners, only Jesus himself did so), this is because he had not fully understood the implications of Jesus's teaching and praxis. It required a further revelation to Peter to get the point across, and thereafter, as Galatians 2:14 makes clear, he did get the point—he ate non-kosher food with gentiles and could even be said to be "living like a gentile."

This radical change did not originate with Paul. Peter was already not living by the Mosaic laws about clean and unclean in Antioch when the confrontation with Paul took place. This being the case, it is far easier to believe that the radical break with some Jewish practices goes back to Jesus himself. But I suspect that what Jesus would have said is the same thing that the author of that profoundly Jewish book Hebrews later suggests—you can't break an obsolete law! With the dawn of the new covenant, with the coming of the Son born under the law to redeem those under it out from under it (see Gal 4), new occasions teach new duties, new wine requires new wineskins.

With the establishing of the eschatological new covenant, the Mosaic covenant, which served an interim purpose in God's redemption plan (again, see Galatians 4), was no longer binding on God's people. Jesus was already moving in this direction by his words and deeds during his ministry, and it is one of the things that led to both animus and, finally, trials and execution.

As Moyise goes on to admit, Jesus's teaching on marriage and divorce in Mark 10 can hardly be called a reaffirmation of the Mosaic permission to divorce in Deuteronomy 24:1–4, the only teaching anywhere in the Mosaic law about divorce. Jesus appeals to God's original creation order over against the Mosaic legislation, which Jesus says was given due to the hardness of human hearts, which is to say, in order to limit sin. It was not God's highest and best vision for marriage. Further, according to Jesus, the one-flesh union of a couple that God has brought together to share is indissoluble. As John Meier exclaims, "Jesus presumes to teach that that which the Law permits and regulates is actually the sin of adultery."[31] Divorce and remarriage is seen as adultery. What best makes sense of this is a recognition that Jesus is not merely intensifying the Mosaic laws demands, he is saying that the time for allowances for hardness of heart has passed now that the eschatological kingdom is breaking in. Now that God's saving activity is coming to a climax, a more rigorous discipleship, grounded in a new covenant, is demanded and enabled based on the eschatological saving activity that is happening.

Moyise also, rightly in my view, points to the discussion about which commandment is the "first" (Mark 12:28).[32] Jesus recites the familiar Shema ("Hear O Israel") but adds the phrase "with all your strength" to it, and goes beyond the scribal question by saying there is a second most important commandment, namely, loving neighbor as self (Mark 12:31). Uniquely, Jesus adds, "there is no other commandment [singular] greater than these [plural]." There are no known parallels to this ranking of commandments as first and second, though, as Moyise points out, there is precedent for citing these two commands together (Testament of Issachar 5:2; Testament of Dan 5:3). Moyise tries to continue to argue that Jesus is just objecting to Pharisaic traditions that limit the full-application of the Mosaic commands and divert them from their original humanitarian intentions.

---

31. John P. Meier, *A Marginal Jew: Rethinking the Historical Jesus; Vol. 4; Law and Love*, AYBRL (New Haven: Yale University Press, 2009), 113.

32. Moyise, *Jesus and Scripture*, 18–19.

But is Jesus merely "against using the 'permission' to divorce in Deuteronomy 24 as a path to adultery"?[33] The answer to this must be no. Jesus is saying no divorce now that the kingdom is dawning—period! (See, rightly, 1 Cor 7:10–11.[34]) He is acting with a sort of authority and freedom in regard to the Mosaic law that was found shocking, already in the very first miracle story in Mark 1 (Mark 1:27). Put another way, Jesus is rewriting the law according to God's creation plan and his current saving activity. And this becomes clear as well when one gets to the issue of the Ten Commandments themselves in Mark 10:19, a discussion that Moyise rightly points to. Here, Jesus: (1) does *not* mention the all-important Sabbath commandment as of continuing validity; (2) rearranges the order of the Ten Commandments, placing honoring parents after murder, adultery, theft, and false witness; and more importantly (3) *substitutes* "do not defraud" for the commandment not to covet. Mark's point is not that Jesus is careless in his citation of the law, or not concerned to recite it precisely. Mark's point is that Jesus had the authority to rewrite the rules!

It is well to remember that Mark's Gospel is our earliest Gospel, and his presentation of Jesus and the law is likely to be closest to the actual contours of the ministry of the historical Jesus himself. Jesus, it would appear, was on a mission to bring in God's eschatological kingdom and new covenant, which was not a covenant without law, nor was it a covenant without some continuity with some elements from the Mosaic covenant. It was, however, a covenant that would leave behind the boundary-defining issues that made it difficult for Jews to associate with and have fellowship with non-Jews—circumcision, food laws, and Sabbath keeping—as well as with sinners and tax collectors among the Jews. You will notice that there are various different stories in different strands of the Jesus tradition about Jesus helping and healing non-Jews during his ministry, including even demoniacs in Gadara, a Syro-Phoenician woman, and gentile centurions, which in some cases involved venturing into gentile territory (see also the visit to Caesarea-Philippi). The sign of the new covenant would be baptism, a gender-inclusive sign, as opposed to circumcision.

Paul was not some maverick blazing trails in directions Jesus never dreamed of. Paul even talks about the "law of Christ" as part of the

---

33. Moyise, *Jesus and Scripture*, 18.
34. I take it that Paul rightly interprets the original logion of Jesus.

new covenant (1 Corinthians 9, Galatians 6), and in Galatians 6 he cites two of the sayings of Jesus and expounds on them as part of this new law, while also reiterating the parts of the Ten Commandments that he believed, as did Jesus, were still binding on the followers of Jesus (see Romans 13:8–10). Notice as well, in Romans 13:8–10, that Paul combines this citation of some of the Ten Commandments Jesus reaffirmed with the love command, in particular the love of neighbor command (having already cited some of the Sermon on the Mount in Rom 12:9–21). This cannot be accidental as this reflects the very discussion of Jesus about the first and second commands as well as the Ten Commandments in our earliest Gospel.[35] There is certainly development of the teaching of Jesus, beyond what he himself said, in the teaching of Paul and the author of Hebrews, but my point would be that they are simply amplifying and pursuing further the trajectory, including the trajectory on the law, that Jesus set in motion from the outset.

When Moyise turns to the presentation of Jesus in Matthew, he notes that Matthew adds some thirty further citations from the OT, while retaining all those found in Mark.[36] Noting the temptation narratives (Matthew 4 // Luke 4), he points out that Jesus imprecisely cites Deuteronomy 6:13, substituting the word "worship" for "fear" in the phrase "fear the Lord," and adding the word "only" to the citation.[37] For Moyise, this suggests Jesus is reaffirming the validity of the Mosaic law, which, in his view, does not require precisely citing that law. No; what is happening here is the same thing we saw in Mark—namely, Jesus's sovereign freedom to alter the law in accordance with the new eschatological situation and covenant. This should have been clear on a reading of the famous antitheses in Matthew 5–7—"you have heard it said, but I say to you"—where Jesus intensifies some commandments (e.g., the one on adultery), interprets the commandment to avoid killing/murder to mean do no violence at all, and completely dismisses the Mosaic rules and permissions about oaths. What is striking about all this is that Jesus is not merely

---

35. Still the best treatment on the love commands is Victor P. Furnish's classic study, *The Love Command in the New Testament* (Nashville: Abingdon, 1972).

36. Moyise, *Jesus and Scripture*, 33.

37. There is an interesting partial parallel to the temptation story, found in Deuteronomy Rabbah 11:5 in which the angel of death quotes Ps 118:17 and 19:2 and Moses responds with Deut 32:1–4. As Moyise says, the written form of this tradition is from centuries later than the Gospels and is hardly a borrowing from or responding to the gospel story. Moyise (*Jesus and Scripture*, 110) thinks the story might go back to Jesus's day as oral tradition. This is not impossible, but it is no more probable than that this story is a response to the Jesus tradition.

interpreting the Mosaic law on some spectrum between rigorist to lenient, he is actually changing the law, which includes offering new ones and making some old ones obsolete.

This brings us to Moyise's treatment of Matthew 5:17–20, which requires more extended comment. First of all, on any showing, Jesus is offering some new teaching, some wisdom in Matthew 5–7. In part, this teaching not only is not found in the Mosaic law, it also at times contravenes what Moses permitted, for example, divorce of two people joined together by God (see Matt 19:1–10) or Moses's rules on oaths.[38] Second, the whole of the Gospel of Matthew is about fulfillment, which is eschatological language: fulfillment of prophecy, fulfillment of the Law, fulfillment of the Writings (e.g., the Psalms, Daniel). When something is fulfilled, it is brought to completion and one is done with it. When a prophecy is completely fulfilled, one doesn't look for further fulfillments, and the same applies to the law, which was viewed by many early Jews, like the rest of Scripture, as prophetic in character. Third, notice that in Matthew 5:17 Jesus doesn't just speak about the law, he speaks about 'the Law and the Prophets' and about not abolishing them. Indeed not! He came to fulfill them. He envisions a day when the law will pass away, but not until it has been entirely fulfilled. But the question has to be asked: *When does he think that will happen?* Does he see that as coming to fruition by means of his own death, fulfilling all of God's righteous requirements in regard to sin and death? Jesus does not say specifically, but if one reads the Last Supper treatments in the Synoptics carefully, one sees that Jesus associates the proper inauguration of the new covenant with his death. Indeed, he passes out tokens of the ben-

---

38. As I have argued at length elsewhere (see Ben Witherington III, *What's in the Word? Rethinking the Socio-Rhetorical Character of the New Testament* [Waco, TX: Baylor University Press, 2009], 103–11), the discussion about the exception clauses has largely been misleading, because what Jesus is talking about is a particular meaning of *porneia*, either prostitution (the root meaning of the word) or more likely incest prompted by the cause celebre that got John the Baptizer beheaded—the incestuous marriage of Herod Antipas to Herodias. In either case, we are talking about a non-marriage, an arrangement where God did not join the two people together, and so not a true exception to the rule. Jesus's view is that when God has brought two people together in marriage and they share a one-flesh union, there should be no divorce, and any further marriage is not only not divinely sanctioned, it is a committing adultery in some form. In other words, Matt 5:19 is not a more lenient teaching on divorce than in Mark 10 and 1 Corinthians 7. To the contrary, as the volatile reaction of the disciples in Matthew 19 to the marriage and divorce teaching ("if that's the way it is between a man and a woman, better not to marry") suggests, Jesus's teaching on marriage and divorce was shocking and went against the permissions by Moses.

efits of his death in advance when he says this is my body broken for you, and this is my blood, the cup of the new covenant.

We must bear in mind that chronologically speaking, the earliest form of the "words of institution" by Jesus are found in 1 Corinthians 11:23–26, and there quite specifically Jesus is depicted as speaking of a new covenant inaugurated by the shedding of his blood. I would say this is how Mark's and Matthew's accounts should be read as well. Paul is simply passing on the earliest tradition we know about this crucial event. Finally, close attention should be paid to what Jesus says in Matthew 5:20: he says that his audience, the disciples, must have a righteousness that exceeds that of the scribes and Pharisees. That higher righteousness is precisely what he is talking about in the Sermon on the Mount, not merely a keeping of the Mosaic commandments more strictly or more leniently as the scribes and Pharisees do; this is what Paul would later call "the law of Christ."[39] This of course includes a reiteration of some Mosaic commandments, but with some additions and subtractions.[40] Matthew is not contradicting Mark, he is simply nuancing the material for his Jewish Christians living in a Jewish ethos or setting.[41] He is certainly not suggesting that Jesus was talking only about the issues of hand washing when he said, "nothing defiles a person that enters their mouths."

It is simply not the case that what Jesus says about oaths represents one point on the spectrum of early Jewish debate on such matters. Yes, the background, as Moyise points out, is Leviticus 19:12, Numbers 30:2, and Deuteronomy 23:21, but Jesus is not merely ruling out false or exaggerated swearing, *he is ruling out oaths altogether, something Moses never did.* This is not a matter of interpretation, whether

39. The "law of Christ" is Pauline terminology, of course, but Jesus's reinforcement of some of the Mosaic commandments demonstrates that he is reapplying some laws, not rejecting law *in toto.*

40. It matters that Matthew's audience appears to be Jewish Christians, which is probably not the majority of Mark's audience. This is why Matthew includes the further clarification about the relationship of Jesus's followers to the Mosaic law, and it may be why he omits the unambiguous declaration from Mark "thus he declares all food clean" in Matthew 15. Jewish followers of Jesus still living in the context of Judaism, perhaps in Capernaum or in the Jewish community in Damascus or say Antioch, may well have, for the sake of their witness to fellow Jews, continued to keep the Mosaic law, as apparently James the brother of Jesus did in Jerusalem. Mark, however, is probably writing to the church in Rome and is more concerned with making clear the radical implications of Jesus's teaching and praxis, making things clearer for gentile followers of Jesus for whom such Jewish debates were nonissues, unless they crossed paths with Torah-observant Jewish Christians (as seems to be the case in light of Romans 14, and Paul's discussion there).

41. See my extended discussion of all these issues in Ben Witherington III, *Matthew,* SHBC 19 (Macon, GA: Smyth & Helwys, 2006).

liberal or conservative; it's about abrogation, and more importantly it should have raised the question, Who does Jesus think he is changing the law, adding to it, subtracting from it, and enfolding what he reaffirms within the context of his own sapiential teaching?[42] As Meier says: "Jesus' shocking teaching, which presumes to revoke some institution or command of the Mosaic Law, probably evoked no little dissent and debate among his Jewish listeners."[43] Just so, and it was one of the things that led to such heated opposition to Jesus during his ministry.

Two further texts are of especial importance in the discussion of Matthew's presentation of Jesus's approach to the Mosaic law. Moyise takes Matthew 23:23–24—where Jesus tells his Jewish audience that the Pharisees neglect the weightier matters of the law, while tithing their condiments—to mean that Jesus affirms the keeping of the whole law: not its abrogation, but that one needs to place the emphasis and the main focus on the weightier matters of the law.[44] This is to ignore that this whole chapter is dedicated to a detailed, emotion-filled critique of the hypocrisy of the scribes and Pharisees, with specific examples cited.

The words of Jesus in Matthew 23:23–24 are directed not to his own disciples, but to the Pharisees themselves, telling them how they should have behaved on the basis of their own presuppositions and approach to the Mosaic law. This tells us *nothing* about Jesus's or his disciples' approach to the law itself. Notice that Matthew 23:1 says that Jesus is speaking to the crowds and also his disciples, but mainly this is addressed to the crowds, and to the Pharisees and scribes within that crowd in Jerusalem. Jesus says to the crowds, "do what the Pharisees say, but do not follow their practice." It is only in the context of Jesus's specific teaching to his disciples (see Matthew 5:1–2) that we see clearly what Jesus wants his own followers to have as an approach to the law. This you cannot deduce from Jesus's detailed critique of Pharisaic hypocrisy in Matthew 23.

Finally, there is the issue of the uniquely Matthean phrase about the two love commandments in Matthew 22:40: "on these two commandments 'hang all the law and the prophets." First of all, notice that Jesus does not say it is simply a summary of "the law." Rather the *whole* of the Law and Prophets (see the earlier phrase about the

42. See Moyise, *Jesus and Scripture*, 36.
43. Meier, *Marginal Jew*, 209.
44. Moyise, *Jesus and Scripture*, 39.

fulfillment of the Law and the Prophets) is at issue. The verb, as Moyise points out, is used figuratively here, of course.[45] But what does it mean? Does it mean all these things are deducible from the two love commandments, or inspired by them? Of these two suggestions, the latter makes better sense. But I would suggest that the verb "hang" here means "depends upon." The whole plan of God, including his salvation plan, is about God setting up a love relationship with God's people and among God's people, a notion that Jesus expands to include *the love of enemies* (Matt 5:43–44), something not suggested in the OT and positively repudiated elsewhere in early Judaism. Very telling is the material at the outset of 1QS, the so-called Community Rule from Qumran that probably comes from just before the time of Jesus, which reads:

> The Master shall teach the saints to live according to the Book of the Community Rule, that they may seek God with a whole heart and soul, and do what is good and right before him as he commanded by the hand of Moses and all his servants the prophets, that they may love all that he has chosen and hate all that he has rejected, that they may abstain from all evil and hold fast to all good, that they may practice truth, righteousness, and justice upon earth and no longer stubbornly follow a sinful heart and lustful eyes, committing all manner of evil. He shall admit into the Covenant of Grace all those who have freely devoted themselves to the observance of God's precepts, that they may be joined to the counsel of God and may live perfectly before him in accordance with all that has been revealed concerning their appointed times, and that they may *love all the sons of light, each according to his lot in God's design and hate all the sons of darkness, each according to his guilt in God's vengeance.*[46]

In sum, Jesus suggests that the interpretation of both the Law and Prophets should be subject to a hermeneutic of love; indeed the right understanding of the whole OT requires reading it through the lens of God's intent to save not just his chosen people, but also even his enemies, even the ungodly, even the notorious sinners, as Jesus demonstrated by his own ground-breaking praxis. (See how Paul puts it in Rom 5:6–11: "Christ died for the ungodly . . . for the sinners . . . for his enemies.")

The discussion of Jesus and the law as presented in Luke's Gospel is necessarily shorter, as there is less to say. Luke only has about

---

45. Moyise, *Jesus and Scripture*, 38.

46. Emphasis added by me. Here I am simply following the translation used in Moyise's book without emendation.

two-thirds of Mark's Scripture quotations. Notably, he leaves out some of the in-house discussions about the details of the Mosaic law, for example about handwashing, corban, and divorce, which means leaving out Genesis 1:27 and 2:24 and Exodus 20:12 and 21:17 on the lips of Jesus. He does, however, include the temptation scene with Jesus's threefold quoting from Deuteronomy.[47]

More than once, Moyise makes something of Jesus's commanding of the leper to go "as Moses commanded and make an offering for your cleansing" (see Mark 1:39–45 and par.).[48] But this need mean no more than that Jesus was compassionately helping the man get reintegrated into his own village life where matters of purity were of great importance. You don't see Jesus requiring this of his disciples he has healed like, for example, Mary Magdalene. In short, this really isn't much of a clue about how Jesus viewed the law going forward, vis-à-vis the praxis of his own fledgling community.

The story in Luke 14:1–6 depicts Jesus as wanting the law to be interpreted in a merciful manner, including the Sabbath law (cf. Luke 6:36 with Matt 5:48). He is shown to be more merciful than the Qumranites (see CD 11:13–17), who did indeed forbid the rescuing of a child or an animal fallen into a well or a ditch on the Sabbath. This approach to the law comports with Jesus's saying that the whole law depends on a hermeneutic of love for its proper interpretation and that love is the chief commandment. But again, Moyise fails to distinguish between Jesus giving advice within the context of early Judaism to Jews who are not his disciples, and his specific teaching to his disciples on the law.

Of more importance is Luke's framing of a saying about the law that relates the law to John the Baptizer's ministry, Luke 16:16a. This is a Q saying found also in Matthew 11:12–13, in the reverse order, and it may seem at first to be unrelated to what comes before, but actually it explains Jesus's hermeneutics rather well. Jesus comes at all of his ethics, including his views of money and marriage, from a sense of the eschatological moment and situation. John the Baptizer is seen as a watershed figure bringing to a climax the age of the Law and the Prophets (see Luke 24:44 on the phrase), for he is the eschatological Elijah that comes before the end times. What is only implicit in the Matthean form of this material is made explicit in Luke (who is prob-

47. And there is an even more drastic truncation if Luke is using Matthew instead of Q, for what that would mean is that he deliberately leaves out various Scripture citations found in Matthew.

48. Moyise, *Jesus and Scripture*, 52 while discussing Luke's presentation.

ably giving us the later form of this material). Luke says rather clearly that the Law and the Prophets were *until* John,[49] but from that time on, the dominion is preached. In the Lukan scheme of things, John is a transitional figure, with one foot in the old era, bringing it to a close, and one foot in the new, an Elijah figure preparing the way and serving as precursor to the messiah (see Luke 1). This saying makes clear Luke's view of where the ministry of Jesus fits in regard to the issue of the Mosaic covenant and its law. In regard to the eschatological dominion or saving activity of God, now breaking into history through the ministry of Jesus, this has already begun, and the Law and Prophets have been or are being fulfilled in the ministry of Jesus, and can be said to be part of the pre-kingdom period brought to its climax in the ministry of John the Baptizer. But what, then, is meant by the rest of that disturbing saying found in Luke 16:16b, included in different order by both Matthew and Luke?

Does it mean that people are pressing or forcing their way into the dominion, or that, with the preaching, are being pressed and persuaded to enter it?[50] Joseph Fitzmyer, for example, inclines to the latter usage in Luke, drawing an analogy with Luke 14:23.[51] Much depends on whether one takes the verb "to force" (which appears in middle or passive form) as having a more active or a more passive sense. Is the dominion somehow suffering violence? This is possible if one is thinking about the violent reaction to John the Baptizer and his beheading, and possibly the rejection and reactions Jesus is receiving from some, especially as he draws closer to Jerusalem.[52] Are we to see those trying to force their way into the dominion as zealots prepared to use force, or perhaps the crowds that are pressing Jesus at every turn?[53] These are possibilities as well. The "all" referred to here is perhaps crucial, indicating the universal scope of the message: "all are

49. On Luke's use of the preposition μέχρι, see Acts 10:30 and Acts 20:7, esp. the latter text. It denotes a delimitation of a period of time, hence "until."

50. On the latter see Robert C. Tannehill, *Luke*, ANTC (Nashville: Abingdon, 1996), 250.

51. Joseph Fitzmyer, *The Gospel according to Luke: Introduction, Translation, and Notes*, AB 28 (Garden City, NY: Doubleday, 1985), 501.

52. See the discussion in Witherington, *Matthew*, 233–34. Martin Culy, Mikeal C. Parsons, and Joshua J. Stigall, *Luke: A Handbook on the Greek Text*, BHGNT (Waco, TX: Baylor University Press, 2010), 527, rightly cautions against renderings that do not do justice to the semantic field of this word—βιάζω means to employ violence or gain something by force in the active sense, and to have violence done to oneself, in the passive sense. The form βιάζονται could be a middle form with active meaning, or a passive form. The negative connotations of the verb suggest we have a middle verb in this verse.

53. One can compare my discussion of this saying and the Zealots in Ben Witherington III, *The Christology of Jesus* (Minneapolis: Fortress, 1990).

being pressed/compelled to enter" (cf. the parable in Luke 14 of the great banquet, where we have the exhortation "compel them to come in").[54] Perhaps what is more important than figuring out this deliberately enigmatic wisdom saying is that Luke adds verse 17. "Luke is anxious to avoid leaving the impression that the law is either irrelevant or, worse yet, broken."[55]

Actually, what he seems to be anxious about is making clear that though the eschatological time has come, and the era of the Law and Prophets is passing away, this does not mean that a *lawless* time has arrived. It is easier for heaven and earth to pass away than for one stroke of the letter of the law to be simply dropped or dismissed. To the contrary, it is an eschatological time when the Law and Prophets are being fulfilled as the dominion comes in and through Jesus (see, e.g., Luke 24:44). This does not mean a legally easier time, but in fact a time of even more intensified ethical demands.

One passage too often neglected in this discussion is Luke 22:35–38. For our purposes, what is most important is the use of Isaiah 53:12 by Jesus of himself: "and he was counted among the lawless."[56] This is given in the context of telling his disciples to now follow a course opposite to what they did during the ministry—now taking a money bag and a traveling bag, and even selling one's robe and purchasing a sword. But Jesus quotes the Scripture and gives this advice to suggest that he is now among lawless persons, the disciples. This is made clear from v. 37b, where he says of Isaiah 53:12, "yes, what is written about me is coming to its fulfillment." The answer to the question, why would Jesus be counted among the lawless, in the first instance must have to do with his association with these disciples. But perhaps it also is Jesus's way of saying that his ministry was associated with lawlessness, in light of what Jesus says in Luke 16:16a–b. It would not be true, but it would be an understandable critique of Jesus, if he seemed to suggest that he had the authority to declare some parts of the law no longer applicable, or already fulfilled in his ministry, or both.

As Moyise says, none of the quotations found on the lips of Jesus in

---

54. See the full discussion of all the options in Darrell I. Bock, *Luke 9:51–24:53*, BECNT 3B (Grand Rapids: Baker Academic, 1996), 1350–54.

55. Craig A. Evans, *Luke*, NIBCNT (Peabody, MA: Hendrickson, 1990), 244.

56. The term itself does not imply a sinner; see Rom 2:12. A person who is "outside the law" or without the Mosaic law may be a sinner, but he may also be a "righteous gentile" who keeps aspects of the law without knowing it since it is written on his heart and he follows his heart. Were this not the case, Paul's argument in Romans 2 would make no sense.

the Synoptics are also found on his lips in John. Furthermore, none of the distinctive quotations that are found on the lips of Jesus in the Fourth Gospel are from the Law.[57] Nevertheless, it is perhaps important that something be said about John 10:35, where Jesus says "the Scripture cannot be λυθῆναι." We have here the verb λύω, which has a wide range of meanings—"loosed, released, destroyed, broken, annulled, contravened." Here the subject is Scripture itself, not, for example, a particular covenant. The thrust of the saying is that God's word must be true, and it always remains true. No one can show that it's been proved false or contravened. So this saying is not about annulling of covenants, or the impossibility of such an annulment or replacement. The earliest followers of Jesus certainly believed that the Law, Prophets, and Writings remained true Scripture, even throughout the comings and goings of multiple covenant administrations and arrangements. It was true and valuable for teaching to followers of Christ (2 Tim 3:16). Perhaps of even greater interest is that Jesus, in this very same context, while strongly affirming the Hebrew Scriptures as God's word, also speaks of "*your law*" (ἐν τῷ νόμῳ ὑμῶν) in the immediately preceding verse. I would suggest this is no accident, nor is it a reflection of later anti-Semitism on the part of a Christian writer. Jesus speaks of "your law," because he believes the Mosaic law and its covenant have been and are coming to fulfillment and completion in himself. The word of God endures forever, but the Mosaic covenant and its law do not, because the kingdom is dawning!

If, in conclusion, we ask about the overall impression of Jesus's use of Scripture, two main things need to be said. As Moyise points out, it is next to impossible to believe that both early Jews and the earliest followers of Jesus followed the practice of citing Scripture to support their arguments and stories, *but that Jesus did not.* In other words, minimalists like Géza Vermes or J. D. Crossan are likely quite wrong in their attempts to minimize Jesus's knowledge of and use of Scripture.[58] Second, all layers of the Gospel tradition, Mark, Q, special M, special L, and John are in agreement that Jesus on occasion referred the Scriptures *to himself,* or suggested they were being fulfilled in his ministry, his words, and his deeds. Again, this involves such a broad example of multiple attestation of an idea that it is hard to doubt it is correct, however much the Gospel traditions have amplified or expanded upon this fact. Third, Moyise's attempt to minimize the

---

57. Moyise, *Jesus and Scripture*, 67.
58. See Moyise, *Jesus and Scripture*, 121.

scandal of the way that Jesus sometimes interpreted Scripture—to testify *against* some of the Mosaic laws—does not work. What Jesus had to say about the Sabbath, about the purity laws, about violence, about oaths, and about marriage and divorce shows that he was not afraid to suggest that the law itself, not merely the interpretation of the law, needed to be changed. Hardness of heart would no longer be allowed as a mitigating factor permitting divorce, oaths, violence, and so on. Jesus was a radical Jew, and part and parcel of this is the way he interpreted the Mosaic covenant and its law, while still accepting that all the Scriptures were God's word.[59]

It is noteworthy that the Gospels depict Jesus as using the Pentateuch, especially Genesis and Deuteronomy, more often than other OT books, except for the Psalms and Isaiah. Moyise notes the following examples of the Pentateuch found on Jesus's lips:

Genesis
1:27: Matthew 19:4; Mark10:6
2:24: Matthew 19:5; Mark 10:7 (also cited elsewhere in the NT)
5:2: Matthew 19:5; Mark 10:6

Exodus
3:6: Matthew 22:32; Mark 12:26; Luke 20:37 (also elsewhere in the NT)
12:46: John 19:36
20:12–16: Matthew 19:18–19; Mark 10:19; Luke 18:20
20:12: Matthew 15:4; Mark 7:10 (also cited elsewhere in the NT)
20:13: Matthew 5:21 (also cited elsewhere in the NT)
21:17: Matthew 15:4; Mark 7:10
21:24: Matthew 5:38

Leviticus
19:12: Matthew 5:33
19:18: Matthew 5:43; 19:19; 22:39; Mark 12:31, 33; Luke 10:27 (also
    found elsewhere in the NT)
24:20: Matthew 5:38

Numbers
30:2: Matthew 5:33

Deuteronomy
5:16: Matthew 15:4; Mark 7:10 (also found elsewhere in the NT)
5:17: Matthew 5:21 (also found elsewhere in the NT)
5:18: Matthew 5:27

59. See at length Witherington, *Christology of Jesus*.

6:4–5: Mark 12:29–30
6:5: Matthew 22:37; Mark 12:30, 33; Luke 10:27
6:13: Matthew 4:10; Luke 4:8
6:16: Matthew 4:7; Luke 4:12
8:3: Matthew 4:4; Luke 4:4
19:15: Matthew 18:16 (also found elsewhere in the NT)
19:21: Matthew 5:38
24:1–3: Matthew 5:31; 19:7; Mark 10:4[60]

This list provides further confirmation for some of what we have already noted, along with a few new insights: (1) the earliest Gospels, Mark and Matthew, provides us with the most examples of Jesus citing the Scriptures from the Pentateuch; (2) there are progressively fewer such citations as we move to Luke, and finally to John, where there is barely one; (3) the most often cited Pentateuch verse is Leviticus 19:18, about loving your neighbor; (4) there are only a few examples of an OT citation found in the triple tradition (i.e., in all three Synoptics). We will have occasion to say more about Jesus's use of "the law" as the study progresses, but what we have pointed out so far needs to be borne in mind as we turn to OT exegesis and the NT use of Pentateuchal texts.

---

60. Moyise, *Jesus and Scripture*, 122.

2.

The Genesis of It All

Archbishop James Usher (1580–1656) published *Annales Veteris et Novi Testamenti* in 1654, which suggested that the Heaven and the Earth were created in 4004 B.C. One of his aides took the calculation further, and was able to announce triumphantly that the Earth was created on Sunday the 21st of October, 4004 B.C., at exactly 9.00 a.m., because God liked to get work done early in the morning while he was feeling fresh. This too was incorrect, by almost a quarter of an hour.

—Terry Pratchett and Neil Gaiman[1]

Genesis has been called the Old Testament of the Old Testament, because of its distinctiveness from the rest of the OT, including even the rest of the Pentateuch.[2] While "Exodus—Deuteronomy narrate the seminal events surrounding the birth of the Israelite people and these events are all framed within the 120-year lifetime of Moses, by far the most important character in the Pentateuch," Moses is nowhere to be found in Genesis.[3] "Some have even called Torah a biography of Moses," but even so, it has a long prequel about his predecessors.[4] Whether it is the story of Adam and then the patriarchs, or

1. Terry Pratchett and Neil Gaiman, *Good Omens: The Nice and Accurate Prophecies of Agnes Nutter, Witch* (New York: Harper, 2006).

2. R. W. L. Moberly, *The Old Testament of the Old Testament: Patriarchal Narratives and Mosaic Yahwism*, OBT (Minneapolis: Fortress, 1992).

3. Joel S. Kaminsky, "The Theology of Genesis," in *The Book of Genesis: Composition, Reception, and Interpretation*, ed. Craig A Evans, Joel N Lohr, and David L Petersen, VTSup 152 (Leiden: Brill, 2012), 635.

4. Kaminsky, "Theology of Genesis," 635.

the story of Moses, there is a lot of narrative in the Pentateuch, apart from Leviticus, of course.

Thus, one of the things that necessarily must distinguish this third volume in this series from the previous two (*Isaiah Old and New* and *Psalms Old and New*) is that we must come to grips with narrative, and the narrative thought-world of the relevant portions of the OT that come up for quotation, allusion, or echo in the NT. It is not really possible to make sense, for example, of what Paul says about Adam or Abraham unless one has a clear sense of the nature and content and import of those stories for the OT itself. The long arc of the story of creation, human sin, and alienation from God, and of God's various acts of redemption and restoration, provides the framework out of which particular OT narratives are drawn on by Jesus and the writers of the NT. As Craig A. Evans puts it: "Genesis is foundational to several major New Testament doctrines, including creation, the fall of humankind, and the covenant with Abraham and his descendants."[5]

In short, the OT narratives must be read forward and in their own contexts, to make sense of how they are read "backward" in light of the coming of the dominion of God, and of Christ thereafter. An exegetically insightful reading of these stories in their own OT settings, then, is an essential prerequisite to dealing with the quotes, allusions, and echoes of the same material in the NT. With OT law itself, context is still important as well, but to a different degree and in a different way, especially when law and narrative are intertwined as they are, for example, in Exodus or Deuteronomy. We must necessarily begin with the discussion of the creation of humanity in Genesis and work forward from there.

One of the more interesting observations that can be made from the outset is that while a prophecy, or the poetry of the Psalms, or even laws may be carefully quoted in the NT, often with citation formulas of various sorts to indicate a quotation is involved, narrative material, on the other hand, is seldom directly quoted, nor are citation formulas regularly used to introduce the quotation. Rather stories tend to be summarized or paraphrased, and so recycled for other purposes and contexts. Thus, we should not be surprised to hear that "approximately thirty verses of Genesis are quoted in the New Testament," but there are more than two hundred uses of material from

---

5. Craig A. Evans, "Genesis in the New Testament" in Evans, *Book of Genesis*, 469.

THE GENESIS OF IT ALL 37

that book in the NT.[6] *Quotations* are but the tip of the iceberg, and more often than not the material is being drawn on as the true back-story to what the author wants to say now about Jesus, his followers, and other relevant topics. Menken and Moyise are right in stressing

> Genesis is functioning in the New Testament more as a *narrative* than as a *text*. In this respect Genesis, largely consisting of stories, differs from prophetic or legal Old Testament books. In the latter case, precise wordings are important, in the former, actors and story lines primarily count. The narrative character of Genesis also explains why the book has strongly influenced the New Testament but is rarely cited in it. More-over, when quotations from Genesis occur, they are in many cases from words spoken by God as a character in the narrative.[7]

Primarily it is the LXX form of the Genesis tradition that is cited or drawn upon in the NT.[8] Because all of the above is true, it will prove less necessary, and in some cases unnecessary, in this volume to cite both the MT and LXX texts when dealing with narrative material, as it is not being quoted directly, but rather mainly alluded to or presup-posed. Nevertheless, the creation of humanity stories proves so cru-cial, and bits of the story are quoted, so we will present them in both versions so we can assess which version is likely being followed in the NT. Here and throughout, I rely on the NIV translation of the Hebrew Masoretic Text (MT) and, for the LXX, on the *NETS*.

---

6. Menken and Moyise, *Genesis in the New Testament*, 1. They list the cited verses as Gen 1:27; 2:2, 7, 24; 12:1, 3; 14:17–20; 15:5, 6, 13–14; 17:5, 8, 10; 18:10, 14, 18; 21:10, 12; 22:16, 17, 18. What this list indicates is that the stories of creation and of Abraham were especially crucial to NT writers and were cited in various ways. Also cited are bits from the story of Isaac (21:10, 12; 22:16–17, 18; 26:4), one verse from the Enoch story (5:24), one verse from the story of Esau and Jacob (25:23), two verses about Jacob (28:12; 47:31), and one about Jacob and Joseph (48:4). The longest salvation history review in Acts, in the speech of Stephen in Acts 7, begins with Abraham and continues on to David, but gives extended treatment to Moses. Compare that to the review in Hebrews 11 that begins with Cain and Abel, gives extended treatment to Abraham and Moses, but mentions only in passing the stories found in Joshua, Judges, and the monarchial period. Elsewhere in the NT, we usually have single story focus, for instance the story of the Exodus and its aftermath in 1 Corinthians 10 or the story of Melchizedek and Abraham that comes up for extended commentary in Hebrews 5 and 7.

7. Menken and Moyise, *Genesis in the New Testament*, 5 (emphasis original).

8. On the text of Genesis in the LXX/OG and the sort of translation issues they faced see Robert J. V. Hiebert, "Textual and Translation Issues in Greek Genesis," in Evans, *Book of Genesis*, 405–26, and in more detail J. W. Wevers, *Text History of the Greek Genesis*, MSU 11 (Göttingen: Vandenhoeck & Ruprecht, 1974).

ADAM AND EVE: THE END AND ENDS OF CREATION

MT

26 Then God said, "Let us make humankind in our image, in our likeness, so that they may rules over the fish in the sea and the birds in the sky, over the livestock and all the wild animals, and over all the creatures that move along the ground."
27 So God created mankind in his own image, in the image of God, he created them; male and female, he created them.
28 God blessed them and said to them, "Be fruitful and increase in number; fill the earth and subdue it. Rule over the fish in the sea and the birds in the sky and over every living creature that moves on the ground."

29 Then God said, "I give you every seed-bearing plant on the face of the whole earth and every tree that has fruit with seed in it. They will be yours for food.
30 And to all the beasts of the earth and all the birds in the sky and all the creatures that move along the ground—everything that has the breath of life in it—I give every green plant for food." And it was so.
31 God saw all that he had made, and it was very good. And there was evening, and there was morning—the sixth day.
2:1 Thus the heavens and the earth were completed in all their vast array.
2 By the seventh day God had finished the work he had been doing; so on the seventh day he rested from all his work.

3 Then God blessed the seventh day and made it holy, because on it he rested from all the work of creating that he had done.

LXX

26 Then God said, "Let us make humankind according to our image and according to likeness, and let them rule the fish of the sea and the birds of the sky and the cattle and all the earth and all the creeping things that creep upon the earth."
27 And God made humankind; according to divine image he made it; male and female he made them.
28 And God blessed them, saying, "Increase, and multiply, and fill the earth, and subdue it, and rule the fish of the sea and the birds of the sky and all the cattle and all the earth and all the creeping things that creep upon the earth."
29 And God said, "See, I have given to you any herbage, sowable, seeding seed which is over all the earth, and any tree that has in itself fruit of sowable seed—to you it shall be for food—
30 and to all the wild animals of the earth and to all the birds of the sky and to every creeping thing that creeps on the earth that has in itself the animating force of life, and all green herbage for food." And it became so.
31 And God saw all the things that he had made, and see, they were exceedingly good. And it came to be evening, and it came to be morning, a sixth day.
2:1 And the sky and the earth were finished, and all their arrangement.
2 And on the sixth day God finished his works that he had made, And he left off on the seventh day from all his works that he had made.
3 And God blessed the seventh day and hallowed it, because on it he left off from all his works that God had begun to make.

Not least, because the creation of humanity story comes up in *crucial* places in the teachings of Jesus and Paul and the author of Hebrews and elsewhere, it is important that we review exegetically some of the material at the beginning of Genesis, starting with the first creation account about human beings, at Genesis existed. I agree, however, that the 1:26.[9] Verse 26 begins the climax of God's creative work, the creation of human beings. The term *'adam*, which here means "earth creature," is a generic and collective term referring to a kind or group, not an individual, as is clear from what follows ("male and female he created *them*"). The reference to "them" also makes clear that the author does not have some sort of androgynous individual in mind in the first place. Only later in the narrative does *'adam* become a name for a particular male individual.

As Bill Arnold stresses, here we have a different sort of divine speech than previously in the chapter. Note that the text says, "let us make," whereas before God has simply spoken things into existence. This "us" and "our" (the plural is present even in the verb) may refer either to: (1) a plural of fullness, that is, God is the equivalent of many and is simply deliberating with himself;[10] (2) a plural of majesty, that is, a royal we as human kings sometimes use; (3) a reference to the heavenly court, that is, God is consulting with the angels;[11] or (4) in later Christian thought, the plural verb was read as a reference to the Trinity. On the basis of OT usage of "we" as applied to God, (2) or (3) is most likely here (1 Kgs 22:19–20; Job 1; Dan 7:10). If (3) is the correct view, as Franz Delitzsch argued, then humans are created in the image of God and angels, and we will have to ask in what sense that is so. The text implies the equality of male and female as in the image of God but the text rules out an androgynous first human. Humanity is made male *and* female, not male-female together. The first creature created is simply male, the female is made out of parts of the first creature.

We must next ask about the meaning of the phrase "image of God" or "likeness of God." Two different Hebrew words, *tselem* and *damuth*, correspond to these two English words. The former can mean either "original image" or "imitation," while the latter means

---

9. See below in the Lexicon of Faith section at the end of this chapter for discussion of things like the echoes of the earlier parts of the creation stories in Gen 1–2.

10. See Bill T. Arnold, *Genesis*, NCBC (Cambridge: Cambridge University Press, 2009), 44.

11. See Claus Westermann, *Genesis 1–11* (Minneapolis: Augsburg, 1984), 144–45; and Gordon J. Wenham, *Genesis 1–15*, WBC (Waco, TX: Word, 1987), 27–28.

"likeness or resemblance." There seems to be little significant difference in meaning between the two words; both refer to a physical resemblance in various contexts, but that is unlikely here. It may be important that *tselem* is also the word used for "idol," so perhaps the author is saying that human beings are God's "idols" on earth, so images of lesser things like animals are inappropriate.[12] Idols were used in worship, and only God should be worshiped, according to our author. Presumably images of animals, like say cave paintings not used for the purpose of worship did not fall under the category of idols. We may note that it is said humans are created *in* the image, not *with* the image, as if it could be assigned to some particular part of a person, in other words, his or her form or "soul." Some have suggested that the image consists in our dominion over the rest of the creatures; however, as Delitzsch said, this dominion is the consequence of being in the image, not its content.

Perhaps the clue is in the phrase "let us make," if this is a reference to the heavenly court. In what regard are we like angels? We share a capacity for relationship with God of a special kind that animals do not have. Because of the image, humankind is not only the representation of God on earth but also his representative, meant to remind all of God's dominion, just as a carved image on a statue or on a coin was intended to indicate who was then ruling. We represent God's presence to and rule over the world. So serious a matter is it to be created in God's image that God takes an attack on his image-bearer as an attack on himself (note the Cain and Abel story). In ANE literature the king is said to bear the image of the deity he serves, and to rule on his behalf, but here it is not just one person who bears the image but humankind in general, so it is not clear that this parallel provides a clue to the content of the image humans bear.[13]

Being in the image of God not only implies a special relationship to God, but also requires of humans a special respect for all other human beings, who are equally image bearers, no matter how badly marred by sin that image may be. Humanity as image is then called to the task of stamping God's impression upon the rest of creation (Ps 8). The word in v. 28 translated "subdue," *kabats*, is a very strong one. Humans are to govern so as to leave a lasting impression on creation,

12. On this point see Sandra L. Richter, *The Epic of Eden: A Christian Entry into the Old Testament* (Downers Grove, IL: InterVarsity, 2008).

13. See the discussion of this much-debated question in J. Richard Middleton, *The Liberating Image: The Imago Dei in Genesis 1* (Grand Rapids: Brazos, 2005).

THE GENESIS OF IT ALL   41

not for their own sake, but for God's glory. Unfortunately, a human being strives as a fallen creature to make his mark for himself, and not for God, and thus perverts the task of representation and being the representative of God. Genesis 1:31 proclaims not merely that what God had made was good, but that what God made in its completion was *tov me'od* or exceedingly good. Gerhard von Rad suggests the translation "completely perfect," just as God designed and planned it.[14] This implies that evil or its consequences were no part of God's creation or plan. God is not the maker or author of evil or evil inclinations or tendencies, much less the author of sin. We will discuss this more in a moment when we turn to Genesis 2:4–3:24.

Genesis 1:26–2:3 concludes with God ceasing from his creation activity. The term so often translated "rested" means "ceased" (*shabbat*, from which we get the words Sabbath and sabbatical). The stress here is on both the absence of activity (though no implication of fatigue is involved) and the presence of satisfaction and joy, since the work was completed and the job was well done. Notice here that there is no concluding, "and there was evening and morning, a seventh day," as on previous days. This is intentional. The seventh day goes on; God continues to be at rest from his *initial* work of creation. This cessation does not imply God is bowing out gracefully and leaving the scene. Quite the opposite. His task of providential governing and intervening for his people begins when the creative task ends. He does not withdraw or take away his interests, his involvement, his governing, his relating, or his helping. As we shall see, this is critical to humanity's ongoing survival.

THE CREATION OF HUMANITY REDUX
(GENESIS 2:4–3:24)

MT	LXX
[4] These are the generations of the heavens and the earth when they were created. In the day that the LORD God made the earth and the heavens, [5] when no plant of the field was yet in the earth and no herb of the field had	[4] This is the book of the origin of heaven and earth, when it originated, on the day that God made the sky and the earth [5] and all verdure of the field before it came to be upon the earth and all herbage of the field before it sprang up,

---

14. Gerhard von Rad, *Genesis: A Commentary*, trans. John H. Marks, OTL (Philadelphia: Westminster, 1961), 61.

yet sprung up—for the LORD God had not caused it to rain upon the earth, and there was no one to till the ground;

⁶ but a stream would rise from the earth, and water the whole face of the ground—

⁷ then the LORD God formed man from the dust of the ground, and breathed into his nostrils the breath of life; and the man became a living being.

⁸ And the LORD God planted a garden in Eden, in the east; and there he put the man whom he had formed.

⁹ Out of the ground the LORD God made to grow every tree that is pleasant to the sight and good for food, the tree of life also in the midst of the garden, and the tree of the knowledge of good and evil.

¹⁰ A river flows out of Eden to water the garden, and from there it divides and becomes four branches.

¹¹ The name of the first is Pishon; it is the one that flows around the whole land of Havilah, where there is gold;

¹² and the gold of that land is good; bdellium and onyx stone are there.

¹³ The name of the second river is Gihon; it is the one that flows around the whole land of Cush.

¹⁴ The name of the third river is Tigris, which flows east of Assyria. And the fourth river is the Euphrates.

¹⁵ The LORD God took the man and put him in the garden of Eden to till it and keep it.

¹⁶ And the LORD God commanded the man, "You may freely eat of every tree of the garden;

¹⁷ but of the tree of the knowledge of good and evil you shall not eat, for in the day that you eat of it you shall die."

¹⁸ Then the LORD God said, "It is not good that the man should be alone; I will make him a helper as his partner."

¹⁹ So out of the ground the LORD God formed every animal of the field and every bird of the air, and brought them to the man to see what he would call them; and whatever the man called

for God had not sent rain upon the earth, and there was not a human to till the earth,

⁶ yet a spring would rise from the earth and water the whole face of the earth.

⁷ And God formed man, dust from the earth, and breathed into his face a breath of life, and the man became a living being.

⁸ And the Lord God planted An orchard in Eden toward the east, and there he put the man whom he had formed.

⁹ And out of the earth God furthermore made to grow every tree that is beautiful to the sight and good for food, the tree of life also in the orchard's midst and the tree for knowing what is knowable of good and evil.

¹⁰ Now a river goes out of Eden to water the orchard; from there it divides into four sources.

¹¹ The name of the one is Phison; it is the one that encircles the whole land of Heuilat, there where the gold is;

¹² now the gold of that land is good, and carbuncle and light green stone are there.

¹³ And the second river's name is Geon; it is the one that encircles the whole land of Ethiopia.

¹⁴ And the third river is the Tigris; it is the one that goes over against the Assyrians. As for the fourth river, it is the Euphrates.

¹⁵ And the Lord God took the man whom he had formed and put him in the orchard to till and keep it.

¹⁶ And the Lord God commanded Adam, saying, "You shall eat for food of every tree that is in the orchard,

¹⁷ but of the tree for knowing good and evil, of it you shall not eat; on the day that you eat of it, you shall die by death."

¹⁸ Then the Lord God said, "It is not good that the man is alone; let us make him a helper corresponding to him."

¹⁹ And out of the earth God furthermore formed all the animals of the field and all the birds of the sky and brought them to Adam to see what he would call them, and anything, whatever Adam

every living creature, that was its name.

20 The man gave names to all cattle, and to the birds of the air, and to every animal of the field; but for the man there was not found a helper as his partner.
21 So the LORD God caused a deep sleep to fall upon the man, and he slept; then he took one of his ribs and closed up its place with flesh.
22 And the rib that the LORD God had taken from the man he made into a woman and brought her to the man.
23 Then the man said, "This at last is bone of my bones and flesh of my flesh; this one shall be called Woman, for out of Man this one was taken."
24 Therefore a man leaves his father and his mother and clings to his wife, and they become one flesh.

25 And the man and his wife were both naked, and were not ashamed.

3:1 Now the serpent was more crafty than any other wild animal that the LORD God had made. He said to the woman, "Did God say, 'You shall not eat from any tree in the garden'?"

2 The woman said to the serpent, "We may eat of the fruit of the trees in the garden;
3 but God said, 'You shall not eat of the fruit of the tree that is in the middle of the garden, nor shall you touch it, or you shall die.'"
4 But the serpent said to the woman, "You will not die;
5 for God knows that when you eat of it your eyes will be opened, and you will be like God, knowing good and evil."
6 So when the woman saw that the tree was good for food, and that it was a delight to the eyes, and that the tree was to be desired to make one wise, she took of its fruit and ate; and she also gave some to her husband, who was with her, and he ate.
7 Then the eyes of both were opened, and they knew that they were naked;

called it as living creature, this was its name.
20 And Adam gave names to all the cattle and to all the birds of the sky and to all the animals of the field, but for Adam there was not found a helper like him.
21 And God cast a trance upon Adam, and he slept, and he took one of his ribs and filled up flesh in its place.
22 And the rib that he had taken from Adam the Lord God fashioned into a woman and brought her to Adam.
23 And Adam said, "This now is bone of my bones and flesh of my flesh; this one shall be called Woman, for out of her husband she was taken."

24 Therefore, a man will leave his father and mother and will be joined to his wife, and the two will become one flesh.
25 And the two were naked, both Adam and his wife, and were not ashamed.
3:1 Now the snake was the most sagacious of all the wild animals that were upon the earth, which the Lord God had made. And the snake said to the woman, "Why is it that God said, 'You shall not eat from any tree that is in the orchard'?"
2 And the woman said to the snake, "We shall eat of the fruit of the tree of the orchard,
3 but of the fruit of the tree that is in the middle of the orchard, God said, 'You shall not eat of it nor shall you even touch it, lest you die.'"
4 And the snake said to the woman, "You will not die by death,
5 for God knew that on the day you eat of it, your eyes would be opened, and you would be like gods knowing good and evil."
6 And the woman saw that the tree was good for food and that it was pleasing for the eyes to look at and it was beautiful to contemplate, and when she had taken of its fruit she ate, and she also gave some to her husband with her, and they ate.
7 And the eyes of the two were opened, and they knew that they were

and they sewed fig leaves together and made loincloths for themselves.

⁸ They heard the sound of the LORD God walking in the garden at the time of the evening breeze, and the man and his wife hid themselves from the presence of the Lord God among the trees of the garden.

⁹ But the LORD God called to the man, and said to him, "Where are you?"

¹⁰ He said, "I heard the sound of you in the garden, and I was afraid, because I was naked; and I hid myself."

¹¹ He said, "Who told you that you were naked? Have you eaten from the tree of which I commanded you not to eat?"

¹² The man said, "The woman whom you gave to be with me, she gave me fruit from the tree, and I ate."

¹³ Then the LORD God said to the woman, "What is this that you have done?" The woman said, "The serpent tricked me, and I ate."

¹⁴ The LORD God said to the serpent, "Because you have done this, cursed are you among all animals and among all wild creatures; upon your belly you shall go, and dust you shall eat all the days of your life.

¹⁵ I will put enmity between you and the woman, and between your offspring and hers; he will strike your head, and you will strike his heel."

¹⁶ To the woman he said, "I will greatly increase your pangs in childbearing; in pain you shall bring forth children, yet your desire shall be for your husband, and he shall rule over you."

¹⁷ And to the man he said, "Because you have listened to the voice of your wife, and have eaten of the tree about which I commanded you, 'You shall not eat of it,' cursed is the ground because of you; in toil you shall eat of it all the days of your life;

¹⁸ thorns and thistles it shall bring forth for you; and you shall eat the plants of the field.

naked, and they sewed fig leaves together and made loincloths for themselves.

⁸ And they heard the sound of the Lord God walking about in the orchard in the evening, and both Adam and his wife hid themselves from the presence of the Lord God in the midst of the timber of the orchard.

⁹ And the Lord God called Adam and said to him, "Adam, where are you?"

¹⁰ And he said to him, "I heard the sound of you walking about in the orchard, and I was afraid, because I am naked, and I hid myself."

¹¹ And he said to him, "Who told you that you are naked, unless you have eaten from the tree of which I commanded you, of this one alone, not to eat from it?"

¹² And Adam said, "The woman, whom you gave to be with me, she gave me of the tree, and I ate."

¹³ And God said to the woman, "What is this you have done?" And the woman said, "The snake tricked me, and I ate."

¹⁴ And the Lord God said to the snake, "Because you have done this, cursed are you from all the domestic animals and from all the wild animals of the earth; upon your chest and belly you shall go, and earth you shall eat all the days of your life.

¹⁵ And I will put enmity between you and between the woman and between your offspring and between her offspring; he will watch your head, and you will watch his heel."

¹⁶ And to the woman he said, "I will increasingly increase your pains and your groaning; with pains you will bring forth children. And your recourse will be to your husband, and he will dominate you."

¹⁷ Then to Adam he said, "Because you have listened to the voice of your wife and have eaten from the tree of which I commanded you, of this one alone, not to eat from it, cursed is the earth in your labors; with pains you will eat it all the days of your life;

¹⁸ thorns and thistles it shall cause to grow up for you, and you will eat the herbage of the field.

19 By the sweat of your face you shall eat bread until you return to the ground, for out of it you were taken; you are dust, and to dust you shall return."

20 The man named his wife Eve, because she was the mother of all living.

21 And the LORD God made garments of skins for the man and for his wife, and clothed them.

22 Then the LORD God said, "See, the man has become like one of us, knowing good and evil; and now, he might reach out his hand and take also from the tree of life, and eat, and live forever"—

23 therefore the LORD God sent him forth from the garden of Eden, to till the ground from which he was taken.

24 He drove out the man; and at the east of the garden of Eden he placed the cherubim, and a sword flaming and turning to guard the way to the tree of life.

19 By the sweat of your face you will eat your bread until you return to the earth from which you were taken, for you are earth and to earth you will depart."

20 And Adam called the name of his wife Life, because she is the mother of all the living.

21 And the Lord God made leather tunics for Adam and for his wife and clothed them.

22 Then God said, "See, Adam has become like one of us, knowing good and evil, and now perhaps he might reach out his hand and take of the tree of life and eat, and he will live forever."

23 And the Lord God sent him forth from the orchard of delight to till the earth from which he was taken.

24 And he drove Adam out and caused him to dwell opposite the orchard of delight, and he stationed the cherubim and the flaming sword that turns, to guard the way of the tree of life.

When we arrive at Genesis 2:4—3:24 we arrive in a different world.[15] The *toledoth* formula in v. 2:4 refers to the "story" or "account" or possibly "offspring (generations)" of the heavens and earth. This is the only time this formula is used to introduce the *generation* of an object rather than a person. The purpose of the formula seems to be to link this older account of human creation in 2:4—3:24 to the previous account.[16] We are about to be told what came forth from the

15. Here is not the place to debate theories of sources (e.g., J, E, P, and D) in regard to the composition of Genesis. Suffice it to say that the character of this story is different enough from the material in Genesis 1 to warrant the conclusion that at least two sources have been drawn on to create this opening to the Bible. As it stands, from the hands of the final editor, the intent seems to be to have the more generic account of all of creation given first, and then an expanded account of the creation of humanity explaining that part of the story in more detail, second. Notice that David Carr's recent study *The Formation of the Hebrew Bible* (Oxford: Oxford University Press, 2011) provides actual historical evidence of ANE scribes and how they worked, how they revised existing traditions and transmitted texts, compared with what we find in the OT. Carr finds clear evidence of preexilic texts within the corpus of the OT dating at least as early as the tenth century BCE and the early monarchy. This whole, more historical methodology is far more useful than source criticism based exclusively on stylistic considerations that ignores possible historical parallels about how scribes operated in that era. For recent discussion on the composition of Genesis, see e.g., Konrad Schmid, "Genesis in the Pentateuch," in Evans, *Book of Genesis*, 27–50; and J. C. Geertz, "The Formation of the Primeval History," in Evans, *Book of Genesis*, 107–35.

16. See Arnold, *Genesis*, 55–56. This older account in vv. 2.4ff. introduces a new designation

earth. The account that follows has often been called a second creation story, and, in a sense, it is. Its focus, however, is not on all of creation but on special creation, the creation of humankind from the dust of the ground. It is not really a duplication or replacement or correction of Genesis 1 but an expansion and explanation of Genesis 1:26–27. It is entirely possible that this narrative was derived from a source other than Genesis 1, and a host of stylistic and content differences suggest this. The structure in Genesis 2 is less poetic than Genesis 1 (though there is some poetic vocabulary), perhaps because it is connected with the history that follows, which suggests the author wishes us to take this narrative as history of some sort.

Here we see humanity's close relationship to the earth. The text plays on the relationship between the term 'adam and 'adamah, and the latter means "earth." Thus, Adam means earth creature until later it is treated as a proper name. In Genesis 1, humanity is distinguished from all the rest of creation in a proper way. Here we see humanity's points of identification with creation and it is tasked to tend the garden (v. 15). Note that we have the beginning of God's special people, and the concern is to show how God had a chosen one or ones from the beginning. This focus on the chosen line almost to the exclusion of all else explains not only the use of Yahweh in this story (God's personal name by which his people knew him) but also why there is no attempt to explain such mystifying questions as where all the rest of humanity came from outside the garden. The author would seem to suggest that God created them as well (cf. the wives of Cain and Abel), but the focus in the story is on the origins of God's people, *not all peoples*. Now we are prepared to examine Genesis 2:4–24 in detail.

From the start, we note that this narrative appears to be presented as a historical account by the author, hence a saga or legend from hoary antiquity, not a creation myth. Thus, Eden is perhaps seen as a country, though the word means "delight" or "paradise" (the English term comes from the LXX). Here Eden is located in the East, and from what follows about the rivers, we are to think of a place either in the Armenian mountains or above the Persian Gulf, in the area of the Fertile Crescent, according to some scholars.[17] The mention of the Tigris and Euphrates clearly locates this place in space and time.

for God in 2.4a: "'the Lord God'" (*Yahweh Elohim*). This connects the God of the ancestors in Genesis 12–36 with the God of Moses to whom God's personal name was revealed. The God of creation is also the God who made covenant with Israel.

17. Derek Kidner, *Genesis: An Introduction and Commentary*, TOTC (Downers Grove, IL: InterVarsity, 2008), 64.

Eden is usually thought of as a garden; *gan*, however, can mean a park or orchard with trees, and while Paradise is originally a Persian word referring to a nobleman's park, *gan* is good Hebrew. The implication is that humanity is getting the royal treatment by God.

God forms 'adam from the ground and gives him the "kiss of life," breathing into his nostrils, as the text says. Humanity is living dust, a true miracle. There is no body-soul dualism in this creation, but body-life dualism.[18] Humanity is distinguished from animals not by being a living being (*nephesh khayah*, cf. Gen 1:21, 24, 30) but by being creatures that can relate to God freely and freely choose to respond to God's will and word. The capacity of special relationship and the power of moral choice set humanity apart, as the story makes clear by what follows.

Two trees are planted in the middle of the garden: one that could lead to everlasting life, the other to death (whether physical or spiritual or both is not made clear). It seems to be implied that Adam was *not* immortal by nature, but that this gift was available to him for the taking. God said he *could* even eat of the tree of life, but not of the tree of the knowledge of good and evil. It is possible as well that the author views Adam and Eve, while vulnerable to being killed, as not inherently, due to their very nature, mortal.

In any case, knowledge (*yada*) here likely implies not mere intellectual knowledge, but the experience of the gamut of good and evil; that is, what the serpent offers. Clearly, God has already defined what is wrong for humankind. Not knowledge itself, but presuming to be the captain of one's own fate, doing what is right in one's own eyes, is at issue here. God's word has defined one thing that is wrong, eating of the tree that leads to death. The experience of all evil or even the knowledge of it (the wages of sin) leads only to death. Note that God did not make evil; it is not a tangible thing. God, of course, knows all that is good and evil, yet God is not tempted or tainted thereby.

God has provided everything humankind needs: a supportive environment, readily available food, a meaningful job of tilling the soil and tending the garden, and a relationship with God. All 'adam lacks is a mate. (Now the Hebrew name refers to the male individual.)

---

18. Arnold, *Genesis*, 58 stresses that *nephesh khayah* refers to the totality of the person. The problem with this explanation is there was already a body formed by God the potter, a body that was not a *nephesh khayah* and it is only when God breathed into that form that a living being existed. I agree, however, that the author is not referring here to the later concept of the "soul."

The "naming of the animals" story indicates that humankind is given power and authority over them. In Hebrew culture, to name is to define, to order, to organize, and not merely to label. Biblical names normally connote something about the nature of the one named. Verse 20b appears to imply that in this process of examining the animal world, 'adam was also looking for a mate. It indicates how close 'adam is to the animals that he would look among them. But, though animals are living beings, they are not to be one with humankind. Only woman is bone of his bone and flesh of his flesh; no animal bears that intimacy and kinship with humanity. God formed them separately.[19]

We must also go on to add that there is no idea of an androgynous Adam in *this* creation story either. Woman is not taken out of man. Rather, she is built up out of a part of him. Adam was looking for his female companion, and she was not simply the other half of his own nature. If man is 'ish in Hebrew, woman is 'ishah, the one who comes out of man. However, as we shall see, calling the woman 'ishah is not giving her a personal name, like later in 3:20, after the fall, when man tries to take control. Adam's exclamation here is not a naming ritual, and so an asserting of authority over the woman but a cry of joy, on finally finding the one for whom you are looking. The key phrase is important here: "it is not good for *man* to be alone," something not said of the woman.

'Adam was made for relationship with God, but also with fellow humans. Adam is made to be a social, not a solitary creature. Indeed, only so can he survive. The phrase goes on, "I will make a helper or companion suitable for (corresponding to) him." Here we should not translate "helpmate." The old King James translation "helpmeet" does not mean a help mate but rather a helper who is "meet," that is, suitable for the task. Woman is not man's maid, nor merely his assistant, but a "suitable companion," corresponding to him. She is the crown of creation, God's last act that makes it all very good.

Woman is just like man in that she shares the same nature ("bone of my bone") and the same capacity for relationship with God. She is also different, a complement that completes human creation, not a duplicate that is redundant. The Hebrew phrase kenegedo implies both similarity (correspondence) and supplementariness. Woman is the mirror in which man recognizes himself for who he truly is, a

19. See the discussion of Venema and McKnight, *Adam and the Genome* in Appendix 2.

special creature made for special relating. It should be stressed that the Hebrew here for "helper" or "companion" is also used of Yahweh himself in the OT as a helper of God's people, so subordination is *not* implied in the use of that term here.[20] As Arnold notes, Adam's "at last" suggests he has been looking among the animals for a mate, and not finding one until Eve appears on the scene.[21]

Various commentators see here the celebration of the first marriage. God brings the woman to the man. Verse 24 suggests this and also indicates that marriage should lead to the one-flesh union, not be preceded by it. Intercourse was the joyous climax of marital sharing, not a result of the fall, and certainly not the content of the knowledge of good and evil. It was something that would be shared without shame. Adam and Eve were able to engage in this total sharing without shame or self-consciousness or loss of identity, unlike fallen creatures. All seems well, until we turn the page and learn of human infidelity.

Let us be very clear about chapter 3. The problem of theodicy, the problem of where evil came from, is not given any full answer here. This chapter is not about the origin of evil but about the original sin, its nature and circumstances. We are not told that the snake is Satan; that notion first occurs in later Jewish literature (see Wis 2:23–24; Sir 21:2; 4 Macc 18:8; see also Rev 1:9; 20:2). The connection is a conclusion one draws in light of later and developing revelation. The snake is called crafty or shrewd (*'arum*), surely a wordplay on the description of humans as naked in the immediately preceding verse (*'arrumim*). The nudes have been duped by the shrewd, and in their desire to be shrewd they discovered the naked facts about themselves.[22] The first question the snake asks the woman, appearing to seek information but trying to plant a seed of doubt, is: "Did God really say you cannot eat of any tree of the garden?" Of course, the answer to this is no, with one exception. The woman's first reply is a case of stretching the truth or exaggerating it. She adds to the divine prohibition about the fruit that *"we must not touch it or we will die."* Problems are already brewing here. We are not told that the fruit in question is an apple.[23] Next, we have the frontal attack on God's word.

---

20. See Arnold, *Genesis*, 60.

21. Arnold, *Genesis*, 60.

22. To modify the playful way Arnold (*Genesis*, 63) renders the story line here; he is following Wenham, *Genesis 1–15*, 72.

23. Here is where basing a translation on the Latin text got various English translators into trouble. One of the Latin words for apple is *"malum,"* which not incidentally is also the word

The serpent pretends to know better than the woman or even than God. This is typical arrogance from the powers of darkness. The serpent insinuates that God is jealously guarding his position as deity. The snake is suggesting that there is no metaphysical difference between God and humanity; it is just that God knows more. The text may perhaps be translated, "will be like gods" since the word for god is the plural *elohim* here. In the context of Genesis, however, *elohim* is normally used of the one true God, so it should likely be taken to mean this here. The woman must choose whether to base her decisions about what is best and true on her own judgment or on God's revealed will. This is still humanity's dilemma. It is clear that the woman is free to choose to resist the temptation and obey God. But her eyes are already opened to the possibilities of sin, taking the fruit. It offers physical satisfaction as food; it has aesthetic appeal, being pleasing to the eye. But the best part is that it is desirable for wisdom.

Adam is the silent partner to her sin. First, he commits a sin of omission. If he was with her, why did he not do something to prevent this? Second, he commits a sin of commission, for he too eats. Their eyes were indeed opened, but what they saw was not their divinity, but the bare facts about their very frail humanity. The fig leaves are a pathetic attempt to hide their most obvious and vulnerable parts that indicate their full humanity. The issue here is not mere nudity but rather shameful nakedness, a combination somehow of desire, self-knowledge, and disobedience.

Our attempt to cover up our nakedness, never mind our sins, is always inadequate and pathetic. Next, we are told that the couple heard the sound of God coming after them (not the sound of God's voice, as some have translated). Their response is fright and flight. Such is always the response of sinful humankind fearful of judgment, not wishing to be revealed or seen for what they are. God does not at this point take a confrontational approach. He simply says, "Where are you?" The creatures God has made personally and specially and given special treatment to are now running from their Maker. It is only sinful humankind who has something to fear from God. Shame is the proper response to sin, but sin also leads to rationalizing.

When humanity is confronted with its sin, rebel humans blame

for bad, or even evil. If this is about a fruit that conveys the knowledge of good and evil, by rendering the original Hebrew or Greek as "*malum*" it was possible to conclude that the author was not merely talking about just any bad or enticing fruit, he was talking about a bad apple.

God or other humans. The man blames God and the woman ("this woman whom *you* gave me"), and the woman blames the snake. The human art of passing the buck has been inaugurated. God judges these three in reverse order, starting with the source of the trouble, the snake, then the first perpetrator of the sin, and finally the accomplice. Genesis 3:15 suggests that world history will be an ongoing enmity and battle between humanity and the powers of darkness.

Notice, however, even in judgment there is mercy, because the seed of the woman will crush the head of evil and its source. This is poetic language and conjures up the image of evil snapping at our heels. Some Christian interpreters have seen here the first proclamation of the gospel remedy for sin (the "seed of the woman" referring, on this view, to Jesus Christ).

Notice also the mercy of God: he does not curse the man or the woman, but gives them "labor pains" in their primary life tasks—the man in working the ground, the woman in childbearing. The woman's punishment is not her desire for her husband, which is not bad, but rather is that sinful man will try to take advantage of her and dominate her. The Greek OT has the sense of it right here: "your desire will be for your man and he will lord it over/dominate you." To love and to cherish degenerates into selfish desire and the will to dominate.

Interestingly, what we have here is literally a case of poetic justice, for the sentencing here is in poetic form.[24] For the man, his work becomes toilsome: the ground will produce not just good fruit, but also thorns and thistles. Thus, work indeed becomes wearying, contributing to the shortening of the lifespan. In any event, implied is the ongoing nature of human life. Though humans will die, they will not completely die out. Also, probably implied in God's judgment is that 'adam is dirt ('adamah) and will return to dust (die), but we are not told whether this involves more than physical death. Painful death, spiritual decay and deterioration, or eternal death may be implied.

And then there is the matter of ongoing struggle—there is wordplay in the verdict on the snake as well—"you will snap [*tensuppenu*] at his heel he will crush [*yesupeka*] your head." Advantage humans. While Judaism saw in 3:15 messianic hope for victory over Satan, the later church fathers Justin and Irenaeus, taking *zera'* (seed) to refer to an individual and therefore not a collective noun, saw this verse

---

24. Westermann, *Genesis 1–11*, 257 notes how verdicts were expected to be in poetry.

as a sort of *protoevangelium*—a foreshadowing of the victory of Christ over Satan (cf. Rom 16:20). It should be clear that the curse on Eve is descriptive of the effects of sin, not prescriptive of how God intends male-female relationships to be.

No sooner does humankind start dying than he also starts killing. Genesis 4 tells the sordid tale of Cain and Abel. Now all of life is "red in tooth and claw." Genesis 5 has as its constant refrain, "and he died, . . . and he died, . . . and he died." The point of all the genealogies is at least in part to remind of God's faithfulness to keep his chosen ones alive and fruitful because from this chosen royal line will come the one who truly crushes the serpent's head. It may be implied in Genesis 5 that Adam is God's viceregent upon the earth; he is to govern the earth until he dies and passes the baton to his descendants.

MARK 10: THE APPEAL TO THE BEGINNING

It is often overlooked, in an age where it is assumed that the newest is the truest and the latest is the greatest, that ancient societies, including that of early Judaism, thought that the opposite was the case. For example, unless a religion or a law or a custom had ancient roots, it was considered suspect. This is why, for instance, Josephus not only names his work *Antiquities of the Jews* but goes out of his way to show just how ancient the Jewish religion really was, even suggesting Greek philosophy and key ideas were indebted to Moses! In that sort of context, an appeal to antiquity, or even the "beginning" of human civilization, was considered a strong appeal indeed, and quite persuasive from a rhetorical point of view. This helps us understand the discussion of Jesus with his fellow Jews in Mark 10, and it is in order to quote the text here.

> Some Pharisees came, and to test him they asked, "Is it lawful for a man to divorce his wife?" [3] He answered them, "What did Moses command you?" [4] They said, "Moses allowed a man to write a certificate of dismissal and to divorce her." [5] But Jesus said to them, "Because of your hardness of heart he wrote this commandment for you. [6] But from the beginning of creation, 'God made them male and female.' [7] 'For this reason a man shall leave his father and mother and be joined to his wife, [8] and the two shall become one flesh.' So they are no longer two, but one flesh. [9] Therefore what God has joined together, let no one separate."
> [10] Then in the house the disciples asked him again about this matter. [11] He said to them, "Whoever divorces his wife and marries another

commits adultery against her; [12] and if she divorces her husband and marries another, she commits adultery."

The essence of this teaching is reiterated by Paul in 1 Corinthians 7:10–11 when Paul affirms that Jesus said "no divorce." Clearly, the Markan form of this discussion seems likely to be closer to the original than that found in Matthew 19. The prohibition of divorce seems to be unprecedented in early Judaism before Jesus offers it. Our interest, however, lies elsewhere, in Jesus's use of the Genesis tradition. There is some justice in Elisabeth Schüssler Fiorenza's remark that

> Divorce is necessary because of the male's hardness of heart [i.e., in this setting only men could divorce], that is because of men's patriarchal mindset and reality—However, Jesus insists, God did not intend patriarchy, but created persons as male and female human beings. It is not woman who is given into the power of man in order to continue "his" house and family line, but it is man who shall sever connections with his own patriarchal family and "the two shall become one *sarx*."[25]

She is on the right track here, but there is more to say.

Jesus is raising the question of what force laws should have, now that the kingdom/divine saving activity is breaking into their midst, laws that were originally written due to the hardness of human hearts, that is, as a concession to human fallenness that has affected everything since the time of Adam and Eve. Jesus seems prepared to appeal to God's original creation intentions and design for marriage over against the later rulings of Deuteronomy 24:1–4, which reflect the sinful human condition. Jesus is paraphrasing several verses here, including Genesis 1:27; 5:2; and 2:24 in Mark 10:6–7. It is probably correct to say that the form of the Genesis text here is closest to the LXX. In fact, Craig Evans claims that the LXX of Genesis 1:27 is followed verbatim here.[26] For example, the quotation from Genesis 2:24 follows the LXX, which has the phrase "the two" as the subject of the end of 2:24 in Mark 10:8a. The MT lacks any designation for "the two" here.[27]

25. Elisabeth Schüssler Fiorenza, *In Memory of Her: A Feminist Theological Reconstruction of Christian Origins* (New York: Crossroad, 1985), 143.

26. Craig Evans, "Genesis in the New Testament," in Evans, *Book of Genesis*, 472.

27. See Stephen P. Ahearne-Kroll, "Genesis in Mark's Gospel," in Menken, *Genesis in the New Testament*, 30, and the discussion in Evans, "Genesis in the New Testament," 472–73. Evans goes on to discuss the fact that the Hebrew of the Genesis text does not explicitly affirm monogamy, and in fact polygamy was practiced by Jews right through the whole biblical era, when it could be afforded. Jesus's teaching then would have been at odds with the

Mark's Jesus says that God made the human race male and female, and because of this duality, a man will *leave* his mother and father and *cleave* to his wife. In that context, the two will become "one flesh" or share a "one-flesh" union (v. 8). The implication seems to be that the one-flesh union is more constitutive of their being than their uniqueness. Jesus takes the following for granted: (1) there was a beginning to the human race, and it involved God making human beings male and female; (2) part of the intent and purpose of that was so that marriage and the fulfillment of the creation command "be fruitful and multiply" could be accomplished; (3) the appeal to something more ancient, near the beginning, has a higher and prior authority than something later like Deuteronomy 24. In particular, the appeal to God's prefallen design and plan trumps later laws that were given due to the fallen condition of humanity, which involves hardness of heart, in particular that of the men who had the power of divorce in a patriarchal society, as Deuteronomy 24 suggests.

> Mark's Jesus uses the double quotation of Gen 1:27 and 2:24 to express the divine intention for male and female, thus he argues for the principle of monogamy as in line with the divine intention. This principle allows Jesus not only to forbid divorce but to equate it with adultery when his disciples ask him in private to elaborate on his teaching about divorce (Mark 10:10–12).[28]

Notice that the use of Genesis 2:24 in Ephesians 5:31 quotes the portion in regard to the "one flesh union" between a man and woman, in the context of making an argument about marriage, but in 1 Corinthians 6:16 surprisingly Paul quotes this verse and applies it to the sexual relationship a man might have with a prostitute, an inappropriate relationship which conflicts with and is contrasted with being "one spirit" with the Lord. Clearly, Paul knows Genesis 2:24 is about marriage, but equally clearly he thinks that other kinds of one-flesh unions are possible and should be avoided if one is a Christian.

---

ancestral traditions on this, as well as on the divorce issue. If marrying a second woman while the first one is alive amounts to adultery and a violation of the one flesh union with the first wife, then it is a combination of Jesus's ideas that leads to the affirmation of monogamy. Contrast Josephus who says that polygamy not monogamy was the ancestral custom (*Ant.* 17.14), and he does not condemn it. In fact, it was not until the eleventh century CE that polygamy was banned by Jewish authorities. See David Instone-Brewer, "Jesus' Old Testament Basis for Monogamy" in *The Old Testament in the New Testament: Essays in Honour of J. L. North*, ed. Steve Moyise, JSOTSup 189 (Sheffield: Sheffield Academic, 2000), 75–105.

28. Ahearne-Kroll, "Genesis in Mark," 34.

Jesus's ruling not only provides more security for women in marriage than does the Deuteronomic legislation by ruling out divorce and so taking away a male privilege, it also shows that now, as the kingdom comes, the original creation-order design is being reinstituted. Moses only "permitted" divorce due to the hardness of men's hearts, he did not command it. Jesus is assuming that the "no divorce" ruling applies to couples "whom God has joined together." He is not commenting on what we would call secular marriage or on relationships that violate other commandments of God (such as the incestuous marriage between Herod Antipas and Herodias, his own brother's [former] wife).

The undergirding assumption of Jesus, based on his reflection on Genesis 1–2 is that God in creation made two distinct but complementary or compatible human genders. God then also brought them together in marriage. Anyone who seeks to divide such a couple is attacking both the one-flesh union of the couple but also the Creator. The Creator and the creation order undergird marriage. There can be little doubt that Jesus believed in an original couple, Adam and Eve, "in the beginning," and not surprisingly, Paul is in complete agreement with this, and knows of Jesus's teaching on marriage and divorce. We must turn to his use of the Genesis tradition.[29]

1 CORINTHIANS 11: THE APPEAL TO THE BEGINNING

Paul's discussion of why women should wear head-coverings includes an argument from the creation of humanity. The clearest allusion is of course to Genesis 2:22–23 in 1 Corinthians 11:8.[30] Paul stresses that the first woman was taken out of the first man (γυνὴ ἐξ ἀνδρός) and he also says she was created διὰ τὸν ἄνδρα. Some have translated this "for the sake of the man" or better "because of the man," and taken this to mean that the phrase implies the subordination of the woman to the man. But since nothing is said about subordination in the Genesis 2 account, it is far more likely that Paul means that since it was "not good for the [original] man to be alone," the woman was created to compensate for the man's need to have a

29. For much more on all this see Ben Witherington III, *The Gospel of Mark: A Socio-Rhetorical Commentary* (Grand Rapids: Eerdmans, 2001), 274–78, and also Witherington, *Women in the Ministry of Jesus: A Study of Jesus' Attitudes to Women and Their Roles As Reflected in His Earthly Life*, SNTSMS 51 (Cambridge: Cambridge University Press, 1984).

30. See Lincicum, "Genesis in Paul," 102.

companion. Nothing is said in Genesis 2 about a woman's need for a companion. Indeed, she is depicted as the crown of creation, after which God stopped creating and declared it all "very good."

David Lincicum suggests that Paul's reading of Genesis 2 controls the way he reads Genesis 1 in 1 Corinthians 11:7. There he speaks of the man being the image and glory of God, while the woman is said to be the glory of man. Lincicum assumes that Paul has read Genesis 1 retrospectively when it speaks of humankind being created in God's image, meaning that Adam was created that way, not Eve. This, however, is hardly plausible, since not only does the Genesis 1:27 passage say that the image involves both male and female, but elsewhere Paul himself uses that very phrase ἄρσεν καὶ θῆλυ from Genesis 1:27 LXX to speak of what is now different in the context of Christ (Gal 3:28). Furthermore, 1 Corinthians 11 goes on to state in v. 12 that ever since the first creation of woman out of man, the process has been reversed such that ὁ ἀνὴρ διὰ τῆς γυναικός. Here διά (with the genitive) means "through," while earlier in the passage διά plus the accusative likely means "on account of" (the woman was created on account of the need of the man).

In any case, the real function of the argument here is to establish several key points: (1) women so long as they wear the head-covering may pray and prophecy in worship; (2) since in worship only God's glory should be evident, and since a woman's hair is her glory and she is the glory of man, that "glory" should be hidden under a head-covering, which head-covering can also double as (3) a sign of her authority to speak in worship; and finally, (4) "because of the angels" indicates that they are the guardians of the proper order of creation and of worship, and the head-covering preserves the affirmation of the male-female distinction while at the same time affirming a woman's right to speak in worship. It is "authority" down from or on her head which all can see, rather like a clergy person wearing a collar today.[31]

Interestingly, NA[27] but *not* NA[28] (see Appendix 1 below) suggests an allusion to Genesis 3:16 in 1 Corinthians 11:3, which would mean that Paul was arguing for hierarchy based on the fall and the curse

---

31. On other aspects of this argument, see Witherington, *Isaiah Old and New*, 361–70. Paul is saying that a woman needs a sign of authority, and the head-covering in 1 Corinthians 11 is that sign, but various other signs are possible, like the clergy collar today. The principle has to do with a sign of authority, not the particular practice of wearing a head-covering, which would symbolize other things today in various contexts, for instance symbolizing the subordination of women to men.

on Eve, but this is unlikely on several grounds: (1) the argument about the κεφαλή is a positive one, not a negative one; it includes a statement about God being the κεφαλή of Christ; and (2) probably the argument here is about source, not hierarchy, which is the other meaning of κεφαλή. There is a play on several meanings of this word in this passage, including the literal anatomical meaning of it.[32] But let's probe a little further and deeper. We should quote the context at this juncture.

> For a man ought not to have his head veiled, since he is the image and reflection of God; but woman is the reflection of man. [8] Indeed, man was not made from woman, but woman from man. [9] Neither was man created for the sake of woman, but woman for the sake of man. [10] For this reason a woman ought to have a symbol of authority on her head because of the angels. [11] Nevertheless, in the Lord woman is not independent of man or man independent of woman. [12] For just as woman came from man, so man comes through woman; but all things come from God.

As I have argued in the first volume in this series, this is in the first instance a discussion about source, not headship—the Father is the source of the Son, the Son, the cocreator with God, depicted as fulfilling the role of personified Wisdom in 1 Corinthians 10–11, is the source of man, and Adam is the source of the woman, Eve.[33] For Paul human duality, maleness and femaleness, is good and to be celebrated, just as the interdependence of male and female is to be appreciated. Maleness and femaleness are part of the good order of creation and are reaffirmed in the new creation.[34]

It is a mistake in interpretation to simply concentrate on vv. 8–10 and ignore the "*nevertheless*" that introduces v. 11. So, on the one hand, Paul affirms that woman comes from man (again Gen 2:4–3:24) and that she was created for the man because "it was not good for the man to be alone." Man had a need that only the woman could meet if there was to be a "one-flesh union" that fulfills the creation order mandate about multiplying. Verse 10 could be taken as a reason for what is said in v. 9, but more likely the phrase "for this reason" is completed by the phrase at the end of that sense unit, "because of the angels." In between, Paul says woman should have a sign of

32. Witherington, *Isaiah Old and New*, 361–70.
33. Witherington, *Isaiah Old and New*, 361–70.
34. See Ben Witherington III, *Conflict and Community in Corinth: A Socio-Rhetorical Commentary on 1 and 2 Corinthians* (Grand Rapids: Eerdmans, 1996), 232–37.

authority/power on her head, a sign of authorization from above, so that she may pray and prophesy in worship. This seems to be especially because there were some Jewish men in the worship service who might expect women to simply be silent during worship.[35] Verse 11 then introduces how things are "in the Lord," namely men and women are interdependent, not least because though Eve came from Adam, ever since then the reverse has been the case, all men have come forth from women; and in any case, since this is a source argument, the thing that really matters is that all things come from God. Human beings are not the ultimate source of their own existence, identity, or authority and power. In short, from start to finish the argument's appeal is based on an *ad fontes* or source assumption, the kind of argument apt to carry weight in a culture where the earlier or older something was, the more likely it was assumed to be true, time-tested, and reliable—especially when it came to matters of religion and philosophy.

THE APPEAL TO THE BEGINNING: 1 CORINTHIANS 15 AND 2 CORINTHIANS 4

A further argument about "beginnings" or origins shows up in the reference to Genesis 1:26 LXX in 1 Corinthians 15:39. Paul says that not all flesh is the same flesh: Humans have one kind, birds another, and so on. This is, as Lincicum points out, probably an argument based on reading the clauses in Genesis 1:26 in reverse, which speaks first of the creation of human beings, then the separate creation of animals. Paul deduces that separate creation suggests "different sorts of flesh." Probably the repeated phrase "according to its kind" (1:11, 12, 21, 24, 25) pointed Paul in that direction.[36] Note that while the Greek word for flesh, σάρξ, does not occur in the LXX text of Genesis 1, it is indeed used in Genesis 8:17 of birds, reptiles, beasts and that latter text otherwise echoes Genesis 1:26–27.

2 Corinthians 4:16 involves another interesting use of the creation story, this time of the command "let there be light" (Gen 1:3–4), which Paul paraphrases, having God say, "let light shine out of darkness" (see similarly John 1:5). While it might not be apparent on first glance why Paul goes on to refer to "the light of the knowledge of

35. Witherington, *Conflict and Community*, 232–37.
36. See Lincicum, "Genesis in Paul," 103.

the glory of God in the face of Christ" on the basis of this allusion to Genesis 1:3–4, this is forgetting that Paul read Genesis 1 in light of the discussion of personified Wisdom in Proverbs 3 and 8 and later in Wisdom of Solomon, a discussion in which Wisdom was cocreator with God, and indeed part of the revelation that comes with and through creation. It is but a short step from there to Paul's notion that Christ himself is the Wisdom of God, manifesting God's presence and glory, the one who with God created the universe itself.[37]

THE APPEAL TO THE FALL: 2 CORINTHIANS 11, 1 TIMOTHY 2, AND ROMANS 8

While Paul does not often refer to Eve directly, at least not by name, clearly in 2 Corinthians 11:3 we find such an appeal: "But I am afraid that as the serpent deceived Eve by its cunning, your thoughts will be led astray from a sincere and pure devotion to Christ." Note that this comes directly after a reference to Christ as betrothed to the church, which comports with his arguments elsewhere in Romans 5 and 1 Corinthians 15 about Christ being the last Adam (see below). It is interesting indeed that both Aquila and Theodotion in their translation of Genesis use the same Greek word for cunning to describe the serpent that Paul uses here.[38] More importantly 1 Timothy 2:14 should be compared with our text here, in both of which it is said that Eve was deceived. Since Paul read the Genesis story in the order in which it is given, it is important to point out that according to Genesis, only Adam received the instruction "thou shalt not eat," and presumably he was responsible for instructing Eve on the matter. Indeed, the Genesis story suggests that Eve was not properly instructed because she tells the serpent that she was not even to touch the fruit, which goes well beyond what the commandment said.

The point of mentioning this is that in Paul's view, people who are not properly or fully and correctly instructed are more prone to *deception*, and exhibit A of this is Eve. The verb used here echoes Genesis 3:13 LXX where Eve complains that the snake "deceived" her (ὁ ὄφις ἠπάτησέν με).[39] The reference to Eve being deceived in

37. See Colossians 1 and the discussion of 1 Corinthians 10 ("'the rock was Christ'") and 1 Corinthians 11 in Witherington, *Isaiah Old and New*, 361–70; see also Witherington, *Jesus the Sage: The Pilgrimage of Wisdom* (Minneapolis: Fortress, 2000).
38. See rightly Lincicum, "Genesis in Paul," 103–4.
39. See the discussion by Philip Towner, "1 Timothy," in *Commentary on the New Testament*

1 Timothy 2 comes in a very different context, the context of the exhortation for high-status women to be quiet and modest, and listen to and submit to the teachings, rather than trying to usurp authority over the legitimate teachers and begin instructing others. They need to be properly instructed, listen and learn first, before they teach. Eve, it will be remembered was not only *not* properly instructed, she made the mistake of giving the fruit to Adam and then he ate it.

Notice as well that Eve is being contrasted with Mary in 1 Timothy 2:14–15, for we have the reference to woman being saved through "the childbearing." The curse is reversed through Mary.[40] That rhetorical comparison leads to a long discussion of the one found in Romans 5:12–21 (see below). It is interesting that while Sirach is prepared to blame Eve entirely for the fall (see Sir 25:24) as does the Apocalypse of Moses: The Life of Adam and Eve (9:2; 14:2; 21:2, 6; 24:1), Paul is not prepared to go there. Indeed, he places the blame squarely on Adam in Romans 5.[41] In 2 Corinthians 11:3, Paul expresses his fear that just as the serpent deceived Eve with his cunning, so also the Corinthians were being deceived by the devil through Paul's opponents. The tradition of the deception of Eve had come to be developed to a remarkable degree in the intertestamental period (see 1 Enoch 69:6; 2 Enoch 36:6; Apocalypse of Abraham 23). In some of this material Eve is said to be seduced by the serpent, but Paul never suggests this either here or in 1 Timothy 2, if it is by Paul. Paul is concerned with the corruption of the minds of the Corinthians.

To judge from the later tradition in 1 Timothy 2:13–14, it suggests not only that Eve was formed after Adam (following the account in Gen 2:4–3:24) but that unlike Adam she was not properly instructed, and hence easily deceived.[42] This, I would suggest, is why Paul consistently blames Adam, not Eve for human fallenness and makes the comparisons he does between Adam and Christ, not Eve and Christ.

Paul does not suggest that women are inherently more susceptible to being deceived than men, unlike Philo (QG 1.23.46). The verb

Use of the Old Testament, ed. G. K. Beale and D. A. Carson (Grand Rapids: Baker Academic, 2007), 894–97.

40. For a detailed exegesis of 1 Tim 2:8–15 see Ben Witherington III, *Letters and Homilies for Hellenized Christians Volume One: A Socio-Rhetorical Commentary on Titus, 1–2 Timothy, and 1–3 John* (Downers Grove, IL: InterVarsity, 2014), 217–32.

41. See Mark A. Seifrid, "Romans" in Beale, *Commentary on the New Testament Use*, 629.

42. See the discussion of the word "'deceive'" which mainly comes up when Eve is mentioned in Paul's letters in Witherington, *Letters and Homilies for Hellenized Christians Vol. One*, 228–29.

"truly deceived" in 1 Timothy 2:14 seems to refer to what happens when one has been misled about something she has been taught, or when one is subject to being misled after the fact because one was not properly taught in the first place. There is in addition an implied contrast between Eve, the mother of all living, and Mary, the woman who produced "the childbearing" (singular) that led to salvation. Eve was first in the fall, but the curse was reversed in Mary who accepted and obeyed the instructions of the angel, becoming the mother of the messiah. The church fathers were later to make much of this "comparison," which is simply hinted at in 1 Timothy 2:15.

One final reference to the fall in a general sense is probably found in Romans 8:20, which likely alludes to the curse in Genesis 3:17–19. In Romans, we hear about how creation was subject to "futility," subjected by God, but in hope of a new creation at the resurrection. The curse, it will be remembered, did not fall on Adam but on the ground itself. Redemption then has both personal and cosmic dimensions, involving more than just human beings.

THE FALL OF ADAM: ROMANS 5
AND 1 CORINTHIANS 15

Though Romans 5 is Paul's chronologically later discussion of Adam, it is best to start with Romans 5:12–21 before turning to 1 Corinthians 15. We can say at the outset that like Jesus, Paul assumes that Adam and Eve were real historical persons, not merely characters in an OT story. It would have been singularly ineffective in a rhetorical comparison such as Romans 5:12–21 to contrast a historical person of the recent past like Jesus with some fictional figure from hoary antiquity, and this is not how a proper *synkrisis* was to be constructed anyway. One would compare and contrast two well-known historical figures. In fact, Quintilian stresses that such comparison should focus on the character of the two persons involved (*Inst.* 4.2.99), in this case one of whom had a negative effect on the human race and the other of whom has a counteractive effect on those who are "in him." Here is Paul's argument:

> Therefore, just as sin came into the world through one man, and death came through sin, and so death spread to all because all have sinned—[13] sin was indeed in the world before the law, but sin is not reckoned when there is no law. [14] Yet death exercised dominion from Adam to Moses,

even over those whose sins were not like the transgression of Adam, who is a type of the one who was to come.

^{15} But the free gift is not like the trespass. For if the many died through the one man's trespass, much more surely have the grace of God and the free gift in the grace of the one man, Jesus Christ, abounded for the many. ^{16} And the free gift is not like the effect of the one man's sin. For the judgment following one trespass brought condemnation, but the free gift following many trespasses brings right-standing. ^{17} If, because of the one man's trespass, death exercised dominion through that one, much more surely will those who receive the abundance of grace and the free gift of righteousness exercise dominion in life through the one man, Jesus Christ.

^{18} Therefore just as one man's trespass led to condemnation for all, so one man's act of righteousness leads to justification and life for all. ^{19} For just as by the one man's disobedience the many were made sinners, so by the one man's obedience the many will be made righteous. ^{20} But law came in, with the result that the trespass multiplied; but where sin increased, grace abounded all the more, ^{21} so that, just as sin exercised dominion in death, so grace might also exercise dominion through righteousness leading to eternal life through Jesus Christ our Lord.

Again, it is impossible to doubt Paul believes he is talking about a historical figure Adam when he says things like "death reigned from Adam to Moses." The two men are viewed as important figures in salvation history. While the logic of this argument will seem strange to modern individuals with an individualistic mindset, in a collectivistic culture this argument made perfect sense: one person can affect the many for ill or for good, and even to a real extent affect or even determine their destiny. Notice that Adam in this argument is viewed as not merely sinning and affecting his own destiny but committing a willful violation of the only law he knew, and therefore *transgressing* against God's express revealed will, an act that affects all his descendants as well, like a person who contracts a deadly and contagious disease and passes it on to others quite apart from their choice. And yet, Paul also wants to make clear there is no unfairness with God because death comes to all persons because they also willfully sinned.

It should be pointed out here, that actually, Paul doesn't spend much time on the story of Moses (though see below on 2 Cor 3:7–18). The story of Moses is not the *generative* narrative for followers of Christ, rather the Adam story, the Abraham story, and the Christ story are.[43] Paul sees the story of Moses, like the Mosaic covenant as *pro tempore*. Paul here is not merely arguing like 2 Baruch 54:15 where it is said that "Adam is not the cause, save only of his own soul, but each of us has been the Adam of his own soul." To the contrary, Paul is arguing that just as one person Adam, affected all his fellow humans negatively, so Christ affects all those in him positively.

It is worth quoting 4 Ezra as well for another point of Jewish comparison, which reads in 7:11–12: "For I made the world for their sake, and when Adam transgressed my statutes, what had been made was judged. And so, the entrances of this world were made narrow and sorrowful and toilsome; they are few and evil, full of dangers and involved in great hardships." The author goes on to lament in 7:48 "Oh Adam what have you done? For though it was you who sinned, the fall was not yours alone, but ours also who are your descendants." Clearly enough, here Adam's sin is seen to have a drastic effect on even creation itself. While Jubilees 3:17–22 blames Adam, Eve, and the serpent equally for sin and death entering the world, and Wisdom of Solomon 2:24 simply blames the devil, Sirach 25:24 and Life of Adam and Eve 3 lay the blame only on the shoulders of Eve. Paul was not alone then in his thinking as expressed in Romans 5:12–21 and one may compare Romans 8:19–20 where Paul says all of creation has been subjected to futility but will one day be liberated at the resurrection. Notably Paul places the major blame on Adam, not Eve, and is only prepared to say Eve was deceived, whereas Adam sinned knowingly and willfully.

The way Paul presents the matter in Romans 5, it appears he is of the view that the human race started over again with Christ. He is the last or eschatological Adam, the last chance for the race to be saved and be in right relationship with God. Now it is important to note about rhetorical comparisons that there is never the suggestion that the two persons are alike in all respects. There are just some points of comparison, and even more importantly some points of contrast. The argument here is a "how much more" kind of argument: "If X is true of Adam, how much more of Christ." Yet at the same time Paul wants to argue "the gift is not like the trespass," eclipsing it in various ways. Notice as well that death is seen here, and in 1 Corinthians 15, as an enemy, not a friend, and death enters the world because of sin

43. See Ben Witherington III, *Paul's Narrative Thought World: The Tapestry of Tragedy and Triumph* (Louisville: Westminster John Knox, 1994).

(though it is not clear whether Paul is talking about spiritual death, or merely physical death, or both).[44]

Romans 5:14 is important because Paul says Adam is but a type of the "coming one."

> Paul sees history as gathering at nodal points, and crystalizing upon outstanding figures . . . who are notable in themselves as individual persons but even more notable as representative figures. These . . . incorporate the human race, or sections of it, within themselves, and the dealings they have with God they have representatively on behalf of their [people].[45]

Wherein lies the difference then of the effect of Adam and Christ? Paul explains in v. 16 that the judgment followed only one misdeed by Adam and resulted in condemnation, whereas the grace gift followed many misdeeds and resulted in acquittal, indeed in salvation. The former outcome was deserved, the latter was entirely gratuitous, undeserved. God's long patience with many sins led not to more condemnation but rather to a radical rescue by Jesus. Thus, there is almost no comparison between the trespass and the gift, except in the profundity of the effect of each.

Christ then is seen as Adam gone right. The former Adam was known for his infamous act of disobedience. Christ, by contrast, was obedient to God even unto death on the cross (v. 19). Adam's act "made" many sinners, but Christ's made many righteous. Christ's death, like Adam's sin affects not merely the human *position* in relationship to God but also the human *condition*. The contrasting element in this comparison is played out more fully in 1 Corinthians 15.

The Adam-Christ analogy comes into play twice in 1 Corinthians 15, once at vv. 20–22 and then again in vv. 45–50.[46] Clearly, in vv. 21–22 Paul treats Adam as a historical person who was responsible for death entering the world, but another Adam, by contrast, brought resurrection from out of the dead ones for those who are "in Christ." Paul does not discuss here the fate of those outside of Christ. The issue here is primarily eschatological rather than christological or personal.

44. I would suggest it is probably the first of these three, in light of what Paul says in Rom 7:11. There Adam's experience is being talked about, but Paul knows perfectly well that Adam doesn't physically die right after he sins. What dies is his positive relationship with God; see the discussion of Rom 7:7–13 below.

45. C. K. Barrett, *From First Adam to Last: A Study in Pauline Theology* (New York: Scribner, 1962), 5.

46. For full discussion see Witherington, *Conflict and Community in Corinth.*

The analogy may not be perfect however since not all are "in Christ" in the same way all are "in Adam."[47]

The contrast between the first and last Adam in vv. 45–48 is that the former only received physical life as a gift (*psyche* refers here to the life or animating principle here, not to the Greek notion of the soul) whereas Christ became a giver of both resurrection and spiritual life. The physically animated life precedes the spiritually animated life in a resurrection body. It is worth stressing that the contrast between a *psychikon soma* and a *pneumatikon soma* is not between a body made out of *psyche* and one made out of "spirit." As Murray Harris stresses, adjectives or qualifiers with the *–ikon* ending normally carry an ethical or functional meaning.[48] Adam's life-breath was decidedly this worldly material, not an immortal or immaterial soul or spirit. *Pneumatikos* has something to do with material, bodily life, not merely spiritual life.[49] In Paul's view the truly "spiritual" person is the one who has been given a resurrection body through the life-giving spirit, namely Christ. Humans bear the natural likeness of Adam, but if they are in Christ they will bear the resurrection likeness of Christ when he returns. Christians then are indebted to both founders of the human race. Paul does not say Adam was made out of the dust of the earth any more than he says the risen Christ was made out of heavenly stuff. Here *ek* indicates character; Adam was earthly in character, Christ heavenly. The assumed similarity is that both Adam and Christ were persons with life in a material body (even after the resurrection, in Jesus's case), but oh how different were their bodies and their effects on others after the big change in their lives (Paul after his sin, Christ after his resurrection).

What one notices about the use of the human creation stories is that the uses by Jesus (and Mark) and Paul are not as extravagant as one finds in some early Jewish literature, for example, in the Enoch literature. The assumption in each case is that Adam and Eve are real human beings, historical figures, who have influenced those who

47. The writers of the Genesis material seem to have assumed they were talking about the ancestor of God's chosen people, Abraham, etc., *not of everyone,* since the story line refers to spouses for Cain and Abel that are not Adam or Eve's offspring, and to people groups outside Eden to whom Cain with his mark could go.

48. Murray J. Harris, *Raised Immortal: Resurrection and Immortality in the New Testament* (Grand Rapids: Eerdmans, 1985), 112–15.

49. See the interesting discussion in Dale B. Martin, *The Corinthian Body* (New Haven: Yale University Press, 1999) in which he makes clear that many of the ancients saw "'spirit'" as gossamer-thin material, not something nonmaterial in nature.

have come thereafter and their actions had to be counteracted by Christ. They were never examples in a positive sense. In any case, now that the kingdom is coming, or as Paul puts it, now that the last Adam has come to refound the human race, the old Adamic order has been eclipsed and is on the way out. It, and its lasting effects, will be fully overcome at the resurrection. This is why Paul in 1 Corinthians 15 brings up the Adam-Christ contrast once more in that text. Adam's story will finally come to a dead end, when the dead in Christ are raised, and they find they are no longer "in Adam."

RETELLING ADAM'S TALE: ROMANS 7:7–13

The problem with interpreting Romans 7 is that you have to be both "wise as serpents" *and* "innocent as doves." There is no more controverted text in all of ancient literature, and in fact no more commented on text from antiquity, than Romans 7. This is the stuff of which whole theologies, not to mention dissertations and scholarly careers, are made. One thing that has characterized the discussion of this text in the twentieth and into the twenty-first century is that until recently scholars have almost universally failed to apply the insights of Greco-Roman rhetoric to the analysis of this text. This is unfortunate because it provides several keys to unlocking the mysteries of this text. For our purposes, it provides a key to understanding how Paul reads the OT, and in particular the crucial story of Adam. Unfortunately, the history of interpretation of this text has often done more to confuse than illuminate the interpretation of this example of intertextuality, and accordingly it is necessary for us to go into considerable detail to unpack this crucial text.

Romans 7 demonstrates not only Paul's considerable skill with rhetoric, but his penchant for using even its most complex devices and techniques. This text proves beyond a reasonable doubt that Paul did not use rhetoric in some purely superficial or sparing way (e.g., using rhetorical questions).[50] To the contrary, the very warp and woof of his argument here reflects, and indeed requires, an under-

---

50. Against several of the essayists in Stanley L. Porter and Dennis L. Stamps, eds., *Rhetorical Criticism and the Bible*, JSNTSup 195 (Sheffield: Sheffield Academic, 2002) who continue to misjudge Paul in this regard, as has rightly also been noticed by Margeret M. Mitchell in several publications; see, e.g., *The Heavenly Trumpet: John Chrysostom and the Art of Pauline Interpretation* (Louisville: Westminster John Knox, 2002); and *Paul, the Corinthians, and the Birth of Christian Hermeneutics* (Cambridge: Cambridge University Press, 2012).

standing of sophisticated rhetorical techniques to make sense of the content of this passage and the way it attempts to persuade the Roman audience. It will repay our close attention at this juncture.

"Impersonation," or *prosopopoia*, is a rhetorical technique that falls under the heading of figures of speech and is often used to illustrate or make vivid a piece of deliberative rhetoric (*Inst.* 3.8.49; cf. Theon, *Progymnasmata* 8). This rhetorical technique involves the assumption of a role, and sometimes the role would be marked off from its surrounding discourse by a change in tone or inflection or accent or form of delivery, or an introductory formula signaling a change in voice. Sometimes the speech would simply be inserted "without mentioning the speaker at all" (*Inst.* 9.2.37).[51] Unfortunately for us, we did not get to hear Paul's discourse orally delivered in its original oral setting, as was Paul's intent. It is not surprising then that many have not picked up the signals (having only Paul's words left to us), that impersonation is happening in Romans 7:7–13.

Quintilian says impersonation "is sometimes introduced even with controversial themes, which are drawn from history and involve the appearance of definite historical characters as pleaders" (*Inst.* 3.8.52). In this case Adam is the historical figure being impersonated in Romans 7:7–13, and the theme is most certainly controversial and drawn from history. Indeed, Paul has introduced this theme already in Romans 5:12–21, and one must bear in mind that this discourse would have been heard *seriatim*, which means they would have heard about Adam only a few minutes before hearing the material in Romans 7.

The most important requirement for a speech in character in the form of impersonation is that the speech be fitting, suiting the situation and character of the one speaking. "For a speech that is out of keeping with the man who delivers it is just as faulty as a speech which fails to suit the subject to which it should conform." (*Inst.* 3.8.51). The ability to pull off a convincing impersonation is considered by Quintilian to reflect the highest skill in rhetoric, for it is often the most difficult thing to do (*Inst.* 3.8.49). That Paul attempts it, tells us something about Paul as a rhetorician. This rhetorical technique also involves personification, sometimes of abstract qualities (like fame or virtue, or in Paul's case sin or grace; *Inst.* 9.2.36). Quintilian also informs us that impersonation may take the form of

---

51. For an earlier version of this discussion, see Witherington and Hyatt, *Letter to the Romans*.

a dialogue or speech, but it can also take the form of a first person narrative (*Inst.* 9.2.37).

Since the important work of Werner G. Kümmel on Romans 7, it has become a commonplace, perhaps even a majority opinion in some NT circles that the "I" of Romans 7 is *not* autobiographical.[52] This however still did not tell us what sort of literary or rhetorical use of "I" we do find in Romans 7. As Stanley Stowers points out, it is also no new opinion that what is going on in Romans 7 is the rhetorical technique known as "impersonation."[53] In fact, this is how some of the earliest Greek commentators on Romans, such as Origen, took this portion of the letter, and later commentators such as Jerome and Rufinus take note of this approach of Origen's.[54] Not only so, Didymus of Alexandria and Nilus of Ancyra also saw Paul using the form of speech in character or impersonation here.[55] The point to be noted here is that we are talking about church fathers who not only knew Greek well but who understood the use of rhetoric and believed Paul was certainly availing himself of rhetorical devices here. Even more importantly, there is John Chrysostom (Homily 13 on Romans), who was very much in touch with the rhetorical nature and the theological substance of Paul's letters. He also does not think that Romans 7 is about Christians, much less about Paul himself as a Christian. He takes it to be talking about: (1) those who lived before the law; (2) and those who lived outside the law or lived under it. In other words, it is about gentiles and Jews outside of Christ.

But I would want to stress that since the vast majority of Paul's audience in Rome is gentile, and Paul has as part of his rhetorical aims effecting some reconciliation between Jewish and gentile Christians in Rome, it would be singularly inept for Paul here to retell the story of Israel in a negative way and then turn around in Romans 9–11 and try to get gentiles to appreciate their Jewish heritage in Christ, and to be understanding of Jews and their fellow Jewish Christians. No, Paul tells a more universal tale here of the progenitor of God's

---

52. See Werner G. Kümmel, *Romer 7 und das Bild des Menschen im Neuen Testament zwei Studien*, TB 53 (Munich: Kaiser, 1974).

53. Stanley K. Stowers, *A Rereading of Romans: Justice, Jews, and Gentiles* (New Haven: Yale University Press, 1997), 264–69.

54. Unfortunately, we have only fragments of Origen's Romans commentary. See the careful discussion by Stowers, *Rereading Romans*, 266–67. Origen rightly notes that: (1) Jews such as Paul do not speak of a time when they lived before or without the law; (2) what Paul says elsewhere about himself (e.g., 1 Cor 6:19; Gal 3:13; 2:20; Phil 3:6) does not fit this description of life outside Christ in Romans 7.

55. See Stowers, *Rereading Romans*, 268–69.

people. But it was clearly possible for Romans 7 to be misunderstood even by some of the most profound of Christian commentators from the early Middle Ages onwards. Much of the discussion of Romans 7 after Augustine was not only indebted to Augustine, it was misled by Augustine.[56]

If the measure of the importance of a text is whom it has impacted in a major way, then in many regards Romans is, perhaps after one or the other of the Gospels, the most important NT book. From Augustine to Aquinas to Erasmus to Melanchthon to Luther to Calvin to Wesley and in the modern era to Karl Barth, Rudolf Bultmann, and many others, the influence has been decisive. But what must be kept squarely in view is that the nature of the impact is in part determined by the way in which, and the tradition from which, each of these persons has read the text, and this is especially the case with Romans.

There is of course a direct line of influence from Augustine to all these other interpreters, who all are in his debt. But it needs to be borne in mind that there were interpreters of Romans, and especially of Romans 7, prior to Augustine, and many of them, including luminaries among the Greek fathers, like Origen and Chrysostom in the East and Pelagius and Ambrosiaster in the West, and they did *not* take Augustine's line of approach to Romans, and in particular Romans 7. It is my view that to a real degree, Augustine skewed the interpretation of this crucial Pauline text, and we are still dealing with the theological fallout, lo these many years later.

Who is the "I" who is speaking here in Romans 7:7–25? In my view the "I" is Adam in vv. 7–13, and all those who are currently "in Adam" in vv. 14–25.[57] Adam, it will be remembered, is the last historical figure Paul introduced into his discourse at Romans 5:12, and we have contended that the story of Adam undergirds a good deal of the discussion from Romans 5:12 through Romans 7.[58] More will be said

---

56. In what follows I am indebted to T. J. Deidun for pointing me in the right direction. See especially his helpful summary of the data, "Romans", in *A Dictionary of Biblical Interpretation*, ed. R. J. Coggins and J. L. Houlden (Philadelphia: Trinity Press International, 1990), 601–4. Also helpful is John D. Godsey, "The Interpretation of Romans in the History of the Christian Faith," *Int* 34 (1980): 3–16.

57. See the lengthy discussion by Gerd Theissen, *Psychological Aspects of Pauline Theology* (Philadelphia: Fortress, 1987), 177–269.

58. On Adam in Romans see Robert Hamerton-Kelly, "Sacred Violence and Sinful Desire: Paul's Interpretation of Adam's Sin in the Letter to the Romans," in *The Conversation Continues: Studies in John and Paul in Honor of J. Louis Martyn*, ed. Robert T. Fortna and Beverly Roberts Gaventa (Nashville: Abingdon, 1990), 35–54; see also Witherington and Hyatt, *Letter to the Romans*, 141–53.

on this below, but suffice it to say here that the old traditional interpretations that Paul was describing his own pre-Christian experience, or alternately the experience of Christians in this text fail to grasp the rhetorical finesse and character of this material, and must be deemed very unlikely not only for that reason, but for others we will discuss in due course.[59]

Here it is important to remind ourselves once more about the Genesis narrative. There are three things that are crucial if one is to understand this text. First of all, Paul believes that Moses wrote the Pentateuch, including Genesis. Second, the "law" in Moses's books includes more than the law given to Moses along with the Mosaic covenant. It would include the first commandment given to Adam and Eve.[60] Third, it appears that Paul saw the "original sin" of coveting the fruit of the prohibited tree as a form of violation of the tenth commandment (see Apocalypse of Moses 19:3).

I would suggest an expansive rendering of vv. 8–11 that takes into account the Adamic story that is being retold here as follows: "But Sin [i.e., the serpent], seizing an opportunity in the commandment, produced in me all sorts of covetousness. . . . But I [Adam] was once alive apart from the law, but when the commandment came, Sin sprang to life and I died, and the very commandment that promised life, proved deadly to me. For Sin [the serpent] seizing an opportunity through the commandment, deceived me and through it killed me." Here indeed we have the familiar primeval tale of human life that began before the existence of the law, and apart from sin, but then the commandment entered followed by deception, disobedience, and eventually death. We must consider the particulars of the text at this juncture.

59. It is telling that some of the most thorough recent treatments of Romans 7, even from the Reformed tradition have concluded that Paul cannot be describing the Christian experience here; see, e.g., Douglas Moo, *Romans*, NICNT (Grand Rapids: Eerdmans, 1996), 443–50; N. T. Wright, "Romans," *NIB* 10:551–55 (who changed his mind from his earlier view that Christians were in view in Rom 7:14–25); Brendan Byrne, *Romans*, SP 6 (Collegeville, MN: Liturgical Press, 1996), 216–26; Joseph A. Fitzmyer, *Romans: A New Translation with Introduction and Commentary*, AB 33 (New York: Doubleday, 1992), 465–73; Charles H. Talbert, *Romans*, SHBC (Macon, GA: Smyth & Helwys, 2002), 185–209. See also Paul W. Meyer, "The Worm at the Core of the Apple: Exegetical Reflections on Romans 7," in Fortna, *Conversation Continues*, 62–84; Jan Lambrecht, *The Wretched "I" and its Liberation*, LThPM 14 (Louvain: Peeters, 1992).

60. It is not surprising that some early Jews saw the commandment given to Adam and Eve as a form of one of the Ten Commandments, specifically the one having to do with coveting; see Witherington, *Paul's Narrative Thought World*, 14. The Genesis stories were read through the lens of later stories about God's covenant with Moses and the Israelites. And indeed, Exodus was even read through the lens of the even later Deuteronomy.

Those who claim that there is no signal in the text that we are going into impersonation at v. 7 are simply wrong.[61] As Stowers points out

> The section begins in v. 7 with an abrupt change in voice following a rhetorical question, that serves as a transition from Paul's authorial voice, which has previously addressed the readers explicitly . . . in 6:1–7:6. This constitutes what the grammarians and rhetoricians described as change of voice (*enallagē* or *metabolē*). These ancient readers would next look for *diaphonia*, a difference in characterization from the authorial voice. The speaker in 7:7–25 speaks with great personal pathos of coming under the Law at some point, learning about desire and sin, and being unable to do what he wants to do because of enslavement to sin or flesh.[62]

It is indeed crucial to see that what we have here is not only a continuation of Paul's discussion of the law, but a vivid retelling of the fall in such a manner that he shows that there was a problem with commandments and the law from the very beginning of the human story. Paul has transitioned from talking about what Christians once were in 7:5–6 before they came to Christ, to talking about *why* they were that way and why the law had that effect on them before they became Christians, namely because of the sin of Adam.[63] This is the outworking of and building upon what Paul says when he compares and contrasts the story of Adam and Christ in Romans 5:12–21.

Furthermore, there is a good reason not simply to lump vv. 7–13 together with vv. 14–25, as some commentators still do. In vv. 7–13 we have only past tenses of the verbs, while in vv. 14–25 we have present tenses. Either Paul is somewhat changing the subject in vv.14–25 from vv. 7–13, or he is changing the time frame in which he is viewing the one subject. The fact that many commentators through the

61. See now the very helpful treatment of Paul's rhetorical use of "'I'" here by Jean-Noël Aletti, "Rm 7.7–25 encore une fois: enjeux et propositions," *NTS* 48 (2002): 358–76. He is also right that Paul reflects some understanding of both Jewish and Greco-Roman anthropology in this passage.

62. Stowers, *Rereading of Romans*, 269–70.

63. Even C. E. B. Cranfield, *A Critical and Exegetical Commentary on the Epistle to the Romans: Volume 1, Introduction and Commentary on Romans I–VIII*, ICC (Edinburgh: T&T Clark, 1975), 337 has to admit that Paul in Rom 7:6 and 8:8–9 uses the phrase "in the flesh" to denote a condition which for the Christian now belongs to the past. It is thus hopelessly contradictory to say on the one hand, "We no longer have the basic direction of our lives controlled and determined by the flesh" (p. 337), and then turn around and maintain that Rom 7:14–25 describes the normal or even best Christian life, even though 7:14 says "we are fleshly, sold under sin," which comports only with the description of pre-Christian life in 7:6 and 8:8–9. This contradicts the notion that the believer has been released from "the flesh" in a moral sense.

years have thought Paul was describing Christian experience, including his own, we owe in large measure to the enormous influence of Augustine, including his influence especially on Luther, and those who have followed in Luther's exegetical footsteps.

What are the markers or indicators in the text of Romans 7:7–13 that the most probable way to read this text, the way Paul desired for it to be heard, is in the light of the story of Adam, with Adam speaking of his own experience? First, from the beginning of the passage in v. 7 there is reference to one specific commandment: "thou shalt not covet/desire." This is the tenth commandment in an abbreviated form (cf. Exod 20:17; Deut 5:21). As we have already mentioned, some early Jewish exegesis of Geneis 3 suggested that the sin committed by Adam and Eve was a violation of the tenth commandment.[64] They coveted the fruit of the tree of the knowledge of good and evil.

Second, one must ask oneself, who in biblical history was only under *only one* commandment, and one about coveting? The answer is Adam.[65] Verse 8 refers to a *commandment* (singular). This can hardly be a reference to the Mosaic law in general, which Paul regularly speaks of as a collective entity. Third, verse 9 says, "I was living once without/apart from the law." The only person said in the Bible to be living before or without any law was Adam. The attempt to refer this to a person being before the time of their bar-mitzvah, when they take the yoke of the law upon themselves at twelve to thirteen years of age, while not totally impossible, seems very unlikely. Even a Jewish child who had not yet personally embraced the call to be a "son of the commandments" was still expected to obey the Mosaic law, including honoring parents and God (see Luke 2:41–52). Remember, the audience in Rome was largely gentiles.

Fourth, as numerous commentators have regularly noticed, Sin is personified in this text, especially in v. 11, as if it were like the snake in the garden. Paul says, "Sin took opportunity through the commandment to deceive me." This matches up well with the story about the snake using the commandment to deceive Eve in the garden. Notice too how the very same verb is used to speak of this deception in 2 Corinthians 11:3 and also 1 Timothy 2:14 (see above). We know

---

64. See 4 Ezra 7:11; b. Sanh. 56b; and on the identification of Torah with the preexistent Wisdom of God see Sir 24:23; Bar 3:36–4:1.

65. See Ernst Käsemann, *Commentary on Romans*, trans. G. W. Bromiley (Grand Rapids: Eerdmans, 1994), 196: "Methodologically the starting point should be that a story is told in vv. 9–11 and that the event depicted can refer strictly only to Adam. . . . There is nothing in the passage which does not fit Adam, and everything fits Adam alone."

of course that "death" was said to be part of the punishment for this sin, but there was the matter of spiritual death due to alienation from God, and it is perhaps the latter that Paul has in view in this text.

Fifth, notice how in v. 7 Paul says "I did not know sin except through the commandment." This condition would only properly be the case with Adam, especially if "know" in this text means having personal experience of sin (cf. v. 5).[66] As we know from various earlier texts in Romans, Paul believes that all after Adam have also sinned and fallen short of God's glory. The discussion in Romans 5:12–21 seems to be presupposed here. It is however possible to take *egnon* to mean "recognize": I did not recognize sin for what it was except through the existence of the commandment. If this is the point, then it comports with what Paul has already said about the law turning sin into trespass, sin being revealed as a violation of God's will for humankind. But on the whole, it seems more likely that Paul is describing Adam's awakening consciousness of the possibility of sin when the first commandment was given. All in all, the most satisfactory explanation of these verses is if we see Paul the Christian rereading the story of Adam here, in the light of his Christian views about law and the Law.[67]

Certainly, one of the functions of this subsection of Romans is to provide something of an apologia for the law. Paul is asking, is then the law something evil because it not only reveals sin but has the unintended effect of suggesting sins to commit to a human being? Is the law's association with sin and death then a sign that the law itself is a sinful or wicked thing? Paul's response is "absolutely not!" Verse 7 suggests a parallel between *egnon* and "know desire," which suggests Paul has in view the experience of sin by this knower. Verse 8 says sin takes the law as the starting point or opportunity to produce in the knower all sorts of evil desires.[68]

The basic argument here is how sin used a good thing, the law, to create evil desires in Adam. It is important to recognize that in

66. C. K. Barrett, *A Commentary on the Epistle to the Romans*, BNTC (Peabody, MA: Hendrickson, 1987), 132 points out the difference between here and Rom 3:20 where Paul uses the term *epignosis* to refer to the recognition of sin. Here he simply says "know."

67. See the earlier discussion of this view at some length by Stanislas Lyonnet, "L'histoire du salut selon le ch. 7 de l'epitre aux Romains," *Bib* 43 (1962): 117–51; and the helpful discussion of Neil Elliott, *The Rhetoric of Romans: Argumentative Constraint and Strategy and Paul's Dialogue with Judaism*, JSNTSup 45 (Sheffield: Sheffield Academic, 1990), 246–50 who comes to the same Adamic conclusion on the basis of rhetorical considerations.

68. Barrett, *Romans*, 132 puts it vividly: "The law is not simply a reagent by which the presence of sin is detected: it is a catalyst which aids or even initiates the action of sin upon man."

Romans 5–6 Paul had already established that all humans are "in Adam," and all have sinned like him. Furthermore, Paul has spoken of the desires that plagued his largely gentile audience prior to their conversions. The discussion here then just further links even the gentile portion of the audience to Adam and his experience. They are to recognize themselves in this story, as the children of Adam who also have had desires, have sinned, and have died.[69] The way Paul will illuminate the parallels will be seen in Romans 7:14–25, which I take to be a description of all those in Adam and outside of Christ.[70]

Paul then is providing a narrative in Romans 7:7–25 of the story of Adam from the past in vv. 7–13, and the story of all those in Adam in the present in vv. 14–25. In a sense, what is happening here is an expansion on what Paul has already argued in Romans 5:12–21. There is a continuity in the "I" in Romans 7 by virtue of the close link between Adam and all those in Adam. The story of Adam is also the prototype of the story of Christ, and it is only when the person is delivered from the body of death, it is only when a person transfers from the story of Adam into the story of Christ, that one can leave Adam and his story behind, no longer being in bondage to sin, and being empowered to resist temptation, walk in newness of life, as will be described in Romans 8. Christ starts the race of humanity over again, setting it right and in a new direction, delivering it from the bondage of sin, death, and the law. It is not a surprise that Christ only enters the picture at the very end of the argument in Romans 7, in preparation for Romans 8, using the rhetorical technique of overlapping the end of one argument with the beginning of another.[71]

---

69. The concept of federal headship and corporate personality is in play here. Paul may or may not have seen Adam as the physical progenitor of the whole human race, but what he certainly believes is that Adam is the head of the whole race, just as Christ is the head of all those who are in him, and this being the case, the whole human race are "in Adam" and have sinned like him, Jew and gentile alike. In both case being "in" the corporate head does not mean being the descendant of that person literally, it means being influenced or affected by their head.

70. It simply complicates and confuses the matter to suggest Paul is also talking about Israel as well as Adam here. Paul is addressing a largely gentile audience who *did not* identify with Israel, but could understand and identify with the head of the whole human race. They were familiar with the Roman "father of the fatherland" concept which refers not to Caesar being the actual progenitor of all Romans, but to his being their "head," such that their very existence was bound up with his. That Israel might be included in the discussion of those who are "'in Adam'" in 7:14–25 is certainly possible, but even there Paul has already described earlier in Romans 2 the dilemma of a gentile caught between the law and a hard place. My point would be that even in vv. 14–25 he is not specifically focusing on Jewish experience, or the experience of Israel.

71. This has confused those who are unaware of this rhetorical convention, and have taken the outburst "Thanks be to God in Jesus Christ" to be a cry only a Christian would make, and that therefore Rom 7:14–25 must be about Christian experience. However, if 7:14–25 is meant to be a narrative of a person in Adam who is led to the end of himself and to the point of con-

Some have seen v. 9b as a problem for the Adam view of vv. 7–13 because the verb must be translated "renewed" or "live anew." But notice the contrast between "I was living" in v. 9a with "but sin coming to life" in v 9b. Cranfield then is right to urge that the meaning of the verb in question in v. 9b must be "sprang to life."[72] The snake/ sin was lifeless until it had an opportunity to victimize some innocent victim, and had the means, namely the commandment, to do so. Sin deceived and spiritually killed the first founder of the human race. This is nearly a quotation from Genesis 3:13. One of the important corollaries of recognizing that Romans 7:7–13 is about Adam (and 7:14–25 is about those in Adam, and outside Christ), is that it becomes clear that Paul is not specifically critiquing Judaism or Jews here, any more than he is in Romans 7:14–25.

Verse 12 begins with *hoste*, which should be translated "so then," introducing Paul's conclusion about the law that Paul has been driving toward. The commandment, and for that matter the whole law, is holy, just, and good. It did not in itself produce sin or death in the first head of the human race. Rather sin/the serpent/Satan used the commandment to that end. Good things, things from God, can be used for evil purposes by those with evil intent. The exceeding sinfulness of sin is revealed in that it will even use a good thing to produce an evil end—death.[73] This was not the intended end or purpose of the law. The death of Adam was not a matter of his being killed with kindness or by something good. Verse 13 is emphatic. The law, a good thing, did not kill Adam. But sin was indeed revealed to be sin by the law and it produced death.

This argument prepares the way for the discussion of the legacy of Adam for those who are outside of Christ. The present tense verbs reflect the ongoing legacy for those who are still in Adam and not in Christ. Romans 7:14–25 should not be seen as a further argument, but as the last stage of a four-part argument that began in Romans 6, all of it being grounded in Romans 5:12–21, and climaxing in Paul's

viction and conversion, then this outburst should be taken as Paul's interjected reply or response with the gospel to the heartfelt cry of the lost person, a response which prepares for and signals the coming of the following argument in Romans 8 about life in Christ. On this rhetorical convention, which can be called chain-link construction, see Bruce W. Longenecker, *Rhetoric at the Boundaries: The Art and Theology of the New Testament Chain-Link Transitions* (Waco, TX: Baylor University Press, 2005).

72. Cranfield, *Romans*, 351–52.

73. Barrett, *Romans*, 136: "Sin in its deceitful use of the law and commandment, is revealed not merely in its true colors but in the worst possible light."

discussion about sin, death, and the law and their various effects on humankind. Finally, it is worth pointing out as Kaminsky does that

> It is far from clear that Gen 3 describes a loss of human immortality because such a reading presupposes that humans were created immortal. . . . Genesis 3 is more properly described as a story about a missed opportunity to obtain immortality [by eating of the tree of life] than about the loss of immortality that humans had originally been granted. One can see that this is the case by noting that the curses God put on humanity in 3:16–19 presume they are mortal.[74]

Adam and Eve must be driven from Eden lest they obtain immortality from the tree of life. If this was Paul's view, then the death he is talking about is spiritual death, not merely physical mortality. The wages of sin is spiritual death, and so the loss of relationship with God, not the immediate loss of physical life.

THE FALLEN ANGELS: GENESIS 6:1–8

This story was the subject of no little focus and attention in early Jewish literature, including in the NT itself. We must deal with the translation first.

MT	LXX
[1] When people began to multiply on the face of the ground, and daughters were born to them, [2] the sons of God saw that they were fair; and they took wives for themselves of all that they chose.	[1] And it came about when humans began to become numerous on the earth, that daughters also were born to them. [2] Now when the sons of God saw the daughters of humans, that they were fair, they took wives for themselves of all that they chose.
[3] Then the Lord said, "My spirit shall not abide in mortals forever, for they are flesh; their days shall be one hundred twenty years." [4] The Nephilim were on the earth in those days—and also afterward—when the sons of God went in to the daughters of humans, who bore children to them. These were the heroes that were of old, warriors of renown. [5] The Lord saw that the wickedness of humankind was great in the earth,	[3] And the Lord God said, "My spirit shall not abide in these humans forever, because they are flesh, but their days shall be one hundred twenty years." [4] Now the giants were on the earth in those days and afterward. When the sons of God used to go in to the daughters of humans, then they produced offspring for themselves. Those were the giants that were of old, the renowned humans. [5] And when the Lord God saw that the wicked deeds of humans were multiplied

74. Kaminsky, "Theology of Genesis," 640.

and that every inclination of the thoughts of their hearts was only evil continually.

⁶ And the Lord was sorry that he had made humankind on the earth, and it grieved him to his heart.

⁷ So the Lord said, "I will blot out from the earth the human beings I have created—people together with animals and creeping things and birds of the air, for I am sorry that I have made them."

⁸ But Noah found favor in the sight of the Lord.

on the earth and that all think attentively in their hearts on evil things all the days,

⁶ then God considered that he had made humankind on the earth, and he thought it over.

⁷ And God said, "I will wipe out from off the earth humankind which I have made, from human to domestic animal and from creeping things to birds of the sky, for I have become angry that I have made them."

⁸ Yet Noah found favor before the Lord God.

This paragraph, as it now stands, concludes the account of Adam's genealogy (5:1) and introduces us to Noah who will be the main character in the next *toledoth* section of the narrative. These two paragraphs demonstrate further what has already been shown to be true in Genesis 3–4, namely that human beings are sinful and deserve to be judged by a righteous and just God.[75] There is not a great deal of difference between the MT and the LXX/OG of this narrative with the following exceptions: (1) those called *Nephilim* in the Hebrew are identified as giants in the LXX/OG and are said to be renown humans, not heroes or great warriors; (2) the Hebrew has God expressing regret he created humans in the first place, whereas the Greek simply says God reconsidered, or he thought over his previous decision; (3) note that both renderings refer to the angels taking wives among the human females, whichever one's they preferred.

While there has been considerable debate about the meaning of Genesis 6:1–8 and whether it referred to cross-breeding between angels and female humans, that is not only the natural way to interpret this text in light of similar accounts of divine-human unions in Babylonian, Egyptian, Ugaritic, Hittite, and Greek literature, it is clearly how the NT writers of Jude and 2 Peter understood this story, and, I would add, the author of 1 Peter as well.[76] The issue here is the violation of the creation order, which is seen as an extreme form of

75. See Arnold, *Genesis*, 89.

76. See Westermann, *Genesis 1–11*, 379–81. For the interesting conjecture that the *"kharem"* or holy war cleansing of the promised land by Joshua and others has to do with the elimination of the descendants of the *Nephilim*, the cross-breeds, rather than Canaanites and other ethnic groups, see now Michael Heiser, *The Unseen Realm: Recovering the Supernatural Worldview of the Bible* (Bellingham, WA: Lexham, 2016). If true, it would certainly change the whole way "holy war" is viewed as a part of OT history.

immorality and rebellion against the Creator. Here a chart or two can be helpful:

The following chart shows how Isaiah and later the author of 1 Enoch recycled the Genesis tradition.[77]

Isaiah 24:21–22	1 Enoch 10:4–6
"In that day the Lord will punish the powers in the heavens above and the kings on the earth below. They will be herded together like prisoners bound in a dungeon; they will be shut up in prison and be punished after many days.	"The Lord said to Raphael, 'Bind Azazel hand and foot, throw him into the darkness.' And he made a hole in the desert . . . and cast him there; he threw on top of him rugged sharp rocks. And he covered his face in order that he might not see the light and in order that he might be sent into the great fire on judgment day."

Turning to the NT itself we find the following further reflections on this tradition—

Jude 6	2 Peter 2:4	1 Peter 3:19–20
And the angels who did not keep their own positions but left their proper dwelling, he has kept in eternal chains in deepest darkness for the judgment of the great Day. (author's translation)	For if God did not spare the angels when they sinned, but fast them into hell [Tartaros] and committed them to chains of deepest darkness to be kept until the judgment. (author's translation)	He [Christ] went and made a proclamation to the spirits in prison, who in former times did not obey, when God waited patiently in the day of Noah. (author's translation)

Were this not enough to keep one pondering for days at a time, to it we may add for a final big bang what is said of the devil himself at the beginning of Revelation 20:

> And I saw an angel coming down out of heaven, having the key to the Abyss and holding in his hand a great chain. [2] He seized the dragon, that ancient serpent, who is the devil, or Satan, and bound him for a thousand years. [3] He threw him into the Abyss, and locked and sealed it over him, to keep him from deceiving the nations anymore until the thou-

---

77. For detailed discussion of these parallels, one may turn to my commentaries on Jude and 1 and 2 Peter in Ben Witherington III, *Letters and Homilies for Jewish Christians: A Socio-Rhetorical Commentary on Hebrews, James and Jude* (Downers Grove, IL: InterVarsity, 2016) and in Witherington, *Letters and Homilies for Hellenized Christians Volume 2: A Socio-Rhetorical Commentary on 1–2 Peter* (Downers Grove, IL: InterVarsity, 2010) and more succinctly in Witherington, *Jesus the Seer: The Progress of Prophecy* (Mineapolis: Fortress, 2014), x–xii.

sand years were ended. After that, he must be set free for a short time. (author's translation)

Here I think we have a parade example of how it is never adequate just to study how the OT is quoted in the NT, or even alluded to or echoed. One needs to see the larger context and how a tradition is developed or diminished over time and in various contexts. In terms of the NT, the earliest form of the development of the tradition is done by someone who is quite cognizant of the trajectory of this material, including its use in apocryphal intertestamental Jewish sources. Let us consider what Jude is doing with the tradition.

With Jude 6 we turn to the play on words using the term "keep" (*tēreō*). In v. 1 it was God who kept or had a firm grasp on believers, here the angels do not keep to their proper domain but rather abandon their abode and come to earth and have relations with women, a much commented on text in early Judaism (see 1 Enoch 6–19; 86–88; 106; Jubilees 4:15, 22; 5:1; 1QApGen 2.1; Testament of Reuben 5:6–7; 2 Bar 56:10–14). As a result, God must keep them in perpetual bondage until the great and terrible day of judgment. The lesson is clear. If believers wish to be "kept" by God they must keep to their proper sphere, and keep God's commandments and keep on relying on Him, not the false teachers. Quite clearly in the background of v. 6 is Genesis 6:1–8. This, however, is not all, it is Genesis 6:1–8 as interpreted, embellished, and added to by various Jewish apocryphal texts. This story is about angels lusting after humans, but the Sodom story will be about humans lusting after angels, and notice how in 1 Enoch 10:4–6 Michael is instructed to bind these angels in chains until the day of judgment. On this one should compare J. N. D. Kelly's and R. J. Bauckham's commentaries, where it is made very clear that Jude is relying on 1 Enoch and also on the Testament of Moses. If we ask what these three examples of judgment have in common, J. Daryl Charles has a ready answer: "all three paradigms—unbelieving Israel, the dispossessed angels, and Sodom and Gomorrah—are for the present purpose of Jude and his audience ongoing examples . . . of divine judgment. The reason is that they *all exhibit an unnatural rebellion*."[78]

It will be well if we move on to 2 Peter 2 at this juncture, and briefly review the very good reasons for seeing 2 Peter as a later use of Jude, rather than vice versa, and instead of assuming they both used a

---

78. J. Daryl Charles, *Literary Strategy in the Epistle of Jude* (Scranton, PA: University of Scranton Press, 2005), 118, emphasis original.

common source. In regard to sources, there are several views: (1) Jude used 2 Peter; (2) both Jude and the author of 2 Peter used a common source; 3) 2 Peter definitely used Jude.[79] In regard to the last view, Ralph Martin gives the following chart:

Jude	2 Peter	Jude	2 Peter
4	2:1–3	11–12a	2:15, 13
5	2:5	12b–13	2:17
6, 7	2:4, 6	16	2:18
8, 9	2:10, 11	17	3:2
10	2:12	18	3:3[80]

Nineteen out of twenty-five of Jude's verses seem to exist in some form in 2 Peter!

In short, almost all the significant material in Jude is taken over, used, and expanded upon or adapted in 2 Peter 2. And just as impressively the material is found *in exactly the same order* in both documents, covering the same themes and topics. This is not a case of just borrowing an idea or two, or a term or phrase or two. The argument here for literary dependence is very strong indeed. Context is important, and so it will be well if we give a more fulsome presentation of the parallels between 2 Peter and Jude.

2 Peter	Jude
False prophets also arose among the people, . . . *denying* the *Master* who bought them . . . , and many will follow their *licentiousness* . . . (2:2)	Certain people sneaked in; . . . impious, they put aside the grace of our God for *licentiousness* and *deny* our only *Master* and Lord Jesus Christ (v. 4)
God did not spare *the angels* who sinned, but cast them into Tartarus *in chains of darkness,* keeping them until *judgment* . . . (2:4)	*Angels* who did not keep their own rank . . . he *keeps* for the *judgment of the great Day,* with eternal *chains of darkness* (v. 6)
God condemned and reduced to ashes the *cities* of *Sodom and Gomorrah,* setting an *example* for those who would be impious (2:6)	*Sodom and Gomorrah* and the *cities* around them, which committed fornication . . . are set forth as an *example,* suffering a punishment of

79. For the view that Jude used 2 Peter, see Douglas Moo, *2 Peter and Jude,* NIVAC (Grand Rapids: Zondervan, 1996), 16–18.

80. Ralph P. Martin, *New Testament Foundations: A Guide for Christian Students; Volume 2; The Acts, the Letters, the Apocalypse* (Grand Rapids: Eerdmans, 1978), 385.

eternal fire (v. 7)

Especially for those who follow the *flesh* in passion for *corruption* and *despise authority*. Bold and arrogant, they are not afraid to *blaspheme the glorious ones* (2:10)	Yet these dreamers *corrupt the flesh* and *set aside authority* and *blaspheme the glorious ones* (v. 8)
Strength and power *do not* bring a *blasphemous judgment* against them from the Lord (2:11)	argued with the Devil . . . *did not* dare *bring a judgment of blasphemy* but said "The *Lord* will rebuke you." (v. 9)

Even on a cursory examination of these two columns, and even examining them in English three things are apparent: (1) they are covering the same ground in the same order; (2) though there is considerable verbal overlap between the two accounts 2 Peter cannot be said to be simply copying Jude's account. Rather the author is adopting and adapting this source for his own purposes and audiences; (3) our author is deeply indebted to the little sermon of Jude, using the vast majority of Jude's material in one way or another, but leaving out the very sectarian material in order to make the source more user friendly for his own broader audience.

Verse 4 begins another typical long cumbersome Asiatic sentence like we find in 1:3–11, and in contrast to what we find in 1:12–21. Further, this present section is full of colorful and un-Petrine vocabulary all of which suggests a different source is being used (Jude of course), but the modification of Jude in a way that works with Asiatic rhetoric is notable. Verse 4 begins by saying, for "If God did not spare." This is not a hypothetical if *(ei)* but a real condition. 2 Peter's treatment of the material differs from Jude in several regards: (1) our author mainly excises the apocryphal material from 1 Enoch 10 and the Testament of Moses; (2) most importantly he adds some positive examples for his audience to follow, unlike Jude; (3) he puts his examples in biblical chronological order. He is thus a careful writer even if his style is rather grandiose and unwieldy. From an epideictic rhetorical point of view this is important as it means that our author is not engaging here in unrelenting invective, but also sets forth some praiseworthy examples too.

Verse 4 also indicates clearly that our author interpreted Genesis 6:1–4 to refer to angels, not men who sinned and were consigned to Tartarus (cf. 2 Enoch 20.2).[81] This is also what one sees in 1 Peter and

---

81. See André Feuillet, "Le péché évoqué aux chapitres 3 et 6,4 de la Genèse : La péché des anges de l'épître de Jude et de la Second épître de Pierre," *Divinitas* 35 (1991): 207–29. Our

Jude. Tartarus was the nether regions of Hades, the very bottom of the pit reserved for disobedient gods and rebellious humans and other creatures presumably. One of the reasons not to translate this word as hell is because it is a preliminary holding tank, not a final destination.[82] The word *serais* presents us with a textual problem, because the original reading may be *sirois* attested by Sinaiticus, A, B, C and other witnesses.[83] The latter word means "pits," the former "chains." In favor of "pits" (literally underground grain silos; it is where we get the word silo) is the fact that in a text like Revelation 20:1–2 we hear of Satan being thrown into a pit. However, if *sirois* was original, it is impossible to explain how the reading *serais* arose. Going in the other direction it is easy to see why scribes would change the original to chains since that is similar to Jude's text. We thus conclude that "pits" is original here. After all, what would gloomy chains mean anyway?

What the author is saying is that these fallen angels are being kept in holding tanks that are gloomy, until the last day. He identifies this place of confinement as Tartarus. Now Tartarus in Greek mythology was a place of punishment for wicked departed spirits, or a place of confinement for the Titans. This was a dungeon or prison (cf. 1 Peter 3) and is in all likelihood not to be identified with the biblical hell. We see here our author's Hellenistic bent. In 1 Enoch 20:2 there was a special angel in charge of Tartarus: Uriel (cf. Rev 20:1–2).

Verse 5 is about God's not sparing the ancient world. Clearly the author of 2 Peter saw the flood as universal, the whole *kosmos* went under the deluge, though of course he is speaking about his own then-known whole world. This example we do not find in Jude. In fact, the two positive examples are also found in Philo (*Moses* 253–65). One of the rhetorical functions of these examples is to provide some relief from the blaming, and cite praiseworthy examples, but even more importantly it allows our author to not only link

author seems to have used the term Tartarus to conjure up the mythological punishment of the Titans in such a gloomy place (see Hesiod, *Theog.* 713–35). See Birger Pearson, "A Reminiscence of Classical Myth at II Peter 2.4," *GRBS* 10 (1969): 71–80. However, as Thomas R. Schreiner, *1 and 2 Peter, Jude*, NAC 37 (Nashville: Broadman & Holman, 2003), 336–37 rightly notes, the term is used by various early Jews and is even found in the LXX (e.g., Job 40:20; 41:24; Prov 3:16; see also Sibylline Oracles 2:302; 4:186; Josephus, *Ag. Ap.,* 2.240; Philo, *Rewards*, 152). However, the parallels between the story about the Titans and the story about these angels may have prompted this usage here, bearing in mind that our author is hellenizing Jude at this point for the sake of his broader audience.

82. Moo, *2 Peter and Jude*, 103. William J. Dalton, "The Interpretation of 1 Peter 3:19 and 4:6: Light from 2 Peter," *Bib* 60 (1979): 547–55.

83. And favored in the Nestle-Aland text of the Greek NT.

his audience to previous righteous ones being assailed by a sea of wickedness, but to give them hope they will prevail over it, and the wicked will be judged.[84] But these little positive examples are meant to remind the audience that "God did not establish commandments, send prophets, and ransom humanity through the death of Jesus in order to maximize the population of hell."[85] Rather his redemptive judgments were all to the end of redeeming the world, just as the warnings of future judgment are to help keep the faithful on the straight and narrow. These particular two examples remind the audience that God could deliver them from even more drastic circumstances than they currently face (see Sir 33:1), and not incidentally Jesus also uses the examples of Noah and Lot back to back as well (Luke 17:26–29).

Notice how he contrasts those whom God does not spare (a recurring verb, cf. vv. 4, 5), and those whom he rescues (also a recurring verb, vv. 7, 9). He is building to the conclusion that: (1) there is plenty of historical precedent for God acting in judgment, and also in redemption in history; (2) these examples are but types of the final judgment, therefore the false teachers and their followers better beware. God protected Noah as one of eight he spared (Gen 8:18). The word translated "deluge" is where we get the word "cataclysm"—an earth-shattering event. Noah is said to be a preacher of righteousness; something also implied in Josephus, *Ant.* 1.3.1. In Wisdom of Solomon 10:4 he is associated with Wisdom, who saves the world. Genesis 6 does not say this but it does imply God allowed a period of repentance. Perhaps our author is drawing on popular Jewish traditions about Noah that he preached to the sinful world before he boarded the ark (see Sibylline Oracle 1.148–498). What then should we make of the material in 1 Peter 3? To it we now turn.

Verse 18 may be said to begin the third major christological reflection in this discourse (cf. 1:18–21 and 2:21–25), possibly drawing on traditional materials.[86] It brings out a further insight into Peter's view

84. Pheme Perkins, *First and Second Peter, James and Jude*, IBC (Louisville: Westminister John Knox, 2012), 183.

85. Perkins, *First and Second Peter*, 183.

86. Peter J. Achtemeier, *1 Peter: A Commentary on First Peter*, Hermeneia (Minneapolis: Fortress, 1996), 240, characterizes 3:18–22 as rambling in style, not recognizing that lengthy and often convoluted sentences are a hallmark of Asiatic rhetoric. His discussion however of the basic possible ways to interpret this passage on pp. 244–46 provides a very helpful summary. See the more thorough discussion in John H. Elliott, *1 Peter: A New Translation with Introduction and Commentary*, AB 37B (New Haven: Yale University Press, 2011), 693–705, on the traditional materials used here.

of the atonement. Isaiah 53:11 LXX is likely in the background here: "The righteous one my servant, shall make many righteous, and he shall bear their iniquities." Verse 18a reminds the listener that even Christ suffered on account of sins, and yet of course, Peter is not just drawing an analogy to his audience's suffering. The use of *hapax* here likely means "only once" (cf. Heb 9:26, 28; see also Rom 6:10; Heb 7:27; 9:12; 10:10) and thus the stress is on the uniqueness of Christ's suffering and death.[87] Here *epathen* likely includes death as in the phrase "suffered under Pontius Pilate." The use of "sins" plural may well suggest that Peter is not using *peri* plus the object to indicate Christ is a sin offering, but just to stress that it was sin that made it necessary, indeed made it God's will for Jesus to suffer. The next phrase "the righteous for the unrighteous," again conjures up Isaiah 53 and clearly refers to a vicarious death by one who did not deserve to die at all, much less to die on a cross. The purpose of the death is clear: to bring people before God, to reconcile them to God, to make it possible for people to come into God's presence even though we are unrighteous. Thus, Christ's death is viewed as an act of pure grace. The term *prosagōgē* means access. Christ's death provided access into the very presence of God (cf. Rom 5:2; Eph 2:17; 3:12). It is perhaps not an accident that this is the same term used to refer to the leading of the animals to sacrifice (Exod 29:10; Lev 1:2). Access comes through sacrifice, in this case the sacrifice Jesus offered in person.

The last clause of verse 18 is difficult to interpret, but clearly it refers to Christ. *Thanatōtheis* implies that Jesus was forcibly put to death and of course *sarka* indicates he was a person of real flesh and blood, fully human. The term *sarka* cannot be instrumental here (i.e., "by his flesh") and this rules out the idea that the parallel phrase means brought to life "by his [the] Spirit." In other words, *pneumati* cannot be a reference to Christ's divine nature since it never died nor could it be said to be brought to life. His human spirit is another matter. It is right to emphasize the parallel construction here and the *men . . . de* contrast. On the one hand, he was put to death in the sphere of

87. I. H. Marshall, *1 Peter*, IVPNTC (Downers Grove, IL: InterVarsity, 1991), 119, points out it could also mean "at one point in time" (i.e., once back then as opposed to now—kind of like the meaning of *pote* in 2:10 or 3:3 or 3:20), but that would be innocuous and furthermore the use of *hapax* in the book of Hebrews also points in the direction of seeing the uniqueness and finality of Christ's sacrifice in this term; cf. Achtemeier, *1 Peter*, 251. Interestingly, Elliott (*1 Peter*, 641) is prepared to translate it "once for all time." In any case the word sets Christ's suffering apart from that of his followers in a crucial way: his alone was for atonement of sins.

the flesh. On the other hand, he was made alive in the sphere of the spirit/Spirit.[88]

But what does *pneumati* means here? Does it mean: (1) in his spirit; (2) in the Spirit; (3) spiritually; or (4) in the realm of or with reference to the Spirit? Notice that there is an intended contrast here: "on the one hand . . . on the other," but in both halves of the contrast we are talking about something that *happened* to Jesus, not something he did. Possibly 4:6b should be seen as a parallel here; dead Christians have been judged in the eyes of humans, they are dead in regard to the flesh, but in God's eyes they are alive in regard to the Spirit. But if 3:18 is talking about the human spirit of Jesus, did it die on the cross or did it merely pass on into God's hands? Sometimes "spirit" means the animating life breath of a physical body (e.g., the *psyche*), but Peter does not seem to mean that here. He is probably not talking about a body/soul dualism here. Normally "made alive" in the NT means resuscitated (see John 5:21; 6:63; Rom 4:17, 8:11) and if this is meant here then clearly Peter is not talking about some spiritual existence Jesus had between death and resurrection. Thus, either *pneumati* refers to the Holy Spirit here, or there is a reference to the realm or sphere of the spirit—the spiritual realm. If it is the latter, then presumably *sarx* here refers to the physical or material realm. Now if Christ's being "made alive" refers to his resurrection, then *pneumati* does not describe Christ's anatomical condition (i.e., that he was nonmaterial at that point), but rather the controlling sphere or factor in his life was the spiritual sphere, not the earthly, fleshly one. This might mean he had a resurrection body but was living in a heavenly or spiritual sphere (i.e., in a realm or condition dominated by God's Spirit). Ernest Best puts it this way:

> The contrast is not between two parts of man's nature, his flesh and his spirit (a contrast which is on the whole foreign to the NT) nor between two parts in Christ (his divine nature could not be said to be made alive in his death), nor is it possible to take "spirit" to mean that Christ went in a bodiless fashion to preach to the "spirits" (verse 19). When spirit is opposed to flesh in the NT the opposition of divine Spirit to human existence is intended; cf. Gal 5:26ff; Rom 8:1ff. . . . Both "flesh" and "spirit," datives without a preposition, are best taken as datives of reference. . . . The phrase then means that Christ died in the human sphere but was made alive and continues alive in the sphere of the Spirit.[89]

88. See Elliott, *1 Peter*, 646–47.
89. Ernest Best, *1 Peter*, NCB (London: Oliphants, 1977), 139.

Unless one wants to argue that Jesus's human spirit being revived is what the second phrase refers to, it is hard to escape the conclusion that the second phrase refers to the resurrection. And the further implication of the grammar here is that Jesus's visit to the spirits in prison took place *after* he was quickened "in the spirit/Spirit."[90] What can be added to this is that the verb *zōopoiētheis* "made alive" is clearly used to refer to the resurrection of Jesus elsewhere in the NT (e.g., John 5:21; 1 Cor 15:22; Rom 4:17; 8:11; Col 2:13; 1 Tim 6:13). The passive voice here and elsewhere makes clear that Jesus did not raise himself, but rather was raised by God.

Furthermore, even texts like Romans 10:7 or Ephesians 4:8–10 do not in fact refer to Jesus going down and preaching to dead human beings. The latter text surely refers to the preexistent Christ's descent to earth, not to Sheol/Hades, and the former text while it may refer to Christ's spirit being in the land of the dead at some juncture, says nothing about preaching to anyone, and in any case, is part of a rhetorical question. Furthermore, Paul is speaking to his own Roman audience in the present tense and believes very clearly that Jesus is not currently among the dead; rather, he is in heaven. Therefore, the rhetorical function of the remark is not to comment on the location of Jesus but instead on the fact that human beings could not go and retrieve Christ from *anywhere* in the spiritual realm. There is no question but that v. 19 follows on from 3:18 and should not be separated from it. However there are at least six hard questions this text does raise:[91] (1) What is the antecedent of "in which"? (2) When did Christ preach to the spirits?[92] (3) Who are these spirits? (4) Where is their prison? (5)What did Christ preach to them? (6) Do 3:16 and 4:6 refer to the same event? In addition to our other problems with this text, it is not clear what Peter's view of baptism is. It has been said by Elliott there are some 180 options for interpreting these complex verses, but still certain issues can be sorted out reasonably clearly.[93] Grammar should have guided the discussion, but in many cases it has not. As

---

90. Achtemeier, *1 Peter*, 258.

91. Indeed, so many questions that even so fine a scholar as Scot McKnight throws up his hands and simply presents the three major options for interpreting this text. See McKnight, *1 Peter*, NIVAC (Grand Rapids: Zondervan, 1996), 215–17.

92. The substitution of Enoch for Christ here by Moffatt and Goodspeed has no textual warrant at all; see the critique in Achtemeier, *1 Peter*, 253–54. This brilliant conjecture that turns *en ho* into Enoch (only one letter different in the Greek) can be traced back to the Greek NT of J. Bowyer in 1763 after which this conjecture took on a life of its own; see Elliott, *1 Peter*, 652.

93. See the laying out of the basic options in Elliott, *1 Peter*, 648–50.

Michaels says "the words *en hō kai* serves to link *zōopoiētheis* closely to the *poreutheis ekēruzen* that follows, making Christ's proclamation to the spirits a direct outcome of his resurrection from the dead."[94] In other words, the preaching, whatever its nature, is surely *not* an activity that took place between death and resurrection.

Of necessity, we must deal with the central thrust of these complex verses, which clearly enough are not primarily focusing on baptism. Attending to question one, which is dealing with the beginning of v. 19, as the commentators have rightly pointed out, when Peter uses the phrase *en hō* its antecedent is always a whole phrase that precedes, not a single word. It is thus unlikely that "in which" means "in the Spirit." Rather it is more likely to mean "in which condition" (i.e., the condition of being made alive by the Spirit or spiritually, which is to say resurrected). Second, we need to answer the question about who these "spirits" (plural) are, who are in some sort of prison.

We may note first that they cannot simply be the dead who are indeed referred to in 4:6 because here these spirits are not said to be all spirits, but only those who are *en phulakē* and furthermore, they are the same spirits who disobeyed in the days of Noah. It needs to be stressed that this language about prison is never used in the NT to refer to Sheol/Hades the land of the dead, much less hell in the NT. It always refers to an incarcerating place for fallen angels or demons (e.g., Rev 18:2; 20:7; 1 Enoch 10:4; 14:5; 15:8, 10; 18:12–14; cf. 2 Pet 2:4). Now if Peter was talking about human beings here he surely would not have chosen the phrase "in prison" or the phrase "spirits who disobeyed," because human beings were neither spirits nor in the Spirit in those days. He would rather have said "the spirits *of those* who once disobeyed," not "the spirits who disobeyed."

Furthermore, the phrase *ta pneumata*, which does not mean "the spiritual ones" is never used elsewhere to refer to human beings who have died with the possible exception of Hebrews 12:23. By contrast we have plenty of evidence of supernatural beings called spirits in the NT (see, e.g., the unclean spirits in Mark 12:23, 26, 27; 3:11). More importantly, in Jude and in 2 Peter the phrase is used of disobedient angels (e.g., Jude 6 and 2 Pet 2:4 and see Testament of Reuben 5:2). In view of this fact, that 1 Peter comes out of the same apocalyptic Jewish Christian milieu as these two books, and that there seems to be a clear drawing on 1 Enoch 6–16 in these sources, and finally since

94. J. Ramsey Michaels, *1 Peter*, WBC (Grand Rapids: Zondervan, 2015), 205–6.

2 Peter 2:4 represents the NT canonical interpretation of our passage (and the one in Jude), then most assuredly what we are dealing with here is angels. Notice how in 1 Enoch 15:8–10 we hear about the giants being born of the union of "spirits and the flesh" (i.e., of angels and human women).

It should be noticed that obviously nowhere in Judaism and also nowhere in early Christianity in the first century unless it is here in 1 Peter do we find the idea of a descent into hell. The first noncanonical mention of the idea of a descent into hell seems to be found in Justin, *Dial.* 72, but it is not associated with the interpretation of this text. That does not come until Clement of Alexandria interprets 1 Peter 3:19 this way, and this then became the dominant interpretation at least by the time of Irenaeus at the end of second century CE.[95] Nevertheless, the first time that the phrase "he descended into hell" appears in any creedal discussion or creed is in about 400 CE in Rufinus's exposition of a Roman creed. It is also worth remarking that the Apostle's Creed does not originally seem to have had this clause, but even if it did, no council ever endorsed this particular early creed unlike the Nicene Creed.[96]

The notion that the preaching was to the disobedient sinners of Noah's generation, giving them a second chance at redemption, so to speak, raises a perplexing question. How exactly rhetorically would that effectively steel the audience of Peter to face persecution and possible death? Wouldn't it rather have the opposite effect? Achtemeier puts it this way: "If God relented on such evil entities, why not rely on the same treatment and deny Christ now to avoid suffering?"[97]

We may also stress with Marshall that there are insuperable problems with the idea that Christ preached to the lost during the time of Noah *in the person of Noah.* As we have stressed, the Greek grammar here favors the view that this proclamation by Christ took place *after* Christ had been "made alive" which is to say "was raised," not before he even took on flesh. Second, the spirit of Christ inspiring OT prophets is one thing, his inhabiting Noah and speaking through

95. See Donald Senior, *1 Peter*, SP15 (Collegeville, MN: Liturgical Press, 2008), 101.

96. See esp. Elliott, *1 Peter*, 706–9 on the history of the *ad Infernos* interpretation.

97. Achtemeier, *1 Peter*, 261. The same problem follows if Jesus is preaching good news to the wicked angels of Gen 6:1–4. The word "'preach'" in itself is not a technical term for "'preach the good news'." Notice how the noun form *kērygma* in Matt 12:41/Luke 11:32 is used of the content of Jonah's message which was closer to that of the Baptist's than Jesus's. Notice the difference with 4:6 where we do indeed have *euangelidzō*; 3:19's verb just means "announce."

him quite another. Were that what the author means, the text should have read "he preached when the spirits disobeyed," but it does not. Third, the spirits in prison would be a very odd way to speak about ordinary human life during the time of Noah.[98] Clearly, we need better exegesis than this of these difficult verses. Notice as well that nothing is said in these verses about Christ going *down* anywhere, much less that he went *down to Hades*. The verb *poreutheis* in v. 19 and in v. 22 describes Jesus's travels and it simply means "he went" or "he has gone" with no direction implied in the verb at all. Only the context will indicate that, if anything does. If v. 22 provides the guiding clue, then this proclamation took place not between death and resurrection but after Jesus experienced resurrection, as v. 18 implies. In other words, it refers to what happened as or while Jesus went to heaven. But there is a much better option than these sorts of exegetical gymnastics and it involves recognizing the influence of 1 Enoch in our text.

If we ask the rhetorical function of this elaborate argument, it would be a further way that Peter is trying to encourage suffering Christians. Don't worry, says Peter, about the powers of evil that motivate such persecutors. They have already been told their doom is sure. Here is where we note the close parallel in 1 Timothy 3:16: appeared in flesh, vindicated by the Spirit, seen by angels (though of course that could refer to seen by nonfallen angels). Presumably we should see this prison as a holding place until the final judgment (cf. Rev 20:1–2), and thus not hell or Sheol. This all comports nicely with the idea that angels and such spirit beings are above, in the air or the heavenlies (cf. the phrase "the prince of the power of the air" or Eph 6:12), though some of the ancients saw Tartarus as "below," but in any case we are talking about in the spiritual realm.[99]

The point of the analogy in v. 20 is that just as God saved his people, though only a few, while the wicked pagans were many in the days of Noah, so will he do with Peter's audience, who are only a few Jews in comparison with a large pagan majority. Jesus's triumphant story is being rehearsed to reassure the persecuted Christians that though they are also going the route of suffering, their triumph afterward will be like Christ's. They need not fear or worry. Verse 21 is one of the more difficult to decipher in this section. First

98. See Marshall, *1 Peter*, 124.

99. See the discussion in Ben Witherington III, *The Letters to Philemon, Colossians, and Ephesians: A Socio-Rhetorical Commentary on the Captivity Epistles* (Grand Rapids: Eerdmans, 2007).

of all, we hear about the "antitype," a term elsewhere found only in Hebrews 9:24 (cf. 2 Clem. 14:3; Polybius *Hist.* 6.31.8 for the use with the dative) to refer to the temple.[100] It must mean something like the waters of Noah's day prefigure the greater judgment and salvation event in Christ that is symbolized in baptism.[101] I would stress that only here in 1 Peter do we have a brief discussion of baptism, and only here in the whole NT do we have a statement that baptism in some sense "saves." It is a mistake to build a whole theology of baptism on the basis of one text that all sides of the discussion admit is obscure, perhaps the most obscure and difficult text in the whole NT canon. What is clear however is that this text draws on Genesis 6:1–8 and the long Jewish history of exegesis of that text to make clear that Christ has triumphed over the powers of darkness.

NOAH COUNT: GENESIS 7

The story of Noah and the flood is one of the most if not perhaps the most familiar of all OT stories to Christians, because it has been celebrated in song, in childrens' toy arks, in story, and in sermons and major films. For our purposes, it is not necessary to recount the whole tale and do detailed exegesis on it all, but the portion of the story about the entering of the ark and the sweeping away of sinful humanity recurs at several junctures in the NT, and so deserves some close scrutiny.

MT	LXX
[11] In the six hundredth year of Noah's life, on the seventeenth day of the second month—on that day all the springs of the great deep burst forth, and the floodgates of the heavens were opened. [12] And rain fell on the earth forty days and forty nights. [13] On that very day Noah and his sons, Shem, Ham and Japheth, together with his wife and the wives of his three sons, entered the ark.	[11] In the six hundredth year in Noah's life, the second month, on the twenty-seventh of the month, on this day all the fountains of the abyss burst forth, and the cataracts of the sky were opened, [12] and the rain came on the earth for forty days and forty nights. [13] On this day Noah, Shem, Ham, Japeth, Noah's sons, and Noah's wife and the three wives of his sons with him, entered into the ark.

100. We now have inscriptional evidence for the word *antitypos* in IGUR 1167.3–4 where it means something like "corresponding." To this should be compared IGUR 1327.5, which refers to an "exact" copy. See the discussion in *NewDocs* 4:41–42.

101. See Senior, *1 Peter*, 104–5.

[14] They had with them every wild animal according to its kind, all livestock according to their kinds, every creature that moves along the ground according to its kind and every bird according to its kind, everything with wings.
[15] Pairs of all creatures that have the breath of life in them came to Noah and entered the ark.
[16] The animals going in were male and female of every living thing, as God had commanded Noah. Then the Lord shut him in.
[17] For forty days the flood kept coming on the earth, and as the waters increased they lifted the ark high above the earth.
[18] The waters rose and increased greatly on the earth, and the ark floated on the surface of the water.
[19] They rose greatly on the earth, and all the high mountains under the entire heavens were covered.
[20] The waters rose and covered the mountains to a depth of more than fifteen cubits.
[21] Every living thing that moved on land perished—birds, livestock, wild animals, all the creatures that swarm over the earth, and all mankind.
[22] Everything on dry land that had the breath of life in its nostrils died.
[23] Every living thing on the face of the earth was wiped out; people and animals and the creatures that move along the ground and the birds were wiped from the earth. Only Noah was left, and those with him in the ark.
[24] The waters flooded the earth for a hundred and fifty days.

[14] And all the wild animals according to kind and all the domestic animals according to kind and every creeping thing that moves on the earth according to kind and every bird according to kind
[15] entered into the ark to Noe, two by two of all flesh in which there is a spirit of life.
[16] And those that were coming in, male and female of all flesh, entered as God had commanded Noe. And the Lord God closed the ark apart from him.
[17] And the flood came for forty days and forty nights on the earth, and the water increased and bore up the ark, and it was raised up from the earth.
[18] And the water was prevailing and increasing greatly on the earth, and the ark was being carried along over the water.
[19] So the water was prevailing very greatly on the earth, and it covered all the high mountains that were under heaven;
[20] the water was raised up fifteen cubits above, and it covered all the high mountains.
[21] And all flesh that moves on the earth—of birds and of domestic animals and of wild animals—died, and every creeping thing that moves on the earth and every human being.
[22] And all things that have a breath of life, and everyone who was on the dry land, died.
[23] And he wiped out everything that rises, which was on the face of the whole earth, from human being to domestic animal and creeping things and the birds of the sky, and they were wiped out from the earth. And only Noe was left, and those with him in the ark.
[24] And the water was raised up on the earth one hundred fifty days.

The description of Noah as "righteous in this generation" (see 6:9 and 7:1) presumably refers to his behavior before entering the ark, and in any case, appears to be comparative, rather than superlative in emphasis. By comparison, Noah and his family were more in accord with God's will than others. According to Genesis 6:19–20 Noah was to admit seven additional pairs of clean land animals and seven pairs of birds (not just two of each), but the reason for this does not become apparent until 8:7–12, as Wenham notes.[102] The extra birds would be let out to reconnoiter to see if the water had receded sufficiently to leave the ark, and the additional land animals were to be used in sacrifice. If only two pairs had been kept, and they were the only types allowed for such sacrifices according to Leviticus, they would have become instantly extinct. The story is told in light of the later distinctions and laws made in Leviticus between clean and unclean animals, although in the Babylonian form of this story, Atrahasis also seems to have included clean animals and winged birds as his cargo.[103] As Exodus 24:18 intimates, forty days and forty nights is a conventional expression for a long time.

Noah and his family simply obey God's commands and survive the flood. It is interesting that the Genesis account plays down Noah's building of the ark, whereas in the Gilgamesh epic the flood hero's efforts are described in detail explaining how he skillfully constructed the ark. Here it is enough to just mention Noah's obedience in doing so. Indeed, Utnapishtim brags about loading all his gold and other resources into the ark, something that is no part of the account in Genesis. It is interesting that Noah's age is noted in v. 6, as six hundred years old, when he entered the ark. The author clearly wants us to see Noah as a real historical figure, something the NT writers take for granted. In fact, as Wenham stresses "the fullness and precision of the dates in the flood narrative are astonishing (7:12, 17, 24; 8:3, 4, 5, 6, 10, 12, 13, 14)."[104] The function of this is probably just to underline the factuality of the events. Notice as well the "on this very day" in v. 13 which sounds like the chronicling of a momentous and memorable event—the procession of humans and animals into the ark (cf. this phrase in Gen 17:23, 26 of Abraham's circumcision, or of the exodus in Exod 12:41, 51; or of Moses's death in Deut 32:18). The sons of Noah are named only here and in 6:9 and 9:18, otherwise we simply hear of "his sons."

The roll call of the animals seems to echo Genesis 1, especially the phrase "according to their kinds/types." There is an interesting contrast between the Gilgamesh account that says that Utnapishtim shut the door himself, whereas here we hear that the Lord shut Noah and the rest in the ark. The flood's effects are described in detail, and the

---

102. Wenham, *Genesis 1–15*, 176–77.
103. Wenham, *Genesis 1–15*, 176–77.
104. Wenham, *Genesis 1–15*, 179.

outcome "all flesh expired" is stated succinctly (vv. 21–22). Life does not simply die here, it is wiped out, swept away, as the NT would have it. In other words, this is a judgment by God. There is a deliberate play on words here between *nh* (Noah) and those wiped out (*mhh*). A verb similar to the form of the name is used. All in all, we are told there were 40 days of rain, followed by 110 days of the waters gradually receding, making 150 total days before the ark settled back onto ground. Genesis 8:1 will make clear that this all stopped because "God remembered Noah." The divine control over the whole process is made very clear, in contrast to the description in the Gilgamesh epic.

As Arnold stresses, the concept of the salvation of the extended family, Noah, his wife, his sons, and their wives as well, all considered part of "the father's household" and all saved because of the righteousness of the head of the extended household, is an important concept that is to play out in various ways in the rest of Genesis. This concept of corporate solidarity in a "head" is an important one, however unfamiliar it may be to modern individualistic societies. It affects the way the story of Adam and Christ is viewed by Paul and others (see above) and it affects the way the story of Noah is viewed by Jesus (see below). The actions or character of one person accrue benefits to all those who are "in him."

Scholars have rightly pointed out that the account (probably originally two different source accounts) in Genesis 6:9–9:29 deliberately echo the creation account, only now we have an undoing of the creation or "uncreation," of the separations, of the distinctions in the original account, now all is swept away, through the elimination of the separation of the waters above and below from the land. But the purpose of the undoing of creation is so a fresh start can be made once more.[105] Salvation in this story of course has to do with rescue from the cataclysmic flood, and the verb *zakar* "remember" as applied to God, means more than just "take note of"; it actually refers to God taking action on behalf of someone or for something (Gen 19:29 for Abraham; Exod 2:24 for Israel). It is not an accident that Jesus chooses this episode in Genesis to draw an analogy with final judgment on the earth when the Son of Man returns, a story to which we now turn.[106]

105. See Arnold, *Genesis*, 102–3.
106. It is disappointing that in his commenting on this difficult text, D. A. Carson basically does not deal with the allusion to Gen 6:1–4 in his "1 Peter," in Beale, *Commentary on the New*

THE BLESSING OF BEING LEFT BEHIND:
MATTTHEW 24

But about that day and hour no one knows, neither the angels of heaven, nor the Son, but only the Father. [37] For as the days of Noah were, so will be the coming of the Son of Man. [38] For as in those days before the flood they were eating and drinking, marrying and giving in marriage, until the day Noah entered the ark, [39] and they knew nothing until the flood came and swept them all away, so too will be the coming of the Son of Man. [40] Then two will be in the field; one will be taken and one will be left. [41] Two women will be grinding meal together; one will be taken and one will be left.

While the first evangelist in Matthew 24 is generally following the earlier account of this speech by Jesus, found in Mark 13, the exception to that rule is the mention of Noah and the flood story as an analogy explaining both the sudden intervention of a divine activity, and the phrase "one taken, and one left." We do not have a quotation of the Genesis story here, but rather an allusion especially to Genesis 7:11–24, which recounts the blotting out of all humanity except Noah and his family. Clearly, by the insertion of the Noah material into the discourse at this point one is meant to think that those left behind are like Noah's family who are left behind after the flood, and so those taken away, are like those swept away in the surging waters of a flood sent to judge the earth. This being the case, "taken" in the aphorisms in vv. 40–41 must mean *taken away* in or for judgment. It has nothing to do with the faithful being raptured out of the world during "the last tribulation" an idea that does not appear in church history before the modern era (perhaps the sixteenth century at the earliest).[107]

A less straightforward reference to the Noah story is found in 1 Peter 3, which we have discussed above. Here again the reference is to the same passage in Genesis 7:11–24 (the only place we hear specif-

---

Testament Use, 1038–39, pleading that the matter is too complex and the space allotted too small. Even less helpful is Craig Blomberg, "Matthew," in Beale, *Commentary on the New Testament Use*, 88–90 who bypasses Matt 24:38–39 altogether, presumably because there is no direct citation. This shows the problems with just dealing with the "quotational" use of the OT in the NT. It's the tip of an iceberg big enough to sink most any hermeneutic about the use of the OT in the NT that ignores the majority of the evidence *that does not involve citation or direct quotation of the OT.*

107. See the discussion in Ben Witherington III, *The Problem with Evangelical Theology Testing The Exegetical Foundations of Calvinism, Dispensationalism, Wesleyanism, and Pentecostalism*, 2nd ed. (Waco, TX: Baylor University Press, 2015).

ically of the eight persons saved, Noah and his wife, and his three sons and their wives). This passage in 1 Peter is the most complex and debated passage, not least because of the analogy between Christian baptism and the flood, an odd analogy at best since Noah and his family rode on top of the water, and were not immersed or even sprinkled by the flood. We have already mentioned the key to understanding the passage, because it seems likely that the spirits in prison who disobeyed in former days is a reference to the bad angels mentioned in Genesis 6:1–4. Also favoring this interpretation is the reference to Christ having angels made subject to him in v. 22.

It is worth pointing out how in the apocalyptic discourse of Jesus that refers to both Noah and Lot (and in the Lukan version even Lot's wife Luke 17:26–35), neither Noah nor Lot are disparaged or set up as negative examples, but the people of Noah's day and the people of Lot's city and even Lot's wife do serve as negative ethical examples of how not to behave since there is a God who judges the world and will do so again in the person of the returning Son of Man. The Matthean form of this material in Matthew 24:36–41 does not include the mention of Lot or Lot's wife and the earlier Markan form of the Olivet discourse has no reference to these figures from Genesis at all. In any case, Peter Mallen is surely right when he says "characters in Genesis, such as Abraham, Lot, and Noah, were considered to be historical figures and the matter of fact way that the story of the flood is treated in Jesus's teaching (Luke 17:26–27) suggests that Luke's audience would hear it in a similar way."[108] In other words, these figures are not viewed as merely literary figures in a story, but rather as historical examples to be heeded. This is equally clear from Matthew 24's use of the same material where what happened in the days of Noah is said to be what will happen again at the coming of the Son of Man, and just as the latter is viewed as on the future historical horizon, so the former provides a previous historical example to heed and avoid (noting the use of ὥσπερ "just as" in Matt 24:37).

Jeannine K. Brown, in her helpful discussion of Genesis references and allusions in Matthew correctly observes:

> The activities assigned to Noah's contemporaries (four periphrastic participles . . . eating and drinking, marrying and giving in marriage) are not drawn from the Genesis flood story and seem, at first to be innocuous actions. Yet "eating and drinking" can have a negative cast in the

---

108. Peter J. Mallen, "Genesis in Luke-Acts" in Menken, *Genesis in the New Testament*, 61.

biblical text (e.g., Exod 32:6) and does so in the immediate context of Matthew 24 (24:49). . . . It is also the case that the language of "marrying and giving in marriage" would likely have evoked the introduction to the flood account (Gen 6:1–4) in which the evil of humanity is illustrated by the intermarriage of "the sons of God . . . [and] the daughters of humans" (6:4). The focus of these activities in Matthew, however, is to emphasis that as the judgment of the flood caught those in Noah's generation by surprise, so the *Parousia* will come unexpectedly. The specific teaching on Noah in relation to the *Parousia* concludes with Jesus' exhortations to be awake and ready (24:42, 44).[109]

For our purposes, what should be noted is that once again, the narrative in Genesis is not being quoted but rather summarized and alluded to, but it is assumed to be just as authoritative as the quotation of a commandment or a prophecy. It provides, not surprisingly, a historical precedent or analogy here, so that Jesus can warn that since God's character and will has not changed, judgment in the future is just as certain as judgment on sin in the past, and will have just as devastating a consequence for those who are not like Noah, righteous among his contemporaries. In other words, *sacred narrative provides a sanction*, making clear the reality of what is coming as described by future prophecy and undergirds the call to present repentance and heeding the words of Jesus.

ABRAHAM OUR FOREFATHER: GENESIS 12–20

Because of the great importance of the Abraham cycle of stories to the writers of the NT, it will be well to do a brief review of the whole story and its function and meaning within Genesis itself.[110] There is in fact no story from here to the end of Genesis more important than this one, to judge from the use of this material in the NT. But this could be said in general just on the basis of the frequent mention of Abraham in the OT itself. For example, outside of Genesis Abraham is mentioned by himself in Ezekiel 33:24; Psalm 47:10; 2 Chronicles 20:7; Nehemiah 9:7–8; and in Psalm 105:42. *He is never mentioned just with Isaac outside Genesis.* He is mentioned once with Sarah in Isa-

---

109. Jeannine K. Brown, "Genesis in Matthew's Gospel" in Menken, *Genesis in the New Testament*, 58.

110. For an interesting study of Abraham and Jesus see R. W. L. Moberly, *The Bible, Theology and Faith: A Study of Abraham and Jesus* (Cambridge: Cambridge University Press, 2000); on Gen 12:1–3 in relationship to NT themes see Moberly, *The Bible*, 120–27.

iah 51:2, and five times with Jacob/Israel in Isaiah 29:22; 41:8; 63:16; Micah 7:20; and Psalm 105:6. He is mentioned together with Isaac and Jacob as the "founding fathers," so to speak, the patriarchal parents of Israel some twenty-six times with some nine of them occurring in Exodus (2:24; 3:6, 15, 16; 4:5; 6:3, 8; 32:13; 33:1) with another eight in Numbers (once) and Deuteronomy (seven times), and the rest occurring in Joshua, 1 Kings, 2 Kings, 1 Chronicles, 2 Chronicles, and Psalm 105:9–10. Surprisingly, there is exactly one use of the triad formula in the prophets: Jeremiah 33:26 (MT, not in the LXX). Finally, the triad often comes in the form "the God of X, Y, and Z," and sometimes is coupled with the promise of the land.[111]

It may also be helpful to note from the outset that one thing that made Abraham all the more useful for a person like Paul in his interaction with gentiles, is that in early Judaism, Abraham was often viewed as the first convert from polytheism and from the religious ethos of what came to be called the gentile world. Abraham figures large in early Judaism precisely because he is seen as the original paradigm of one converted from idolatry to the true worship, service, knowledge of, and faith in the true God (see e.g., Testament of Job 3–5; Josephus, Ant. 1.155–56).

Genesis 12–50 as a whole has been called "the Old Testament of the Old Testament" because it plays a relationship to all that follows in the Hebrews Scriptures much like the OT as a whole plays in relationship to the NT. "As the New Testament considers Jesus of Nazareth the fulfillment of the divine promises of the Old Testament, so God's deliverance of Israel from Egypt, the covenant at Sinai, the conquest of the promised land, etc. all fulfill the promises made to Abraham in the ancestral covenant of Genesis 12–50," promises of progeny, land, blessing.[112] At the same time the Abraham saga looks back to and has a relationship with the Primeval Narrative in Genesis 1–11, Noah in the tenth generation from Adam provides the story of a righteous man through whom the race is rescued, and in the tenth generation from Noah, Abraham is that righteous man through whom God begins and then rescues and blesses a people. In fact, one can even see a typological reversal of the curse in the garden in the story of Abraham. The curse affected the land, the progeny, the blessing, but now in Abraham there is a renewed promise of land,

---

111. See the discussion by Thomas Römer, "Abraham Traditions in the Hebrew Bible outside the Book of Genesis," in Evans, *The Book of Genesis*, 161.

112. Arnold, *Genesis*, 127.

progeny, blessing.[113] Yet the shadow of the curse keeps dogging the steps of Abraham, whose wife Sarai is barren.

How you assess Genesis 12–50 depends on what kind of literature you see Genesis 12–50 as being. Is it history, myth, legend, saga, or some combination of all of these? The material in Genesis is presented as history with a theological interpretation that incorporates poetry and prose and various other literary types. For our purposes, it is sufficient to say that the OT writers/editors of this material present it as some sort of theological history chronicle, and this is how the NT users of the material take it as well, including Jesus, Paul, and the author of Hebrews.

The authors/editors of Genesis 12–50 intend us to see this material as similar to Genesis 1–11, as it deliberately links the two periods by genealogies and other allusions from the former period. Thus, for instance, the genealogies in Genesis 1–11 that begin in Mesopotamia with Shem end in the same region with Abram who is from "Ur of the Chaldees." Certain editorial notes in Genesis indicating that the author/final editor lived significantly later than the events. Certainly, there are decisive hints that Moses did not write the Pentateuch *in toto*, though he may have been responsible for some important parts of it.

First, Moses obviously did not write the material about his own death in Deuteronomy 34, despite Philo and Josephus trying to find a way around this. Second, note that Moses is never "I" in these books, not even when he participated in the events (even Numbers 33 is in the third person). Third, Genesis 36:31–43 definitely suggests someone who edited the work when there *were* Israelite kings (1020 BCE on), and we simply do not know how long after that the editorial process went on. Was it finished during the monarchy, when there were scribes who could undertake such a task?[114] Fourth, other phrases that suggest a time later than Moses for the book's final form include: (1) reference to Canaanites in the land as a past fact (Gen 12:6; 13:7); (2) the phrase "as far as Dan" (Gen 14:14), since Dan is the Israelite name of a city or territory that did not yet bear such a name; and (3) the phrase "beyond the Jordan" (Deut 1:1) may even suggest composition in the land of Jordan.

113. See Michael Fishbane, *Biblical Interpretation in Ancient Israel* (Oxford: Oxford University Press, 1988), 372–73.
114. Karel van der Toorn, *Scribal Culture and the Making of the Hebrew Bible* (Cambridge: Harvard University Press, 2009).

Moses lived *at least* five or six hundred years after Abram. For instance, if Israel was in Egypt 430 years (Exod 12:40), and we place the exodus somewhere between 1280 BCE and 1447 BCE (dates suggested by various OT scholars), *at the very least* Abraham, who must date in the early second millennium, lived six hundred years before Moses. Thus, a certain amount of anachronism and/or editorial explanations are to be expected so that Genesis 12–50 will make sense to a much later age that lived after the exodus.

The stories involving Abraham really begin with the genealogy in Genesis 11:27–30. It is obvious the author desires to separate between now and then and appears able to do so. It is also obvious he is dealing on a limited scale with family history, not world history. It is clear that the Abraham saga has been carefully edited for it officially begins with God speaking to Abram and telling him to "go" followed by a prepositional phrase in Genesis 12:1 and it is rounded off in 22:2 with the command to "go to the land of Moriah." This is the first and last time God speaks to Abraham, and it is the only time in the whole OT that we have this grammatical construction of the verb "go" attached to a prepositional phrase.[115] This is surely not an accident.

Before we begin to examine Abraham's call in 12:1, we need to look at his roots as mentioned in 11:27–31. First of all, the home of Abram is said to be Ur of the Chaldees. Ur is the Babylonian city of dynastic and governmental significance on the Euphrates River. Abram may have lived there during the Third Dynasty of Ur, 2060–1950 BCE, or possibly at the end of the Second Dynasty if he migrated as early as 2009 BCE. It is also the city where the moon god Sîn was worshiped. Here also the Arameans have roots, for the Chaldeans are an Aramean people, from which we get the word and language Aramaic. Haran not only had trade but also religious links with Ur because it too was a place where Sîn, the moon god, was worshiped, and several of Abram's relatives have names associated with the moon (Sarah, Milchah, Terah). This may mean that the reason Terah set out for Canaan but "settled" in Haran was because they were moon worshipers. We should not be surprised if this is so prior to Abram's call, and we cannot assume that Abram began by worshiping Yahweh just because he descended from Noah. Descendants can go astray (cf. Josh 24:2, 14).

---

115. See rightly Arnold, *Genesis*, 130.

1. THE CALL OF ABRAM

The call of Abram is recorded in Genesis 11–12. Abram's call is not located in time in Genesis 11–12, but Acts 7:2–8 suggests he received the call prior to going to Haran. If so, then he did not embark on the final pilgrimage to Canaan until his father died. Notice in 12:4 the indication of a separate trip starting from Haran. Finally, what about the relationship of Sarai and Abram? We are told in 11:30–31 that Nahor married his niece Milcah, the daughter of his brother, and apparently it was the custom for Terah's descendants to marry this way (cf. 20:12, 24:3–67, 29:19). At 20:12 we are told that Sarai is Abram's half-sister, the daughter of his father and another wife who was not Abram's mother. This proves important for what happens in 12:10–20, 20:1–18. Also, we are told Sarai was barren and had no children (11:30), which is crucial to the story that follows because of the promise made to Abram in 12:1–9. Notice how the genealogy prepares us for this narrative.

The Abram cycle may be distinguished from what precedes it in one very important respect: the promises made to Abram are not made to anyone before him. To be sure there is the blessing of fruitfulness for Adam and Noah, but not a promise of the promised land, or the promise that Abram and his seed will be a blessing to those around, part of the major theme of this cycle of material. The promise theme runs throughout the rest of Genesis like a clear and ever-present stream, giving life and hope to the story. It is the very heart of the narrative around which all else revolves and can be explained. The patriarchal stories illustrate the numerous obstacles that stood in the way of accepting the promise and the extreme lengths to which Yahweh went in order to fulfill the promise. It is not the case that the promises can be seen as a later icing on the cake; without it there is no cake.

Derek Kidner says that chapter 12 is the beginning of the story of redemption, for we have the story of the promise.[116] Abram is simply told, "Leave your country, people, and household, and go to an as yet undisclosed destination." Here is the classic example of moving on faith, not on sight. Thus, Abram becomes exhibit A in Hebrews 11's "hall of faith and faithfulness." Notice that God offers something that could be said to compensate, or at least replace, what Abram was

---

116. Derek Kidner, *Genesis: An Introduction and Commentary*, TOTC (Downers Grove, IL: InterVarsity, 2008).

giving up (12:2–3). He leaves a country and is made into a nation. He leaves his people, but is promised progeny. He leaves a household, but becomes a household word, a blessing to all peoples. Canonically speaking, the NT parallel is Mark 10:28–31, where Peter and the disciples are said to give up all but gain more of the same in due course. Note how the command continues to narrow down what is to be left—country, relatives, immediate family, as the call to obedience becomes more difficult.

While it is possible that the move from Ur to Haran was part of a larger nomadic enterprise, here we are talking about the calling of an individual and his family to move; not because of economic or political reasons, but due to divine purpose. Abram is like a touchstone or representative of God (12:3). How he is treated will determine how they will be treated by God, as if Abram was God's special representative. It will become clear that the text does not see Abram as merely a nomad, much less a donkey caravaner; he is or becomes a ruler and a father of rulers (cf. 23:5, 17, 20), a prophet (20:7), and a priest who sets up altars to God (12:8 and other places in the book).

Not until Abram arrived near the place where Shechem would later be does he receive the word, "to your offspring I'll give this land." Notice God does not say he would give this land *to Abram* (neither does 12:1–3), and the land was not wholly possessed by Abram at any time personally. He would not receive the full benefit of this promise. We have here a theophany, a God appearance, after which time Abram built an altar to honor and worship the God who promised this, despite appearances to the contrary, for "the Canaanites were *then* in the land." God affirms the truth of his word to Abram, he was present even in a pagan land; Yahweh was not a local deity tied to a shrine. If Genesis 12:1–9 is about *fide* (faith), then 12:10–20 is about perfidy. The author, if he is attempting to glorify Abram and whitewash his story, could not have included this narrative, which has all the earmarks of a historical event.

Further, there is ambiguity from the outset in the narrative. Take for instance Genesis 12:3. Should we take the form of the verb bless (בָּרַךְ [bārak]) to be a passive form, and therefore a rare form of the verb and so we translate "all the families of the earth will be blessed" by or through Abraham, or should we look to the later renderings of the verb in Genesis 22:18 and 26:4 as a *hithpael*, in which case the verb is reflexive: "all the families of the earth will bless themselves by or through Abraham." The former rendering more clearly conveys the idea that Abraham and his descendants will be a conduit of blessing to the other nations/families of the world. But it is even possible to take this to mean that other nations will receive blessing in direct proportion to how they treat Abraham and his offspring. On the whole, Genesis 18:17–19 seems to support the understanding that Abraham is seen as a means of blessing for the other nations.[117] But not only so. Abraham is not merely an instrument God uses to bless other people groups, he and his descendants are in fact the object of God's calling and blessing themselves as well.

The purpose of Israel's election, the reason they are blessed is not merely so they can be a blessing to others. This fact is underscored by Paul's argument in Romans 9–11 that God is not finished with Israel, even though many gentiles are being saved through faith in Christ. No, God intends to save "all Israel" as well. I suspect Paul would have nodded in agreement with Kaminsky when he says

> The God of the Hebrew Bible has an ongoing relationship with his people Israel, and thus, one needs to be cautious in employing the metaphor of service in a heavy-handed fashion that ignores the relational elements at the root of Israel's election theology. God's special favor toward Israel involves a mysterious act of divine love that precedes any call to service and persists even when Israel fails to respond to God properly. Most importantly, in all these texts Abraham and his chosen descendants, the people of Israel, remain God's elect.[118]

This is true even when his people keep making mistakes, as we see in Genesis 12:10–20 and elsewhere.

There are close parallels in Genesis 12:10–20 to Genesis 20 and 26, which tell a similar story. We can only say in regard to Genesis 26, "like father, like son"; and in regard to Genesis 20, "it worked once, so it might work twice." In Genesis 20 we are given the excuse of Abram, "there is no fear of God in the land, so to protect my hide, I did this." In short, these stories are about a fear of human beings by Abram (and Isaac) that does not comport with a fear of God. Whatever the interrelationship of these stories, which may have been edited to appear in similar form by the final editor, we see an Abram who is at least in part a man of fear and calculation.

---

117. On this see Kaminsky, "Theology of Genesis," 644–46.
118. Kaminsky, "Theology of Genesis," 647.

2. THE JOURNEY INTO EGYPT

If there was famine it was common to go to Egypt, where the Nile still watered the land, to get food.[119] The famine is said to be heavy. Before Abram and Sarai ever enter the land, Abram decides what he will do to take advantage of his beautiful wife's looks. Abram tells her: "Say you are my sister so I will be treated well, and my life will be spared." Abram wishes to profit by this trip. Verse 16 says he acquired sheep, camel, donkeys, servants, and camels, because Abram loaned Sarai out even to pharaoh. In short, he was willing to compromise his wife's virtue to make money and save his own skin. Abram himself has endangered the promise by giving away his wife. We are to see deceit going on here, for though Sarai is his half-sister, she is also his sole wife, and he is properly reprimanded by Pharaoh when this becomes known. We are not told how Pharaoh knew, but Abram has no response, since he knows he is in the wrong. Did Abram perhaps think that since his wife seemed barren, there would be no complications from this deceit?

Pharaoh provides Abram an escort out of the country because of his untruth and lack of faith. Abram becomes a curse, not a blessing, to the nation of Egypt and foreshadows what happens to future Israelites and pharaohs in that land. It is not implied that the escort was hostile; rather, pharaoh is trying to make sure Abram goes, to appease God's wrath and send its cause out of the land.

What is the point of this? Notice how the story is not told for its own sake. Rather, the point concerns God's wish to be faithful, to protect, and to be true to his promises despite sinful human nature and the obstacles Abram puts in the way. God's sovereignty and control, despite his own peoples' fears and immoralities, overcomes all obstacles. God is the central actor, and the narrator's intention is to show how God brought about his will even through and in spite of scoundrels. It is a word of encouragement to God's people later: "The one who called you is faithful and he will do it." God and his word are vindicated despite the sinfulness of his chosen one. Even the patriarchs were sinners, and what they had they also had by the sheer mercy of God, which they sometimes believed in and accepted. If even an Abram can stumble and still be used by God, then there is hope for all of God's people.

---

119. John Skinner, *A Critical and Exegetical Commentary on Genesis*, ICC (Edinburgh: T&T Clark, 2000), 248, refers to inscriptional evidence.

3. ABRAM AND MELCHIZEDEK (GENESIS 14)

Genesis 14 brings Abram in touch with tribes and peoples beyond his own. Abram returns as the victorious conqueror and is met by the priest-king Melchizedek and the king of Sodom, who sees him as a notable conqueror. Note that Abram had 318 men of his household in his military entourage, clear evidence that we are dealing with his tribe, not just a lone individual. Melchizedek is a mysterious figure. We are given no history about him, and he disappears after this story. Precisely because of this lack of backstory or sequel the author of Hebrews feels led to say he was "without father, mother or genealogy having neither beginning of days nor end of life, but resembling the Son of God, he remains a priest forever" (Heb 7:3). He is seen as a prototype of Christ by the author of Hebrews, but even in Hebrews, Melchizedek is not seen as a preexistent appearance of Christ himself.

Melchizedek provides hospitality and food for the weary conqueror (v.18); the bread and wine are part of any normal meal and probably have no sacramental significance. What then is the purpose of this narrative in its original setting? Obviously, it is not told for its own sake; since we are not told anything more than is absolutely necessary about this mystery man, Melchizedek. Two things become evident: (1) Abram prospers only when he does God's will; and (2) even pagan kings and priests must reckon with the works of Yahweh and the validity of his servant Abram. Perhaps we also see how other pagan nations are blessed or bless themselves through Abram, the conquering hero. We will have occasion to say a lot more about this when we look at the use of these traditions in Hebrews.

In his final reflections on the use of the Abraham/Melchizedek material in Hebrews, Moyise rightly notes that what our author is doing with the materials in Genesis 14 is a form of typology that is somewhat different from Paul's Adam-Christ typology in Romans 5 and 1 Corinthians 15. The author of Hebrews is not arguing that the work of Christ supercedes or undoes the work of Melchizedek, but rather that he is of the same priestly order and everlasting priesthood. These two priests have no place in the Levitical priesthood, and yet they are legitimate, indeed set apart by God. He also rightly adds that there are similar things going on in the Qumran use of the Melchizedek stories, indeed one may even say the use of the material in 11Q13 (11QMelch) 9–10 is even more otherworldly than that in Hebrews for *there* Melchizedek seems to be a heavenly figure who will act as judge at the end of days, and by combining Genesis 14 with Psalm 82:1 Melchizedek can even be said to be called *Elohim*. While the author of Hebrews is definitely prepared to say these sorts of things about Christ, he is not saying this about Melchizedek who is but a historical foreshadowing of Christ in some respects.[120]

4. THE COVENANT (GENESIS 15)

The narrative is pivotal in many ways in the Abram cycle of stories because it brings to light covenantal theology in a way we have not seen before (except perhaps with Noah). Covenantal theology has been seen by many OT scholars as the unifying thread that ties together the OT itself, and the OT with the NT. We can say, looking at matters from a canonical perspective, that Paul in Galatians 3–4 saw a definite connection and continuity between the Abrahamic and the new covenant, though of course there are obvious differences (circumcision vs. baptism, etc.). Here as in the Noah narratives, it is God who initiates, stipulates, and confirms the covenant and its sanctions. Abram is the passive recipient of its benefits.

He was in need of more assurance than just a promise, and thus God performed a sacred rite that sealed the promises and made clear that Yahweh was determined to make them come true. Much is learned by studying ancient lord-vassal treaties (Assyrian, Hittite; see *ANET*). Such treaties are not between two parties that are equals, but, as the treaty title implies, there is a hierarchical relationship involved, so that the lord dictates terms and benefits. This is, of course, what we find here. God makes promises and by a ceremony swears to be faithful to them. There are curse and blessing sanctions in such treaties, curses if the treaty stipulations are not performed, and blessings if they are.

Genesis 15:6 is, of course, very significant to NT theology, since Paul draws on it in Galatians and Romans to enunciate the principle of righteousness by faith. It will be well if we provide a rendering of both the MT and LXX form of the text, as it is one of those rare incidences where a narrative sentence is actually quoted in the NT.

---

120. See the discussion in Moyise, *Old Testament in the New*, 156–58.

MT	LXX
Abram believed the LORD, and he credited it to him as righteousness.	And Abram believed God, and it was reckoned to him as righteousness.

The sentence is Abram's response to the promise God enunciates in vv. 4–5 that he will indeed have "seed," indeed countless seed. The Hebrew is clear enough: v. 6b is a result of Abram's trust/belief expressed in v. 6a. Verse 6a means both that Abram trusts God and therefore trusts that his promise will come true. Since the verb in v. 6a is in the perfect tense, it may imply continuing action—"he kept on believing" as he had done in the past. In other words, this response to God is characteristic of how Abram responded to God, it is not a singular or momentary thing. And how did God respond to that response? "Using a computational accounting metaphor ('count', 'calculate', 'reckon' *hsb*) the narrator asserts that Abram's faith counts in God's economy as that moral quality so greatly needed—righteousness or a right relationship with God."[121]

While technically the "it" in "it was reckoned" could refer to Abram reckoning that God's word of promise was an expression of God's righteousness, the immediate context does not favor this conclusion and the NT writers certainly do not interpret the verse that way.[122] Note that Abram is responding to a special revelation of God to him at this juncture in the narrative. This is not blind faith but response to a special revelation that reassures Abram about progeny. This verse has its own intertextual effect in the OT as can be seen in Psalm 106:31 in reference to Phinehas's intercession that is reckoned as righteousness, and it may well be related to Habakkuk 2:4b "the righteous live by their faith," as well as the postexilic confession in Nehemiah 9:7–8.

To sum up and reiterate, Genesis 15:6 indicates the following: (1) the verb means "believe in," or "trust in," and thus is not referring to a set of doctrines Abram believed, but rather indicates his trust in Yahweh to do as Yahweh said; (2) *tsaddiq* "righteousness" can be a relational term implying right-standing with God, being in a right relation with God, but it can also refer to moral character. Abram's righteousness is in any case something he receives, not something he achieves, and he receives it through trusting God; (3) the verb

121. Arnold, *Genesis*, 156.
122. See Arnold, *Genesis*, 156 and the discussion there.

here translated "reckoned" or better "credited" is from the language of commerce, of credits and debits. There is no indication here, or in the NT for that matter, that we are dealing with an *exchange* of one person's righteousness for another's. It is Abram's trust that is reckoned as Abram's righteousness or right-standing. We will have much more to say about this in due course when we discuss the use of this material particularly in Galatians and Romans.

Again, notice that Abram believes there will be an heir on the basis of a promise. In the narrative, which begins in v. 7 (if this is a second narrative added here), the discussion is about possessing a land, not an heir, and it is about this promise of land that Abram requires further assurance: "Can I know I will gain possession of it?" To this God responds with a covenant ratification rite, indicating an implied curse should it be unfulfilled.

5. FOLLOWING THE COVENANT (GENESIS 17)

It has been said that to come to God costs nothing, but to follow him requires everything. We see this same idea of total discipleship in the two narratives of Genesis 15 and 17, and it is in the latter that the obligations of the covenant incumbent upon Abram are made clear. The point of concluding the covenant at this juncture is that Abram is indeed about to undergo a life-changing event in a year. Isaac will be born and Abram's own identity as father of a multitude will finally be on the way to being established.

God appears to Abram and says, "I am *El Shaddai*." We are told at Exodus 6:3 that this was the signature name that God revealed to Abraham, Isaac, and Jacob before he revealed his personal name of Yahweh. Unfortunately, it is not clear what *El Shaddai* means. Some scholars believe it is derived from *sadu* meaning God of the Mountains (cf. the Psalms and the Song of Moses in Deuteronomy 32 that call God "the rock"). This derivation is uncertain. What is more certain is that the word is usually used in situations where God's people are hard-pressed and need assurance (Gen 17:1, 28:3, 35:11, 43:14, 48:3, 49:25). This may suggest it is an assertion of God's sovereignty or might, hence the translation "almighty."

In regard to the changing of Abram's and Sarai's names to Abraham and Sarah, probably the change of name marks both a new era and a new status and is consistently used in subsequent narratives perhaps rather like an ancient king's assumption of a special throne name. However, here it is God who gives the name and the point is that *God* is establishing their identity. There is probably a word play in v. 5. Abram seems to mean "exalted father" while Abraham, if it is not a mere lengthening of the same name, means "father of many." As so often in the OT, the name signifies something God is about to or has done for a person or some attendant circumstance involved in a special event in one's life (cf. Isaac, Jacob).

No one else in the OT or NT is given this name. Abraham alone is the father of many for the Hebrews. Abraham is to walk before God in a blameless way (i.e., he is to act in accordance with God's word and will). This is not like Enoch's or Noah's walking with God, which implies a special closeness or relationship. Here the emphasis is on behavior in God's sight. The word *tamim* means whole or perfect, and here the meaning seems to be "acting without ulterior motives," wholeheartedly following God's way and word. It indicates complete surrender, not moral perfection. In regard to Sarai's new name Sarah, we can only say that it, like Sarai, seems to mean princess, implying royalty (note Abraham is called a prince in 23:6, which would strengthen the parallel to the taking of royal names). It is said in 17:6 that kings (17:20b) will come from Abraham, again implying a royal identity.

When God appears to Abraham, Abraham responds like a servant, with complete obeisance, falling flat down on his face. In v. 7 we are told it will be an everlasting covenant (*berith 'olam*), and we are immediately told how so: this is a covenant not just with Abraham but also with his descendants. If it is for Abraham and his family, then the sign of the covenant must likewise be for all, regardless of age or stage or status. Possibly the kind of covenant we are dealing with here is not just master-servant but high king to vassal king who will serve the high king. The vassal king is under the high king. He has special obligations and duties as well as privileges involved in his position. When it is applied to God and his royal servant, Abraham, the following may be said:

> The *berith* is neither a simple divine promise to which no obligation on man's part is attached . . . nor is it a mutual contract in the sense that the failure of one party dissolves the relation. It is an immutable determination of God's purpose, which no unfaithfulness of man can invalidate;

but it carries conditions, the neglect of which will exclude the individual from its benefits.[123]

This conclusion however would make the covenant a unilateral and unconditional one, which is not how such covenants worked in antiquity. They were always bilateral, and if they were not "kept" by the subordinate party, there were curse sanctions applied, and the covenant could be ended by the dominate party.

What then are we to make of this circumcision to be performed not on those who believe but on all of Abraham's male family and descendants? We probably have here the principle of household inclusion in the covenant, in light of the collectivist nature of this ancient culture. Faith is expected of Abraham and his descendants but before they are even able to respond, God includes them. Thus, their initial inclusion rests primarily on God's election, not the human response, though the latter must necessarily follow or else the covenant is broken. Possibly circumcision here is seen as the oath-sign (i.e., a sign by which one invokes a curse upon oneself if one does not do as the other requires). The curse is related to the promise. If the promise is progeny, the curse is the cutting off of progeny, symbolized by the act of circumcision. The idea is "if I do not per-form this covenant, may I and my descendants be cut off from God's people."

In verse 14 we have a word play: any uncircumcised one (one without flesh cut off) will be cut off from God's people, by which is meant excommunication, not execution. Elsewhere in the Penta-teuch, we have the phrase "cut a covenant" (*karath berith*). Since cir-cumcision is the covenant sign, cutting and covenanting go together in another sense as well (Jer 34:18; Gen 15:10). The act of circum-cision consecrated someone to the Lord. The point is that one must be willing to accept the consequences (the curse) if one wishes to receive the blessings. Persons are addressed as responsible humans. Some were circumcised before they could exercise such responsibil-ity; however, they are made accountable to God from the start by this act.

What is Abraham's response to the promise of a child? He laughs, asking, "Can old maid Sarah now give birth when she could not pre-viously?" Abraham offers to God a more reasonable option: "Why not just bless my son Ishmael?" But what seems reasonable to us is not

---

123. Skinner, *Genesis*, 298.

always what is right in God's plan. God promises to do this, but here we see that not all the ones that God blesses are God's chosen line. Indeed, he promises that Ishmael will be the father of a great nation, but that is not necessarily the sign that God is with them in the sense of being with a chosen people. Prosperity is no clear guide to one's standing with God, even in the OT.

From this narrative, we again see the humanness of Abraham and his seeming disbelief at such stupendous promises. His view of God was too small, for the narrative stresses that nothing is too hard for God. The narrative is also about God's elective purposes, which precede human response and make that response necessary and possible. We see, too, that the covenant involves blessing and curse, promises and obligations, and assumes human responsiveness and responsibility. But God's elective purposes do not require ability; in some cases, they may create it.

6. THE SACRIFICE OF ISAAC (GENESIS 22)

All of the Abrahamic cycle has been straining toward the point when Isaac, the promised child, will be born. This great joy is recorded in Genesis 21 with the child being named Isaac, that is, "he laughs," for obvious reasons. In a very real sense, Abraham's life story has gone from the incomprehensible to the incomprehensible. He begins by obeying God and setting out for he knows not where, then he comes to the twilight of his life and God tells him to sacrifice the one child he had been continually promising him. There have been other tests along the way, but here Abraham is called to act against his life-long dream and ambition, against his love and affection for his only child born of Sarah. To be sure, there are interesting parallels between Isaac and Jesus, *but at the crucial juncture Isaac is not sacrificed whereas Christ is*. Thus, if you draw parallels, some may ask, is God more merciful to Isaac than to his own son, Jesus? But this is the wrong question to ask. Further, the lamb that is substituted here is not said to be a sacrifice for sin; there is no interest in sin or substitutionary atonement in the Abraham story at all.

We must not turn this story into a Christian allegory and miss its real meaning in its original context. Indeed, one has to look quite hard to find evidence of the influence of this story in the NT. Even the Psalms and Isaiah's discussions of the righteous sufferer come up more frequently in the NT than the example of Isaac. The reason for this is probably because Isaac is *not* sacrificed in the end, nor would his death have been seen as an atoning sacrifice either. There is no hint of that in the Genesis story. And last, God intervenes and stops the sacrifice, providing a ram in a thicket.[124] Thus, the analogy between Christ and Isaac breaks down at various points and is limited to the fact that both stories involve a beloved or only son, and both stories have God commanding a sacrifice of the beloved. That is all.

We are told in v. 1 that God is testing Abraham. This forewarns us as readers, but Abraham did not know that. It is noticeable that Abraham obeys quickly. It is clear that God knows how important this child is to Abraham: "take your son, your only son, the one whom you love." The redundancy indicates that God knows precisely what is at stake for Abraham. The way the narrative proceeds is indirect. It does not psychologize Abraham or peer into his inner thoughts; we know him only by what he says or does. Isaac is a young boy now, old enough to help with chores, but he could hardly expect that the wood he was carrying would be for his own funeral pyre. Even here we see Abraham's tender care of him to the last. Abraham takes the knife and the fire, which would be dangerous to handle while climbing a mountain. Notice again how Abraham is not told which mountain to go to: "it is one I will tell you about." Not all God's instructions come up front, but often after a person is moving in obedience. It is difficult to explain v. 5. Is it merely said so the servants won't follow and interfere, or does Abraham really believe (on the basis of the promise) that he will return with Isaac?

The action of the story slows down almost unbearably from v. 6 on. The dialogue between father and son is especially gut-wrenching. Again v. 8 is ambiguous. Is Abraham really hopeful or sure God will provide a substitute, or are these words simply meant to silence his son's thoughts and questions? Perhaps Abraham speaks more truth than he realizes, but even if he is expressing his belief, it is clear he thinks only divine intervention will stop this inexorable process. The words, "and the two went on together" (vv. 6b, 8b), are a poignant refrain. It is clear Abraham has resolved to go all the way with God's command, and the messenger of Yahweh only intervenes after he has taken the knife to slay his son. Only then come the words "do not lay a hand on the boy," and only then does Abraham look up and

---

124. One could almost say there are more parallels between Christ and the ram than there are between Christ and Isaac.

see a ram in a thicket. Verse 14 indicates that Abraham names the spot, something that would be appropriate. Perhaps it means "in the mountain it will become clear," or perhaps "in the mountain it will be provided." God reveals himself in his own place and time and in his own way. His will may seem inscrutable on many occasions and very trying, but there will come a time when the truth will become clear. Now we see through a glass darkly. The testing is a most extreme one.

In Genesis 12 Abraham had to cut himself off from his whole past. In chapter 22 he is called to give up his whole future and trust God will provide. Some have seen in this story the mystery of life, apparently so contradictory to the existence of a loving God, yet in this story it is God who provides the apparent contradiction. Clearly, the story implies God will test us, even to extreme degrees, but as 1 Corinthians 10 says, with the test he will provide a way out. There is something more important than life, and that is obedience to God and the personal integrity of living "with fear of the Lord." Perhaps the best commentary on this is Micah 6:6–8:

> With what shall I come before the Lord? Shall I come before him with burnt offerings, with calves a year old? Will the Lord be pleased with thousands of rams, with ten thousand rivers of oil? Shall I give my first-born for my transgression, the fruit of my body for the sin of my soul? He has showed you, O humankind, what is good; and what does the Lord require of you but to do justice, and to love kindness, and to walk humbly with your God?

Abraham now has the promise of greatness and land reaffirmed. He has finally passed God's ultimate test. He has grown much since he left Ur of the Chaldees, and so have the hearers of these tales if they have journeyed with him on his pilgrimages in Genesis.

JOHN AND FATHER ABRAHAM

A textbook example of what can happen when one is trying to study the use of the OT in the NT but only focuses on quotations or partial citations and does not treat the broader use of the OT stories, characters, ideas in the NT is shown by closely scrutinizing John 8:31–59, an intra-Jewish debate between Jesus and his audience about pater-

nity, the seed of Abraham, who Jesus is, and related matters.[125] It will
be well to cite this text in full here, to indicate just what an oversight
this is:

[31] To the Jews who had believed him, Jesus said, "If you hold to my
teaching, you are really my disciples. [32] Then you will know the truth,
and the truth will set you free."

[33] They answered him, "We are Abraham's descendants and have
never been slaves of anyone. How can you say that we shall be set free?"

[34] Jesus replied, "Very truly I tell you, everyone who sins is a slave
to sin. [35] Now a slave has no permanent place in the family, but a son
belongs to it forever. [36] So if the Son sets you free, you will be free
indeed. [37] I know that you are Abraham's descendants. Yet you are looking for a way to kill me, because you have no room for my word. [38] I
am telling you what I have seen in the Father's presence, and you are
doing what you have heard from your father."

[39] "Abraham is our father," they answered.

"If you were Abraham's children," said Jesus, "then you would do
what Abraham did. [40] As it is, you are looking for a way to kill me, a
man who has told you the truth that I heard from God. Abraham did not
do such things. [41] You are doing the works of your own father."

"We are not illegitimate children," they protested. "The only Father
we have is God himself."

[42] Jesus said to them, "If God were your Father, you would love me,
for I have come here from God. I have not come on my own; God sent
me. [43] Why is my language not clear to you? Because you are unable to
hear what I say. [44] You belong to your father, the devil, and you want to
carry out your father's desires. He was a murderer from the beginning,
not holding to the truth, for there is no truth in him. When he lies, he
speaks his native language, for he is a liar and the father of lies. [45] Yet
because I tell the truth, you do not believe me! [46] Can any of you prove
me guilty of sin? If I am telling the truth, why don't you believe me? [47]
Whoever belongs to God hears what God says. The reason you do not
hear is that you do not belong to God."

[48] The Jews answered him, "Aren't we right in saying that you are a
Samaritan and demon-possessed?"

[49] "I am not possessed by a demon," said Jesus, "but I honor my Father
and you dishonor me. [50] I am not seeking glory for myself; but there is
one who seeks it, and he is the judge. [51] Very truly I tell you, whoever
obeys my word will never see death."

125. Notice the complete lack of treatment of John 8:31–59 in Andreas Köstenberger,
"John," in Beale, Commentary on the New Testament Use, 458–59. If you are going to offer a
book on the "use" of the OT in the NT, and not merely the "citation" of the OT in the NT,
then clearly John 8:31–59 should have come in for considerable comment, which it doesn't in
the whole of that large volume.

[52] At this they exclaimed, "Now we know that you are demon-possessed! Abraham died and so did the prophets, yet you say that whoever obeys your word will never taste death. [53] Are you greater than our father Abraham? He died, and so did the prophets. Who do you think you are?"

[54] Jesus replied, "If I glorify myself, my glory means nothing. My Father, whom you claim as your God, is the one who glorifies me. [55] Though you do not know him, I know him. If I said I did not, I would be a liar like you, but I do know him and obey his word. [56] Your father Abraham rejoiced at the thought of seeing my day; he saw it and was glad."

[57] "You are not yet fifty years old," they said to him, "and you have seen Abraham!"

[58] "Very truly I tell you," Jesus answered, "before Abraham was born, I am!" [59] At this, they picked up stones to stone him, but Jesus hid himself, slipping away from the temple grounds.

The OT text is not really cited here, but if one doesn't know the backstory of Abraham, and in fact various episodes of the backstory, it becomes difficult to parse out the logic of the argument here in John. Richard Hays gives a very brief treatment of this text, and he is right that the whole saga of Genesis 12–22 is presupposed here, not quoted, not cited, but presupposed. Both Jesus and his audience assume that Abraham is understood to be the father of the people of Israel, and being his children is associated with both freedom and having a legitimate claim to being part of God's chosen people. Especially difficult if you don't know the backstory is what Jesus means when he says in John 8:39, "if you really were the children of Abraham, you would do the works of Abraham." This seems to mean, as the text moves along, that they should have received Jesus in the same way Abraham was glad to see "Jesus's day," or is this a reference to Abraham's famous hospitality to the supernatural visitors (Gen 18:1–15), contrasted with the lack of positive reception of Jesus by this audience?[126] In any case, Hays is right that the discussion in John 8 about who counts as "seed of Abraham" is in some ways similar to the discussion in Galatians 3–4 (on which see below).

More helpful is the more detailed discussion by Menken on John 8:31–59, which we need to dialogue with at this juncture.[127] First

---

126. Richard B. Hays, *Echoes of Scripture in the Gospels* (Waco, TX: Baylor University Press, 2016), 290.

127. Maarten J. J. Menken, "Genesis in John's Gospel and 1 John," in Menken, *Genesis in the New Testament*, 91–95.

of all, this passage in John is the climax of the debate in the temple precincts between Jesus and his interlocutors there. The debate involves not only the identity of Jesus but the identity of his debate partners as well. Notice that in v. 31, this group of persons is said to believe in Jesus in some sense. One of the major motifs in this Gospel is to make clear the inadequacy of some forms of belief in Jesus that do not include understanding where Jesus came from, namely the Father, and where he is going, namely back to the Father. One character after another in the narrative professes some kind of belief in Jesus (he is a miracle worker and God is with him [Nicodemus]; he is a great prophet [Samaritan woman]; he is the messiah [Martha]) that are true assertions far as they go, but they are inadequate to really grasp the full identity of Jesus. It is this issue that is being wrestled with here. The identity of the audience is revealed by how they react to the identity claims of Jesus, vis-à-vis Abraham. And note as well that here is another story in John where not knowing where Jesus comes from (see John 1) and is going means not knowing who he really is.

Note that Abraham comes up repeatedly again and again, as the red thread that ties this whole discussion together (vv. 33, 37, 39–40, 52–53, 56–58).[128] The audience is claiming (v. 33) both something positive and something negative: (1) "we are seed of Abraham"; (2) "we have never been slaves of anyone." The expression "seed of Abraham" only rarely occurs in the OT (but see Isa 41:8; Ps 105:6; 2 Chr 20:7; and in the form "your seed" and "his seed" Gen 12:7; Neh 9:8). The phrase "seed of Abraham" comes to mean not just the immediate physical descendants of Abraham, but more broadly, God's chosen people in general (see Psalms of Solomon 9:9; 3 Macc 6:3; Luke 1:55; Heb 2:16). As Menken concludes, the phrase "seed of Abraham" then is an allusion not to a particular OT text, but to a key biblical theme, a theme that should not be missed when one is trying to discuss the use of the OT in the NT.[129]

The claim "we have never been slaves of anyone" seems astounding for a people who celebrated the exodus-Sinai events every year at Passover. Jesus of course is talking not about those events but about bondage to and liberation from sin, a kind of darkness that prevents one from seeing Jesus for who he is, and from even seeing oneself as

128. For an extended treatment of this passage and its use of the Abraham traditions see Tineke de Lange, *Abraham in John 8:31–59: His Significance in the Conflict between Johannine Christianity and Its Jewish Environment* (Amsterdam: Amphora, 2008).

129. Menken, "Genesis in John's Gospel," 92.

one truly is. But according to Genesis 15:13–14, even Abraham was informed in advance in a vision that his offspring would one day be enslaved. In vv. 34–35 the contrast is made between a slave and a son in a household. The audience is indeed enslaved to sin, whereas Jesus is the Son in the household of God. Though the evangelist does not say so, this is not far from the Pauline idea that Jesus, and not the audience, is the genuine seed and heir of Abraham.

While Jesus seems to admit in v. 37 that the audience is indeed the physical seed of Abraham, the real question is who is their spiritual father. Underlying this discussion is the whole previous discussion in John 3 (and even alluded to before that in John 1) that even devout Jews "must be born again" if they are to understand Jesus, much less enter the dominion of God later on. The audience affirms strongly (v. 39) "Abraham is our father!" (cf. Josh 24:3; Isa 51:2; Luke 1:73; Josephus, *Ant.* 1.158; m. Ta'an. 2:4–5).

It is at this juncture that Jesus says, "if so, you should be doing the works of Abraham," but instead they are trying to kill Jesus. You can know the tree by the fruit it bears. Or, put another way, not all physical descendants of Abraham are true Israelites. Obviously, Abraham gladly received and trusted the messages from God and it was credited to him as righteousness, and he even received the mysterious messengers from God, but the audience of Jesus neither receives his message, nor welcomes him. The implication of the argument in John 8 is that were Abraham around when Jesus showed up, he would have received him gladly, would have rejoiced to see his day, indeed did so rejoice, seeing it from afar.

The discussion turns truly polemical in vv. 42–47 when the audience claims God in fact is their father (ironic since Jesus is implying that he is the one who truly has God as Father, being his only begotten Son) but Jesus counters by saying, no, "the devil is your father" as is evidenced by their hostility toward Jesus. Verses 52–53 has the audience noting that "Abraham died long ago" (see Gen 25:8 LXX) and Jesus is not yet fifty, so clearly Jesus could not have run into Abraham earlier in life. They ask if Jesus is claiming to be greater than Abraham. In his helpful discussion, Menken notes that in the early Jewish discussions of the Abraham stories, Genesis 15 was taken to mean that God revealed the eschatological things to Abraham (see 4 Ezra 3:14; 2 Baruch 4:4); he even sees the new Jerusalem (Apocalypes of Abraham 15–30). Jubilees 14:21 even says that Abraham rejoiced when he saw these things. "John has apparently made use of extant

Jewish rereadings of Genesis 15, and 'christianized' these by making Jesus' day the object of Abraham's vision of future things and of his joy."[130] But perhaps it is also true that Jesus himself had reflected on these Abraham stories in messianic ways.

The discussion in any case is fraught, because Jesus just speaks of Abraham having seen Jesus's *day*, whereas the audience thinks Jesus is talking his being old enough to have encountered Abraham himself. And then of course the final rebuttal comes: "before Abraham was, I am." Is this a contrast between the temporal existence of Abraham, who died, and the eternal being of the Son, as Menken suggests? Not necessarily, though that is possible. It is also possible to read this as a claim to preexistence, the notion that Jesus as God's Wisdom and Word preexisted and was encountered in that form by Abraham. Could this be an allusion to Jesus being the shadowy Melchizedek figure to whom Abraham tithed, and who blessed Abraham? That too could be alluded to here. In any case, Menken is surely right that Genesis 15 is the main part of the Abraham saga that lies behind this discussion. "Genesis 15 contains many elements that were apparently interesting to early Jewish and early Christian readers. Abraham's vision, his faith, the promise of a son, and numerous offspring, Abraham's sacrifice, God's announcing slavery and exodus, God's covenant with Abraham."[131] And we are the poorer, and have less understanding, if we ignore these sorts of uses of the OT in the NT.

PAUL AND FATHER ABRAHAM

It may seem strange, to those who know of the preoccupations of early Jews with Moses, including its great thinkers such as Philo, that Paul, the former Pharisee devotes considerable time and space to Abraham and his story (Romans 4; 9:6–15; 11:1; Gal 3:6–18; 4:21–31) but gives Moses far less ink. For Paul, Abraham is the critical example of faith prior to the time of Christ. Paul mentions Abraham some eighteen times in three letters (Galatians, 2 Corinthians, Romans), which accounts for one quarter of the references to Abraham in the NT.[132] Galatians 3:8 emphasizes: "And the Scripture, foreseeing that God would set right the gentiles by faith, declared the gospel

130. Menken, "Genesis in John's Gospel," 94.
131. Menken, "Genesis in John's Gospel," 95.
132. Evans, "Genesis in the New Testament," 481.

beforehand to Abraham." Abraham is both prototype and exemplar of Christian faith, or at least of the process that came to be called "justification by grace through faith." He heard the first preaching about trusting God and it being reckoned to him as righteousness or at least right-standing with God and he responded appropriately. Abraham is in effect seen by Paul as the ancestor and model for both Jew and gentile. Even gentiles share in the faith of Abraham (Rom 4:16) and with Jewish Christians become his heirs and beneficiaries of the promises given to him through Christ (Gal 3:14). The differences between the treatment of the very same Genesis text in Galatians 3 and Romans 4 provide for us a good clue to the kind of rhetorical adjustments Paul made to his source material to make them words on target for each audience he is addressing. Let's examine the texts side by side.

Galatians 3:6–9

Romans 4:1

Abraham trusted God and "it was credited to him for righteousness"

so you believers are also descendants of Abraham

The Scripture foresaw God would set right the Gentiles by faith, and it declared the Good News to Abraham in advance saying "the Gentiles will be blessed in you"
(v.9) Therefore, those who believe are blessed with believing Abraham.

What was gained by Abraham our ancestor according to the flesh? Was he set right by works?
No, the Scripture says "Abraham trusted God and it was credited to him as right-eousness'"

(Explanation of the differ-ence between something cred-ited and something earned as wages by working).

In both of these passages, Genesis 15:6 is quoted and the story of Abraham is drawn upon. But in Galatians, Paul is stressing how the gentiles were included on the same basis as Abraham, by faith, and indeed were included in the chosen people due to a promise made to Abraham himself. Works of the Mosaic law did not enter into the discussion at all; they came later in the time of Moses. In Romans, the point is somewhat different on several scores. Notice first the ref-erence to Abraham, our ancestor according to the flesh. Here Paul, probably ironically, is reminding the largely gentile audience that they are not Jews and not Abraham's descendants by heredity. They have no such claim on Abraham, unlike the Jewish Christians in Rome and Paul himself. They only have a claim through faith to be Abraham's offspring. Paul is trying to put the gentiles in their place and elevate the status and honor rating of Jewish Christians in Rome, as Romans 9–11 will go on to make very clear. Paul has no such concern in Galatians. Indeed, he is trying to make the gentile converts in Galatia see what an exalted status they already have in Christ and thus have no need to get themselves circumcised and keep the Mosaic covenant. The differing audiences and situations lead to differing rhetorical usages of the Abraham story in these two texts and reveal some of the differences between Galatians and Romans.

True, Paul always looks at the Abraham story as he does all such stories through christological, and to a lesser degree ecclesiological glasses, but that is not the whole story. The story elements that come to the fore are those that are most germane to his particular Christian audiences. What he omits from the story of Abraham (the sacrifice of Isaac, the Sodom and Gomorrah story, the entertainment of the angels, the Melchizedek incident) is as revealing as what he includes.[133] Paul's urgency is to show that Abraham is a paradigm of faith and that the promises to him are fulfilled in Christ, and in Christ's people, who become Abraham's heir.

One of the most important aspects of the Abraham story for Paul is of course its chronology. It is crucial not only that he was promised many offspring in Genesis 12:2–3 but also that God's covenant of promise with Abraham is already initiated in Genesis 15. Of course, for Paul Genesis 15:6 then becomes *the crucial verse:* "And he believed the Lord, and the Lord reckoned it to him as righteousness." All of this happens prior to any discussion of circumcision as a covenant sign, which we find in Genesis 17. Notice as well that the story of Sarah and Hagar does not show up until after Genesis 15 as well (in Genesis 16; 21:8–21). This ordering of those events allows Paul to appeal to God's original dealings with Abraham over against the later ritual of circumcision whether connected with the Abrahamic or late Mosaic covenant.

This linear or chronological reading of the story of Abraham leads to the conclusion we find in Romans 4:11–12 that circumcision is only the seal or sign of the righteousness or right-standing Abraham

---

133. This omission of Melchizedek from the Abraham story Paul tells is a very clear clue that he is not the author of Hebrews, for that writer's imaginative use of the Melchizedek story generates a whole new approach to christology, with Melchizedek seen as a type of Christ the high priest.

had already obtained through faith in God. Paul also concludes from this sequence of events that Abraham can be the father of gentile as well as Jewish believers, for like them he believed without having been circumcised and was accepted on that basis (Rom 4:1). He is not the forefather of all believers according to the flesh but rather on the basis of faith.[134] As Paul thinks through the further implications of this argument he is also able to conclude that not all of Abraham's physical descendants are true children of God, true Israelites, for it is not the children of the flesh but the children of the promise who are the true descendants (so Rom 9:6–7).

In Romans 4:23–24, Abraham is depicted as exhibit A of relating to God on the proper basis of eschatological faith: "Now the words 'it was reckoned to him' were not written for his sake alone, but for ours also. It will be reckoned to us who believe in him who raised Jesus our Lord from the dead." Since this story is a scriptural story it is not seen as merely analogous to the story of Christians but in fact the model or paradigm for the Christian story in regard to the issue of faith. Galatians 3:16 shows that in Paul's telling the story can take surprising twists, thus apparently on the basis of his reading of Genesis 17:6–7 (the promise to Abraham and his offspring [singular] that kings will come from him), Paul is able, in a rhetorical *tour de force,* to argue that Christ is the offspring in question, just as he is the king in question. Of course, as Romans 9:6–7 shows, Paul knows that the term "seed" is a collective noun, but the larger context of Genesis 17 allows him to focus on the most important Jewish king who is Abraham's descendant. But there is also the point that Paul sees Christ as an incorporative personality, one in whom many can dwell or abide. Christ is *the seed,* but his offspring are also present in him, and so they become Abraham's heirs through being in the seed who is Christ. Thus, the term "seed" in Galatians 3:16 has both an individual and a collective sense, just as it did with Abraham, for "in Abraham" Isaac and subsequent descendants also received the promise.[135]

134. Or is he? If Paul is thinking of Abraham as initially a pagan, and then a Hebrew, it is not impossible he saw Abraham as "our forefather according to the flesh" for both gentile and Jew.

135. It is instructive to compare the way Paul argues on the basis of the Abraham story and the way he argues on the basis of the Adam story. Notice, he does not speak about "the seed of Adam." Heredity is not the primary issue with Adam, rather it is his behavior as representative of all humans that affects the rest of the race. Adam sinned, and all humanity felt the effects, due, apparently, to the curse. But in the case of Abraham, heredity is absolutely of importance for the later people group called Israel and her messiah, Jesus. However, even in the case of Abraham, it is by having similar faith to Abraham's that one is incorporated into Christ, just as it is by committing similar sin to Adam's that we like Adam all die spiritually, and then physically.

Of absolutely crucial importance for mapping out the lines of Paul's narrative thought world is the connection Paul makes between the Abrahamic and the new covenant, particularly in Galatians 3–4. The Abrahamic covenant is seen as being fulfilled in Christ, and so the new covenant is the consummation of the Abrahamic one. Both of these covenants involved both the circumcised and the uncircumcised, and thus circumcision ceases to be seen as the crucial thing. Genesis 15 precedes Genesis 17 and so faith takes precedent over circumcision in Paul's thought world. Both the Abrahamic and the new covenant involve children given by the grace of God, both involve an everlasting covenant, both promise that all the nations of the earth will be blessed (see Gen 17:6). In terms of the larger scheme of Paul's narrative a high price is paid for closely linking the Abrahamic and the new covenant, namely it means that the Mosaic covenant in all its glory must be seen nonetheless as a temporary or interim arrangement, a parenthesis between the promises given to Abraham and their fulfillment in Christ. This does not mean that the Mosaic law is seen as a bad thing, only a temporary one. In fact, it is seen as like a childminder, a *paidagogos*, a guardian who keeps God's people in line until messiah comes and they reach the adult stage of their existence.

In sum, when Paul thinks of Adam he thinks of the entire story of sin and the fall, when he thinks of Abraham he thinks of a faith-based divine initiative, a faith-based covenant and the promises that went with it; but when he thinks of Moses, he thinks of the law and in particular the law as something given for a specific purpose and a specific period of time, whose time is up when Christ comes. When Christ came, the relationship of God's people with the law was supposed to change: "But when the fullness of time had come, God sent his Son . . . born under the law in order to redeem those who were under the law, so that we might receive adoption as children" (Gal 4:4–5). The Mosaic covenant is not seen as opposed to the promises or as annulling the Abrahamic covenant (Gal 3:17–21); it was simply given for a later and temporary period of time and for specific purposes.

One more story, already alluded to, deserves some scrutiny in light of the remarkable allegorizing of the story of Sarah and Hagar we find in Galatians 4. By using the term ἀλληγορούμενα, Paul has alerted his audience that he will not be using the OT story in a usual or expected way. Here is the portion of the Genesis story, from Genesis 21, not from the earlier account of the impregnating of Hagar in Genesis 16, that Paul has in mind:

MT	LXX/OG
[8] The child grew and was weaned, and on the day Isaac was weaned Abraham held a great feast. [9] But Sarah saw that the son whom Hagar the Egyptian had borne to Abraham was mocking, [10] and she said to Abraham, "Get rid of that slave woman and her son, for that woman's son will never share in the inheritance with my son Isaac." [11] The matter distressed Abraham greatly because it concerned his son. [12] But God said to him, "Do not be so distressed about the boy and your slave woman. Listen to whatever Sarah tells you, because it is through Isaac that your offspring will be reckoned. [13] I will make the son of the slave into a nation also, because he is your offspring." [14] Early the next morning Abraham took some food and a skin of water and gave them to Hagar. He set them on her shoulders and then sent her off with the boy. She went on her way and wandered in the Desert of Beersheba. [15] When the water in the skin was gone, she put the boy under one of the bushes. [16] Then she went off and sat down about a bowshot away, for she thought, "I cannot watch the boy die." And as she sat there, she began to sob. [17] God heard the boy crying, and the angel of God called to Hagar from heaven and said to her, "What is the matter, Hagar? Do not be afraid; God has heard the boy crying as he lies there. [18] Lift the boy up and take him by the hand, for I will make him into a great nation." [19] Then God opened her eyes and	[8] And the child grew and was weaned, and Abraam made a great banquet on the day his son Isaak was weaned. [9] But when Sarra saw the son of Hagar the Egyptian, who had been born to Abraam, playing with her son Isaak, [10] then she said to Abraam, "Cast out this slave-girl and her son; for the son of this slave-girl shall not inherit together with my son Isaak." [11] Now the matter seemed very hard in the sight of Abraam on account of his son. [12] But God said to Abraam, "Do not let the matter be hard in your sight on account of the child and on account of the slave-girl; whatever Sarra says to you, obey her voice, for in Isaak offspring shall be named for you. [13] And as for the son of the slave-girl, I will make him also into a great nation, because he is your offspring." [14] Then Abraam rose in the morning and took bread loaves and a skin of water and gave them to Hagar and put them on her shoulder, along with the child and sent her away. And when she departed she began wandering about the wilderness over against the well of the oath. [15] Then the water from the skin gave out, and she cast the child under a silver fir. [16] And after departing she sat down opposite him a good way off, about a bowshot, for she said, "I will not look upon the death of my child." And she was seated opposite him, and the child cried out and wept. [17] And God listened to the voice of the child from the place where he was, and God's angel called Hagar from the sky and said to her, "What is it, Hagar? Do not be afraid, for God has given ear to the voice of your child from the place where he is. [18] Rise, take the child, and hold it fast with your hand, for I will make him into a great nation." [19] And God opened her eyes, and she saw

she saw a well of water. So she went and filled the skin with water and gave the boy a drink. ²⁰ God was with the boy as he grew up. He lived in the desert and became an archer. ²¹ While he was living in the Desert of Paran, his mother got a wife for him from Egypt.	a well of living water. And she went and filled the skin with water and gave the child a drink. ²⁰ And God was with the child, and he grew up. And he dwelt in the wilderness and became an archer. ²¹ And he dwelt in the wilderness of Pharan, and his mother got a wife for him from the land of Egypt.

The text of the passage in Galatians reads as follows:

²¹ Tell me, you who want to be under the law, are you not aware of what the law says? ²² For it is written that Abraham had two sons, one by the slave woman and the other by the free woman. ²³ His son by the slave woman was born according to the flesh, but his son by the free woman was born as the result of a divine promise.

²⁴ These things are being taken figuratively: The women represent two covenants. One covenant is from Mount Sinai and bears children who are to be slaves: This is Hagar. ²⁵ Now Hagar stands for Mount Sinai in Arabia and corresponds to the present city of Jerusalem, because she is in slavery with her children.

To this we need to add v. 30 the only direct quote from the passage in Genesis 21:

³⁰ But what does Scripture say? "Get rid of the slave woman and her son, for the slave woman's son will never share in the inheritance with the free woman's son."

Of considerable interest for our discussion is the fact that in Jubilees 16, a document that surely must predate Galatians, the author sees Ishmael as representing Abraham's gentile progeny, while Isaac represent the Jewish progeny. Thus, Abraham is seen as the father of all nations in Jubilees. But this way of reading Genesis 21 leads to the anomaly that Abraham is seen as the father of gentiles, *before he is the father of Jews*. The further problem with this reading of course is that Genesis 21:10 says that Ishmael *shall not inherit*. Jubilees 16:17–18 then says

All the seed of [Abraham] sons should be gentiles, and be reckoned among the gentiles. For he should become the portion of the Most High, and all his seed had fallen into the possession of God, that it should be unto the Lord a people for possession above all nations and that it should become a kingdom of priests and a holy nation.

The account in Jubilees does not involve allegorizing, unless one counts the identification of Ishmael as the protogentile, and in any case, clearly Paul is not indebted to this particular approach to Genesis 21. Philo most certainly does allegorize the text as thoroughly as Paul (*Prelim. Studies* 11) and there are similarities in the two treatments, though Philo's main point is that Ishmael represents elementary teaching, while Isaac represents more advanced approaches to wisdom and virtue. As Hays has observed, in the LXX version of the story, Sarah is nowhere called "the free woman," and yet both Paul and Philo highlight the contrast between the slave and the free woman, a contrast that is not *explicit* in the Genesis text in either the Hebrew or Greek versions of the text.[136]

It seems clear enough from Galatians 4:31 that Paul means to suggest that the agitators and perhaps their adherents need to be cast out of the Galatian assemblies, as they are playing the role of Hagar and her offspring. On this reading, Paul himself is the "free woman" like Sarah and the Galatians are his legitimate offspring.[137] The big switch from the reading in Jubilees is that Paul is saying that the gentiles are part of the *legitimate* seed of Abraham, through Christ, the seed. The voice of Sarah is the voice of Paul quoting her in v. 30. Paul offers his audience a tale of two covenants, the Abrahamic and the Mosaic ones, and only the former is seen as being directly connected with the new covenant. He makes clear to his converts that they have no need to get themselves circumcised and to keep the Mosaic covenant, as they already have the blessings of Abraham through Christ his seed.

As I have said in an earlier context,

> Against the idea that Paul is simply engaging in exegetical sleight of hand here, it must be recognized that ancient allegory and allegorizing follows its own rhetorical conventions and should not be judged on the basis of whether or not the argument measures up to modern canons of historical critical interpretation. Paul was not attempting to provide a historically grounded interpretation of a portion of the OT here. As a pastor, he was using a widely recognized rhetorical manner of handling

136. Richard B. Hays, *Echoes of Scripture in the Letters of Paul* (New Haven: Yale University Press, 1989), 112.

137. On which see Beverly Roberts Gaventa, *Our Mother St. Paul* (Louisville: Westminster John Knox, 2007).

a text so as to contemporize it. This falls under a homiletical or rhetorical use of the text, not a historical interpretation of it.[138]

As a *rhetorical technique*, it should be compared to Philo's handling of the text, as we suggested above. It needs to be stressed that like homiletical uses of the OT in general, allegorizing is not an attempt to undercut or deny the historical basis of the original narrative, so there is no need at all to defend what Paul is doing here as just typology rather than allegorizing. Paul is quite capable of typology and this is not what it looks like, especially when he wants to argue that the Judaizing Jewish Christians are actually like the offspring of the slave woman, and that earthly Jerusalem along with Mt. Sinai falls into the category with them, in contrast to the Jerusalem which is above.[139] If we want to see what classic typology looks like, we should turn to Hebrews, which we now intend to do.

HEBREWS AND FATHER ABRAHAM

Paul is hardly the only NT writer enamored with Abraham and his story. The most notable figure in the Hebrews 11:1–12:3 "hall of faith" who gets even more play than Jesus is Abraham. Consider the following:

> By faith Abraham obeyed when he was called to set out for a place that he was to receive as an inheritance; and he set out, not knowing where he was going. [9] By faith he stayed for a time in the land he had been promised, as in a foreign land, living in tents, as did Isaac and Jacob, who were heirs with him of the same promise. [10] For he looked forward to the city that has foundations, whose architect and builder is God. [11] By faith he received power of procreation, even though he was too old—and Sarah herself was barren—because he considered him faithful who had promised.[12] Therefore from one person, and this one as good as dead, descendants were born, "as many as the stars of heaven and as the innumerable grains of sand by the seashore."
> [17] By faith Abraham, when put to the test, offered up Isaac. He who had received the promises was ready to offer up his only son, [18] of whom he had been told, "It is through Isaac that descendants shall be named for you." [19] He considered the fact that God is able even to raise someone from the dead—and figuratively speaking, he did receive him back.

138. Witherington, *Grace in Galatia*, 327–28.
139. Moisés Silva, "Galatians," in Beale, *Commentary on the New Testament Use*, 807–8 misses the point largely because he does not recognize the rhetorical approach Paul is taking here.

Our author in vv. 8–19 uses the example of OT faith par excellence, Abraham, choosing three episodes from his life. Of course, this is not the first time he has used Abraham as an example (see 6:13–15).[140] Four times the "by faith" phrase is applied to him (vv. 8, 9, 11, 17). But our author also pauses to generalize the lesson about the virtues and example of Abraham in vv. 13–16 where he reflects on the life of faith as the life of an alien or sojourner upon the earth.[141]

Our author stands in the line of a long Jewish tradition that set forth Abraham as an ideal or paradigm (e.g., Genesis 12–22; Sir 44:19–21; Wis 10:5; 1 Macc 2:52; Philo in his two treatises on Abraham; Gal 3:6–9; Romans 4; Acts 7:2–8; 1 Clem. 10:1–7). As to where our author stands in this tradition it is clear enough that the sapiential stream of this tradition is the one our author is most indebted to, a stream that looks for ways to use this story to inculcate virtues and good behavior. But it is equally clear that our author stands on the Christian side of the interpretation of these stories, for like Paul he stresses Abraham's trust or faith as leading to his acceptability to God, whereas in some Jewish treatments Abraham's *obedience* is that which was said to lead to his right standing with God.[142]

Abraham's faith is seen as demonstrated in his obedience to what God commanded him to do as well as his trust in God's promise. His trip to the promised land and his nomadic existence there our author takes as a sign that Abraham knew there was a greater reality, a city with real foundations above. Notice that our author in v. 8 deliberately uses the term "place" rather than "land" to speak of what was promised to Abraham, a term which had already been used in this sermon with positive effect (1:2 ,4, 14; 6:12, 17; 9:15; 11:7).[143] Our author is not alone in interpreting the promises to Abraham as involving a city. Philo, for example, says that Abraham's motivation for what he did involved "a city good and large and prosperous" (*Alleg. Interp.* 3.83). Later tradition in 2 Baruch 4:1–4 speaks of a city prepared by God before the beginning of time and shown to Adam, Abraham, and Moses. Our author stands in the same line of thinking as we find in 4 Ezra 7:26, 8:52, 10:27, 13:36; Galatians 4:26; and Revelation 21:2–19 that refers to a heavenly city that will come down

---

140. See Richard N. Longenecker, "The 'Faith of Abraham' Theme in Paul, James and Hebrews," *JETS* 20 (1977): 203–12.

141. See Fred B. Craddock, "The Letter to the Hebrews," *NIB* 12:135.

142. See the discussion in Witherington, *Grace in Galatia*, on Galatians 3–4.

143. Craddock, "Hebrews," 136.

to earth (see Ps 87:1; cf. Ps 47:9 LXX of the earthly Jerusalem whose foundations are said to be laid forever).

Verse 9 calls the holy land the "land of promise" an interesting phrase found only here in Scripture. It may be worded this way because our author sees the holy land not merely as a place where some divine promises come true but also as the land that figures forth a greater place in which God intends for his people to dwell. This interpretation is confirmed when we consider v. 10 where we are told flatly that the promise to Abraham was not completely fulfilled by taking possession of a piece of dirt (cf. Ps 105:11). No, a city designed and built by God would be the ultimate fulfillment of the promise. Notice the poignant contrast between the temporary tent home of Abraham and the permanent city he was looking forward to.[144] Our author's perspective is especially clear from the use of the term *paroikein*, which means to reside as an alien. Our author is actually saying that Abraham resided as an alien in the promised land, clear proof that he "still hadn't found what he was looking for."[145] Abraham immigrated to a land of promise but lived in it as if he had still not reached his destination, as if the land belonged to another. Typical epideictic praise rhetoric for cities involved praising their founders and fortification (see Quintilian, *Inst. Or.* 3.7.26–27), just as we find here.

The second episode from his life that is seen as an example of faith is the trust both Abraham and Sarah had to have in order to conceive a child by normal means, despite their great age and Sarah's barrenness. Interestingly the word translated "as good as dead" is also found applied to Abraham in Romans 4:19 another hint they both shared a common tradition or more likely that our author, as I have already suggested, had read or knew some of Paul's letters, specifically Galatians, 1 Corinthians, and Romans. There is an issue here of how v. 11 ought to be rendered, and the translations vary considerably between those that indicate faith is ascribed to Sarah (e.g "by faith Sarah was enabled to conceive") and those that suggest that she is only mentioned in passing (e.g. "by faith Abraham received power

144. George W. Buchanan, *Hebrews: Translation, Commentary, and Conclusions*, AB 36 (Garden City, NY: Doubleday, 1972), 188–89, has actually suggested that the author of Hebrews is envisioning repossessing the land of Israel and rebuilding earthly Jerusalem. Our author however, gives no hint that the city is at present destroyed, but Buchanan is right in one sense; while our author does not envision the rebuilding of the city, he does envision a heavenly city coming down to earth, presumably centered in the holy land. He is not envisioning the promise to Abraham being fulfilled "in heaven."

145. To borrow a phrase from Bono and U2.

of procreation even though he was as good as dead, and Sarah herself was barren").[146]

The factors that should lead to a decision on this matter are as follows: (1) literally v. 11 reads "received power for the laying down of seed" which under any normal circumstances refers to the male act of procreation (cf. Greek Apocalypse of Ezra 5:12); (2) in Genesis 18 (see especially vv. 11–18) Sarah is hardly portrayed as an example of faith; (3) there is uncertainty as to whether the noun Sarah is in the nominative or the dative case, the difference only being a subscript iota, which would not have been in the original manuscript anyway since it had all capital letters and no such markings; (4) if it is a dative of accompaniment, then it can be rendered "together with barren Sarah, he received power to procreate"; (5) Sarah is mentioned first after *pistei* so on first blush, it would appear that she is at least included in the statement "by faith," but Abraham is equally clearly the subject of v. 12 as the gender of the term "one" there demonstrates.[147] One must conclude then that while the focus is on Abraham's faith, Sarah is included in the statement about being empowered to have a child.

Verse 12 paraphrases Genesis 22:17 and it is worth comparing the use of the text here with Romans 4:16–18 where the reference is seen as including gentiles, but our author mentions no such thing focusing entirely on Jews in this hall of faith. Verse 12b simply amplifies by two analogies the nature of the promise of descendants. They will be as numerous as the stars in the sky or the grains of sand on the beach. What is unstated but perhaps implied is that our author is referring to those who like Abraham exhibit faith and faithfulness.

There is a sense in which Abraham by receiving Isaac received a foretaste of the promise, or a first installment, but in v. 13 our author is willing not only to say that these patriarchs died in faith but he is also willing to make a generalization that all those thus referred to who had died in the past had not properly speaking received the promise, but only seen it and saluted it from afar, thereby indicating they were strangers/foreigners and settlers/Bedouins upon the earth (cf. Gen 23:4; 24:37; 1 Chr 29:15; Ps 39:12; 1 Pet 2:11 on Christians being strangers).[148] All the above is taken as evidence that they were

146. For all the scribal emendations and conjectures see James. Swetnam, *Jesus and Isaac: A Study of the Epistle to the Hebrews in the Light of the Aqedah*, AnBib 94 (Rome: Pontifical Biblical Institute, 1981), 98–101.

147. On all of this see J. Harold Greenlee, "Hebrews 11:11: Sarah's Faith or Abraham's?" *Notes* 4 (1990): 37–42.

148. This concept of Christians being resident aliens upon the earth was to continue to

still seeking the true fatherland, and will not inherit except when all do at the eschaton (see v. 40). Thomas Long tells the story of how in the Middle Ages pilgrims from France who were journeying over the Pyrenees into Spain heading for the Cathedral of Saint James vied for the front position in the group of travelers so that whoever got the first glimpse of the great cathedral could shout, "my joy."[149] This same sort of cry of joy of the pilgrim when finally he glimpses his destination can already be seen in Virgil's *Aeneid* 3.524. Something similar is in view here in v. 13. Craddock is right that our author takes a salvation-historical perspective and he does not allegorize the OT stories, unlike Philo. But it is true to say that the promises actually made to Abraham and the other patriarchs are relativized and seen to be not the full meaning of what God had in mind for them, and apparently we are meant to think that Abraham realized this when he chose to live in the promised land as though it were just the land of future promises.[150] What is especially noteworthy is how these stories are interpreted in light of a much more robust theology of the after-life, both in heaven and on earth. *This is a major difference from the way the stories are presented in the OT.* Material promises become less important or are transformed in the light of the world to come.

In verse 15 we have a hypothetical conditional remark: had they Mesopotamia in mind they would have simply returned to their earthly home but they were looking for a greater place. This counter-factual argument helps establish the point that the patriarch's considering of themselves as aliens was not because they longed to return to their homeland but because they aspired to or yearned for a better heavenly city where God wouldn't be ashamed to be called their God (v. 16).[151] This whole concept of God being proud or ashamed of his people tells us something significant about our author's worldview, where honor and shame were far more important categories than life

---

develop well after NT times as a way of helping Christians live with a sense of detachment from the dominant cultural value system and at the same time a sense of anticipation of longing for something better that was yet to be seen on earth. We see this clearly enough in the postapostolic era document Epistle of Diogenetus 5.5, which says that Christians "inhabit their own lands, but as resident aliens; they take part in all things as citizens, but they endure all things as aliens. Every foreign land is a fatherland, and every fatherland is a foreign land." See the discussion in David A. DeSilva, *Perseverance in Gratitude: A Socio-Rhetorical Commentary on the Epistle to the Hebrews* (Grand Rapids: Eerdmans, 2000), 402.

149. Thomas G. Long, *Hebrews*, IBC (Louisville: Westminster John Knox, 1997), 119.

150. Craddock, "Hebrews," 137.

151. Harold W. Attridge, *The Epistle to the Hebrews*, Hermeneia (Philadelphia: Fortress, 1989), 331.

and death. Better to die in the good graces of God prematurely than live a long life of which God was ashamed. In this case God is not ashamed of the patriarchs because they did not settle for an ordinary inheritance but in faith looked forward to a better one.[152]

In verse 17 we have the third episode from Abraham's life that shows faith: the willingness to sacrifice Isaac his only begotten son. The verb *proseneuoxen* here may be an inceptive imperfect, "he began to offer." The Jewish traditions about the *aqedah* or binding of Isaac (see Wis 10:5; Sir 44:20; Jubilees 17:15–26; 18:16; Judith 8:25–26; 4 Macc 13:12; 16:20; Philo, *Abraham* 167–207; m. 'Abot 3:5) do not appear to be reflected here for our author says nothing about this offering being some kind of atoning work.[153] Notice however the use of "only son" here rather than "beloved son" as in Genesis 22:2. The promise could only be fulfilled through Isaac, the only legitimate son, and so this was a severe test, as v. 18 makes clear, because it seemed to go flatly against the divine promise made about Isaac in Genesis 21:22. We may compare the handling of this story in James 2:21–23.[154] God put Abraham to this test.

Why then did Abraham go through with it if it was so contrary to God's previous promise (here Gen 21:12 is partially cited)? Because, says our author, Abraham reckoned that God could raise Isaac again from the dead. This conclusion is based on the sentence where Abraham tells his servants that he and Isaac would return from the mountain. This may amount to allegorizing, or our author may really have seen a portent of Christ's death and resurrection in this act in which case the *aqedah* could be alluded to here.[155] At this juncture we may note that Paul in Romans 4:17–21 refers to the birth of Isaac as life from the dead.[156] The word "parable" here has its rhetorical sense and means "figuratively speaking," but Abraham did really, not merely

152. See Craig R. Koester, *Hebrews: A New Translation with Introduction and Commentary*, AB 36 (New York: Doubleday, 2001), 490.

153. It is interesting that in Jubilees it is not said to be God who tested Abraham but rather an evil figure; see Koester, *Hebrews*, 491.

154. See Donald A. Hagner, *Encountering the Book of Hebrews: An Exposition* (Grand Rapids: Baker Academic, 2002), 150. On the *aqedah* tradition see Robert J. Daly, "The Soteriological Significance of the Sacrifice of Isaac," *CBQ* 39 (1977): 45–75.

155. See Markus Bockmuehl, "Abraham's Faith in Hebrews 11," in *The Epistle to the Hebrews and Christian Theology*, ed. Richard Bauckham, Daniel R. Driver, Trevor A. Hart, and Nathan MacDonald (Grand Rapids: Eerdmans, 2009), 364–73, who calls this the clearest reference to the *aqedah* in the NT. If so, these ideas are not much in play in the NT.

156. Craddock, "Hebrews," 138.

figuratively, receive Isaac back.[157] Abraham received him back from the dead in that the ram became the substitute for the required sacrifice and was sacrificed. Alternately our author may mean this act "prefigured" the coming great resurrection of Christ.[158] In any case the testing was severe; "by leaving his father's house, Abraham gave up his past; by sacrificing Isaac, Abraham would give up his future."[159] Precisely because the analogy between Isaac's situation and that of Christ is so imprecise (there are as many differences as similarities), the analogy tends not to be pressed in the NT.

Finally, Wenham, in searching high and low for echoes of Genesis 22 in the NT is able to come up with the notion that it is the imagery and the language about offering the beloved son that the NT writers latch onto:

> The NT writers develop this imagery in a very striking way. For them Abraham and Isaac are types of God the Father and Jesus. But whereas Abraham did not quite sacrifice Isaac, Jesus did actually die. So his death is a perfect and fully effective atoning sacrifice, whereas Isaac's near sacrifice merely prefigured our Lord's and could not redeem mankind. This typology is very widespread in the NT and therefore must be extremely early and probably reflects Jesus' own self-interpretation of his mission. When Paul says "If God is for us, who is against us? He who did not spare his own Son but gave him up for us" (Rom 8:31–32), the echoes of Gen 22:12, 16 "you have not withheld your son, your only child", are obvious. John 3:16 "For God so loved the world that he gave his only Son" makes the same comparison. . . . The heavenly voice at Jesus' baptism and transfiguration says "This is my beloved Son." Though this terminology could be linked with Isa 42:1; Ps 2:7, it is even closer to Gen 22:2, 12, 16 in wording, for the LXX translates only by ἀγαπητός, "beloved."[160]

While some of this is suggestive, what Wenham fails to note is that the analogy would mean that God, in regard to his Son, is acting like Abraham, not the reverse, a very interesting analogy indeed, and so God is testing himself, or proving faithful, or both, by offering his only begotten Son as a sacrifice.

---

157. Notice how in his exposition Chrysostom recognizes that "parable" here means "rhetorical figure" in *Hom. Heb.* 25:3.

158. See Attridge, *Hebrews*, 335.

159. Koester, *Hebrews*, 499.

160. Gordon J. Wenham, *Genesis 16–50*, WBC (Grand Rapids: Zondervan, 2015), 117.

JAMES AND FATHER ABRAHAM

It is frankly impossible to discuss James in isolation from the subsequent history of the interpretation of Paul and James, especially in the modern era, as if they were dueling banjos, playing different tunes though often using the same notes. As a ground-clearing exercise, and before we can look directly at how James handles the stories of Abraham, we need to attend to the subsequent discussion that has so often obscured rather than clarified both what James is saying about Abraham, and for that matter, what Paul is saying as well.

The church fathers before the Reformation indeed saw there was at least an apparent tension here between Paul and James when it came to interpreting Abraham and his faith, but resolved it in a way that did not dismiss or ignore the insights of James, and without, for the most part, relegating James to the noncanonical dustbin. For example, Chrysostom says, "even if someone believes rightly in the Father and the Son, as well as the Holy Spirit, if he does not lead the right kind of life, his faith will not benefit him at all as far as his salvation is concerned . . . we must not think that merely uttering the words is enough to save us. For our life and behavior must be pure as well" (*CEC* 15). Bede cleared up the fact that Paul is talking about initial justification, which is by grace and through faith. "What Paul meant was that no one obtains the gift of justification on the basis of merit derived from works performed beforehand, because the gift of justification comes only from faith. . . . James here [in 2:14–26] expounds how Paul's words ought to be understood" (*On James* 93.22).

Augustine got a little tired of those critics who simply thought James and Paul were contradicting one another. He argues: "Holy Scripture should be interpreted in a way which is in complete agreement with those who understood it and not in a way which seems to be inconsistent to those who are least familiar with it! Paul said that a man is justified through faith without the works of the law, but not without those works of which James speaks" (*On the Christian Life* 13). The distinction was made between prebaptismal faith, which was by grace and through faith alone, and postbaptismal faith, which is combined with works.[161]

---

161. It is interesting to hear this same opinion expressed in almost the same way in the modern discussion by Ralph P. Martin, *James*, WBC (Waco, TX: Word, 1988), 81: "Paul denies the need for 'pre-conversion' works and James emphasizes the 'absolute necessity of post-conversion works.'" Here he is quoting and following Douglas Moo. The assessment is correct,

Andreas adds, "For the same Abraham is at different times an example of both kinds of faith" (*CEC* 16). Oecumenius makes the same point and distinction in his *Commentary on James* 119.481, of course ignoring that Abraham was never baptized. Finally, Chrysostom, seeking to balance the ledger, stresses that "faith without works is dead, and works without faith are dead as well. For if we have sound doctrine but fail in living, the doctrine is of no use to us. Likewise, if we take pains with life but are careless about doctrine, that will not be any good to us either. It is therefore necessary to shore up the spiritual edifice in both directions" (*Hom. Gen.* 2.14).

It would be my judgment that the gist of this discussion, especially as perceived by Chrysostom and Augustine, was on the right track. James is not talking about how one comes to Christ, or receives initial justification or salvation *at all*. Even when he uses the language of "righteousness," it is final vindication or justification at the eschaton he is referring to. He is addressing those who are already Christians about how they should live. At the same time, Paul is equally clear that postconversion behavior can affect whether one is vindicated in the end, at the final judgment. Both James and Paul are quite sure that moral apostasy is possible and a real danger for the Christian. They are also in agreement that obedience and working out one's salvation after initial salvation is not optional for the Christian. The modern discussion, not surprisingly, surpasses the preoccupation of the ancient one in trying to sort out the differences between James and Paul on these sorts of matters. For example, consider the following quote from Peter Davids:

> These data mean that neither the works which James cites nor the justification which results are related to Paul. Rather, the works are deeds of mercy (which therefore fit with the opening verses of this section) and the ἐδικαιώθη refers not to a forensic act in which a sinner is declared acquitted (as in Paul), but to a declaration by God that a person is righteous, *ṣaddîq* (which is the implication of the "Now I know" formula of Gn. 22:12; cf. Is. 5:23 . . .). Adamson is correct in seeing that a moral rather than a primarily judicial emphasis is intended (although of course there is some judicial tone in any declaration of standing by "the judge of all the earth").[162]

---

but commentators were saying this well before the Reformation. In other words, this is not an insight unique to the Protestant tradition.

162. Peter H. Davids, *The Epistle of James*, NIGTC (Grand Rapids: Eerdmans, 1982), 127.

Or consider the remarks of Ropes:

> In the discussions of the Apostle Paul the contrast is the same in terms, but its real meaning is different and peculiar. Paul's lofty repudiation of "works" has nothing but the name in common with the attitude of those who shelter their deficiencies of conduct under the excuse of having faith. Paul's contrast was a novel one, *viz.* between the works of an old and abandoned system and the faith of a newly adopted one. His teaching was really intended to convey a doctrine of forgiveness.
>
> Our author, on the other hand . . . is led to draw the more usual contrast between the faith and works which are *both* deemed necessary under the *same* system. Hence, while faith is the same thing with both—an objective fact of the Christian life, the works of which they speak are different—in one case the conduct required by the Jewish law, in the other that demanded by Christian ethics. That the two in part coincided does not make them the same. One was an old and abandoned failure, impotent to secure the salvation which it was believed to promise, the other was the system of conduct springing from and accompanying a new life.[163]

I am in agreement with Alfred Plummer that we also must not see James 2:14–26 as a *direct* response to what we find in Galatians (or Romans for that matter). As Plummer says

> Had St. James been intending to give the true meaning of either or both of these statements by St. Paul [i.e., Rom 3:28; Gal 2:15–16] in order to correct or obviate misunderstanding, he would not have worded his exposition in such a way that it would be possible for a hasty reader to suppose that he was contradicting the Apostle of the Gentiles instead of merely explaining him. He takes no pains to show that while St. Paul speaks of works of the law i.e., ceremonial observances, he himself is speaking of good works generally, which Paul no less than himself regarded as a necessary accompaniment and outcome of living faith. . . . It is most improbable that if he had been alluding to the teaching of St. Paul, St. James would have selected the unity of the Godhead as the article of faith held by the barren Christian. He would have taken faith in Christ as his example.[164]

---

163. James H. Ropes, *A Critical and Exegetical Commentary on the Epistle of St. James*, ICC (Edinburgh: T&T Clark, 1916), 204 (emphasis original).

164. Alfred Plummer, *The General Epistles of St. James and St. Jude* (London: Hodder & Stoughton, 1891), 142, 152. See his telling exposition of Luther's own comments on pp. 147–48 where he shows that if Luther himself were consistent, he would have seen that Paul equally with James believes that faith without works is dead.

This last point about James's stress on the oneness of God is of course right, and it shows among other things that James is surely speaking to Jews in this homily, in this case Jews who follow Jesus, who took monotheism for granted, and indeed as the great earmark of their profession distinguishing them from all others in the diaspora.

Plummer rightly notes that both Abraham and Rahab were favorite topics of discussion when it came to the matter of faith and works in early Judaism.[165] The discussions in Wisdom of Solomon 10:5 or Sirach 44:20 or 1 Maccabees 2:52 should all be consulted, and we may mention Hebrews 11:17 and Matthew 1:5 from the Christian writings as well. James's discussion of Abraham is closer to the earlier Jewish one than to the later Pauline one, for the good reason that not only does James focus on the binding of Isaac story, but he also stresses that Abraham is an example of faith that manifests itself in action, in obedience to God.

James is pursuing the same line of discourse that we find in Matthew 12:37: a person is vindicated, or even "justified" or accounted righteous, as a result of what they have done or said.[166] This is a different matter than the discussion of the basis of initial justification or salvation. Clearly enough, James is more likely drawing on the earlier Jewish discussion of these figures of faith than on the later Pauline one. And once and for all we must stress that when Paul speaks of works of the Mosaic law, in fulfillment of the Mosaic covenant, he is talking about something very different than James's discussion of works that come forth from and express Christian faith. "James and Paul simply do not mean the same thing when they write of 'works,' and interpreters who write as it they did distort the thought of both."[167]

All of this however does not rule out the possibility that James is dealing with some issues raised by Jewish Christians from what they have heard, and perhaps misunderstood, about the teaching of Paul in its early stages in the early 50s when there were in fact Judaizers from Jerusalem going behind Paul in Antioch, Galatia, and perhaps elsewhere trying to add observance of the Mosaic covenant to the Pauline gospel even for gentile Christians.[168]

165. Plummer, *General Epistles*, 156–58.
166. See the helpful discussion in Douglas Moo, *The Letter of James*, PNTC (Grand Rapids: Eerdmans, 2000), 133–36.
167. Willima F. Brosend, *James and Jude*, NCBiC (Cambridge: Cambridge University Press, 2004), 81.
168. See rightly Moo, *Letter of James*, 121; Martin, *James*, 95–96.

It may also be said that both James and Paul were concerned about what later came to be called "dead orthodoxy," faith without its living expression in good works. While it may be true that "'faith without works' spares individuals the embarrassment of radical disruptions in their lives and relationships," the truth is that both Paul and James were all about radical disruptions in the lifestyles people had previously been accustomed to.[169] James here is busy deconstructing various prevailing social customs and habits and offering up in sacrifice various sacred cows, but Paul did the same thing in his own way.

Sharyn Dowd suggests that "James is using Paul's vocabulary but not his dictionary," which is clever but not quite right.[170] They are both drawing on previous Jewish usages of this sort of vocabulary, and when one considers even just the Abraham stories in Genesis 12–22 one discovers a range of meaning of the term faith as well as emphasis on the importance of obedient deeds, not to mention possibilities for the range of meaning of the *tsaddiq* language. Yet there is some force in the point Dowd makes when she says

> Paul never uses *pistis/pisteuō* to mean a mental agreement with a theological construct that has no implications for behavior. In fact, he never uses a *hoti* clause after the noun. . . . But even more important is the fact that Paul would have been incapable of constructing a sentence analogous with James 2:19 in which correct faith is attributed to demons. In Paul's writings, the subject of *pisteuein/echein pistin* is always one for whom "Jesus is Lord" (Rom 10:9), a confession only possible under the influence of the Holy Spirit (1 Cor 12:3). The fact that James can speak of the "faith" of demons shows he knows a use of the term that is foreign to Paul's thinking.[171]

The problem with this point is twofold: (1) it very well may be that the person speaking is the interlocutor not James; James may be being *accused* of being one who believes God is one, just as the demons do. (2) James also thinks that purely mental or even verbal faith is dead faith or useless faith, not real living Christian faith. What Dowd's argument however provides further support for is the contention that in fact James doesn't know Paul's letters and the common way he expresses such matters.[172]

169. Perkins, *First and Second Peter*, 13.
170. Sharyn Dowd, "Faith that Works: James 2:14–26," *RevExp* 97 (2000): 202.
171. Dowd, "Faith that Works," 202.
172. Here we may bring up a further possible point. When Paul met with James and Peter in Jerusalem after his conversion, what language did they speak? It could of course have been

I am in agreement with Brosend that we may assume Paul and James knew something of each other's gospel both from personal conversation and hearsay, but *not* from reading each others letters. Along with him I think it is right to conclude that "it is probably true that Paul and James did not think or worry about each other nearly as much as interpreters of James think and worry about Paul but about as much as interpreters of Paul worry about James . . . the history of interpreting James using Paul as the measuring rod always inhibits appreciation of James."[173]

It is a very sad irony that when Luther comes to discuss faith in his preface to his Romans commentary, he unwittingly provides an apt summary for much of what James is trying to say about faith and works here in James 2:

> O it is a living, busy active mighty thing, this faith. It is impossible for it not to be doing good things incessantly. It does not ask whether good works are to be done, but before the question is asked, it has already done this, and is constantly doing them. Whoever does not do such works, however, is an unbeliever. He gropes and looks around for faith and good works, but knows neither what faith is nor what good works are. Yet he talks and talks, with many words about faith and good works.[174]

Martin is correct that we do indeed have connections between the first and second half of James 2. Both vv. 1–13 and vv. 14–26 use the diatribe style, choosing some polemical examples to punctuate the points being made, and the underlying problem of mistreatment of the poor believers surfaces in both parts of the chapter as well. In both sections faith and works are seen as inevitably and intimately connected and in both sections impartiality is seen as a hallmark of real faith.[175]

Sadly, the perceived intertextuality between James (thought to be later) and Paul (thought to have been writing earlier) and the whole complicated subsequent history of discussion of these materials has impeded a straight forward reading of James in its original context,

Greek, but it surely is more likely to have been in Aramaic, the primary language of discourse for Jews in Jerusalem, and a language which Paul will have learned since he moved to Jerusalem many years before as a youth (see Acts 22:3; 26:4–5). This in turn would mean that James had never heard Paul express his views on faith in Greek.

173. Brosend, *James and Jude*, 79–80.

174. I am following the translation of Moo, *Letter of James*, 144 here.

175. Martin, *James*, 79.

and how he draws on the Abraham material. To this we must now turn.

Before we consider the text in detail it is important to note how several aspects of this portion of the discourse reinforce the point that our author is indeed a Jewish Christian talking to Jewish Christians:

1. His reference to Abraham, our father, in v. 21;

2. His midrashic treatment of the OT stories of Abraham and Rahab;

3. His emphasis on works and the sort of righteousness that results from doing good deeds, and especially deeds of charity;

4. His reference to Abraham as the friend of God—a popular Jewish designation of Abraham (cf. 2 Chr 20:7; Isa 41:8 to the later literature, e.g., Philo, *On Sobriety* 56, which renders Gen 18:17 with the phrase "Abraham my friend");[176]

5. His anthropology: a human being as body and breath, or body and spirit, not soul (*psuchē*) and body, nor as a trichotomy.

All of this likely implies that James thinks that at least some of his Jewish Christian audience knew well these OT stories and their context, if not also the way they were interpreted in Jewish circles. Joseph B. Mayor has a fascinating rabbinic quote that embraces the very sort of so-called faith James is inveighing against: "As soon as a man has mastered the thirteen heads of the faith, firmly believing therein . . . though he may have sinned in every possible way . . . still he inherits eternal life" (Mekilta on Exod 14:31).[177]

It would be hard to overestimate how strongly the issue of faith and works and salvation is stressed here. Some nine of the twenty uses of the term *pistis* in James occur in this passage, as are twelve of the fifteen uses of the term *ergos,* and one of the five uses of the verb *sōdzō.* In other words, twenty-five of the words in this brief passage (217 total Greek words) are these three words, or some 12 percent of the passage.[178]

James begins in v. 14 by asking his Christian audience whether or not a faith without works is useful or useless. To ask about the profit, use, or benefit of something is a common question in deliberative

176. Joseph B. Mayor, *The Epistle of St. James* (London: MacMillan, 1910), 107.

177. Mayor, *St. James,* 96.

178. See Brosend, *James,* 72–73.

rhetoric. The nature of the conditional sentence here show he thinks this question might well arise. The second remark is also a question. "Is your faith able to save you?"—a rhetorical question to which the answer implied is "no," if by faith is meant that type of faith which James is attacking. James has here broadened the previous discussion to the more expansive topic of faith and works. Crucial to understanding this verse is recognizing the use of the anaphoric definite article before the word "faith" here. The question should be translated "Can 'that (sort of) faith' save him?"[179]

James is following here the rhetorical advice that suggests that one should stick with, and reiterate, one's strongest point the longest (see Rhet. Her. 4.45.58) precisely because all of the rest of the argument rests on this crucial point about the necessary connection between living faith and good works. Notice that the discussion here has moved on from talking about visitors to the assembly of faith, to "brothers and sisters" (one of the few occasions of the use of the term adelphē in the NT in a nonphysical sense).[180] Christian treatment of fellow Christians is at issue here.

There follows a little parable in vv. 15–16, also begun by ean indicating a condition that is future but probable. Just as was the case in the first half of this chapter, the ratio takes the form of an example. It differs from the earlier example in that here the rhetorical question expects a negative answer. Notice that the deliberative topic of "what profits a person" is being raised here (Rhet. Alex. 7.1428b.10–20). Certainly, there were plenty of destitute Christians in the first century needing aid from the community. We see a scantily clad and hungry brother or sister; gymnoi need not imply naked, but rather under or poorly clothed, rather than unclothed.[181] This person is so indigent he does not even have enough food for today.[182] The response in v. 16 is meant to seem shaky and shallow. It sounds pleasant enough, even concerned in a superficial way: "hope you are well fed and clothed." But in fact, this is an anti-Christian and unloving response that is unacceptable. Beneath the surface is the idea that deeds of mercy are not an option but an obligation for those who profess and have real faith.

179. See rightly Moo, Letter of James, 123.
180. Brosend, James and Jude, 73.
181. See P. Wisconsin 73, which is a letter containing the lament by a woman that "she has nothing to wear" (gymne estin, lines 19–20); see NewDocs, 2:79.
182. On tes ephemerou trophēs as daily sustenance see Matt 6:11; Luke 11:3; probably the phrase is an echo of the Lord's prayer. See Martin, James, 84.

"Go in peace" is what the person says to the indigent man. It could mean, as Mayor suggests, "have no anxiety," but in fact it was a stereotyped parting formula, and often meant no more than "good-bye," though it could have the fuller sense of "blessings" (cf. Gen 15:15; Exod 4:18; Judg 16:6; 1 Sam 20:42; Mark 5:34; Luke 7:50).[183] This seems more likely here. It appears also that we should trans-late *thermainesthe kai chortazesthe* in v. 16 as middles, not passives, in which case it means "warm yourself," and "feed yourself," not "be warmed," "be filled," as a sort of wish. If this is right, then the per-son in question is being very callous indeed. He is juxtaposing warm words with cold deeds.[184] He, like so many others since, is saying in effect "pull yourself up by your bootstraps" or "do it yourself."

To this behavior, James rejoins, "if you say you have faith and fail to help—of what use is it? What good does it do you or anyone else?" Possibly, in v. 17, we should translate *kai* as "even," and read "so (or in the same way) *even* faith, if it does not have works, is dead by itself." James has thus made two key points: (1) living faith necessarily entails good deeds and (2) faith and works are so integrally related that faith by itself is useless or dead, unless coupled with works or as Mayor puts it, the sort of "faith" James is critiquing is "not merely outwardly inoperative but inwardly dead."[185]

Davids summarizes well:

For James, then, there is no such thing as a true and living faith which does not produce works, for the only true faith is a "faith working through love" (Gal 5:6). Works are not an "added extra" any more than breath is an "added extra" to a living body. The so-called faith which fails to produce works (the works to be produced are charity, not the "works of the law" such as circumcision against which Paul inveighs) is simply not "saving faith."[186]

To the believer who prides himself on right belief (and clearly in vv. 18, 19 faith means something else than what it usually means for James, not trust in or active dependence on God, but rather mere belief that God exists), James says to such a mere believer, "so you say you believe God is one. Good for you, however so do demons and they are shuddering in their belief—fearing the wrath of God to

183. Mayor, *St. James*, 97; Ropes, *St. James*, 107.
184. Mayor, *St. James*, 99.
185. Mayor, *St. James*, 126.
186. Davids, *James*, 122.

come. A lot of good that faith did them." The sarcasm in v. 19 is hard to miss.[187]

In v. 20 James becomes even more sarcastic: "So you want evidence, O empty headed one [cf. Rom 2:1; 9:20], that faith without works is useless/without profit [argos]—let's turn to the Scriptures." Another way of translating argos here would be workless—faith without works is workless, or as I would prefer to put it, faith without works won't work![188]

The two examples from Scripture that James cites were very standard examples of true faith among the Jews. He is choosing the most stellar example (Abraham) and in some ways the most scandalous example, Rahab the harlot. James probably knows how much Abraham was idolized in the Jewish tradition. For example, Jubilees 23:10 says, "Abraham was perfect in all his deeds with the Lord, and well-pleasing in righteousness all the days of his life." Sirach 44:19 says, "no one has been found like him in glory." More important of course is 1 Maccabees 2:51–52, which says Abraham was reckoned righteous not on the basis of his faith but as result of passing the test and remaining faithful and obedient when he was asked to sacrifice his son. Clearly James does not push his use of the exemplary Abraham to these extremes, but he stands in the tradition of seeing Abraham as the exemplum par excellence. It is of more than passing interest that the use made of Genesis 22 here is closely similar to the use made in Hebrews 11:17–19, which says that it was by faith that Abraham, when tested brought forth Isaac and offered his son. This may suggest that there were some standard interpretations of the key OT figures that circulated in Jewish Christian circles.

James refers to two separate texts in Genesis: the promise in 15:6 and also Genesis 22:12–16, the story about the offering of Isaac. As is frequent in midrashic exegesis, the two texts are combined. James is stressing that it was on the basis of his obedient offering of Isaac, that is, his deed of obedience, that he was edikaiōthē—justified or vindicated. Principally, he is thinking of Genesis 22:16 where God promises his blessing as a result of his having done what he did. This may be compared to the word of blessing in Genesis 15:6. Robert Wall may be right that this one climactic example of obedient faith may be a shorthand reference to all ten of the tests Abraham passed,

187. See Brosend, James and Jude, 75.
188. See Dowd, "Faith that Works," 199.

which led to this conclusion of vindication.[189] In any event, in v. 22 the verb *sunergei* should be seen as an iterative imperfect, which implies that faith was working along with works at the same time side by side, or put another way, it implies these two things coexisted in Abraham's life over a period of time.[190] Davids ably shows the Jewish train of James's thought here:

> But there is a larger issue because even in Genesis 15, Abraham's believing entailed ensuing obedience—he did what the Lord told him in going to Canaan, in bringing his son for sacrifice, and in so many other ways. His was not a faith separated from works of obedience. His point is that *even* in the case of believing Abraham, his works were essential as an expression of faith. In what sense was he vindicated? His trust in God was vindicated for he dared to offer his son trusting God to provide or take care of the situation. If this is what James takes *edikaiōthē* to mean, it is very different from Paul's notions. Abraham trusts in God that he already had been or was vindicated when he offered Isaac, and there was divine intervention. In a real sense, faith was made perfect by his trusting obedience.[191]

So, James can go on to say, "You see that faith cooperates with his works, and by works his faith was perfected. The two go together hand in hand, works perfecting faith, which is by implication imperfect without it." The concept of righteousness here at least in v. 21 seems to be Jewish, not "counted righteous" or considered righteous but declared to *be* righteous, that is, righteous by means of deeds. Abraham's belief was belief in action.

The point of James's argument, then, has nothing to do with a forensic declaration of justification; the argument is simply that Abraham did have faith, which here unlike other places in James means monotheistic belief. For this Abraham was famous in Jewish tradition, but he also had deeds flowing from that faith. Thus, James is not dealing with works of the law as a means to become saved or as an entrance requirement. Notice he never speaks of "works of the law." He is dealing with the conduct of those who already believe. He is talking about the perfection of faith in its working out through good works. "Work out your salvation with fear and trembling" was how Paul put it, or better in Galatians 5:6 Paul speaks of faith working

---

189. See Robert W. Wall, *Community of the Wise: The Letter of James* (Valley Forge, PA: Trinity Press International, 1997), 136.

190. See Dowd, "Faith that Works," 201.

191. Davids, *James*, 127–28 (emphasis original).

itself out through love, while James speaks of faith coming to mature expression or its perfect end or goal in works. These two ideas are closely similar.[192]

This still leaves us with the difficulty of v. 24, a statement Paul would never have made. However, if, as we should, we take the vindication in v. 24 as referring to that final verdict of God on one's deeds and life work, then even Paul can be said to have agreed. Even he speaks of a final justification/vindication that is dependent on what believers do in the interim (see Gal 5:5 and what follows it).[193] It is this final vindication or acquittal in view here. Paul would agree that one cannot be righteous on that last day without there having been some good deeds between the new birth and that last day in the spiritual pilgrimage. Thus v. 24b only apparently contradicts Paul, not least because not even Paul thought faith alone kept one in the kingdom, though it did get one into it.

As a secondary and more daring example that is intended to illustrate the same ideas (*homoios* makes this clear, "similarly") James turns to Rahab, who entertained the Hebrew spies and chucked them out (hence *ekbalousa,* literally "cast out") the back window when the enemy approached. The point here is if everyone from Abraham to Rahab received final vindication because of faith *and* works, so shall the followers of Jesus. Rahab's faith is not mentioned but it was widely held to by Jews.[194] We may also think that the rhetorical strategy here involves forestalling the objection: "But I am not a towering figure of faith like Abraham," to which the proper reply is "at least you could follow the example set by Rahab!"[195] The last example then removes all excuse for doing nothing and shames the audience into action. Finally, one can also suggest that since both Abraham and Rahab are examples of those who exercised faith and hospitality, which contrasts nicely with the first example in this section where no

192. As the church fathers noted; see Luke Timothy Johnson, *The Letter of James: A New Translation with Introduction and Commentary,* AB 37A (New York: Doubleday, 1995), 243.

193. It is a mistake to think that "final justification" means declared innocent, or acquittal here. Rather it has to do with God's recognition that someone has behaved in a way that can be called right or righteous, and at the last judgment those acts are vindicated to be righteous. Against, Moo, *Letter of James,* 138–40 who is following Joachim Jeremias, "Paul and James" *ExpTim* 66 (1955): 368–71.

194. See the discussion in A. T. Hanson, "Rahab the Harlot in Early Christian Tradition," *JSNT* 1 (1978): 53–60.

195. Plummer, *First and Second Peter,* 163.

hospitality is shown to the poor, this may in part explain why these two historical examples are cited here.[196]

James is not dealing at all with the question on what basis do gentiles get to enter the community of faith, but rather what is the nature of the faith, of true Christianity? Does it necessarily entail deeds of mercy? It is of course possible that James got wind of some sort of perverted or garbled Pauline summary that had been heard by his audience, but even this is not a necessary assumption. Jews were fascinated with Genesis 22 and the story of Abraham and much of the common terminology is to be explained by both James and Paul drawing on the same OT text, possibly both relying on the LXX version. This discussion has taken us in various directions, and above all it demonstrates once more just how crucial the Abraham cycle of stories in Genesis was to the earliest Christian writers, writers such as Paul and James. They use the traditions in differing ways, but always with appreciation of "father Abraham" who presages the very meaning of faith, trust, obedience for the earliest Christians.

THE LEXICON OF FAITH: THE BROADER USE OF GENESIS

It should have struck us as odd that the most famous patriarch other than Abraham, namely Jacob/Israel, *the one for whom the whole people were named*, shows up *almost nowhere* in the NT.[197] And, in fact, where it does show up in a quote of Isaiah 59:20–21 at Romans 11:26–27 the reference is to the "impiety" of Jacob. Of course, this is a reference to the people Israel in general and not just to Jacob in particular, but still the impression is clear: Jacob was no hero of the faith, unlike Abraham. Notice as well how Jacob is treated in Stephen's speech in Acts 7:8–18. It is admitted that Jacob was the father of the twelve patriarchs, and that he sent family members to get grain during a famine, but the story is told in a way to highlight the accomplishments of Joseph, whose jealous brothers sold him "into Egypt" (v. 9), but God was with him and rescued him. Later Joseph revealed himself to his brothers when he was a great official in Egypt, and it was Joseph who

---

196. See Johnson, *Letter of James*, 249; Moo, *Letter of James*, 143, and the passage in 1 Clem. 12:7 may support this suggestion.

197. In this section of this and subsequent chapters we are looking at partial quotations, allusions, and echoes of some consequence that do not show up in the discussions of the major figures and texts already discussed.

invited Jacob and seventy-five family members to come to Egypt and survive the famine. The story is told from the point of view of Joseph, and to his advantage, leaving out the bit about the trickery involving the cup and Benjamin after the first visit of the brothers to Egypt. On this showing we might have expected more to be said about the accomplishments of Joseph in the NT because God was with him, perhaps even a mention of his famous judgment spoken to his brothers "what you intended for harm, God intended for good."

In fact, however, apart from a passing reference that mentions both Jacob and Joseph in Hebrews 11:20–22, there is nothing of substance to be found elsewhere in the NT. Here is what Hebrews 11:20–22 says:

> [20] By faith Isaac invoked blessings for the future on Jacob and Esau. [21] By faith Jacob, when dying, blessed each of the sons of Joseph, "bowing in worship over the top of his staff." [22] By faith Joseph, at the end of his life, made mention of the exodus of the Israelites and gave instructions about his burial.

This should have struck us as quite odd. First, we hear not of Jacob but of Isaac invoking blessings for the future of Jacob and Esau, and then the text passes on to Jacob invoking blessing on each of the sons of Joseph. Then nothing is said of the life and accomplishments of Joseph, other than at the end of his life he mentioned the exodus from Egypt and gave instructions about his own burial. When we compare and contrast this with what is said about Abraham and then Moses both in Hebrews 11 and Acts 7, the contrast is stark, especially in regard to the near silence about Jacob, and the more surprising lack of mention of Joseph. Let's look a little more closely at this paragraph in the hall of faith.

Hebrews 11:20–22 concludes this paragraph with the reference to Isaac's blessing of his two sons, Jacob's blessing of his two grandchildren while at the end of his life while leaning on his staff (partially citing Gen 48:15–16), and finally Joseph who foresaw the exodus from Egypt and so asked his bones to be carried back to the promised land when that happened (Exod 13:19; Josh 24:32; Acts 7:16).[198] The

---

198. This bowing could be seen as a gesture of worship; see Koester, *Hebrews*, 493. It is worth adding that the text in Gen 48:15 has Jacob *claiming* the two sons of Joseph as his own, which might explain the reference to the grandchildren rather than the blessing on the children of Jacob. Whether Jacob was leaning on his staff or in bed is one of those cases where the issue becomes the pointing of the MT. The same consonants (*mth*) can produce the word "bed" or the word "staff"; the LXX of Gen 47:31 follows the latter reading.

key link between these three examples is that blessing requires faith that there will be a future, as does giving orders about one's future dead bones.[199] As Long puts it Joseph "staring into the grave, . . . saw grace."[200] "From these aspects of the patriarch's life, the addressees are to learn that God's promise is more certain than death, and that the person of faith need not flinch before any hardship."[201] However, as Hagner says, it is surprising that we have the reference to the blessing of the *grandchildren* where Jacob once more plays favorites rather than the blessing of his twelve sons.[202]

Even in the hall of faith, Jacob is up to his old tricks, playing favorites. Perhaps this is why the author leads with a reference to Isaac, a less objectionable patriarch, rather than with his son Jacob, even though the nation would be named after the son. One gets the impression that Jacob makes it into the hall of faith on the coattails of Isaac and Joseph, his father and most famous son. The impression of the silence in the NT about Jacob should be compared to a document like the Testament of the Twelve Patriarchs, from approximately the same period, where we have interesting elaborations on each of the sons of Jacob, but there is no real focus on Jacob himself. Were early Jews embarrassed about the legacy of Jacob himself?

But perhaps you are saying, "Wait a minute." What about the discussion of Jacob and his well at Sychar in John 4? First of all, consider where Jesus is—in Samaria. In John 4 it is a Samaritan woman that is bragging about "our ancestor Jacob" and she even asks, apparently in mocking tones, the question, "Are you greater than our father Jacob, who gave us the well and drank from it himself, as did also his sons and his livestock?"

The answer is of course, "Yes much greater, I give living water, the water of everlasting life, not merely well water." Jesus will go on to say: "You Samaritans worship what you do not know; we worship what we do know, for salvation is from the Jews." Notice that Jesus does not say "salvation comes from the patriarchs" or from our ancestor Jacob. No, it comes from the Jews (i.e., not the Samaritans). Thus, in this story, Jacob at best provides a foil for the claims of Jesus. Jacob can provide no more than mundane water, water that cannot quench the deepest thirsts of humankind and requires repeated use.

199. DeSilva, *Perseverance in Gratitude*, 404 rightly notes how closely our author is following the LXX of Gen 50:26 even in his choice of words to speak of Joseph's "dying."

200. Long, *Hebrews*, 121.

201. DeSilva, *Perseverance in Gratitude*, 405.

202. Hagner, *Encountering Hebrews*, 151.

But Jesus offers something far more substantial and life-giving, living water that provides everlasting life. Even in John 4, Jacob comes up short, and is eclipsed by a greater one, just as was the case in the "Bethel" reference in John 1:51. Whether at Sychar or at Bethel, Jesus as the Wisdom of God come in the flesh, as the living presence of God, turns out not merely to be greater than Jacob, he turns out to be the Bethel in whom one encounters God.

Let us walk through the other passing references and allusions to the material in Genesis in Hebrews 11. Since he could not use Adam and Eve as examples of faith, the author begins with the first figure in Genesis that could be said to be such an example: Abel. Abel offered a greater sacrifice than Cain. Genesis 4:2–10 of course does not say his sacrifice was *greater*, nor does it mention his faith. How are we to understand "greater"? Greater in quantity or simply better? Some have conjectured that more was meant, some have thought that a more adequate sacrifice was offered because it was a blood sacrifice (cf. Philo *Sacrifices* 88; Josephus, *Ant.* 1.54), but as F. F. Bruce says, this sacrifice was more adequate because of the faith and righteousness involved not due to quantity or type of sacrifice.[203] God's pleasure in the gift shows that it was offered in the right spirit, the acceptance of the sacrifice attested that he was a righteous one (cf. Testament of Zebulun 5:4). As DeSilva suggests, it is the virtue behind the sacrifice, the trust in God, that makes it acceptable and that makes Abel a model of such virtue in our author's eyes.[204] His example still speaks to us though he is dead, says the author.[205] There is perhaps an interesting echo of the Genesis story, which says that Abel's blood cried out from the ground to God (cf. Gen 4:10; Heb 12:24), but here it is his example of faith and righteousness that continues to speak after his death.[206]

---

203. F. F. Bruce, *The Epistle to the Hebrews*, NICNT (Grand Rapids: Eerdmans, 1990), 285–86.

204. DeSilva, *Perseverance in Gratitude*, 388.

205. It is interesting, as Koester, *Hebrews*, 476 points out, that our author assumes Abel is still dead, even though he is an exemplar of faith. This speaks volumes about our author's theology of the afterlife, which does not primarily consist in the concept of "dying and going to heaven." Enoch is seen as exceptional under this schema of afterlife thinking. Here DeSilva (*Perseverance in Gratitude*, 389) is mistaken in seeing Abel as an example like Enoch of one who lives on in heaven. The text reads literally "through it [i.e., faith], having died, yet it speaks."

206. On the interpretation of the Cain and Abel story in early Judaism and beyond see John Byron, "Cain and Abel in Second Temple Literature and Beyond" in Evans, *Book of Genesis*, 331–51. Cain, as the first murderer, became a type of the wicked, while Abel became a type of the righteous, even though Abel is not called righteous in either the MT or LXX account; see, e.g., Wis 10:1–21; Philo, *Sacrifices* 10, 14; Deuteronomy 32; and esp. Josephus, *Ant.* 1.53.

Notice how in Matthew 23:35 Abel is also referred to as righteous (cf. 1 John 3:12). It would appear that in both texts he is viewed as the first example of a righteous martyr. But while there is a foreshadowing of Jesus here, as Long says Hebrews 12:24 reminds us that Jesus offered a better word than the blood of Abel: "Abel's blood cries out for revenge, but Jesus' blood brings an end to vengeance and grants forgiveness (9.22; 10.10)."[207] Walter Moberly however suggests that in fact Abel's blood, if he is seen as a prototype of Christ here, cries out for mercy on his brother Abel, a mercy that God shows Cain, just as Christ's blood pleads for mercy on us all. One must ask in what sense does Abel's blood still speak today, as our author says? If we do indeed compare Hebrews 12:24 closely, the most reasonable suggestion is that Christ's blood speaks a "better word" in the sense of a more comprehensive and effective plea for mercy. Our author right through the discourse has been comparing what is good with what is better (e.g., angels and Christ, Moses and Christ), and this sort of comparison may well be in play between Abel's and Christ's blood.[208] That our author says "Abel speaks" may suggest he, like Philo, has the view that Abel is still alive. Philo says the righteous like Abel "live an incorporeal life" (QG 1.70).

Next in line for comment in v. 5 is Enoch whom the Bible says walked with God (which means obeyed him, followed his ways) and was taken up from earth without experiencing death (see 1 Enoch 12:3; 15:1; 2 Enoch 22:8; 71:14; Jubilees 4:23; 10:17; 19:24–27; Josephus, *Ant.* 1.3.4).[209] Our author seems to know not only Genesis 5:24, which he partially quotes, but perhaps also the various traditions about Enoch found in Sirach 44:16; 1 Enoch 70:1–4; Wisdom of Solomon 4:10 and elsewhere, though he shows far more restraint in what he does with this tradition than in 1 and 2 Enoch (cf. also 1 Clem. 9:2–3).[210] Our author says he was pleasing to God as is obviously shown by his "translation" to heaven.[211] It is the LXX text that speaks of his being pleasing. This in turn is the basis of assuming

---

207. Long, *Hebrews*, 116.

208. See R. Walter L. Moberly, "Exemplars of Faith: Abel," in Bauckham, *Epistle to the Hebrews and Christian Theology*, 353–63.

209. See Attridge, *Hebrews*, 317–18.

210. See Craddock, "Hebrews," 133.

211. Notice the emphasis on being "taken up," the root form of the word appearing three times in v. 5. This is not surprising since Enoch is a prototype of Christ whose "translation" is also stressed in Hebrews.

Enoch must have had faith, since as our author is about to say, without faith, one cannot please God,

One may debate whether brief references to characters and stories in Genesis deserve to be called citations, allusions, or echoes, especially when there is nothing like a verbatim citation. The impression one gets again and again is that the stories are not cited, they are just rehearsed in the speaker's own diction. At the same time, the reference to Abel in Hebrews 11:4, the very first example cited in the so-called hall of faith (stretching from Abel to Jesus) is hardly just an allusion or echo. The author says, "by faith Abel offered a better sacrifice than Cain did." The term "better" or "greater" (πλείων) is a repeated refrain used by the author of Hebrews to compare and contrast many things, including the new and old covenants, the new and old sacrifices, the various priesthoods, and so on.[212] What is interesting in the use of the Abel example from Genesis 4:4–5 is that what is said in that text involves not a comparison, but a contrast—between a sacrifice that was acceptable to the Lord, and one that was not. This is perhaps clearer in the LXX than in the MT, for the former has καὶ Αβελ ἤνεγκεν καὶ αὐτὸς ἀπὸ τῶν πρωτοτόκων τῶν προβάτων αὐτοῦ καὶ ἀπὸ τῶν στεάτων αὐτῶν καὶ ἐπεῖδεν ὁ θεὸς ἐπὶ Αβελ καὶ ἐπὶ τοῖς δώροις αὐτοῦ followed immediately by a contrasting "but Cain . . ."

There is in addition the deduction that Abel must have been a righteous person since his sacrifice was acceptable to God, which is an inference also found in other early Jewish texts such as 1 Enoch 22:7; Testament of Abraham 12:2–3 (cf. Matt 23:35; 1 John 3:12). Notice as well that the notion that Abel was still "speaking" after his death is an allusion to Genesis 4:10 about his blood crying out to God, a text that is clearly alluded to in both Hebrews 11:4b and again importantly at 12:24. But in what sense does Abel still speak today, especially since the author at 12:24 compares Abel's sacrifice to the much greater one of Christ?

Some commentators, such as Pamela Eisenbaum, have suggested that the verse should be interpreted to mean that Abel himself still lives to testify because the Scripture still testifies to the validity of his sacrifice and God's approval of it.[213] The "righteous" live on, as Daniel 12:2–3 says. She also rightly notes that our author has in a sense

212. On this see Witherington, *Letters and Homilies for Jewish Christians.*
213. Pamela M. Eisenbaum, *The Jewish Heroes of Christian History: Hebrews 11 in Literary Context*, SBLDS 156 (Atlanta: Scholars Press, 1997), 149.

"denationalized" these OT heroes by emphasizing qualities in their lives that are more universal and could be emulated by the Jewish Christian audience of Hebrews: faith, righteousness, pleasing God. Notice how in Matthew 23:35 as well we hear about the "blood of righteous Abel" who will testify against the scribes and Pharisees who have been hypocritical, condemning the prophets and sages and others that God has sent to his people. It is probably relevant to this discussion that the LXX heightened the difference between Cain's and Abel's sacrifice by not only using different words for "sacrifice" in each case but by calling Abel's offering a "gift." Possibly too, righteous Abel, as the first martyr to shed innocent blood in the Bible is meant to foreshadow another righteous person's death—Jesus, whose righteous blood is betrayed (Matthew 27:4). The reference to all the martyrs from A to Z (Abel to Zechariah ben Barachiah) is meant to encompass all those recorded in the OT narratives from Genesis 4 to 2 Chronicles 24.[214]

It comes as something of a shock that the only OT passage explicitly used by the author of 1 John, at 1 John 3:12, is the story of Cain and Abel. Why? Menken plausibly suggests that the behavior of the secessionists from the Johannine community reminded the author of the behavior of Cain toward his brother Abel. The secessionists belong to the world, which is under the sway and guidance of "the Evil One," just as Cain was, according to 1 John 3:12. The secessionists are motivated by hate for their brothers and sisters, just as Cain was (cf. 3:12 to 4:20).

But it is not just the OT text of Genesis 4:1–16 that the author of 1 John is following. No, he is drawing on the early Jewish readings of that material. Saying that Cain is "from the evil one" is not in the Genesis text, but you do find it in the Apocalypse of Abraham 24:5: Cain was "led by the Adversary to break the Law" (but see also 1 Enoch 22:5–7; 4 Macc 18:6–9; Jubilees 4:1–6; Testament of Benjamin 7:1–5, the last of which also suggests Satan inspired Cain's action).[215] Josephus likewise calls him very evil (*Ant.* 1.53). By contrast, Abel is called "righteous" not in Genesis but in Matthew 23:35; Hebrews 11:4; and here in 1 John 3 his deeds are said to be righteous. Both Josephus (*Ant.* 1.67) and the author of 1 John use the word "mur-

---

214. This is assuming that the Hebrew canon concluded with 2 Chronicles, as indeed was later the case; see Brown, "Genesis in Matthew's Gospel," 52n53.

215. See the discussion by D. A. Carson, "1 John," in Beale, *Commentary on the New Testament Use*, 1066–67.

der" to describe the action of Cain against Abel. In other words, 1 John 3 reflects not just a use of Genesis but the early Jewish history of the interpretation of the text. For our author, it was an important text, because "those who went out from us" were causing havoc, and their true character needed to be unmasked, through an analogy with Cain.[216] A present problem prompted a pregnant analogy to a Genesis text.

There is a very interesting and uniquely Matthean allusion to the story of Lamech in Genesis 4:23–24, who follows the example of Cain and takes it much further.[217] The LXX has it this way: ὅτι ἑπτάκις ἐκδεδίκηται ἐκ Καιν ἐκ δὲ Λαμεχ ἑβδομηκοντάκις ἑπτά. This should be compared to Jesus instruction to Peter about the number of times one should forgive in Matthew 18:22 where Jesus says, Οὐ λέγω σοι ἕως ἑπτάκις, ἀλλὰ ἕως ἑβδομηκοντάκις ἑπτά. The ministry of forgiveness is meant to break the cycle of violence, reverse the curse, replacing revenge with forgiveness. As Hays says, Jesus's words are surely a deliberate echo of the Lamech text for these are the only two places in Scripture where the number seventy-seven, or perhaps seven times seventy, are to be found.[218] This comports with the regular theme in Matthew of mercy and forgiveness (Matthew 6:9–15; 9:12–13; 18:23–35) a theme emphasized by the citing of Scripture.[219] "It is likely that the phrase connotes unlimited forgiveness just as Lamech's words imply unlimited revenge."[220]

In the next verse of relevance in Hebrews, 11:5, we find a use of Genesis 5:24 and in particular the notion applied only to Enoch in the OT that "Enoch was not found because God took him up." This unique claim sparked no little interest among early Jewish interpreters of Genesis, including the author of Hebrews. This, again is not a literal translation, it is a mixture of citation, allusion, and the author's own words, linking his being taken up to his faith (or "walking with God").[221] What Genesis actually says is that Enoch "pleased"

216. See Menken, "Genesis in John's Gospel," 95–98.
217. It is odd that nowhere in the massive *Commentary on the New Testament Use of the Old Testament,* even in the Matthew portion, is this text discussed, and yet it is so fundamental to Matthew's view of Jesus.
218. Presumably, seventy-seven is what is meant, as this is the clear meaning of the Hebrew original, something the translator of the LXX knew perfectly well.
219. Hays, *Echoes of Scripture in the Gospels,* 124–25.
220. Brown, "Genesis in Matthew's Gospel," 51.
221. See Susan Docherty, "Genesis in Hebrews," in Menken, *Genesis in the New Testament,* 140.

God (Gen 5:22). The elaboration of this profile of Enoch is considerable in early Jewish literature.[222]

The third example held up for emulation in the hall of faith is
Noah, again with a brief summary alluding to Genesis 6:13–22.
Unlike the two prior examples, Noah is explicitly said to be righteous
in the OT text: "Noah was a righteous man, being perfect in his
generation; Noah was pleasing to God" (Gen 6:9; cf. 7:1; see the
LXX Νωε ἄνθρωπος δίκαιος τέλειος ὢν ἐν τῇ γενεᾷ αὐτοῦ τῷ θεῷ
εὐηρέστησεν Νωε). This profile of course conveniently overlooks the
story of Noah's drunkenness and possible other misadventures after
the floodwaters receded.

Noah, according to v. 7, was instructed concerning the coming
judgment, and so he built an ark that saved his family. Notice that
sōtēria here has the sense of rescue or keep safe. It does not refer to
eternal salvation here.[223] This comports with the notion in Hebrews
that salvation brings rest. Also, *eulabētheis* here suggests that Noah
reacted to God's word to him about judgment with reverence or religious awe—with the fear of the Lord that prompts godly and obedient action.[224] But Noah's "folly" turned out to be a symbol of God's
judgment on the rest of the world.[225] This is very similar to the argument in 1 Peter 3:19–22 that refers to those who were by faith righteous and so are inheritors. Noah is not here however portrayed as a
preacher of repentance as we find in 2 Peter 2:5 and 1 Clement 7:6.
Here the seed idea found in Habakkuk 2:4 is reused again in a fashion
somewhat similar to Paul's usage. It is interesting that here alone is
the "unseen" something that is threatening, namely judgment, rather
than something that is promising. But it is analogous with the situation of the audience of Hebrews, for our author has warned them
that they live in the shadow of the coming "day" of judgment (10:25,
36–37).[226]

This analogy reminds us once more that our author is primarily
holding out for his audience an eschatological prospect of recompense or judgment, not otherworldly compensation. "Like Noah, the
addressees are to use their time and resources in this life to prepare

---

222. See Lloyd R. Bailey, *Noah: The Person and Story in History and Tradition* (Columbia: University of South Carolina Press, 1989).

223. See DeSilva, *Perseverance in Gratitude*, 391.

224. Attridge, *Hebrews*, 319.

225. On Noah's righteousness see Gen 6:9; 7:1; Ezek 14:14, 20; Sir 44:17; Wis 10:4. Here it
would appear that it is his faith in God that is the judgment on the world.

226. DeSilva, *Perseverance in Gratitude*, 391.

for salvation at the day of judgment, at the return of Christ."[227] The phrase at the end of the verse, "he became an inheritor of the righteousness that comes by faith" certainly sounds Pauline, and while *kata pistin* is used here instead of the Pauline *ek pisteos* we still probably have a hint that our author is familiar with Galatians and/or Romans.[228] This becomes all the more likely when we consider the next example chosen: Abraham. Note that here "righteousness" probably refers to the right-standing one obtains on the last day—in other words final justification or righteousness.

Acts 3:25b involves a partial quotation from some Genesis text, but which one? The promise to Abraham shows up in many places and in several forms: Genesis 12:3 ("in you all tribes will be blessed"); Genesis 18:18 ("all nations"); Genesis 22:18 ("all nations blessed in your seed"); or Genesis 26:4 (nearly identical to 22:18). Luke in any case has changed the text to refer to "families" rather than tribes or nations, which could be seen as his way of using a more inclusive term that might suggest both Jews and gentiles. This can be contrasted with b. Yebam. 63a, which says the nations will be blessed for Israel's sake, or even that Israel in the days of the messiah would destroy the nations (Num. Rab. 2.3)![229] Peter's point would seem to be that God's blessing is for Jews through Jesus, and by extension for others as well, but to the Jew first.[230]

Genesis 28:10–22 provides us with one of the most famous of all stories in the Jacob saga, the story of angels descending and ascending on a ladder to heaven, and Jacob proclaiming the place "the house of God" (Bethel) and even "the gateway to heaven." But how is this material used in John 1:51? Whereas Jacob is speaking of a place where there is a divine manifestation, Jesus speaks of *himself* as the Bethel, the gate of God. It is on him that the angels descend and ascend. But in Jacob's vision it is God himself who speaks to him. Is this through the angels, God's messengers? Jesus in the Johannine

227. DeSilva, *Perseverance in Gratitude*, 391.
228. See Ben Witherington III, "The Influence of Galatians on Hebrews," *NTS* 37 (1991): 146–52. It may even be the case that the term *dikaiosynē* has the sense of "'right-standing'" that it has in Paul (see Rom 3:21–26) at various points in Galatians and Romans, rather than the more sapiential use of the term we find in James. Alternatively, this phrase may mean that Noah's faith enabled him to live righteously and obediently to God. But if that was meant we would hardly expect the term "inherit" here, which suggests a future obtaining of some thing or some condition or status.
229. See Ben Witherington III, *The Acts of the Apostles: A Socio-Rhetorical Commentary* (Grand Rapids: Eerdmans, 1996), 189.
230. See I. H. Marshall, "Acts," in Beale, *Commentary on the New Testament Use*, 549.

account tells Nathaniel that there is something greater about the Son of Man than just that he is the Son of God, the King of Israel. The only thing greater is the suggestion that the Son of Man is the incarnation of God's presence on earth, which is why the angels are coming to and going from him (with messages?). Jacob's Bethel vision was great, but behold a greater sight will be available to Nathaniel in due course. Hays puts it well:

> Jesus now takes over the temple's function as a place of mediation between God and human beings. . . . Jesus has become the nexus between heaven and earth—the role previously ascribed to the temple as the site of God's presence. . . . In this mysterious utterance the Son of Man is not himself the figure who moves between the two realms; rather, the angels are the heavenly messengers, while Jesus is the intermediary figure which makes the connection possible.[231]

Sometimes an echo of a particular OT text is especially apt because there is a parallel between the person speaking it in the OT and the person reiterating it, or saying something very similar in the NT. Consider the case of Rachel in Genesis 30:23 who says when she finally conceives "God has taken away my disgrace" and Elizabeth in Luke 1:25 who speaks of God looking with favor on her "to take away my disgrace." Are we meant to think of Elizabeth drawing on the story of Rachel and making the parallel with her own plight as a pious Jewish woman might do, or is this just Luke's attempt to give the narrative in Luke 1–2 a thoroughly Jewish feel?

Scholars have often noted just how much Luke's way of framing stories and his very diction are full of "Septuaginisms," and this is clear even in small ways as well as large ones. Let us take a couple of examples from Genesis 46. In 46:2 God speaks to Jacob in a night vision saying "Jacob, Jacob" to which he responds "Here I am." Jacob then is called or encouraged to go down to Egypt, where God will make him "a great nation" and go with Jacob. Acts 9, 22, and 26 have the same double calling of the name, but in Saul's story he has to ask who is speaking before, in the Acts 26 account, Saul is commissioned on the spot. Interestingly, Paul characterizes his encounter as a heavenly vision (26:19), and notice that he says that God promises to rescue him from both his people and from the gentiles. In both the story of Jacob and Saul the words of assurance are meant to overcome fear.

---

231. Hays, *Echoes of Scripture in the Gospels*, 313, 333. See also Jerome H. Neyrey, "Jacob Traditions and the Interpretation of John 4:10–26," *CBQ* 41 (1979): 419–37.

Even more interesting as an echo is Luke 2:29, the famous *Nunc Dimittis*, "Lord now dismiss thy servant in peace," that Simeon utters immediately after he sees and holds the baby Jesus, "my eyes have seen your salvation" he adds. This surely echoes the words of Jacob himself in Genesis 46:29–30 where Joseph throws himself into the arms of his father Jacob, and Jacob says, "I'm ready to die now because I have seen your face and you are still alive!" What makes this poignant moment even more parallel to Luke's account is that it is Joseph who rescued Jacob's family from famine, providing "salvation" OT style.

Genesis 47:11 shows up in Hebrews 11:21 and it seems clear the author is following the LXX version of the text. Since we have already discussed this text, we will simply note here that the NT writers are perfectly willing to see some Greek translation of the OT as God's word, and base exegetical conclusions on the Greek text of the LXX/OG *even when the Hebrew is either ambiguous or different from the Greek,* why exactly should those reading the OT as Christian Scripture give precedence to the text of the Hebrew original?

That many of the authors of the NT books had long meditated on, learned from, and even memorized a good bit of the OT, few would dispute. Leaving aside their quoting of the OT, their very vocabulary reflects a mind saturated with OT ideas, phrases, key terms, and the like. So when we come to a text like Mark 11:2–4, most scholars will point to a text like Zechariah 9:9 LXX as standing in the background and informing the choice of words, but a good case can be made for Genesis 49:11 LXX playing a role as well.

Genesis 49:11 LXX doesn't just mention a "foal" using the word πῶλος, it says "binding his foal to a vine, and his donkey's foal to a tendril" and so the issue of binding or tying up of the animal is present in both texts. The context of course is the final charge and blessing of Jacob on his offspring, a text not infrequently seen in a messianic light, and the phrase in question says literally in the Hebrew "he washed the colt of his donkey, binding his foal to the choice vine." This is part of the promise that the scepter will not depart from the person or persons under discussion.

This allusion to Genesis 49 simply adds more context to the already pregnant nature of the account in Mark 11, for only here in the Gospels does Jesus deliberately elevate himself above the crowds or his disciples, and notice he does not ride into town on a war horse, but rather in a fashion associated with the peaceable king alluded to in

Zechariah. As Ahearne-Kroll says "it makes sense that Zech 9:9 and Gen 49:11 contribute to the royal messianic depiction of Jesus and nuance it significantly to show Jesus in a humble light rather than as a conquering, militaristic king."[232] What is not so often noted is that Zechariah 9:9 seems to be a relecture of the blessing in Genesis 49:11 and the whole prophetic sign act of this particular mount and riding would seem to undermine some traditional assumptions of what the Davidic king would come and do when Jerusalem was territory under the control of a foreign power.[233] It is odd that there is no discussion by Brown, when focusing on Matthew 21 where Zechariah 9:9 is clearly cited as the prophetic text used to comment on Jesus's triumphal entry, about the possible *additional* allusion to Genesis 49:11 because it is especially in this latter text that it is *made clear* that two animals are in view, something Matthew famously takes for granted to the extent that he says that Jesus "sat on *them*" during his ride.[234] This is especially an oversight if Zechariah 9:9 is a reframing of the blessing promise in Genesis 49:11.[235]

While the NA[28] mentions Acts 7:16 as possibly drawing on Genesis 50:12, in fact vv. 15–16 seem to be a telescoping of several patriarchal burial accounts that took place in Hebron and Shechem (cf. Genesis 23, 49–50; Josh 24:32). Genesis 50:12 refers to Jacob's burial in the cave of Macpelah in a field near Mamre, a field purchased from Ephron the Hethite. Stephen however refers to Shechem and a tomb bought from the sons of Hamor. This may well be based on some oral tradition, but in any case, the reference to Shechem was bound to annoy Stephen's audience since it was in Samaritan territory in his day. As I pointed out some time ago, the use of the OT in this longest of all Acts speeches, is by way of allusion with the occasional quote from the LXX or some unknown Old Greek version, but it is clear that Stephen is adding some things to the mix from early Jewish tradition, for example the reference to angels mediating the law (cf. vv.

232. Ahearne-Kroll, "Genesis in Mark," 36.

233. See Deborah Krause, "The One Who Comes Unbinding the Blessing of Judah: Mark 11:1–10 as a Midrash on Genesis 49:11, Zechariah 9:9, and Psalm 118:25–26," in *Early Christian Interpretation of the Scriptures of Israel: Investigation and Proposals*, ed. Craig A. Evans and James A. Sanders, JSNTSup 148 (Sheffield: Sheffield Academic, 1997), 149–50. Krause however goes too far in suggesting that the story in Mark 11 is simply constructed out of those OT passages.

234. But see the discussion in Brown, "Genesis in Matthew's Gospel," 42–59.

235. Neither the Lukan nor the Johannine accounts of the triumphal entry allude to Gen 49:11, unless one allows for a very faint echo in John 12:15 in combination with Zech 9:9 and also Isa 40:9; see Köstenberger, "John," 418.

38, 53 to Gal 3:19; Heb 2:2; Jubilees 1:29 Testament of Dan 6:2; Josephus, *Ant.* 15.136; and the LXX of Deut 33:2).[236]

Finally, it is worth noting how the book of Revelation draws on various ideas and themes of the book of Genesis, but really is not doing exegesis of Genesis. John's Scripture-saturated imagination naturally draws on some of narratival elements of the book: the tree of life, the serpent, Sodom and Gomorrah as places of sin, the lion of Judah. Moyise suggests that John is more influenced by the trajectory of Jewish interpretation of these elements (for instance in 1 Enoch) rather than the actual Genesis texts.[237] It is not clear to me that this is entirely so. Yes "the serpent," described as a slanderer and deceiver in Genesis 3 is shown to have a worldwide role in Jubilees 11:5, 1 Enoch 54:6, and 2 Enoch 7:18, an idea further developed in Revelation. Thus, while demonology in Revelation owes something to the earlier Jewish discussion, what is more evident is how the author's understanding of christology and even the story of Christ (see Revelation 12) has affected the way he views the stories in Genesis.[238] In other words, it's more the Christian foreground than the early Jewish trajectory of interpretation that seems to most influence things. For example, the tree of life in Revelation is the tree of everlasting life, which only those who embrace Christ and live and die bearing witness to him are worthy of partaking of. And nowhere in the early Jewish interpretive schemas is it said that the Lion of Judah is also the Lamb who takes away the sins of the world. Various forms of the afterlife theology, which is absent from Genesis, show up in both early Jewish literature and early Jewish Christian literature such as Revelation.

CONCLUSION

There is so much more that could be said about Genesis and its influence on the books of NT, as even a glance at the NA[28] index in Appendix 1 will show, but this must suffice to demonstrate the importance of tracking down the citations, allusions, echoes, and simple language usage of Genesis in the NT, as well as the importance of Genesis in its own right as the leading book of the Hebrew

236. See Witherington, *Acts of the Apostles*, 265.
237. Steve Moyise, "Genesis in Revelation" in Menken, *Genesis in the New Testament*, 179.
238. See G. K. Beale and Sean M. McDonough, "Revelation," in Beale, *Commentary on the New Testament Use*, 1125.

Scriptures that had considerable influence on those that follow it in the OT. We noted especially how the prophets seem to draw on Genesis and its stories in their oracles and visions. Most importantly, Genesis established once and for all the notion of a singular creator God who cared not merely about nature but also human nature, not merely about natural history, but above all about human history, and a relationship with those creatures especially created in his image. All subsequent reflection of a biblical nature would have to be concerned about creation, history, ethics, the relationship between God and his people, to mention but a few topics. But it would also have to be concerned about the human propensity to sin, and how that affected all the aforementioned subjects. Exodus immediately takes us to a dark place, a place of bondage and slavery, a place of brutal overlords, and the need for redemption. That story would not make sense were it not for all the threads and themes woven together in Genesis.

3.

The Exodus and the Entrance

The mandate we have as Jews is for the story of the Exodus from Egypt to be retold every generation.

—Ilan Stavans

Jews read the books of Moses not just as history but as divine command. The question to which they are an answer is not, "What happened?" but rather, "How then shall I live?" And it's only with the Exodus that the life of the commands really begins.

—Jonathan Sacks

After Genesis, Exodus is perhaps the most important OT book in terms of the impact of the events it records. It is clear that in the events that take God's people from Egypt to Sinai, they were shaped and set on a course of unique destiny. Unlike Genesis, which tells the story of many individuals and families, the material in the book of Exodus involves Moses from beginning to end. Genesis concludes with the story of Joseph, the child of Rachel and Jacob, but Exodus begins with, and the Pentateuch begins to focus on, the descendants of Jacob by Leah, that is, Moses and David. Thus, there is a shifting from Genesis 50 to Exodus 1. On closer inspection, it becomes clear that the entire rest of the Pentateuch, after Genesis, is telling the story of Moses from birth to death, and whatever else is in these four books is there because of its connection with the story of Moses, one way or another. Some have even suggested that the Torah is the biography of Moses, with a long prequel in Genesis.

Traditionally there have been two schools of thought about dating the Exodus from Egypt (and thus dating Moses). One school has dated the Exodus around 1290 BCE or a little after, while the other school dates it somewhere around 1450 BCE. Whatever the modern debates, including the view that the Exodus never happened, it is clear that the final editors of the Pentateuch were quite sure these events not only happened but were of historic importance for the formation of Israel and its subsequent history. Furthermore, the writers of the NT also assume these events actually happened in some form and fashion. Since our concern is with the meaning of these texts in their original contexts and their subsequent use in the NT, we will not linger to engage in the unresolved debates about the historical substance of this material, but it is the working assumption of this author that there *is* historical substance in and undergirding these remarkable stories, whatever degree of later editing and elaboration they also reflect, a process perhaps beginning already in the time of David.

EXODUS 1–4: THE TALE OF
THE RELUCTANT REDEEMER

Exodus 1 is merely a transitional passage. Verse 8 mentions a new pharaoh coming to power who did not know or favor Joseph and his Semitic descendants. If Joseph was in Egypt during the Hyksos period, this is understandable not only because the Habiru were despised, but also because the Hyksos were despised. If Ramesses II is in view here, the ruler traditionally said to be the pharaoh of the exodus, we must assume that soon after he came to power, he oppressed the Jews and forced them to build Pithon and Rameses, the storage cities. There is nothing improbable about this, and it could have happened about 1289 or so. Problems arise, however, when we hear in Exodus 2:23 that after a long time, pharaoh died *before the exodus*. Clearly, Ramesses II did not die before the exodus. His dates are 1290–1223 BCE. Let us then consider the possibility that the Ramesses for whom the town is named in Exodus 1:11 is Ramesses I (ca. 1306–1305?). There is a possible clue to all this in the very name "Moses," which is not a Semitic name per se. Could he have been named after Ra-Meses, or closer still Thut-mose?[1] In any case, *mose* in Egyptian, like *ben* in Hebrew, means "son."

Let us examine briefly Moses's birth story, found in Exodus 2:1–10. This story has certain notable echoes in later biblical birth stories, especially that of Jesus, where an infant's life is being endangered by a cruel ruler. The first evangelist (Matthew) may have edited his birth story in a way to show its similarity to Exodus 2. The story also has echoes of the earlier story of the birth of Sargon, as the hero abandoned in a little boat of reeds in a river, who is then rescued and goes on to become a ruler.[2]

Moses's parents do not wish to abandon him; their actions are a ruse to save his life. The sister is sent as a lookout to make certain Moses is found by an Egyptian and adopted. We may note the loving care with which the child is protected; the little ark, made of interwoven papyrus reeds, is made water-tight with bitumen so it will stay afloat. The word *tebah,* ark, used here, only occurs elsewhere in the Bible in the flood story. Perhaps the word is deliberately chosen to draw a parallel. Notice that this little ark also has a top that must be opened to see the baby. The use of the term "Hebrew" is significant; it is a term first found on the lips of the princess, and in general it is not the term Jews called themselves (Gen 39:14). It likely comes from the name Eber, a descendant of Eber. It is perhaps not to be confused with Habiru, which is a social term, not an ethnic or religious term, although the Hebrews when they were in Egypt and enslaved were likely considered Habiru, by which was meant despised, poor, common people.

There are numerous call narratives in the OT, perhaps the most familiar of which are those in Isaiah 6 and Ezekiel 1. It is the nature of this call narrative, found in Exodus 3:1–4:17, that sets Moses off from the patriarchs mentioned in Genesis and sets him in the line of the prophets. Moses, unlike the patriarchs, is not merely called to go and to do, to bless and be a blessing, to receive and believe in the promise and its fulfillment. He is also called upon to proclaim God's word even to an inhospitable audience, to perform miraculous deeds and wonders, and to lead his people home, to set them free. As a prophet, Moses is much like his descendants, Isaiah, Jeremiah, and Ezekiel, but

1. See the discussion in Thomas B. Dozeman, *Exodus*, ECC (Grand Rapids: Eerdmans, 2009), 81–82. Notably, in a hypocoristic name like "Moses" the divine component that would come first is left out.

2. See *ANET*, 119 and the discussion in Dozeman, *Exodus*, 83–84. The same sort of rags to riches story is told of Cyrus the Persian by Herodotus, *Hist.* 1.107.1–113.3.

he is also unlike them in that he is a liberator, not just a proclaimer, nor just a claimer of God's promises. Dozeman notes that the two sections of 3:1–15 and 3:18–4:18, while they focus on the motif of divine commission, are bound together by Moses's repeated resistance to the divine commission.[3] Notice how the identity and mission of Moses is bound up with the identity and purposes of Yahweh.

Moses is out in the Sinai peninsula tending sheep and appears to be "looking for better pasture" when he comes to Mt. Horeb. Horeb appears to be just another name for Sinai, and already here it is called the mountain of God. If this is Jebel Musa, it is an impressive seven thousand five hundred feet high. It is surely no accident that the very mountain where God will reveal his will and presence to his people *later* is where he reveals his will and presence to Moses now. Moses is simply minding his father-in-law's business, having escaped from Egypt and settled into a situation of comfortable domesticity. He is not seeking any close encounters of the third kind with a deity. Moses went to the back of the desert (to the west). Semitic peoples reckoned directions by facing east, not north, and so west was behind or back of the way one was facing.

The *mal'ak Yahweh* appears to Moses. Several commentators suggest that this messenger of God is God himself, that is, it is not merely God's angelic representative. The *mal'ak Yahweh* or angel/messenger of Yahweh appears in the older parts of the historical books of the OT directly (e.g., Judg 2:1, 4, 5;23, 6:11–18). The peculiarity of seeing a bush burn without being consumed intrigues Moses and so he draws closer. God's presence as a flame would seem to imply his holiness (see v. 5) and purifying force, but perhaps also his miraculous power. Any being that can set a bush on fire and not destroy it is a unique being. This bespeaks harnessed energy and power inexplicable in merely human terms. This event does not seem to be depicted as a supernatural vision (unlike Ezek 1), but rather a miraculous natural occurrence happening outside of Moses's psyche. Notice the probable word play between the word bush *seneh* and the word Sinai, employing the same Hebrew consonants.[4]

God calls Moses by name two times, indicating a certain urgency, and Moses responds immediately, "Here I am." Throughout this discussion, while Moses complains about his inability to be a public speaker, he shows himself more than capable of carrying on a dia-

3. Dozeman, *Exodus*, 119.
4. Dozeman, *Exodus*, 124.

logue with God at length, and we have to bear in mind that the earlier stories about Moses in Egypt in these earlier chapters also do not suggest he had any problems with speaking. Verse 5 should be translated "stop coming near (as you are doing)." God does not want Moses to experience a premature ministerial burnout, so to speak. The point is that Moses is not ready yet to come into God's presence; he must be prepared and know with whom he is dealing. This he finds out in v. 6.[5]

The place is called a holy place because God is there, not because it is inherently sacred or hallowed ground. This *holiness* characterizes the story of God and his people in Exodus in a way that is not true in Genesis. God is holy, and he requires a holiness and strictness of his people's behavior in a way that is at least not made explicit before the Mosaic era. The taking off of sandals may be because they were dirty, or it may simply be Middle Eastern practice in God's presence to be without various articles of clothing.

Beginning with 3:7, God explains that he has not ignored the cries of his people. Rather, he has both heard them and has come down to do something about their suffering. The story makes clear that it is God, not Moses, who is the prime rescuer of his own people: "I have come down to rescue them . . . and bring them up out of that land." He also plans to provide a homeland for them, a land presently inhabited by various other peoples and groups. Further, it is not just any land, but a good and broad land, "flowing with milk and honey." Actually, as various commentators point out, "oozing with milk and honey" would be a better translation here. The image is of a verdant land that enables bees to produce lots of honey, and cows lots of milk.

Moses's initial response is understandable; he is overwhelmed. He intimates it is too great a task for one who is only a simple shepherd, and, in any case, he is unworthy of such a job: "Who am I that I should go to Pharaoh?" Moses is not yet making excuses but simply sees himself as inadequate to the task. But has Moses forgotten his previous history altogether? Probably not. In any case, it is not the adequacy of Moses or his worthiness that is at issue, since God, who is fully adequate and worthy, will be with him. Moses's own shortcomings will not prevent God from using him.

5. Exod 3:6, and 15 with the phrase "the God of Abraham, Isaac, and Jacob" is one of the most cited verses in the NT, e.g., Matt 22:32; Mark 12:26; Luke 20:37; Act 3:13; 7:32 (closest to the exact words of Exod 3:6), and see also Heb 11:16 "God is called their God." On the use of the triadic phrase about the patriarchs in the OT in detail, see Ben Witherington, *Convergence: A Biblical Theology* (Grand Rapids: Baker, forthcoming).

The first part of God's answer is simply "I will be with you." This is perhaps a play on God's name, *Yahweh* from the Hebrew word הָיָה [*hayah*] (vv. 14–15). The second part of God's two-fold answer to Moses in vv. 13–15 is one of the greatest storm centers of controversy in all of OT studies. What is God's name? What does it mean? What sort of question is Moses asking?

The matter is extremely complex, but the evidence leads us to the following conclusions. First, in v. 12 God had said to Moses, "I will be with you" (the verbal form אֶהְיֶה [*'ehyeh*]).

Second, in v. 14 we have the same form of the verb from הָיָה [*hayah*]. The paranomastic use of this verb in v. 14 suggests that we are being told something about God's *activity* or self-revelation in his activity, not something about his *being* or essence. It is probably incorrect then to translate אֶהְיֶה אֲשֶׁר אֶהְיֶה [*'ehyeh 'asher 'ehyeh*] in v. 14 as "I am that I am" and interpret it to mean God is a self-existent, self-contained being.

Third, normally when God was going to act or had just revealed himself, he is given a new title or name (Gen 16:13). Notice that Moses does not say, "Who are you" or even "Who shall I say you are," but rather he expects to be asked "What is his name" (מַה-שְּׁמוֹ) by which is likely meant, "What new revelation have you received from God?" or "Under what new title has he appeared to you?"[6]

Fourth, Moses's question is not posed as a merely hypothetical one, but as the natural and expected reaction of the oppressed Israelites. The authenticity of Moses's mission is linked to a revelation of the divine name, confirming that God is going to do something. Verses 14b–15 do not suggest that אֶהְיֶה אֲשֶׁר אֶהְיֶה [*'ehyeh 'asher 'ehyeh*] is taken to be a refusal of God to reveal himself. It cannot be a totally enigmatic response. Further, vv. 14b–15 should be seen as parallel explanations or responses, and v. 15 is clear enough. It is the God of their forefathers who is speaking to them and promising this.

Fifth, it is probable that the tetragrammaton YHWH (the four consonants in God's name) is a shortening of the whole phrase *'ehyeh 'asher 'ehyeh* into a personal name, which as Dozeman argues, should be translated "I will be who/what I will be."[7]

As Exodus 4 progresses, it becomes increasingly clear how much Moses is looking for a way out of this, until finally he exclaims, "Send

---

6. See R. Alan Cole, *Exodus*, TOTC 2 (Downers Grove, IL: InterVarsity, 2008), 69–70.
7. Dozeman, *Exodus*, 132–34.

someone else to do it" (v. 13). Though the question in 4:1 is "What if they [the Israelites] do not believe me [Moses]?" it is clear the real issue is whether Moses is willing to believe and trust Yahweh. It is Moses, not just Israel, that needs convincing here. God more than adequately provides a way for Moses to answer the Israelites' disbelief with three miraculous signs. God's power is obvious; the only thing left for Moses to do is begin making excuses (v. 10, "I am not eloquent, I am heavy of mouth"). Is Moses lying or just showing lack of faith in God? There may be an implied rebuke, however, when Moses adds that his condition has not changed since this revelation began (v. 10b). God's answer is proper and final: "Who has set a mouth in humankind?" God is obviously angry with Moses's excuse-making and says, "Now go and I will teach you and help you speak." So finally, Moses must decide what to do; he can evade the matter no longer with questions.

Even given Moses's plea and God's anger, God in his mercy takes part of the burden off Moses by providing his brother Aaron to help him and be his mouthpiece. Moses will speak for God and Aaron will speak for Moses. Moses provides Aaron with the revelatory message and thus it is "as if you were God to him," that is, Aaron does not get the revelation directly, but through Moses. God will use Moses whether he likes it or not. It is clear enough that later interpreters of this story saw right through Moses's excuse-making. In the book of Acts, in the longest of all the speeches in Acts, Stephen reviews the whole history of Israel. In the midst of this review he says the following at Acts 7:20–22: "At that time Moses was born, and he was no ordinary child. For three months, he was cared for by his family. [21] When he was placed outside, Pharaoh's daughter took him and brought him up as her own son. [22] Moses was educated in all the wisdom of the Egyptians and was powerful in speech and action." Notice that last bit, "*powerful in speech*." But modern scholars have come to the very same conclusions. Consider for example the analysis of Sandra Richter:

> Moses had been raised in the royal court. As a result, he is literate and has been groomed for administration and diplomacy. He was at least bilingual, he has been trained to lead, and he knows what to do with a weapon. He knows how to organize large groups of people. These are definitely not the standard skills of a slave, but will be essential for the new rebel leader of the Israelite cause. He is, culturally, an Egyptian. And more than likely his function in Egyptian society was to bridge the

gap between the Egyptian elite and their Hebrew work force. But when he comes to adulthood, Moses' true loyalties emerge when he strikes down an abusive Egyptian foreman. The result is that he is exiled from Egypt, finds asylum with the nomadic pastoralists of Midian, and after a generation of training as a shepherd in the Sinai wilderness, is waylaid by the God of his fathers to return to Egypt and rescue his people from Pharaoh. An impossible situation at best.[8]

All of the above raises some interesting questions about the influence of the Moses's story on the NT presentation of Jesus, on the discussion of the divine name and numerous other topics. Let us first consider the presentation of Jesus in Matthew's Gospel; is he being depicted as a new Moses? The answer seems to be yes . . . and no. On the one hand, there is no doubting that the story about the slaughter of the innocents in the Matthean birth narrative alludes to the similar event in Egypt when the angel "passed over" the Hebrews and killed Egyptian children. But even in the context of telling that story and the escape to Egypt of the holy family, when Hosea 11:1b is cited "out of Egypt I called my Son" the reference in Hosea is to Israel, not to Moses, and so, as various commentators have noted, the citation in Matthew has to do with a parallel between Israel and Jesus, not Moses and Jesus.

Or again, analogies have been drawn between the five books of Moses, and what are thought to be the five discourses of Jesus: (1) Matthew 5–7; (2) Matthew 10:1–11:1; (3) Matthew 13:1–52; (4) Matthew 18; and (5) Matthew 24–25. The problem with this analogy is that surely Matthew 23 deserves to be seen as a separate discourse. Jesus offers six discourses, not five, and surely the point is that Jesus is one greater than Moses, indeed he is greater than all the patriarchs, prophets, and kings of Israel for he is depicted in Matthew as Immanuel, God with us, as the Son of God, as the Christ, as the Son of Man of Daniel 7 fame, and so on. On the Mount of Transfiguration Moses and Elijah are the secondary figures, but Christ is central, the one who fulfills both the Law and the Prophets.

Furthermore, the Sermon on the Mount should not be seen as a "new law." It is clearly framed by wisdom material (beatitudes and parables), and is part of the larger portrait of Jesus as both a Jewish sage, and indeed as God's Wisdom come in the flesh. A sapiential reading of Matthew is essential to understanding that Gospel, and the treatment of commandments or "laws" is done within the context of

8. Richter, *Epic of Eden*, 166-67.

wisdom literature. Torah is seen as a form of wisdom and takes on its original meaning: instruction, whether in the form of parables, proverbs, aphorisms, riddles, or imperatives.⁹ In short, Jesus is clearly portrayed as one greater than the patriarchs, Moses, David, and the prophets in Matthew's Gospel, and the analogies with Mosaic stories should not be over-pressed. There are echoes and allusions, but as part of the larger tapestry of weaving together all sorts of OT material to present a compelling portrait of Jesus as God's Incarnate Wisdom in a Gospel.¹⁰

The lengthy retelling of the story of Moses in Acts 7 in the speech of Stephen is worth taking a close look at. Here is the text itself.

At that time Moses was born, and he was no ordinary child. For three months he was cared for by his family. ²¹ When he was placed outside, Pharaoh's daughter took him and brought him up as her own son. ²² Moses was educated in all the wisdom of the Egyptians and was powerful in speech and action.

²³ "When Moses was forty years old, he decided to visit his own people, the Israelites. ²⁴ He saw one of them being mistreated by an Egyptian, so he went to his defense and avenged him by killing the Egyptian. ²⁵ Moses thought that his own people would realize that God was using him to rescue them, but they did not. ²⁶ The next day Moses came upon two Israelites who were fighting. He tried to reconcile them by saying, 'Men, you are brothers; why do you want to hurt each other?'

²⁷ "But the man who was mistreating the other pushed Moses aside and said, 'Who made you ruler and judge over us? ²⁸ Are you thinking of killing me as you killed the Egyptian yesterday?' ²⁹ When Moses heard this, he fled to Midian, where he settled as a foreigner and had two sons.

³⁰ "After forty years had passed, an angel appeared to Moses in the flames of a burning bush in the desert near Mount Sinai. ³¹ When he saw this, he was amazed at the sight. As he went over to get a closer look, he heard the Lord say: ³² 'I am the God of your fathers, the God of

9. There is now a considerable body of literature on a sapiential reading of both Matthew and John's Gospel. On Matthew one can consult the works of M. J. Suggs (*Wisdom, Christology, and Law in Matthew's Gospel* [Cambridge, MA: Harvard University Press, 1970]), C. Deutsch (*Hidden Wisdom and the Easy Yoke* [Sheffield: Sheffield Academic Press, 1987]), M. D. Johnson (*The Purpose of the Biblical Genealogies*, 2nd ed. [Eugene, OR:Wipf & Stock, 2002]), and my interaction with that body of literature in Witherington, *Jesus the Sage*, as well as in Witherington, *Matthew*. On John as a wisdom Gospel see Witherington, *John's Wisdom: A Commentary on the Fourth Gospel* (Louisville: Westminister John Knox, 1995).

10. Against, e.g., Dale Allison, *The New Moses: A Matthean Typology* (Minneapolis: Fortress, 1993) and Ulrich Luz, *Matthew 1–7: A Commentary*, Hermeneia (Minneapolis: Augsburg, 1989), 127–55.

Abraham, Isaac and Jacob.' Moses trembled with fear and did not dare to look.

[33] "Then the Lord said to him, 'Take off your sandals, for the place where you are standing is holy ground. [34] I have indeed seen the oppression of my people in Egypt. I have heard their groaning and have come down to set them free. Now come, I will send you back to Egypt.'

[35] "This is the same Moses they had rejected with the words, 'Who made you ruler and judge?' He was sent to be their ruler and deliverer by God himself, through the angel who appeared to him in the bush. [36] He led them out of Egypt and performed wonders and signs in Egypt, at the Red Sea and for forty years in the wilderness.

[37] "This is the Moses who told the Israelites, 'God will raise up for you a prophet like me from your own people.' [38] He was in the assembly in the wilderness, with the angel who spoke to him on Mount Sinai, and with our ancestors; and he received living words to pass on to us.

[39] "But our ancestors refused to obey him. Instead, they rejected him and in their hearts turned back to Egypt. [40] They told Aaron, 'Make us gods who will go before us. As for this fellow Moses who led us out of Egypt—we don't know what has happened to him!' [41] That was the time they made an idol in the form of a calf. They brought sacrifices to it and reveled in what their own hands had made. [42] But God turned away from them and gave them over to the worship of the sun, moon, and stars. This agrees with what is written in the book of the prophets:

"Did you bring me sacrifices and offerings
forty years in the wilderness, people of Israel?
[43] You have taken up the tabernacle of Molek
and the star of your god Rephan,
the idols you made to worship.
Therefore I will send you into exile beyond Babylon."

[44] Our ancestors had the tabernacle of the covenant law with them in the wilderness. It had been made as God directed Moses, according to the pattern he had seen.

The speech of Stephen is the longest of all the speeches in Acts and the main reason for that length is that Stephen spends considerable time, some twenty-five verses, retelling the story of Moses. I have demonstrated elsewhere that this speech is neither temple critical, nor law critical, but rather "people" critical, and more specifically it is critical of those Jews who down through the ages have rejected God's prophets and their messages. Nor is this speech an apologetic attempt by Stephen to defend himself against charges. The speech itself is a neat piece of forensic rhetoric for a hostile audience, and the speaker is using the rhetorical device of *insinuatio*, the indirect method of criticizing one's opponents. Stephen shares a common history with his audience, and he will rehearse it in a way favorable to his interpretation of salvation history and to his critique of some of his own people. The point is to make clear that those rejecting Jesus and the good news are just further examples of a longstanding pattern of some Jews having uncircumcised or hard hearts, refusing to listen to God's messengers.

There is an extensive use of the LXX in this speech, but not just that, for Stephen also draws on later Jewish traditions about Moses in the part of the speech with which we are concerned. Stephen is critical of neither Moses himself, nor of the law, which he calls the living oracles of God (Acts 7:38). He could hardly afford to be very critical of the Pentateuch since his cases largely rests on portions of those books—the case proving Israel has a long history of not merely grumbling but of rejecting God's messengers and their messages. In fact, Stephen largely makes his case by citing texts from the Pentateuch some ten times, largely from Genesis and Exodus. Notice as well that Stephen's final and most telling indictment of his audience is they don't keep the law (v. 53).

It can also be argued that Stephen is drawing on the familiar Deuteronomistic view of Israel's history which follows the pattern: (1) repeatedly disobedient Israelites are (2) admonished by God's prophets and other messengers, but (3) their words are rejected, and so (4) God brings judgment on his own people (cf. 2 Kgs 17:7–20; Neh 9:26; 2 Chr 36:14–16 on this pattern.)[11] The notion that the speech is temple critical, largely based on the contrast between things made with human hands and things made by God, is flawed, especially when there is an attempt to say this contrast is paralleled by a contrast between the tabernacle and the later temple. But alas, both of those entities were things made with human hands. The issue is not tent vs. house, but rather true vs. false thinking about God's presence with his people. Stephen is arguing that God transcends human structures, not that God's presence can't be encountered in temples, or tents for that matter. The verb "dwell in" here means God is not confined to, or limited to, or contained by tents or temples. Furthermore, a belief that the temple will be destroyed (by Jesus and various

---

11. The classic study on this is Odil Steck, *Israel und das gewaltsame Geschick der Propheten: Untersuchungen zur Überlieferung des deuteronomistischen Geschichtsbildes im Alten Testament, Spätjudentum und Urchristentum*, WMANT 23 (Neukirchen-Vluyn: Neukirchener Verlag, 1967), see esp. 66–77.

of his followers) because of unbelief, is a criticism of unbelief, not of the temple itself, as Craig Hill long ago made clear.[12]

There has been some debate over what version of the OT Stephen is following when he quotes or alludes to it, with one suggestion being he is following the Samaritan Pentateuch, but it seems clear this speech is composed in Greek, and reflects a Greek version of the OT, but with the speaker paraphrasing where he feels the need, hence there are places where no extant translation is being quoted or strictly followed. The reference to angels mediating the law shows in addition that the speaker is drawing on later Jewish tradition as well (see Jubilees 1:29; Testament of Dan 6:2; Josephus, *Ant.* 15.136; the LXX of Deut 33:2; and in the NT, Gal 3:19 and Heb 2:2).

Stephen indicates that Moses was born at a time of crisis and that he was beautiful in God's eyes which seems to mean without physical or mental defect, which becomes relevant in what follows when Moses makes excuses for why he shouldn't return to Egypt and speak for God. Interestingly, Stephen divides the story of Moses up into three forty-year periods. The OT does not record it, but Stephen speaks of Moses's education in Egyptian ways and wisdom (see Philo, *Moses,* 1.21–24). He became powerful in word and deed (cf. the same idea in Acts 6:8 of Stephen himself and Acts 2:22 of Jesus).

The second forty years are depicted in vv. 23–29 when Moses is a ruler and judge of God's people, and protects them, striking down an Egyptian. Also, he tries to reconcile Israelites to each other. Verse 25 is crucial because it is nowhere to be found in the Exodus account of these things. Rather it reflects Stephen's own views. Notice the motif of misunderstanding. Moses assumed his people would understand he was acting on their behalf and that God was using him to rescue them, but they do not understand this at all. They even report his killing of an Egyptian, which in turn causes him to flee to Midian. Notice the total omission of the Exodus recounting of Moses's trying to avoid doing what God wanted him to do. The portrait of Moses here is strictly positive.

Notice also how at verse 35 the discourse becomes more pointed, using the phrase "this Moses" repeated some five times. We are probably meant to hear an echo of Acts 3:13–15 where essentially the very same thing is said about the rejection and vindication of Jesus by some of his fellow Jews. There is a repeated pattern not only of

---

12. Craig C. Hill, *Hebrews and Hellenists: Reappraising Division within the Earliest Church* (Minneapolis: Fortress, 1992).

God sending messengers to his people, but also of his people's rejection of the messengers and the message. It is not until verse 37 that it begins to become clear where this discourse is going, namely predicting the coming of Jesus: this Moses prophesied that God would raise up a prophet from among Israel for you. This verse echoes Deuteronomy 18:15 and applies it to Jesus as is also done in Acts 3:22.[13] Moses is being presented as the original founder of the true religion, where God's word is proclaimed in the midst of the *ekklesia*, the assembly of God's people and in the presence of God. Yet sadly, shamefully, Moses and his word were pushed aside, and instead God's people made idols with their own hands. The contrast here is between true and false worship, not hand-made vs. God-made. This part of the story of Moses is left at the juncture of the idolatry and immorality at the base of Mt. Sinai.[14]

The third section on Moses begins at v. 30 but it is not completely clear where it ends (v. 44?). It tells of an angel appearing to Moses in the wilderness of Sinai at the burning bush (cf. Exod 3:2 LXX). The point is not merely to demonstrate that there are holy places outside the temple, but rather that holy is by definition wherever God manifests the divine presence, and that presence sanctifies whatever it touches. Moses is portrayed here as a pious man who averts his eyes, knowing that no one can look on God and live. This portrayal of the Moses story and the covenant he inaugurates does not have the implied criticism of Moses or his covenant that we find elsewhere in the NT (e.g., 2 Corinthians 3, and in Hebrews). The speech is Israel-critical but not Moses and the law or temple-critical.

Here we must interact with I. H. Marshall's analysis of the speech in Acts 7 and its use of the OT. As he notes from the outset, while we have here one of the most dense "webs of OT material" it is only at the end of the speech that there are recognizable quotations from the OT, in Acts 7:42 and 48.[15] This should have warned us from the outset, that it is not sufficient to only examine clear citations when evaluating the use of the OT in the NT, but also woven into these webs is later Jewish reflections on the history of God's people from intertestamental Jewish sources. The intertextual situation involves the OT, intertestamental sources, and the take on all these sources by the NT author.

13. We will have occasion to deal with that text in depth in our Deuteronomy chapter, pp. 294–98 below.

14. On the exegesis of this important text see Witherington, *Acts of the Apostle*, 259–72.

15. Marshall, "Acts," 556–72.

Marshall notes how, from the outset, Stephen identifies Abraham as "our father" (7:2). Notice that while Genesis 24:10 identifies the locale of the revelation as Aram Naharim = Mesopotamia, Stephen calls it "the land of the Chaldeans" (Gen 11:31; 15:7, with the MT having "Ur of the Chaldeans"). Note that the term Mesopotamia from the fourth century BCE on was taken to include the region near the Persian Gulf where Ur was located, and Stephen is following this later intertestamental view. While Genesis 11:31–12:5 seems to indicate that Abraham is already in Haran when he receives this revelation, Genesis 15:7 (cf. Neh 9:7) seems to suggest he had a previous one in Ur, and this seems to be the view of both Philo (*Abraham* 71) and Josephus (*Ant.* 7.1).

Time and again, what one sees in this speech is a synthetic or blended use of Pentateuchal history plus later Jewish reflection on it, plus one other factor—the use of materials not in Genesis or Exodus to talk about the stories in those books. For example, take the phrase "not even a foot length" (Acts 7:5). This phrase is not found in the first two books of the Bible, but it is a close echo of Deuteronomy 2:5 where God says he will not be giving them any of Edom, "not even enough to put your foot on." We are dealing with a speech or a speaker relying on memory to compose the speech, and the memory incorporates much more than just the content of Genesis and Exodus.

As Marshall notes, Acts 7:6–7 is a partial citation of some combination of Genesis 15:13–14 LXX with a dash of Exodus 3:12 thrown in for good measure. Again, whether we are dealing with the Hellenistic Jew Stephen, or Luke, there are differences from the LXX in various ways that probably should be attributed to memory rather than some other OG text. "The changes show that Luke (or Stephen) was not tied to the wording of the LXX and was perhaps citing from memory rather than copying from a text."[16] Just so, but one wonders if this is not often the case with NT figures and writers, and given that many of them feel free to paraphrase, or add things based on the tradition, perhaps we need a new word other than "intertextuality," an approach that assumes people have texts in front of them, or memorized. In a largely oral environment, like the world of the people of the OT and NT, orality is primary and texts are secondary. Sometimes our obsession with texts and intertextuality leads us to underplay or downplay the historical situation in which these texts were generated. The proper question is: How do texts, and especially sacred

16. Marshall, "Acts," 558.

texts function in a largely oral environment? What is the interaction between later religious oral traditions and sacred text, and so on?

Notice for instance the use of the term "patriarchs" for Abraham, Isaac, and Jacob in Acts 7:8. This term is not drawn from any text in the OT but rather reflects the later usage in 4 Maccabees 7:19; 16:25 (see also the Testament of the Twelve Patriarchs). What this should tell you, is the composer of this speech is not simply composing it out of the reading he has done in the OT, but rather it reflects the later milieu of early Judaism and a knowledge of its oral traditions and texts.

Acts 7:14, which refers to seventy-five kin of Jacob in Egypt, follows the LXX of Genesis 46:27 (cf. Exod 1:5 LXX; 4Q13; Philo, *Migration* 199). But the MT has seventy (cf. Deut 10:22) followed by Jubilees 44 and Josephus, *Ant.* 2.176–183 (he follows the exact list in Gen 46:8–27). In short, this speech is following some form of the Greek translation of this tradition.[17] But there are problems at several junctures in the speech. Acts 7:16 attributes the purchase of the tomb at Shechem from the sons of Hamor to Abraham, unlike Genesis, which says it was Jacob. Further, the text seems to insist that Jacob was buried in the same tomb as his sons in Shechem rather than in the cave of Macpelah. Perhaps we must be satisfied with the suggestion that this is simply an example of conflation of stories, not unlike the conflation of the call of Abraham in Ur and Haran.[18]

We've had occasion to say something already about Acts 7:22, but here I would stress that the text is drawing on a tradition not found in the OT but apparently known to Philo (*Moses* 1.21–24) about Moses's education in Egypt, and then another tradition that suggested Moses was powerful in word and deed found in Sirach 45:3 (and note that the phrasing echoes what is said of Jesus in Luke 24:19). Stephen is being portrayed as knowledgable, and speaking to an audience where they *are* in the history of the development of traditions about the patriarchs and Moses. Again, *this is not just about the use of the OT in the NT,* it is about the use of the OT with value-added material from early Jewish traditions and texts. Then there is the further problem, especially when it comes to Acts, namely Christian scribes amplifying and fiddling with the text.

For example, at Acts 7:24 Stephen seems to be paraphrasing Exodus 2:11b, but then there is this phrase "went to his defense [i.e., of the

---

17. Marshall, "Acts," 559.
18. Marshall, "Acts," 560.

Hebrew being attacked by the Egyptian slave-driver] and avenged him" which is not in Exodus while the phrase "by killing the Egyptian" is taken from there; and then in Codex Bezae (D) the phrase is added "and hid him in the sand." It is right to be very suspicious of numerous of the additions to the text of Acts (sometimes called the Western text of Acts) from this and related papyri and codexes.[19]

In Acts 7:30, Stephen simply has "angel" for the "angel of the Lord" as in Exodus, but it becomes clear that the Lord is meant in both Exodus and in Acts. Again, at some points in this speech, some phrases may suggest the use of the Samaritan Pentateuch, or a familiarity with its traditions.[20]

At Acts 7:35 we have a cessation of partial citations and direct allusions or paraphrases, and a move to comment so the text becomes even more allusive, and thus elusive for those keen on source criticism. One of the more interesting additions in the evaluation of Moses by Stephen is the use of the phrase ἄρχοντα καὶ λυτρωτήν to describe the roles of Moses himself. The latter terms is used only of God in the LXX of the Psalms (18:15 and 77:35 LXX numbering). The former term is not used elsewhere to describe Moses's role. This is all part of the laudatory traditions in early Judaism where the roles and halos of the ancient heroes are polished to some degree.[21]

Acts 7:38 provides us with another example of conflation, in this case the conflation or linking of Deuteronomy 18 with the giving of the law, something already seen in the Samaritan Pentateuch (which indeed conflates Exod 20:21–22 with Deut 18:18; cf. 4Q175; 4Q158). Notice as well here that Moses is said to be with the angel who spoke to him on Mt. Sinai (and at 7:53 it is angels plural, which makes it unlikely this is another example of angel = angel of the Lord = Yahweh). Most importantly, Stephen is in no way devaluing the revelation to Moses, he calls it "living oracles," a description of the Mosaic law also found in Romans 3:2 (cf. the phrase used of Christian teaching in Heb 5:12; 1 Pet 4:11). This idea is also found in Numbers 24:4; Deuteronomy 33:9; and Psalm 119.[22]

Fast-forwarding to Acts 7:51 where we finally have the direct

---

19. See the discussion in Bruce M. Metzger, *A Textual Commentary on the Greek New Testament: A Companion Volume to the United Bible Societies' Greek New Testament (Third Edition)*, 2nd ed. (New York: United Bible Societies, 1971), 259–72 and cf. Ben Witherington III, "The Anti-Feminist Tendencies in the 'Western' Text in Acts," *JBL* 103 (1984): 82–84.

20. See Marshall, "Acts," 562.

21. See Marshall, "Acts," 563. From a rhetorical point of view, this is called amplification.

22. Marshall, "Acts," 564.

accusation by Stephen against his audience, calling them a "stiff-necked" people, and so like the wilderness wandering generation (cf. the application to rebelling Israelites in Exod 33:3, 5; 34:9; Deut 9:6, 13; see also Bar 2:30). Then there is the phrase "uncircumcised in heart and ears"(!), which owes something to Leviticus 26:41; Jeremiah 9:26; and Ezekiel 44:7, 9 (the "ears" part coming from Jer 6:10). This very same sort of phrasing used to critique recalcitrant Jews is found at Qumran (1QS V, 5; 1 QpHab XI, 13; Jubilees 1:7, 23). This then is not a Christian polemic against Judaism, but rather an in-house critique by one group of sectarian Jews of another. The same must be said of the accusation in 7:52 about them being prophet-killers, a common theme (1 Kgs 19:10, 14; 2 Chr 36:16; Neh 9:26; Jer 26:20–24) further amplified in the NT, especially in the Gospels (see esp. Matt 23:29–36 and par.).

In this brief survey, based on the acute and detailed observations of Marshall, we have concentrated on the resonances with the OT and early Jewish literature and traditions, but it is also true that this speech is tailored in ways to emphasize that the first Christian martyr follows a path similar to, and is in character much like his master, Jesus. There is always a danger, when just focusing on the intertextual aspects of the material, that one misses the large design and purpose of the material. And even if one's focus is just on the use of the OT in the NT, one needs to attend to echoes, allusions, key ideas, and phrases, and not just citations, to assess the full impact of the OT in the NT material.

Also interesting is the very attenuated recounting of elements from the story of Moses in Exodus in the hall of faith chapter in Hebrews 11. It reads as follows

By faith Moses' parents hid him for three months after he was born, because they saw he was no ordinary child, and they were not afraid of the king's edict.

[24] By faith Moses, when he had grown up, refused to be known as the son of Pharaoh's daughter. [25] He chose to be mistreated along with the people of God rather than to enjoy the fleeting pleasures of sin. [26] He regarded disgrace for the sake of Christ as of greater value than the treasures of Egypt, because he was looking ahead to his reward. [27] By faith he left Egypt, not fearing the king's anger; he persevered because he saw him who is invisible. [28] By faith he kept the Passover and the application of blood, so that the destroyer of the firstborn would not touch the firstborn of Israel.

[29] By faith the people passed through the Red Sea as on dry land; but when the Egyptians tried to do so, they were drowned.

Here we have a much more Christianizing use of the story of Moses, with v. 26 even saying that Moses did something "for the sake of Christ." In vv. 23–28 the example of Moses is held up at some length, and it is quite clear that our author is following the LXX version of the exodus story (note the mention of *parents* not just mother in v. 23 as in the MT, and also the beauty of the child is only mentioned in the LXX of Exodus 2). Moses and Abraham are clearly the two major figures held up as examples of faith, and in each case, both by the formula "by faith" mentioned four times, and by mentioning four specific acts of faith.[23]

Verse 23 is of course not about Moses's faith but that of his parents.[24] The question is what to make of the word ἀστεῖος found only here and in Acts 7:20. In the LXX it is part of a phrase "beautiful before God" which suggests not simply physical beauty but being well-pleasing to God as Acts 7:20 may also suggest. We are perhaps then meant to think that Moses's folks saw something special in him and so hid him, defying the edict of Pharaoh. Chrysostom assumes physical beauty is meant and adds

> The very sight of him drew them on to faith. Thus, from the beginning—yes from the very swaddling clothes— great was the grace that was poured out on that righteous man, this not being the work of nature. For observe, the child immediately on its birth appears fair and not disagreeable to the sight. Whose work was this? Not that of nature but of the grace of God. (*Hom. Heb.* 26.3)

We must also bear in mind that Moses has already been held up as a paradigm of faithfulness at Hebrews 3:2–5, and once again in this subsection we have the phrase "by faith" reiterated four times.[25]

---

23. Craddock, "Hebrews," 140.

24. DeSilva, *Perseverance in Gratitude*, 406 is right to note that our author does not even mention the Mosaic covenant or Moses's giving of the law, which would have suited his supercessionist views. Rather he chooses to use Moses as a positive example rather than as a foil for Christ the greater one.

25. A few later Greek MSS insert between v. 23 and v. 24 the following: "By faith Moses, when he was grown up, killed the Egyptian, because he observed the humiliation of his people." While our author likely knows various of the postbiblical stories about Moses (cf. Josephus, *Ant.* 2; Philo, *Moses* 1) this addition is not likely original and seeks to make the connection between v. 23 and v. 24 clearer; see Craddock, "Hebrews," 141. As Attridge, *Hebrews*, 338 says, this incident is hardly a good example of the faithful endurance being inculcated in this paragraph.

Verse 24 indicates a deduction on the basis of the fact that Moses identified with the oppressed Israelites, and took up the cause of one who was beaten, even though he had become a son of Pharaoh's daughter and so a royal heir (Exod 2:10). The direct refusal of a title is not mentioned in the OT. Moses in v. 25 is seen as a figure who refuses short-term gains or the short-lived pleasure of sin but rather chose hardship with his people. The term συγκακουχέω is a *hapax legmenon* perhaps coined by our author and refers to being maltreated with others (see the simple form of this verb at 11:37 and 13:3).[26] Notice that sin here refers to turning one's back on the plight of one's own people and choosing instead to live in luxury; whereas faith and faithfulness is living in solidarity with God's suffering people. The relevance of this as part of the implied exhortation being given to the Jewish Christians in Rome is obvious.[27]

Verse 26 is clearly anachronistic. There is nothing to suggest that Moses considered the disgrace of Christ as the cause of his identifying with his people's plight and refusing the wealth of Egypt. It would appear this verse is echoing what is said in Psalm 88:51–52 LXX, which includes the keywords reproach, anointed one, and reward. These echoes do not suggest our author is seeing Moses's as some sort of anointed one, but perhaps he is viewed as a visionary who foresaw the anointed one and his coming suffering, for the next verse will even say he saw the invisible God.[28] The point our author is trying to make is that Moses "by faith" identified with the greater purposes of God, "looking to the reward," considering it greater to suffer, as in time even Christ would, in the service of a just and godly cause than to receive the earthly rewards he would have gotten from remaining in the Egyptian court. In principle, as Hagner says, suffering disgrace for God was like suffering for Christ or like the suffering of Christ.[29] "Hebrews says that one's relationship with Christ is its own reward, even when it entails suffering."[30]

It is most unlikely that our author is saying that Moses suffered as God's anointed, since it was Aaron and not Moses who was anointed. Rather the meaning is Moses was suffering disgrace like the anointed/Christ. Moses suffered such disgrace, because, says our author, he looked forward to a greater reward. The point is his trust in God and

26. Attridge, *Hebrews*, 340.
27. See DeSilva, *Perseverance in Gratitude*, 408–9.
28. Attridge, *Hebrews*, 341–42.
29. Hagner, *Encountering Hebrews*, 152.
30. Koester, *Hebrews*, 503.

forward-looking faith in God's promises. It is important to bear in mind the degree to which this material has been shaped so it will be a word on target for the Christians under fire in Rome, who themselves will be called upon to suffer like Christ (cf. 11:25 to 13:3, 13). As Long puts it "the Preacher's assessment of Moses's choice is actually his verdict on the congregation's option: Moses faithfully and wisely chose 'rather to share ill-treatment with the people of God than to enjoy the fleeting pleasures of sin' (11:25)."[31]

It is not certain which of Moses leavings is in view in v. 27. Some see here a reference to the time he fled to Midian, but against this is that on this occasion the OT text says he did flee out of fear (Exod 2:11–15). More likely he has in mind the exodus itself, though he then backtracks to talk about the Passover. We may note that our author doesn't preserve any strict chronology in v. 32 (or 11:8–19) either, so he need not do so here. It is also not to the point to say pharaoh was not angry when Moses left, since he ordered him to leave after the last plague. In fact, pharaoh's pursuit of Moses shows he was angry indeed. We are told he remained constant or stead-fast as seeing the unseen. Some have thought this was a reference to the burning bush, but it could as easily be a reference to the pillar of smoke and fire that lead out of Egypt. The point is to stress his faith in the invisible God. So great was that faith that it was as if he saw God. The reference to God as the invisible one is not found in the LXX but it becomes a commonplace in early Christian texts, in particular Pauline ones, some of which our author may have known (cf. Rom 1:20; Col 1:15; 1 Tim 1:17).[32]

Verse 28 refers to the first Passover and the pouring of the blood on the door mantle to avoid the destroyer, that is, the angel of death (Exod 12:1–28). Long says, "If in the first Passover the blood of the lamb kept God from touching the flesh of the faithful, in the new Passover God through the Son became human flesh so we might not fear his touch, so that we might not dread destruction but 'may receive mercy and find grace in time of need' (4:16)."[33] But our author does not make these connections explicit.[34] It is possible how-ever that he expected his audience to already know of such corre-spondences, as Paul does when he speaks of "Christ our Passover who

31. Long, *Hebrews*, 122.
32. See Craddock, "Hebrews," 142.
33. Long, *Hebrews*, 123.
34. See Koester, *Hebrews*, 504–5.

has been sacrificed for us" without elaboration (1 Cor 5:7–8). The concern of our author is to reveal the character of Moses as something worth emulating. As Aristotle put it "character is that which reveals moral choice" and character is revealed by what "a person chooses or avoids in circumstances where the choice is not obvious" (*Poetics* 1450B). What this subject has made clear is that in almost every case it is the more difficult choice that is the faithful and better one.

In her interesting and provocative study, Pamela Eisenbaum suggests that the presentation of the heroes in the hall of faith in Hebrews 11 is intended to denationalize biblical history, that is, they are presented as being marginalized and criticized by their own people, the nation of Israel. Thus, the author of Hebrews is using Moses and the others as excellent examples for Jewish Christians who themselves are struggling with marginalization. The net effect of the use of these "heroes" such as Moses here would be that it gives the audience a positive ongoing claim on, and sense of oneness with, their biblical ancestry, without encouraging them to see this in a nationalistic way, and so withdraw from their Christian community and back into non-Christian Judaism, perhaps in order to avoid persecution. The warning then here is that like Moses, they would only suffer criticism and rejection if they made such a move.[35]

EXODUS 20: THE TEN WORDS OF GOD

Interestingly enough, the first actual reference in the Bible to the phrase "Torah of Moses" comes not in the Pentateuch itself, but in Joshua 8:30–34, which reads:

> Then Joshua built on Mount Ebal an altar to the Lord, the God of Israel, [31] just as Moses the servant of the Lord had commanded the Israelites, as it is written in the book of the law of Moses, "an altar of unhewn stones, on which no iron tool has been used"; and they offered on it burnt offerings to the Lord, and sacrificed offerings of well-being. [32] And there, in the presence of the Israelites, Joshua wrote on the stones a copy of the law of Moses, which he had written. [33] All Israel, alien as well as citizen, with their elders and officers and their judges, stood on opposite

---

35. See Eisenbaum, *Jewish Heroes*, and see the comment by George H. Guthrie, "Hebrews," in Beale, *Commentary on the New Testament Use*, 992. This comports nicely with my conclusion about the provenance of Hebrews (see Witherington, *Letters and Homilies for Jewish Christians*) that the author is writing to marginalized Jewish Christians, probably in Rome, who are feeling pressure and thinking about retreating back into non-Christian Judaism.

sides of the ark in front of the Levitical priests who carried the ark of the covenant of the Lord, half of them in front of Mount Gerizim and half of them in front of Mount Ebal, as Moses the servant of the Lord had commanded at the first, that they should bless the people of Israel. [34] And afterward he read all the words of the law, blessings and curses, according to all that is written in the book of the law. [35] There was not a word of all that Moses commanded that Joshua did not read before all the assembly of Israel, and the women, and the little ones, and the aliens who resided among them.

Of course, the debate is what exactly, or how much of the Mosaic legislation, does this refer to? Does it refer to "the Ten Words" alone, the so-called Ten Commandments? The reference to blessing and curse sanctions makes it likely it refers to whole original covenant statement with its preamble, promises, stipulations/commandments, curse and blessing sanctions, and concluding remarks. One of the things that makes the Mosaic covenant standout from other ANE treaty documents is the fact that all sin is seen as committed not just against one or another fellow human being, but against God.[36]

That is, sins are not viewed as merely social problems between human beings, they are viewed as a violation of one's covenantal relationship with God, and one is answerable to God, as well as human beings for such transgressions. This significantly contrasts with the Sumerian Code of Ur-Nammu (ca. 2100–2050 BCE), and the more famous Babylonian Hammurabi Code (ca. 1720 BCE). Almost half of the latter deals with human contracts of one sort or another. Not so the Mosaic code. It is worth mentioning in addition that in some of these ANE treaty/covenant documents the king plays a crucial role (e.g., in the documents found at Ugarit), which merely punctuates the fact that Israel was originally a theocracy, and so there is no mention of a king in the Mosaic codes. In other words, the covenant was not with or through a human king, but directly with God the King or Sovereign. It has been said, probably rightly, that no area of OT

---

36. On the entire scenario and content of Exodus 19–24 see the more detailed treatment by Thomas Dozeman, *God on the Mountain: A Study of Redaction, Theology, and Canon in Exodus 19–24*, SBLMS 37 (Atlanta: Scholars Press, 1989). He is especially concerned to show that "this study calls into question the opposition that is frequently advocated in biblical theology between Sinai and Zion, Moses and David, law and temple. Our redaction-critical study of Exod 19–24 would suggest that Sinai and Horeb must be interpreted as theological qualifications of Zion, and furthermore, that Sinai has actually come to represent a tempered priestly theology" (201). Perhaps this may be said more aptly of Deuteronomy than of this Exodus material, but the basic point is correct.

study has benefited more by comparisons with other ANE literature than the study of law in the OT.[37]

If we consider for a moment the history of OT scholarship on law, including the Decalogue, it has gone through various permutations and combinations, even suggesting at one point that there were two categories of OT law, casuistic and apodictic, with the Ten Commandments falling into the latter category since they involve imperatives, whereas casuistic law was conditional in character and provided a rationale or cause for the directives. Rather clearly, a comparison between the Exodus and Deuteronomy forms of the Decalogue suggest that the code developed over time, or was adapted as the times changed. For example, the division into two tables does not occur in Exodus 20, but first in Exodus 34 and Deuteronomy 5. Furthermore, the reference to "Ten Words" does not appear in Exodus 20 but first in Exodus 34:28; Deuteronomy 4:13; and Deuteronomy 10:4. In the Exodus 20 form of the table, "covet" seems to have an original connotation of action but in Deuteronomy 5:21 (cf. vv. 12 and 15), it is clear that the emphasis is being placed on the intention or inner attitude.

It is however characteristic of OT law in general to juxtapose positive and negative imperatives (cf. Exod 34:14–18; Lev 19:14–19; Deut 14:11–21). The strictly apodictic style of the Ten Commandments is unlike what we find elsewhere in the Pentateuch where case law or casuistic style law is mixed with the apodictic (cf. Exod 22:15–20; Lev 19:3–10). The generalized form of these commandments, which have little or no reference to historical specifics or contextually specific concepts and ideas, made them readily transferrable and applicable to many different contexts, including those in the setting of Jesus and Paul.

None of these laws are trivial, rather all of them deal with matters that chart out the ethical boundaries of the covenant community, including its religious or worship boundaries (the affirmation of monotheism, the rejection of idolatry, the affirmation of the Sabbath command).

To transgress is not to commit a misdemeanor but to break the very fibre of which the divine-human relation consists. . . . The Decalogue serves not only to chart the outer boundary, but also to provide the positive content for life within the circle of the covenant. The Decalogue

---

37. See Dale Patrick, *Old Testament Law* (Atlanta: John Knox, 1985), 8.

looks both outward and inward; it guards against the way of death and points to the way of life.[38]

The Decalogue is not addressed to just one class of God's people (e.g., the priests), but rather to all of God's people. It seems obvious, at least to this observer, that the Exodus form of the Decalogue is the earlier and more primitive one, which is why we are concentrating on it. These laws presuppose a relationship between God and his people, and it should be clear that they have a correlation to the two great commandments to love God and neighbor, with commandments among the ten in essence falling into one or the other of these two spheres. Idolatry is a violation of the love of God, whereas keeping Sabbath is a form of loving God with one's whole being. By contrast adultery is a violation of loving neighbor, and avoiding the inclination to covet is a way of respecting and loving one's neighbor.

Here is a useful summary of what the *entire* Mosaic law code seems to have contained:

> The content of the Law is spread among the books of Exodus, Leviticus, and Numbers, and then reiterated and added to in Deuteronomy (*deutero-nomy* is Latinized Greek for "second reading of the law"). This includes:
>
> * The Ten Commandments
> * Moral laws: on murder, theft, honesty, adultery, and so on
> * Social laws: on property, inheritance, marriage and divorce
> * Food laws: on what is clean and unclean, on cooking and storing food
> * Purity laws: on menstruation, seminal emissions, skin disease, and mildew, and so on
> * Feasts: the Day of Atonement, Passover, Feast of Tabernacles, Feast of Unleavened Bread, Feast of Weeks, and the rest
> * Sacrifices and offerings: the sin offering, burnt offering, whole offering, heave offering, Passover sacrifice, meal offering, wave offering, peace offering, drink offering, thank offering, dough offering, incense offering, red heifer, scapegoat, first fruits, and the rest

---

38. In this part of the discussion I am following the helpful reflections of Brevard Childs, *The Book of Exodus: A Critical, Theological Commentary*, OTL (Philadelphia: Westminster, 1974), 388–401, here 398.

- Instructions for the priesthood and the high priest including tithes
- Instructions regarding the tabernacle, which were later applied to the temple in Jerusalem, including those concerning the holy of holies containing the ark of the covenant (in which were the tablets of the law, Aaron's rod, the manna)
- Instructions and for the construction of various altars
- Forward-looking instructions for time when Israel would demand a king[39]

Exodus 20 is perhaps the chapter of the OT that has been most central to Israel's faith and has had the most effect on Christians. The critical problems raised by this chapter are both greater and lesser than elsewhere in the Torah. They are greater because this material is so crucial, and thus proper interpretation is so vital, and there is less margin for error here; lesser because it is generally agreed by perhaps the majority of OT scholars that this material in some form goes back to Moses, though most would insist it has been amplified and edited along the way. There is nothing in the Ten Commandments that could not have originated with Moses. It does not show, as some other supposed decalogues do, the influence of an agrarian background such as we would expect if it originated after the entrance into Canaan. There is also nothing in it that is clearly cultic.

Almost everything has been disputed, from how many commandments there are and how we divide them up to what they mean. Note that while extrabiblical treaties (especially the Hittite suzerainty treaties) are helpful in our study of the form of Israelite covenants in general, we have in Exodus 20 at best a truncated form in comparison to such treaties, and many of the typical characteristics (such as being told where to store and read the treaty) are not found here. These analogies are more helpful with Deuteronomy as a whole than the Decalogue. The treaty form is little help in understanding the content of these verses. At most we can say that the parallels may show a common treaty form, which suggests the antiquity of this covenant and others in the Pentateuch.

In regard to the Decalogue, note that these verses are not called commandments: we are simply told, "God spoke all these words." Properly speaking, they should be called the Ten Words, not the

---

39. This helpful summary is found in an excellent short article on Wikipedia: http://tinyurl.com/ybbbgzvd. Many scholars would see the "forward-looking legislation referencing a king" to be a later addition to the code.

Ten Commandments. Here we have general principles, not specific case-by-case rulings, which cover the whole gamut of relationships with God and humanity. They can be divided into two categories dealing with loving God and loving neighbor. The form of these is simple imperatives, and in the Hebrew often it involves just TWO words, (e.g., no killing, no stealing). They are not casuistic or conditional remarks, in other words, "If you do this, then this." They are givens, not options, and there are no statements about punishments or rewards if they are broken or kept. Scholars call this form apodictic. As I said, here the general principles are laid down that will be worked out later in the book of the covenant (Exod 20:18–31:18) and applied to specific situations.

The division of the Decalogue into two tablets does not come here, but at Exodus 34 and Deuteronomy 5, and it is in Exodus 34:28 and Deuteronomy 4:13, 10:4 that it is first called "The Ten Words." There are only two positive imperatives: honoring parents and remembering the Sabbath. All the rest are negatives in the form "you shall not." What we seem to have here are remarks necessary for the survival of God's people if they wish to remain his people and remain distinct from the pagan world. There is little internalization of these words. Most of them have to do with deeds, not attitudes (though see below on covetousness). Here then are the first principles on areas of vital importance for religious life. Most of the Ten Words can be paralleled outside the OT, except perhaps for the first two. They are not totally unique, but their combination here and their link to serving Yahweh as one's only God is unique. These Ten Words are addressed to each individual, (i.e., "you shall not" is in the singular, not plural). They are not just words for general community behavior collectively, but are applicable to each of God's children individually. It would be wrong, however, to take the Ten Words as God's blueprint for all laws in any nation. The presupposition is that these are words for God's chosen people, not everyone, though it would be nice if everyone would obey them. However, the last eight commandments must not be taken out of the context of the first two. They are the things that those who worship the true God are to do or refrain from doing. They are principles for believers. Nonetheless, they are so general that they proved applicable to numerous ages of believers and various of them are reaffirmed in the NT. In this regard, they appear to be viewed by the writers of the NT at least as valuable ongoing guiding principles, unlike what follows in the book of the covenant and in Leviticus. I wish to stress once more that what we have here are principles, not laws. They are the basis on which all laws were and could be grounded and extrapolated.

Several general comments about the NT use of this material are important at this point. There can be no doubt that the Ten Commandments, along with the love commandments about God and neighbor were seen as the most important touchstones of the Mosaic law. They recur in many forms in early Judaism, and in the NT, even in places where the OT is not being directly quoted, but assumed to provide principles for Jewish living. For example, in Luke 13:14 the indignant synagogue ruler rebukes Jesus for healing on the Sabbath, indirectly, by telling the people observing his act of healing: "There are six days for work. So, come and be healed on those days." This of course is an echo of Exodus 20:9, "six days you shall labor and do all your work," only there it involves an imperative from God, whereas in Luke it is taken to be a principle for living. In other words, God is commanding a six-day work week, whereas the synagogue leader assumes that is the norm.

According to the earliest Gospel, Jesus explicitly reaffirms the fifth through ninth words of the Decalogue (see Mark 10:1–19). In the Sermon on the Mount, he intensifies several of these, notably that on adultery and murder. Second, Jesus seems clearly to reject various Levitical distinctions of clean and unclean (Mark 7:1–15), or at least Mark was sure that he did (see the parenthetical remark in 7:15). Instead, Jesus wanted concentration on moral purity in light of the Decalogue. One should examine Mark 7:21–22, where he expands words five to nine and adds various attitudes besides covetousness to the list of prohibitions. Third, it will be noted that neither Jesus nor Paul enjoins the Sabbath on his followers. Indeed, in Mark 2:28 Jesus appears to change the rules about what is appropriate on such a day and indicates that the Sabbath was meant for our aid and fulfillment; we were not created to fulfill it. This tells us something fundamental about Jesus's attitude, namely, that he saw all such words as meant for human well-being. They are not eternal principles in the sense that we will always have need of all of them in their OT form.

Jesus felt free to modify, fulfill, qualify, add to, and delete from them as he saw fit, because he was bringing in a new eschatological kingdom situation to which new, as well as some old, rules would apply. In the eschatological age, not all of the Mosaic material was going to be directly applicable, though one can still learn of God's nature and what he wants in general of his children even from that which a Christian is no longer bound to, such as Sabbath observance. One must also realize that believers will hardly need such "thou shalt nots" when the kingdom fully comes on earth. So, in a real sense, the Ten Words are interim ethics until then. Thereafter we will do by nature what now we must strive to do by will and choice and effort. One cannot help but think that much of what Moses said is based on the premise that we are all fallen creatures, and in some cases, as Jesus makes clear about Mosaic laws on divorce, it allows for human hard-heartedness in a way Jesus does not (cf. Matthew 5 and 19 and par.).

We will be following the Jewish and Protestant, not Catholic, division of the Ten Words, that is, the second commandment begins "you shall not make a graven image." The prologue is very brief. The first phrase could be read, "I, Yahweh, am your God," but more likely is the translation, "I am Yahweh your God." God identifies himself in v. 2b and reminds them that he revealed who he was in the exodus deliverance. This gracious act of deliverance precedes this covenanting, and it was not performed on the basis of any covenant or stipulations. The deliverance was pure grace. Thus, we should not see even here the intention of God to provide a way to salvation in these principles. Rather, it is the means of living for those who have already been rescued by God's activity in Egypt.

WORD ONE

The translation of v. 3 is problematic because of the final prepositional phrase. Had the sentence simply read "You shall have no other gods," it would be easier to interpret. The phrase *al-panay* has been translated in the following ways: "before me," "to my face," "beside me," "over against me," "in defiance of me." If this phrase has a hostile connotation, the meaning would be, "You shall not prefer other gods to me." If we take the phrase "to my face" literally, it may imply no other gods in my presence, and some have related it to the prohibition of setting up idols in Yahweh's presence. More likely it is a general statement meaning "I will be your only God." This word does not deny the possibility of other real gods existing. This comes later, especially in prophetic literature (cf. Isa 45:6, 14, 21). The point is not to debate monotheism, but to state that whatever else anyone may do or have, Israel will have no other gods. Thus, Israel is confined to and defined by monotheism, which made them stand out in the ancient world. They were seen as a peculiar people indeed.[40]

WORD TWO

This word follows logically upon the previous one. The word *pesel* means an image carved from stone or wood, and it later included metal or molten images as well (Isa 40:19; 44:10). Deuteronomy 4:9–20 clearly interprets this word to refer to images of God. It is of course true that making of images of false gods would also be unacceptable, but this verse seems to deal with the true God. The point is that this is an improper response to God's self-revelation. God has revealed himself in words and in deeds, but not in an image or a form. The attempt to create such an image is the attempt by human religious imagination to define and delimit God. This is both unnecessary and incorrect. God has revealed himself in his own way; human beings must accept him on his own terms, not create an image of him as we would like him to be.

We know that at least initially Israel took this commandment to heart. When they invaded and took over Canaan, the archaeology shows that late in the thirteenth century an anti-iconic people entered the land. We must not, however, overlook the fact that the central issue here is the nature of the human response to the true God, (i.e., the nature of legitimate worship). Thus, images of the prophets or Jesus or OT or NT saints or even angels in stained glass are not in themselves prohibited here. What is prohibited is the use of images as objects of worship, or objects used to define, delineate, or control God (a regular ancient magical practice). It is an open question what one does with an image or painting outside a worship context, or even in a worship context if it is not used as an object of worship.

WORD THREE

The taking of the Lord's name in vain has often been misunderstood. The key verb *saw'* means "swear falsely," but its root meaning is "to be empty" or "groundless." The term almost always has a pejorative connotation. However, it appears from Leviticus 19:12 that "You shall not swear falsely in my name" seems to be the primary

40. See Childs, *Exodus*, 402–4.

meaning of Exodus 20:7 as well. Thus, what is being ruled out here is not all use of God's name (literally it reads "the name") but only its abuse. Oaths in OT times were clearly not forbidden. Jesus, however, changed this in the Sermon on the Mount. False or worthless swearing or oaths using God's name are clearly ruled out here. God will not ignore such abuse; he will hold people accountable for it.

WORD FOUR

More attention has been given to this commandment by scholars than any other. It is the longest of the ten words and the first positive word. At the outset, we notice the different way this word is given here and in Deuteronomy 5:12–15. The word "observe" is used instead of "remember" here. Deuteronomy adds, "as the Lord your God commands you." In addition, in Deuteronomy the animals are enumerated in a more detailed way. Then too the motive in Deuteronomy 5:15 for Sabbath observance is different: there it is "you shall remember that you were a servant in the land of Egypt and the Lord your God brought you out there with a mighty hand." In our text, the reason for keeping the Sabbath is God's rest from his work of creation. The etymology of the term *shabbat* remains uncertain, but probably the noun *shabbat* comes from the verb meaning "rest, cease from work." The major thrust of the word is the stress on hallowing, and here the verb means "make holy" or "remember to make holy" and thus it involves deeds, not just an attitude, and requires an effort. It implies the cessation of normal activities for a special day because the *shabbat* belongs to Yahweh in some undefined way or sense that other days do not.

The question then becomes, Is this ordinance also for God's NT people? The vast majority of Christians celebrated worship on the first day of the week, calling it "The Lord's Day," presumably because it was the day the Lord rose. Neither Jesus nor Paul commands the Sabbath of their followers. Paul in fact makes quite clear that it is acceptable to observe one day as sacred or all days alike; each should do as his or her conscience dictates (see Rom 14:5–7; Gal 4:10). These earlier observances are viewed as shadows of things that were to come; the reality, however, is found in Christ. In short, Christ's coming has changed the situation in regard to such ordinances. Thus, the Christian is not bound to them anymore.

WORD FIVE

Here we have the second positive word; however, unlike the fourth word, it does not give a theological rationale for the word but rather includes a promise. Frequently, this commandment has been interpreted to mean that parents are the visible representatives of God for the exerting of his authority. While this interpretation has tended to go far beyond the biblical text, nevertheless it can lay claim to a certain biblical warrant. The command appears to mean that you are to honor your parents whether you yourself are a child or an adult. Many see this commandment as the transition between the commandments involving love of God and love of neighbor.

The promise that goes along with this word is important. It is unlikely the Israelites had a full doctrine of eternal life at this point, so extension of natural life was considered one of the greatest blessings God could offer. Here, however, the promise is tied to making it into the land and living in it. So now the context suggests that God's promise is to get his people into the land and allow them to enjoy it when they get there. It is thus a promise tied to the specific context of physical Israel as a land and is a heritage of living in one's own land. It is, however, altered in the NT at Ephesians 6:2–3 to "the earth" (cf. Deut 5:6). It is thus applied in a way that does not confine it to the Israelites and their link to a land.

WORD SIX

There are numerous prohibitions against the taking of life in the OT (Exod 21:20; Lev 24:7; Deut 27:24). There are also numerous crimes for which the death penalty is commanded, not to mention the endorsement of the concept of holy war in the OT. Thus, whatever the sixth word means, it is unlikely to be a prohibition *against all killing*. In fact, it has long been recognized that the Hebrew radical *rsh* refers to a special kind of killing. We cannot simply translate it "murder" here or elsewhere. It appears that in many cases, this verb has to do with the matter of blood vengeance and the role of the avenger (see Numbers 35), including both the initial slaying and the retaliation, as well as the execution of the initial murderer. However, and it is a big however, this verb sometimes refers to accidental killing (Num 35:11; Deut 19:4; Josh 20:3), which by any normal definition is *not* murder. But more often the term does refer to what we would call murder (Hos 6:9; Isa 1:21). Murder involves intent. But clearly here in the Decalogue accidental killing cannot be to the fore, because the brief imperative surely does not mean: "Don't accidentally kill someone"![41] D. A. Carson notes that this verb is regularly used for the killing of one person by another, but never in a judicial or military context.[42] In any case, as we shall see, Jesus is prohibiting his own disciples from even getting angry with other people, never mind killing them.

WORD SEVEN

The verb *na'ap* means "to commit adultery." It is obviously the purpose of this commandment to protect the institution of marriage in an environment that was profligate. It is usually pointed out that the man can only commit adultery against another person's marriage, and a woman only against her own, due to the nature of ancient patriarchal marriage. We have no mention of punishment here for this crime, but Deuteronomy 22:22 indicates the death penalty for it. Notice that the punishment for fornication with an unmarried woman is not the same (cf. Exod 22:16; Deut 22:28–29), and it suggests this is considered a lesser crime.

Some have suggested that premarital intercourse is never prohibited in the OT, but clearly enough in Exodus 22:16–17; Deuteronomy 22:28–29 we are told that the law about premarital sex requires the couple to marry and it does not allow for divorce.[43] One should not infer from its lesser penalties that it was seen as acceptable behavior, not least because these were honor and shame cultures and the protecting the virginity of young nubile women prior to marriage was an important part of avoiding sexual shame. It may be that its condemnation was so obvious it went without an explicit prohibition. Sexual sin was so serious a matter that even King David falls under the death penalty for his adultery with Bathsheba. Various texts indicate that adultery is also a sin against God, since he created and

---

41. See Walther Zimmerli, *Old Testament Theology in Outline*, trans. David E. Green (Edinburgh: T&T Clark, 1978), 134–35.

42. D. A. Carson, "James," in Beale, *Commentary on the New Testament Use*, 1001. He also notes how James at least reverses the order of the commands, mentioning killing first and adultery second.

43. See Dozeman, *Exodus*, 494.

protects monogamous marriage (Gen 20:6; 39:9; Ps 51:4). As is well known, Jesus expands the definition of adultery in Matthew 5 to include attitudes or actions that lead to or lead another into adultery. Further, he also includes divorce and remarriage as adultery.

WORD EIGHT

The verb *gnb* can have as its object either a person or a thing. This particular word is distinguished from other words for theft in that the element of secrecy is involved here. Thus, what is meant is a taking by stealth. Since the word has no object, it must mean that the taking of anything by stealth is prohibited.

WORD NINE

This word deals with the matter of legal procedures and is a prohibition against giving false testimony. Bearing false witness was a very serious matter in the ANE. Two things were done to discourage false witness. In the Code of Hammurabi, false witness was punishable by death, while in the OT, false witnesses were dealt with by the *lex talionis* (the law of the tooth, "an eye for an eye," etc.). Revenge-taking was to be comparable to what the witness was trying to do to the person he was bearing false witness against. In the OT, no one could be put to death on the testimony of just one witness (cf. Num 35:30; Deut 19:15). Notice how in Leviticus 19:11 the prohibition against false swearing is linked to stealing, lying, and dealing falsely. The prophets also saw this connection (e.g., Hos 4:2, Jer 7:9).

WORD TEN

This commandment concludes the list, and here especially, attitudes rather than actions are in the foreground. The verb *khamad* is repeated with several objects. *Khamad* means literally desire, and in itself is a neutral word. In regard to the objects coveted here, house can mean household, which would include not merely the tent, but also the occupants, perhaps especially the wife. Thus, this word may be related to the seventh commandment. Ox and ass are characteristic of Bronze Age peasant or seminomadic societies; slaves are the other prime form of movable progeny. Childs points out that this list of objects is ancient, which argues for the antiquity of this list of Ten Words in general. The list is intended to be comprehensive, in the sense that it is to include all *types* of things that could be stolen, not all possible items. It is very interesting indeed that when Paul draws on this commandment, in this case toward the end of Romans 7, he leaves out any object of desire. As my old mentor C. K. Barrett used to say, this is because the real problem is the sinful desire itself, not the object of desire.

We have now examined the Ten Commandments and seen them in context as a comprehensive set of principles that stand behind all OT laws intended for God's covenant people. We must be cautious how we handle this vital material. We have now worked our way through some of the most crucial parts of the Pentateuch. In a very real sense, all that follows in the OT is a development of what we have already examined. If we keep in mind the major ideas and developments in the Pentateuch thus far, what follows will make a great deal more sense.[44]

The NT handling of the "Ten Words" is interesting in various respects, not the least of which is that nine of the ten commandments are explicitly reaffirmed, but not the Sabbath commandment. Indeed, there is even a warning against anyone judging a Christian in regard to what they eat or in regard to "new moons and Sabbaths" in Colossians 2:16–17. These things are called shadows of which the reality is found in Christ. But the first interesting thing to note from the citation of various of these commandments by Jesus is that Jesus seems to replace the commandment about coveting with one about defrauding another, but defrauding is a manifestation of coveting, and perhaps this way of framing the matter was because Jesus is dealing with someone who is wealthy, and in a position to take advantage of others (cf. the use of ἀποστερέω in Mal 3:5; Sir 4:1; 34:22).[45]

As Rikk Watts points out, the list of commandments comes from the so-called second table of the Decalogue (cf. Philo, *Decalogue,* 121) and is given in the Hebrew order, employing *mē* plus the subjunctive, which is unlike the LXX order and its use of *ou* plus the indicative. In other words, this suggests we are not dealing with Mark's later framing of these words for a Greek-speaking audience. Notice as well that

---

44. For an interesting modern treatment of the Ten Words, see Joy Davidman's *Smoke on the Mountain: An Interpretation of the Ten Commandments* (Philadelphia: Westminster, 1985).

45. See Witherington, *Gospel of Mark,* 282.

Jesus moves the commandment about honoring parents to last place in the list, perhaps for emphasis. It is the only commandment that comes with a promise. It is also one of the commandments that one might wonder if Jesus fully lived into and up to, considering texts like Mark 3:21, 31–35. What it is important to realize is that Jesus feels free to modify, adapt, intensify, and even let fall into abeyance various of these commandments.[46]

If we look at the Nestle-Aland index more closely here are the references to the Decalogue in the NT

20:4	Revelation 5:3
5	John 9:2
9–10	Luke 13:14
10	Matthew 12:2; Mark 2:27
10–11	Luke 23:56
11	Acts 4:24; 14:15; Revelation 10:6
12	Matthew 15:4; 19:19; Mark 7:10; Ephesians 6:2
12–16	Mark 10:19; Luke 18:20
13	Matthew 5:21
13–14	James 2:11
13–15	Revelation 9:21
13–16	Matthew 15:19; 19:18
13–17	Romans 13:9
14	Matthew 5:27
17	Matthew 5:28; Romans 7:7

Several things emerge from close scrutiny of this. The Decalogue is only quoted or clearly alluded to in the Gospels and Acts and in Revelation, with exceptions in: (1) Romans 13:9 where we have a form of Exodus 20:13–17; (2) in Ephesians 6:2 where honoring parents is mentioned; and one other exception in (3) James 2:11 where the commands about adultery and murder are mentioned (and note that the order adultery . . . murder, which follows the LXX).[47]

46. But see the discussion in Rikk Watts, "Mark," in Beale, *Commentary on the New Testament Use*, 199–200.

47. See Dozeman, *Exodus*, 468.

Furthermore, John 9:2 is not a citation of Exodus 20 but simply an allusion to the notion of hereditary guilt and punishment. Otherwise, there is no reference to the Decalogue or its context in either the Gospel or the Epistles of John. Surprisingly there is nothing in the Petrine literature, Hebrews, or Jude despite the paraenetic emphases of those works.

The four commandments that get the most attention in the NT are honoring parents (the most citations), Sabbath keeping, and the prohibitions of murder and adultery. Note that the Sabbath commandment comes up for discussion in various places, but is not clearly reaffirmed even by Jesus. The other three most discussed commandments are indeed not only reaffirmed, but in various ways intensified (e.g., adulterous feelings count as adultery, any sort of violence or harm to another is prohibited). The Ten Commandments in the NT have been edited down, beefed up, intensified, and added to by Jesus and others, and this sovereign freedom in dealing with the Ten Words should come as something of a surprise if one pays close attention to Deuteronomy 5:22, which says that these commandments God proclaimed on Sinai to the whole nation "and he added nothing more. Then he wrote them on two stone tablets." This surely implies the finality of these commandments and that they were not to be added to. It is probably where the idiom "written in stone," meaning unchangeable, comes from. Thus, when one gets to the treatment of these commandments in the NT it becomes apparent that we are talking about commandments for a new and different covenant, some of which reiterate parts of the Ten Words, some of which add to or intensify the original form of the commands. We will have a good deal more to say about these commandments when we examine the Deuteronomistic form of them later in this study. We will reserve some of the more important observations for that discussion.

EXODUS 34: OF VEILS AND GREATER GLORY

It would be hard to overestimate the importance of Exodus 34 both in its own context, and in the context of Paul's *synkrisis* between the ministries of Moses and himself and between the old and the new covenant as articulated in 2 Corinthans 3. This text has had a rather amazing effect on Christian art in regard to Moses, for example Michelangelo's famous statue of Moses with horns (see below).

The Hebrew *qaran 'or* may mean "shining skin," but if one derives the term from *qeren* it could mean the "sprouting of horns," which is exactly how the Vulgate took it, and so did subsequent translations based on the Vulgate.[48] Clearly, an unlikely translation is capable of leading to interesting, if misleading art. Childs is on the right track by suggesting the translation of *qaran* as "ray of light," a translation supported not only from the LXX translation ("his face had become glorified") and Philo's treatment of the matter (*Moses* 270), but also from Paul, as we shall see. Also problematic is the translation of the Hebrew noun *masweh* usually rendered veil, which occurs only here in the Hebrew Bible, and there are no related stories about this "veil," but veils did indeed play a role in the ANE, and its function was apparently always to shield someone's face from being viewed.[49] It is well to keep in mind that "face" and "saving face" and "giving face" and "losing face" were important notions in ancient honor and shame cultures. In the case of Moses, the function seems to be protecting the sinful people from the possible negative effects of God's glory.[50]

As we shall see, particularly interesting is comparing and contrasting Exodus 34:29–35 and 2 Corinthians 3:12–16, which has prompted no little discussion by Moyise, Hays, and others. As always, our discussion must begin with dealing with the text of Exodus 34 in its own original context, both in the Hebrew text and in the LXX.

48. See the discussion in Elisabeth L. Flynn, "Moses in the Visual Arts," *Int* 44 (1990): 265–76; and Dozeman, *Exodus*, 752.

49. See Karel van der Toorn, "The Significance of the Veil in the Ancient Near East," in *Pomegranates and Golden Bells: Studies in Biblical, Jewish, and Near Eastern Ritual, Law, and Literature in Honor of Jacob Milgrom*, ed. David P. Wright, David Noel Freedman, and Avi Hurvitz (Winona Lake, IN: Eisenbrauns, 1995), 327–39.

50. I am unconvinced by the arguments of Dozeman, *Exodus*, 752–53 and others that we should see the veil as a mask meant to obscure Moses's identity from the leaders of Israel. Surely his voice and the tablets in his hands would have been a dead giveaway. Notice that Moses himself is unaware that he is radiating light.

Fig. 3.1. Statue of Moses (detail), by Michelangelo (1513–1515); Church of San Pietro in Vincoli, Rome. Commons.wikimedia.org.

MT

LXX

1 The Lord said to Moses, "Cut two tablets of stone like the former ones, and I will write on the tablets the words that were on the former tablets, which you broke.

2 Be ready in the morning, and come up in the morning to Mount Sinai and present yourself there to me, on the top of the mountain.
3 No one shall come up with you, and do not let anyone be seen throughout all the mountain; and do not let flocks or herds graze in front of that mountain."
4 So Moses cut two tablets of stone like the former ones; and he rose early in the morning and went up on Mount Sinai, as the Lord had commanded him, and took in his hand the two tablets of stone.
5 The Lord descended in the cloud and stood with him there, and proclaimed the name, "The Lord."
6 The Lord passed before him, and proclaimed, "The Lord, the Lord, a God merciful and gracious, slow to anger, and abounding in steadfast love and faithfulness,
7 keeping steadfast love for the thousandth generation, forgiving iniquity and transgression and sin, yet by no means clearing the guilty, but visiting the iniquity of the parents upon the children and the children's children, to the third and the fourth generation."
8 And Moses quickly bowed his head toward the earth, and worshiped.
9 He said, "If now I have found favor in your sight, O Lord, I pray, let the Lord go with us. Although this is a stiff-necked people, pardon our iniquity and our sin, and take us for your inheritance."
10 He said: I hereby make a covenant. Before all your people I will perform marvels, such as have not been performed in all the earth or in any nation; and all the people among whom you live shall see the work of

1 And the Lord said to Moses, "Cut for yourself two stone tablets, just like the first ones, and ascend to me onto the mountain, and I will write upon the tablets the words that were on the first tablets that you shattered,
2 and be prepared for the morning, and you shall come up onto the mountain, Sinai, and shall stand there for me on the top of the mountain.
3 And let no one come up with you or be seen in all the mountain. And do not let the sheep and the cattle graze near that mountain."
4 And he cut two stone tablets, just like the first ones. And when it was early in the morning, Moses went up onto the mountain, Sinai, just as the Lord instructed him. And Moses took with him the two stone tablets.
5 And the Lord descended in a cloud, and he stood beside him there, and he called in the name of the Lord.
6 And the Lord passed by before his face, and he called, "The Lord, the Lord God is compassionate and merciful, patient and very merciful and truthful
7 and preserving righteousness and doing mercy for thousands, taking away acts of lawlessness and of injustice and sins, and he will not acquit the guilty person, bringing lawless acts of fathers upon children and upon children of children, upon the third and fourth generation."
8 And quickly, bowing down to the earth, Moses did obeisance
9 and said, "If I have found favor before you, let my Lord go together with us. For the people are stiff-necked, and you shall take away our sins and lawless acts, and we will be yours."
10 And the Lord said to Moses: "Look, I am making a covenant with you. Before all your people I shall do glorious things that have not happened in all the earth and in any nation. And all the people among whom you are will see the works of the

the Lord; for it is an awesome thing that I will do with you.

11 Observe what I command you today. See, I will drive out before you the Amorites, the Canaanites, the Hittites, the Perizzites, the Hivites, and the Jebusites.

12 Take care not to make a covenant with the inhabitants of the land to which you are going, or it will become a snare among you.

13 You shall tear down their altars, break their pillars, and cut down their sacred poles

14 (for you shall worship no other god, because the Lord, whose name is Jealous, is a jealous God).

15 You shall not make a covenant with the inhabitants of the land, for when they prostitute themselves to their gods and sacrifice to their gods, someone among them will invite you, and you will eat of the sacrifice.

16 And you will take wives from among their daughters for your sons, and their daughters who prostitute themselves to their gods will make your sons also prostitute themselves to their gods.

17 You shall not make cast idols.

18 You shall keep the festival of unleavened bread. Seven days you shall eat unleavened bread, as I commanded you, at the time appointed in the month of Abib; for in the month of Abib you came out from Egypt.

19 All that first opens the womb is mine, all your male livestock, the firstborn of cow and sheep.

20 The firstborn of a donkey you shall redeem with a lamb, or if you will not redeem it you shall break its neck. All the firstborn of your sons you shall redeem. No one shall appear before me empty-handed.

21 Six days you shall work, but on the seventh day you shall rest; even in plowing time and in harvest time you shall rest.

22 You shall observe the festival of weeks, the first fruits of wheat harvest,

Lord because the things that I will do for you are awesome.

11 Mind all the things that I command you. Look, I am casting out from before you the Amorite and Canaanite and Hittite and Perizzite and Hivite and Gergesite and Jebusite.

12 Mind yourself, lest you make a covenant with those dwelling on the land that you are entering into, lest it become a stumbling block for you.

13 Their altars you shall tear down, and their steles you shall break, and their groves you shall cut down, and the cast images of their gods you shall burn with fire.

14 For you shall not do obeisance before another god. For the Lord God, a jealous name, is a jealous God,

15 lest you make a covenant with those dwelling on the land and they go fornicating after their gods and they sacrifice to their gods and invite you and you should eat their sacrifices

16 and you should take from their daughters for your sons and from your daughters you should give to their sons and your daughters go fornicating after their gods and they lead your sons to fornicate after their gods.

17 And you shall not make for yourself molten gods.

18 And the feast of unleavened bread you shall keep. Seven days you shall eat unleavened bread, according as I have commanded you, during the time in the month of the new things. For in the month of the new things you came out of Egypt.

19 All that opens the womb, the males are mine, firstborn of a cow and firstborn of a sheep.

20 And you shall redeem the firstborn of a draft animal with a sheep. Now if you do not redeem it, you shall give a price. Every firstborn of your sons you shall redeem. You shall not appear before me empty-handed.

21 Six days you shall work, but on the seventh day you shall rest. In seedtime and harvest you shall rest.

22 And a feast of weeks you shall make for me during the beginning of the wheat

and the festival of ingathering at the turn of the year.

²³ Three times in the year all your males shall appear before the Lord God, the God of Israel.

²⁴ For I will cast out nations before you, and enlarge your borders; no one shall covet your land when you go up to appear before the Lord your God three times in the year.

²⁵ You shall not offer the blood of my sacrifice with leaven, and the sacrifice of the festival of the Passover shall not be left until the morning.

²⁶ The best of the first fruits of your ground you shall bring to the house of the Lord your God. You shall not boil a kid in its mother's milk.

²⁷ The Lord said to Moses: Write these words; in accordance with these words I have made a covenant with you and with Israel.

²⁸ He was there with the Lord forty days and forty nights; he neither ate bread nor drank water. And he wrote on the tablets the words of the covenant, the ten commandments.

²⁹ Moses came down from Mount Sinai. As he came down from the mountain with the two tablets of the covenant in his hand, Moses did not know that the skin of his face shone because he had been talking with God.

³⁰ When Aaron and all the Israelites saw Moses, the skin of his face was shining, and they were afraid to come near him.

³¹ But Moses called to them; and Aaron and all the leaders of the congregation returned to him, and Moses spoke with them.

³² Afterward all the Israelites came near, and he gave them in commandment all that the Lord had spoken with him on Mount Sinai.

³³ When Moses had finished speaking with them, he put a veil on his face;

³⁴ but whenever Moses went in before the Lord to speak with him, he would take the veil off, until he came out; and when he came out, and told

harvest, and a feast of gathering in the middle of the year.

²³ Three times per year every male of yours shall appear before the Lord, the God of Israel.

²⁴ For whenever I cast out the nations from before you and enlarge your borders, no one shall desire your land whenever you go up to appear before the Lord your God three times per year.

²⁵ You shall not slaughter the blood of my sacrifices near leaven, and sacrifices of a feast of pascha shall not lie until morning.

²⁶ The first products of your land you shall bring into the house of the Lord your God. You shall not boil a lamb in its mother's milk."

²⁷ And the Lord said to Moses: "Write for yourself these words. For on the basis of these words I have made a covenant with you and Israel.

²⁸ And Moses was there before the Lord for forty days and forty nights. He did not eat bread and he did not drink water. And he wrote these words on the tablets of the covenant, the Ten Words.

²⁹ And as Moses was descending from the mountain, the two tablets also were in Moses' hands. Now as he was descending from the mountain, Moses did not know that the appearance of the skin of his face was charged with glory while he was speaking to him.

³⁰ And Aaron and all the elders of Israel saw Moses, and the appearance of the skin of his face was charged with glory, and they were afraid to come near to him.

³¹ And Moses called them, and Aaron and all the rulers of the congregation turned to him, and Moses spoke to them.

³² And after these things all the sons of Israel drew near to him, and he commanded them all the things that the Lord said to him on the mountain, Sinai.

³³ And when he stopped speaking to them, he placed a covering over his face.

³⁴ But whenever Moses would enter in before the Lord to speak with him, he would remove the covering until coming out. And when he came out, he would tell

the Israelites what he had been commanded,
³⁵ the Israelites would see the face of Moses, that the skin of his face was shining; and Moses would put the veil on his face again, until he went in to speak with him.

all the sons of Israel what the Lord commanded him.
³⁵ And the sons of Israel saw the face of Moses that it was charged with glory, and Moses put a covering over his face until he went in to converse with him.

There are few passages in the OT that better illustrate the mixed genre nature of the Torah, involving both narrative and law or commandments intermingled, than Exodus 34. The narrative provides *context* for the law, but it also provides clues as to the *content* of the law as well. The main thrust seems to have been to provide laws to prevent Israel from committing idolatry and immorality by having too close a relationship with the tribes and peoples they lived in the midst of. Proximity is seen as religiously and ethically dangerous to Israel, and to judge from what their prophets were to say, especially in the monarchial period, that is correct. Fraternizing with polytheistic foreigners is viewed as a way Hebrews could be led down the garden path.

This story, of course, is about the second giving of the stone tablets with the law by God to Moses, and his second descent to convey God's word to his people. The tablets here are uniquely called the two tablets of testimony (v. 29). If we ask the function of the story in its original context it seems likely to be meant to convey the authority of Moses, describing the process by which he got that authority, and the way the people reacted to this fact. Notice that the original story does not mention the fading of the glory on the face of Moses. What it does reveal is that Moses, unlike his people, is able not merely to survive a close encounter with God, as was already shone in the burning bush episode, but to be empowered and validated by such an encounter. The warning that no one can see God and live would seem to even apply to the reflected glory on Moses's face when he encounters his people.

Notice as well the difference between Exodus 34:34–35 and Numbers 7:89. In both cases Moses enters an enclosure to speak with God and presumably also to receive a "late word from God," a fresh revelation, but the enclosure in Exodus is identified as the tent of meeting, whereas in Numbers it seems to have become identified with the tabernacle located at the center of the camp of the Israelites (see Numbers 7:1, 5). Furthermore, in the later recension in Numbers, there are clarifications, for instance that God spoke from between the cherubim (over the ark of the covenant), and that the content of the revelation had to do with the role of the Aaronic priesthood in the tabernacle (8:1–4), and the role of the Levites outside it (8:5–26). This is not evident in Exodus.[51] Finally, while it is true that neither in Exodus, nor anywhere else in the Pentateuch do we hear of the fading of the glory on Moses's face. Nor is it suggested that Moses glowed for the rest of his life and had to wear a veil permanently after his second trip down from Sinai. Some silences in the OT do not imply something went on forever.

There is a remarkable amount of intentional repetition in Exodus 32–34, for instance the two accounts of the broken tablets both emphasize that the words on them were God's words (32:16; 34:1) and were the same words on both sets of tablets, both times engraved in stone. As J. Alec Motyer suggests, this is a metaphor of permanence and indelibility (see 32:16 and 34:1 and 4a). In the first account Moses comes down from the mountain with the tablets (32:15) and in the second he goes up to receive them (34:1–3). Between these two events some things have, and some things have not, changed. The people still disobey, and will not wait on the word of God.

"So what did the Lord do when his law was broken, his character denigrated and his people shown to be unable, unfit and unwilling? The answer is that he reiterated what he is in his holiness (34:3) and repeated his word unchanged (34:1, 4a). He adjusted neither his holy character nor his holy law to suit the sinfulness and weakness of his people."[52] The "Ten Words" take on especial probity not just because they are from God in a general way but because Moses had a mouth-to-mouth conversation with God (Num 12:8) and not just once. The intimacy of Moses's relationship with God is contrasted with the distance God's people wish to keep from their deity. It thus comes as something of shock when Paul in 2 Corinthians wants to suggest that granted the intimacy Moses had with God, it pales in comparison to what Christ's followers can *all* have when it comes to intimacy and glimpsing the glory.

At this juncture, we must turn to Paul's use of Exodus 34 and here an extended translation is in order.

---

51. See the discussion in Dozeman, *Exodus*, 755–57.

52. J. Alec Motyer, *The Message of Exodus: The Days of Our Pilgrimage*, BST (Downers Grove, IL: InterVarsity, 2005), 305. As we shall see in our discussion of Deuteronomy 24, Jesus doesn't quite agree with this conclusion, though it doesn't involve adjusting things. Jesus will simply say some of the laws were given in the first place due to hardness of the people's hearts.

¹ Are we beginning to commend ourselves again? Surely, we do not need, as some do, letters of recommendation to you or from you, do we? ² You yourselves are our letter, written on our hearts, to be known and read by all; ³ and you show that you are a letter of Christ, prepared by us, written not with ink but with the Spirit of the living God, not on tablets of stone but on tablets of human hearts.

⁴ Such is the confidence that we have through Christ toward God. ⁵ Not that we are competent of ourselves to claim anything as coming from us; our competence is from God, ⁶ who has made us competent to be ministers of a new covenant, not of letter but of spirit; for the letter kills, but the Spirit gives life.

⁷ Now if the ministry of death, chiseled in letters on stone tablets, came in glory so that the people of Israel could not gaze at Moses' face because of the glory of his face, a glory now set aside, ⁸ how much more will the ministry of the Spirit come in glory? ⁹ For if there was glory in the ministry of condemnation, much more does the ministry of justification abound in glory! ¹⁰ Indeed, what once had glory has lost its glory because of the greater glory; ¹¹ for if what was set aside came through glory, much more has the permanent come in glory!

¹² Since, then, we have such a hope, we act with great boldness, ¹³ not like Moses, who put a veil over his face to keep the people of Israel from gazing at the end of the glory that was being set aside. ¹⁴ But their minds were hardened. Indeed, to this very day, when they hear the reading of the old covenant, that same veil is still there, since only in Christ is it set aside. ¹⁵ Indeed, to this very day whenever Moses is read, a veil lies over their minds; ¹⁶ but when one turns to the Lord, the veil is removed. ¹⁷ Now the Lord is the Spirit, and where the Spirit of the Lord is, there is freedom. ¹⁸ And all of us, with unveiled faces, seeing the glory of the Lord as though reflected in a mirror, are being transformed into the same image from one degree of glory to another; for this comes from the Lord, the Spirit.

There has been no little controversy over how to interpret 2 Corinthians 3:6–18, but I want to state clearly from the outset that it does not appear to me that Paul is talking about a *spiritual reading* of the OT as opposed to a literal or legalistic one. In other words, the primary issue here is *not hermeneutics*.[53] Paul is not talking about how to read the OT, he is talking about the ministry of Moses as compared to his own ministry, and the old Mosaic covenant as opposed to the new one. As vv. 7–18. make evident, he is not thinking about just any laws, but in fact about the very heart of the Mosaic covenant, the revelation written in stone on Mt. Sinai, the Ten Commandments.

---

53. Otherwise Hays, *Echoes of Scripture in the Letters of Paul*, 122–53.

Paul is not one who administers and applies the Mosaic law to his converts, not even the Ten Commandments as part of the Mosaic covenant. No, he reiterates some of these commandments (see e.g., Rom 13) *but as part of a new covenant,* not as an enforcement of the old one. In the main, here he portrays himself as a minister who proclaims and dispenses the Holy Spirit. The ministry of the letter, that is the Mosaic law, is death-dealing rather than life-giving in its effect on fallen human beings (Romans 6–7). While the law is good and holy in itself, its fault is that it cannot enable people to keep it. It can tell one what to do, but not enable one to do it. That requires the Holy Spirit. Thus, tragically the intent of the law is one thing, but its effect on fallen people is another.

Paul both here and in Romans 9:4 is perfectly willing to say that the law came attended with glory. His point is however that its day has passed and its glory has been surpassed by the even more glorious new covenant, just as the glory of Christ exceeds the glory Moses briefly had on his face when he came down from encountering God on Sinai. In verse 7 Paul begins with a conditional statement that assumes that the administration in engraved stone was instituted in glory. Then he moves on to the effect of that administration on Moses himself, which was that his face shone so that the people of Israel were not able to stare at or look intently at his face (ἀτενίζω means more than just look or gaze on briefly). Paul develops the idea of the glorious face by speaking of the greater glory of the face of Christ, which is the very mirror in which followers of Christ see God and God's glory, since Jesus, unlike Moses, is the very image, the full human representation of God. It is likely that Paul is here drawing on Wisdom of Solomon 7:26 where Wisdom is said to be "a spotless mirror of the working of God." Jesus, for Paul, is the embodiment of all the good things Jews had previously said about personified Wisdom.[54]

While the Israelites couldn't bear to look on Moses's face (not having the Spirit), hence the need for the veil, Christians can look intently at the face of Christ with the effect that they can be transformed into the glorious likeness of Jesus (v. 18). They become what they admire to some extent. Paul says that the glory on Moses's face was to be annulled (vv. 7, 13). This verb καταργέω is sometimes translated "transient," and of course it is true that the glory on Moses's face did not last forever, but in Paul's letters this verb normally refers

54. On which see Witherington, *Jesus the Sage.*

to what has been invalidated or annulled or is being replaced (cf. 1 Cor 1:28; 2:6; Rom 3:31) as Hays rightly notes.[55] Some have suggested that Paul is using the Jewish form of argument called *qal wayyomer* or from the lesser to the greater, but in fact that is also the standard way Quintilian and others say one should argue when making a *synkrisis* or rhetorical comparison such as we have here, or say in Romans 5:12–21.

In verse 9, Paul contrasts the administration of condemnation, which was called an administration of death in v. 7, with that of righteousness. He is once more contrasting the effects of the two covenants. The first one led to spiritual death and condemnation because fallen people could not fulfill it. The new covenant by contrast led to right-standing with God (δικαιοσύνης). Probably we should read v. 11 to be contrasting the glory of the annulled and so temporary, covenant with that of the abiding one (τὸ μένον). Notice that the neuter participle τοῦ καταργουμένου "annulled" (v. 13) agrees with "that which was glorified" in v. 10 and so applies to *the whole of the old covenant symbolized by Moses*. This leads to the proper conclusion that what is said to be annulled in Christ in v. 14 is probably the old covenant, rather than the veil.

It is because of the character of the new covenant that Paul is able to use free and open speech (παρρησία v. 12) in contrast with what is veiled and obscure (v. 13). Paul felt that the style of his speaking should match the character of his message—free, open, bold, clear, honest.

In verse 13 Paul says Moses put a veil over his face so the Israelites would not see the τέλος of what was being annulled. Here again "annulled" is in the neuter and so does not refer to the glory on Moses's face or to the law but rather to the whole administration of the old covenant. It was being annulled and replaced now that the new covenant had come and new era had dawned. Τέλος here most likely means "end" as in Romans 10:4, not fulfillment, aim, or goal.[56] The point is that Israelites are blind to the fact that the law has had its day, they are oblivious to the end of the annulled covenant.

Then, at verse 14 Paul adds a new thought—the Israelites were blind because their minds had been hardened (v. 14). This was part of

---

55. Hays, *Echoes of Scripture in the Letters of Paul*, 133–35.

56. See rightly Victor P. Furnish, *2 Corinthians: Translated with Introduction, Notes, and Commentary*, AB 32A (Garden City, NY: Doubleday, 1984), 207 against Hays *Echoes of Scripture in the Letters of Paul*, 137, who translates the word as "aim" here.

the problem, and part of the reason for the veil over Moses's face. But in a very clever turning of the metaphor in another direction, Paul sees that the hardening is a sort of veiling of the minds or hearts of the Israelites, and he believes they are still in this condition as he writes 2 Corinthians. In Romans 11 he will add that the hardening is temporary, until messiah returns, but he adds that "now" the veil is sadly not lifted when the old covenant is read in the synagogue. Here we have the very first reference to any portion of the Hebrew Scriptures being called "the old covenant."[57]

Verses 13 and 15 suggest a parallel between the veil over Moses's face and the Israelites of Paul's day who are "veiled in heart." Paul is not suggesting a veil over the Torah in v. 14, as if it were obscure, but rather as is clear from v. 15, the veil is over the hearts of the Jewish listeners. It is the hearts that have been made dull, not the revelation that has been made difficult or obscure. In other words, the metaphor does not change from v. 14 to v. 15. The veil over the heart of the Israelites is only removed when they turn to the Lord, just as Moses unveiled himself when he turned and went into the Lord in the tabernacle (v. 16). Verse 17 is difficult, but the least problematic way of reading it is as an epexegetical remark—Paul is saying, "Now when I say 'Lord' here, I mean the Spirit." That is, it is the Spirit of the Lord that unveils the human heart and lays it open to receive the truth and to gaze intently on the face of Christ. The Israelites must turn to the Spirit, the Spirit of the Lord, if they wish to change, for only the Spirit gives life and freedom. The term "Lord" here could refer to either Christ or God, but in either case Paul is asserting the need for internal transformation in order to see Christ in true perspective.[58]

But further light can be shed on this complex text by listening to the echoes of several other OT texts as Carol Stockhausen has suggested.[59] For example, it is clear enough that though Paul doesn't quote Jeremiah 38:29–34 (LXX, Jerermiah 31 in the MT), and Jeremiah 39:27–42 LXX, he is certainly thinking of these passages. In the first of these passages there is the clear contrast between the old and the new covenant, the latter of which is specifically called a "new covenant" and said to be "*not* according to the covenant which I made

---

57. The next noteworthy use of the phrase is in Melito of Sardis in the second century. Clearly here Paul is talking about a written text that includes, but is not limited to, the Ten Commandments; see P. Grelot, "Note sur 2 Corinthiens 3.14," *NTS* 33 (1987): 135–44.

58. For more along these lines see Witherington, *Conflict and Community in Corinth*, 178–82.

59. Carol Kern Stockhausen, *Moses' Veil and the Glory of the New Covenant*, AnBib 116 (Rome: Pontifical Biblical Institute, 1989).

with their fathers." Explaining the difference, Jeremiah says that this new covenant will involve law, but not an external one, rather a law written on the mind and on their hearts. Later, in the next chapter in v. 39 it is said they will be given another heart to revere God continually, and the very next verse promises an "everlasting" covenant. As Stockhausen goes on to show, Paul is also thinking of Ezekiel 11:19 and 36:26 where we find the phrase "hearts of flesh," a phrase that occurs only in 2 Corinthians 3:3 in the NT. The first of these passages in Ezekiel also speaks of God giving his people a heart transplant ("I will put a new heart within them") and putting a new spirit within them as well, "and will extract the heart of stone from their flesh, and give them a heart of flesh" (v. 19) a theme reiterated at 36:26, where v. 27 makes clear that God is promising to put his own spirit in them (not merely renew their spirits).[60] It is not unusual for Paul not only to mix his metaphors, but to combine his scriptural references, so, for example, the phrase "stone tablets" is to be found in the LXX in Exodus 31:18; 32:15; 34:1–4 and the parallels to these texts in Deuteronomy 4:13; 9:10–11; 10:1, 3.

The upshot of the use of these several texts together is that clearly Paul is contrasting not only the Mosaic covenant with the new covenant but the heart of the Mosaic covenant, the Ten Words written on stone, with the essence of the new covenant, the Holy Spirit in and transforming the heart of the believers. Paul believes the time for the new covenant has already been inaugurated by the Christ event, particularly by Christ's death, and that the Spirit has already been dispensed into the hearts of the believers, but that sadly, many Jews who have not accepted the gospel, still have hearts of stone, and their minds are still blind or veiled to these facts about Christ and the Spirit.[61]

60. See Stockhausen, *Moses' Veil*, 47–49.

61. It is only in Paul and in the Lukan account of the Last Supper that we clearly have the phrase "new covenant" however the textual variants from the parallel accounts in Matthew and Mark also have the word "new" with the reference to the covenant. Most importantly is the account in 1 Corinthians 11, especially vv. 23–25 where Paul says he is only passing along the tradition he had already received about a "new covenant" in Christ's blood. This is our chronologically earliest reference to a new covenant, and it is specifically associated with the coming death of Jesus. It should be noted that the Qumranites also thought along some of these lines calling themselves the "men of the new covenant" as distinguished from others Jews (see 1 QHa which also speaks of the law written on the heart). Note as well the extended citation of Jeremiah 31 (i.e., 38 in the LXX) in Heb 8:8–12, and the phrase "new covenant" stands alone in 9:15 and 12:24. Hebrews makes even more explicit than 2 Corinthians 3 that the Mosaic covenant is seen as obsolescent, or as Paul puts it, having a fading glory.

Stockhausen goes on to argue that Paul is contrasting a written covenant with a spiritual one, but the contrast has to do with *where* the covenant is written by the Spirit, and where it was written by the finger of God—on hearts vs. on tablets of stone. Yes, Paul is also talking about the gift of the Spirit of life to the Corinthians, but in this context the focus is on where the covenant is written by that Spirit, and more importantly what the effect of the Spirit is on the person as opposed to what the effect is of "the letter." One gives life, the other kills or has a deadening effect.[62]

Paul is clearly not contrasting a law-free covenant with a purely spiritual one since elsewhere he speaks about the law of Christ (see, e.g., 1 Corinthians 9 and Galatians 6) nor is he contrasting a purely external covenant with a purely internal one either. What he is talking about is the effect of each covenant. The Spirit enables the believer to obey God and keep his commandments, and also to participate in external celebrations whole-heartedly such as the Lord's Supper. Paul is then also not contrasting the ritual law with the moral law, to the detriment of the former. His is an eschatological and christological argument contrasting two covenants and two ministries, not an exercise in hermeneutics (spiritual vs. literal interpretation).

A little more should be said about the use of Exodus 34:29–35 in the second half of this remarkable argument found in 2 Corinthians 3:7–18. Stockhausen is right that here in particular a "from the lesser to the greater" kind of argument is in play (which is not the case in the Exodus text itself).[63] If the Mosaic covenant came with glory, albeit a glory that fades, how much more the new covenant? But there are also allusions to the theme of Israel's hard heart found in Isaiah 6:9–10 and 29:10–14, as Stockhausen notes. Paul's Scripture-saturated mind draws in ideas and passages from various places in the OT to make his argument here, and as we have noted before, since the focal text, Exodus 34 is narrative, it is not cited or quoted with or without a citation formula, it is simply assumed and taken up into the argument.

Even more important than that is the fact that Paul is not just comparing and contrasting two covenants, one of lasting quality, one that is coming to an end, he is comparing and contrasting himself with Moses.

62. But see Stockhausen, *Moses' Veil*, 77–79.
63. Stockhausen, *Moses' Veil*, 91–92.

> Paul is both like Moses and unlike Moses. Paul is not like Moses because he may be bold and does not need to veil himself in either shame or humility. Paul is like Moses because he too has a share in the glory which is given to a minister of God's covenant with Israel. . . . Because Paul is the minister of a superior new *covenant*, he shares in Moses's glorification. Because Paul is the minister of a *superior* new covenant, he need not veil that glorification.[64]

This sort of argument makes very good sense when one realizes that in 2 Corinthians, at various points, Paul feels the need to defend his apostolic ministry, and contrast it with that of the pseudoapostles that seem to be bewildering the Corinthians (see esp. 2 Corinthians 10–13). As 2 Corinthians 3 says at its outset, the Corinthians themselves should see themselves as exhibit A, as a letter of reference, that Paul's ministry is authentically from God.

While this is basically correct, there are two problems with this reasoning: (1) the glory that Paul is talking about comes from the face of the resurrected and glorified Christ, and it is an unfading glory, involving the transformation of the viewer on an ongoing basis. It is thus not the same thing as the temporary glory Moses received from gazing on Yahweh's back or encountering God on the mountain; (2) the new covenant Paul is talking about is not simply with Israel. The good news is indeed for the Jew first, but also for the gentiles such that the new covenant community can be said to involve "neither Jew nor gentile in Christ" (see Gal 3:28). That is, the new covenant is not simply with Israel, and the new covenant community is quite clearly *not* Israel, for Israel has mostly rejected her messiah, as Romans 9–11 so poignantly and painstakingly describes. The reason why the *ekklesia* is not simply called "Israel" is because God still has a plan for incorporating "the full number of Israelites" back into the people of God, Jew and gentile united in Christ, when Christ, the Redeemer, returns from heavenly Zion and turns away the impiety of Jacob (Rom 11:25–27). The recipients of the old covenant are said by Paul in 2 Corinthians 3:7 quite specifically to be "the sons of Israel" but there is no such delimitation with the new covenant.

Stockhausen is also right to point to the further parallel between Exodus 34 and 2 Corinthians 3:16–18—namely that when Moses went into the tent of meeting he unveiled his face to have intimate conversation with God. But according to Paul, all (not just himself

---

64. Stockhausen, *Moses' Veil*, 94 (emphasis original).

as a minister of the new covenant) who turn to the Lord may look upon him with unveiled faces and be transformed. But there is more. The veiling, in the case of Moses, was apparently, according to Paul, because the people could not bear direct contact with God's glory. Now Exodus 34 doesn't quite say that, it simply says they were afraid to do so (34:30–35).[65] Stockhausen is also right that since all five books of the Pentateuch were seen as from Moses, the assumption was that reading the Pentateuch was "reading what Moses said" in the "Law" or Torah. "The figure, Moses, had in a sense become the book."[66]

Thus when Paul speaks of the "fading glory of Moses" (an idea not explicit in Exod 34) what he really means is the fading glory of the Mosaic covenant, which still has glory in his own day, but has been eclipsed by a better covenant with a greater glory. Paul's justification for such a notion comes from his understanding of Jeremiah 31 (38 LXX) with its discussion of the new covenant written on human hearts and minds. But there is one thing more of note. Paul speaks here of "free speech," the ability to speak plainly and directly and openly with both God and his people. This stands in contrast not only with the ministry of Isaiah as described in Isaiah 6 but with the similar statement made by Jesus about his public ministry with his fellow Jews in Mark 4 and parallels. Jesus's public discourse was in dark speech, in parables, precisely because, as Isaiah learned, God's people's hearts were hard. Paul, by contrast can use direct speech because the Spirit of the new covenant has been given, allowing free and unfettered discourse with both God and his people. Indeed, as Romans 8 tells us, the Spirit enables the believer to have even deep speech with God when words fail him or her.

It is perhaps worth mentioning however, that if one takes 2 Corinthians 3:16 as a pesher on Exodus 34:34, then the reference to "the Lord" is a reference to Yahweh and his Spirit, not a reference to the identification of Christ with the Holy Spirit or even the identification of the experiencing of the Spirit with the experiencing of Christ. I think this argument, long ago laid out in detail by James D. G. Dunn, is correct, but it is not the end of the story.[67] It is not the

---

65. See the discussion in Stockhausen, *Moses' Veil*, 98–100.
66. Stockhausen, *Moses' Veil*, 100.
67. James D. G. Dunn, "2 Corinthians 3:17: The Lord is the Spirit," *JTS* 21 (1970): 309–20.

end of the story because in Paul's view Yahweh's spirit is one and the same with the Holy Spirit now dispensed to the believer.[68]

What 2 Corinthians 3 testifies to is the complexity of Paul's use of the OT, mixing together ideas from narrative and prophecy, from a variety of sources, primarily Exodus 34, but also from Jeremiah 31, and Isaiah 6 and 29. None of these texts are directly cited as scriptural texts but all of them are assumed to be God's word, and proper quarries from which Paul may build his complex argument here. As Stockhausen shows in detail, the argument is logical, not capricious, and it follows the most basic dictums of early Jewish exegesis of the period—namely that Scripture is its own best interpreter, and that all of it is prophetic, all of it God's word, and all of it capable of contemporary application *in some way*. This observation must be set alongside the clear fact that Paul is contrasting two covenants here, one with a fading glory on the way to obsolescence, and one with an everlasting glory. The new covenant cannot be seen as simply a renewal of the old one. Paul's covenantal theology in no way negates his belief that while his converts are no longer under the old covenant and its commandments and rules, nonetheless, all of that is still God's word, still capable of ongoing application, though in various different ways and by different means. The stories about Moses and even the law of Moses provide lessons, even when some of the stipulations of the Mosaic covenant are no longer binding on believers because they have not been taken over and reaffirmed in the new covenant.

THE LEXICON OF FAITH:
THE BROADER USE OF EXODUS

The echoes of Exodus loom both small and large in various places in the NT, and sometimes it is mainly at the level of a concept. For example, at Exodus 4:12 Moses is reassured by God that when the time comes God will help him speak and teach him the words to say. Similarly, Jesus reassures the disciples in Matthew 10:19 that they are not to worry when they are arrested and probed, for they will be given the words to say. The same basic notion is in play in Mark 13:11 but in Matthew it is closer to Exodus 4:15 perhaps.

Of the numerous echoes of the Mosaic story in Matthew's Gospel, one of the more interesting ones is found in Exodus 4:19 and

---

68. See the further discussion in Stockhausen, *Moses' Veil*, 133–37.

Matthew 2:20. In the former text, Moses is told to take his family
and go back to Egypt for the ones who wanted to kill him are dead,
whereas by contrast in Matthew 2:20 Joseph is told to take his family
and leave Egypt and go back to Israel for the ones who wanted Jesus
dead are themselves dead; and of course, Matthew 2:15 quotes Hosea
11:1 "out of Egypt I called my son," which in turn is an allusion to
the exodus events, but this at most can only count as an indirect use
of Exodus in Matthew.

Again, purely at the level of concept or key phrase we find the
notion of God hardening someone's heart in both Exodus 4:19 and
Romans 9:18. Exodus 7:11 provides the background for 2 Timothy
3:8. The Exodus text tells us Pharaoh summoned sorcerers and magicians to counter Moses's miracles, but no names are given to them in
Exodus. They are called Jannes and Jambres in 2 Timothy 3:8. The
Damascus Document at Qumran mentions Satan raising up Jannes
and his brother against Moses. But this tradition must have circulated
widely because even Pliny the Elder in *Nat.* 30.11 mentions Moses
and these two brothers as well-known ancient magicians. Interesting, but less likely as a source, is Origen's claim that Paul was quoting
the apocryphal book of Jannes and Jambres. This book only exists in
some Greek fragments in the Chester Beatty Papyrus XVI, as well as a
complete Ethiopic version that was discovered in 2015. This reminds
us once more, that the NT writers often remembered the OT stories
not just in the original form, but as filtered through the literature of
early Judaism that they had heard or read at some juncture. This is
why merely studying the use of the OT in the NT without attention to the literature of the intervening period is not an adequate
approach to intertextuality if one wants to figure out what exactly
the NT writers are quoting, alluding to, or echoing. It is not even
enough to deal with the citations and the clear allusions and echoes.

Not surprisingly, the plagues in Exodus 8–11 provide some ideas
and imagery for later scenes of judgment in the NT, perhaps particularly for three sets of seven judgments in Revelation 6–19. Again,
nothing is quoted or directly alluded to, and in apocalyptic visionary
material in any case the language is metaphorical and often hyperbolic, but nonetheless, the influence is clear enough. To take but
one set of examples, a careful reading of Revelation 16 provides us
with references to boils, water turning to blood, a plague of darkness,
impure spirits that look like frogs, and so on. John of Patmos is not
saying "this is that" or even "this is a fulfillment of that"; he is saying

"this is reminiscent of, or like, that previous judgment of God." Mark 13:19, with its reference to unprecedented or never before seen levels of distress and trauma, is echoing a regular refrain in the plague chapters (cf. Exod 9:18; 11:6).

While the echoes of Exodus 12 are obvious in the accounts of the Last Supper, there is something that is rather surprising about those accounts, and it's not just the words of institution "this is my body," "this is my blood." *There is no recital of the Passover story*, nor for that matter any traditional interpretation of the elements (e.g., the bitter herbs represent the bitterness of bondage) in the NT accounts. This is one reason why it has actually been debated whether the Last Supper should be seen as a Passover meal. After all, no lamb is mentioned in the Last Supper accounts, and of course the Johannine account (John 13) is even less connected to the Passover with its ritual of foot-washing, and no words of symbolic interpretation of anything. One also gets the impression from the earlier account of the Lord's Supper in 1 Corinthians 11, that even in its origins, the story was going to be about Jesus and his betrayal and death, not a rehearsal of the elements of Passover or it's story.[69]

The consecration of the firstborn male unto the Lord is mentioned in Exodus 13:2 with the insistence "the firstborn of every womb among the Israelites belongs to me." This text, perhaps coupled with Exodus 13:12 is quoted in Luke 2:23 in regard to the dedication of Jesus in the temple. There is some irony in this citation since Mary's child already belongs to the Father as the tale is told in Luke 1–2, whether Mary offered him back to God or not. What needs to be recognized is that Luke is actually combining three separate ceremonies that are recording in the OT Scriptures: the purification of a woman forty days after child birth (Lev 12:2–6); the presentation of the firstborn to God (Exod 13:2–16; 34:19; Num 18:15–16); and finally, the dedication of the first born for service to God (see 1 Samuel 1–2).[70] The cited text however is clearly Exodus 13. There is one further irony as well. Exodus 13:15 speaks of *redeeming* the firstborn son. But the Son referred to in Luke 2 did not need to be redeemed, he would do the redeeming himself.

Sometimes a series of chapters in Exodus (and other parts of the

69. Nevertheless, it is still worth noting the connections; see the classic study of Joachim Jeremias, *The Eucharistic Words of Jesus* (Philadelphia: Fortress, 1966); see also the broader discussion in Witherington, *Making a Meal of It.*

70. See Darrell I. Bock, *Luke: The NIV Application Commentary from Biblical Text to Contemporary Life*, NIVAC (Grand Rapids: Zondervan, 1996), 92.

Pentateuch) will show up as the source of a capsule summary that is not a quotation but a condensed version of the narrative, retooled for other purposes. Two good examples of this can be found in 1 Corinthians 10, which draws on Exodus 13–17, as well as other texts, and Hebrews 12:18–29, which draws on Exodus 19, among other texts. It will be useful to look in some detail at how these texts are used in the NT. We will consider the latter text and its source material first.

Hebrews 12:18–24 are in fact one long *ou . . . alla* contrast, the essence of which is that we have not come up to Sinai, but to Zion. The main verb that controls the contrast is interesting. It is the verb *proseleluthate* (from *proseuchomai*) from which we get the word "proselyte." Thus, the sense of "coming up to" or "approaching" may have overtones of conversion—the believers have now converted to the covenant that comes from Zion not Sinai. More probable however is the suggestion of Long, who stresses that in fact this word should simply be translated "approach" since this is its sense at 4:16; 7:25; and 10:22. In each of these former examples the reference is to approaching God or the throne of grace or the house of God which is very similar to the discussion here.[71] As Craddock says, the term is cultic in this sort of context and refers to one's approach in worship to the divine.[72] In any case the perfect tense of the verb is significant; it means to approach and remain near, an ongoing state of being.[73]

The image is of a pilgrimaging people of God, who after a long trek are now at the edge of the holy mount awaiting the final worship service, the final divine-human encounter, and should not be thinking of going back to Egypt again.[74] Here I think we see the basis of what our author has earlier said about seeing the heavenly reward or the promises from afar. He has this spatial image of the mount of God in view, and with it the final theophany when God will come down and be with his people, once and for all. "This does not mean that listeners have arrived at the heavenly city in any physical sense. . . . The

---

71. See Long, *Hebrews*, 138.

72. Craddock, "Hebrews," 158.

73. Koester, *Hebrews*, 544 is right to stress that our author does not believe that the audience has yet "arrived" at the eschatological destination. Rather they have just drawn near and still hope for "the city that is to come" (13:14).

74. As such then, it is not about "entering" anything, not even heaven. The verb is all about drawing near to God in worship.

portrayal of a city that transcends experience gives listeners incentive to persevere in the earthly city where they live."[75]

Now it is quite clear that our author is no Marcionite; it is the same living God who has manifested himself on both mounts, as v. 29 indicates emphatically, "our" God, who also was and is the God of Israel, is an all-consuming fire. Yet still the character of the old and new revelation differs. The former revelation on Sinai is said to be awesome and terrifying to God's people, who in fact asked for at least the aural part of it to cease. By contrast the revelation from Zion is more like a giant celebration and party than like coming into contact with a tornado or a fifty thousand volt electrical wire. Craddock says about the Sinai theophany, "the writer's point is unavoidable: the condition under which the old covenant was given were dread, fear, distance, and exclusion (Exod 19:23). The old tabernacle, with its curtain, preserved the features of distance, exclusion, and inaccessibility."[76]

Verses 18–21 are based on several key texts, in particular Deuteronomy 4:11; 5:22–25; Exodus 19:12–19; 20:18–21. The partial quotation in v. 20 comes from the LXX of Exodus 19:12–13. The word terrified is found in a slightly different context at Deuteronomy 9:19, for it is not said either that Moses was terrified or trembled at Sinai, but later when the people rebelled in the wilderness, Moses feared God's anger.[77] The image here is meant to convey something ear-splitting, eye-popping, and mind-blowing, in short something totally overwhelming.

So holy was God that the people in fact dared not directly approach him. Indeed, if even a wild animal came on his mount it had to be destroyed. It was like it had come into contact with nuclear waste or a dreaded and deadly disease that kills on contact. But that, after all, is what it is like to be in the presence of a holy God when one is a sinner. It is an unbearable, frightening experience that can be lethal, unless an adequate means of the two parties relating is provided. The Israelites are said to have asked God to stop speaking to them it had so terrified them. We are meant to contrast this with those gathered at Mt. Zion who are encouraged to listen when the divine voice speaks.

75. Koester, *Hebrews*, 550.

76. Koester, *Hebrews*, 550.

77. There may be here an implicit argument from the lesser to the greater. If even Moses was frightened by the theophany how much more should the hearers of this discourse be frightened as well; see Koester, *Hebrews*, 550 on the point.

"Thus Sinai is deliberately set forth in an unappealing way in order to sharpen the contrast with what our author calls Zion."[78]

One other point about this description is crucial. The word *pselaphomenos* refers not merely to the material but to the palpable. It is used in Exodus 10:21 for the "palpable darkness" in Egypt as the plagues were happening.[79] Our author then is contrasting the tangible effect of the first theophany with the currently intangible effect of drawing near to the second theophany. He is not making a straightforward material vs. spiritual contrast here because he believes that when the better resurrection happens it will be a contrast between temporary and permanent rather than material and spiritual that will characterize the final revelation.

At verse 22 our author turns to the positive side after having made Sinai and its theophany as ominous, gloomy, and frightening as possible. It would appear from the fact that the images our author will use are also found both in Revelation 21 and in Galatians 4:24–31 that he is drawing on a common and perhaps well-known stock of Jewish Christian images. He says "we have come up" to or approached Mt. Zion, but believers have not in fact inhabited it, nor has it come down to them yet. The perfect tense refers to a past coming that has lasting impact on the present. Hagner however is wrong that this is a description of a present enjoyment of a glorious status.[80] No, the joy has been set right before them, but they have not yet enjoyed or taken possession of it. The angels are already celebrating, but then they are in heaven with God. The point our author is making is that believers are on the verge or edge of the consummate reality God has in mind for them, and so it is much too late to talk about turning back now. They must remain forward-looking and act like the church expectant, having neither entered the final rest yet, nor received final salvation with all its benefits and rewards yet. Zion does not stand for the new covenant and its already realized benefits. It stands for the final reconciliation of God with his people when God in Christ comes down to earth. Our author paints a vivid picture of that final theophany so the audience can almost see it. But they have not yet partaken of it or participated in it.

The imagery may be seen to develop: first he speaks generally of

78. Hagner, *Encountering Hebrews*, 162. I am unconvinced however that our author is comparing the present experience of salvation by the audience with the past experience at Sinai. Their present experience did not involve theophany or voices from heaven.

79. See Koester, *Hebrews*, 543.

80. Hagner, *Encountering Hebrews*, 162.

Mt. Zion, then he speaks of the city set on that hill, the city already mentioned in 11:10, 16 as Abraham's true goal. He then calls this city the heavenly Jerusalem, and makes even more clear that he is not speaking about some already extant material destination like the material Mt. Sinai when he adds that we have come to myriads of angels in festal gathering. Festivals were a normal part of Israel's worship (e.g., Hos 9:5; Amos 5:21). Even more to the point, references to myriads of angels clearly recalls descriptions of divine theophanies, not merely life in heaven (cf. Deut 33:2; Ps 68:17–18, both referring to the Sinai theophany). When one knows this tradition, it becomes even more clear that two theophanies are being compared here.[81]

There is considerable debate about how to interpret the rest of vv. 22b–23. First of all, there is a problem in regard to whether the word *panegyrei* goes with what precedes it or what follows it. In view of the *kai* that precedes "myriads" and the *kai* that follows *panegyrei* it is most natural to take this word grammatically with what precedes, thus it refers to a festal gathering of myriads of angels who are prepared to celebrate. This is one of the groups of inhabitants of the heavenly city. Verse 23a refers to the "*ekklesia* of the first born" enrolled in heaven. Now in view both of the term "enrolled," which is never predicated of angels (see Luke 10:20; cf. Rev 13:8; Dan 12:1), and the *kai* that separates this group from what precedes and from the reference to God that follows (whether one reads the latter as "God who is judge over all" or "to the judge which is God over all," either being possible), *ekklesia* is likely seen as a separate group from the angels. But the question is who these people are. Are they the OT saints? Are they the church? Are they both together? Are they all the saints in heaven? Are they the Christian martyrs? Whoever they are, they are not the audience of Hebrews, who has only come to see this assembly; they are not yet a part of it. On the whole I suspect this refers to all the deceased OT saints such as those listed just prior to this in Hebrews 11. This suggests that those referred to in v. 23 as spirits are a more specific group, namely the martyrs, perhaps particularly the Christian martyrs (cf. Rev 6:9–11).

It will be remembered that in Hebrews 11 our author said that the one group would not be perfected without the other, but he did not thereby amalgamate the two groups. Now it might be thought that the word *ekklesia* must definitely point to the church except for sev-

81. See Attridge, *Hebrews*, 374.

eral factors: (1) this is the normal LXX term for the OT assembly or congregation of God's people; (2) in the term's only other use in this homily it refers to God's OT people in a quote in Hebrews 2:12 of Psalm 22:22; (3) the reference to "first born" might well be taken as a reference to the precedence the OT saints have over Christians in the city. As Hagner admits, if *ekklesia* refers to Christians, this is the only place it does so in Hebrews.[82]

It might be objected that 11:40 might count against this idea where it would seem the OT saints' perfecting is held up till Christians come along and get theirs as well. But being firstborn and being first-perfected are two different concepts and we have two different groups mentioned. It may further be noted that we have a human group, OT saints, followed by a reference to an individual, God the Judge, then another and likely different partial group "the spirits of just persons made perfect," and another individual, Christ. As Christians would more naturally be associated with the latter, the OT saints might more naturally be associated with the former, though I would not rule out a more specific reference to Christian martyrs whose spirits have been perfected. Let us consider this phrase in a little more detail.

Many would see "the spirits of just persons made perfect" as the OT saints (see 1 Enoch 22:9), or possibly the martyrs among them. I would first call attention to the word "spirits" here; those in question have been made spiritually perfect, or complete, or complete in spirit. Thus, our author in this phrase is envisioning what has happened already above in heaven, not what will happen at the end of history after the last resurrection. That these spirits have been made complete suggests not only that they are in heaven, but in view of the strong emphasis in this document on the connection of completion through suffering, or at least completion of Christians by and after death, we are led to think of these persons being Christians, perhaps particularly Jewish Christians, who are the exemplars for the present audience. Hebrews 13:7 may even suggest this is a reference to the leaders of the Roman church who have been martyred, such as Peter and Paul.

At this juncture, we may point to Revelation 6:9 that speaks of the spirits of the martyrs. I would urge then that this group refers to the church triumphant, and perhaps in particular the martyrs who are in the heavenly Jerusalem, and if it is even more specific this could be a reference to the Jewish Christian leaders who have given their life for the faith, perhaps particularly those connected with the Roman

82. Hagner, *Encountering Hebrews*, 163.

church (13:7).[83] It needs to be borne in mind that in early Judaism and among those who had a more robust theology of the afterlife there was still more than one opinion on what happened to the spirits of the righteous at death. Some texts suggested they entered heaven at once (Wis 3:1), but more simply suggested that these spirits of the deceased were preserved until the final judgment (1 Enoch 22:3–7; 4 Ezra 7:99). As Koester stresses "Hebrews provides no clarity about a person's state between death and final judgment."[84] There is certainly no emphasis here or elsewhere in this discourse on believers dying and following Jesus directly to heaven. On the one hand, the language about all being perfected together would suggest all believers will reach the final state of affairs at the same time. On the other hand, the image of both the community of the firstborn and the spirits of the righteous being with the angels suggests they are coming from heaven to the theophany. Whatever else one can say, it becomes clear that our author, like Paul and the author of Revelation, sees heaven as at most an interim stopping off place on the way to the kingdom of God coming fully on earth.

Craddock rightly points out that calling God the judge of all here doesn't necessarily convey the sense of condemnation, one who will judge you in a negative sense, because of course in biblical tradition God vindicates and exonerates as well as condemns, and for believers what God as judge does is pronounce the final no condemnation. They can expect from God fairness and impartiality and a keeping of his promises.[85] Judgment in the biblical sense implies moral examination and discrimination, which can lead either to commendation or condemnation.

It must be borne in mind that our author is saying that he, and his audience, and by extension all Christians on earth, have come up to this Mt. Zion but they are not yet on it as are the angels, the assembly, and the spirits, and God, and Christ. They have drawn nigh unto this great assembly and theophany; they are not yet part of it, hence the exhortation not to draw back, but to go on and join the myriad who praise him in his presence.

Verse 24 speaks of Jesus (again the human name is stressed and put emphatically last) as the mediator of the "new" (meaning recent here, only our author uses *neas*, which refers to new in time as opposed to

---

83. But see W. J. Dumbrell, "The Spirits of Just Men Made Perfect," *EvQ* 48 (1976): 154–59.
84. Koester, *Hebrews*, 546.
85. Craddock, "Hebrews," 158.

THE EXODUS AND THE ENTRANCE 219

new in character, but the two adjectives seem to have overlapped in meaning by this point in history).[86] It is only appropriate he mentions Christ as mediator of the new covenant as he is in fact describing the final theophany event, the final covenant-making event, which because of Jesus's earthly work believers may take part in. Verse 24b makes a contrast between the blood of sprinkling (here Christ's, seen as the blood that is sprinkled on the mercy seat making atonement and thus pleading for forgiveness for us; cf. 10:22 and 1 Pet 1:2 and Heb 9:13–21) and the blood of Abel, which it will be remembered cried out for vengeance from the dust of the ground (cf. Gen 4:10). Here, as throughout Hebrews, our author has maintained that the chief difference between the old and new order is that the new order promises and delivers something that is better, *kreitton*. This is the last time he will mention this term which is so key in this homily, for it indicates our author's hermeneutic, his view of the relative merits of the Mosaic vs. the new covenant.

Verse 25 picks up on the note of the blood speaking in v. 24, and he says make sure you don't disregard that speaking. Our author then develops another of his *a fortiori* arguments: for if those who were part of the old covenant could not escape when they ignored the covenant warnings, warnings that were given upon earth, how much more trouble will believers be in if they ignore the warnings that come forth from the heavenly Jerusalem and turn away from its revelation. This is like some of the previous warnings at 2:1–3; 6:6–8; and 10:28–29 about apostasy, which is what we should expect in a peroration where there is reiteration and amplification of earlier major themes. In fact, it is the same kind of warning against apostasy that we will also find in 1 Corinthians 10 (see below).

Finally, our author must end with the warning that the audience be careful to receive (the participle here is in the present). They are in the process of receiving this kingdom, but have not fully done so, and if they pull out before the end there will be hell to pay—literally. Here is the only mention of receiving a kingdom, but it is an unshakeable one that comes as a gift that should prompt the believer's gratitude, worshiping with reverence in a fashion that is acceptable to God. There are probably echoes here of Daniel 7:18–22, which

---

86. *Kaine* is used at 8:8, 13; 9:13. This way of referring to the new covenant in this verse is unique in all Christian literature. I agree with Attridge, *Hebrews*, 376 that we are merely dealing with stylistic variation, as is typical in an epideictic piece of rhetoric, particularly in the summing up in the peroration where changing the terms but not the meaning shows one's skills in "invention" and amplification.

is significant because there the kingdom is given to the saints once the Ancient of Days comes down for final judgment in a theophany in favor of the saints and against the beastly nations, and they finally possess this kingdom—on earth, not in heaven.[87]

Here the theophany involves believers worshiping with a sense of awe about all this, and our author has attempted to reinculcate that sense of awe by the imagaic discussion that has just preceded. The term *latreuō* used of worship is the technical term for the priestly service already discussed in 8:5; 9:9; 10:2; 13:10 that suggests that this Christian worship is the fulfillment of the previous Levitical service (cf. 9:14).[88] Notice as well the word *deos* translated awe, which occurs only here in the NT but in the LXX shows up in scenes of terror, holy or otherwise (2 Macc 3:17, 30; 12:22; 13:16; 15:23). Our author on the one hand wishes to say God will be more accessible but he does not wish to suggest that God ceases to be God or ceases to deserve worship and absolute awe and respect at the eschaton. This is why he adds v. 29.

Finally, our author ends the discussion, as A. Lincoln points out, with an *inclusio*; he began at v. 18 with a discussion of fire on the mount; he closes with a reference to the fact that our God is a consuming fire whom believers certainly would not want to be on the bad side of (drawing on Deut 9:3).[89] This is the same God the OT people encountered, but now operating through a more gracious mode and covenant. Long stresses:

> This statement is ambiguous. Should we sing the doxology or hide under the pew? The Preacher wants to leave the image undefined, since God's fire both refines and devours, purifies and incinerates. God's word is a two-edged sword both severing and saving, and it all depends on whether or not we enter the sanctuary "by the new and living way that Jesus opened for us."[90]

Our author sees this final salvo as a panacea "for a church plagued by neglect, apathy, absenteeism, retreat, and near the point of apostasy."[91] It is well to add however that the allusion to the consuming fire is a reminder of coming final judgment (cf. Isa 33:14; Wis 16:16;

---

87. See Attridge, *Hebrews*, 382 on this allusion.

88. See Hagner, *Encountering Hebrews*, 167

89. A Lincoln, "Lecture on Heb. 11–12" (class lecture presented at Gordon-Conwell Theological Seminary, 1976).

90. Long, *Hebrews*, 141.

91. Craddock, "Hebrews," 160.

Psalms of Solomon 15:4) when Christ returns. It thus nicely rounds out the treatment of the final theophany.

Portions of Exodus 12–34 provide the basis for the capsule summary that Paul offers in 1 Corinthians 10, which reads as follows

> [1] For I do not want you to be ignorant of the fact, brothers and sisters, that our ancestors were all under the cloud and that they all passed through the sea. [2] They were all baptized into Moses in the cloud and in the sea. [3] They all ate the same spiritual food [4] and drank the same spiritual drink; for they drank from the spiritual rock that accompanied them, and that rock was Christ. [5] Nevertheless, God was not pleased with most of them; their bodies were scattered in the wilderness.
>
> [6] Now these things occurred as examples to keep us from setting our hearts on evil things as they did. [7] Do not be idolaters, as some of them were; as it is written: "The people sat down to eat and drink and got up to indulge in revelry." [8] We should not commit sexual immorality, as some of them did—and in one day twenty-three thousand of them died. [9] We should not test Christ, as some of them did—and were killed by snakes. [10] And do not grumble, as some of them did—and were killed by the destroying angel.
>
> [11] These things happened to them as examples and were written down as warnings for us, on whom the culmination of the ages has come.

Exodus 32:6 is quoted at 1 Corinthians 10:7, however much of the summary above comes from earlier in Exodus, though not just Exodus in itself but Exodus through the filter of Wisdom of Solomon, where the rock is Wisdom, a subject we have discussed at length in the first volume in this series, *Isaiah Old and New*.[92] Here Paul is viewing the Exodus text typologically, which assumes that the events described actually happened, and they could happen again to Paul's audience if they behave like the wilderness wandering generation. At the heart of the analogy here is the fact that the miraculous event of the Red Sea crossing and the miraculous gift of manna and water in the wilderness didn't prevent many of the audience from ending up dead outside the promised land.

Paul intimates that Christian baptism and partaking in the Lord's Supper will not prevent the possibility of apostasy and exclusion from entering the kingdom if the Corinthians behave badly. *Paul is not doing exegesis of the Exodus text* but rather using it as a taking off point for an ethical warning to his audience, making an ominous comparison. One of the things that makes this argument work is that Paul

92. See Witherington, *Isaiah Old and New*, 361–70.

assumes that Christ preexisted and was actually playing the role of Wisdom, providing resources for the Israelites. His point is that the Israelites had the same sort of benefits, indeed benefits from Christ, as the Corinthians do, and even this did not prevent most of them from perishing in the wilderness.

The actual progress of the capsule summary starts with an allusion to Exodus 14:19–22, Paul then moves on to Exodus 16:4–30 and Exodus 17:1–7 // Numbers 20:2–13, the latter being the famous story of water coming forth from the rock. It is worth pointing out as well that there was a rabbinic tradition (see b. Sukkah 3a–b and 11a–b), probably from as early as Paul's day about Miriam's well being shaped like a rock and following the Israelites in the wilderness, providing water when needed (cf. Num 21:16–18).

Notice that in v. 3 Paul calls the manna "spiritual food," which presumably means food miraculously provided by God, not food with a heavenly texture or taste. Likewise, it is normal water spiritually provided. The direct quotation of Exodus 32:6 comes of course from the golden calf story, a text of special relevance to his argument since it is a text about both idolatry and sexual immorality, precisely the thing Paul is warning his audience about, urging them to stay out of pagan temple feasts where these two things are assumed to go on (cf., e.g., Josephus, *Ant.* 18.65–80). Notice that the allusion to snakes comes from Numbers 21:5–6 and the grumbling likely alludes to Numbers 14:2, 36; and 16:41–49. The destroyer mentioned in 1 Corinthians 10:10 presumably is the destroying angel of Exodus 12:23 LXX.[93]

What becomes clear as one works through the use of the Pentateuch in this Pauline passage is that Paul is drawing on several passages, mentally combining them into a summary and probably quoting the one verse from Exodus from memory. This is not an exercise in exegesis of the Pentateuch, it is the building of argument with an ethical intent and focus, drawing on the OT stories meant to stop his audience from committing idolatry and immorality in the context of pagan temple feasts.

The intensification of some laws or apodictic statements by Jesus can be seen in Matthew 5:21–22 where, alluding to Exodus 21:12, Jesus not only says no killing, he also says if one is even angry with his brother or sister one will be subject to judgment. Or again in Matthew 5:38–39, partially quoting Exodus 21:24, Jesus says that no revenge or retaliation is to be taken, one is to turn the other cheek,

---

93. See the detailed discussion in Witherington, *Conflict and Community in Corinth*, 218–24.

even if the slap was just to shame a person, he is to allow his garment to be taken, and if someone impresses a disciple into service for a mile, one is to go with them two miles. Jesus is not merely limiting revenge, retaliation, or the attempt to recover things taken, he is eliminating such activities. This is not merely an intensification of the law, this is a reversal of its policies in the opposite direction. This comports with the more detailed discussion about forgiveness without limit in Matthew 18.

Of considerable importance is the phrase "the blood of the covenant" that appears in Exodus 24:8 in the story of how Moses took the blood of a bull, and put it in bowls and splashed half of it against the altar, and the other half he took and sprinkled on the people saying, "This is the blood of the covenant that the Lord has made with you in accordance with all these words." Not to be missed is the echo of or allusion to this scene in Mark 14:24; Matthew 26:28; Luke 22:20; 1 Corinthians 11:25; and Hebrews 9:20 and 13:20. The Mosaic scene is about the inauguration of a new covenant between God and his people. In the Gospels and in Hebrews 13 the reference is to the new covenant which Christ inaugurated by the shedding of his own blood, and Hebrews 13 goes so far as to call the new covenant the eternal one, in contrast to the obsolescent earlier covenants including the Mosaic one. In light of the Mosaic background, the Gospel writers, Paul, and the author of Hebrews seem to be clear enough in their affirmation that what Jesus depicted at the Last Supper and did on the cross was not about a renewal of the Mosaic covenant but rather the inauguration of a final eternal covenant, a genuinely new covenant.

As Watts points out, Exodus 24 is the only place where blood of the covenant is connected with a meal, so it is especially apropos that Jesus uses the phrase he does from Exodus 24, combining it with a partial citation of Isaiah 53:12, which refers to the substitutionary sacrifice. It is the sacrifice and the shedding of the blood that inaugurates the new covenant between God and his people (and Mark 10:45 had prepared for what we find in Mark 14:24).[94] Pao and Schnabel are surely correct, in commenting on Luke 22:20, that the reference to the blood of the new covenant is not a reference to the blood of the Passover lamb, which is never described as the blood of a new covenant, whereas obviously this is the implication of Exodus 24.[95] It

94. See Watts, "Mark," 229–30.
95. David W. Pao and Eckhard J. Schnabel, "Luke," in Beale, *Commentary on the New Testament Use*, 382.

is of course Luke and Paul who make clear that the discussion is about a "new" covenant, and Paul is our earliest witness to the original form of the words of institution.

Exodus 29:18 speaks of the burning of a whole ram on the altar as a burnt offering to God, and it is said to be "a pleasing aroma, a food offering presented to the Lord." Paul in Philippians 4:18 speaks of the gifts the Philippians sent to him by means of Epaphroditus as "a fragrant offering, an acceptable sacrifice, pleasing to God." Paul is drawing an analogy between himself and God receiving gifts, except that ultimately the sacrifice they made on behalf of Paul is really a sacrifice offered and pleasing to God.

Exodus 32:32 has Moses saying to God after the golden calf debacle "please forgive their sin, but if not blot me out of the book you have written." This should ring a bell with students of the NT familiar with Paul's passionate words in Romans 9:3: "for I could wish myself cursed and cut off from Christ for the sake of my people, those of my own race, the people of Israel." Paul is willing to make the same sort of sacrifice as Moses to save his people.

The image and idea of "the book you have written" is further developed in the OT in reference to God's book of life, where life refers to mundane existence, not everlasting life. A similar idea of God having a ledger in heaven shows up in Luke 10:20 where Jesus tells his disciples they should rejoice that their names are written in heaven. More telling still is the reference in Revelation 3:5 where there is a warning about being blotted out of the book of life by Christ himself, and there the reference is surely to the book of everlasting life, not merely ordinary physical existence.

There is an interesting possible allusion in John 15:15 to Exodus 33:11 that refers to God speaking to Moses face to face, as to a friend. In John however, it is Jesus speaking candidly and openly with his disciples and calling them friends. This is not a paralleling of Jesus and Moses, but rather of God and Jesus. Note that in the OT, only Abraham and Moses are said to be friends of God (cf. 2 Chr 20:7; Isa 41:8). Jesus extends the friendship circle to all the disciples, who demonstrate their friendship by following Jesus's command to love one another, and even be prepared to lay down their lives for one another.[96]

Something similar is going on in the famous saying in Matthew 11:28 where Jesus beckons people to come unto him and he will give

96. See Köstenberger, "John," 493.

them rest, a rather clear allusion to Exodus 33:14 where God reassures Moses, "My presence will go with you and I will give you rest." Again, Jesus is speaking like God speaks in Exodus. One may as well see an interesting contrast where in Exodus 33:18 Moses asks to see God's glory, but instead God says that only his goodness will pass in front of Moses, but Moses is not allowed to see God's face, because he would not survive it. Contrast this with John 1:18 where the author boldly states that we have seen his glory, the glory of the one who is the Word, who in turn is in fact God the only begotten Son.

There are no citations or allusions to Exodus 35–39 in the NT, which discusses the tabernacle, the priests, the furniture in the tabernacle, especially the ark of the covenant. The writers of the NT were not interested in reestablishing either a tabernacle or a tent or for that matter a temple in the wake and in light of the Christ event. Such means of atonement and contact with God were seen as obsolete. Nevertheless, in texts like Revelation 8:3 and 9:13, the descriptions of the earthly tabernacle and incense altar are used to describe the heavenly tabernacle and its equipment (cf. Exod 30:1–7). Or the same sort of cultic language about the jewels in the breastplate described in Exodus 28:17–21 are used to describe the beauty of the new Jerusalem in Revelation 21:12–19. Compare this to the fact that the description of the curtain in the tabernacle in Exodus 26:31–33 seems to have provided a blueprint for the curtain in Herod's temple (cf. Mark 15:38; Matt 27:51; Luke 23:45), and in both cases the curtain in question is separating the holy of holies from what is outside it.

Finally, since we have been dealing with the theme of glory, it is worth noting that the account of the transfiguration in Mark 9:7 seems rather clearly indebted to the description of the glory cloud descending on the tabernacle at the end of the book of Exodus (Exod 40:34) and an even more clear echo of that conclusion of Exodus is found in Revelation 15:5, 8 where interestingly the language is used to describe the tabernacle which John sees *in heaven,* not on earth.

CONCLUSIONS

Though the book of Exodus does not figure as prominently as Genesis does in the NT, it nonetheless has a major impact on the thinking, writing, quoting, and alluding of the NT authors in various ways. There is first of all the figure of Moses himself, who provides a point of analogy when Paul wants to talk about his ministry, or when the first evangelist wants to compare Jesus to the greatest figures in the OT, only in order to make clear that Jesus is even greater. It is however something of a major surprise that in Paul's narrative thought-world, Moses, *does not* play the sort of dominant role we might expect in the writing of a former Pharisee, a surprise that is until we remember that Paul believes that the crucial covenant which Moses ushered in is obsolescent, having been eclipsed by the new covenant. In a *tour de force* argument in Galatians 4 Paul is prepared to say that the Mosaic law covenant was an interim arrangement by God, until the time had fully come to send forth his Son. The book of Hebrews is even more emphatic about the new covenant not being a mere renewal or fulfillment of the Mosaic covenant.

Nevertheless, various of the Ten Commandments figure prominently in the NT, in the teaching of both Jesus and Paul, and so some of the individual commandments carry over into the new covenant—not however the Sabbath commandment any more than the food laws or circumcision commandment does. Paul's own extended discussions about the Mosaic law of course depend on the assessment of the holy and good Mosaic law as a whole, and its intended function, but then also its actual *effect* on fallen human beings, humans not enabled by the Holy Spirit to keep those laws. For Paul, the law is a collective entity that stands as one, circumcision is the entre into the keeping of some 613 or so commandments. But law is part of a larger thing called covenant, and the covenant theology he advances, as we also find it in Hebrews, is one that suggests that the new covenant is not a renewal of the Mosaic law covenant. In general, the hermeneutic applied to the OT and its interpretation, vis-à-vis how it might or might not continue to be directly applicable to followers of Christ, is determined by what one believes about the Christ event and the resulting new covenant.

But Moses the man, the Mosaic law, and the Ten Commandments are by no means the only way the book of Exodus turns up in the NT. You might not really know this if you focused solely on direct quotations of Exodus in the NT or cameo appearances of Moses as a mediator or prophetic figure in that book. As we have observed at several points, *narrative* from the Pentateuch is seldom the subject of an OT direct quotation in the NT whereas a law, or a direct statement by God much more often is. Narrative functions differently than quoted laws or sayings from the OT.

For one thing, narrative serves as assumed backstory, for the writers of the NT assume that they are still telling the story of God's people. For another thing it serves as analogy, used to make both ethical or theological points. For example, in Matthew 24 Jesus alludes to the Noah story to warn his audience that they too could be taken away in judgment if they don't repent. Or consider 1 Corinthians 10 where Paul warns his converts that they shouldn't think that just because God had blessed them with "sacraments" that they are exempt from the sort of fate the Hebrews suffered in the wilderness who had a "dry" baptism in the Red Sea and then miraculous manna in the desert, but committed idolatry and immorality, like some Corinthians were doing in the pagan temples in Corinth. But sometimes the arguments turn decidedly theological, the story of Abraham and his faith reckoned as righteous provides the analogy for understanding how one gains right standing with God through faith in Christ.

Precisely because narrative could be used in a variety of ways, often quite creatively (see, e.g., what Paul does with Sarah and Hagar in Galatians 4) it often turns up not just in rehearsals of salvation history such as in Acts 7, it also turns up in arguments, in sermons, and in letters because it could be assumed that someone out there in the audience was familiar with the narrative thought world of the OT. In an oral culture, it is often the stories of the past, in this case the OT stories, that would be told and retold with various elaborations, embellishments, and truncations perhaps far more often that OT imperatives.

In the discussion of Acts 7 we brought up the fact that intertextuality is too narrow a category to account for all the use of the OT we find in the NT. For one thing, we are sometimes talking about the impact not of a text, but of a remembered series of characters, ideas, and words from the OT on the new thing that a NT writer wants to talk about. He is not quoting, or directly alluding to some particular text or texts, he is creating something new out of OT parts, thoughts, rituals, or practices. For example, consider the use of the language of the plagues in Egypt to talk about very different and eschatological judgments in Revelation.

There is furthermore the issue not only of the use of intertestamental texts and ideas along with OT ones in the NT (though it is worth nothing that the only quotes *directly cited* as Scripture in the NT are from thirty-nine books of the OT, unless Jude's reference to 1 Enoch is an exception). There is also the issue of the function of sacred texts in an oral culture, not to mention the paraphrasing of OT texts. In the latter case, we cannot assume that the speaker or writer is using some alternative ancient translation; he may be just doing his own rendering of the text. In the former case, we could well have examples in a text like Acts 7 where Stephen has mushed together several OT stories and ideas, based entirely on memory, a not entirely precise memory. If that is what is going on and Luke is just reporting it, then we should stop talking about Luke misquoting the OT. In his most recent major work E. P. Sanders comes to the conclusion that even a literate person like Paul is likely quoting the OT from memory the vast majority of the time, not looking up texts. The problem with too many intertextuality studies is they assume that we are *just* talking about the interaction between texts, when it fact we may be talking about the interaction between memory (faulty or good), oral traditions (recent or long-standing), and sacred texts.[97]

As we have had several occasions to note in these three volumes, very often the authors of the NT are *not doing exegesis of OT texts.* They are making homiletical uses of OT texts, not infrequently for different purposes than their original functions. They are doing this knowing full well that they are not offering a *literal* rendering of the original meaning of this or that text. Even so typology prone a writer as the author of Hebrews is careful not to say things like Jesus is the angel of the Lord in the OT, or Melchizedek was Jesus in disguise in the life of Abraham. The NT writers should not be accused of being bad citers or bad interpreters of the OT if they are (1) not attempting to quote an OT text verbatim, but may just be borrowing language or paraphrasing; and (2) are not attempting to explain the original contextual meaning of these OT texts.

One of the real benefits of reading OT texts both forward and backward, both in their original contexts, and as they are used in the NT, is it becomes clear that a wooden literalistic lament about the misuse of the OT by NT writers presupposes criteria of evaluation that should never have been applied to what they are attempting to do in the first place.

Precisely because the OT sacred text is a given, the writers of the NT feel free to improvise using just this idea, or that element, or that saying, or this analogy on the basis of it. Like a jazz musician who presupposes a familiar stable text (e.g., John Coltrane and the song "My Favorite Things") precisely because there is a known stable original text which is not altered by a creative, even artistic use of it for

97. E. P. Sanders, *Paul the Apostle: Life, Letters, and Thought* (Minneapolis: Fortress, 2015).

other purposes, the person in question feels free to use the material in fresh ways. Yes, we do have what counts as exegesis of OT texts sometimes in the NT, but unless we take into account the *whole spectrum of ways the OT is used in the NT,* and not just focus on citations or quotations or clear allusions, we will never fully understand the full impact of the OT on the thought world of the writers of the NT and on their theologizing and ethicizing.

Finally, it is well to keep steadily in view that evaluation of the use of OT commandments and of narrative, which is primarily what the Pentateuch offers up to our NT writers, requires of any evaluator some rather different assumptions and criteria than if one was evaluating the use of either prophetic, or musical poetry from Isaiah or the Psalms. Prose narrative is a more indirect way to theologize or ethicize on some topic than say prophecy. Even commandments which can sometimes be read and used in a more straightforward ethical manner in the NT ("no adultery" still means "no adultery"), if they are commandments that don't have to do directly with the point the author is wanting to make, can be used creatively to speak to a different though related issue, as we shall see when we consider later why Paul thought a saying about not muzzling oxen might have some relevance for the discussion of feeding working apostles!

4.

Cracking the Levitical Code and Counting Up the Numbers

Entering the house of God to dwell with God, beholding, glorifying and enjoying him eternally, I suggest, is the story of the Bible, the plot that makes sense of the various acts, persons and places of its pages, the deepest context for its doctrines.

—L. Michael Morales[1]

Without love even the most radical devotion to God is of no value to Him. Let me make sure that sinks in. . . . You can gain all the spiritual gifts in the world. You can take the most radical steps of obedience. You can share every meal with the homeless in your city. You can memorize the book of Leviticus. You can pray each morning for four hours like Martin Luther. But if what you do does not flow out of a heart of love—a heart that does those things because it genuinely desires to do them—it is ultimately worthless to God.

—J. D. Greear[2]

The Lord said to Moses, [23] "Tell Aaron and his sons, 'This is how you are to bless the Israelites. Say to them:
[24] "The Lord bless you
and keep you;
[25] the Lord make his face shine on you

---

1. L. Michael Morales, *Who Shall Ascend the Mountain of the Lord? A Biblical Theology of the Book of Leviticus*, NSBT (Downers Grove, IL: InterVarsity, 2015), 21.

2. J. D. Greear, *Gospel: Recovering the Power that Made Christianity Revolutionary* (Nashville: Broadman & Holman, 2011), 17–18.

and be gracious to you;
²⁶ the Lord turn his face toward you
and give you peace."

—Numbers 6:23–26

Because Leviticus and Numbers are comparatively minor sources of material for quotations allusions and echoes in the NT, we will treat the material from these two books together in one chapter. It is however true that the book of Hebrews in particular draws rather heavily on the priestly institutions discussed in these sources to make his points about the greater and heavenly high priest—Jesus.

LEVITICUS

From the outset of this chapter, it is wise to note a point made strongly by Steve Moyise, namely that by and large the portions of Leviticus that are quoted or alluded to in the NT come *not* from the material aimed specifically at the priests, but from the portion aimed at the people of God as a whole, namely the holiness code found in Leviticus 17–26, with Leviticus 19 coming in for special use due to its injunction to love one's neighbor. What this suggests is that the NT authors are seeing a parallel between instructions to Israel and those to the church, rather than between instructions to Israel's priests and the leaders of the NT community.[3] This doesn't prevent the author of Hebrews from doing a dramatic comparison and contrast between OT priests and the heavenly high priest Christ.

It is clear enough that Leviticus was a very important book in early Judaism, as is shown by a careful study of the some seventeen Leviticus scrolls found at Qumran or Masada. Only the Psalms, Deuteronomy, Isaiah, Genesis, and Exodus have more representation among the Judean desert scrolls. Peter Flint in fact makes clear it was widely used and discussed not only at Qumran but in general in early Judaism.[4] At Qumran we find Leviticus manuscripts in two Hebrew scripts (paleo and square) and in no less than three languages: Hebrew, Aramaic, and Greek. Not accidentally or incidentally, many

---

3. Steve Moyise, *The Old Testament in the New, An Introduction*, 2nd ed. (London: Bloomsbury, 2015), 169–70.
4. See the helpful essay, Peter Flint, "The Book of Leviticus in the Dead Sea Scrolls," in *The Book of Leviticus: Composition and Reception*, ed. Rolf Rendtorff and Robert A. Kugler, VTSup 93 (Leiden: Brill, 2003), 323–41.

of these manuscripts show the same kind of strong interest in the Holiness Code for individuals in Leviticus 17–26, just as we find in the NT, but in fact all the chapters of Leviticus are quoted or alluded to somewhere in these scrolls.[5] Relatively few of the Qumran scrolls were written in Greek but of those most are Pentateuchal books, including two Leviticus manuscripts (4Q119 [4QLXXLeva] and 4Q120 [4QpapLXXLevb]).[6]

And there is evidence, from the *targumim* and elsewhere that a text like Leviticus 18:5 was taken in early Judaism to be speaking not only about this life but about "the life to come" (see Tg. Onq. Lev. 18:5; Tg. Ps-J. Lev. 18:5; cf. Sipre Lev. 337a; b. Mak. 23b; Midr. Exod. 30:22).[7] This prepares us for what we find in the NT use of Leviticus 18:5. One more comment is in order before we get down to texts.

> "The Hebrew text tradition of Leviticus had basically achieved a uniform state, to judge from the extant sources, by the second half of the Second Temple period . . . this contrasts with the pluriform state of Exodus and Numbers, which display two or more literary editions. . . . The OG of Leviticus is the most literal of Pentateuchal translations, perhaps due to its unique nature.[8]

LEVITICUS 18:5: OBEDIENT LIFESTYLES

Our first text for close scrutiny must be Leviticus 18:5, which is drawn on in Matthew 19:17; Luke 10:28; possibly Romans 2:26; more clearly Romans 7:10; and 10:5; and also Galatians 3:12. In these latter two texts, Leviticus is partially quoted.

5. See the chart in Flint, *Book of Leviticus*, 338–39. By my count eight of these Qumran manuscripts have a strong focus on the Holiness Code chapters. Some of these scrolls actually have parts of more than one Pentateuch book, and in the traditional order Exodus, Leviticus, Numbers, so, e.g., 4Q17 (4QExod–Levf). They provide evidence of the Pentateuch bound together as a collection; see Flint, *Book of Leviticus*, 329.

6. Flint, *Book of Leviticus*, 330.

7. See the discussion by Seifrid, "Romans," 655–56 in the context of his discussion of the citation of Lev 18:5 in Romans 10; Paul modifies the LXX here as he did in Galatians.

8. Sarianna Metso and Eugene Ulrich, "The Old Greek Translation of Leviticus" in Rendtorff, *Book of Leviticus*, 267. Note also the judgment of Jacob Milgrom that the variant readings in the LXX and MT of this book are few and almost always insignificant; Jacob Milgrom, *Leviticus 1–16: A New Translation with Introduction and Commentary*, AB 3A (New York: Doubleday, 1991), 2.

MT	LXX
Keep my decrees and laws, for the person who obeys them will live by them. I am the Lord.	And you shall keep all my ordinances and all my judgments, and you shall do them; as for the things a person does, he shall live by them; I am the Lord your God.

καὶ φυλάξεσθε πάντα τὰ προστάγματά μου καὶ πάντα τὰ κρίματά μου καὶ ποιήσετε αὐτὰ ἃ ποιήσας ἄνθρωπος ζήσεται ἐν αὐτοῖς ἐγὼ κύριος ὁ θεὸς ὑμῶν

The verb here in the Hebrew, translated "keep" indicates that the human will must be exercised so one can "do" the commandments. Notice in this verse that "keeping" certainly applies to both laws and decrees, and the decrees at least are to be practiced continually until they become ingrained, or just a normal way of life. "Keeping" commandments is said to provide life (Lev 26:3–13; Deut 28:1–14). John Hartley insightfully points out that since disobedience to a commandment was the "original sin" that led to the expulsion from the garden of Eden where the tree of life was, now a new way to life has been made available through keeping commandments.[9]

Life here refers to a good life here on earth in positive relationship with God, in this case so one can thrive in the promised land. It is unlikely this refers to everlasting life in its original context, but at the same time what is being spoken of is not mere existence here, merely surviving. What is spoken of here is a vision of "the good life." Keeping the law is the path or "walk" to divine blessing, to a happy and fulfilled existence.[10] Notice that this law is given a solemn sanction in two ways: (1) the Hebrew word *mishpat* means a formal legal decision, even a sentence passed by a judge; (2) the closing clause "I am the Lord" indicates this is given by no ordinary judge; it is spoken and vouched for by God himself, the Lord who has the right to rule over his people in this fashion. In other words, doing this is of supreme importance if you want to have a good life.

In regard to the final statement "I am the Lord," as W. H. Bellinger points out, this is the formula of self-revelation, and as such is meant to make clear there can be no gainsaying or modifying of what is urged here. The Israelites must not live like the idolaters of whatever nation, plain and simple. Instead they must keep the laws and decrees

9. I am simply following John E. Hartley, *Leviticus*, WBC (Dallas: Word, 1992), 293.
10. See rightly Gordon J. Wenham, *The Book of Leviticus*, NICOT (Grand Rapids: Eerdmans, 1979), 253.

of their specific God—the Lord. Bellinger adds that the verb (*shmr*) translated "keep" has to do with guarding, watching over, being sure to implement or do.[11]

In the NT, this concept appears, and this verse is quoted partially (e.g., Rom 10:5; Gal 3:12) to indicate that if anyone can keep this law, he or she will enjoy or at least inherit everlasting life. Jesus himself says in Matthew 19:17 to the inquiring young man, "if you want to enter life, keep the commandments."[12] Notice that the original question has to do with "everlasting life"; the young man was already experiencing "the good life," indeed he was wealthy. In the Lukan parable of the good Samaritan, Jesus in Luke 10:28 responds to the rehearsal of the great love commandments with "You have answered correctly, do this and you will live." Notice here as well the question is not how may I live the good life here and now, but "what must I do to inherit eternal life." This sort of response comports completely with the various texts in the OT which suggests one may find life if one keeps the torah (cf. Lev 18:5; 25:18–19; 26:3–5; Deut 5:33; 6:2; 11:8–9; 1 Kgs 3:14; Neh 9:29; Ps 16:11; 91; 119; Prov 6:23; Isa 1:19; Ezek 3:21; 18:5–9; 20:11; Amos 5:4–6; Mal 2:4–5).[13]

Paul characterizes the "doing of the Law" as "the righteousness that comes from the law." He paraphrases "the person who does these things will live by them." In Galatians 3:12 Paul uses a portion of Leviticus 18:5 to assert that the law is not based on faith, but rather requires doing it, indeed living by it. Moises Silva quite candidly says

> From a theological point of view, the most difficult problem in the quotations found in Gal 3:6–14 and perhaps in the whole Pauline corpus is the opposition between Hab 2:4 (Gal 3:11) and Lev 18:5 (Gal 3:12). The problem is exacerbated by the way Paul introduces the latter: he states that "the law is not of faith." . . . It goes without saying that Paul's contemporaries would have viewed the Lev 18:5 . . . in a totally positive way.[14]

Notice that the contrast between Habakkuk 2:4 and Leviticus 18:5 in the LXX is exacerbated by similarity of syntax in the two passages; both have subjects with the definite article ("the righteous," "the

11. W. H. Bellinger Jr., *Leviticus, Numbers* (Grand Rapids: Baker, 2001), 110, 114.
12. Note that this is not in the parallel in Mark 10, so this is part of the Matthean portrait of Jesus, which in effect is a re-Judaizing of the picture Mark paints. See the discussion in Witherington, *Matthew*, 368–69.
13. See Watts, "Mark," 200.
14. Silva, "Galatians," 800.

doer"); both have short prepositional phrases ("from faith/ faithful-ness," "in/by them"). Both also have the very same main verb, ζήσεται. Paul in fact alters the LXX text of Leviticus 18:5, omitting the relative pronoun and adding an article to the participle ("the one doing") and dropping the now unnecessary word "man." As Silva goes on to say, for Paul's argument to work in Galatians 3:10–14, Galatians 3:11–12 must reflect Paul's view of some kind of contrast between faith and law, at least in regard to how one obtains right standing with God.[15] More importantly, Silva is quite right that what is going on here is part of Paul's larger argument (see 3:16–17) about chronological redemptive-historical distinctions, namely that the Abrahamic covenant based on Abraham's trusting God came prior to the Mosaic covenant.

To say that "the law is not of faith" "is to claim that the Mosaic covenant belongs to a different redemptive epoch than does the Gospel."[16] Exactly. The new covenant is connected to the Abrahamic covenant, whereas the Mosaic covenant is connected to neither the Abrahamic nor the new covenant by Paul (see Galatians 4). It is seen as an interim arrangement *pro tempore*, until the time had fully come and God sent his Son to redeem people out from under the Mosaic law. This is not because the law itself is bad in any way, nor because keeping the law is somehow antithetical to having faith in God, indeed it can be an expression of such faith. It is because keep-ing the law is not a means of saving faith or right standing with God. Romans 7:10 finds the speaker saying that the commandment which was intended to bring life, actually brought death. The speaker here is likely Adam, telling about the outcome of his disobedience to the one commandment he was given.[17]

One of the problems with reading a passage like Leviticus 18:5 through the lens of Paul is that Paul of course sees Leviticus as part of a covenant, the Mosaic covenant, that his audience should not be committing themselves to. He uses portions of the Mosaic covenant to talk about the situation that now exists for followers of Jesus in the new covenant, for instance in contrasting faith in Christ, with the keeping of the Mosaic covenant. This is not an antinomian approach to "law" *itself*, but rather an emphasis on what is the case now that

---

15. Silva, "Galatians," 803.

16. Silva, "Galatians," 804.

17. On the rhetorical issue of impersonation or speech in character being used here in Romans 7, see Witherington and Hyatt, *Letter to the Romans*, 179–92. The "I" here clearly enough is not Paul the Christian, see Phil 3:6 and discussion in ch. 2, above.

Christ has redeemed those under the law out from under the Mosaic law (Galatians 4). Christians are now beholden to the new covenant and the law of Christ (see Galatians 5). But as for the basis of salvation or inheriting everlasting life or receiving the Holy Spirit (Galatians 3), that comes not by keeping the Mosaic law but through faith in Christ.

It is worth adding as well that in both cases where Jesus alludes to Leviticus 18:5 he also is prepared to talk not about mundane life, but about entering or obtaining or inheriting everlasting life. But in both the Matthean and the Lukan texts, Jesus is a Jew speaking to Jews in the context of the keeping of the Mosaic covenant. Both the young man and the lawyer were law-abiding Jews, and the discussion is not about "living by or in the law," but rather about life that one can enter or obtain through the keeping of the law. In other words, both of these pious Jews are looking for something *more* than just the good life here and now, which presumably they already have as law-abiding Jews. No, they are asking about everlasting life.

LEVITICUS 19:18: LOVE THY NEIGHBOR

Our second major text from Leviticus requires extended discussion. I am referring of course to Leviticus 19:18, which is drawn on a remarkable ten times in the NT: Matthew 5:43; 19:19; 22:39; Mark 12:31, 33; Luke 10:27; Romans 12:19; 13:9; Galatians 5:14; and James 2:8. The command to love one's neighbor is found in numerous early Jewish texts, some of which insist that it is the foundation of the whole of Torah (e.g., b. Shabbat 31a; t. Pe'ah 4:19).[18] Certainly the command is reiterated at Qumran and elsewhere (1QS VII, 8–9; Sibylline Oracles 8:481). What is notable about some of the later reflections on Leviticus 19:18 is that sometimes there is not merely the assumption that it refers just to fellow Israelites, but that *foreigners and Samaritans are explicitly excluded from the love obligation* (Mek. Exod. 21:35), while proselytes to Judaism could be included (Sipra Qed. 8).

Was there a precedent for combining the love of God and love of neighbor commands in early Judaism? Possibly, at least in the form of a command to worship just one God and love neighbor (see

---

18. On this see E. P. Sanders, *Judaism: Practice and Belief, 63 BCE–66 CE* (Philadelphia: Trinity Press International, 1992), 258.

Testament of Issachar 5:2; 7:6; Testament of Dan 5:3; Philo, *Spec. Laws* 2.63) *but* in none of these cases are the two texts of Deuteronomy 6:5 and Leviticus 19:18 explicitly quoted or alluded to, and in any case dating the Testament of the Twelve Patriarchs is difficult, though perhaps most scholars think it predates the time of Jesus.

MT	LXX
"'Do not seek revenge or bear a grudge against anyone among your people, but love your neighbor as yourself. I am the Lord.	And your own hand shall not take vengeance, and you shall not be angry against the sons of your people, and you shall love your neighbor as yourself; it is I who am the Lord.

καὶ οὐκ ἐκδικᾶταί σου ἡ χείρ καὶ οὐ μηνιεῖς τοῖς υἱοῖς τοῦ λαοῦ σου καὶ ἀγαπήσεις τὸν πλησίον σου ὡς σεαυτόν ἐγώ εἰμι κύριος

It is the second half of this saying, specifically, that recurs repeatedly in the NT. Interestingly, Hartley suggests the proper way to render the original Hebrew is "you shall love your companion as yourself. I am Yahweh." The verb here is *'ahab* which should not be confused with the concept of *khesed,* loving kindness (a word which does not usually mean covenant love, or insider love in any case).[19] Here the construction is such that one could render it "to show love to your companion," and some scholars have thought this simply means to treat kindly, but that is questionable. Notice that in the LXX the verb is ἀγαπήσεις and in every single case in the NT, the LXX rendering is followed.

It is possible that in Leviticus the "neighbor" reference originally has in part to do with, or at least includes, strangers or non-Hebrews who live in the promised land in close proximity. The term in question, רֵעֲךָ [*re'aka*] was general or vague enough that it raised questions as to who counted as a neighbor, as could the Greek term πλησίον (see of course Luke 10:27), which at root simply refers to someone who is near or proximate. Bellinger argues: "The love of neighbor consists of commitment to the welfare and best interest of another person, whether citizen or sojourner. Verses 17–18 contrast hate and vengeance with honest relationships and love. The climax of this section is the call to love one's neighbor, companion, or friend."[20]

More clearly, Jesus will have nothing to do with defining neighbor

19. See the discussion of this key term in Witherington, *Psalms Old and New,* 132–62.
20. Bellinger, *Leviticus, Numbers,* 118.

too narrowly, for example, so as to exclude potential enemies, like Samaritans. To make this even more clear, Jesus simply flatly tells his disciples to love their enemies, obliterating the notion of setting up limits to "neighborliness." It is worth stressing that in Leviticus there is no combining of the command to love God with the command to love neighbor, using exactly the same word for both activities as we find, for example, in Mark 10:31, 33 or Luke 10:27. In the former text, it is Jesus juxtaposing the commands, and even suggesting it is one great commandment to love God and neighbor but in Luke 10 it is the lawyer who mentions both love commands. Pao and Schnabel rightly note that Leviticus 19:18 combined with Deuteronomy 6:5 also show up in Mark 12:28–31 and Matthew 22:34–40 in a different setting, much later in Jesus's ministry, and there the issue is not who is a neighbor but rather what is the greatest commandment.[21] Nor is the person who cites the Scriptures the same in Luke as in Mark and Matthew, so perhaps Jesus discussed these texts more than once.

Luke's citation of Leviticus 19:18 follows the LXX verbatim. Notice that while in Mark and Matthew the two commandments are listed as first and second in order, in Luke the two commands are merged into a single command, which comports with the implication in Mark 12:31 when Jesus says, "there is no other commandment [singular] greater than these [plural]." Jesus's comments reflect the larger debate of what counts as neighbor, with Jesus taking a particularly broad approach to the definition.

It should be kept in mind that while the OT does not commend hating one's enemy, the saying in question in Leviticus 19:18a does urge not to seek revenge against any of *one's own people*, which is then juxtaposed with the command to love neighbor. I agree with the suggestion that the *preceding* context of Leviticus 19 strongly favors the view that "neighbor" here is assumed to be fellow covenant-keeping Hebrew. Leviticus 19:18 builds on the call for God's people to be holy as God is holy found in Leviticus 19:2, and in fact 19:18 summarizes the subsection of 19:11–18.[22] The natural inference from this might well be that "neighbor" in the second part of the saying might well be *limited* to one's own people or countrymen. Leviticus 19:34–35 however suggests the mandate must be extended further, "The alien among you shall be to you as the citizen among you; you shall love the alien as yourself." If there is any ambiguity in Leviticus 19, Jesus

21. Pao and Schnabel, "Luke," 319.
22. Pao and Schnabel, "Luke," 320.

will allow no narrowing of the meaning of neighbor when it comes to his teaching. Jesus is urging his disciples to love in a way that goes considerably beyond in-group love, indeed it is a love not conditioned by kinship circles or normal cultural or reciprocity conventions.

In the partial citation of Leviticus 19:18 in Matthew 5:43 notice first the dropping of the phrase "as yourself." The MT of Leviticus 19:18 is translated quite literally in the LXX, and for the most part the NT use of this verse seems to follow the LXX verbatim.[23] In Targum Pseudo-Jonathan on Leviticus 19:18, the negative golden rule is added to this commandment "so what is hateful to you, do not do to him" (i.e., your neighbor; cf. Matthew 7:12; and Rabbi Hillel's famous dictum b. Shabbat 31a; Gen. Rab. 24:7). Sipre Deuteronomy 186/7; 235 even suggests that failure to love one's neighbor eventually leads to murder! Jesus is prepared however to go further than all these spinning out of the implications of Leviticus 19:18, applying it even in regard to enemies. Notice as well that in later Christian literature, Leviticus 19:18 is connected to the Golden Rule "do unto others." (e.g., Did. 1.2; Letter of Aristeas 207). The Golden Rule, however, is not about setting up a reciprocity cycle, doing something good for the other which then obligates them to respond in kind.[24]

Too few commentators have noticed not merely the indebtedness to Matthew 5–7 shown in the second portion of Romans 12 and 13, but the actual character of what Paul says in Romans 13:8, namely "the one who loves has fulfilled *the other law*." It does not say "the one loving the other fulfills the law." The Greek word order and the definite article with the word "law" rule out that translation.[25] What Paul is talking about is the law of Christ (see Galatians 5 and 1 Corinthians 9). The heart of Jesus's ethic is whole-hearted love of God, neighbor, and even the enemy, including praying for the enemy. The first table of the Ten Commandments is summed up in love of God, the second in love of neighbor, as seen in Leviticus 19:18, to which Jesus adds love of enemy. Neither Paul, nor Jesus is saying that love trumps or outweighs law; indeed, it is the heart of the law. Nor is Paul in Romans 13 suggesting that love completes the law, like a sweet icing on a cake . What Paul is saying, following the lead of Jesus is, another law has replaced and fulfilled the heart of the Mosaic law, namely the

---

23. See Blomberg, "Matthew,"29.
24. Rightly Pao and Schnabel, "Luke," 297.
25. Contra Seifrid, "Romans," 682.

law of the new covenant, the law of Christ. Love in action is not a substitute for law, it is rather the perfect expression of and fulfillment of the law's intentions and purposes.[26]

LEVITICUS 24:16: STONE THE BLASPHEMER!

Less well known but still important is the use of Leviticus 24:16 at Matthew 26:66; Mark 14:64; John 10:33; 19:7; and 2 Timothy 2:19.

MT	LXX
Anyone who blasphemes the name of the Lord is to be put to death. The entire assembly must stone them. Whether foreigner or native-born, when they blaspheme the Name they are to be put to death.	Whoever names the name of the Lord—by death let him be put to death; let the whole congregation of Israel stone him with stones. Whether a guest or a native, when he names the name, let him die.
	ὀνομάζων δὲ τὸ ὄνομα κυρίου θανάτῳ θανατούσθω λίθοις λιθοβολείτω αὐτὸν πᾶσα συναγωγὴ Ἰσραηλ ἐάν τε προσήλυτος ἐάν τε αὐτόχθων ἐν τῷ ὀνομάσαι αὐτὸν τὸ ὄνομα κυρίου τελευτάτω

There is a notable difference between the Hebrew and the LXX text of Leviticus 24:16, namely that the latter seems to be talking about actually *saying* the divine name of God, whereas the former is talking about blaspheming that name, but Leviticus does not expand on what constitutes blasphemy. Is it "taking the Lord's name in vain"? Is it using God's name in some sort of curse? Is it claiming to be God and therefore defaming the actual deity? It seems clear from Leviticus 24:10–23 that we are dealing with legal cases involving a blasphemer. Verse 11 suggests that the offense is not simply uttering the holy name of Yahweh, nor is it merely cursing by itself, but rather using the holy name of Yahweh in a curse. In other words, this law is some form of the third commandment found in Exodus 20:7 (cf. Exod 22:28).[27]

Some of the mystery about this becomes clearer when we realize that in this ANE culture it was believed that blessings (see the story

---

26. See the detailed discussion in Ben Witherington III, *The Indelible Image: The Theological and Ethical Thought World of the New Testament; Volume One; the Individual Witness* (Downers Grove, IL: InterVarsity, 2009), 258–59.

27. See Wenham, *Leviticus*, 311.

of Jacob and Esau) and curses were viewed not as mere words but rather as actions that did something to the listeners. Thus blasphemy "brings guilt on those who hear it as well as on the blasphemer himself. To rid themselves of this guilt the hearers had to lay their hands on the blasphemer's head" according to verse 14. The death of the blasphemer then followed, and this event atoned for both the hearer's sin in listening as well as the speaker's sin. Wenham rightly observes that unlike in other ANE cultures, religion and family crimes are viewed as the most heinous ones, whereas economic crimes such as theft lead to lesser penalties.[28] While ignorance comes into consideration in various legal situations in Israel, it is to be noted that the law referred to in Leviticus 24:16 applies equally to Israelites and also to resident aliens (though presumably not to people just visiting or passing through).[29] There are in fact a whole series of laws, including this one, applied to foreign residents in Israelite territory (e.g., Exod 12:19, 49; Lev 16:29; 17:15; 18:26; Num 9:14; 15:30).

A few particulars on Leviticus 24:16 are in order. The plural verb in the Hebrew indicates that each and every member of the community is to participate in the stoning. Further, the prepositional structure of the Hebrew sentence makes clear that the foreign residents are on the same footing and under the same obligation in regard to this law. Note that the LXX adds the phrase "of the Lord" at v. 16c to the words "the name." What is especially clear in the Hebrew is that offenses against God are seen as the most serious sorts of offenses.

Hartley in his discussion of vv. 15–16 offers a somewhat different take on the text than Wenham. He says the following:

> The first two laws state the penalty for blasphemy distinguishing between cursing God or gods and misspeaking the name of Yahweh. The former act carries an indefinite penalty; i.e., a person who commits such a sin must be held responsible for his sin. The latter offense carries the death penalty. The distinction between these two laws rests on two issues. First, they use different terms for God. . . . The second distinction is that the first law uses . . . "curse" and the second law . . . "misspeak a name." The first law therefore is general; if a person, an Israelite or a foreigner, curses God or the gods, the god he has cursed will punish that person's brazen presumption. . . . The second law rules that no person,

---

28. Wenham, *Leviticus*, 311.

29. Bellinger, *Leviticus, Numbers*, 146 compares Deut 23:7–8, but the point here is different. The point is that blasphemy within God's community, by whomever, is such a very serious violation of the holy nature of God, such a besmirching of his character, that it must be dealt with severely, regardless of who uttered the offending words.

neither an Israelite nor a foreigner, may distinctly speak in a light or disparaging manner the name Yahweh, the revealed name of God."[30]

The punishment for this was stoning by the whole community.

What is perhaps equally important is that these laws were understood to imply, during the Second Temple period, that Yahweh's name was so sacred that Jews had best not even pronounce the name. Even today, orthodox Jews, when they come across the name "Yahweh" in the text will say instead "the Name" or "my Lord." What seems clearly to be implied at least by v. 16 is very strict monotheism, such that anyone claiming to be Israel's God, or seeming to claim equality with Israel's God, would be considered in violation of the blasphemy law. It is this implication that seems to be in play in the various NT texts where Leviticus 24:16 directly or indirectly shows up.

Matthew 26:66 // Mark 14:64 bring the trial of Jesus before the Sanhedrin to a climax. Leviticus 24:16 is not cited but rather implied by the judgment "he is worthy of death." But what precisely had Jesus said that invoked the blasphemy statute? It was not the claim to be the Anointed One, the Son of the blessed. As Andreas Köstenberger says, "in both the OT and other Jewish literature the claim of being God's son need not be blasphemous and may refer to the anointed king of Israel (2 Sam 7:14; Ps 2:7; 89:26–27) or to the Messiah (4Q174; cf. John 1:49). Even Israel could be called God's 'son' (Exod 4:22; Hos 11:1 cf. John 10:33–38)."[31]

The reaction of the high priest does not come after Jesus affirms the truth of the priest's question (in Mark), or at least gives the suggestion of affirming it by saying "you say so," or perhaps better "it is as you say" (Matthew). No, the blasphemy comes from the next part of Jesus's response: that they will see the Son of Man sitting on the right hand of the Almighty and coming on the clouds of heaven. Why would this be considered blasphemy, especially when Jesus avoided saying, much less mispronouncing the tetragrammaton? The answer has to do with the implication that: (1) Jesus is the Son of Man who will, (2) be seated at God's right hand, and equally importantly, (3) come on the clouds to judge the world, which of course the OT says repeatedly is Yahweh's job, on the *Yom Yahweh*. Jesus is turning the tables on the high priest and in effect saying "You think you are

30. Hartley, *Leviticus*, 410.
31. Köstenberger, "John," 500.

judging me, but in fact the Son of Man will be returning and judging you!" In other words, it is the implied claim to be the Son of Man figure of Daniel 7 that constitutes the blasphemy.

But notice that, unlike the case with Stephen, those present abuse Jesus, but *do not take him out and stone him.* They do not fulfill the requirements of the law in Leviticus 24:16. Perhaps this is because of when this hastily convened trial took place, namely during the Passover season, or perhaps it is because they wanted Jesus to die, but not at their own hands when so many Jews could be watching, many of them Jesus sympathizers or followers. That we are on the right track in reading the high priest's reaction to what Jesus says is confirmed when we read in m. Sanh. 7:5 that the high priest's tearing of his robes would be an appropriate response to hearing blasphemy. Matthew 26:66 // Mark 14:64 then has the high priest asking the council to pass a formal judgment, based on the statute in Leviticus 24:16.[32]

The two relevant texts in John, 10:10 and 19:7, are of particular importance to the overall assessment of the christological picture in that Gospel. In 19:7 the Jewish officials say to Pilate that they have a law (i.e., Lev 24:16; cf. Num 15:30–31; Deut 21:22) that indicates Jesus should suffer the death penalty "because he claimed to be the Son of God," which presumably is taken here to be a violation of the divine name, that is, of monotheism. In John 10:33 the implication is the same. The crowd is prepared to stone Jesus for blasphemy, and what constituted the blasphemy is not the way he used the divine name, but the implied claim to be God—perhaps especially the claim "I and the Father are one" (v. 30).[33] As Hays astutely notes, the Jewish authorities in John 19:7 are not claiming that Jesus is in violation of Roman law here, but of Jewish law, and that scene probably looks back to John 10:33–38.[34]

Of a whole different ilk is 2 Timothy 2:19b. Here we have some kind of citation or paraphrase, apparently, which says, "Everyone who confesses the name of the Lord must turn away from wickedness." This actually seems to be a conglomeration or echo of many different texts: Sirach 17:26; Numbers 16:26; Leviticus 24:16; and Isaiah 26:13 LXX in the first half of the citation and the latter half seems to owe something to Psalm 6:8 and Isaiah 52:11 and to the parallel

32. See the discussion in Witherington, *Matthew*, 498–99.
33. Köstenberger, "John," 464.
34. Hays, *Echoes of Scripture in the Gospels*, 437n105.

passages in Luke 13:27 and Matthew 7:23 (cf. 2 Cor 6:17).[35] Taken as a whole, since the term Lord in v. 19b here seems likely to refer to Jesus the risen Lord (though in v. 19a it seems to refer to God the Father who is laying the foundation), because of the reference to the resurrection and the two men who have departed from the Christian faith (cf. v. 8), *then Paul would be counseling the precise behavior that early Jews thought was blasphemy and worthy of death.* Wickedness in this case is not making such a confession but something one turns from if one does confess Jesus is Lord.

What this amounts to is a reuse of OT ideas in some very different ways than the text was understood either in antiquity or in early Judaism. What once was deemed blasphemy is now considered "the good confession" of Christians. This idea of confessing Jesus as Lord as part of confessing one's belief in the true God (and so the opposite of blasphemy) comes out clearly in Paul's modification of the Shema in 1 Corinthians 8:5–6, and more clearly where confession is specifically spoken of in Romans 10:9, indeed that very confession is the key to being saved at all.[36]

THE LEXICON OF FAITH:
THE BROADER USE OF LEVITICUS

The use of Leviticus in the NT reminds me of an old star of 1950s and 1960s Hollywood Westerns; his stage name was Slim Pickens. There really isn't much, once one gets beyond the love commandment. In some ways, this is unsurprising. The writers of the NT were not reinstating a religion of priests, temples, and sacrifices, at least not in the usual sense of those terms. For one thing, the only priesthoods in the NT are the heavenly high priesthood of Christ as discussed in Hebrews, and the priesthood of all believers as mentioned in 1 Peter, Revelation, and perhaps elsewhere.

For another thing, early Christians thought that the death of Christ made unnecessary any more literal sacrifices, particularly sacrifices for sins. The language is spiritualized and there is talk about offering oneself as a sacrifice (Rom 12:1–3) or offering one's praise and the like (see Heb 13:15; cf. Lev 7:12) but no literal sacrifices are

---

35. See Witherington, *Letters and Homilies for Hellenized Christians Vol. One*, 338.
36. See the discussion in Witherington and Hyatt, *Letter to the Romans*, 262–63.

encouraged.[37] Definitely there was to be no building of literal temples, not when Jesus himself claimed to be the believer's temple (John 2), or Saint Paul insisted that the believer's own body was their temple (see 1 Cor 6:19) or perhaps the body of Christ corporately was the temple where God dwells (1 Corinthians 12).

In any case, with theology like the aforementioned, the book of Leviticus becomes less useful for the new Christian movement. It is only later, during the Constantinian period and beyond, that the notion of ministers as priests, church buildings as temples, the Lord's Supper as a literal sacrifice of sorts, and Sunday as the Sabbath becomes a prominent theology of the church either in the East or the West. In other words, Leviticus took on new life in the church when these sorts of OT hermeneutical moves became prominent and even dominant in post-Constantinian Christianity.

But it will not be inappropriate to spend a little time considering how the author of Hebrews talks about the institution of the priesthood, comparing it to and contrasting it with the heavenly high priesthood of Christ. While we could have discussed this in our Genesis chapter when Melchizedek and Abraham came up for scrutiny, in some ways this location is more appropriate for such a discussion, since Leviticus is the one book that devotes so much discussion to priests and their duties, and the Levitical priesthood is the one institution the author of Hebrews wants to make clear that Jesus and his priestly work made entirely obsolete.

The one truly unique concept in Hebrews that makes it stand out from all other NT documents is our author's vision of Christ as the heavenly high priest. If one has an understanding of this major issue, most of the rest of the homily falls into place rather readily. It is difficult to say what sparked our author to write about Christ in this way. It may have been his penetrating study of the OT and its institutions. He may have been looking for a way to say that Christ fulfilled their intention and indeed eclipsed and replaced them. But it is also possible that he was familiar with the varieties of messianic speculation in early Judaism, which at Qumran and perhaps elsewhere included the idea of a priestly messiah.[38]

---

37. Not surprisingly, it is Hebrews that most often alludes to Leviticus in the NT, e.g., when he is describing Moses sprinkling of the blood to make atonement for sin in Heb 9:21, he is surely echoing Lev 8:15, 18; Heb 5:3 is surely echoing Lev 9:7 in the discussion about priests atoning for their own sins, something the priestly Jesus never had to do.

38. Not surprisingly the literature on this subject is vast, most of it focusing on Hebrews 7. See e.g., Robert H. Culpepper, "The High Priesthood and Sacrifice of Christ in the Epistle to

Whatever his state of knowledge of the speculation about a priestly messiah, our author certainly goes beyond what we know of these concepts from these other sources, for he is going to insist not only that Messiah died but that he was both perfect high priest and unblemished sacrifice offered by the priest. There was also of course a Melchizedek speculation before the time of Jesus, as the Qumran documents show clearly enough. There was then certainly a Jewish speculation about messiah being a priest before our author wrote.

When our author wishes to describe Jesus as high priest he uses as his main basis the messianic interpretation of Genesis 14 and Psalm 110, *not Leviticus*. Now it must be understood that the whole idea of priesthood in the OT is dependent on the idea of covenant. The shape that a priesthood takes depends on the shape and stipulations of the covenant or treaty that God's people are called upon to live by. The way our author is going to show that the Levitical priesthood is obsolescent is by showing. (1) There was a *higher and prior* priesthood in the case of Melchizedek, and Jesus is connected to that sort of priesthood which is an eternal one. (2) The very fact that the Levitical priesthood is linked to heredity (and thus is dependent on death and descendants to determine who will next be priest) is in our author's mind a clear sign of the inadequacy of the Levitical priesthood. (3) The inferiority of the Levitical priesthood is also shown by the fact that Abraham the forebear of Levi was blessed by and tithed to Melchizedek. In all of this our author, like Jesus before him, operates with the idea that the earlier idea or institution has precedence and thus a higher claim to authority. But a text like Hebrews 7:27, or 9:28, makes quite clear that our author is no slave to previous concepts, for he goes on to talk of Jesus voluntarily offering himself up as sacrifice. Hebrews 9:28 seems to refer to Isaiah 53:12, and perhaps more than any other NT writer, except perhaps the author of 1 Peter, our author has been affected by reflection on Isaiah 53.

Now it is quite true also that from texts like 4 Maccabees 6:29 there was the idea that a martyr such as a Maccabee could offer an atoning sacrifice, and in the case of Eleazar he was a priest. Yet there is a difference here for a death as atonement is not quite the same as

the Hebrews," *TTE* 32 (1985): 46–62; Fred L. Horton, *The Melchizedek Tradition: A Critical Examination of the Sources to the Fifth Century A.D. and in the Epistle to the Hebrews*, SNTSMS 30 (Cambridge: Cambridge University Press, 1976); Jerome H. Neyrey, "'Without Beginning of Days or End of Life' (Hebrews 7:3): Topos for a True Deity," *CBQ* 53 (1991): 439–55; Deborah W. Rooke, "Jesus as Royal Priest: Reflections on the Interpretation of the Melchizedek Tradition in Heb 7," *Bib* 81 (2000): 81–94.

a deliberate sacrifice of atonement, and more to the point, the Maccabean concept is tied up with the idea of the suffering of the righteous, which doesn't seem to be in the foreground here. Our author operates out of the concept of cultic sacrifice, not martyrdom for a cause, per se.

One of the essential elements in understanding the high priestly concept in Hebrews is that the Son of God *had to be* a human being to be a priest. In other words, all of this reflection on Christ as high priest tells us a lot about his perfect humanity and his human roles, but very little if anything about his divinity. The latter ideas are bound up with our author's presentation of Jesus as also God's unique and preexistent Son and Word. Jesus is the perfect human being, and thus is the perfect candidate to be a perfect sacrifice. But he is also a perfect high priest and thus is the perfect one to freely offer such a sacrifice, and when he does so he is perfected in his intended vocation. It is not that his going to heaven perfects him in any moral sense, but what is meant is that he completes his vocation to perfection in heaven. The language of perfection in application to Christ is sometimes thought to be cultic (i.e., in terms of consecration rather than moral sanctification), but I am not at all convinced on this score. Again, we must remember that the discussion of priesthood in Hebrews is not primarily indebted to discussions in Leviticus. Yet it is also true that in this homily we learn of Jesus's moral perfection as well, for he was tempted like all humans in every regard save without sin. This resistance to sin is conceived of as part of the way he fulfilled his vocation and so could be both perfect high priest and sacrifice.

But there is more to this than one might imagine, for in fact Christ is able to forgive sins and be the perfector/completer of faithfulness for believers leading them on to maturity/completion in their vocation only because he was in a position both to have compassion, knowing their temptations, but also successfully passing such tests so he is in a position to judge sin and offer forgiveness, which he himself did not need to receive.

Now the claim that Jesus was sinless is not very meaningful unless it means he voluntarily and willingly resisted temptation, that is, that it was possible for him to have done otherwise. By definition temptation is not tempting unless one is actually inclined and could attempt to do what one is tempted to do. Thus, we must take seriously statements like we find in Hebrews 2:17 or 4:15 and assume that Jesus was subject to all the common temptations, including sexual ones, that we are, yet he had the victory over them.

We are also told at Hebrews 5:8 that Jesus learned obedience. This of course means he learned through experience, and it may be that he knew it prior to that conceptually, but the point is that Jesus, as a human, learned things through experience just as we do. His life manifested a normal development and progressive consciousness. What is the connection between learning obedience through death and being made perfect through suffering? Simply this, that Jesus fulfilled God's will for his life that he die on Golgotha and so he completed the task that would not have been made perfect and complete without that death.

Our author is able to talk of Jesus as a human being having faith (12:2), indeed being our pioneer or model for faith and faithfulness. One of the key things that sets apart Jesus's work as high priest and all previous such attempts is the unique character of his sacrifice. It is said to be *once for all time*, unlike the previous repeated sacrifices (which shows that they at most only had temporary and limited efficacy, and in fact it appears our author would dispute they even had much of that value). There is a great deal in Hebrews that could lead one to the conclusion that our author was anti-ritual, and/or that he has spiritualized the very material promises in the OT about rest, land, and other things. Against this sort of conclusion, it must be argued that our author in fact maintains that there is only one sacrifice that is and was truly cultic—the sacrifice of the human will of Jesus, and by extension the call for believers to make that same sort of sacrifice through the praise of their lips and lives (cf. Hebrews 13).

It is not the abolition of ritual but its perfection in human form that our author is about, for God ultimately wants the obedience and self-giving of humans, the highest form of his creation; the only form of it that can be in personal relation with its maker, the only form of it that could have Psalm 8 spoken about it. Furthermore, our author does not simply spiritualize the OT like say Philo does in the service of his higher philosophy. Quite the contrary, our author believes that God's promises are now fulfilled in heaven, but that this reality will one day come to earth as well and transform earth. Nor is our author's perspective simply that the OT merely has to do with externals and imperfection. Our author says nothing of the OT being imperfect; he does say it is partial, piecemeal, a shadow, and inadequate finally to deal with human sin. But one must also remember he affirms the essential spiritual promises of God such as those found in Jeremiah 31, and furthermore there is the whole matter of the eternal priesthood of Melchizedek, who is more than a mere shadow; he is a likeness of Christ.

Our author's complaint *is not with the OT per se nor with ritual per se but with a particular ritual system—the Levitical one—which was inadequate.* He never says it was bad or incorrect in its intent, just inadequate to meet human needs. Our author's terminology when he discusses Old and New is comparative, not merely positive—the old is a shadow *in comparison to* the new reality in Christ. Yet there is of course the matter of discontinuity as well, the *once for all* aspect (Heb 9:12). This means that Jesus not only fulfills all the OT priesthood, but he goes beyond it and overcomes its inadequacy.

What is striking about all this high priest language is that our author in this one concept has a way to bridge both the earthly and heavenly work of Christ, for Christ offers the sacrifice on earth, then takes the blood into the heavenly sanctuary and intercedes for us on an ongoing basis, as well as proclaiming sins forgiven. Herein we see the picture of the OT priest sacrificing the animal outside the temple, then taking the blood and pouring it on the altar, and going into the holy of holies on Yom Kippur, and then coming back out and pronouncing forgiveness of sins and reconciliation between God and his people.

Leviticus 16, about the Day of Atonement, is not really cited in the NT, but the material in it comes up repeatedly and is drawn on extensively, for example: v. 2 can be compared to Hebrews 6:19 and 9:7; v. 4 can be compared to Hebrews 10:22; v. 6 can be compared to Hebrews 5:3; v. 12 can be compared to Hebrews 6:19 (cf. Rev 8:5); vv. 14–15 can be compared to Hebrews 9:7; v. 15 alone can be compared to Hebrews 6:19; v. 17 can be compared to Hebrews 5:3; vv. 18–19 can be compared to Hebrews 9:7; v. 20 can be compared to Hebrews 8:2; and finally v. 27 can be compared to Hebrews 13:11.

It is the genius of our author's conceptualizing of things that he is able to bridge the past and the ongoing work of Jesus for believers, as a human being. Our author does seem to operate with the well-known ancient concept of the earth as the vestibule of the heavenly sanctuary. One enters the heavenly sanctuary by passing through the earthly one, and he envisions the sacrifice of Christ as offered in that earthly portico of the heavenly sanctuary, after which he enters into the sanctuary with the blood to sprinkle.

Of course, the analogy with OT practice should not be pressed too far. Does our author really think Jesus took a bowl of his blood with him to heaven? Is there really an altar or curtain in heaven where he sprinkled it? Probably not, but the point is that Jesus effected on earth and in heaven what these ritual acts symbolized: atonement for sin, placation of God's wrath, cleansing of the sinner, reconciliation with God. He conveys these profound concepts by using the OT picture language. In contrast to earthly priests, Jesus is a priest forever, thus forestalling anyone else ever being, or needing to be a priest (this of course has implications for one's view of the pastoral ministry) in this sense. Christ is a priest forever because he lives forever, and as 7:25 says, he always lives to make intercession for believers. Oscar Cullmann sums up his masterful investigation of Christ as high priest in Hebrews by saying the following "The High Priest concept offers a full Christology in every respect. It includes all three fundamental aspects of Jesus' work: his once for all earthly work, his present work as the exalted Lord, and his future work as the one coming again. Yesterday, today and forever."[39]

In closing one might wish to ask how the second coming fits into this schema. The answer intimated by our author is that the high priest had to come forth again from the temple to proclaim to the people the results of his work and the benefits. So also, Christ will come again from the heavenly sanctuary. Thus, we see the single most comprehensive christological concept in the NT, which exalts the perfect human work of Christ the believer's high priest.

After this high ground, much of the rest of what we have to say about the use of Leviticus in the NT will seem rather mundane, but there are a few allusions and echoes worth noticing. In the course of discussing grain offerings in Leviticus 2:13, the writer reminds the listener not to forget to season with salt their offering to God. Mark 9:49 has Jesus say, "Everyone will be salted with fire . . . have salt among yourselves and be at peace with each other." Now the first half of this saying is textually problematic. There are three different variants: (1) everyone will be salted with fire; (2) every sacrifice will be salted with fire; and (3) a combination of both (1) and (2). It seems clear that the combined reading in (3) is surely later, an attempt to

39. Oscar Cullmann, *The Christology of the New Testament*, rev. ed. (Philadelphia: Westminster, 1989), 103–4.

reconcile the two textual traditions. The first rendering, supported by B, L, Δ, and various minuscules has the edge as being original because the second rendering, found in Western texts (D, itb, etc.) reflects the attempt to clarify what Jesus meant by relating it directly to Leviticus 2:13. In Metzger's *Textual Commentary*, we hear this:

> The history of the text seems to have been as follows. At a very early period a scribe, having found in Lev 2.13 a clue to the meaning of Jesus' enigmatic statement, wrote the Old Testament passage in the margin of his copy of Mark. In subsequent copies the marginal gloss was either substituted for the words of the text, thus creating reading (2) or added to the text, thus creating reading (3).[40]

But what is Jesus actually saying? The first bit of the saying seems to be about the coming testing "as through fire" of his disciples. Since salt was also used as a preservative, perhaps the second half of the saying is about having a properly mature or seasoned relationship with other believers, being at peace with one another. But there may also be the lingering overtone that disciples of Jesus are sacrifices offered to God. It depends on how loud the echo of Leviticus 2:13 really is here. Or perhaps one should take this whole discussion of an enigmatic saying of Jesus with a pinch of salt. Obviously, the scribes who copied the aphorisms here had a hard time figuring out what was meant.[41]

Leviticus 7:6, 15 speaks of the privilege of the males in a priest's family to participate in a food offering made by the priest, but they must eat it in the sanctuary area for it is most holy, and v. 15 insists it must all be eaten on the day of the sacrifice itself. It is just possible that this text is echoed in 1 Corinthians 10:18 when Paul reminds his converts that those who eat sacrificial meat are, like priests, "participants in the altar." Paul's point is that if you eat it in the temple, as is described in Leviticus 7, then in fact you are participating in the worship of that deity. It is a holy act, not just another meal eaten in the dining halls of the pagan temple. Paul's concern here is one of venue, not menu, as the rest of the discussion in 1 Corinthians 8–10 makes clear.[42]

Possibly Luke 24:50 is echoing the Aaronic act of blessing with raised hands in Leviticus 9:22, but if so the third evangelist doesn't

---

40. Metzger, *Textual Commentary*, 103.
41. See the whole discussion by Watts, "Mark," 195.
42. See Witherington, *Conflict and Community in Corinth*, 186–230.

make much of it, and in any case praying with lifted up hands, or presumably blessing with the same gesture, was exceedingly common in the ANE and in the world of the NT writers (see, e.g., 1 Timothy 2:8).[43] John the Baptizer is portrayed as following Levitical (or more specifically Nazaritic?) rules in regard to diet (cf. Lev 11:21–22 to Mark 1:6; Matt 3:21). The Pharisees as well, who seem to have wanted all pious Jews to follow the bulk of the Levitical law, are said by Jesus in Matt 23:24 to "strain out gnats" from their drinks, an allusion to Leviticus 11:4.

More important is the command "I am the Lord your God who brought you up from out of the land of Egypt, therefore be holy as I am holy," which we find in Leviticus 11:45 (cf. v. 44) and also in Leviticus 19:2; 20:7–8, 26 and this is of course reiterated in various forms in the NT (see, e.g., 1 Pet 1:16). Note that in the Leviticus text, God's redemptive act is said to be the indicative on which the imperative is based. God's people have been redeemed and they are to mirror his character, however the basic concept of "holiness" in Leviticus is being set apart or distinct from the lifestyles and behavior of the larger non-Hebrew culture. The emphasis is on behavior and praxis, not primarily on a moral condition or a level of sanctification, though that is probably implied.[44] That which is holy is set apart for God, and by God.[45]

What is remarkable about the NT usage of the language of holiness is that it is not exclusively applied to Jews, indeed in various of the letters of the NT it is applied to audiences that are likely mainly gentiles (e.g., 1 Thessalonians). In other words, Jew and gentile united in Christ are now called to be set apart from non-Christ followers (cf. 2 Cor 6:14–7:1). The holiness code has now been applied not just to a broader audience including a few gentile proselytes or God-fearers, but to a majority gentile audience with some Jews included as well. This of course raises the question as to who the people of God are according to the writers of the NT. Paul, in Romans 9–11, insists that God has not forsaken his first set apart or holy people, but that eventually, when Christ returns, they must be integrated back into the people of God through God's mercy, and by grace and through faith in Jesus. Meanwhile, the ethical standards of the new community of

43. See Pao and Schnabel, "Luke," 402.
44. See the discussion in e.g., Carson, "1 Peter," 1017–18 and by Jeffrey A. D. Weima, "1 and 2 Thessalonians," in Beale, *Commentary on the New Testament Use*, 876.
45. See Bellinger, *Leviticus, Numbers*, 76. He is right that holiness involves avoiding uncleanness, but much more is entailed as well.

Jesus are to be even higher or more demanding than those required in the OT in various regards (see Matthew 5–7).

Leviticus 12:3 lays down the rule that Hebrew males are to be circumcised on the eighth day after birth, which is said to be exactly what happened to John at Luke 1:59, but also to Paul in Philippians 3:5. The point is they come from devout, law-abiding Jewish families.[46] Luke 2:24, as part of a conglomerate citation of ideas alludes to Leviticus 12:8, and in this case, it is Jesus's parents who are being portrayed as Torah-true Jews.

Sometimes much has been made of Jesus in Luke 5:14 sending a formerly leprous person to the priest once he has healed the man, following the rules of verification of purity found in Leviticus 13:12–23, (especially v. 19). But this healed man is *not a follower of Jesus*, and Jesus simply wants him to be reintegrated into his normal village life. It is an act of compassion. This is not evidence that Jesus thought his own disciples should follow the rules of clean and unclean in Leviticus. He never tells a disciple, even an ill one, to do this.

The discussion in Mark 7, including the commentary by Mark himself at 7:19, suggests Jesus was not reinforcing such purity laws. Note that we have no evidence at all that Jesus ever used a *mikveh*. Further, anyone who says that nothing that enters a person defiles them, rather it is what comes out of their heart that can defile them, is certainly taking a radical approach to purity laws, as Mark rightly concluded. As with many things, the disciples did not understand Jesus's aphorism at this point, and it took further revelations (see, e.g., Acts 10:9–15 in the case of Peter) for the full implication of Jesus's teaching to become apparent. Matthew 8:4 and Mark 1:44 share a similar background, perhaps primarily in Leviticus 14:2–32 in this case should be evaluated the same way.

Leviticus 15:25 says this: "when a woman has a discharge of blood, for many days at a time, other than her monthly period, or has a discharge that continues beyond her period, she will be unclean as long as she has the discharge, just as in the days of her period." The Hebrew word translated "discharge" indicates a "flowing" or even "gushing forth," and so an abnormal discharge, and so some commentators have suggested that this is a reference to gonorrhea or venereal disease or perhaps more probably obstetric fistula.[47] This is

---

46. This same Levitical text may be alluded to in John 7:22 when Jesus mentions circumcision happening on a Sabbath, presumably because it was that child's eighth day.
47. See http://tinyurl.com/y8lfft2d and Bellinger, *Leviticus, Numbers*, 97.

of direct relevance to the understanding of Mark 5:25 and Matthew 9:20. The woman in question who encounters Jesus on the way to Jairus's house is perpetually unclean. Why? The woman has tried various doctors and is now in desperation, wanting contact with "the great physician," and she is healed. Unlike the case with the lepers, Jesus says nothing to her about going and showing herself to the priest, and perhaps her situation was less dire, since it was not a visible, tangible matter, unlike the case with people with skin diseases, but if venereal disease is alluded to then she might well have carried an unpleasant odor, and her condition been known. This might be why she seems to be operating with some caution, trying to avoid drawing attention to herself. In any case, Jesus wants to make clear to her that magic from a holy cloth did not heal her, rather her faith healed her. What is important in this story is twofold: (1) The woman probably did follow the Levitical laws, but no cleansing in a *mikveh* was ever sufficient since she kept on bleeding. It is possible as well that if she lived in a small village and consulted various doctors, her condition was known to others. But unlike lepers, Leviticus doesn't counsel such a woman to go around shouting "watch out, I'm unclean and can make you unclean by touch." (2) Thus, she may not have been shunned, or been worried about being in a crowd watching the passing Jesus.

The prohibition against eating animal blood in Leviticus 17:10–14 is sometimes thought to explain the similar prohibition in Acts 15:20, and that may be correct, however the prohibitions in Acts 15 are in a group and they involve "the pollutions of idols," "things strangled," as well as blood and sexual immorality; and the context of Acts 15, as well as the content of 1 Corinthians 8–10 suggests the subject is about where one would find these four things together, namely in pagan temple feasts. Leviticus 17:10–14 is not about dining in a pagan temple where one would find all four of these things, and in Leviticus the prohibition is because "the life is in the blood" and meat with blood in it is what is in view there.[48] So, in this case the NA^{28} is perhaps wrong to suggest such an allusion.[49]

The primary source of the NT use of the exhortation "be holy as I am holy" seems likely to be Leviticus 19:2 at 1 Peter 1:16 (but see below). Less convincing is the suggestion of the NA^{28} that this verse

---

48. See Bellinger, *Leviticus, Numbers*, 107–8.

49. See my full discussion in Ben Witherington III, *What's in the Word: Rethinking the Socio-rhetorical Character of the New Testament* (Waco, TX: Baylor University Press, 2009), 89–101.

is the background to "be ye perfect . . . " in Matthew 5:48, much less the exhortation "be ye merciful/compassionate" in Luke 6:36. Leviticus 19:12 is one of those examples where Jesus contrasts his own teaching with that of the Holiness Code. Matthew 5:33 indicates that swearing should be avoided altogether, not merely false swearing.

Leviticus 19:15 is worth citing at this juncture: "do not pervert justice; do not show partiality to the poor or favoritism to the great, but judge your neighbors fairly." This sounds rather clearly like the opposite of talk about "a preferential option for the poor," though there are plenty of places in the Pentateuch that talk about taking care of poor widows and orphans. The Hebrew verb in this verse usually translated partiality, actually speaks of "lifting of the face," a gesture showing favor or even favoritism.[50] NA[28] thinks that this text may stand in the background behind Acts 23. More clearly James 2:9 seems to draw on this Levitical teaching in saying that if you show favoritism (in this case to the rich) you sin and are being convicted by the law. This teaching is juxtaposed with a quoting of the love your neighbor command Leviticus 19:18 just before it in James 2:8, where the command is called "the royal law" that is "according to Scripture."

James, it should be remembered, is speaking to Jewish-Christian groups outside the holy land, groups where Leviticus would be known and respected. As Carson points out, the verb used here is not the usual one for "keep," it is in fact τελέω.[51] He rightly points out the contrast between vv. 8 and 9: "If you really fulfill the royal law. . . . But if you show favoritism." I agree with the suggestion that "king's" or royal law here probably points to Jesus's repristinizing of the love commandment, in view of the fact that some twenty times in this document there is a repurposing of the teaching of Jesus, chiefly from the Sermon on the Mount.[52]

Leviticus 20 is alluded to or echoed twice in 1 Peter 1, once at v. 16 where 20:7 seems to be in view, and in the very same Petrine verse, 20:16 comes to the fore. While these are rules about the consecration and holiness of priests, Peter, because he affirms the priesthood of all believers, is applying them to his whole audience.

Leviticus 20:9 refers to the penalty for cursing one's parents. But do the Gospels cite this verse? First, we note that there is a very interest-

50. Bellinger, *Leviticus, Numbers*, 118.

51. Carson, "James," 998.

52. On this particular text and on the discussion of the reuse of Jesus's teaching in James see Witherington, *Letters and Homilies for Jewish Christians*, 459–60 for this text, and 394–95 for a listing of the reuse of Jesus's teaching in James.

ing difference between the Matthean and Markan citings of the OT at this point. In Matthew 15:4 Jesus says "and God says 'honor . . . ,'" whereas Mark 7:10 has "and Moses says 'honor. . . .'" It is surprising that the first evangelist would alter the Markan text in this way, unless of course he is really not all that concerned about pursuing a comparison/contrast of Jesus and Moses.

In fact, we find this same imperative in Exodus 21:17, and the Matthean and Markan versions seem to be citing the LXX version of that verse. Both Matthew and Mark have Ὁ κακολογῶν πατέρα ἢ μητέρα θανάτῳ τελευτάτω, and the LXX of Exodus 21:17 is ὁ κακολογῶν πατέρα αὐτοῦ ἢ μητέρα αὐτοῦ τελευτήσει θανάτῳ. Notice that the LXX of Leviticus 20:9, like the Exodus example, also has the word "his" before father and mother but neither of the Gospel texts have that modifier. On the whole, it appears the LXX, not the Hebrew, is being followed in these Gospel texts, and in particular it is the LXX of Exodus 21:17 rather than of Leviticus.

Falling into the category of background material is Leviticus 20:10, which speaks of what is to be done when a man commits adultery with his neighbor's wife. The penalty is the death of both of them. This is likely the text alluded to in John 8:5, though obviously it is being used selectively, since only the woman is being brought forth for stoning. Jesus is being tested in that scene, but in fact he perceives that his testers are misusing the Levitical text to try and trap him into condemning the woman in question. The elders of the community were responsible for the rectitude of the community, and selective enforcement of the law was unacceptable. Where was the man caught in adultery? Hence, Jesus accuses the moral arbiters in this case by saying, "let those without sin [in this matter] cast the first stone." Here knowing the Levitical text condemns both the adulterer and adulteress to death makes clear that the law was not being upheld on this occasion, and Jesus will not be a party to such selective application of the law. Notice however that he is far from condoning the woman's action either: "go and sin no more."[53]

Probably Leviticus 20:13 and 18:22 lie in the background of Paul's comment in Romans 1:27 condemning same sex sexual activity between men, having already condemned the same activity between women in Romans 1:26. But Leviticus only refers to the former, not the latter. The phrase "even their women" in 1:26 makes evident the subject is gentile women, a case not treated in Leviticus, which

53. See the detailed discussion in Witherington, *John's Wisdom*, 362–66.

focuses on Hebrew males and their behavior. In other words, Paul is going beyond the clear strictures in Leviticus in Romans 1. John the Baptizer, in objecting to the incestuous union between Herod Antipas and Herodias, his brother's wife, seems to be drawing on Leviticus 20:21. What we see in this rather varied use of Leviticus 20 is that, as Moyise pointed out, the Holiness Code portion of Leviticus is seen as still applicable to the followers of Jesus.

Leviticus 21:9 is the source of the description of judgment on Babylon the harlot in Revelation 17:19, as in both cases the prostitute is to be burned. John of Patmos clearly enough had a detailed knowledge of the whole of the Pentateuch, including Leviticus, and it provided material for his apocalyptic descriptions of coming judgment, among other things.

Leviticus 23:29 appears to be cited in Acts 3:23, but the original context is about denying oneself and those who refuse to do so shall be cut off from God's people, whereas Peter is talking about anyone refusing to listen to the prophet Moses spoke about. That person will be cut off from God's people. Now clearly enough Deuteronomy 18:15–19 is also in view in Acts 3:19, but it says nothing about excommunicating someone who does not listen to the prophet (though v. 19 mentions God holding persons accountable for not listening). So, this would appear to be another conglomerate citation or allusion. Here the detailed discussion by Marshall is helpful.[54] While some have speculated about the use of a *testimonia* here, presumably by Luke, it is surely just as likely that we are dealing with a conglomerate paraphrase from memory.

While one could argue that John 12:13 alludes to Leviticus 23:40, the latter is talking about a very different festival, the fall festival after crops have been gathered, not the Passover. Far more likely is the fact that palm branches were waved to celebrate the Maccabean victory in retaking Jerusalem, though of course that full celebration became the postbiblical Hanukkah festival.

Leviticus 24:4–9 is the backdrop to the discussion in Mark 2:26, Matthew 12:4, and Luke 6:4. The original text of course speaks about bread for Aaron and his sons, not for King David, and not during the reign of Abiathar as high priest either. An incident from 1 Samuel 21 is in the foreground in these Gospel texts. Abiathar was certainly the more famous of the priests in that era, and Maurice Casey has pro-

---

54. See Marshall, "Acts," 546–48.

vided a helpful explanation for this text.[55] One associated an era with
the most famous figures in the era, in this case David and Abiathar.
The shewbread was meant for priests, but Jesus thinks that David's
action, in a time of need, was appropriate. The *chreia* ends with the
statement "humankind was not made for the Sabbath, but the Sabbath for humankind." That is, the laws were written to benefit human
beings, not to prevent them from receiving such benefits. What better day to make sure that hunger and other needs "cease" than the
Sabbath, just as Jesus would suggest what better day to give people
relief from disease or demon possession—isn't this the very essence of
Shabbat shalom—wholeness?

We have discussed the blasphemy punishment procedures above,
but it is in order to point out now that Leviticus 24:14, not just 24:16,
is alluded to in an odd assortment of places: Mark 15:20; Acts 7:58;
and Hebrews 13:14. The oddest of the bunch is the exhortation in
Hebrews 13:13 to go outside the camp and bear the shame with Jesus
of being a blasphemer, presumably alluding to Mark 15:20. This is a
very different sort of intertextual echo between two NT texts or at
least an event in the life of Jesus and a later NT text. Leviticus 24:17
is important because Jesus cites it as a basis for forbidding killing
entirely. Unlike texts in Exodus or Deuteronomy, here in Leviticus
the prohibition seems to be absolute, and no exceptions are listed in
the immediate context for private individuals. Judicial punishments,
for example of blasphemers, are taken to be a separate issue.

The echo of Leviticus 25:10 in Luke 4:19 has led to elaborate theories about Jesus bringing in a year of Jubilee through his ministry.[56]
But Jesus's message is about the coming of God's dominion on earth,
not just a periodic sabbatical year for the people and the land. Nevertheless, some of the agendas of the Jubilee are said to be coming true
in the ministry of Jesus.

While the Paul of the letters doesn't much have recourse to Leviticus, it is interesting that in Acts 14:17, Paul is depicted as turning a
promise of God in Leviticus 26:4 into an indicative statement of what
God has done. Leviticus 26:11–12 is paraphrased in 2 Corintians 6:16,
though a unique citation formula is used ("as God said"). It is not

55. See my discussion of Maurice Casey, *Aramaic Sources of Mark's Gospel*, SNTSMS 102
(Cambridge: Cambridge University Press, 1998) and his retrojection of this back into Aramaic
(which he assumes was the original), in Witherington, *Gospel of Mark*, 130. Much depends on
how one takes the preposition ἐπί here.

56. Sharon Ringe, *Jesus, Liberation, and the Biblical Jubilee: Images for Ethics and Christology*
(Eugene, OR: Wipf & Stock, 2004).

found elsewhere in the NT. While the quotation in Corinthians is in the third person, the OT text is in fact in the second person, the LXX as well as the Hebrew, with the LXX reading: "And I will place my tent among you, and my soul shall not abhor you. And I will walk about among you and will be your God, and you shall be a for me a nation." Paul has in fact combined two texts, with the latter part of the quotation coming from Jeremiah 32:38 though with reverse order of the clauses. Obviously talk about a particular nation would not suit Paul's mixed audience of Jews and gentiles in Corinth. There may even be a third text in Paul's mind, Ezekiel 37:27.

Such composite citations suggest strongly that Paul is just quoting from memory and the texts have been blended together in his mental Cuisinart. Of course, there is a difference between saying "I will live amongst them" and "I will set my tabernacle/dwelling place amongst them," the latter referring to a specific dwelling place, not just a general divine presence among God's people.[57] What this should tell us is that Paul is not doing contextual exegesis of the OT, even when he offers a conglomerate citation or paraphrase. He is using key ideas from the OT text, and applying them in a new way to his own audience. Actually, Revelation 21:3, 7 is in some ways closer to Leviticus 26:12 than the Pauline text.

NUMBERS

If the cupboard was relatively bear in the case of Leviticus when it comes to its use in the NT, this is much more the case with the book of Numbers. No lengthy passages in Numbers come up for any major treatment in the NT. We will have to content ourselves with a few notable uses, and some minor examples of the use of names, terms, ideas, or allusion to OT events here and there.

THE SEVENTY: NUMBERS 11:16–17

Numbers 11:16–17 has Moses being told by God to bring him seventy elders and officers of the people and they are to take them to the tent of meeting where, "I will come down and speak with you there. I will take some of the Spirit who is on you and put the Spirit on

57. See the helpful discussion by Peter Balla, "2 Corinthians," in Beale, *Commentary on the New Testament Use*, 769–72.

them. They will help you bear the burden of the people, so that you do not to have to bear it by yourself." This on first glance seems to be the background for Luke 10:1, except that unfortunately we have a textual problem. Major Alexandrian and Western witnesses have seventy-two rather than seventy (p75, B, D), as do most of the old Latin and Sinaitic Syriac manuscripts. On the other hand, Aleph, L, Δ and numerous other important manuscripts support the number seventy. Kurt Aland argues strongly for seventy-two, not least because it is the more difficult reading.[58] There are several problems with this conclusion. For one thing, Luke in Luke 9:49–50 seems to have just alluded to Numbers 11:24–30 where Eldad and Medad are not to be stopped by Joshua from prophesying just because they are not part of the group of seventy elders. It makes sense that he would continue the trend at the beginning of Luke 10. It needs to be remembered that the seventy are appointed in addition to the Twelve.

In a forthcoming commentary on the Gospel of Luke, Amy-Jill Levine and I argue as follows:

"The use of numbers in the Gospels can be symbolic, and that the manuscript tradition records both the numbers 70 and 72 suggests that early scribes did think of the number as symbolic." [Metzger, *Textual Commentary*, 150] Determining what it symbolizes cannot, however, be done with mathematical precision. The number "70" itself shows up 77 times in the Christian Bible (NRSV), and any text can be seen as informing this scene, whether Luke intended the allusion or not. The number 70 recollects the seventy members of Jacob's family (Gen 46:27b mentions that "all the persons of the house of Jacob who came into Egypt were seventy") and so can suggest that the disciples reflect the people Israel. According to Exod 24:9, 70 elders accompanied Moses and Aaron to see God on Mt. Sinai. The Mishnah, Sanh. 1:6, perhaps following this notice, states that the "Great Sanhedrin," the Jerusalem court, had 71 members. In Num 11:16–30, Moses appoints seventy men to be filled with the spirit, but then two more receive the gift as well—Eldad and Medad. Luke's 72 could then allude to the people who saw God on Mt. Sinai, or who were filled with the spirit in the wilderness, or who served as leaders of the earlier community. Josephus states that the Zealots, whose primary purpose was to expel Rome from the land of Israel, had 70 judges (likely in imitation also of Numbers 11; see *War* 4.336). Luke, who may have been familiar with Josephus's writings, can be seen as offering a counter-revolutionary model: Jesus's 70 are not to engage in violent struggle; theirs is another model for another Kingdom.

58. In Metzger, *Textual Commentary*, 150–51.

Alternatively, the 70 might suggest the traditional view that there are 70 nations of the world (Gen 10:2–31; see also *Jubilees* 44.34). The Septuagint states that there are 72 nations, and the *Letter of Aristeas* 46–50 records that 72 scribes translated the Torah into Greek, so the third evangelist, who knew the Septuagint, or copyists, may have adapted the number to fit the Greek texts and so anticipate the gentile mission. Or again, Luke may have been looking for a number that suggested fullness or completion, or even critical mass.[59]

Since Luke says nothing about these seventy or seventy-two evangelizing gentiles a reference to the table of nations in Genesis 10–11 seems less likely than an allusion to Numbers 11.[60]

THE SNAKE ON A STICK: NUMBERS 21:8–9

Numbers 21:8–9 is the famous "snake on a stick" story, where the image on the pole is to be gazed upon in order to cure snakebite, and we are told this method had a 100 percent success rate. The story is interesting in several respects. First of all, this incident provides us with the last of the examples of the rebellions of God's people due to impatience in having still not arrived in the promised land (see 20:14–21). They once more complain, "why have you brought us to the desert to die," and then moan that the manna is miserable. In response to this God sends them venomous snakes and many Israelites die as a result of being bitten. The evidence, as we have it, suggests that there were indeed numerous different poisonous snakes in that desert: horned vipers, puff-adders, cobras, and the very lethal carpet viper.[61] While the word *nahash*, the general word for serpent, is used at the outset of the story, when one gets to the bit about the bronze snake on the pole a different word, *sarap* is used, which refers to a poisonous snake whose bite burns, hence the old translation "fiery serpents." The story should be compared to the one in Numbers 11 where deaths also occurred, apparently as a judgment for rebellion.

The Israelites then repent, but God does not remove the snakes, instead he instructs Moses to make a bronze snake and stick it up on a pole where all can see it, and apparently by gazing intently at it, one can be healed or at least one is allowed to go on living. This is

---

59. Amy-Jill Levine and Ben Witherington III, *The Gospel of Luke*, NCBC (Cambridge: Cambridge University Press, forthcoming).

60. Pao and Schnabel, "Luke," 316–17.

61. R. Dennis Cole, *Numbers*, NAC 3B (Nashville: Broadman & Holman, 2000), 347.

supposed to remind the people to both confess and to turn to God for healing. While God removed the problem after the repentance in earlier rebellions, *here he does not do so*. Is the snake supposed to remind the people of their previous idolatries? Is it some kind of aversion ritual meant to give power over the snakes and their bites? Is it an example of sympathetic magic, which is to say the controlling of an adversary through manipulation of a replication? Perhaps it is best to say we don't know and let sleeping snakes lie. The story in Numbers does not make this matter clear, but in an interesting sequel in 2 Kings 18:1–8 we hear of King Hezekiah removing Moses's bronze serpent, called *Nehushtan* from the temple because the people had come to treat it as an idol! This will have transpired several hundred years after the time of Moses.[62]

This is, of course, the background to John 3:14, and in that Gospel there is at least a double entendre involved in the use of the phrase "lifted up": namely lifted up on the cross, like the snake on the pole, but also, lifted up into heaven by God thereafter and so exalted to the right hand of God. Köstenberger's remarks are apt:

> Nicodemus, on the basis of the analogy of Num 21, was called to turn to Jesus for new birth in much the same way as the ancient Israelites were commanded to turn to the bronze snake for new life. . . . Jesus' adduction of the account in Num 21 and John's inclusion of this instance of Jesus' use of Scripture in his Gospel are part of a very broad exodus typology or Moses/exodus typology that pervades much of this Gospel.[63]

More insightful is Hays observation that the verb "lifted up" is not to be found in the Numbers 21 text. Moses is told to "set" the serpent image on the pole; the text relates that he put it there. Why then does John 3 use the verb? Because he is also drawing on Isaiah 52:13–53:12 where we do indeed here about the lifting up of the servant (52:13 LXX). Hays calls this a case of complex intertextual overlay: "The three images of Son of Man [from Daniel 7], bronze serpent, and Suffering Servant are projected on top of one another and all together interpreted as prefigurations of the Gospel story of Jesus' death and resurrection." John 12:31–33 confirms this reading of what is happening here.

It would appear that John has performed an astonishing intertextual

---

62. See the discussion in Bellinger, *Leviticus, Numbers*, 261.
63. Köstenberger, "John," 437.

fusion of Daniel 7:13–14, Numbers 21, and Isaiah 52:13. The intertextual fusion *occurs entirely in the hidden realms of allusion and echo, without any explicit quotations of the Old Testament textual precursors.* Yet the theological result of this fusion is explosive: it generates an interpretation of Jesus' death on the cross as the triumphant exaltation of the Son of Man.[64]

Hays is quite right, and it is a cautionary reminder that merely studying the direct citations of the OT in the NT does not give one the full impression or impact of the OT on the NT, and on the thinking and writing of the NT writers.[65]

"LIKE SHEEP WITHOUT A SHEPHERD": NUMBERS 27:17

Numbers 27:17 with its phrases "bring them in and bring them out" and "like sheep without a shepherd" is one of clearest verbal echoes of all in the NT that derives from the book of Numbers. We may compare Mark 6:34, Matthew 9:36, and John 10:9. The phrase is prefaced by a reference to "the Lord's community" and the Lord in question in the three Gospel allusions is of course Jesus rather than Yahweh. John 10:9 draws on the "coming and going" part of the Numbers text whereas the earlier Gospels draw more directly on the more familiar phrase "like a sheep without a shepherd." It is a mystery to me why anyone should think that the two Synoptic passages primarily allude to Ezekiel 34:5 that speaks of sheep scattered due to a lack of a shepherd.[66] The implication of the use of the phrase in Matthew and Mark is that Jesus is the one God appointed to lead his sheep, which should be clear since in Numbers the issue is compassion through a leader who can gather the sheep.[67]

---

64. Hays, *Echoes of Scripture in the Gospels*, 335 (emphasis added).
65. Many scholars think this reflects John's theology of Jesus rather than Jesus's creative use of the OT. See, e.g., Moyise, *Jesus and Scripture*, 73–74. I am not sure he is correct, in view of the very creative way Jesus drew on Ps 110:1. Perhaps it is a both/and rather than either/or situation here. John has made explicit something that Jesus left more implicit about such texts.
66. But see Blomberg, "Matthew," 35. There is no discussion at all by Watts of the Mark parallel in the same volume.
67. At least this issue is clearer than the famous conundrum of Num 25:9 compared to 1 Cor 10:8 where the former texts says 24,000 died and the latter text says 23,000. Paul could just be citing from memory, but it is not compelling to appeal to the fact that he is using round numbers. So is the author of Numbers, but it's a different round number. The LXX of Num 25:9 has τέσσαρες καὶ εἴκοσι χιλιάδες, whereas Paul clearly has τρεῖς χιλιάδες. Is he thinking of Num 26:62? But if so, that is a different matter.

THE LEXICON OF FAITH:
THE BROADER USE OF NUMBERS

Numbers 6 provides the rules about Nazaritic vows that is assumed and alluded to vaguely in texts like Acts 18:18 and Acts 21:24, 26 both in reference to temporary Nazaritic vows like the one Paul undertook and more permanent ones, like John the Baptizer took. In fact, Numbers 6:3 is briefly quoted in Luke 1:15 in regard to the beverage restrictions to be observed by John the son of Zechariah.

Numbers 9:12, a reiteration of Exodus 12:46, refers to the restrictions in regard to the Passover lamb: "they may not leave any of it until morning, or break any of its bones." The third person usage in both Numbers 9:12 and John 19:36 but not in Exodus 12:46 makes the former text the primary one being draw on from the Pentateuch here, but the exact verbal form in John 19:36 is found in Psalm 33:21 LXX, συντριβήσεται. This provides background for the citation in John 19:36 where we are told that what happened to Jesus on the cross fulfilled this Scripture. This of course is part of the larger picture of Jesus as the Passover lamb of God already announced near the beginning at John 1:36. While Hays finds curious that a Gospel that says Moses wrote about Jesus (5:46) would make so little use of the Pentateuch as christological prophecy, at least here at John 19:36 we find some evidence of it.[68] Psalm 34:20 is also in view here, a text that says that God will protect the bones of the righteous sufferer. Once again John offers a conglomerate citation. So, near the beginning of his Gospel Jesus is compared to the snake in the desert as well as the Lamb of God, and at the end those two images hover in the background again when Jesus is lifted up on the cross but has no bones broken.[69]

Numbers 12:3, which informs us that Moses was the most humble man on the face of the earth, may be the text that is partially echoed in Matthew 11:29, the famous yoke saying. This seems likely for a variety of reasons: (1) Jesus's yoke is being compared favorably with that of Moses; (2) Jesus himself, like Moses is said to be humble of heart.

Numbers 19 and the discussion about purification comes up in Hebrews 9 in that author's contrast between the effectiveness and

68. Hays, *Echoes of Scriptures in the Gospels*, 286–87.
69. See the discussion by Köstenberger, "John," 503–4. Whether it is right to call this typology or not can be debated; prefigurement might be a better term.

benefits of the Mosaic covenant and that of the new covenant. The point, particularly in Hebrews 9:13–28, is made by the phrase "how much more." The sacrifice of Christ provides more—and more lasting—benefits than the Mosaic rituals. The author does not say there was no efficacy to what Moses did, he simply says it has been eclipsed and supplanted by the actions of Christ. But in fact, it is primarily Exodus 24, rather than Numbers 19, that our author is thinking of here.[70]

The story of Balaam, told in Numbers 22–24, and then with a coda in Numbers 31, stands in the background of the assertions in 2 Peter 2:15 and Revelation 2:14 but there is no quotation in either case, and it is not clear that either of these texts is alluding to the brief references in Numbers 31. It seems more likely the fuller story in Numbers 22–24 is in mind. Probably Numbers 23:19 lies in the background of Hebrews 6:18 because in both texts there is a reference to the impossibility of God lying, and that same Numbers verse includes the notion that God does not change his mind either. Yes, Psalm 110:4 is also probably alluded to in Heb. 6:18.[71]

The expression "a thorn in my side" draws on Numbers 33:55, and as familiar as that is, it probably should not be seen as the background to 2 Corinthians 12:7. For one thing, the LXX of the verse in Numbers is βολίδες ἐν ταῖς πλευραῖς ὑμῶν, whereas Paul has σκόλοψ τῇ σαρκί so there is no direct verbal echo. For another thing, Paul is talking about Satan, not mere human adversaries, and the highly metaphorical quality of Numbers 33:55 is rather different from the actual pain in the flesh Paul is alluding to.

Finally, Numbers 35:30 seems to stand in the background of Hebrews 10:28 though it is not directly cited. The idea here is that no one should be put to death on the testimony of just one witness, indeed Hebrews says it requires two or three witnesses before judgment without mercy could be executed. Numbers 35:30 is more specific: a murderer is the subject of the discussion, and notice that the assumption is that the person in question did actually commit murder, but that without the testimony of more than one witness, he should not be executed. One wonders if this policy did more to protect the guilty than the innocent victims of such a crime, but in either case it makes clear just how seriously the law viewed the deliberate taking

70. See Guthrie, "Hebrew," 974–75.
71. See Guthrie, "Hebrew," 966–67.

of human life. There was not even an atoning sacrifice that could be offered for such a "sin with a high hand."

CONCLUSIONS

While it was quite easy to see the obvious influence of Genesis and Exodus on the writings of the NT, this was not the case when dealing with Leviticus and Numbers, with rare exceptions. There are a host of reasons for this. For one thing, Numbers reads like the further similar adventures of God's people to those already recorded in Exodus. Second verse, same as the first, when it comes to rebellions and wanderings; and the Exodus stories were more seminal and formative on an ongoing basis for the character of God's people. One may wonder why more is not made of the rather telling and even humorous stories about Balaam in the NT, but one must remember that if we look at the types of literature we find in the NT, there is only one book of prophecy, the book of Revelation. Otherwise, figures like Balaam, however notorious, only come up for passing reference when a NT writer is dealing with things like false teachers and pseudoprophets of his own era. Still, we have found a few tales in Numbers, especially the "snake on a stick" story, that caught the eye of NT writers and were drawn upon to make clear the full significance of Christ and the Christ event.

It is proper to add as well that since Numbers is basically a book for a people that are a nation of sorts, and involved in what we might call national politics (land claims, battles, laws for the newly settled, etc.), it is no surprise that not much of this carries over into the NT. The followers of Jesus were not an ethnically specific entity. They did not seek to be a nation with their own piece of land to live in as a collective entity. Their battles were not military ones, and they did not choose to use such weapons for resolving the human conflicts they did have. Indeed, there was an entirely new ethic, the one we find summarized in Matthew 5–7 and Romans 12–13, that the followers of Jesus were trying to live into, and to live by. This made the substance of many of the chapters in Numbers only tangentially relevant to their own faith journeys and lives.

The silence of the NT about Numbers 24:17, "I see him, but not now; I behold him, but not near, a star will come out of Jacob, a scepter will arise out of Israel" might be surprising if the NT was written in the second century CE, for this was the signal prophecy adopted and applied to Simon bar Koseba in the 130s CE during the second Jewish revolt, and the text was already quoted at Qumran as a messianic prophecy in the War Scroll and elsewhere, but not so in the NT. The writers of the NT were not looking for another military leader to "crush Moab," or in this case, Rome. Neither Matthew 2:2 (the magi see a star in the east), nor Revelation 22:16 (Jesus as the morning star) likely allude to that prophecy. The first deals with an astrological sign, not a written prophecy, the second refers to Jesus as the morning star, which *might* allude to the text in Numbers in passing, but it must not be forgotten that Martial (*Epigrams* Book 8) during the very era when Revelation was written had called the Emperor Domitian himself the morning star, and the criticism of Domitian in Revelation seems pretty clear. He's not the morning star, he is the antichrist figure! This could be another example in the NT of Christ is the reality of which the emperor is but a sad parody.[72]

As for Leviticus, yes there were some central commandments such as the love command that Jesus and his followers could and did draw on for a community ethic, but there was also an alien character to Leviticus, of a different sort than with Numbers, that made it a book more difficult to adopt and adapt for Christian purposes. For one thing, the new religious praxis of the followers of Jesus did not involve a class of human priests, or literal sacrifices, or temples, or tabernacles, or tents. Indeed, there was a growing and profound theology in the NT, especially in evidence in Hebrews, but not absent in Paul and 1 Peter and elsewhere, that the whole Mosaic sacerdotal system had been eclipsed, and indeed been made obsolete by the life, death, and resurrection of Jesus, especially his once for all persons, once for all sins, sacrifice on the cross. That being the case, the use of a book like Leviticus could involve images, ideas, language, but not a wholesale appropriation of the pith and substance of the book applied to a different group of people. The priesthood of all believers, both Jew and gentile, and the heavenly high priesthood of Christ made unnecessary a special class of male Levitical priests, later called clergy.

There is some irony, but also tragedy, in the fact that when Christianity was finally allowed to be a public religion from the time of Constantine on, the church of deacons and elders and bishops and prophets and teachers and evangelists which met in caves in Cap-

---

72. See Ben Witherington III, *Commentary on Revelation*, NCBC (Cambridge: Cambridge University Press, 2003) on Rev 22:16.

padocia, or in homes throughout the Roman Empire well and truly turned into a church of priests, temples, and sacrifices, just like their Greco-Roman counterparts. Just as in the OT times when God's people longed to be a nation like other nations with a proper king, at the expense of the original theocracy, so when the opportunity arose, God's NT people longed to be a religion like other ancient religions, and the character of ministry and worship and service was changed forever. This is what happens when the original more radical vision of a Jesus or a Paul or a John in regard to the relationship of the OT institutions to the newly arriving dominion of God, is domesticated, and a different sort of OT hermeneutic is substituted for what we find in the NT itself.

By this I mean, "the church above ground" by and large appropriated the OT in a very different way than the Jesus movement had done in the first three centuries of its existence, as witnessed in all the chapters of these three books on intertexuality. Ministers became priests, the Lord's Supper became a sacrifice of the Mass, meeting places became temples or "churches," Sunday became the Sabbath, the rules about Levitical priests dictated that women could not serve in those capacities going forward in the "public church," and so on. In other words, the profound "forward" reading of the OT into the NT and its religious praxis and ministry eclipsed the original profound backward reading of the OT in light of the Christ event.

The loss of eschatological vision in regard to the new roles of women and men in the new movement, and the loss of understanding of what the *ekklesia* was meant to be was profound.[73] To a considerable extent, this loss of eschatological vision happened because of a loss of understanding of the role the OT actually played and was meant to play in the writings of the NT and in the communities formed by those writings.

But all of this should not be laid at the doorstep of Constantine and his successors. As Ramsay MacMullen showed several years ago, there had always been a "second church," a group of Christians not prepared to give up on various aspects of their Greco-Roman religion in order to be followers of Christ.[74] They had continued to practice celebrations with the dead in graveyards, and so continued the "cult of

---

73. See the discussion in Ben Witherington III, *Women and the Genesis of Christianity* (Cambridge: Cambridge University Press, 1990).

74. See Ramsay MacMullen, *The Second Church: Popular Christianity A.D. 200–400*, WGR-WSup 1 (Atlanta: Society of Biblical Literature, 2009).

the ancestors." They had practiced proxy baptism for their departed loved ones. They had felt that syncretism between the early Jewish character of the Jesus movement and some aspects of Greco-Roman religion could be appropriate, without compromising the essentials of the new faith.

This syncretism had gone on, and been fought against repeatedly in the first three centuries of church history, and the NT itself bears witness to the ongoing struggle to be something different from "religion" as it was then known and practiced, whether Greco-Roman or Jewish sacerdotal religion. Part of the battle, since God's people are people of a sacred book, was how to interpret the sacred book, and we must never forget that the only "Scripture" the earliest Christians had at first, was the OT itself.

Yet, the story of how they drew on and handled those OT texts at the outset of Christianity is a story involving a very different sort of hermeneutic than we see beginning to raise its head with figures like Ignatius of Antioch, or with some of the other Apostolic Fathers or later Clement of Alexandria and others. In some ways, it appears that perhaps Marcion and the Gnostics forced the issue of deciding what sorts of use could or should be made of the OT by Christians. Consider for a moment the words of Ptolemaeus, the second century Valentinian Gnostic, in his Letter to Flora:

> For it is clear that the Law, which is secondary, was not ordained by the perfect God and Father, since it is imperfect, lacks completion [by Christ] and contains commandments alien to the nature and purpose of such a God. Again, the Law cannot be attributed to the injustice of the Adversary, for it opposes injustice. Both of these opinions follow from not attending to what was said by the Savior. . . . Again that part of the Law which is from God himself is divided into three parts: (1) into pure legislation, free from evil, which is rightly called Law and which the Savior "came not to destroy but to complete" (for that which he fulfilled was not alien from him, or it could not have been perfected); and (2) into that part bound up with lower things and injustice, a law which the Savior abrogated as alien to his own nature; and it is divided also (3) into that part which is typical and symbolical, legislated as images of spiritual and better things, which the Savior transformed from the sensible and phenomenal into the spiritual and invisible. And that pure Law of God free from evil is none other than the Decalogue.[75]

75. Here I am drawing on the translation of the Letter to Flora, probably written to Christians in Rome in the second century, by Robert Grant, *Second Century Christianity: A Collection of Fragments*, 2nd ed. (Louisville: Westminster John Knox, 2003), 63–65.

This bears witness to the struggle even in the Roman church in the second century to figure out exactly how and what parts of the OT could be appropriated and used by the church, and in what ways. Ptolemaeus is prepared to suggest that some of the OT is not really sacred Scripture for Christians, but rather is manmade. The writers of the NT suggest nothing of this sort. The matter was not settled in the second century, but the hermeneutic was already shifting.

Leviticus was to rise to prominence again as a guide for Christian priesthood. Numbers was to become important again, because the church needed to eliminate false prophets, and focus on its legitimate day-to-day ministers of the sacrifices. Indeed, some felt it needed to silence the voices of prophets altogether.[76] Theologies of sacred zones and locales would once again become important, despite Jesus's teaching that "neither on Mt. Gerizim nor on Mt. Zion," but whenever and wherever worship was practiced in Spirit and in truth would be true worship. To their credit, the writers of the NT boldly went through the doors cracked open by the ministry of Jesus and the writings of such early Christians as Paul and the anonymous author of Hebrews, probably a Pauline protégé. Their approach to the OT is consistently respectful, but also creative and meant to be in accord with the new thing God had done in the Christ event, the new covenant that he had inaugurated.

We must turn now to the last of the Law, the so-called "second law," Deuteronomy, and we will discover that this book had far more impact on the writers of the NT than Leviticus and Numbers, indeed more than Exodus, and in some ways slightly more even than Genesis. It is important that we fully take into consideration the plethora of uses of Deuteronomy in the NT. In some ways this is unsurprising, because Deuteronomy had already become the go-to book of the Law for many early Jews.

---

76. For a creative and entertaining take on the attempts to silence the voice of prophecy in the "official" medieval church see Umberto Eco's classic novel *The Name of the Rose* (Boston: Mariner, 2014).

5.

Deuteronomy and the Demise of Moses

And finally, it was Deuteronomy that brought about the historical result of Josiah's reformation.

—Julius Wellhausen[1]

Perhaps it comes as something of a surprise that Deuteronomy is the third most used book of the OT when it comes to quotations, allusions, and echoes in the NT, behind Isaiah and the Psalms. It becomes somewhat less of a surprise if in fact the Deuteronomistic form of the law was the "go to" source after the exile and in early Judaism, rather than Exodus, when it came to law and the making of legal rulings. Two observations about Paul, our chronologically earliest NT writer, help us to begin to understand what is going on here.

First, note that some of Paul's letters have no explicit OT quotations (i.e., 1 Thessalonians and Philippians) and then there are the two that have the most such quotations (Galatians and Romans), both of which are preoccupied with the question of "works of the Mosaic law" and their possible application to the life of the follower of Christ, or not. That is, law *qua law*, is discussed by Paul when the issue is which covenant is the follower of Christ, Jew or gentile, now under; which laws must one keep? Paul is well aware of the importance of "the law" for his fellow Jews and Jewish Christians, which may help explain the fact that, as Carol Stockhausen points out, Paul often begins his arguments with texts (or events) from the Law, and

---

1. Julius Wellhausen, *Prolegomena to the History of Israel*, trans. J. Sutherland Black and Allan Envies (Edinburgh: Adam & Charles Black, 1885), 48.

clarifies then with texts from the Prophets and/or the Writings, using a pesher-type of contemporizing exegesis to bring out the meaning for his own audience—and it is Deuteronomy that comes to the fore at the outset of these sorts of arguments.[2]

One of the problems however with the study of the use of the OT, especially in Paul, Hebrews, and Acts, is the failure by many scholars to understand that the authors are forming *rhetorical* arguments with the help of OT material. They are following rhetorical conventions, in which citing accepted and recognized preexisting authorities, especially preexisting materials from the Torah portion of the OT, is considered one of the strongest sorts of proof of one's case, an inartificial proof, or one based in a revered ancient source, not a proof made up by the speaker's own imagination. I suggest this is why stories from Genesis about Adam and Abraham and Melchizedek, stories about Moses from Exodus, and laws, chiefly in their Deuteronomistic form, are brought forward in the arguments we find in these sources as strong evidence to back the larger argument.

Yes, it is true in a text like Galatians 3 Paul appeals first to experience, then to the Torah, then to custom, but this is likely because his audience is largely, if not almost entirely gentile, and for them the appeal to experience is the strongest appeal because they cannot deny their own experience ("did you receive the Spirit by hearing with faith or by doing works of the Mosaic law") but they may not yet find appeals to "the Torah" quite as compelling.

Deuteronomy brings the Moses cycle to a conclusion, and as such it is not simply a recycling or rehearsing of earlier Pentateuchal material, a fact that is particularly evident in its final chapters (Deuteronomy 27–32) with the special blessings and cursing of Moses and the famous Song of Moses that includes a theme to be picked up frequently in the NT, the possibility of universal salvation, at least in so far as the divine intent and side of the equation is concerned. We will see the influence of Deuteronomy 32 in various places such as Hebrews 10–13 and the book of Revelation. Strikingly, the integrity formula from Deuteronomy 4:1–2 and 13:1 is picked up at the end of Revelation at 22:18–19 turning Revelation, like Deuteronomy, into a "binding religious document to be safeguarded, intended to fend off idolatry and false prophecy."[3]

---

2. Stockhausen, *Moses Veil*.

3. M. J. J. Menken and Steve Moyise eds., *Deuteronomy in the New Testament*, LNTS 358 (London: T&T Clark, 2008), 4.

We will turn to the use of Deuteronomy in early Judaism in a moment, but perhaps a few general statements are in order before we get down to the detailed treatment of particular texts. Most scholars have come to the conclusion that in so far as a written text of Deuteronomy is concerned, the authors of the NT are following the LXX or some Old Greek text similar to the LXX. In other words, by and large, they are not doing their own translations of the Hebrew text. Having said this, when it comes to the most familiar material from Deuteronomy, such as the Decalogue or the Shema, this may have reached the various NT authors mainly through the collective memory of the Jewish community, rather than directly from a text. We must remember that those two texts are found together in the phylacteries discovered in the Judean desert, and in regard to Deuteronomy 8, it was used as a grace after meals in early Judaism.[4] NT writers do frequently quote from memory rather than look up a citation, and what makes things even more difficult is that they are sometimes just paraphrasing a text, which makes it hard to figure out the source of the quotation or allusion. As we have already intimated, the closing chapters of Deuteronomy take on especial significance for the writers of the NT in various ways, not least because Deuteronomy 18 and later texts in the conclusion look forward to a day when a "prophet like unto Moses" will arise and help God's people. Last, Deuteronomy itself already raises the question of which commandments should be prioritized, a discussion we find again in the NT in both the Jesus and the Pauline traditions.[5]

DEUTERONOMY IN EARLY JUDAISM

The word "Deuteronomy" means "a second law" and it serves in the LXX as a translation of two Hebrew words *mishneh* and *torah,* which in turn is taken from a phrase in Deuteronomy 17:18. The phrase in question refers to "a copy of this law/teaching," in this case the ruler's copy. The LXX's turning of two words into a newly coined word "is semantically significant, as it implies an understanding of the original meaning of the book as another law; that is a law in addition to . . . the one that was given to Moses on Mount Horeb (28:69) . . . the second law covenanted with Israel on the plains of Moab."[6]

4. See Lim, "Deuteronomy," 14.
5. On all this see again the comments of Menken and Moyise, *Deuteronomy*, 4.
6. Lim, "Deuteronomy," 7.

This becomes especially significant if, as many scholars do, one identifies the law code in Deuteronomy 12–36 as that discovered by Hilkiah the high priest in the temple during the reign of King Josiah (640–609 BCE; see 2 Kgs 22:8). Equally important, the LXX, following what is said in Joshua 8:30–35 about the renewal of the covenant on Mt. Ebal, indicates at Joshua 9:2 that the law of Moses in question that was the basis of this renewal was "the second law." The Hebrew title for the book is taken from its opening lines and refers to "the speeches of Moses," pointing to 1:1–4:43; 4:44–28:68; and 28:69–30:20, which are identified internally as three Mosaic speeches that in turn provide us with the basic overall structure of the book, except for its very ending, which comes across as final words by a later editor about the farewell and death of Moses (31:1–34:12).

There has been endless scholarly chicken and egg sorts of debates about the relationship of Exodus and Deuteronomy (did the latter draw on the former, or vice versa), but fortunately for us, we do not need to settle this issue in order to do the kind of contextual study we are doing here. For my part, it seems clear enough to me that Deuteronomy reflects a later form of the law code than we find in Exodus, but one must remember that the whole of the Pentateuch seems to have been edited and shaped in light of Deuteronomy in various ways. What is clear is that while Deuteronomy itself is a rather heavily edited volume, through many centuries, the writers of the NT treat it as a coherent whole, even when it ostensibly reflects both the time of Moses when he overlooked the land ("these are the words of Moses that he spoke to all Israel 'beyond' Jordan") and also the later perspective of an editor who is within the land itself (Deut 1:1; 3:8, 20, 25; 4:41, 46; 11:30).[7]

For the Qumran community, as for various NT writers, Deuteronomy seems to have been the go-to form of the Law of Moses that would be used or appealed to. There have been fragments of some thirty-one Deuteronomy scrolls found in the caves at Qumran itself, and three more found at Wadi Murabba'at, Naḥal Ḥever and on Masada. The earliest of these scrolls seem to date from perhaps 200 BCE, the latest, not surprisingly from the non-Qumran sites, come from the first century CE.[8] With twenty-nine clear copies of Deuteronomy found at Qumran, only the Psalms with some forty copies is more well represented. Amazingly, these Qumran scrolls

---

7. Lim, "Deuteronomy," 9 makes this point quite clearly.
8. See the chart in Lim, "Deuteronomy," 10.

attest to some three hundred years worth of copying Deuteronomy on either skin or papyrus and ranging from paleo-Hebrew from perhaps 200 BCE (4Q46 [4QpaleoDeut]) to the square-formed characters dating from the first centuries BCE and CE. The very best preserved of these twenty-nine scrolls is 4Q30 which has 120 verses of the book drawn from nineteen different chapters. It has been identified as a proto-Masoretic text that largely agrees with the later "received" form of the text. In some ways more interesting is 4Q29 because it provides a glimpse of what may be the text behind the LXX form of Deuteronomy. This is thought to be the case because the LXX and this text agree in a few clear errors.[9]

One of the difficulties in dealing with the evidence at Qumran is that we have "testimonia" or collections of excerpted partial texts. For instance, 4Q175 (also called 4QTestimonia, "the Messianic Anthology") has exactly four paragraphs composed of: (1) Deuteronomy 5:28–29 and 18:18–19; (2) Numbers 24:15–17; (3) Deuteronomy 33:8–11; and (4) an apocryphal source called the Apocryphon of Joshua (4Q379 [4QapocrJoshb]), frag. 22 col. 2. The latter is in fact an interpretation of Joshua 6:26 LXX. Notably, (1) above is also found in the Samaritan Pentateuch at Exodus 20:21b. The Apoocryphon text follows the LXX, but otherwise some Hebrew text is followed. There is no commentary on (1)–(3), but there is on (4). What were the functions of testimonia? Lim suggests they had various functions: for study, for apologetical use in controversies, and for liturgical purposes.[10] It is not clear why (4) above was added to the first three, for the first three have to do with speculation about messianic figures: a prophetic one like Moses, a royal one based on Balaam's prophecy, or a priestly one.

Phylacteries and mezuzot have become an important additional source of information about the forms of biblical texts in early Judaism. For example, while later rabbinic tradition suggested four texts for a phylactery (Exod 13:1–10, and 11–16; Deut 6:4–9; 11:13–21), the some thirty-one phylacteries found mainly at Qumran tell a different story. There is the addition of Exodus 12:43–51 in some, the addition of Exodus 13:1–16 in others, and Deuteronomy 10–11 in still others. The scroll 4Q141 (4QPhyl N) has only Deuteronomy 32. But in no less than eight phylacteries we have the

---

9. See Julie A. Duncan, "Deuteronomy, Book of," in *The Encyclopedia of the Dead Sea Scrolls*, ed. Lawrence H. Schiffman and James C. Vanderkam (Oxford: Oxford University Press, 2000), 1:198–202; and Lim, "Deuteronomy," 12.

10. In all of this I am following Lim, "Deuteronomy," 13.

addition of the Decalogue. Perhaps these reflect sectarian practice at Qumran especially, but probably not.[11] A combination of the Shema and the Decalogue makes perfectly good sense as a collection of some of the very most important and most memorized texts from Deuteronomy. Interestingly, however the text of the Decalogue found in the Nash Papyrus, Philo, 4Q134 (4QPhyl G), 8Q3 (8QPhyl 3), and 4Q149 (4QMez A) is closer to Exodus than Deuteronomy and to the LXX than to the MT.[12] Of equal interest are mezuzot that according to later tradition included Deuteronomy 6:9 and 11:20, but at Qumran they could include all of Deuteronomy 6:4–9 and 11:13–21. We do not know how old the tradition recorded in m. Tamid 5:1 is, but it does tell us that the Decalogue and the Shema were recited together with the daily blessing in the temple and on the Sabbath.

The good news about the LXX of the book of Deuteronomy is that on the whole the translator (somewhere in the third century BCE) was conservative, more conservative than the person who rendered Genesis into Greek. In fact, one could call it almost a literal translation of the proto-Masoretic text of the Hebrew. Even Hebrew idioms that do not find good equivalents in Greek are rendered rather woodenly into Greek (cf., e.g., Deut 20:3 MT and LXX). Furthermore, Lim admits "there is no overarching theological *Tendenz*" detectable in the translation.[13] The most one can say is that the translator adds some clarifying or harmonizing words from time to time. There is little translator embellishment in Deuteronomy 1–11, only a few technical divergences in Deuteronomy 12–26 (e.g., ruler is substituted for king in 17:14). For our purposes, it is important to note that the interpretive notes and additions are most numerous for Deuteronomy 27–34.

Contrary to what one might hope, Josephus is not much help in figuring out the Greek form of the text of Deuteronomy in the first century, for while he promises to add nothing to the biblical text, in his recounting of it in *Ant.* 4.176–331 he systematizes the discussion of subjects, gathering material from various places in the Pentateuch including Exodus 20 and Leviticus 19 and 21, and even from Numbers as well in 4.270–314. In other words, he has categorized

11. See Lim, "Deuteronomy," 16–17.
12. Innocent Himbaza, "Le Décalogue du Papyrus Nash, Philon, 4QPhyl G, 8QPhyl 3 et 4QMez A," *RevQ* 79/20 (2002): 411–28.
13. Lim, "Deuteronomy," 19.

things, and combined things. He does not help us with the issue of
Exodus vs. Deuteronomy in terms of the earliest form of some of the
key texts. Philo is even less help because he combines biblical interpretation with Greek philosophizing using an allegorical method of
interpretation. In addition, he goes out of his way to emphasize
God's sovereignty in his interpretation of Deuteronomy 1:17 (see *On
Dreams* 2.17–30, esp. 2.24).[14]

So pervasive is the general influence of Deuteronomy in early
Judaism that one can even talk about the Deuteronomistic ethos
in which the Pentateuch is interpreted. For instance, 4Q252 interprets Genesis with various references to Deuteronomy. Or take the
example of the famous Temple Scroll (11Q19 [11QTa] and 11Q20
[11QTb]), dating from the Herodian period. "The Temple Scroll
according to 11QTSa [11Q19], is a systematic rewriting of the biblical text of Exodus and Deuteronomy according to a thematic order.
. . . The whole of the Temple Scroll is shot through with the influence of the book of Deuteronomy." Deuteronomy is the base text of
the Temple Scroll, following the basic order of Deuteronomy 12–26,
with additions from elsewhere.[15] In this sort of environment, and
with these sorts of precursors or contemporary uses of Deuteronomy,
it is not a surprise it comes up a lot in the NT, and we must turn to
that usage now.

DEUTERONOMY QUOTED . . . AND REPURPOSED

What are the kinds of texts from Deuteronomy that are quoted somewhere in the NT? What is their subject matter? Let us first provide a
quick list of the quoted texts

Deuteronomy 5:6–21: Decalogue
Deuteronomy 6:4–5: love command
Deuteronomy 6:13–16: Fear the Lord
Deuteronomy 8:3: manna
Deuteronomy 9:3–4, 19: God goes before you as a consuming fire
Deuteronomy 10:20: Fear the Lord and worship him
Deuteronomy 17:6–7: Testimony of two witnesses
Deuteronomy 18:15: the prophet like Moses
Deuteronomy 19:15: testimony of two witnesses
Deuteronomy 19:21: eye for an eye

14. Lim, "Deuteronomy," 23–25.
15. Lim, "Deuteronomy," 22–23.

Deuteronomy 21:23: cursed is the one who hangs on a tree
Deuteronomy 25:4: Do not muzzle the ox
Deuteronomy 27:26: Cursed is the one who does not put this law into
    practice
Deuteronomy 29:3: you saw the signs and wonders
Deuteronomy 29:17: idols made of wood, gold, silver, and so on
Deuteronomy 31:6, 8: Be strong and of good courage, the Lord will go
    with you
Deuteronomy 32:4: The Rock, all his ways are just
Deuteronomy 32:21: They have provoked his jealousy by idols
Deuteronomy 32:35–36, 43: Vengeance is mine, I will repay, vindicate
    my people.

What strikes one at first glance is the reference to strict monotheism, and God taking vengeance on his people's foes and vindicating them. There is also a good deal about witnesses at a trial where death might be the outcome, but at the other end of the spectrum is the love command, and also the promise of a great leader, a prophet like Moses. But it is the famous Ten Words given to Moses that first attract the attention of NT writers when they turn to the book of Deuteronomy. There can be little doubt that later evaluation of Deuteronomy saw Deuteronomy 5–6 in particular as the centerpiece of this entire book.[16] The composer of the book deliberately sets off this material with a framework involving Deuteronomy 5:1–5, 22–33; and 6:1–3 that separates this material from what follows it, noticing how the opening words in 5:1 are echoed in the concluding words in 6:3. But at the same time v. 1 points forward beyond the Ten Words and the Shema to the statutes and ordinances in Deuteronomy 12–26 that spin out the implications and applications of those crucial and fundamental teachings. Moses speaks in the present tense about statutes and ordinances, but the Ten Words were spoken in the past at Horeb.[17]

ANOTHER TEN WORDS: DEUTERONOMY 5:1–22

The popularity of Deuteronomy in early Judaism, including among the followers of Jesus has quite rightly led to the supposition that it is the Deuteronomic forms of things like the Shema and the Ten Commandments that are drawn upon in the NT. It will repay us to consider closely the form of these texts. In short, the statutes and

16. See rightly Patrick D. Miller, *Deuteronomy*, IBC (Louisville: John Knox, 1990), 65.
17. Miller, *Deuteronomy*, 66.

ordinances grow out of the basic covenant with its Ten Words. The effect of all this is to make clear that even the Ten Words are not merely directives for the past, they address God's people in the present, the present generation. This hermeneutical move of contemporizing a previous revelation is not unlike what we find in the use of the OT in the NT and provides a precedent for it. "The covenant was made not with our ancestors but with us, we, these ones, here, today, all of us, living."[18]

MT

LXX

[1] Moses summoned all Israel and said: Hear, Israel, the decrees and laws I declare in your hearing today. Learn them and be sure to follow them.

[2] The Lord our God made a covenant with us at Horeb.
[3] It was not with our ancestors that the Lord made this covenant, but with us, with all of us who are alive here today.
[4] The Lord spoke to you face to face out of the fire on the mountain.

[5] (At that time I stood between the Lord and you to declare to you the word of the Lord, because you were afraid of the fire and did not go up the mountain.) And he said:
[6] "I am the Lord your God, who brought you out of Egypt, out of the land of slavery.
[7] "You shall have no other gods before me.
[8] "You shall not make for yourself an image in the form[19] of anything in heaven above or on the earth beneath or in the waters below.

[9] You shall not bow down to them or worship them; for I, the Lord your God, am a jealous God, punishing the children for the sin of the parents to the third and fourth generation of those who hate me,
[10] but showing love to a thousand

[1] And Moses called all Israel and said to them: Hear, O Israel, the statutes and judgments that I am speaking in your ears this day, and you shall learn them and be watchful to perform them.
[2] The Lord your God established a covenant with you at Horeb.
[3] Not with your fathers did the Lord establish this covenant, but with all of you here alive today.

[4] The Lord spoke with you face-to-face at the mountain, from the midst of the fire,
[5] and I stood between the Lord and you at that time, to report to you the words of the Lord, for you were afraid because of the fire and did not go up into the mountain, saying:
[6] I am the Lord your God who brought you out of the land of Egypt, out of a house of slavery.
[7] You shall have no other gods before me.
[8] You shall not make for yourself a carved object or likeness of anything whatever is in the sky above and whatever is in the earth beneath and whatever is in the waters under the earth.
[9] You shall not do obeisance to them, nor are you to serve them, because I am the Lord your God, a jealous god, repaying the sins of fathers upon children to the third and fourth generation to those who hate me,
[10] and doing mercy unto thousands,

18. Miller, *Deuteronomy*, 67.
19. It is interesting, as Richard D. Nelson, *Deuteronomy*, OTL (Louisville: Westminster John

generations of those who love me and keep my commandments.

11 "You shall not misuse the name of the Lord your God, for the Lord will not hold anyone guiltless who misuses his name.

12 "Observe the Sabbath day by keeping it holy, as the Lord your God has commanded you.

13 Six days you shall labor and do all your work,

14 but the seventh day is a Sabbath to the Lord your God. On it you shall not do any work, neither you, nor your son or daughter, nor your male or female servant, nor your ox, your donkey or any of your animals, nor any foreigner residing in your towns, so that your male and female servants may rest, as you do.

15 Remember that you were slaves in Egypt and that the Lord your God brought you out of there with a mighty hand and an outstretched arm. Therefore, the Lord your God has commanded you to observe the Sabbath day.

16 "Honor your father and your mother, as the Lord your God has commanded you, so that you may live long and that it may go well with you in the land the Lord your God is giving you.

17 "You shall not murder.

18 "You shall not commit adultery.

19 "You shall not steal.

20 "You shall not give false testimony against your neighbor.

21 "You shall not covet your neighbor's wife. You shall not set your desire on your neighbor's house or land, his male or female servant, his ox or donkey, or anything that belongs to your neighbor."

22 These are the commandments the Lord proclaimed in a loud voice to your whole assembly there on the mountain from out of the fire, the cloud and the deep darkness; and he

for those who love me and keep my ordinances.

11 You shall not take the name of the Lord your God in vain. For the Lord will never acquit the one who takes his name in vain.

12 Keep the day of the Sabbaths to consecrate it, as the Lord your God commanded you.

13 Six days you shall labor and do all your labor,

14 but on the seventh day there is Sabbath to the Lord your God; you shall not do in it any labor—you and your son and your daughter, your male slave and your female slave, your ox and your draft animal and any animal of yours and the guest within your gates so that your male slave and your female slave may rest as well as you.

15 And you shall remember that you were a domestic in the land of Egypt, and the Lord your God brought you out from there with a strong hand and with a high arm; therefore, the Lord your God instructed you to keep the day of the Sabbaths and to consecrate it.

16 Honor your father and your mother, as the Lord your God commanded you, so that it may be well with you and that you may be long-lived in the land that the Lord your God is giving you.

17(18) You shall not commit adultery.

18(17) You shall not murder.

19 You shall not steal.

20 You shall not testify falsely against your neighbor with a false testimony.

21 You shall not covet your neighbor's wife; you shall not covet your neighbor's house or his field or his male slave or his female slave or his ox or his draft animal, or any animal of his or whatever belongs to your neighbor.

22 These words the Lord spoke to your whole gathering at the mountain, from the midst of the fire—darkness, blackness, tempest, a loud voice—and he did not

---

Knox, 2002), 75 points out, that many witnesses including 4Q31 (4QDeutn), Sam., OG, Vulg., and Syr. adjust the text here to match Exod 20:4, "nor any shape." This would go against the assumption that Deuteronomy was consistently being used to norm the earlier parts of the Pentateuch, particularly Exodus, by NT times, when it comes to such crucial texts as this one.

| added nothing more. Then he wrote them on two stone tablets and gave them to me. | add. And he wrote them on two stone tablets and gave them to me. |

It will not be necessary to go into as much exegetical detail here as with the Exodus material, except insofar as this text deviates from the form of the Ten Commandments found in Exodus, which we have already considered at some length.[20] But some general remarks from Peter Craigie here will help get us oriented:

> The law was legally binding, but not in a restrictive sense; it was representative of God's love for [humankind] and it called in turn for a response of love (6:4–5). The Decalogue was representative of God's love in that its injunctions, both negative and positive, led not to restriction of life but to fullness of life. It demanded a response of love, not because obedience would somehow accumulate credit in the sight of God, but because the grace of God, experienced already in the liberation from Egypt and in the divine initiative in the covenant promise, elicited such a response from [humankind] in gratitude.[21]

As has often been noted, most of the Ten Commandments are straightforward prohibitions, without qualifications, even in the later statutes portion of Deuteronomy. The exception to this is the commandment not to kill, which is later qualified in some ways. Notice these prohibitions do not list with them the consequences or penalty for disobedience. "Disobedience is not ameliorated by the exacting of some penalty."[22] At the same time, the Ten Words confine themselves to certain basic areas of life, leaving large areas of life up to freedom of human choice. Naturally, this freedom is further qualified by the statutes and ordinances that follow. Note that all this material sets up a community ethic, so while each commandment here is in the second person singular, making clear it applies to every single Israelite, it applies to them as a member of a specific community in covenant with a specific deity. While these commandments are basic guidelines, they are not mere abstractions or suggestions, they are the law of the community and enforcement is expected. The prologue makes clear that these commandments are the appropriate response to a grace-rescuing God who plucked the Hebrews out of bondage in Egypt. As Patrick Miller puts it, "Setting free the oppressed is the

20. See pp. 185–92 above.
21. Peter Craigie, *The Book of Deuteronomy*, NICOT (Grand Rapids: Eerdmans, 1976), 150.
22. Miller, *Deuteronomy*, 73.

will of a compassionate God. Life in community and obedience is the consequent demand of that same God."[23]

Note also that the Ten Commandments are distinguished from the statutes and ordinances in both Exodus and Deuteronomy and therefore given priority, greater weight and authority, not least because they reflect direct revelation from God, in contrast to statutes taught by the mediator, Moses. This is further underscored by the fact that while the Ten Words are virtually the same in Exodus and Deuteronomy (with the exception of the Sabbath commandment) there is considerable variation in the statutes and ordinances found in Exodus 21–23 and Deuteronomy 12–26.[24]

The command to hear (v. 1), often present in ancient treaty texts, has the sense of "hear and obey" in such contexts.[25] Notice the idiom "spoke face to face," one used of God and Moses in Exodus 33:7–25, and in both cases indicating speaking directly, in this case to the people of God. The preamble to the Ten Words establishes the authority of the Ruler to make such a treaty, and the basis of the demands themselves, namely God's gracious rescue of his people from Egypt. "Thus the 'Exodus' is the 'gospel' placed at the head of the law . . . it was law for a people already redeemed, not designed per se to redeem the people."[26]

To draw an analogy, the Ten Words are like a fundamental constitutional law that cannot be changed, whereas the attempts to apply it to different situations is what we find in the statutes and ordinances. This makes it all the more striking that various NT writers were to insist that even one of the Ten Words might not be "written in stone" for the followers of Jesus, namely the Sabbath commandment. This is because the new covenant was viewed as not a mere renewal of the Mosaic covenant but a genuinely fresh start, a different covenant. This caused no little furor, since the Sabbath commandment in particular was viewed as the very center and heart of the Mosaic Ten Commandments, providing a transition from the part which deals with our relationship to God to the part that deals with our relationship with each other.

Here is perhaps a good place to note that there is no general agreement about the enumeration of the Ten Commandments, by which

23. Miller, *Deuteronomy*, 75.
24. Rightly, Miller, *Deuteronomy*, 69.
25. See Duane L. Christensen, *Deuteronomy 1–11*, WBC (Waco, TX: Word, 1991), 111.
26. Craigie, *Deuteronomy*, 151.

I mean, for instance, that the Jewish tradition sees the prologue in v. 6 as the first commandment, which in turn makes the prohibition of polytheism and idol worship together the second commandment. Roman Catholics and Lutherans follow this lead, but in the Reformed tradition the first commandment is the one against polytheism and the second is the prohibition of images.[27] Finally, note that the order of the commandments is like the ordering of the "great commandment" namely things dealing with one's relationship with God come first, followed by things dealing with our relationships with our neighbors or fellow human beings.

The command in vv. 6–7 to have no other gods "before me" has parallels in other ANE treaties and involves a demand for exclusive loyalty to the god in question. Other gods are not to be acknowledged or served by God's people. What would seem clearly to be implied, though not stated (though it would be said elsewhere and later in the OT) is that Yahweh is the only real or living God; these other beings, whatever they may be are not deities.[28] There is good reason given for them to do so—it was Yahweh who delivered them from bondage in Egypt.

The first commandment quite naturally leads to the second in vv. 8–10—namely not making idols, in this case one may ask if images of Yahweh or of other gods are in mind. In my view, the reference to things above and below would seem to be an odd way to refer to God, though some have seen this as a reference to his domain. But the issue here is "graven images" of some deity, not of creation. So, it makes better sense to see this as a reference to alternative deities.

It is certainly true that human beings are the image of God on this earth, which is yet another reason why no alternative images of God should be made, but this is not the focus here.[29] A sanction clause is given as to why such an action is forbidden. Yahweh is a jealous God who can brook no rivals, and just as importantly God is faithful to keep his word about judging and blessing his people, about showing loving kindness to those who keep his Word.[30] That

27. See Miller, *Deuteronomy*, 71–72.

28. In other words, this is not really an affirmation of henotheism, Yahweh being the "most" high or best God in the pantheism of deities. It is possible, but unlikely that "before my face" refers to other cult statues of other deities placed in the holy place where the true God was worshiped; see Craigie, *Deuteronomy*, 152. On the belief in other supernatural beings not considered gods by the Hebrews see Heiser's recent study, *Unseen Realm*.

29. But see the discussion in Richter, *Epic of Eden*.

30. Miller, *Deuteronomy*, 76 is right to insist that we are not talking about divine insecurity or about an irrational passion on the part of God. What "jealousy" means here is that God expects

is, God's people should be exclusively faithful to God just as God is to them. If the commandment is dealing with the prohibition of images of Yahweh, then the point is Yahweh is spirit, and does not have a physical form and should not be so represented. The real problem with images and idols is that they can subtly become the object of worship rather than a tool to prompt worship of something greater.[31]

The third commandment in v. 11 is about the misuse of God's name, not in the modern sense of "taking the Lord's name in vain," but rather in trying to use the powerful name to achieve some end that does not comport with God's will. In other words, to use God's name as if it were an idol, a talisman, a power tool of sorts. In short, the prohibition involves the avoidance of a magical use of God's name for personal benefit or other sorts of worthless purpose, and by the same token, avoiding this temptation helped God's people be free from the influence of magic.[32] God's people are to relate to God as a person, not as a powerful thing. Notice that no specific penalties are mentioned for not observing these commandments, but a general warning is given about the consequences of noncompliance.

The Sabbath commandment in 5:12–15 is stated positively first, but it is coupled with a reminder of the Genesis story, and the prohibition of work on the Sabbath, a prohibition even for the servants and the animals. It could not be much clearer: keeping the Sabbath holy involves avoiding work by any member of the family or any property of the family (servants, animals). It is however worth stressing that whereas in the Exodus parallel text the doctrine of creation dominates the explanation for the commandment, here in Deuteronomy it is mainly the doctrine of redemption that provides the rationale. But there is a connection: the Exodus was used by God to create a people—Israel, whereas Genesis is about the creation of the first human beings and what makes for their well-being, namely rest.[33] Miller states the difference this way: "in the case of Exodus, the community is called to remember and to obey out of that memory; in the Deuteronomic form, the community obeys to keep alive the memory

to have an exclusive relationship with his people, exclusive just like a marital relationship, and it means he will be zealous to maintain its exclusivity. Just as Israel shall have no other gods at all, so Yahweh will have no other people with which he has such a relationship.

31. On God's loving kindness, see the older study of Nelson Glueck, *Hesed in the Bible* (Eugene, OR: Wipf & Stock, 2011). Unfortunately, while the word in question can speak about loving kindness in a covenant relationship, it does not refer exclusively to that, in fact it often does not refer to that at all in the OT; see the discussion in Witherington, *Psalms Old and New*.

32. See Craigie, *Deuteronomy*, 156.

33. Craigie, *Deuteronomy*, 157.

of redemption and to bring about the provision of rest from toil for all members of the community."[34]

There are other differences between the way this commandment is stated in Exodus and here. For instance, here in v. 12 the key verb is *shamor*, which basically means "take care to," but in Exodus 20:8 it is *zakor*, which means "remember" or "remembering." In other words, the Exodus form of this is meant as a memory prompt, a reminder not to forget the basis of this command in God's past actions.[35] Some have suggested that the reason "wife" is not listed among those who are not to "work" on the Sabbath is due to the assumption that the law did not apply to ordinary domestic activities. This is probably reading too much into the silence. In any case, this commandment and praxis seems to be distinctive of Israelite culture. There is no clear evidence of other ANE cultures observing a Sabbath day, or a six-day work week.[36]

The fifth commandment about honoring parents provides another positive commandment, and this one comes with the rationale of "in order that your days may be prolonged and it may go well with you." This should be compared to Deuteronomy 4:40 where the "bene-fits" of covenant-keeping in other regards are stated similarly. The debate on whether this commandment should be grouped with the preceding or following ones need not be settled here. It is proba-bly over-reading the text to suggest that parents are standing in for God in the family structure, and so children are to relate to parents in a way similar to the way they relate to God. The text says nothing of this, and worshiping God is one thing, honoring parents another. On the whole, this command surely belongs with the following ones that deal with interpersonal relationships. Honoring here implies sub-mission to authority, in this case the authority of the parent (cf. 1 Sam 15:30; Ps 86:9).[37] Contrast Deuteronomy 21:18–21 and 27:16. What is true is that this commandment, like the others, is addressed to adults, not primarily to children, and may primarily have in view the

---

34. Miller, *Deuteronomy*, 80.

35. Craigie, *Deuteronomy*, 156.

36. Craigie (*Deuteronomy*, 158) is right to note the parallel between this and the Christian observance of the Lord's Day as a celebration of God's liberation wrought through the raising of Jesus from the dead. In other words, different covenants generated by different acts of redemp-tion, celebrated on different days. Besides the absence of the circumcision requirement in the NT, this change as well should have made very clear that the new covenant is not a renewal or perfecting of the Mosaic covenant.

37. See Nelson, *Deuteronomy*, 83.

responsibility of adults to take care of their elderly parents.[38] This scenario comes up in the famous discussion of corban by Jesus in Mark's Gospel.

It is interesting to see how the Markan portrayal of Jesus intensifies the commandment about honoring parents by way of associating it with other material in the Pentateuch (see Mark 7). Steve Moyise puts it this way: "the commandment to honor father and mother is intensified by being linked to the command that those who speak evil of father and mother should be put to death [Exod 21:17; Lev 20:9]. Depriving one's parents of the necessities of life [through a pronouncement of something being corban] is apparently equivalent to cursing them."[39] This is all the more striking because of what Jesus had already said about who his real mother and siblings are in Mark 3:31–35. He also rightly notes that perhaps the reason Mark has placed the "honor parents" commandment last of the ten (followed by Matthew and Luke) is because the citation comes in the context of the query of the young man, who will say just after the listing that he has kept all these since his youth.[40]

The sixth commandment is indeed a prohibition of murder, whether premeditated or accidental.[41] The subject of capital punishment or war is treated separately (cf. Deut 17:2–7 and 19.:2; and on war Deut 20–21), but in the same larger Pentateuchal context. This differs from the way the subject is handled by Jesus. He does not affirm either capital punishment or war, and indeed, he rules out his disciples even from unrighteous anger and instead urges nonresistance. It is right to note that the normal general Hebrew word for "kill," *harag*, is not found here. Instead we have *ratsakh*, which normally refers to murder, premeditated murder of another individual. But the term can also be used more broadly to refer to accidental slaying (Num 35:25–28), which has led to the dilemma of how to translate this term into good English. The singular form here of the verb suggests that the focus is on personal violence by a Hebrew individual against another individual.[42]

Is this really the only one of the Ten Commandments that implies

38. See Nelson, *Deuteronomy*, 84, "honoring" parents in this sense creates the social context in which parents and their offspring can live long in the land together, hence the unique connection here with the promise.

39. Steve Moyise, "Deuteronomy in Mark's Gospel," in Menken, *Deuteronomy*, 29.

40. Moyise, "Deuteronomy in Mark's Gospel," 32.

41. See rightly Blomberg, "Matthew," 21.

42. Miller, *Deuteronomy*, 87.

exceptions? Certainly, the prohibition of theft and adultery do not imply any exceptions, nor do the positive commandments. The prohibition here then would seem to deal with actions of individuals, but even so it is hard to reconcile this command with the "law of the tooth," the law of limited reciprocity when it comes to harm, which certainly does deal with individuals in the covenant community taking actions against others. Umberto Cassuto long ago pointed out that commandments six through eight are found in every civilized society, but what is unusual here is the absolute, and unqualified form of the commandment, giving the impression that it is an eternal principle.[43]

The seventh commandment prohibits adultery, which according to Genesis 20:9 is a "great sin." Deuteronomy 22–25 deals with other sexual sins. Probably betrothed girls were considered equivalent to married women in regard to this matter (see Deut 22:23–24).[44]

> The reason why adultery is singled out for attention in the Decalogue is because adultery, more than any other illicit sexual behavior, has to do with unfaithfulness in a relationship of commitment. . . . The crime of adultery was the social equivalent to the religious crime of having *other gods* (5:5); both offenses involved unfaithfulness and both were therefore reprehensible to the God of the covenant, whose character was to be totally faithful.[45]

In other words, being unfaithful to one's wife was a form of unfaithfulness to God and the covenant agreement with God. Again, this contrasts with ANE law elsewhere, for instance the Code of Hammurabi, where adultery is viewed as basically an offense against the husband. The connection between faithfulness to God and to one's spouse is also assumed by the use of adultery as a spiritual metaphor by the OT prophets when speaking of Israel's unfaithfulness to God.

It is worth adding that this commandment pushes the needle in the direction of exclusive monogamy to the exclusion of polygamy, for if any sexual act outside of the one-flesh union of marriage is seen as adultery, then starting another marriage or adding another wife to the fold would seem to be a clear breach of this commandment. Polygamy is not endorsed in the OT, though it was certainly practiced by various OT persons. Not incidentally this seems to be how

43. See Umberto Cassuto, *Commentary on the Book of Exodus* (Jerusalem: Magnes, 1967).
44. Christensen, *Deuteronomy 1–11*, 124.
45. Craigie, *Deuteronomy*, 160.

Jesus understood the prohibition, for he says that even a person who divorces his wife and marries another is committing adultery. The implication is that the first relationship was exclusive, and continues as such even with a formal divorce. This probably goes beyond the intent of the law here, but the trajectory Jesus is tracing is understandable.

While the eighth commandment is often read in a very broad and general way and certainly stealing in general is prohibited (see Exod 22:1–13), it appears that what is mainly in focus here is the theft of another person, namely kidnapping, or better said enslaving. Deuteronomy 24:7 (cf. Exod 21:16) then provides a further exposition of what is meant here, stealing a person and selling them for personal gain (see the story of Joseph in Gen 37:22–28).[46] But there are broader implications of this commandment as well: "Any act that involves the manipulation of another human being for personal gain is tantamount to the crime."[47] In a sense then, this commandment parallels the prohibition of the use of images, which is an attempt to manipulate God. The absoluteness of the commandment of course means that the theft of ordinary property is in view, but it may not be accidental that this command comes hard on the heels of the one about adultery, which could be said to be an example of theft, stealing a neighbor's wife.

The ninth commandment seems to envision a legal situation in which false testimony really matters. The situation envisioned is a false testimony against a fellow believer, and may well be what stands behind what Paul says in 1 Corinthians 6. Deuteronomy 19:15–21 spells out in more detail what this prohibition entails and why it is important. It is especially concerned to prevent false testimony in a capital case that might lead to a person's death.

The tenth commandment prohibits coveting, and so an attitude. Duane Christensen is probably correct that this commandment deals with the motivator of violations six through nine, namely self-interest prepared to do others a wrong to get what one wants.[48] Some have argued that what is meant is an attitude that leads to an action, otherwise how would the community even know about it, but Patrick Nelson refutes this when he says "apparently the verb does not extend to include actual attempts at appropriation. This conclusion is indi-

46. See Craigie, *Deuteronomy*, 161.
47. Craigie, *Deuteronomy*, 162.
48. Christensen, *Deuteronomy 1–11*, 124.

cated by the need to add a further verb to describe such attempts
(7:25). Perhaps the connotation can be captured by 'plan to appropriate' or 'scheme to acquire.'"[49] But since the verb *khamad* is paralleled
here with the word for strong desire *('awah)*, which means only deep
or strong desire, not desire in action, this possibility seems ruled out.
It would seem likely this prohibition seeks to get at the root cause
of various violations in the second table of the Ten Commandments.
Since love is also commanded (Deut 6:4), it is simply not correct to
suggest that God does not seek to regulate attitudes and even feelings as well as actions through his law. The conclusion of the passage
stresses that these are commandments straight from God, originally
spoken from the theophany cloud.

Any close reading of this text will show the differences it has from
the Ten Words in Exodus 20:11. A few points are worth noting: The
accentuation of the importance of the Sabbath and "keeping the Sabbath" is shown by the fact that in Deuteronomy in contrast to Exodus
20:11, "sanctifying" is always presented as a human rather than divine
activity (15:19; 22:9). God's holy people are to sanctify things, including the holy day. Notice too that the operative verb in v. 12 of our
text is "keep" as opposed to the use of "remember" in Exodus. The
Sabbath is at the center of commands, and is one of only two positive
commands. Notice as well the addition of more animals who are to
keep the Sabbath holy: ox and donkeys, whereas Exodus only mentioned cattle.[50] It is hard to doubt that the Deuteronomic form of the
Ten Words is the later one, reflecting later praxis. Sinai is now clearly
in the rearview mirror. The audience has to be told in Deuteronomy
to "remember" their slavery in Egypt and so keep the Sabbath (Deut
10:19; 15:15; 16:12; 24:18, 22). Notice too in the coveting commandment how Deuteronomy changes the order of things found in the
Exodus text so that the sequence "wife" and then "house" reflects the
order of the commandment about adultery and theft.[51]

Nelson helpfully points out that while the Decalogue is said to
have been given in the past at Horeb/Sinai, the laws in Deuteronomy
12–26 are located as part of the ongoing revelation to Moses and
God's people between Horeb and the crossing of the Jordan. Nelson
also notes the careful construction such that this early passage in
Deuteronomy 5 is echoed in Deuteronomy 27:14–26 where one

49. Nelson, *Deuteronomy*, 76.
50. Nelson, *Deuteronomy*, 82–83.
51. Nelson, *Deuteronomy*, 84.

hears about the twelve curses that cover the same topics: idols, parents, the neighbor's life, and property. Thus, the extreme importance of the Decalogue is emphasized in this way, but also by the fact that it was said to be given to Moses "face to face" and nothing more was to be added (vv. 4 and 22) and then of course it is only these commandments that are then stored in the ark (10:1–5).[52]

The role of Moses is accentuated more in Deuteronomy than in Exodus as the intermediary with God par excellence. Yahweh is the God of the Exodus, and Moses is the human intermediary who led them out, and led them to know their God was Yahweh (cf. Deut 6:12; 7:8; 8:14; 13:6, 11). Finally note that the term "commandment" in v. 31 is in the singular, but it refers to the whole Deuteronomic law (cf. 6:1, 25; 7:11; 8:1; 11:8, 22). The body of law given by Moses, both the Ten Words and the statutes and ordinances stand together and should be taken as a whole. Herein lies the background for the later use of the term "law" by Paul and others in a comprehensive sense, not least when Paul warns the Galatians that if they submit to circumcision, they will also be obligated to keep all the rest of the Mosaic law as well.

It will be well at this juncture to point out the various way the Ten Commandments are cited and arranged in the Bible.

Exodus 20:12–17	Deuteronomy 5:16–21	Mark 10:19	Matthew 19:18–19	Luke 18:20	Romans 13:9
honor	honor				
adultery	Adultery	murder	murder	adultery	adultery
theft	Murder	adultery	adultery	murder	murder
murder	Theft	theft	theft	theft	theft
false witness	false witness	false witness	false witness	false witness	
covet	Covet				covet
		defraud			
		honor	honor	honor	
			love neighbor		love neighbor.[53]

52. Nelson, *Deuteronomy*, 76–77.
53. Following Moyise, "Deuteronomy," 32.

One may wonder where the "do not defraud" variation or substitute for no coveting comes from, but we find this imperative exactly the same in Sirach 4:1 and perhaps in a few manuscripts of Deuteronomy 24:14 (A and F) in the LXX, but this seems to reflect the later Christian alteration of the LXX to assimilate it to Mark. It has to be borne in mind that the second-century church (and later) largely took over the production and use of the LXX while Jews were largely abandoning it, so it is not always possible to tell which is the chicken and which is the egg when it comes to the citations of the LXX in the NT. Are they citing the earlier versions of the OG, or are we looking at the later Christianizing of the LXX in some of the NT manuscripts?

Among the variety of places some or all of these Ten Words occur in the NT is Romans 13:8–10. Note how there the citation of Deuteronomy 5:17–19 and v. 21 is followed by a citation of Leviticus 19:18, and those two source texts together are surrounded by the assertion that love in action fulfills the Law (Rom 13:8b, 10b). Notice that the order of the commandments in Paul (adultery, murder, stealing) is the same order as is found in LXX MS B, the Nash Papyrus, Philo, Mark 10:19 (MS A), Luke 18:20, and James 2:1. The order in the MT in both Exodus and Deuteronomy (including in 4Q28–4Q44 and LXX MS A) is murder, adultery, stealing. The order murder, stealing, adultery is found in Exodus LXX MS B and in Mark 7:21–22 in both A and B.[54] Paul omits the commandment about false witness (Deut 5:20) and shortens the coveting commandment, leaving out its object. At least here in Romans 13 Paul also omits the commandment about honoring parents (but cf. Ephesians 6).

It is something of a surprise that few seem to notice that whether we are talking about Paul or James or even Jesus, none of them reaffirm the commandment about the Sabbath for their disciples. Nor for that matter do they reaffirm the circumcision requirement either. Nor do they even suggest food laws are still required. While some silences are not pregnant or meaningful, these certainly are. The reason is because they are dealing with a new covenant, not the renewal of the Mosaic one.[55]

54. See Roy E. Ciampa, "Deuteronomy in Galatians and Romans," in Menken, *Deuteronomy*, 113.

55. The failure to recognize that Jesus is inaugurating a new covenant, distinct from the Mosaic one in various ways, leads to misunderstanding of the Gospel portrayal of Jesus as appealing, e.g., to the creation order, over against divorce laws of Moses that allow for hardness of heart (Deuteronomy 24). Jesus is not pitting one Scripture against another in the arguments in Mark 10 // Matthew 19 (pace Moyise, "Deuteronomy," 30–31). He is suggesting that the Mosaic covenant was from the outset a concession to human fallenness, to hard-heartedness, in

THE LOVE COMMAND: DEUTERONOMY 6:4–5

This familiar passage is in fact the beginning of the direct teaching of God's people by Moses, having passed along the direct revelation of the Ten Words. In a sense this is the bridge between the Ten Words, and the later statutes and ordinances that begin in Deuteronomy 12. As Miller notes, the reason Jesus (Matt 22:40) can say all the commandments hang on these words here is because quite literally the later statutes are spinning out the implications of the Ten Words and the love command as given here.[56] In turn, these words here can be seen as a summary of the Ten Words. Put another way, Deuteronomy 6:4–5 summarize the essence of the Ten Words and provide the basis for the spinning out of the implications of this great commandment in statutes and ordinances that follow this passage. The Shema begins by dealing with the same issue as the first two of the Ten Commandments, and continues by dealing with the rest of them in the command to love one's neighbor. Notice how often we find the language of the Shema juxtaposed with the prologue and first two commandments' language in Deuteronomy: 6:12–15; 7:8–10, 16b, 19b; 8:11, 15, 19; 9:1; 10:12–13; 11:1, 13, 16, 18–22, 28b; 13:2–5, 6, 10, 13; 18:9; 26:16–17; 29:26; 30:2b, 6, 8, 10, 16–17.[57] The Shema itself begins as a sort of confession that makes a claim on the confessor, and then leads to a command.

Notably, the phrase that introduces this material is the same as the one that introduces the Decalogue, namely "Listen up Israel," the introduction to the text that came to be called the Shema because of the initial verb. It is as though the writer wishes to make clear how very important these two pieces of tradition are.

MT	LXX
Hear, O Israel: The LORD our God, the Lord is one.	And these are the statutes and the judgments, which the Lord commanded to the sons of Israel in the wilderness as they were coming out from the land of Egypt. Hear, O Israel: The Lord our God is one Lord.

various ways, and so did not reflect God's highest and best for humankind at times. The new covenant however, will repristinize the original creation order design for marriage, forbidding divorce. As Paul was later to say rather clearly, the Mosaic covenant was pro tempore, a temporary arrangement until the new covenant should be inaugurated. This nuance of Jesus's teaching the author Hebrews understood as well.

56. Miller, *Deuteronomy*, 97.
57. Miller, *Deuteronomy*, 98.

⁵ Love the LORD your God with all your heart and with all your soul and with all your strength.
⁶ These commandments that I give you today are to be on your hearts.

⁵ And you shall love the Lord your God with the whole of your mind and with the whole of your soul and with the whole of your power.

⁶ And these words that I command you today shall be in your heart and in your soul.

καὶ ταῦτα τὰ δικαιώματα καὶ τὰ κρίματα ὅσα ἐνετείλατο κύριος τοῖς υἱοῖς Ισραηλ ἐν τῇ ἐρήμῳ ἐξελθόντων αὐτῶν ἐκ γῆς Αἰγύπτου ἄκουε Ισραηλ κύριος ὁ θεὸς ἡμῶν κύριος εἷς ἐστιν
καὶ ἀγαπήσεις κύριον τὸν θεόν σου ἐξ ὅλης τῆς καρδίας σου καὶ ἐξ ὅλης τῆς ψυχῆς σου καὶ ἐξ ὅλης τῆς δυνάμεώς σου

Verse 4 is the call to attention, and the reminder about the unique nature of Israel's God. There has been enormous debate about how exactly to translate the Hebrew of this verse, and whether or not the LXX is a good rendering of it. I have printed the Greek text above so one can see immediately that the word κύριος comes up twice at the end of v. 4, so the question becomes do we translate this "the Lord our God is one Lord," or "the Lord our God is (the only) Lord," or "the Lord our God is a unique Lord." What is the significance of the word "one"? Does it stress unity or uniqueness, or both? And why would the "unity" of Yahweh even be an issue? Is there a stress on this God being solitary, numerically One? The words themselves *Yahweh 'ekhad,* as opposed to say *Yahweh lebad,* have led some to suggest since *'ekhad* normally have to do with unity while *lehad* has more to do with uniqueness, this might point the discussion in a particular semantic direction, but the larger context and historical situation has to be taken into account as well.[58]

The polytheistic environment in which this pronouncement emerged would favor the conclusion that it was asserting that Yahweh is the only God, and as such it would not be a statement about the unity or nature of God per se, not a statement about his ontological make up, but rather a statement that Yahweh is the only living or true God.[59] The older rendering "Yahweh is our God, Yahweh is One" is on the right track, and does not settle the issue of what "one" might mean here.[60] Christensen, along with others,

58. See Miller, *Deuteronomy,* 99.

59. See the discussion in Richard B. Bauckham, *Jesus and the God of Israel: God Crucified and Other Studies on the New Testament's Christology of Divine Identity* (Grand Rapids: Eerdmans, 2008).

60. See Craigie, *Deuteronomy,* 168, following Cyrus H. Gordon.

suggests the rendering of the Hebrew as "Yahweh (is) our God, Yahweh alone."[61] This rendering of course would not rule out that other peoples might have other deities, but for Israel it would be solely Yahweh.[62] Miller suggests:

> To confess, therefore, that the Lord is "one" is to claim that the One who receives ultimate allegiance and is the ground of being and value is faithful, consistent, not divided within mind, heart, or self in any way. The reality of God in one time and place is wholly conformable with all other movements and experiences. . . . In purpose and in being God is one and the same.[63]

Whichever way one renders it, it is clear that this is as close as one gets to fundamental doctrine or dogma for ancient Israel. The relationship between God and his people is exclusive, and Yahweh is a unique deity, who will brook no rivals. When one compares this passage to the Decalogue itself there is considerable overlap in the whole exclusivity indicated when it comes to the way God's people are to view, relate to, and worship the one true living God. Not surprisingly, when we turn to v. 5, what God requires of his people is exclusive and whole-hearted allegiance, love, loyalty, and faithfulness to this unique deity who stands alone in a world thought to be populated by many gods.[64]

The point is not merely that God is the "most High" or top dog deity in a henotheistic pyramid, but rather that Yahweh is the only genuine deity, and there are no other real contenders, only pretenders. This did not prevent either OT or NT writers from suggesting that there were other supernatural beings out there, angels and demons, as they came to be called. Indeed, Paul in 1 Corinthians 10 will be quite explicit that monotheism doesn't evacuate the heavens of all other supernatural entities. Paul even calls the pagan deities

61. Christensen, *Deuteronomy 1–11*, 142; see also Nelson, *Deuteronomy*, 86.

62. Christensen, *Deuteronomy 1–11*, 142.

63. Miller, *Deuteronomy*, 101.

64. Nelson, *Deuteronomy*, 89 is right in saying that there is no general agreement among scholars as to how to translate v. 4 on two grounds: (1) syntax, and (2) the meaning of "one." Zech 14:9 would support the understanding that "one" means something like "unique," i.e., the only God for God's people. It would not then be a comment at all on God's interior or ontological nature. It is also possible to conclude that 2 Sam 7:23 provides the clue, the meaning being God is unrivaled and unparalleled "Yahweh is the one, the only Yahweh" (i.e., true God). Is this a claim that Yahweh has a unique relationship with his people, or that the other supernatural beings are not true God, or both? Either way, it would not be a comment on Yahweh's constitutional makeup. The idea however entails the notion that the one real God, Yahweh, has given his exclusive allegiance to his people, and they should reciprocate.

"demons" (10:21). The point is, they are not nothings, they are spiritually dangerous and so idolatry must be avoided for some very good reasons.

The love command itself in v. 5 is in effect a command to love the true God with one's whole being (cf. 4:9, 29; 10:12). Total commitment is what is implied by the combined phrases. This requires not just emotional attachment but real commitment of the whole person, affecting their thoughts, words, deeds, relationships, work habits, worship, and much else besides. It has been said that the whole book of Deuteronomy is in a sense a commentary on this verse, showing Israel what shape this love should take, and the shape is law-shaped, it involves keeping the law (cf. 10:12–13; 11:1, 3; 19:9; 30:16, 20, in short "if you love me you will keep my commands").[65] It should be stressed that the language about loving God was not characteristic of ANE treaty documents or covenants.[66] This is something that is distinctive of the nature of the relationship between Yahweh and his people. The injunction to love is based on the prior demonstration of love by God both in creating and in redeeming a people out of bondage. "Heart" here refers to the center of thought and intention, whereas *nephesh* refers to the inner self with its emotions, its deepest commitments.[67] The uniqueness of Yahweh as the real God calls for a unique and unconditional commitment to the real God by his people, hence all the warnings about idolatry, hence all the judgments for infidelity.

One of the more interesting differences between the Synoptic treatments of the love command is that whereas in Matthew 22:24–40 and Mark 12:28–34 the two great love commands (loving God, loving neighbor) are juxtaposed by Jesus himself, by contrast in Luke 10:25–28 it is the lawyer who combines Deuteronomy 6:5 with

---

65. See Craigie, *Deuteronomy*, 169.

66. Yes, William L. Moran, "The Ancient Near Eastern Background of the Love of God in Deuteronomy," *CBQ* 25 (1963): 77–87 has shown that the language of love is in some respects reminiscent of treaty language, but when one gets down to cases, the language about loving God, exclusively, is not drawn directly from the treaty terminology. See Ronald E. Clements, *God's Chosen People: A Theological Interpretation of the Book of Deuteronomy* (Valley Forge, PA: Judson, 1969), 83.

67. Nelson, *Deuteronomy*, 91.

Leviticus 19:18, though Jesus unequivocally endorses his answer.[68] But there are other oddities about the use of this material in the NT.

For instance, in Mark 12:29–33, after Jesus cites the text, the scribe he is talking with then repeats Jesus's answer, *but in a different form.*

> Beginning with an affirmation ("You are right Teacher; you have truly said that") and an oddly familiar reference to God ("he is one"), he adds "and besides him there is no other," possibly taken from Deut 4:35. He then abbreviates the four faculties to three by omitting "soul" and substituting "understanding" for "mind," deducing that this is much more important than all the whole burnt offerings and sacrifices (absent from Matthew and Luke) which Mark regards as a wise answer (12.34).[69]

I would suggest that the reason for the variance between Jesus's citation and what the scribe says, is that the scribe is demonstrating his independence from Jesus's wisdom, without being adversarial. In other words, he does not come off as simply a disciple of Jesus, parroting back the master's words. It has to be remembered that scribes were teachers, theologians and ethicists in fact, and as such they might speak in their own manner.[70]

FEAR THE LORD: DEUTERONOMY 6:13–16

This passage is important chiefly because of its mandate that God's people should "fear the Lord." But what does that really amount to? The instructions in Proverbs 1:7 tell us that it is the beginning of wisdom, but what sort of wisdom is it? Is the writer really talking about "live in fear or holy terror of God, because if you stray to other gods, he will get angry and exterminate you?" The rhetoric of fear, and God's wrath has often been read that way, and it can be coupled with the notion that God's people are to be holy, set apart, just as God is holy, set apart from other so-called gods.

68. Hays, *Echoes of Scripture in the Gospels*, 209 suggests that this difference means that Luke is portraying Jesus as bringing no new revelation, but is simply reinforcing what the teachers of Israel say. Yes and no. Luke portrays Jesus as offering an ethic in Luke 6 that does bring new revelation, but he also reaffirms some of the standing interpretation of Torah by others. There was in any case partial precedent for combining the love commands, cf. Testament of Issachar 5:2, "love the Lord and your neighbor"; and Testament of Dan 5:3, "love the Lord and one another with a true heart." The form of the double commandment is clearly different in these other sources.

69. Moyise, "Deuteronomy," 34–35.

70. Notice that only Luke 10:27 also has "strength" like Mark, but this surely just a variant of the Deuteronomic use of "might."

The theme of the fear of the Lord is already present in Deuteronomy 4:10 and 5:29, and it will be given strong emphasis again at
Deuteronomy 10:12. It is a regular motif in this sort of apodictic literature. Some scholars have quite reasonably suggested that what is
meant is to "revere" God, treat God with the respect, awe, and reverence due such an awesome and awe-inspiring being. One needs to
consider carefully what is put in parallel with the verb for "fear" here
and elsewhere, namely, the loving of God, and also the walking in
God's ways, obeying him. As we learn in the NT, there is no craven
fear in love, in fact real love casts out all fear (1 John 4:18). It must be
then seen as unlikely that the command here amounts to "be afraid,
be very afraid of Yahweh." Micah 6:8 suggests that "fearing the Lord"
equals doing justice, loving kindness, and walking humbly with one's
God. In other words, in all that one does, one keeps one eye on God
and what would both please God and comport with God's very character.

Christensen makes the helpful point that the nature of the servant
and his service is determined by the nature of the master. If the master
is, say, pharaoh, a ruthless dictator, then the service becomes a form
of slavery. If however the master is Yahweh, then the service is not
onerous, indeed it amounts to having the honor to worship God in
all one does.[71] Craigie is even more helpful. He notes that there is a
deliberate contrast and word play between "you shall serve" (ta'abod)
Yahweh, which is contrasted with "the house of slavery" ('abadim).
"Both words are derived from the same root and contrast vividly the
old and new masters of Israel."[72]

Another thing, the language about God being a jealous God and
a consuming fire (see Deut 4:24) that we find in various places in
Deuteronomy is tantamount to telling us that God is a lover of his
people, and like any good lover, he is zealous to protect the exclusive-
ness of the relationship.[73] Yes, the rhetoric is somewhat hyperbolic,
but it is not meant to portray God as some sort of insecure and mean-
spirited being. It is meant to portray him as a passionate maintainer
of his special relationship with his people, especially so because he is
both holy and has an exclusive relationship with that people.

In all of this we see a picture of a God with deep feeling, or as

---

71. Christensen, Deuteronomy 1–11, 47–48; and cf. pp. 205–6.
72. Craigie, Deuteronomy, 173.
73. See Craigie, Deuteronomy, 138.

Abraham Joshua Heschel long ago stressed, a God of pathos.[74] The notion of God's unchanging nature has to do with God's moral character, not whether God is "impassable" in the later Greek sense of the term. The God of the Bible most certainly has what we would call emotions, there is much he is passionate about, and to judge from Jesus, we would expect it to be no otherwise, for Jesus was one of the most passionate and emotional persons in Jewish history. One more point, the incarnation makes clear that God can incorporate change into the divine being without his character changing. Both Yahweh and Jesus, in regard to character, can be said to be the same yesterday, today, and forever.[75] The problem with reading the Pentateuch as portraying God in a primitive way and then reading the NT as though it portrayed God in some more "sophisticated" way is that it isn't really true. God is a God of both justice and mercy, of both holiness and compassion, of both purity and love in both testaments, Old and New. God is at least equally passionate in both collections of books.

The old caricature of the God of the OT being a God of wrath, and the God of the NT being a God of love is just that—a caricature. Nor is Christ portrayed in the NT as somehow less interested in justice and righteousness than Yahweh in the OT. Indeed, it is the slain lamb in heaven according to Revelation 5 who is the only one said to be worthy to judge the earth, a process recounted from Revelation 6–19. But this is hardly different from something like Mark 14:62 when Jesus tells the high priest that the Son of Man will be back, riding on the clouds to judge the very people currently judging him! If you think this is an exceptional picture of Christ, take a look at 2 Thessalonians 2! I could go on to point out that Jesus has more to say

74. See the classic book Abraham Joshua Heschel, *The Prophets* (New York: Perennial, 2001).

75. We will not attempt to address here the related philosophical conundrum as to whether God can change his mind on something. Certainly, God is depicted as doing so in the Pentateuch on some occasions, but since God is omniscient, philosophers have rightly asked questions about this. Perhaps God only appears to change his mind, but all along he knew where the conversation with, e.g., Abraham, was going? There is need for caution in such discussions because God is depicted in various anthropomorphic ways in the Bible, e.g., when God gets angry, the Hebrew sometimes says "his nose burned" or we would say, "God got red in the face." This is of course a metaphor, since God doesn't have a nose, or for that matter a face. So the question becomes: How does one read the anthropomorphic language of the Pentateuch? Is this just reporting how things appeared from the human point of view, e.g., how it appeared to Abraham or Moses? A further complication is this: the Bible depicts God as a God of divine condescension, he comes down to the human level in order to relate to his people in a loving and intimate way. See the fresh attempt to address these sorts of issues from a literary point of view by A.K. Knafl, *Forming God: Divine Amthropomorphism in the Pentateuch* (Winona Lake, IN: Eisenbrauns, 2014).

about Gehenna = hell than any other figure in the NT except perhaps the author of Revelation.

Perhaps here is a good place to note that Matthew's Jewish audience gets a full dose of Jesus using Deuteronomy, including in this chapter, more than in the other three Gospels by a lot. Maarten J. J. Menken is able to point to the following fifteen examples:

Matthew 4:4=Deuteronomy 8:3
Matthew 4:7=Deuteronomy 6:16
Matthew 4:10=Deuteronomy 6:13;10:20
Matthew 5:21=Deuteronomy 5:17 or Exodus 20:13
Matthew 5:27=Deuteronomy 5:18 or Exodus 20:14
Matthew 5:31=Deuteronomy 24:1, 3
Matthew 5:33=paraphrase of Deuteronomy 5:11, 20 ; 23:22
Matthew 5:38=Deuteronomy 19:21 or Exodus 21:24 or Leviticus 24:20
Matthew 15:4b=Deuteronomy 5:16 or Exodus 20:12
Matthew 18:16=Deuteronomy 19:15
Matthew 19:7=Deuteronomy 24:1,3
Matthew 19:18–19a= Deuteronomy 5:17–20, 16 or Exodus 20:13, 16
Matthew 22:24=Deuteronomy 25:5
Matthew 22:37=Deuteronomy 6:5[76]

What one notices immediately about this list is: (1) the heavy concentration in the first chapter of the Sermon on the Mount, Matthew 5; (2) the absence of any use of Deuteronomy in the ten chapters between Matthew 5 and Matthew 15; (3) the frequent use of material from Deuteronomy 5:16–20 and to a lesser degree from Deuteronomy 24; (4) the lack of use of any material between Deuteronomy 9 and 19. Now some of these uses are not citations, and some may in fact reflect use of Exodus rather than Deuteronomy, though there are some good reasons to think Deuteronomy is to the fore, especially on the lips of Jesus himself. As Menken notes, the use of Deuteronomy between Matthew 15–22 comes in controversy or pronouncement stories where Jesus is arguing or dialoguing with his discussion partners.[77] Matthew 18:16 is however an exception where Deuteronomy is used to norm relationships between Jesus's followers.

Matthew, on the whole reflects the same tendency of the NT writers in general, in using Isaiah, the Psalms, and Deuteronomy as his go-to texts. Note that Matthew's Deuteronomy material comes from

76. Maarten J. J. Menken, "Deuteronomy in Matthew's Gospel," in Menken, *Deuteronomy*, 42.

77. Menken, "Deuteronomy in Matthew's Gospel," 42.

all his sources: Mark, Q, and his special M material, especially the first and last of these sources (though Matthew 4:4, 7, 10 can be attributed to Q, unless of course Luke is using Matthew and not Q). To some extent this discussion of the discrete use of Deuteronomy by Matthew is a bit off the mark, because Matthew never cites the book Deuteronomy under that title, indeed it is always introduced by things like Moses said, or "it is written" and in general the author is typical of many in seeing the whole Pentateuch as a single unit of the "Law."

If we ask whether in general Matthew is using the LXX/OG form of these texts the answer seems to be yes, and note in particular that the expansion of Deuteronomy 8:3 in Matthew 4:4 points to the LXX as does the unidentified quote of Deuteronomy 19:15 in Matthew 18:16, though as Menken points out, elsewhere he seems to be using a later version of the LXX that has been corrected to conform more closely to the original Hebrew text when he uses books *other than Deuteronomy*, such as Isaiah and the Psalms.[78] The overall impression of the use of Deuteronomy in Matthew is that Matthew is drawing almost exclusively on the legal regulation material, not on the narratives. Menken allows that Jesus sometimes radically alters or interprets Torah, but he is also said to fulfill it, however the fulfillment saying is not just about the Law, but about the Law and the Prophets, and the language of fulfillment has to do with bringing to its intended eschatological conclusion, not merely keeping or obeying it. But Menken is right that the evangelist is writing to a group of Jewish Christians very interested in the ongoing use of Torah by followers of Jesus.[79]

NOT BY BREAD ALONE: DEUTERONOMY 8:2–3

MT (see below in the paragraph)

LXX
2 And you shall remember all the way that the Lord your God has led you in the wilderness so that he might distress you and test you and discern the things in your heart, whether you would keep his commandments or not.
3 And he distressed you and let you hunger and fed you with manna with which your fathers were not acquainted in order to announce to you that man shall not live by bread alone, but by every word that goes out through the mouth of God man shall live.

78. Menken, "Deuteronomy in Matthew's Gospel," 61.
79. Menken, "Deuteronomy in Matthew's Gospel," 62.

The OT text here deals with a reminder about the wilderness wandering period and God's provision of miraculous bread—manna, which means something like "what is it?," the response of a befuddled people who were starving. But more importantly, the passage is about God testing his people. "To 'test' (*nāsâ* v. 2) is to bring someone into a critical situation in order to observe reaction and behavior. Testing provokes a decision that proves character and faith" or the lack thereof if one fails the test.[80] While it is fine for God to test his people, the reverse is not fine because it involves not taking a totally trustworthy deity at his word. In this case

> The test involved humbling with hunger, and then feeding with manna (v. 3). Manna taught dependence because it came directly from God . . . Yahweh brings about both satiety and hunger. Israel must remember this lesson when good times bring about inappropriate self-confidence, but also may confidently trust divine providence when bad times threaten despair.[81]

As Miller stresses, the real issue here is not material food vs. spiritual food so much as obedient trust in God's provision as opposed to some sort of self-reliance.[82] The lesson of the wilderness wandering period was that God's people must always and ever be dependent on God for everything, even the mundane things in life. Therefore, God's people must live their lives by keeping the commandments, keeping and obeying the words God has given them, which is the key to ongoing life, even abundant life.

The famous temptation scene of Jesus that is found in Matthew 4 and Luke 4 has, without doubt, its background in Deuteronomy 8:2–3, which says

> Remember that the Lord your God led you on the entire journey these forty years in the wilderness so that he might humble you and test you to know what was in your heart, whether or not you would keep his commands. He humbled you by letting you go hungry, then he gave you manna to eat, which you and your fathers had not known so that you might learn that man does not live by bread alone but by every word that comes from the mouth of the Lord.

---

80. Nelson, *Deuteronomy*, 111.
81. Nelson, *Deuteronomy*, 111.
82. Miller, *Deuteronomy*, 116.

At the implicit level, bread is likely being compared to God's word here, or the author is saying that mundane food is not enough, for actual living one has to also take the word into one's life.[83]

One of the striking things about this, when we compare the story about Jesus being tempted in the wilderness is, that while it is true that Deuteronomy 8:3 is partially quoted in the account in the Gospels, it is also true that the preexisting narrative in Deuteronomy 8 has shaped the way the story of Jesus's temptation is framed. Consider for a moment the Matthean account: "Then Jesus was led up by the Spirit [of God] into the wilderness to be tempted by the Devil. After he had fasted for 40 days and forty nights, he was hungry." Notice as well that Matthew has the fuller quote from Deuteronomy 8:3, for Luke does not add "but by every word that comes from the mouth of God."[84] It is rare, in the many places that quotes or allusions show up in the NT, where not only a command is quoted but it's narrative context also shapes the NT text itself. But let's be clear; again, this is not exegesis of the OT text. It is drawing an analogy between the experience of Israel and that of Jesus. We can call this typology if we choose, but what we really are talking about is historical precedent that foreshadows later events, a foreshadowing that the NT writer noticed, and then allowed the context to shape how he told the Jesus story. I agree with Richard Hays assessment that "in Matthew's telling of the story, the Devil seeks to lure Jesus to *worship* him, but this would be a disastrous reversal of the true order of reality, in which Jesus himself is the proper object of worship—as demonstrated by Matthew's other uses of προσκυνεῖν. It follows, of course, that if only God is to be worshiped—as the quotation affirms—Jesus himself must be God."[85]

It is interesting that in Luke-Acts, only the characters in the narrative such as Jesus, quote Deuteronomy, or for that matter the OT in general with only one exception: Luke 2:23, 24 where we find Exodus 13:2, 15 and Leviticus 12:6–8. For that matter, as Dietrich Rusam points out, those quotations are always by a reliable character in the narrative, apart from Luke 20:28 = Deuteronomy 25:25–26.[86] We

83. See Hays, *Echoes of Scripture in the Gospels*, 118–20.

84. Notice that neither Matthew nor Luke have the final phrase found in the LXX: "man shall live."

85. Hays, *Echoes of the Scripture in the Gospels*, 396n52. Emphasis original. Cf. Menken, "Deuteronomy," 46n21.

86. Dietrich Rusam, "Deuteronomy in Luke-Acts," in Menken, *Deuteronomy*, 64. Satan is also an unreliable character in the narrative, but he used the Psalms rather than Deuteronomy to tempt Jesus.

may assume that reliable characters also reflect the views of the evangelist. Notice however that in regard to the quotations Luke takes over from his sources, such as Mark, all of them appear in controversy narratives between Jesus and his interlocutors, except in Acts 3:22 and 7:37 (Deuteronomy 18:15–29) where they appear in Peter and Stephen's apologia. In other words, overall the Scripture is being used to defend the new Jesus movement. It is the LXX that Luke is following in such quotations, as is evidenced by the fact that in Luke 18:20 he reverses the order of the commandments about adultery and murder found in Mark 10:19 to comply with the order in the LXX. Perhaps Luke's audience knew the LXX.[87]

FEAR AND WORSHIP: DEUTERONOMY 10:20

Perhaps it will not be amiss to deal here with Deuteronomy 10:20, another verse Jesus quotes in his battle of Scripture quotations with the devil in Matthew 4 // Luke 4. One of the things that is striking about this is that while the devil is singing the same old song, namely the Psalms, Jesus is sticking to the Pentateuch, the law as it is found in Deuteronomy. Here is the text itself—

MT	LXX
"You are to fear the Lord your God and worship him"	"You shall fear the Lord your God, and him you shall serve"

For good measure here is the Greek of the LXX:

κύριον τὸν θεόν σουφοβηθήσῃ καὶ αὐτῷ λατρεύσεις

Matthew 4:10 Κύριον τὸν θεόν σου προσκυνήσεις καὶ αὐτῷ μόνῳ λατρεύσεις.

Luke 4:8 Προσκυνήσεις Κύριον τὸν Θεόν σου καὶ αὐτῷ μόνῳ λατρεύσεις.

The OT text itself of Deuteronomy 10:20 picks up the language of fearing and serving from the lists in vv. 12–13, and then repeats Deuteronomy 6:13, but with the additional idea of "clinging," a verb more naturally applied to humans, indeed to spouses or lovers (cf. Gen 2:24; 34:3; 1 Kgs 11:2). While a modern person might think that

---

87. See Rusam, "Deuteronomy in Luke-Acts," 64–65. For much more detail see Rusam's larger study, *Das Alte Testament bei Lukas*, BZNW 112 (Berlin: de Gruyter, 2003).

love and fear, or even worship and fear do not belong together, this would not be the view of the biblical writers. The LXX here might seem to provide a more natural conjunction of slave-like behavior—you fear the master and you serve him. But the Hebrew is not talking about terror, or abject fear. God's people are to revere God highly, so highly that they worship Yahweh alone. The adding of a word here in the NT citations is quite natural.

Both Matthew and Luke have an additional word not found in either the MT or the LXX, namely "only"/"alone"; and notice that neither Matthew nor Luke mention *fear*, instead they speak of worshiping the Lord God and serving only him. Probably as we have already said however, the term "fear" in the original text should be rendered "revere" and so is close to the concept of worship. This is one of the cases where the agreement of Matthew and Luke (though Luke is closer to the word order in the LXX than Matthew) against any known ancient text of Deuteronomy 10 should be seen as an argument for either the existence of a Q source used by both evangelists, which had the word "only" at this point, or for the case that Luke used Matthew. I am unconvinced of the arguments for the latter, not least in this case because one has to ask: Why would Luke reorder the arrangement of the words in Matthew?

What should be asked about this whole scenario is how do these two evangelist's view Jesus?[88] Is he just another human figure like Job beleaguered by temptations by the devil, or is something more going on here? Is Jesus just playing out a script already seen in part in the life of Moses who was forty days and nights on Mt. Sinai and ate and drank nothing, or the similar trial of Elijah in the desert? The answer to this is no.

These temptations in Matthew and Luke should have struck the reader as odd. They are no ordinary temptations. While I've known some human beings who could turn bread into stones, I've never met a sane one who was "tempted" to turn stones into bread. Similarly, while I've met some people who thought they could do remarkable things, like leap the Grand Canyon on a motorcycle, I've never met a sane one who thought they could defy gravity altogether, or simply call on God's angels to bail them out when they foolishly jumped off a high precipice without a rope or bungee cord tied to their leg. Finally, while there have been some unhinged megalomaniac human rulers who thought they could rule all the kingdoms of the known

88. See the discussion in Hays, *Echoes of Scripture in the Gospels*, 118–19.

world by conquest (e.g., Alexander), none of them are said to have tried to strike a Faustian bargain with the devil, so that he would simply give these kingdoms to them in exchange for worshiping Satan.

My point is, these temptations are of the sort that only a divine Son of God might face if he was tempted to draw on the divine power he had in order to solve his personal problems and get out of difficult situations. Jesus did have the power to turn stones into bread, to call on an angelic entourage, and he was even destined to rule the nations, though not by means of a satanic shortcut. What is really happening here is that Satan is tempting Jesus to push his God button, but if he did that, he would no longer be 100 percent human; he would no longer be a person his disciples could model themselves on, for they did not have a God button to push. So, instead, Jesus draws on the resources any faithful person has, the word of God and the Spirit of God, to resist and reject the temptations of Satan. He acts as a true human being, even though he actually also is the divine Son of God. In due course, in Luke's narrative it will become apparent that Jesus is indeed the divine Son of God, worthy of being worshiped by his disciples, as Luke 24:52 indicates. As Rusam notes, only Jesus and God are to be worshiped as Luke's second volume, as Acts 7:43 and 10:25 indicate.[89]

This long theological reflection then leads to the question why did Jesus say, "you shall not tempt the Lord your God"? Is Jesus referring to *his own* temptation to tempt God himself, or, more likely, is he referring to the devil, who is doing the tempting here, tempting Jesus as the divine Son of God? Jesus, in this scenario, would be the "Lord" of the devil whom the devil should not be tempting. Notice that Satan does not say, "If you are a genuine human being following God then . . ."; no, he says, "If you are the [divine] Son of God, then . . ." But at the same time, and still drawing from Deuteronomy, Jesus also says, "a human being shall not live by bread alone."

In other words, Jesus intends to live as a fully human being, and indeed like any normal such being, he gets hungry and wants bread, but if he turns stones into bread, then he is doing something no mere mortal can do. Hence, these temptation scenes depict Jesus as both truly human and also truly divine, and his temptations are not normal human ones. This will also prove to be the case in the garden of Gethsemane when Jesus is tempted to avoid becoming a ransom for the many by dying on a cross. Again, this is no ordinary human

89. Rusam, "Deuteronomy," 66.

temptation. This is a temptation only a person who really could provide atonement for sins could undergo. In other words, the portrait of Jesus as both human and divine in these two Synoptic Gospels is not radically different than the one we find in John where Jesus states plainly that he and the Father are one, and the prologue tells us that God is not too big a word to apply to Jesus.[90]

THE PROPHET LIKE UNTO MOSES:
DEUTERONOMY 18:14–22

The promise of a prophetic figure like Moses was an important one, especially in early Jewish contexts where the focus was almost entirely on the Pentateuch, for example, in the case of the Samaritans (see, e.g., John 4). The Essenes clearly enough expected an eschatological prophet based in part on this text (cf. 1QS 9.1 and 4Q175). In addition, John 1:25 seems to suggest that the Pharisees expected a coming prophet.[91] It is no surprise then that Peter is depicted in Acts 3:22–23 as indicating that these very verses find their own prophetic fulfillment in Jesus (on which see below).

The discussion in Deuteronomy 18:14–22 needs to be seen in the larger context of what has just been prohibited, namely that Israelites are not to be using magic, or consulting sorcerers, using divination, or practicing necromancy (vv. 10–11). How then was Israel to get a late word from God? By listening to a true or genuine prophet. But how could one tell if this or that person was a genuine prophet? After the fact, one might discover he was or wasn't telling the truth, so one would have to wait and see what came to pass. Speaking truth, even speaking truth to power, was the final criteria that validated a true prophet.[92] This passage tries to address those sorts of questions in a general way. To some extent the point of this passage is to assure continued guidance from God for God's people after Moses was deceased. "But in addition, the passage is in itself prophetic as the New Testament interpretation makes clear."[93]

---

90. This is one of the more major important points Hays makes in *Echoes of Scripture in the Gospels*. There is no so-called "low christology" in those earlier Gospels.

91. The classic study on this matter is Howard M. Teeple, *The Mosaic Eschatological Prophet*, Journal of Biblical Literature Monograph 10 (Philadelphia: Society of Biblical Literature, 1957).

92. Miller, *Deuteronomy*, 152.

93. Craigie, *Deuteronomy*, 262.

MT	LXX
¹⁴ The nations you will dispossess listen to those who practice sorcery or divination. But as for you, the LORD your God has not permitted you to do so.	¹⁴ For these nations that you are about to dispossess, these will hear omens and divinations, but as for you, the Lord your God has not granted you to do so.

¹⁴ The nations you will dispossess listen to those who practice sorcery or divination. But as for you, the LORD your God has not permitted you to do so.
¹⁵ The LORD your God will raise up for you a prophet like me from among you, from your fellow Israelites. You must listen to him.
¹⁶ For this is what you asked of the LORD your God at Horeb on the day of the assembly when you said, "Let us not hear the voice of the LORD our God nor see this great fire anymore, or we will die."
¹⁷ The Lord said to me: "What they say is good.
¹⁸ I will raise up for them a prophet like you from among their fellow Israelites, and I will put my words in his mouth. He will tell them everything I command him.
¹⁹ I myself will call to account anyone who does not listen to my words that the prophet speaks in my name.

²⁰ But a prophet who presumes to speak in my name anything I have not commanded, or a prophet who speaks in the name of other gods, is to be put to death."
²¹ You may say to yourselves, "How can we know when a message has not been spoken by the LORD?"
²² If what a prophet proclaims in the name of the LORD does not take place or come true, that is a message the LORD has not spoken. That prophet has spoken presumptuously, so do not be alarmed.

¹⁴ For these nations that you are about to dispossess, these will hear omens and divinations, but as for you, the Lord your God has not granted you to do so.
¹⁵ The Lord your God will raise up for you a prophet like me from among your brothers; you shall hear him.
¹⁶ According to all that you requested of the Lord your God at Horeb on the day of the assembly, saying: "We shall not any more hear the voice of the Lord our God and again see this great fire—and we shall not die."
¹⁷ And the Lord said to me: "They are right in all that they have said.
¹⁸ I will raise up for them a prophet just like you from among their brothers, and I will give my word in his mouth, and he shall speak to them whatever I command him.
¹⁹ And the person who does not hear his words, whatever the prophet may speak in my name, I will exact vengeance from him.
²⁰ But the prophet who acts impiously by speaking a word in my name that I have not ordered to speak and who speaks in the name of other gods, that prophet shall die."
²¹ But if you say in your heart, "How will we know the word that the Lord has not spoken?"
²² whatever the prophet might speak in the name of the Lord but the thing does not take place and does not happen, this is the word that the Lord has not spoken. That prophet has spoken it in impiety; you shall not spare him.

The first criteria to be met for someone to be a legitimate prophet who follows Moses and continues to speak God's word to his people is that they have to be a fellow Israelite (v. 15). They could not be, for instance, a Balaam, from another cultural and ethnic context. The mediators referred to in vv. 9–14 are foreigners, who are not to be sought out or consulted. It shows a measure of extreme desperation that a king of Israel, like Saul, would ban such consultation and then in the end go consult the medium of Endor (1 Sam 28:3–25).

It may be asked why exactly God's people couldn't just hear from God directly, but it should be remembered that God's people were afraid to listen to God's voice directly, hence the need for a mediator, in the first case Moses, then prophets (see Deut 5:23–27). Genuine prophecy is a top down process. The prophet must wait on a revelation from God. There is no process or ritual that the genuine prophet can use to manipulate God and force an answer. Notice that since the word of the prophet is actually the word of God, and thus spoken with divine authority to ignore it or fail to obey it leads to divine judgment (v. 19).

Verses 20–22 turns to the matter of distinguishing true and false prophecy, an ongoing problem in the ANE. Clearly false prophecy was a problem, and so here we learn of the sanction for doing it—capital punishment. "But in order to know whether to obey the prophetic word, and in order to condemn the false prophet, criteria had to be established by which a distinction between true and false prophets could be made."[94] The distinction could be easy, for example, if the prophet spoke in the name of some deity other than Yahweh, which in addition would be a violation of the first commandment (also punishable by death). But what if a prophet spoke a false word in the name of the true God? This was more difficult to deal with, and two criteria are mentioned for discerning whether the prophet is telling the truth or not: (1) In the Hebrew is says "the word is not," that it literally, the word has no substance, no basis in reality, is not so. One could perhaps tell this by comparing what had just been said, to the sorts of things God had clearly said previously. (2) "The word does not come to pass." This is surely referring to prophetic words of a predictive or immediately judicial nature (e.g., "God will now strike you down with leprosy"). Christians would later add additional criteria to these two, for instance, if an itinerant prophet overstays his welcome in a particular place or asks for money then he is a false prophet (see Did. 11:10–12).[95] But even elsewhere

---

94. Craigie, *Deuteronomy*, 262.
95. There is some ambiguity in the text of the Hebrew, and some scholars have actually suggested that Deuteronomy has a purely negative view of possible later prophets. Compare the point and counterpoint on this issue by Hans M. Barstand, "The Understanding of the Prophets in Deuteronomy," *SJOT* 8 (1994): 236–51 (prophets after Moses are viewed negatively) and by Knud Jeppesen, "Is Deuteronomy Hostile towards the Prophets?," *SJOT* 8 (1994): 252–56 (not negative on the whole).

in the OT there are additional criteria for discerning a true prophet, such as consistency of his or her word with what true prophets had said in the past (but cf. Deut 13:1–5), evidence they were operating purely under the compulsion and direction of God, and often against their personal desires (cf. Jer 26:16–19; and 28:6–9) or it could even be asked if they participated in the divine council and so "overheard" God's word at the source (Jer 23:21–22; 1 Kgs 22:19–22; Isa 6:1–13, see esp. v. 8).[96]

Speaking of a prophet "like Moses" does not mean a prophet *equal* to Moses in all respects but like him in receiving and conveying God's inspired word. Like Moses, he is an authorized intermediary or even mediator for God with his people. Yahweh puts his word in the very mouth of the prophet (see Jer 1:9), so the prophet is not only not speaking on his own authority, he is speaking someone else's words, like a press secretary reading a leader's own words to the public.[97] Hence the regular formula used by Biblical prophets "thus says Yahweh."[98]

Not surprisingly, this material from Deuteronomy 18 crops up in the NT when a NT writers wants to suggest that Jesus was the eschatological prophet foreseen in the OT by Moses. For example, in Acts 3:22–23, Deuteronomy 18:15–20 comes up for citation, along with Leviticus 23:29, and the upshot is that Jesus and his followers are to be seen as the fulfillment of such prophecies. This is not because Luke desires to pursue a "Jesus is a prophet like Moses" typological schema.[99] Luke's agenda is rather to make clear that God's larger salvation historical schema for Israel and gentiles is coming to fruition in Jesus and his community.[100] Notice that Luke omits Deuteronomy 18:16–18 here, while the added sentence reflects Deuteronomy 18:19. He also adds the word "you" to the clause "you must listen to whatever he tells you." Otherwise, the LXX is closely followed here.[101] The omission seems to be because that material doesn't fit the context in Acts, and Luke is also suggesting that the prophecy spoke "to you," the immediate audiences of both Peter and Luke. Note that Deuteronomy is used as imperative or norm in the Gospel, but in

---

96. Miller, *Deuteronomy*, 153.

97. See Nelson, *Deuteronomy*, 235.

98. On this whole matter see Witherington, *Jesus the Seer*.

99. In fact, it might be better to say he is pursuing a "Jesus is like the prophet Elijah schema"—see Luke 7:16.

100. See Hays, *Echoes of Scripture in the Gospels*, 353.

101. Rusam, "Deuteronomy," 78.

the two places Luke has quotes from this source in Acts, it is used prophetically.[102]

The Markan framing of the transfiguration story in Mark 9 alludes to Deuteronomy 18:15 in the heavenly declaration "This is my Son, the Beloved: listen to him." Compare this to the LXX: "The Lord your God will raise up for you a prophet like me from among your own people; you shall listen to such a prophet" (προφήτην ἐκ τῶν ἀδελφῶν σου ὡς ἐμὲ ἀναστήσει σοι κύριος ὁ θεός σου αὐτοῦ ἀκούσεσθε). In light of the comment following in Mark 9:9–10 about the raising of the Son of Man, it is even possible that the language about "raising up" the prophet would still be alluded to, though now with a different sense of "raising up."

CURSED BE HE WHO HANGS UPON A TREE: DEUTERONOMY 21:22–23; 27:26

MT	LXX
[22] And if there is a man who has committed a crime incurring the death penalty, and he is put to death, and you hang him on a tree,	[22] Now if there is in someone sin, a judgment of death, and he dies and you hang him on a tree,
[23] his body shall not remain overnight on the tree, but you shall be careful to bury it on that same day, for a hanged man is an object accursed by God; and you shall not pollute your land, which the Lord God is about to give to you as an inheritance.	[23] his body shall not sleep upon the tree, but with burial you shall bury him that same day, for anyone hanging on a tree is cursed by God. And you shall not defile the land that the Lord your God is giving you as an allotment.
[27:26] Cursed be he who does not elevate the words of this law by doing them! And all the people shall say Amen!	[27:26] "Cursed be any person who does not remain in all the words of this law to do them." And all the people shall say, "May it be!"

The Greek of the LXX reads:

ἐὰν δὲ γένηται ἔν τινι ἁμαρτία κρίμα θανάτου καὶ ἀποθάνῃ καὶ κρεμάσητε αὐτὸν ἐπὶ ξύλου

οὐκ ἐπικοιμηθήσεται τὸ σῶμα αὐτοῦ ἐπὶ τοῦ ξύλου ἀλλὰ ταφῇ θάψετε αὐτὸν ἐν τῇ ἡμέρᾳ ἐκείνῃ ὅτι κεκατηραμένος ὑπὸ θεοῦ πᾶς κρεμάμενος ἐπὶ ξύλου καὶ οὐ μιανεῖτε τὴν γῆν ἣν κύριος ὁ θεός σου δίδωσίν σοι ἐν κλήρῳ

ἐπικατάρατος πᾶς ἄνθρωπος ὃς οὐκ ἐμμενεῖ ἐν πᾶσιν τοῖς λόγοις
τοῦ νόμου τούτου τοῦ ποιῆσαι αὐτούς καὶ ἐροῦσιν πᾶς ὁ λαός
γένοιτο

Galatians 3:10, 13:

Ὅσοι γὰρ ἐξ ἔργων νόμου εἰσὶν, ὑπὸ κατάραν εἰσίν, γέγραπται γὰρ
ὅτι Ἐπικατάρατος
πᾶς ὃς οὐκ ἐμμένει πᾶσιν τοῖς γεγραμμένοις ἐν τῷ βιβλίῳ τοῦ
νόμου τοῦ ποιῆσαι αὐτά.
Χριστὸς ἡμᾶς ἐξηγόρασεν ἐκ τῆς κατάρας τοῦ νόμου γενόμενος
ὑπὲρ ἡμῶν κατάρα, ὅτι γέγραπται Ἐπικατάρατος πᾶς ὁ κρεμάμενος
ἐπὶ ξύλου,

It is quite clear from the context in Deuteronomy 21 that this is not
a saying about crucifixion, nor even about dying while tied or nailed
to a tree or a wooden post (the Hebrew noun can mean tree or just
wood, and so a wooden object such as a pole or post; cf. 16:21). It is
about exposure of a dead person, surely for shaming by public viewing, after they have died (cf. Gen 40:19; 1 Sam 31:10; 2 Sam 4:12).
According to this text, the shaming is not to go on for long, the body
should not remain on the tree overnight but rather be buried the same
day "for a hanged man is an object accursed by God"; to leave it on
the tree overnight is to pollute the land.

In other words, the concern is not for the honor of the dead person,
but rather for the danger of ritual impurity in the land as a result of
a corpse being left above ground too long, not to mention the actual
danger of contagion and disease.[103] But one must also not forget that
permanent denial of burial was considered a huge affront, even a sin
(cf. 2 Sam 21:8–14; Jer 22:18–19). Such an act would not only bring
shame on oneself and one's people, but would amount to disobedience to God.

What then does it mean about the curse? The Hebrew could be
rendered so as to indicate that God is the one who is doing the cursing (a subjective genitive), but if one takes it as an objective genitive then we are talking about an offense or affront *against* God.
But what does one do with the word *Elohim* here? The curse might
involve creating a situation where a corpse's lengthy exposure leads
to the ghost of the diseased plaguing or cursing those who neglect

103. See Nelson, *Deuteronomy*, 262.

their duty to the dead.[104] Finally, are we being told that the body is accursed because it is the corpse of a person who committed a capital crime, or is the curse due to the fact that this person has been stripped of his honor, being displayed on a tree for public reviling? In either case, it is the deceased in all likelihood that is seen as cursed.

Besides public shaming, the hanging of the dead person in plain view was meant as a deterrent to serious crime by others, a warning that some crimes did carry the death penalty. This practice was certainly also used in military operations (see Josh 8:29; 10:26–27) but the context in Deuteronomy is judicial not military. One may presume that after a battle this practice had the same purposes of deterrent, warning, and shaming as in the judicial situation. As Craigie explains "the body was not accursed of God (or lit. 'curse of God') because it was hanging on a tree; it was hanging on a tree because it was accursed of God. And the body was not accursed of God simply because it was dead (for all [persons] die), but it was accursed because of the reason for the death."[105] In other words, this outcome was the evidence that the person had been cursed by God. It is not hard to see how this verse might be later used to conclude that a crucified Jesus had likewise been cursed by God.

If we ask the question whether the material in Deuteronomy might have led some early Jews to think the application was not just to hanging on a tree after execution, but in fact to hanging on a tree as a means of execution, the answer to the question is absolutely *yes*, and Paul is hardly the first person to make such an application. We see this already at Qumran in 11Q19 LXIV 10–12.[106] And we can lay to rest the false assumption that Paul in Galatians 3 means the law itself is the curse from which Christ liberated people. As Hays said some time ago: "When Paul's allusion to Deuteronomy is taken fully into account, one time-worn issue of Pauline exegesis solves itself: 'the curse of the law' from which Christ redeems us (Gal 3:13) is not the Law itself regarded as a curse, but the curse that the Law pronounces in Deuteronomy 27."[107] Like many another in early Judaism, Paul interprets Deuteronomy 21 in light of the later material in Deuteronomy 27, associating the two texts because of

104. Nelson, *Deuteronomy*, 255.

105. Craigie, *Deuteronomy*, 285.

106. This is helpfully discussed by Francis Watson, *Paul and the Hermeneutics of Faith* (London: T&T Clark, 2004), 420.

107. Hays, *Echoes of Scripture in Paul*, 203–4n24.

the shared language about the curse of God.[108] In Deuteronomy 27 we actually find the word for curse Paul substitutes in this quote (cf. 27:15–26) many times over. This helps assimilate the Deuteronomy 21 text to the opening words of Deuteronomy 27:2 (cited in Gal 3:10), so clearly Paul wants us to associate the discussion about the curse in these two texts. The curse recorded in the law is not to be distinguished from the curse of God that fell on Christ who took the place of sinful humanity on the cross.[109] If the curse sanctions of the Mosaic covenant have been exhausted, used up, in the judgment on Christ on the cross, then what follows from that (see Gal 3:10) is one is no longer obligated to keep "all the words of the Mosaic law." In the ANE when the curse sanctions had been executed, normally on the ones who had violated or broken the treaty or covenant, then that covenant and its laws were over and done with, null and void. The very language of Deuteronomy about curses prefigures how it would be that God would inaugurate a new covenant even after his people were expected to endure the curse sanctions of the old one, due to disobedience.[110]

NO OX MUZZLING PLEASE! DEUTERONOMY 25:4

MT	LXX
You shall not muzzle an ox while it is threshing out the grain.	You shall not muzzle a threshing ox.

LXX Greek:

οὐ φιμώσεις βοῦν ἀλοῶντα

1 Corinthians 9:9–10:

ἐν γὰρ τῷ Μωϋσέως νόμῳ γέγραπται Οὐκ ημώσεις βοῦν ἀλοῶντα. μὴ τῶν βοῶν μέλει τῷ Θεῷ; 10 ἢ δι' ἡμᾶς πάντως λέγει; δι' ἡμᾶς γὰρ ἐγράφη,

This piece of legislation in Deuteronomy has neither parallels nor any real evident connection to its immediate context, though I suppose

108. See the discussion of Watson, *Paul and the Hermeneutics*, 422 and Ciampa, "Deuteronomy," 103–5.
109. Ciampa, "Deuteronomy," 104–5.
110. See Hays, *Echoes of Scripture in Paul*, 44.

one could connect it to the general concern for animals expressed in the Sabbath commandment. But here the issue is not rest but food. The idea is that the ox should be allowed to eat a bit of the grain as he is threshing it out. There were two means of threshing, one is having the ox simply trample the grain, and the other is having the ox pull a sledge that does the threshing.[111] This command, like many another, seeks to connect work or action with appropriate consequences. The animal, who has previously plowed the field and is now threshing the harvest crop it helped to make possible, should be allowed to benefit from its labor.[112] Paul of course famously wants to suggest that the same principle, *mutatis mutandis*, should apply to apostles like himself: they should get some benefit from their apostolic labors.

In his discussion of Paul's use of this verse, Hays says

> Even the most mundane apodictic pronouncements in Scripture gain unforeseen spiritual gravity when read with the ruling conviction that Scripture must speak to us and must speak of weighty spiritual matters. . . . The commandment of Deut 25:4 cannot merely be a helpful tip on the care of livestock, because it is written . . . on account of us . . . and it concerns *us* . . . he speaks entirely for our sake. . . . Paul reads the text as bearing direct reference to his own circumstances and reads this commandment of the Law of Moses as a word addressed directly to Gentile Christians.[113]

Yes and no. Yes, he certainly thinks that this text is of relevance to his own situation and that of his converts in Corinth, vis-à-vis whether they are obligated to support his apostolic labors or not. But I would suggest this is not an allegorizing of this text, nor is the issue merely how Paul *reads* the text. Rather, Paul actually believes that this text has as its foundation a principle, namely that any kind of worker, animal or human, deserves to be compensated for his work. He should be able to receive the basic necessities of life for what he does, in this case food. This is a meaning that underlies or undergirds the particular application of the principle to the situation of the threshing oxen. In other words, Paul is not reading something into the text that is not there, nor is he allegorizing the text, but as Hays suggests, he does believe that the Scripture, even mundane texts such as this one, if carefully studied and applied, does still have a word from God for

111. See Craigie, *Deuteronomy*, 313.
112. Nelson, *Deuteronomy*, 297.
113. Hays, *Echoes of Scripture in Paul*, 165–66.

himself and his audience. More helpful are Miller's remarks that in 1 Corinthians 9:9 and 1 Timothy 5:18

> Torah is cited as Scripture, not as a literal regulation for Christian conduct but as indicative of a general principle that one who works deserves to be properly rewarded. That principle is indeed part of the force of the original regulation in Deuteronomy [i.e., one didn't have to spiritualize the rule to get that out of it], but its use in the New Testament illustrates how principles operative in these Old Testament statutes continued to guide the Christian community whether or not they may have been followed literally.[114]

In other words, the general principle is latent in and implied by the specific command, and is seen as applicable to persons and animals, perhaps even more applicable to persons than animals, as Paul suggests.

1 Corinthians 9 is not however the only place in the Pauline tradition that a quote of Deuteronomy 25:4 shows up. It also shows up in 1 Timothy 5:18, with slightly different word order, but again, otherwise close to the LXX text, in fact closer to the LXX text than the Pauline citation in 1 Corinthians 9:9 in that we find the same verb here in 1 Timothy 5:18 as in the LXX. For this reason, as well as for the reason of word order, it is unlikely that this use of Deuteronomy 25:4 is simply cribbed from 1 Corinthians 9; it is an independent citation of the LXX text.[115]

To this is appended a different saying, "the worker is worthy of his hire," which presumably goes back to a saying of Jesus, and is found in a different form in 1 Corinthians 9:14 where it is specifically attributed to Jesus, unlike here. Here the discussion has to do with supporting elders in particular, and the word τιμή may in fact refer to pay, rather than to honor, but that is uncertain.[116] It is interesting that this is perhaps the only clear quotation from the OT in the Pastoral

---

114. Miller, *Deuteronomy*, 171.

115. Here is not the place to enter the lists of long debate about the authorship of the Pastorals. It is my view that they were written by a Pauline coworker, probably Luke, and at Paul's behest while he was under arrest in Rome in the mid-60s and before his death. There are some forty vocabulary words and phrases found in the Pastorals and in Luke-Acts and nowhere else in the NT. The person who composed these documents is not a slavish imitator of Paul, but has his own style and way of putting things; see Witherington, *Letters and Homilies for Hellenized Christians Vol. 1.* I like to put it this way, the voice is the voice of Paul, but the hands are the hands of Luke.

116. See the discussion by Gerd Hafner, "Deuteronomy in the Pastoral Epistles," in Menken, *Deuteronomy*, 138–44.

Epistles, and yet it is precisely in the Pastorals that we find the dramatic statement about the inspiration, authority, and profitability of the teaching of the OT in 2 Timothy 3:16–17.

VENGEANCE IS MINE! DEUTERONOMY 32:35–36, 43

MT	LXX
35 To me belongs vengeance and recompense For the time when their foot shall slip Because close is the day of their calamity And impending doom hastens up them.	35 In a day of vengeance, I will repay, in a time when their foot slips, because near is the day of their destruction and things prepared for you are at hand.
36 For the Lord will vindicate his people And will have compassion upon his servants, When he sees that their strength is exhausted And become nothing, for slave and free alike. . . .	36 For the Lord will judge his people and be comforted over his slaves. For he saw them paralyzed, both failed under attack and enfeebled. . . .
43 Praise his people, o nations, For he will avenge the blood of his servants. And he will return vengeance to his adversaries And make atonement for the land of his people.	43 For he will avenge the blood of his sons and take revenge and repay the enemies with a sentence, and he will repay those who hate, and the Lord shall cleanse the land of his people.

Though the form of the English translation above will not make this clear, this is Hebrew poetry and is part of the final Song of Moses, helping to bring the story of Moses and the book of Deuteronomy to a close, leaving only the obituary about Moses's death at the very end of the book. It should be said at the outset that this poem has many words found nowhere else in the OT, and it is often difficult to properly translate. Most scholars suggest the poem is probably very ancient indeed, and I concur. The song does not speak about particular events, but gives a general prognosis about the future both in terms of blessing and in terms of judgment. It is generally prophetic in character, and, in that regard, can be said to be like the poetic prophecy in Second Isaiah.

What characterizes the prophecy here is long lines and skilled forms of poetic parallelism. The poetic character of the material makes it stand out from what precedes it in Deuteronomy. The song bears witness to, and celebrates the renewal of the covenant with God's people, and his ongoing promise to deal with their enemies and vindicate them. The verses we are concerned with that recur in the

NT deal quite specifically with that subject.[117] Note that the song's pattern of argument seems like or similar to that of the covenant lawsuit that God prosecutes with his people through his prophets from time to time.[118] More certainly, God is depicted as the divine warrior here who defends (but also judges) his people, and deals with their adversaries and enemies. Because God will faithfully judge, there is no need for Israel to take personal revenge. Verse 43 circles back to the opening theme and promise of divine vindication of God's people.

Harold Fisch has helpfully reminded us of the way poetry like this works when it is sung repeatedly by God's people:

> It will . . . act as a mnemonic, an aid to memory, because during the intervening period it will have lived unforgotten in the mouth of the reader or hearer, ready to come to mind when the troubles arrive. Poetry is thus a kind of time bomb, it awaits its hour and then springs forth into harsh remembrance. . . . It will live in their minds and their mouths, bringing them back, whether they like it or not, to the harsh memory of the desert sojourn. Once learned it will not easily be forgotten. The words will stick, they will be importunate, they will not let us alone.[119]

As Miller rightly stresses, the imagery about God as the divine warrior is using the language of the day to convey the notion that God is sovereign and will see justice done, in particular in the form of vindicating the oppressed, the poor, the disenfranchised. As Miller says, we are talking about vindication not vindictiveness here, not irrational angry lashing out.

> It is the exercise of God's power for the protection of God's people and the accomplishment of God's purpose, the executive action of the deity to effect moral order and just rule in the universe. . . . The manifestation of that vindication may be the undoing of the corrupt and wicked. . . . It may also be the lifting up of the weak and the powerless, the hurt and the suffering. . . . Indeed, the Lord's vindication may be an act of both lifting up for some and putting down for others . . . the positive or negative character of the divine vengeance is shaped by the circumstances.[120]

117. Craigie, *Deuteronomy*, 373–78.
118. See Nelson, *Deuteronomy*, 369.
119. Harold Fisch, *Poetry with a Purpose: Biblical Poetics and Interpretation*, ISBL (Bloomington: Indiana University Press, 1988), 51.
120. Miller, *Deuteronomy*, 233.

This is what some scholars have called redemptive judgment, whereby the same act vindicates some and judges others. It can even, like the exodus, involve deliverance for some by means of judging others. Miller is also right to add that the implication of "vengeance/vindication is mine" is that it is not *ours*, it is not for God's people to usurp God's role in such matters as final justice or vindication. Romans 12:19 among other NT texts makes especially clear that this matter should be left exclusively in God's hands.[121]

In order to fully appreciate what is going on in those verses we need to look at the *other* allusions to the earlier and later parts of this song in the NT. There is first of all the praise of God in v. 4 that reads "The Rock—his work is perfect; all his ways are just. [He is] a faithful God without bias, he is righteous and true." 1 John 1:9 picks up the phrase "faithful . . . and righteous" and uses it of the same subject as it is used of in Deuteronomy 32. In other words, the language is not transferred to Jesus, even though his atoning death is mentioned in the immediate context. So this is not an example of transferring the terminology to Jesus. Revelation 15:3–5 is a whole different story. It is a paraphrase of Moses's Song. Consider here the parallels:

Deuteronomy 32:3–4	Revelation 15:3
I will proclaim the name of the Lord.	Lord God Almighty.
Oh, praise the greatness of our God! 4 He is the Rock, his works are perfect, Just and true are your ways, A faithful God who does no wrong,	Great and marvelous are your deeds, and all his ways are just. upright and just is he.

But here's the catch. The Song in Revelation 15 is identified as not only the Song of Moses but also the Song of the Lamb. To use a phrase from the world of music, Moses's song has been "sampled" and inserted into a song that praises both God and the Lamb. And actually, this is often the kind of way Deuteronomy is used in the NT. Its language, its images, its ideas, its phrases are sampled, and made part of a different larger whole. Sometimes the subject is the same as in Deuteronomy, sometimes it is not. In this case, it is partially the same. But the starting point for John is the new reality involv-

---

121. Miller, *Deuteronomy*, 234–35.

ing Christ, which transfigured how he saw and read and used the OT Scriptures.[122]

Deuteronomy 32:5 critiques God's people as a devious and crooked generation, a critique that crops up in various places in the NT with slight variations. The LXX has the phrase as γενεὰ σκολιὰ καὶ διεστραμμένη. We find on the lips of Jesus in Matthew 17:17 // Luke 9:41 a similar phrase Ὦ γενεὰ ἄπιστος καὶ διεστραμμένη, the difference being the accusation of unbelief rather than being devious or warped. Acts 2:40 has the even shorter echo, τῆς γενεᾶς τῆς σκολιᾶς ταύτης. Interestingly, it echoes the first of the two adjectives in the phrase in Deuteronomy 32 not the second one, unlike the Gospels. Now this sort of phrase is found in various places in the accusations against God's people in the OT, but because of the heavy use of Deuteronomy 32 in various places in the NT, it is probably the primary source for such language in the NT. A slight variation of this same phrase crops up in Deuteronomy 32:20 where the generation is called perverse and unfaithful (οὐκ ἔστιν πίστις ἐν αὐτοῖς). So now it becomes apparent that the allusion in the Gospels is a composite one to several places in the Song of Moses.

The notion that God set boundaries on the earth for various different people groups is found not only in Deuteronomy 32:8 but also in Paul's speech at the Areopagus in Acts 17:26. It is interesting to compare Deuteronomy 32:11 where God is depicted as like a great eagle hovering over the nest of baby birds, catching them when they fall, carrying them on his wings to the image of Jesus as a hen who would gather and protect his Jerusalem chicks, but they would not come to him (Matt 23:37 // Luke 13:34). Why the difference in imagery? I would suggest it is because Jesus often portrayed himself as Wisdom, which was a female image in Proverbs 3, 8 and in intertestamental literature like Wisdom of Solomon.[123]

There are only two notable references to "demons" using the basic term τὰ δαιμόνια outside the Gospels and Acts, namely in 1 Corinthians 10:20 (the only use of the term in Paul) and Revelation 9:20 (the only use in that book as well). Is this an intertextual echo? As it happens the LXX of Deuteronomy 32:17 reads ἔθυσαν δαιμονίοις, they sacrificed to demons, a reference to the false gods that Israel should never have worshiped, indeed beings that were not gods at

---

122. See the discussion in Michael Tilly, "Deuteronomy in Revelation," in Menken, *Deuteronomy*, 172–74.

123. For a detailed discussion on this point see Witherington, *Jesus the Sage*.

all, though they were real beings. This seems to be another example of drawing on Deuteronomy 32. As Rosner points out, Psalm 106:37 extends this critique of idolatry complaining "they sacrificed their own children to demons."[124]

Deuteronomy 32:21b is in fact quoted in some form in Romans 10:19, and note that the quotation is attributed by Paul to Moses. Let's compare the LXX with what Paul has

LXX κἀγὼ παραζηλώσω αὐτοὺς ἐπ' οὐκ ἔθνει ἐπ' ἔθνει ἀσυνέτῳ παροργιῶ αὐτούς
Romans 10:19 Ἐγὼ παραζηλώσω ὑμᾶς ἐπ' οὐκ ἔθνει, ἐπ' ἔθνει ἀσυνέτῳ παροργιῶ ὑμᾶς.

The only major difference is the use by Paul of the second person here rather than the third person, which makes it seem more like a direct address. The point of the quote is to punctuate the idea that God's saving of gentiles was in part meant to make Israel jealous so they too would turn back to God. In 1 Corinthians 10:22 Paul uses the language of the first half of that same verse from Deuteronomy 32 to ask if the Corinthians by their sinful behavior involving idol feasts were not provoking God to jealousy.

Deuteronomy 32:39 may be alluded to in John 5:21 in the claim "to make alive," but it is hard to tell since that evangelist tends to rephrase and repurpose his use of OT texts and in any case Deuteronomy 32:39 is not the only place God is said to be able to give and take life (cf. Neh 9:6; Eccl 7:12; 2 Kgs 5:7; and see the citation of Deut 32:39 in 4 Macc 18:19).[125]

Not to be overlooked are the various uses of Deuteronomy 32:43 in the NT. It is quoted twice and alluded to in three other places. Here is the LXX text of that verse

LXX εὐφράνθητε οὐρανοί ἅμα αὐτῷ καὶ προσκυνησάτωσαν αὐτῷ πάντες υἱοὶ θεοῦ εὐφράνθητε ἔθνη μετὰ τοῦ λαοῦ αὐτοῦ καὶ ἐνισχυσάτωσαν αὐτῷ πάντες ἄγγελοι θεοῦ ὅτι τὸ αἷμα τῶν υἱῶν αὐτοῦ ἐκδικᾶται καὶ ἐκδικήσει καὶ ἀνταποδώσει δίκην τοῖς ἐχθροῖς καὶ τοῖς μισοῦσιν ἀνταποδώσει καὶ ἐκκαθαριεῖ κύριος τὴν γῆν τοῦ λαοῦ αὐτοῦ

124. Brian Rosner, "Deuteronomy in 1 and 2 Corinthians," in Menken, *Deuteronomy*, 130.
125. See Michael Labahn, "Deuteronomy in John's Gospel," in Menken, *Deuteronomy*, 90–91. In general, Labahn (88) is able to show that the one chapter in John that seems to have various allusions to Deuteronomy 5 is in fact John 5 (he cites Deut 5:5, 21, 31–34, 37, and various other places in 5:20–37).

This needs to be compared to Romans 15:10 and Hebrews 1:6. The latter text is so very clearly drawing on the LXX because the Hebrew text does not mention angels praising but the LXX clearly does.[126] In fact Hebrews only has the one clause "let all God's angels praise him" and none of the rest of that verse. Romans 15:10 needs to be quoted in full:

καὶ πάλιν λέγει Εὐφράνθητε, ἔθνη, μετὰ τοῦ λαοῦ αὐτοῦ.

Paul has chosen this text and this phrase from this text because it mentions both gentiles and Jews separately, and it speaks about gentiles rejoicing with Jews about the mercy and grace of God.[127] Indeed, he strings together several texts from the OT that mention gentiles to make the point—the first quotation may be from some form of 2 Samuel 22:50, but more likely it is from Psalm 18:49, only using a different verb. The second quotation is the one mentioned above. The third one, at Romans 15:11 is drawn from Psalm 117:11, a call for all the nations to praise the biblical God, and the fourth one comes from Isaiah, this time connecting the coming of the root of Jesse with both the ruling of the gentiles and also their placing their hope in him (Isa 11:10). What connects them all is not just the mention of gentiles, but the gentiles having some sort of relationship with both the biblical God and his Jewish people.

This provides backing for the exhortation of Romans 15:7 to his largely gentile audience to embrace the Jewish Christians in their midst, "for I say that Christ became a servant of the circumcised on behalf of God's truth, to confirm the promises to the fathers, and so that Gentiles may glorify God for his mercy." As it turns out, God is the God of both Jews and gentiles and they both enter the new covenant community on the same basis: the mercy of God, by grace through faith in the Lord Jesus whom God raised from the dead.

This brings us to our main texts, quoted above about the vengeance of God, and we must deal with them in some detail, because the ideas in those verses are so important to understanding what the NT says about vengeance and vindication by God.

126. In particular, it is following the form of the LXX text found in Codex Alexandrinus. See Gert J. Steyn, "Deuteronomy in Hebrews," in Menken, *Deuteronomy*, 156.

127. As Ciampa, "Deuteronomy," 114–15 notes, Paul is following the LXX, which is much longer than the MT version, which has only four lines. More importantly the LXX version "reflects a more positive attitude towards the Gentiles than that which is found in the MT," which may help explain why Paul is following it here.

Hays discussion of Paul's use of the Song of Moses in Romans 10 and 15 is helpful at this juncture.

> Deuteronomy fits the profile of the other texts given the greatest canonical weight in Paul's Scriptural interpretation, because—on Paul's reading—it renders an account of God's mysterious action through the word to bring the whole world, Jew first and also the Greek, to acknowledge his unconditional lordship. . . . Deuteronomy parallels Isaiah's crucial hermeneutical turn: both texts have already read the history of Yahweh's dealing with Israel typologically as a prefiguration of a larger eschatological design.[128]

Right there in the Song of Moses was the notion of God making Israel jealous, of Israel's lack of faith and yet final return to the fold, and even of the gentiles coming to praise Israel's God. But is this mere typology, where what the author of Deuteronomy says has an application in his own day, which foreshadows a bigger and better application or fulfillment in a later eschatological day? Perhaps. But if we ask when did something as described in Isaiah 66 or Deuteronomy 32 ever happen in the history of Israel, the answer would seem to be—*never*. That being the case, Paul may be saying that what was spoken of back then finds its first and only real fulfillment in the series of eschatological events already transpiring in his own day.

Ross Wagner, in his detailed look at this same material, is absolutely right in saying that "the use Paul makes of Deuteronomy 32:43 in Romans 15:10, then provides striking confirmation of my argument that Paul reads the Song [of Moses] as a whole as a narrative of God's faithfulness to redeem Israel and through Israel, the entire world."[129] He rightly points to the way the Song material shows up right through the powerful argument found in Romans 9–11, meant to demonstrate that God has not forsaken his first chosen people, and that they will yet have a future in Christ. So, for example, Deuteronomy 32:4 is echoed in Romans 9:14 and possibly Romans 11:1 as well; then Deuteronomy 32:21 is quoted in Romans 10:19 and then further alluded to in Romans 11:1–19; and then in Romans 12:19, Deuteronomy 32:25 is quoted; and then finally there is our text in Romans 15. "There, Paul appeals to Deuteronomy 32:21 in order to demonstrate that Israel's present resistance to the Gospel is an integral part of God's

---

128. Hays, *Echoes of Scripture in Paul*, 164.

129. J. Ross Wagner, *Heralds of the Good News: Isaiah and Paul in Concert in the Letter to the Romans* (Leiden: Brill, 2002), 317.

plan to effect salvation for the Gentiles and, in the end, to redeem Israel as well."[130]

When one sees the larger pattern of how Paul is using the Song of Moses in these chapters it becomes impossible to argue that Paul means the church, or for that matter Christ, by Israel in these discussions. No, Israel is still Jacob (see Rom 11:26–27), and the Redeemer will have to come again from heaven and turn away the impiety of Jacob before "all Israel may be saved (11.25-25)."[131] This brings us to a crucial point in our study. How one views Israel as discussed in the NT dramatically affects how one views the hermeneutics of the NT writers' use of the OT. If one thinks either Christ or the church or both is signified by the term Israel in the NT, this certainly changes how one evaluates the use of the OT in the NT by these early Christian writers. If the writers think God is not done with non-Christian Israel yet, then the way they apply the OT to the church is definitely affected, indeed in some cases determined by that conviction.

It cannot be an accident that a figure like Paul wants to connect the new covenant with the Abrahamic one and not with the Mosaic one. Paul says Christ brought to an end, or conclusion any sort of righteousness that could be obtained by the keeping of the Mosaic law covenant (Rom 10:4). And yet, God is not done with Israel the people, because God is faithful to his own character and plans for Israel. But they, temporally broken off from the people of God if they have rejected Christ, must reenter the people of God on the same basis as the gentiles—by grace through faith in a merciful God who sent forth his Son so there could be Jew and gentile united in Christ. This means that for Paul some of the prophecies and promises of God are still awaiting fulfillment for Israel. There are not two peoples of God following two different covenantal destinies, studying two different sets of biblical texts.

Ultimately all must be one in Christ through the new covenant, but there is an already and not yet dimension to the kingdom, to the church, to the fulfillment of prophecy and promise in the OT, and so too to the interpretation of the OT. God is not finished with Israel yet. The "oracles," (see Rom 9:1–5), or, as we call them, the OT Scriptures, have not been snatched from the hands of Israel and

---

130. Wagner, *Heralds of the Good News*, 316.

131. On which see the exegesis of Romans 9–11 in Witherington and Hyatt, *Letter to the Romans*, 236–79.

given to another people who then can simply apply them to themselves while ignoring their meaning for Israel. No indeed.

The church is the heir of Israel, not its replacement, and so the Scriptures belong now to both Israel and the church and have meaning for both groups. The Christ is not Israel but rather the Redeemer of Israel and also of the nations. It is this sort of theological mindset that best explains the use of the OT in the NT by early Jewish Christians like a Paul or a James or a Peter or the author of Hebrews.

Here it is worth suggesting a theory as to why there are more than thirty quotations, allusions, or echoes to the Song of Moses in the NT. My suggestion would be the same as I have made about some of the Psalms: these songs were memorized by early Jews, including early Jewish Christians and sung by them. They were sung right along with the new christological hymns we find fragments of in places like Philippians 2:5–11 or Colossians 1 or Hebrews 1 or John 1. Indeed, Ephesians 5:19 encourages Christians to recite and sing "psalms, hymns, spiritual songs" to one another as part of their worship. I would suggest that this included the Song of Moses, which could be adopted and adapted in various ways, hinted at in Revelation 15.[132] As I said in the book on the Psalms, one of the main reasons that song material crops up so often in the NT is because it was the most familiar, being the only part of the OT that was taught, preached, memorized, recited, and sung in worship. It's liturgical character and its frequent use not only in teaching but in worship, and its poetic form that made it so memorable and memorizable, also made it something that readily came to the mind of the earliest Jewish Christians when they wanted to express their faith and adoration of God.

So what then should be made of Deuteronomy 32:32–35, 43b? In the first place, the discussion is about what will happen to the adversaries of Yahweh, who are also the enemies of Israel. While there are plenty of places in the OT where we hear about God's judgment beginning with the household of God (cf. Jer 25:29 and 1 Pet 4:17), this is not one of them. There is some deliberate paradox in our verses. Yes, God could use Israel's foes as an instrument to judge Israel's sin, but they would remain responsible for their own actions. Israel here is told not to retaliate but to leave the matter in God's hands. When justice is not immediately done to Israel's foe the expression is that they are storing up wrath for the future. Here a similar sort of language is used: "Is that not stored up with me, sealed up

132. See Witherington, *Psalms Old and New*.

in my treasure houses? To me belong vengeance and recompense, for the time when their foot shall slip; because close is the day of their calamity and impending doom hastens upon them. For the Lord will vindicate his people."

Several different ideas are at work here. Vengeance here is not the modern concept of an irrational and passionate act, spawned out of anger because of some perceived wrong or slight. No, here we are dealing with the idea of the administration of justice, not personal revenge-taking. The principle of a fair recompense, and of the punishment fitting the crime is underlying all this, but more importantly what is really assumed is that only an omniscient and entirely fair and just God is really capable of assessing complex human situations and truly doling out justice. Ultimately, God reserves the right to be the judge of the earth, and finally only God has the insight and power to see it through to a just conclusion.

Another idea here in play is of course the idea of God being the protector of his people and the guarantor of the covenant or treaty he has with them. This entails the notion that an attack on God's people is an attack on their covenant God. This is the very same idea that comes into play in say Acts 9 when Jesus confronts Saul on the Damascus Road and asks why Saul is persecuting Jesus. To mess with God's people is to mess with God, and God will vindicate his people without any human irrational vindictiveness.

And this brings us to one further key OT idea: namely, the idea of redemptive judgment, already mentioned briefly. The very same act of God, namely bringing judgment on Israel's foes also brings redemption and vindication to God's people. So, for example, the liberation of the Hebrews from Egypt was accomplished by the judgment of Yahweh on Egypt the oppressor. In such a case, the same actions serve as acts of compassion for one group, and acts of judgment on another. Redemption and judgment in the Bible are not always two distinct things; they often go together.[133]

Deuteronomy 32:35 is quoted in Romans 12:19 as an imperative given to the Roman Christians. They are not to avenge themselves but to leave room for God to take care of that. "Paul follows early Jewish tradition in applying this promise to personal offenses suffered at the hands of ungodly neighbors and enemies (1QS X.17–18; CD

---

133. See Craigie, *Deuteronomy*, 387–89.

IX.2–5; T. Gad. 6:7; 2 Enoch 50:4; Ps. Phoc. 77).”[134] Paul of course now applies this to even gentiles within the Christian community.

Here perhaps is a good juncture to deal with the varied use of Deuteronomy in the book of Hebrews. A brief chart will show what I mean—

Hebrews 1:6	Deuteronomy 32:43 (Moses's Song)
Hebrews 10:28	Deuteronomy 17:6
Hebrews 12:3	Deuteronomy 32:35–36 (Moses's Song)
Hebrews 12:15	Deuteronomy 29:17 (18)
Hebrews 12:18, 19	Deuteronomy 4:11, 12
Hebrews 12:21	Deuteronomy 9:19
Hebrews 12:29	Deuteronomy 4:24/9:3
Hebrews 13:5	Deuteronomy 31:6[135]

Notice that all the quotations here are short, even fragmentary, and so Gert Steyn is right to ask: Is the author quoting from memory? And if so, should we be spending so much time trying to figure out which version of the OT he is using, when he could be paraphrasing in his own language? Importantly, Steyn points out that unlike his Psalms and Jeremiah quotations, the use of Deuteronomy does not involve extended quotations, nor are the Deuteronomy quotations cited with reference to divine authority. Could this be because our author, while recognizing Deuteronomy as Scripture believes the Mosaic covenant is no longer binding on his audience per se, and particularly because he doesn't want these Jewish Christians retreating back into non-Christian Judaism under pressure or persecution is being careful how he uses the Law? In any case, he clearly believes the Mosaic covenant has been superseded by a better covenant, the new covenant. Further, what explains the fact that apart from Hebrews 1:6, all of the citations come between Hebrews 10:28 and 13:5? Even of these nine found within those parameters, only four are clearly explicit quotations, Deuteronomy 32:43 (LXX Ode 2) in Hebrews 1:6; Deuteronomy 32:35–36 in Hebrews 10:30–31; Deuteronomy 9:19 in Hebrews 12:21; and Deuteronomy 31:6 in Hebrews 13:5.

134. Ciampa, "Deuteronomy," 112.
135. I have modified the chart from Steyn in "Deuteronomy in Hebrews," 153.

In a different work, I have pointed out at some length how the book of Hebrews likely reflects familiarity with several of Paul's letters, for instance Galatians.[136] A good case could be made for his knowing several other Pauline letters, for instance 1 Corinthians, and I would also say Romans. Steyn's observation provides some substance to this suggestion:

> The unknown author of Hebrews quotes from the context immediately preceding a quotation (Deut 9:3 in Hebrews and Deut 9:4 in Romans [10:6a]) and also alludes to the following context of a quotation that occurs in Romans (Deut 29:17 in Hebrews and Deut 29:3 in Romans). Furthermore, from all the books in the NT which contain quotations from Deuteronomy [Mark, Matthew, Luke-Acts, Romans, Hebrews], it is only Hebrews and Romans that explicitly quote from Deuteronomy 32, the "Song of Moses."[137]

Among other things, the possible connection between a letter of Paul written to Romans (mostly to gentiles), and the sermon called Hebrews also likely written to Romans (mostly to Jews) should also be considered.

In my view, the most likely scenario is that the author of Hebrews, writing some years after Romans was written, knew the latter document when he wrote his masterpiece. It should be remembered that the Song of Moses seems to have been exceedingly popular in early Judaism, for instance, it is found at the end of the corpus of the Psalms in Codex A of the LXX, and the Testament of Moses, a document probably from the early second century CE is built around Deuteronomy 31–34.[138] Note that it is mostly the song material and the farewell material at the end of Deuteronomy that our author uses, not the legal material, and he does not use it to argue for the imposition of the old laws on his audience; and here is where we note that our author places Deuteronomy 32:35–36 on the lips of Jesus, and Deuteronomy 31:6 as the direct words of God, with Deuteronomy 32:43 referring to the Son.[139]

There is great value, as Steyn's work shows, in evaluating in a comprehensive manner how a particular author uses a particular OT book in his own work. From such study, some patterns begin to emerge, and lead to the asking of better questions of the use of OT in that

136. Witherington, "Influence of Galatians," 146–52.
137. Steyn, "Deuteronomy in Hebrews," 154.
138. Steyn, "Deuteronomy in Hebrews," 154–55.
139. Steyn, "Deuteronomy in Hebrews," 168.

particular work. The author's own theology and ethics affect how he uses the OT, and which parts he focuses on, but there is evidence as well that his use of the OT has been influenced by Christian predecessors, such as Paul.

THE LEXICON OF FAITH:
THE BROADER USE OF DEUTERONOMY

There are many allusions and echoes of Deuteronomy in the NT, and we will not be attempting to be comprehensive in our dealings with them, but rather are giving a representative sampling of how the book is used and applied in the NT. In some ways, it is no surprise that there are more quotations from Deuteronomy than several of the earlier books in the Pentateuch, which are largely comprised of narrative materials. Narrative, as it turns out, is seldom quoted verbatim, or with a citation formula in the NT. Laws and prophecies are far more likely to be quoted in this way. This does not prevent the considerable assumption of narrative background, or the allusions to particular stories and characters in the OT stories in the NT documents, but we have to bear in mind that *narrative was mostly used differently than prophecy or poetry or commandments.* We will work through Deuteronomy in canonical order to examine the different types of uses of the book when it doesn't involve quotations. Much of it, as we shall see, simply involves the influence of the language of Deuteronomy on the way the NT writers frame or express their thoughts.

For example, Deuteronomy 1:7 uses the phrase "the great river Euphrates," a phrase that is picked up and used in a very different context (talking about the work of angels) in Revelation 9:14. This is simply an example of language influence. And sometimes the connections are flimsy. Deuteronomy refers to God's people inheriting the promised land (Deut 1:8, 21) Jesus speaks of the meek inheriting the earth (Matt 5:5), a rather larger promise. Another possible example of mere language influence on a NT writer can be seen when one compares Deuteronomy 1:13 to James 3:13. The former speaks about appointing wise, understanding leaders, the latter about the need for the audience to be wise and understanding.

Sometimes knowing the use of a phrase from Deuteronomy can help solve a crux in interpreting something said in the NT. For example, in Deuteronomy 3:26 (LXX) God gets frustrated with Moses and lets him know he's done with what Moses is saying, and then we have the phrase ἱκανούσθω σοι "that's enough!" as an exclamation. This provides us with the necessary clue as to how to interpret Jesus's exasperated response when his disciples say "we have two swords" and Jesus says in Luke 22:38 Ἱκανόν ἐστιν! Jesus is not saying, "Why that's plenty enough swords for the purpose." Jesus is saying, "That's enough of that!" just as God said to Moses.

Deuteronomy 4:2 warns Israel "you must not add anything to what I command you or take anything away from it," which can be compared to the very end of the Bible at Revelation 22:18 where we hear similarly that whoever adds to or subtracts from the words of prophecy in Revelation, that God will add to him the plagues mentioned in the book. The tone of this warning indicates the seriousness of the matter, and it also indicates the prophetic authority John believes his words carry. They come from God, just as much as the direct speech in Deuteronomy 4:2.

The description of Mt. Horeb as blazing with fire and enveloped in a black cloud in Deuteronomy 4:11 LXX (καὶ τὸ ὄρος ἐκαίετο πυρὶ ἕως τοῦ οὐρανοῦ σκότος γνόφος θύελλα) probably serves as the background to the similar description in Hebrews 12:18 (καὶ κεκαυμένῳ πυρὶ καὶ γνόφῳ καὶ ζόφῳ καὶ θυέλλῃ) of the same event at the same locale. Or again in Acts 9:7 the companions of Paul when Jesus appears to him are said to hear a sound, but do not see anyone. Similarly, at Deuteronomy 4:12 the theophany is described as involving hearing the sound of the words but not seeing a form. Even closer to Deuteronomy 4:12 is the accusation of Jesus against his audience, "You have not heard his voice at any time nor seen his form" at John 5:37. In other words, they could not claim to be of the same ilk as the Israelites at Mt. Horeb.

The description of idolatry and what people made images of (creatures that fly, creatures that crawl, creatures that swim) in Deuteronomy 4:15–18 is probably in the mind of Paul in his excoriation of idolatry in Romans 1:23. Despite all the talk about how Paul's Areopagus speech in Acts 17 reflects various Greek philosophical notions (and there is some of that), in fact the main background to major parts of that speech is found in Deuteronomy 4:28–29 in its critique of idolatry: "There you will worship man-made gods of wood and stone which cannot see, hear, eat or smell. But from there you will search for the Lord your God, and you will find him when you seek him with all your heart and all your spirit." This should be compared to Acts 17:29, 27, which reads, "We shouldn't think that the divine nature is like gold, or silver or stone, an image fashioned by human art and imagination. . . . He did this so that they might seek God and perhaps they might reach out and find him, though he is not far from each one of us."[140]

For the most part, even when there are some quotations from Deuteronomy, they are brief snippets, key phrases rather than a marked quotation. For example, in Hebrews 12:29 the phrase about God as a consuming fire is picked up from Deuteronomy 4:24, or again the half phrase "the Lord is God, there is no other besides him" is picked up and paraphrased in Mark 12:32 in the response of the scribe to Jesus when he says, "He is the One, and there is no one else except him." Or consider Deuteronomy 7:6, which speaks of God choosing "you to be his possession out of all the peoples" (and cf. Deut 14:2) and compare that to Titus 2:14 where it is said of Jesus that gave himself for us "to redeem us from all lawlessness and to cleanse for himself a people for his own possession."

One of the more interesting cases of allusion without clear citation can be found in Mark 13, the Olivet discourse, where, as Moyise points out, there are a series of allusions to Deuteronomy, for instance one may compare Deuteronomy 4:32 to Mark 13:19, although the former is talking about former ages, the latter about latter days. Or one may compare more fruitfully Deuteronomy 13:1–2 about false prophets with the false prophets saying in Mark 13:22. Here there is real correspondence. The promise of gathering God's people from the diaspora in Deuteronomy 30:4 may lie in the background of Mark 13:27, but there it is angels and not God doing the gathering. One may also compare Deuteronomy 13:6 to Mark 13:12 about brothers betraying each other. As Moyise says, Mark 13 actually alludes to a wide variety of OT texts including of course Daniel, but the number of allusions or echoes to Deuteronomy is notable, and comports with evidence elsewhere that Jesus used Deuteronomy regularly.[141]

One of the incidental echoes of Deuteronomy comes at Deuteronomy 8:15 where in the course of recounting the experiences of the

---

140. On the background to this speech, see Witherington, *Acts of the Apostles*, 521–35.

141. See Moyise, "Deuteronomy," 38–39; on Jesus's use of the OT see pp. 12–33 above. Certainly, this comports with the regular mention of Moses by name (e.g., Mark 1:44, "Moses commanded"; Mark 7:10 "Moses said"; Mark 10:3 "Moses commanded"; Mark 12:19 "Moses wrote"; and Mark 12:19 "read Moses") often in conjunction with material from Deuteronomy, as Moyise notes.

wilderness wandering generation we hear, "He led you through the great and terrible wilderness with its poisonous snakes and scorpions, a thirsty land where there was no water." This must be compared to Luke 10:19 where we hear of the triumphant return of the seventy (or seventy-two) from their initial ministry foray, and Jesus says "Look I have given you the authority to trample on snakes and scorpions and over the power of the enemy, nothing at all will harm you." The disciples of Jesus are not merely guided through the hostile land and protected from harm, they are even given the power to trample on dangerous creatures. Since this saying comes in a context where just before Jesus says he saw Satan fall like lightning from heaven (v. 18) and just after Jesus warns the disciples not to rejoice if "the spirits/demons submit to you" (v. 20), is Jesus referring to actual scorpions and snakes, or is he, as Paul in Romans 16:20, talking about the crushing of the powers of darkness, particularly Satan, under God's feet (through his emissaries?)?

The reference to the two tablets of stone on which God himself wrote "with his finger" the Ten Words is mentioned in Deuteronomy 9:9–10, and Paul will pick up this description in order to contrast the Mosaic covenant and its central tenants with the new covenant that is written on tablets of human hearts (2 Cor 3:3). But in fact, the whole rhetorical *synkrisis* (comparison by contrast) between these two covenants is played out at length with the stone/heart contrast (see vv. 7–10) remaining prominent. The implied contrast is also between the ministry of Moses, and the ministry of Paul, which he quite specifically characterizes as the ministry of a new covenant (v. 6), the one Jeremiah, not Moses, talked about.

Hebrews 12:21 hardly seems like a quote of Deuteronomy 9:19, which has Moses saying, "I was afraid of the fierce anger the Lord had directed against you, for he was about to destroy you." Hebrews 12:21 reports Moses's reaction to the theophany on the mountain and it says, "the appearance was so terrifying that Moses said, 'I am trembling with fear.'" But the latter is about the appearance, the former is about God's anger itself and the potential destruction of the sinful people of God. The LXX is a bit closer to Hebrews 12:21: "And I was terrified on account of the wrath and the anger, because the Lord had been provoked against you to destroy you utterly." This is not a quotation or even a clear allusion, but it does in all these contexts properly convey the fear of Moses that God would judge his people.

The exhortation to "circumcise your hearts" is found in Deuteronomy 10:16a, a phrase that Paul clearly picks up and uses in a different context to talk about the "inward" Jew, who has experienced circumcision of the heart by means of the Holy Spirit (Rom 2:29). The difference here is striking; on the one hand Moses exhorts the people to circumcise their own hearts and stop being stiff-necked. Paul by contrast, believes this "inward" circumcision is the work of God's Spirit, not of the person of faith. He contrasts the work of the Spirit with that of the "letter," presumably in this case the letter of the law, which can inform a person about what they should do, but not enable them to do it.

Deuteronomy 10:17 is of interest for two very different reasons. On the one hand, it speaks of God as "God of Gods and Lord of Lords," a modified form of which occurs twice in Revelation: once at Revelation 17:14 and once at 19:16. In the former text, the rider on the white horse wears a robe with the inscription "King of Kings, and Lord of Lords." In the latter text, the inscription is the same and it is written both on the robe and on the rider's thigh. But this very same verse brings up the subject of God's impartiality and that God takes no bribes. This is a very important theme that will crop up in various ways and places in the NT, for instance in Galatians 2:6 and in Acts 10:34. The theme is important because it counterbalances the notion of possible unfairness in God because he has a chosen people and seems to favor them in various ways.

Deuteronomy 11:29 is of interest for the study of the Samaritans, who, it will be remembered, thought the Pentateuch was the whole of God's revelation to his people, and in fact had their own version of the Pentateuch. But all the versions of this verse mention both Mt. Gerizim and nearby Mt. Ebal, the former being the place where God's people should proclaim the blessing that they had entered and been given the promised land. This is of course important to understanding the theological discussion between Jesus and the Samaritan woman in John 4, especially in regard to John 4:20. Here the woman has the better of the argument, because Moses does not mention Jerusalem as a holy hill on which worship should take place, but he certainly mentions Mt. Gerizim. Notice as well that the woman says "you Jews" in regard to Mt. Zion, which may even here mean "you Judeans." Probably not however, since Jesus was a Galilean.

The divisions between and rival theologies of these two Jewish sects are plainly revealed in this interesting dialogue. It is probable as well that when the woman speaks of a messianic figure, the prophet like unto Moses is in view (Deuteronomy 18), noticing that she says to Jesus "I perceive you are a prophet" as well as saying that she knows the messianic figure who will reveal all things is coming. This, again, is based on Samaritan expectations that the messianic figure, the Taheb, the restorer, would come and among other things help the Samaritans find the sacred vessels on Mt. Gerizim. The evangelist who wrote John 4 knew his early Jewish theology well, and knew that sadly Jews and Samaritans really disliked each other, even to the point of not offering each other hospitality (see John 4:9).[142]

It is possible that some of the so-called Jubilee rules (cancellation of debts once every seven years, the prophecy/promise that there should be no poor among you, Deut 15:1–4) were something that the earliest followers of Jesus thought should be followed, now that the kingdom was coming as a result of the Christ event. This would perhaps explain why Luke's emphasis in the summaries at the end of Acts 2 and 4 especially stresses that the Jerusalem Jesus community could say, "for there was not one needy person among them"; the reason was those who had property or goods that could be sold, did so when a need arose, to take care of the poor. Notice in Deuteronomy 15 it is said that there would not be poverty because God was going to bless the land and its people. Did Jesus proclaim the year of Jubilee in his inaugural sermon (Luke 4)? Scholars will debate this, but it seems clear that the earliest Christians thought that the OT dictums about widows, orphans, and the poor should absolutely be taken seriously in the new community of Jesus.

It is quite possible that 2 Corinthians 9:7–8 reflects the influence of Deuteronomy 15:9–11. Paul says, "God loves a cheerful giver. God is able to make every grace gift overflow to you, so that in every way, always having everything you need, you may excel in every good work," and then we have a quote of Psalm 112:9. In Deuteronomy 15:9–10 there is this warning about being stingy to the poor. "Give to him, and don't have a stingy heart when you give, and because of this the Lord your God will bless you in all your work and in everything you do." Paul seems to be paraphrasing this, but he is not the only one, because it goes on to say in v. 11, "for there will never cease to be poor people in the land." This it would appear is the background for what Jesus himself says in the famous anointing story in Mark 14:3–11 ("the poor you will always have with you"). Taken in

---

142. On all of this see Witherington, *John's Wisdom*, 115–30.

context, one could never have understood Jesus to mean that it was unimportant to look after the poor. To the contrary, the saying in Deuteronomy 15 meant that there would always be a need to be generous and look after the poor!

The legal requirement that no one should die unless two witnesses have testified to the capital crime (remembering as well that the penalty for perjury could be that you received the death penalty!) comes into play clear enough in Mark 14:56 and John 8:17 and interestingly in Hebrews 10:28 where it is specifically noted that the rule came from Moses. The text in question is surely Deuteronomy 17:6–7 and the punishment prescribed is stoning, with the witnesses being the first to do so. The second of these verses is the background to the stoning of Stephen in Acts 7:58, and in John 8:7; the last clause of Deuteronomy 17:7 shows up in some form in 1 Corinthians 5:13 where Paul says "remove the evil person from your midst." You will notice however that Paul is urging expulsion from the community not extinction by the community. Why? I would suggest there is a very specific reason: Jesus forbade killing, even judicial killing (see Matthew 5). Indeed, he even forbade anger against a brother or sister, or hate toward an enemy.

The rules about the Levitical priests being entitled to eat from the sacrifices on the altars found in Deuteronomy 18:1–3 is used as an analogy or basis for Paul's argument in 1 Corinthians 9:13–14 that "in the same way the Lord commanded that those who preach the gospel should earn their living by the gospel." Matthew 10:8–10 seems to be lurking in the back of Paul's mind here, in particular the saying "the worker is worthy of his food" (v. 10), an instruction Jesus gives to the Twelve before they go out on mission to their fellow Jews. Does Paul think he is a priest? Does he think that Jesus thought so? Probably the most one can get from this is that Paul thinks that the same principle applies by analogy to gospel workers as applied to the Levitical priests, namely they shouldn't have to do something other than the Lord's work to make a living and survive.

We have already had occasion to speak about the rule that capital punishment required the testimony of two witnesses, but here it is important to add that this rule, either in a quote or in an allusion is perhaps the most frequently cited or used portion of Deuteronomy in the NT. Deuteronomy 19:15 shows up in one form or another in Matthew 18:16; Mark 14:56; Luke 7:18; John 8:17; 2 Corinthians

13:1 (which as we will see in a moment is extraordinary); 1 Timothy 5:19; and 1 John 5:7.

The text of Deuteronomy 19:15 is cited by Jesus himself in Matthew 18:16 as the rationale for dealing with a sin of one brother against another, and the one sinned against is to take two or three witnesses with him to confront the offender. Mark 14:56 merely alludes to the rule and explains why Jesus was not condemned by witnesses. Luke 7:18 may obliquely allude to the rule, but in this case the witnesses are John's disciples and what he wants is confirmation not of a crime but of whether it was true that Jesus was "the one who is to come." John 8:17 of course is Jesus again appealing to the rule but astoundingly Jesus is saying that he can testify on behalf of himself and that the second witness is God the Father! Clearly, Deuteronomy 19 has two or three human witnesses in mind, but presumably Jesus is working on the principle of analogy. Paul applies the rule strictly in instructing Timothy in 1 Timothy 5:19, saying that no accusation against an elder should be accepted unless supported by two or three witnesses.[143] Just as we saw in John 8:17, we seem to have divine witnesses involved in 1 John 5:7, only in this case the witnesses are the Holy Spirit plus the incarnation and death of Jesus, symbolically referred to as "the water and the blood."[144]

We've saved the most astounding use of Deuteronomy 19:15 for last. In 2 Corinthians 13:1 Paul says, "This is the third time I am coming to you: 'Every matter must be established by the testimony of two or three witnesses.'" But Paul is referring to himself visiting Corinth and witnessing to them three different times.[145] This is most definitely not what Deuteronomy 19:15 had in view. Perhaps here we may also draw attention to the text of the first and last of these uses of Deuteronomy 19:15 by Jesus and Paul (if he is the author of 1 Timothy).

The LXX of Deuteronomy 19:15 says

ἐπὶ στόματος δύο μαρτύρων καὶ ἐπὶ στόματος τριῶν μαρτύρων σταθήσεται πᾶν ῥῆμα
Matthew 18:16: ἵνα ἐπὶ στόματος δύο μαρτύρων ἢ τριῶν σταθῇ πᾶν ῥῆμα·

143. As to whether this is more of an allusion than a quotation here see Hafner, "Deuteronomy in the Pastoral Epistles," 144–47.

144. On this exegesis see Witherington, *Letters and Homilies for Hellenized Christians Vol. One*, 542–46. The subject here is not baptism and the Lord's Supper; the issue has to do with the false teachers who deny "Jesus come in the flesh."

145. See the discussion in Rosner, "Deuteronomy in 1 and 2 Corinthians," 133–34.

2 Corinthians 13:1: ἐπὶ στόματος δύο μαρτύρων καὶ τριῶν σταθήσεται πᾶν ῥῆμα.

Interestingly, the quote by Paul is closer to the LXX original than the quote in Matthew 18:16. The Hebrew is somewhat different in any case, saying that "a thing/matter must be established by the testimony of two or three witnesses." In other words, none of the examples in the NT seem to be following the Hebrew. For one thing, the Hebrew speaks only of "a matter" not "all things/matters." For another thing, notice how the reference to the witnesses comes before the reference to the thing in question in the three Greek texts above. This brings up a further point: This law was already mentioned in Deuteronomy 17:6, and *there* the reference to the witnesses, as in these Greek texts, precedes the reference to the matter at hand. Are we simply dealing with memory citations that combined bits of Deuteronomy 17:6 and 19:15? It is possible. In any case, multiple witnesses were required in the Jewish tradition to establish the truth of most anything important, and especially if someone's life was on the line.

Deuteronomy 17:7 comes into play at 1 Corinthians 5:13, or at least the exhortation "expel the wicked person from among you" is derived from a regular theme found in Deuteronomy 17:7, 19:19, 21, 21, 22, 21; and 24:7. The text of 1 Corinthians 5:13 and the LXX of Deuteronomy 17:7 are in fact mostly identical, and it is notable that the strong verb "expel" (ἐξάρατε) is found only here in the NT. Paul does not introduce this quotation with a citation formula, perhaps because he wants the words to be seen as an expression of his own apostolic authority over his converts. Interestingly, this imperative becomes a theme that we find variations of in vv. 2, 5, 7, and 11 leading up to the quotation.[146]

At Deuteronomy 20:6 we find the rhetorical question, "Has anyone planted a vineyard and not begun to enjoy its fruit?" and Paul's version of this, in the course of justifying that an apostle deserves to benefit from his apostolic labors is, "Who plants a vineyard and does not eat its fruit?" (1 Cor 9:7). This is part of a series of rhetorical ques-

---

146. See rightly Rosner, "Deuteronomy in 1 and 2 Corinthians," 122–23. Rosner makes a reasonable case that 1 Corinthians 5–7 is indebted in various ways to various texts in Deuteronomy that deal with incest, marriage, exclusion from the covenant, and theological subjects such as monotheism. But Paul is adopting and adapting such ideas for a different and eschatological community that is not under the Deuteronomistic law covenant.

tions meant to provide a rationale for the dictum a worker is worthy of his hire.

At Matthew 11:19 // Luke 7:34, we have a Q saying where Jesus is accused of being a glutton and a drunkard, and also a friend of tax collectors and sinners. The former charge has a special resonance, as it comes from the legislation in Deuteronomy 21:20 where a rebellious son is brought to the elders in the city gate and said to be precisely this "a glutton and a drunkard." The accusation has behind it the statement that this son does not obey his father and mother and doesn't even listen to them after they discipline him. Now one wonders if this accusation against Jesus was not *just* a commentary on his dining habits, but also a commentary on his refusal to come home when his mother and siblings came out to get him according to the account in Mark 3:21–35? Was Jesus seen as a rebellious son? Did the hometown folks mentioned in Mark 6 think so? Does this have anything to do with the saying that a prophet is without honor within his immediate kinship circle, or with the statement in John 7:5 that Jesus's brothers didn't believe in him? The larger context of Deuteronomy 21 urges us to ask those kinds of questions.

Mark 2:23 // Matthew 12:1 present us with disciples gleaning a few heads of grain from a nearby field on the Sabbath. The law in this case clearly permitted them to do so, and we find it in Deuteronomy 23:25. One was allowed to glean a bit, but not to put the sickle in and take someone else's whole crop. Though as Moyise says, nothing is said about the Sabbath in that text.[147] The question became, does this activity count as work, and so should it be forbidden on the Sabbath. The law itself does not say whether or not it could be undertaken on the Sabbath. The Pharisees clearly see this counting as work, and they object. Jesus appeals to the case of David, when he was hungry, even eating food meant for the priests, and then reminds that the Sabbath was made for the benefit of humankind. We regularly find Jesus debating his fellow Jews about the meaning of specific teachings in Deuteronomy. There is also the famous saying about Jesus being the lord of the Sabbath as well, which suggests either that he is free to suspend the rules, as David did, or determine what constitutes works, or even say that such rules don't apply to his disciples now that the kingdom is breaking into human history.[148]

147. Moyise, "Deuteronomy," 36.

148. The reluctance of Moyise ("Deuteronomy," 37) to see Jesus as radical in the way he handled the law is a consistent trait in his work, but it does not always match up well with what

The famous discussion about marriage and divorce found in Mark 10 // Matthew 19 is, in the case of Jesus's inquisitors, based on the law found in Deuteronomy 24:1 that permits divorcing of a wife by means of writing her a certificate of divorce. Jesus concludes this law was given by Moses due to the hard-heartedness of some men (and it is men in particular he is talking about since they alone, according to the law, had the right to divorce a spouse). The problem with the law in Deuteronomy 24 was what one made of the clause 'er-wat dabar translated "some unseemly thing." This could be interpreted variously, from trivial offenses like burning a meal to a serious matter like adultery—and Jesus will have none of it. According to both our earliest Gospel (see Mark 10) and according to our earliest NT writer, Paul (see 1 Corinthians 7) Jesus said, "no divorce," which in turn meant the male privilege of divorce had been withdrawn now that the kingdom was coming.

It has been argued that Jesus was just intensifying the Mosaic prohibition, but in fact that is not quite correct. Jesus forbids what Moses permits. If applied, this ruling would have given women more security in their marriages. Notably, even in Matthew 19 where there is an exception clause (which does not refer to "marital infidelity"), the disciples go ballistic protesting Jesus's strict ruling and say "if that's the way it is, then better not to marry." Jesus then calmly gives them the option of being a eunuch for the sake of the kingdom, in other words, single, like Jesus.[149] The variant forms of the tradition in Mark and Matthew (in Mark Jesus asks what did Moses command; in Matthew he talks about Moses permitting and his interlocutors about what he commanded), reflect the different audiences Mark and Matthew are addressing, the latter would better make sense to a Jewish Christian

---

the text actually tells us were Jesus's views, and because we do not have other contrary sources on these matters, this seems like special pleading.

149. I have dealt with these passages elsewhere in great detail in many places. See, e.g., Witherington, *Matthew*, 359–66. It is very unlikely that *porneia* in the exceptive clauses in Matthew 5 and 19 refer to marital infidelity. The word for that is *moixeia*, adultery, a word used elsewhere in Matthew 5 in distinction from *porneia*. The latter word comes from the Greek word for prostitute, and often refers to prostitution, but it could also refer to incest, and does so in 1 Corinthians 5. Sometimes the word refers to a whole panoply of sexual sins, but that makes no sense of Matthew 19 where the disciple's reaction makes clear that Jesus is being more strict, not less, than Moses. It is possible Jesus is commenting on the incestuous marriage of Herodias and Herod Antipas, as his cousin John did, who lost his head for doing so. If this is in view, then Jesus would be saying in effect no divorce, except in cases where the relationship wasn't a marriage in God's eyes in the first place, not something God joined together. In any case, Jesus's teaching is no divorce, which is a ruling Deuteronomy 24 does not suggest or affirm.

audience, the former to a largely gentile one in a context (probably Rome) where women could actually divorce.[150]

The flogging rule in Deuteronomy 25:3 of no more than forty lashes, led in turn to the practice of only using thirty-nine lashes to make sure one didn't lose count and go beyond the limit, which was said to degrade or dehumanize the person in the sight of the punishers. Perhaps some also saw thirty-nine lashes as a sign of mercy or leniency. However it was viewed, Paul of course says that he experienced this punishment (2 Cor 11:24) no less than five times by the time he wrote 2 Corinthians. This must surely mean that he kept going to the synagogues as he went from town to town, and suffered this specifically Jewish punishment again and again. This not only illuminates his clear statement that the gospel is for the Jew first in Romans 1, but it also gives credence to the portrait of Paul going first to the synagogues in each town in the book of Acts.

Deuteronomy 25:5 shows up partially in Mark 12:19. But Jesus's response doesn't have much to do with the partial citation by the Sadducees. In fact, what is going on here is Jesus suggesting that prooftexting is not enough, one must have the hermeneutical sophistication to compare OT texts and know how they relate to one another.[151] Rusam points out that formally this discussion about Levirate marriage is like the temptations of Jesus in that a Scripture is used to test Jesus, and here again we find an unreliable character in the narrative using Scripture for the test.[152]

Deuteronomy 27:26 says that anyone who does not put the "words of this law" into practice is cursed. Paul concludes from this in Galatians 3:10–13, perhaps in part because Deuteronomy 27:26 is the conclusion of all the curse sanctions in that chapter (vv. 9–26), that the reference here is to putting into practice "everything written in the book of the law," and this is surely correct. In fact, he may be mainly thinking of Deuteronomy 28:58 where this is stated perfectly clearly. This in turn rules out the notion that the phrase "works of the law" in Galatians 3:10 refers only to the boundary defining laws of circumcision, food laws, and Sabbath laws. No, it refers to "everything in the book of the law," by which Paul means the whole of Deuteronomy!

Deuteronomy 30:11–15 presents God's people with a life or death choice. We are told that the command of God (presumably

---

150. These variations show that the Gospel writers had some degree of freedom to modify or edit their Jesus tradition sources to best speak to their current audience.

151. See the discussion by Moyise, "Deuteronomy," 33.

152. Rusam, "Deuteronomy," 74.

commands written in this book, see v. 10) is not too difficult or beyond the audience's reach. They do not need to go up to heaven to find it and bring it back down and proclaim it, nor cross the sea to find it either. "But the message is very near to you, in your mouth and in your heart so you may follow it." Students of Paul will find that all of this sounds very familiar, only the subject matter in question is rather different. Here in Deuteronomy it is the law that is being spoken of. In Romans 10:6–8 we read:

> But the righteousness that is by faith says: "Do not say in your heart, 'Who will ascend into heaven?'" (that is, to bring Christ down) [7] "or 'Who will descend into the deep?'" (that is, to bring Christ up from the dead). [8] But what does it say? "The word is near you; it is in your mouth and in your heart," that is, the message concerning faith that we proclaim: [9] If you declare with your mouth, "Jesus is Lord," and believe in your heart that God raised him from the dead, you will be saved. [10] For it is with your heart that you believe and are justified, and it is with your mouth that you profess your faith and are saved.

Whereas Moses was speaking (for God) in Deuteronomy 30, here "the righteousness from faith" is speaking, it would seem, and what he/it is saying is one doesn't have to go up into heaven or down into the abyss to bring Christ to the listener; no, the message about Christ is near you, in your mouth, even in your heart. Thus, a text that was originally about the law of Moses and its accessibility is now about the message about Christ, and the confession of lips and belief in the heart in Him. Here some interaction with the helpful discussion by Hays will profit us, but it should be already apparent that Paul is not doing any kind of exegesis of Deuteronomy 30, contextual or otherwise. Rather, by contrast he is using the same language found in Deuteronomy 30 to talk about an entirely different message, different subject, namely Christ.

As Hays observes:

> Paul's citation of Deut 30:13 diverges from any known textual tradition. Whereas both the MT and the LXX speak of crossing the sea to find this commandment, Paul's citation reads "Who will go down into the abyss?" This is the sort of divergence from the scriptural text that encouraged Sanday and Headlam to venture the opinion that Paul was not really interpreting Deuteronomy. In fact, however, this deviant quotation is not just a careless Pauline paraphrase, it is . . . a textual overlay that is decidedly interpretive in effect. M. Jack Suggs has demon-

strated convincingly that Paul's formulation reflects conventions associated with the personified figure of Sophia in Jewish Wisdom tradition."[153]

Hays is right about this, and there are phrases about Wisdom where she speaks about herself and says in Sirach 24:5, "Alone I have made the circuit of the vault of heaven, and I have walked in the depths of the abyss." A further development of the same tradition is found in Baruch 3:29–30 where the language of Deuteronomy 30 is repurposed to describe Wisdom: "Who has gone up into heaven and taken her, and brought her down from the clouds? Who has gone over the sea and found her, and will buy her for pure gold?" The significance of the latter quote becomes more apparent when one realizes that Baruch 4:1 identifies Wisdom with Torah. The point seems to be that righteousness by faith doesn't annul law qua law, but rather brings it to its proper goal or fulfillment: "for the word of faith which we preach is Jesus Christ [who is incarnate Wisdom and the goal/end of the law]."

The problem with Hays reading of this whole schema is that he assumes that because Paul does not overtly identify Christ with Wisdom, only the most learned and subtle of readers would conclude this. Paul in fact does make such an identification in various places in 1 Corinthians (see, e.g., 1 Corinthians 1 and the reference to Christ as the rock in 1 Corinthians 10, following the identification in Wisdom of Solomon and Philo of Wisdom as the rock). More to the point, the whole critique of pagan culture in Romans 1 comes right out of wisdom literature such as Wisdom of Solomon, and Paul no more identifies his source there than here in Romans 10. It is part of Paul's strategy in Romans 9–11 to offer such a text-rich argument that the only way most of the gentiles in Paul's audience could understand it, *is with the help of Torah-skilled Jewish Christians in Rome.* The whole of Romans is intended to bring some rapproachment between gentile and Jewish Christians in Rome, and one of the rhetorical strategies of Paul to accomplish that aim is to deal with the "Israel" problem in such way that members of Israel would have to help gentile Christians of a pagan background catch the implications and nuances of the refutation argument in Romans 9–11.[154]

Is it then true that Paul is suggesting that the latent sense of

153. Hays, *Echoes of Scripture in Paul*, 80.

154. See the detailed discussion in Witherington and Hyatt, *Letter to the Romans*, on Romans 9–11.

Deuteronomy 30 becomes patent and clear in the gospel? Hays goes on to maintain, "Paul's interpretation presupposes what it argues and argues what it presupposes: that the real meaning of Deuteronomy 30 is disclosed not in law-keeping but in Christian preaching."[155] Is Paul actually saying, "the real meaning all along of Deuteronomy 30 is Romans 10:8b–9"? In fact, the answer to this is no because what Paul is talking about is what is true in the new covenant situation, not what was true in the old covenant situation. One's hermeneutics is dictated by one's covenant theology.

Paul does not think (1) the new covenant is simply a renewal or completion of the Mosaic one; (2) that the church is Israel; (3) that all along Deuteronomy was furtively and obscurely talking about the good news about Jesus's death, resurrection, and the confession thereof; (4) that the righteousness that comes from doing the Mosaic law is the same thing as the righteousness from faith. Watson, from a slightly different angle also rejects Hays reading of this passage. He says Moses is not named as the source of this quotation because, "Paul has no intention of citing this text in the form in which Moses wrote."[156] He urges that Paul is rewriting the text so that it may testify about the righteousness of faith and against the righteousness that comes from the law. In any case, Ciampa is right that Paul is not doing a simple exegesis of Deuteronomy 30 here, as is demonstrated by the contrast between what Moses writes in v. 5, and what the righteousness of faith says in vv. 6–10. Much more ought to have been made of the fact that Paul introduces the quote from Deuteronomy 30 by citing a different text, namely Deuteronomy 9:4 "do not say in your heart." In short, the listener is not to say in his heart that God's word is far off, unapproachable, unretrievable. On the contrary, the word of the "righteousness of faith" is as near as the proclamation of the gospel.[157]

Paul thinks that things are *foreshadowed* in the law that are only filled out later in light of and by means of the gospel . In other words, what Moses said in Deuteronomy 30 foreshadows to some degree but is not identical with what Paul does with the use of the language of Deuteronomy 30 in Romans 10. The righteousness from faith is not the same thing as the righteousness from the law. There is analogy, and it is appropriate to use the same scriptural language of them both,

155. Hays, *Echoes of Scripture in Paul*, 82.
156. Watson, *Paul and the Hermeneutics*, 338.
157. Ciampa, "Deuteronomy," 106–7.

but unless one gets the picture that Paul is talking about two different covenantal situations, one involving Mosaic law, the other involving the law and righteousness of Christ, then one has misunderstood what is happening in this remarkable *tour de force* argument. In short, Paul is not doing a *reading* of Deuteronomy 30 and saying "to everyone's surprise *this is that*"; rather he is reusing and repurposing the language of Deuteronomy 30 for a different covenantal situation and time.

The charge of Moses in Deuteronomy 31:6–8 to the people to be strong and courageous, coupled with the promise that God will be with them, indeed the comforting words, "he will not leave you nor abandon you" should be compared to Hebrews 13:5, which reads, "I will never leave or abandon you." It is one of the most interesting features of the book of Hebrews that often the author not only puts scriptural phrases in the first person, making it sound like God is speaking directly to his immediate Jewish Christian audience, but he even places OT quotes on the lips of both the Father, and the Son, and even the Spirit. In this fashion, the text is contemporized for his own audience.

One of the verses in Jude that has caused no little controversy is Jude 14: "Look! The Lord comes with tens of thousands of his holy ones," a prophecy that is said to be spoken by the prophet Enoch. But it in turn is surely drawing on Deuteronomy 33:2, which says, "the Lord came from Sinai . . . and came with ten thousand holy ones." Much has been made of Jude quoting an extracanonical *book,* but in fact Jude says nothing about a *book,* he says that a prophet named Enoch said this, from which one *cannot* deduce that he was endorsing the whole book of 1 Enoch as inspired or canonical, or the like, and especially not since the verse in question is a rerun of Deuteronomy 33:2.

Finally, there is not much use of the last chapter of Deuteronomy, Deuteronomy 34, but there is this. You will perhaps remember that Moses goes up to Mt. Nebo from which he can view the entire holy land, and God says to him, "This is the land I promised Abraham, Isaac, and Jacob, I will give it to your descendants. I have let you see it with your own eyes, but you will not cross into it." This should be compared to Matthew 4:8 where Satan is said to take Jesus up to a very high mount, and shows him the kingdoms of this world and says to Jesus, "I will give you all these if you will fall down and worship me." There is not merely a contrast here between God forbidding Moses from entering the promised land, and Satan offering to give the kingdoms of the world to Jesus, but also some ambiguity. Satan is elsewhere called the "ruler/prince of this world" by Jesus himself (John 12:31). Did he really have those kingdoms to give to Jesus? Or should we hear the intertextual echo with Deuteronomy 34 as a straight contrast between what God can offer and what Satan offers? It could be read either way. In any case, Jesus and Moses stand together in reliance upon and belief in God's word.

CONCLUSIONS

We have once again ranged far and wide in our study of the quotations, allusions, and echoes of another Pentateuch book in this chapter: Deuteronomy. Deuteronomy does indeed come up for the most direct use or quotation in the NT of all the books in the Pentateuch, and this comes as no surprise considering the popularity of the book in early Judaism, as witnessed at Qumran and elsewhere. Jesus himself is recorded as resorting to this book not just for teaching his fellow Jews, but even for refuting Satan. The suggestion lies not far at hand that the Gospel writers would have their audiences follow this kind of practice when confronted with challenges and temptations natural or supernatural.

We noted at some length that the Deuteronomistic form of the Ten Words seems to have been the primary form of those commandments used in the NT, except, notably the commandment about the Sabbath, which in neither of its forms (Exodus or Deuteronomy) is reapplied to the disciples of Jesus. The book of Deuteronomy could be used theologically for discussions about the coming messianic prophet (John 4 and elsewhere) but primarily the book is used to discuss ethics, or even ministerial praxis (don't muzzle that apostle, let him benefit from his work). I would point out, as Miller does, that we are not talking about a spiritualizing even of a saying like "do not muzzle the ox." We are talking about the perception of an underlying principle that the NT writer believes still applies in his own day. The principle is the same, the particular application of it varies. The issue here is not merely a way of reading the OT, or for that matter reading into it something that is not there.

The issue involves the following: (1) It is believed that the OT text is rich, sometimes even multivalent, especially if it's poetry, and in any case, it has fundamental theological and ethical principles and truths to still teach a Christian audience. (2) Because there is a stable, well-known text of the OT (both in Hebrew and Greek), the writers of the NT can afford to quote from memory, paraphrase at times, and do creative improvisations with the text. This latter I call a homiletical use of the OT, not a rather weak or poor attempt at exegesis of an OT text. This becomes especially clear when one actually does the contextual exegesis of the OT text and sees how differently the material is being handled and used in the NT. (3) While popular books like Deuteronomy are still viewed as Scripture, with much to teach the followers of Jesus, this does not lead to the conclusion that Christians are still under the Mosaic covenant. No, the material is viewed and used with the assumption that there is a new covenant, and this changes how one should view or use a book like Deuteronomy, especially when Jesus himself had laid down teaching that made clear some of the material in that Mosaic covenant needed to be left behind, for example, "the law of the tooth," or the rules about oaths, or the divorce permission in Deuteronomy 24. (4) It is interesting that the go-to texts from Deuteronomy in the NT prove to be either the Ten Words or the poetic Song of Moses, or some of the other notable commandments in Deuteronomy. Missing in action is much of the narrative from that book, including surprisingly the narrative at the end of Deuteronomy about Moses's demise. Even so, it is law in particular that comes to be viewed and applied most differently in the NT than it is in Deuteronomy itself. This is in part because the earliest Christians are not setting up a nation, engaging in political activities such as the allotting of parcels in the promised land, and so on. No, the earliest Christians view themselves as resident aliens on the earth, looking toward a better kingdom, brought in by God in Christ himself, in part now, and in full later. (5) This did not mean that the writers of the NT thought God had replaced one people of God with another, or that God had reneged on his promises to Israel. Israel falls under the heading of "unfinished business" in the NT when it comes to God fulfilling his promises and prophecies. The writers of the NT not only read the OT with christological spectacles, they read it with eschatological ones as well, not least because they are convinced they live in the age of fulfillment of both the Law and the Prophets. Even the repristinized form of the Mosaic covenant found in Deuteronomy can, at the end of the day, be compared and contrasted with "the righteousness from faith" as voices that speak to God's people, and at the end of the day it is the righteousness that comes from faith in

Christ, and the obedience that flows from that, rather than the right-eous attempt to keep all the particulars of Deuteronomy that is said to have soterological value and effect.

Christ is the end of the old law as binding covenantal law that pro-vides a means of living righteously before God, but because it is also God's word, Holy Writ, it can be taken up into the new covenant, often in different and fresh ways and used as a way of responding to the good news in Jesus Christ. Jesus, after all, was indeed that prophet like unto Moses promised in Deuteronomy 18, but he was also so much more than that. The glory that came with Moses and the Ten Words coming down from Mt. Sinai is eclipsed by the resurrection glory of Christ, whom all believers can behold, and be transformed by, into his likeness. Second Corinthians 3, Galatians 4, and texts like Hebrews make very clear that it is the new covenant hermeneutic that so affects the way the NT writers interpret and apply Deuteron-omy and the other books of the Pentateuch. But we will leave the further spinning out of the insights and possibilities of this study for the final conclusions, which follow directly hereafter.

6.

Coda: Final Reflections

How one views Israel as discussed in the NT dramatically affects how one views the hermeneutics of the NT writers' use of the OT. If one thinks either Christ or the church or both is signified by the term Israel in the NT, this certainly changes how one evaluates the use of the OT in the NT by these early Christian writers. If, however, one thinks God is not done with non-Christian Israel yet, and I am convinced that is the view of the writers of the NT, then the way they apply the OT to the church is definitely affected, indeed in some cases determined by that conviction.

—Ben Witherington III

I do believe that Israel is covenant land. That's very controversial, but I read the Bible literally, and I believe that God gave them that land, all the way back to Deuteronomy.

—James Dobson[1]

Christians must be Jews. The truth of what we believe depends on the truth of Judaism, depends on the first covenant.

—Michael Novak

Our study began with a brief dealing with the terminological confusions having to do with the term "torah," especially at the juncture when it began to be translated as νόμος in the LXX and in other contexts, which seems to narrow the semantic field, focusing more on the apodictic or imperatival side of law. But it would be incorrect to suggest that "torah" meant no more than "instructions" in earlier

1. Interview on *Larry King Live*, November 22, 2006; http://tinyurl.com/ybxy5xty.

Hebrew contexts. Plenty of the material in the Pentateuch falls into the category of "laws," laws that were meant to be enforced, not mere instructions or hypothetical advice. The casuistic or apodictic law, for example, the law dealing with blasphemy, shows a clear judicial context in which these laws would be adjudicated and enforced under certain circumstances. But this in turn reflects a people settled in a particular place, where there was a regular process for laws to be enforced, and officials to make sure it was enforced.

But I would be remiss if I did not stress that a good half of the Pentateuch is not law in the narrow sense at all—it is narrative. It tells the story of God's people from Adam through Moses with particular emphasis in the last four books on Moses. Indeed, some have even called Exodus through Deuteronomy a sort of biography of Moses the great lawgiver. No evaluation of the Pentateuch that does not take into account the huge amount of narrative and ask how it relates to the narrower category of law will ever adequately deal with what we find in the Pentateuch. Narrative not only provides the backstory about the origins and nature of God's people and their God, it also provides the context that best explains the character of the law we find in the Pentateuch. It is covenantal law, which is to say, it is a binding part of the covenantal relationship between God and his people that also determines the appropriate relationship between various individuals within that people group.

Presupposed is that Yahweh really did exist, really did create all things and so is the owner of all things (see the Sabbath discussion in the Ten Words in Exodus), really did intervene in the life of the Hebrews, really did bring them up out of Egypt (see the Sabbath discussion in the Ten Words in Deuteronomy), really did give them commandments to live by on Sinai, and really did guide Moses in all of this long process—not to mention the insistence that Yahweh was indeed well and truly the one and only true or "living" God. From a legal point of view there isn't really a people before Sinai and the Mosaic covenant is cut. There are ancestors, patriarchs, and predecessors who related to the God of the Bible, but there is no Israel before the people are properly formed into a community with a law and governing principles. Just from a historical point of view, obviously, there are no twelve tribes of Israel before there were the sons of Jacob, and before Jacob there was no one called Israel. Hebrews yes, Israel no.

This needs to be stressed because of course early Jews also read their Hebrew Scriptures backward just as did early followers of Jesus, by which I mean they asked questions like, "Which of the Ten Commandments was the one given to Adam?" and they saw the Abrahamic covenant and the circumcision provisions in that early covenant in light of the later Mosaic one. Unlike Paul they did not privilege the chronologically prior "Abraham trusted God" over the later command of circumcision. The Abrahamic covenant was over- laid with and read in light of the later Mosaic one. Paul and other earlier followers of Jesus said no to this hermeneutical maneuver.

The other side of this torah coin is the Ten Words that were foun- dational for the rest of the law and served as the undergirding guiding principles of the torah. It should be stressed that we are dealing with a specifically religious kind of law for a very religious people, a law that even regulated what they say about and how they relate to God, and not just how they relate to each other. In no case is any of the law we find in the Pentateuch simply like modern secular law. One's relationship with God norms one's relationship with one's neighbor, hence the later combining of the two love commandments, seen as the heartbeat of the law. I stress all this because later Christian dis- cussions about Mosaic law seen in a negative light, and in particu- lar the accusation of legalism, or legal chicanery or hypocrisy tend to obscure what exactly is said and meant by law in the OT.

It is all the more shocking then that some early Jews, beginning with Jesus and continuing on through his earliest Jewish followers, were prepared to say not only that the eschatological inbreaking of God's final reign changes the covenantal situation, and sets aside the casuistic law about stoning adulterers, or the legitimacy of divorce, or oath taking under certain circumstances, and a host of other things, but also to say that the foundational guiding principles in the Ten Words needed to be rethought, and in the case of the Sabbath com- mand, no longer to be imposed on all believers now that the new covenant is being offered, and Jews and gentiles are both involved.

At the beginning of the study we examined how law was viewed in early Judaism as well, and moved on to discuss Jesus's approach to law in that context. While some scholars continue to want to suggest (1) Jesus was not much a quoter or user of the holy writ; or (2) or on the other side of the coin Jesus was torah-true and did not take a rad- ical approach to things like the food or Sabbath or purity laws, nei- ther of these views is *adequate* or likely to be historically accurate. It is no accident that our earliest Gospels, Mark and then Matthew, regularly depict Jesus in scriptural debate with his contemporaries. This does not likely *just* reflect later polemics between followers of Jesus and their Jewish contemporaries. Jesus was viewed as a radical teacher in his own day, one that prompted much controversy in both Galilee and in Judaea.

True enough, the implications of Jesus's own teaching about the Mosaic and new covenants for gentile inclusion in the *ekklesia* were not made clear or brought out into the open before Paul and the gentile mission, but it needs to be noted that Galatians 1–2 indicates that there was a fundamental agreement between Paul and the pillar apostles in Jerusalem as to what the gospel message was (and ought to be) concerning Jesus himself and salvation. The difficulty was in the details of how, in terms of meal praxis, circumcision, Sabbath keeping, this was all to work, especially since there were many Jewish followers of Jesus who wished to remain torah-true, perhaps especially to be a witness to their fellow Jews. James the Just, the brother of Jesus, is exhibit A of this approach. Nonetheless, no right hand of partnership between Paul and the pillars could have happened at all if there was fundamental disagreement as to what the substance of the good news about Jesus and the thrust of his teaching was. It was however Paul who seems to have first realized the full implications of the radical character of that good news vis à vis whether the Mosaic covenant was to be seen as ongoing or obsolete. Herein lay the rub. Others, such as the author of Hebrews, were to push further to make clear just how new the new and "better" covenant really was, and how necessary it was to stick with the new covenant when pressure and persecution came from fellow Jews or others.

Was the new covenant indeed just a renewal of the old Mosaic covenant with its law, or was it indeed a new covenant, connected to Abraham—one that was *not to be viewed as the early form of the Mosaic covenant?* This was the debate that swirled around Paul and the gentile mission, and led to passionate responses and attempts to "correct" the Pauline praxis by those who came to be called Judaizers. Acts 15 provides one version of how the crisis was resolved, but of course it is not the whole story, because obviously, various Jewish followers of Jesus who remained torah-true (the predecessors of the Ebionites perhaps), were not wholly satisfied with that sort of compromise.

They likely sensed that it meant: (1) that gentiles did not need to become Jews to be full participants in the community of Jesus; and that (2) this in turn meant that in due course the community would become not merely another sectarian form of Judaism, but a different sort of religious community with Jew and gentile united in Christ on equal footing in various respects; and even (3) that as Paul deduced (1 Corinthians 9), keeping the Mosaic provisions was a blessed option but not even an obligation for Jewish followers of Jesus anymore.

My point at this juncture is this: this sort of radical departure from the Mosaic law covenant ultimately goes back to Jesus and his reading of the torah in light of what he believed about the new eschatological situation and what he believed about himself. Paul was not the inventor of this departure. I have taken time to lay out this historical scenario because I am convinced it best explains what we actually find in the NT when it comes to the handling of the OT in the NT. The hermeneutics of Jesus provide the starting point for the hermeneutics of his earliest followers, though they were to pursue the trajectory much further than Jesus did during his ministry.

But note that there is absolutely no evidence that the writers of the NT were in agreement with Marcion or some of the later Gnostics about the OT not being Holy Writ, or at best being a mixed bag of revelation from God and merely human propositions, much less that the OT was a revelation of a lesser, and less friendly or loving deity, the demiurge. No, they believed that the whole corpus of the Hebrew Scriptures were God's living oracles, and this included even the arcane in the Pentateuch.

The challenge then was to figure out how to interpret and apply it in the new eschatological situation, especially if the Mosaic covenant was, or was becoming, obsolete. One key hermeneutical move, inaugurated by Jesus himself, was to say that the Mosaic legislation was in various cases given by God himself with a full cognition of the hardness of human hearts, but that this was not God's highest and best for his creatures. In the new eschatological situation, the original creation design and intent should be returned to. This led to the conclusion by Paul and others that those portions of the Mosaic covenant that were not reapplied or repristinized or re-commanded by Jesus and the early apostles to their followers were no longer binding on the followers of Jesus. Since the Mosaic law stood or fell together as a collective entity, this meant that the Mosaic covenant as a whole was no longer in force, though individual commandments were reaffirmed.

This conclusion was also based on the fact that some of the new teaching of Jesus not only intensified some aspects of the law (e.g., the adultery provisions), it also set up paradigms that went in a different direction from the Mosaic law. The banning of divorce and oaths, the command to love one's enemies, the insistence on nonviolence and no revenge taking and instead on perpetual forgiveness, and possibly the denial that there was unclean food, could not be simply said to be a "going beyond the Mosaic law" in the same direction. Intensification is one thing, fulfillment or nullification is another. Some of that law was being set aside, and new principles were being instituted. We see the working out of the implications of all this in the way the OT is handled in the NT.

In our study of the use of Genesis in the NT we noticed several key factors: the narrative portions of Genesis set up a paradigm of creation followed by disobedience and sin, followed by various acts of redemption, and the writers of the NT take this paradigm as a given. It is not argued for, it is assumed, and theological and ethical conclusions are based on the assumption. The core of the stories are assumed to be historical, whether one is talking about Adam, or Noah, or Abraham, or Joseph, or later Moses. And just as importantly, that backstory is seen as part of the bedrock foundation of biblical faith. The religion of Israel presupposes a historical foundation and relationship with the God who created it all, a God who also redeemed the Hebrews and in essence founded Israel through the mediator Moses.

This religion then would be grounded not chiefly in some theological mythology but in the words and deeds of Yahweh in human history. While the Hebrews did interact with and adopt and adapt various concepts from the ANE, they were not by and large a myth-making people. Thus, it is not surprising that the writers of the NT take a basically historical orientation to the OT texts, in the sense that they assume that the ongoing revelation of God has to do with the ongoing salvation history of God's people. The revelation is progressive, and the relationship is ongoing. These facts are taken for granted, and again it affects how the OT is viewed and used by the writers of the NT.

Much of the handling of Genesis has to do with the recycling of the narrative material, for example, to use as an analogy. The story of the flood and Noah is used as analogy with the coming maelstrom of final judgment by Jesus. Or again, the story of Abraham is used as a paradigm for how right-standing with God is obtained by Paul, and so on; law qua commandments really does not figure so much in the handling of Genesis in the NT, which is to say that the use of Genesis is more about theology and history than about ethics. This cannot be said when it comes to the other four books of the Pentateuch, where at least in the case of Exodus and Deuteronomy it is more about law, instructions, and commandments and less about narrative.

Nevertheless, it would be wrong to underestimate the importance of the Exodus telling of the story of Moses, and the rescue of God's people from bondage in Egypt, and the wilderness wandering tales for the writers of the NT. Not only do they use these as cautionary tales to warn their audiences "go and do otherwise" (see 1 Corinthians 10), there is in addition much reflection on what human sin and redemption means on the basis of the stories in Exodus, just as the story of Adam and Eve in Genesis provides foundational elements for a reflection on the fall and redemption in Romans 5:12–21 and elsewhere.

The focus of the NT writers when it comes to Exodus is not much different than it was elsewhere in early Judaism—a strong concentration on the Ten Words is found in abundance, though it appears that the Deuteronomistic form of the Ten Words is more often influential. The encounter of Moses at the burning bush and the revelation of the divine name are assumed to be critical for understanding God. As I have stressed throughout, much of the use of Exodus and the other Pentateuch books by the writers of the NT is not exegetical but rather homiletical in character. While there is some spiritualizing of language to allow the texts to speak to other and later concerns, mostly this is not the case. Rather, creative *relecture* and reapplication is mainly what we find.

The writers of the NT seem to presuppose a stable text of the OT, on the basis of which they may paraphrase, improvise, and reapply the material. We also stressed that the oral nature of these cultures makes it difficult to tell when a writer is using an alternate text or translation for some portion of the Pentateuch, or when they are just quoting from memory or paraphrasing. We noted that the *narrative* in the Pentateuch is seldom *cited* as Scripture in the NT, but this hardly tells us how important it was to the thought world of the NT writers. We lamented that one of the real problems with "intertextuality" studies is that it presupposes texts interacting, but in fact sometimes it is just memory or oral tradition or deliberate paraphrasing interacting with the OT text.

This also brought to the fore the deficiencies of just looking at clear citations or allusions when one wants to assess the influence of the OT on the NT, or its reuse in the NT. As I have said, citations are the tip of the iceberg, and where the deficiency of this approach is clearest is with narrative, which is not usually directly cited. Though a volume like *A Commentary on the New Testament Use of the Old Testament* is enormously helpful as a starting point for dealing with direct or approximate citations of the OT in the NT, time and again the use of narrative in nonquotation modes and ways comes up for no discussion at all. This leads to an incomplete, and in some ways inadequate, picture of the function of the Pentateuch in the NT.

Leviticus is an excellent test case when it comes to the hermeneutics of the NT writers in regard to the essence of pentateuchal law and praxis. As we noted in chapter 3, there is not much direct citation of or allusion to Leviticus in the NT, and for very good reason. Apart from the famous love command, and a few other bits in Leviticus, the laws about priests, temples, and sacrifices, about priestly orders and tabernacles are not on the tips of the tongues of the writers of the NT. Why not? Because the writers of the NT did not see the Jesus movement as an attempt to reinstitute or set up a new sacerdotal religion involving priests, temples, and sacrifices. The only priesthood the NT is prepared to talk about is the heavenly high priesthood of Christ (in Hebrews), which eclipsed and makes obsolete all previous priesthoods, temples, and sacrifices, or the priesthood of all believers (see 1 Peter and Revelation). This meant that much of the legislation in Leviticus was of no direct application to the followers of Jesus, and could only be used for its language in talking about presenting oneself as a living sacrifice or the sacrifices of praising God and the like. The followers of Jesus had no interest in, and did not attempt to set up, a new all-male priesthood like that found in Leviticus, probably for a host of reasons, not least of which is their theology of the sufficiency the ministry and death of Jesus to handle the sin problem. But there is more.

The writers of the NT were indeed convinced that something eschatological and new had happened in the Christ event, and at least some of them understood this to mean that the schema of this world is passing away to be replaced by the new creation, and part of that schema was the fallen institutions of patriarchy and slavery and the like. We get a glimmering of the attempt to change the narrative within the Christian household when we examine the household codes in Colossians 3–4 and Ephesians 5–6 over against parallel codes in the Jewish and Greco-Roman world, and we get a clearer glimpse of where the discourse was going on slavery when we arrive at Philemon and Paul says not only that Onesimus should be manumitted, but because he is a brother he should no longer be seen or treated as a slave.

In short, there was some social dynamite when it came to the social implications of the gospel and the coming of the one who "makes all things new," and this definitely affected how the NT writers approached such venerable institutions as marriage, patriarchy, slavery, an all-male priesthood and the like. True, often the implications of the new covenant were not always fully understood or spun out by the writers of the NT, but you can see in the very ways they handle a book like Leviticus what a Copernican revolution was going on in their thinking. One can also see it in the references to women teachers, prophetesses, and apostles in the NT, but that is a story I've told at length elsewhere.[2]

The book of Numbers also comes up for slender use in the NT, and one may be a bit surprised that in light of the problems with false teachers and pseudoprophets we don't find these writers saying much about Balaam, which was a regular topic of conversation for early Jews in other settings, or for that matter about the star prophecy in Numbers, which may come up once perhaps in the NT at the very end of the canon in Revelation 22, but as we noted there, John may simply be casting shade on the emperor, who was called morningstar by Martial in the very time period Revelation was likely written. On the other hand, the rather amazing and somewhat comical tale of the snake on the stick is surprisingly used in the Gospel of John to provide profound theological reflections about "the lifting up of Christ." We suggested as well that so little of Numbers is recycled in the NT because it is mostly reruns, more tales of woe about the wilderness wandering generation and their various rebellions.

The study of Deuteronomy in the NT is an important one, not least because it is the third most cited or alluded to OT book in the NT, after Isaiah and the Psalms. In part this reflects the great emphasis on this book in early Judaism. But that is not the only reason. It would appear that Jesus himself used Deuteronomy in various ways more than, for instance Exodus, when he was commenting on his

---

2. See Ben and Ann Witherington, *Women and the Genesis of Christianity*.

358 TORAH OLD AND NEW

own ministry. This may have provided a precedent, or opened a door for his followers to walk through thereafter.

There are several hundred quotations, allusions, or echoes of Deuteronomy in the NT, and interestingly, one of the most-used portions is the famous Song of Moses in Deuteronomy 32. In light of our study of Isaiah and the Psalms, this should not surprise us. Old Testament poetry seemed to be more easily appropriated, far more approachable and flexible a material for *relecture*, reuse, and reapplication in various ways. It was inherently multivalent, and open to open-ended sorts of recontextualizing.

Again, most of the use of Deuteronomy in the NT does not amount to what we would call contextual exegesis, but this does not make it examples of exuberant over-reading of the OT text, reading things that are not in touch with what was actually there, at least by implication or as an underlying principle. Even the "do not muzzle the ox" saying is not an example of gerrymandering the OT for later purposes, for as Miller pointed out, there is the underlying principle of a worker deserving some personal benefit for his or its work. When the NT writers want to allegorize something, they tell us (Galatians 4), and when they use typology they also tell us (Melchizedek). But by and large these techniques do not describe the usual ways the OT is used in the NT.

We noted that there seems to be little interest in the NT in the postscript to the Pentateuch found at the end of Deuteronomy. In fact, we noted that the story of Moses and his demise is not even used as a foil for or analogy to the end of the story of Jesus really, even though many early Jews believed that Moses, like Enoch and Elijah, had been taken up into heaven in the end, though the OT does not say so. We noted as well how, as in Acts 7 and Hebrews 11, the writers of the NT were perfectly prepared to draw on later Jewish traditions about Moses and his mediatorial role, referring to the wisdom he gained in Egypt, or to the angels conveying the Ten Words to Moses, and the like. But nothing is said about the exaltation of Moses compared to that of Christ, unless the transfiguration story implies such a thing. I would suggest this is because the NT writers had a mixed view of the legacy of Moses, not so much as a man (his attempt to pass off his calling onto Aaron is not discussed), but Moses as the lawgiver of laws, many of which made too many concessions to human hard-heartedness. But those concessions could not be part of the final and eschatological new covenant and new creation. New occasions were to teach new duties, and the renewed ones were reconfigured within the context of "the law of Christ," the next teaching of Jesus and his apostles and prophets and teachers. It cannot be emphasized enough that the Shema in Deuteronomy 6 as well as the recounting and recalibrating of the Ten Words of Moses shaped both the monotheistic theology of the NT writers, and their essential ethics about how to relate to God and one's fellow human beings.

We have still not plumbed the depths of the use of especially Deuteronomy in the NT but kudos to all those who have labored long in the vineyard of intertextuality, especially Richard Hays, Ross Wagner, Steve Moyise, and others who point out the riches, depths, and complexity of the interesting and creative uses of the OT in the NT.

Studying the OT material found in the NT is like looking at a rich and complex and colorful tapestry. At times, it is frustrating and one feels like one is looking at the backside of the tapestry and only see-ing the loose thread and knots that went into making up the tapestry and not the larger design and patterns of it. But at times, one seems to get glimpses of the front side of the tapestry and its design, or at least the light dawns in a way that, while still standing at a distance and behind the tapestry, we get glimpses of the larger design and beauti-ful patterns on the other side through looking at the matter through the eyes of the NT writers who are creatively using their sacred texts to tell the story of the Christ event and its sequel. Perhaps we also get a glimpse of how they thought about the larger issue of creating a new biblical theology and ethic based on the Christ event and its ongoing impact. But that is a story for another day, and I hope to get to it, God willing and the "Noahic creek don't rise!"

Appendix 1
Citations, Allusions, and Echoes of the Pentateuch in the NT according to Nestle-Aland²⁸

From the critical apparatus of the Eberhard Nestle and Kurt Aland, eds., *Novum Testamentum Graece*, 28th ed. (Stuttgart: Deutsche Bibelgesellschaft, 2012). Used by permission.

Genesis
ß
Ch. 1 : Heb 11:3
1:1 : John 1:1
2.6.9 : 2 Pet 3:5
2f. : 2 Cor 4:6
11f. : 1 Cor 15:38 Heb 6:7
14 : Acts 17:26
20.24 : 1 Cor 15:39
24 : Acts 10:12
24.30 : Acts 11:6
26f. : Acts 17:28 Rom 8:29 1 Cor
    11:7 Jas 3:9
27 : *Matt 19:4 Mark 10:6*
28 : Acts 17:26
31 : 1 Tim 4:4
2:2 : *Heb 4:4*.10
4 : Matt 1:1
7 : Luke 3:38 John 20:22 *1 Cor*
    15:45.47
7.22 : 1 Tim 2:13
9 : Rev 2:7; 22:2
10 : Rev 22:1
17 : Rom 5:12; 7:10 Heb 5:14
18 : 1 Cor 11:9
22f. : 1 Cor 11:8

24 : *Matt 19:5 Mark 10:7 1 Cor*
    6:16 Eph 5:31
3:1 : Matt 10:16 Rev 12:9
1–7 : Matt 4:3
3 : Rev 2:7
5 : Heb 5:14
6.13 : 1 Tim 2:14
13 : Rom 7:11 2 Cor 11:3
14–19 : Rom 8:20 Rev 12:9
15 : Rev 12:17
16 : 1 Cor 14:34 Eph 5:23 1 Tim
    2:12
17f. : Heb 6:8
19 : Rom 5:12 Heb 9:27
22.24 : Rev 2:7
4:4f. : Heb 11:4
7 : John 8:34
8 : 1John 3:12 Jude 11
8.10 : Matt 23:35 Luke 11:51
10 : Heb 11:4
24 : Matt 18:22
25f. : Luke 3:38
5:1 : Matt 1:1 1 Cor 11:7
1–8 : Luke 3:38
1–32 : Luke 3:36
2 : *Matt 19:4 Mark 10:6*
3 : 1 Cor 15:49

3–18 : Jude 14
24 : Heb 11:5
6:1–3 : Jude 6
1–4 : 2 Pet 2:4
2 : Luke 20:36 1 Cor 11:10
5–12 : Luke 17:26
8 : Luke 1:30
11–13 : Matt 24:37
12 : Rom 3:20
13–22 : Heb 11:7
7:6–23 : Luke 17:27
7 : Matt 24:38
13 : 2 Pet 2:5
13.17.23 : 1 Pet 3:20
21 : 2 Pet 3:6
8:17 : 1 Cor 15:39
18 : 2 Pet 2:5
21 : Phil 4:18
9:2 : Jas 3:7
3 : 1 Tim 4:3
4 : Acts 15:20
6 : Matt 26:52
19 : Acts 17:26
Ch. 10 : Luke 10:1 Acts 17:26
11:10–22 : Luke 3:35
24–26 : Luke 3:34
30 : Luke 1:7
31 : Acts 7:2
32 : Acts 7:4
12:1 : *Acts 7:3*
1.4 : Heb 11:8
2f. : Heb 7:6
3 : Acts 3:25 *Gal 3:8 Rev 1:7*
5 : Acts 7:4
8 : Heb 11:9
13:12 : Heb 11:9
15 : *Gal 3:16*
14:17 : Heb 7:10
17–20 : *Heb 7:1*
18 : Mark 5:7 Luke 8:28
19 : Heb 7:6
19.22 : Rev 10:6
20 : *Heb 7:4*
35 : Luke 8:8
15:1 : Matt 5:12
5 : Rom 4:13.*18*

6 : *Rom 4:3 Gal 3:6 Jas 2:23*
7 : Acts 7:2 Rom 4:13 Heb 11:8
8 : Luke 1:18
12 : Acts 10:10 Rev 11:11
13f. : *Acts 7:6*
15 : Luke 2:29
16 : 1 Thess 2:16
18 : Rev 9:14
16:1 : Acts 7:5
11 : Luke 1:13.31
15 : Gal 4:22
17:5 : *Rom 4:17*
7 : Luke 1:55.72
8 : *Acts 7:5 Gal 3:16*
10–12 : John 7:22
10.13 : Acts 7:8
11 : Rom 4:11
12 : Luke 1:59
16 : Gal 4:23
17 : Luke 1:18 Rom 4:19
19 : Luke 1:13.31 Gal 4:23 Heb
   11:11
18:2–33 : Heb 13:2
4 : Luke 7:44
6 : Matt 13:33
10 : *Rom 9:9*
11 : Luke 1:7.18
12 : 1 Pet 3:6
14 : Matt 19:26 Mark 10:27 *Rom 9:9*
18 : Acts 3:25 *Gal 3:8*
19 : Matt 22:16 Mark 12:14
20 : Rev 18:5
20f. : Luke 17:28
19:1–3 : Heb 13:2
3 : Luke 24:29
4–9 : Luke 10:12
4–25 : Jude 7
7–9 : 2 Pet 2:7
15–29 : Luke 17:29
16.29 : 2 Pet 2:7
17 : Luke 9:24; 17:31
19 : Luke 1:58
24 : Rev 14:10
24f. : Matt 10:15 2 Pet 2:6
26 : Luke 17:32
28 : Rev 9:2

21:1 : Luke 1:38
2 : Gal 4:22 Heb 11:11
2f. : Luke 3:34
4 : Acts 7:8
8 : Luke 5:29
9 : Gal 4:29
10 : *Gal 4:30*
12 : *Rom 9:7 Heb 11:18*
17 : John 12:29
Ch. 22 : Heb 11:17
22:22 : Mark 12:6 Luke 3:22
2.9 : Jas 2:21
16 : Rom 8:32 Heb 6:13
17 : Rom 4:13 *Heb 6:14*; 11:12
18 : *Acts 3:25*
23:3–20 : Acts 7:16
4 : Heb 11:9.13 1 Pet 2:11
24:3 : Matt 11:25; 15:22 Mark 5:7
7 : Matt 11:25 *Gal 3:16*
25:21 : Luke 1:7
22 : Luke 1:41
23 : *Rom 9:12*
24 : Luke 1:57
26 : Matt 1:2 Luke 3:34 Acts 7:8
33f. : Heb 12:16
26:3 : Luke 1:73
4 : *Acts 3:25*
5 : Luke 1:6
12 : Luke 8:8
27:27–29 : Heb 11:20
30–40 : Heb 12:17
39f. : Heb 11:20
28:12 : *John 1:51*
14 : *Rev 1:7*
15 : Heb 13:5
29:29–31 : Luke 16:13
31 : Luke 1:7
32 : Luke 1:48
35 : Matt 1:2 Luke 3:33
30:13 : Luke 1:48
23 : Luke 1:25
34 : Luke 1:38
31:30 : Luke 22:15
32:13 : Heb 11:12
31 : 1 Cor 13:12
33:4 : Acts 20:37

19 : Acts 7:16
34:26 : Luke 21:24
35:2 : Heb 11:9
11 : Heb 7:5
19 : Matt 2:18
22–26 : Acts 7:8 Rev 7:5
36:6 : Rev 18:13
37:9 : Rev 12:1
11 : Luke 2:19 Acts 7:9
20 : Mark 12:7
28 : Acts 7:9
38:8 : Matt 22:24 Mark 12:19
    Luke 20:28
12–30 : Matt 1:3
24 : John 8:41
29 : Luke 3:33
39:2f. : Acts 7:9
4f. : Matt 24:45
21, 23 : Acts 7:9.10
40:14 : Luke 23:42
41:42 : Luke 15:22
43 : Acts 7:10
46 : Luke 3:23 Acts 7:10
54 : Acts 7:11
55 : John 2:5
42:2 : Acts 7:12
5 : Acts 7:11
45:1.3 : Acts 7:13
4 : Acts 7:9
8 : Acts 7:10
9–11 : Acts 7:14
14f. : Acts 20:37
16 : Acts 7:13
18 : Acts 7:14
26 : Luke 24:11
46:2 : Acts 9:4
3f. : Acts 7:15
27 : Acts 7:14
30 : Luke 2:29
47:27 : Acts 7:17
31 : *Heb 11:21*
Ch. 48 : Heb 11:21
48:1.5 : Rev 7:6
4 : *Acts 7:5*
7 : Matt 2:18
22 : John 4:5

49:9 : Rev 5:5
10 : Heb 7:14
11 : Rev 7:14
33 : Acts 7:15
50:13 : Acts 7:16
24f. : Heb 11:22

Exodus
𝔊

1:5 : Acts 7:14
6 : Acts 7:15
7 : Acts 7:17
8 : *Acts 7:18*
9–11 : Acts 7:19
16 : Acts 7:19
22 : Acts 7:19 Heb 11:23
2:2 : Acts 7:20 Heb 11:23
3 : Acts 7:19
3.5.10 : Acts 7:21
11 : Acts 7:23 Heb 11:24
11f. : Acts 7:24
13 : Acts 7:26
14 : Luke 12:14 *Acts 7:27.35*
15 : Acts 7:29 Heb 11:27
22 : Acts 7:6.29
24 : Luke 1:72
3:1f. : Mark 12:26 Luke 20:37
2 : Acts 7:30
3f. : Acts 7:31
4 : Acts 9:4
5 : *Acts 7:33*
6 : *Matt 22:32* Mark 12:26 *Luke 20:37 Acts 3:13; 7:32* Heb 11:16
7s.10 : *Acts 7:34*
12 : Acts 7:7
14 : Rev 1:4
15f. : Matt 22:32 Mark 12:26 Luke 20:37 Acts 3:13; 7:32
4:12 : Matt 10:19
15 : Mark 13:11
16 : Heb 2:17
19 : Matt 2:20
21 : Rom 9:18
22 : Rom 9:4
31 : Luke 1:68
6:1.6 : Acts 13:17

23 : Luke 1:5
7:1 : John 10:34
3 : Acts 7:36 Rom 9:18
9 : John 2:18
11 : 2 Tim3:8
17–21 : Rev 16:3.4
17.19f. : Rev 11:6
20 : Rev 8:8
22 : 2 Tim3:8
8:3 : Rev 16:13
4.24 : Acts 8:24
15 : Luke 11:20
9:10f. : Rev 16:2
12 : *Matt 27:10*
16 : *Rom 9:17*
18 : Mark 13:19
23–25 : Rev 8:7
24 : Rev 11:19; 16:18
28 : Acts 8:24
10:12 : Rev 9:3
14 : Mark 13:19
16 : Luke 15:18
17 : Acts 8:24
21 : Rev 8:12
22 : Rev 16:10
11:6 : Mark 13:19
12:6 : Mark 14:12 Luke 22:7
10 : *John 19:36*
11 : *Luke 12:35*
14 : Luke 22:19
14f. : Luke 22:7
14–20 : Matt 26:17 Mark 14:12
15.18 : Luke 2:43
19 : 1 Cor 5:7
21 : Acts 5:21 1 Cor 5:7
21–23 : Heb 11:28
23 : Heb 11:28
24–27 : Luke 2:41
40f. : Gal 3:17
46 : *John 19:36*
48 : Heb 11:28
51 : Heb 11:27
13:2 : *Luke 2:23*
5 : Rom 9:5
7 : 1 Cor 5:7
9 : Matt 23:5

12 : Luke 2:22
15 : *Luke 2:23*
16 : Matt 23:5
21 : Rev 10:1
21f. : 1 Cor 10:1
14:13 : Matt 9:2 Mark 6:50
21 : John 14:1 Acts 7:36
22 : 1 Cor 10:1 Heb 11:29
27 : Heb 11:29
15:1 : Rev 15:3
4 : Acts 7:36
11 : Rev 13:4
14 : Rev 11:18
16 : 2 Cor 7:15 Rev 11:11
23 : Rev 8:11
16:2f. : 1 Cor 10:10
4 : John 6:31 1 Cor 10:3
4f. : Luke 11:3
7 : Rom 9:4 2 Cor 3:18
10 : Luke 9:34 Rom 9:4 2 Cor 3:18
15 : John 6:31
18 : *2 Cor 8:15*
19 : Matt 6:34
32–36 : Rev 2:17
33 : Heb 9:4
35 : Mark 1:13 Acts 13:18 1 Cor
   10:3
17:1–16 : Heb 3:16
2 : Acts 15:10
6 : 1 Cor 10:4
7 : Heb 3:8
18:3f. : Acts 7:29
4 : Acts 12:11
17–23 : Acts 6:2
19 : Heb 5:1
25 : Mark 3:14
19:3 : Luke 6:12
4 : Rev 12:14
5 : Titus 2:14
5f. : Heb 8:9
6 : Rev 1:6; 5:10
10 : Rev 7:14
12 : Heb 12:18
12f. : Heb 12:20
14 : Rev 7:14
16 : Rev 1:10; 4:5
16–19 : Heb 12:19

18 : Heb 12:26 Rev 9:2
24 : Rev 4:1
20:4 : Rev 5:3
5 : John 9:2
9f. : Luke 13:14
10 : Matt 12:2 Mark 2:27
10f. : Luke 23:56
11 : *Acts 4:24; 14:15* Rev 10:6
12 : *Matt 15:4; 19:19 Mark 7:10*
   Eph 6:2
12–16 : *Mark 10:19 Luke 18:20*
13 : *Matt 5:21*
13f. : *Jas 2:11*
13–15 : Rev 9:21
13–16 : Matt 15:19; *19:18*
13–17 : *Rom 13:9*
14 : *Matt 5:27*
17 : Matt 5:28 *Rom 7:7*
18 : Heb 12:19
26 : Acts 6:13
21:12 : Matt 5:21
17 : *Matt 15:4 Mark 7:10*
24 : *Matt 5:38*
32 : Matt 26:15
37 : Luke 19:8
22:10 : Heb 6:16
21f. : Mark 12:40
22 : Luke 18:3
27 : John 10:34; 18:22 *Acts 23:5*
28f. : Luke 2:22
23:4f. : Matt 5:44 Luke 6:27
12 : Mark 2:27
14–17 : Luke 2:41
20 : *Matt 11:10 Mark 1:2 Luke 7:27*
22 : Rev 1:6
24:1 : Luke 9:28; 10:1
1–3 : Luke 6:12
1.9 : Mark 9:2
3–8 : Heb 9:19
7f. : Gal 4:24 1 Pet 1:2
8 : Matt 26:28 Mark 14:24 Luke
   22:20 1 Cor 11:25 *Heb 9:20;*
   13:20
12–18 : Luke 6:12
15f. : Mark 9:2
15–18 : Luke 9:34

17 : 2 Cor 3:18
18 : Mark 1:13 Luke 4:2; 9:34
25:9 : Acts 7:44
10–22 : Heb 9:4
18.20 : Heb 9:5
23.30f. : Heb 9:2
31.37 : Rev 1:12
39f. : *Heb 8:5*
26:31–33 : Matt 27:51 Mark
    15:38 Luke 23:45
31.33 : Heb 9:3
27:2 : Rev 9:13
21 : Acts 7:44
28:1 : Heb 5:4
17–20 : Rev 21:19
21 : Rev 21:12
36 : Rev 13:16
29:18 : Phil 4:18
33 : Matt 7:6
37 : Matt 23:19
38 : Heb 7:27
30:1 : Rev 8:3
1–3 : Rev 9:13
1–10 : Heb 9:4
7 : Rev 8:3
7f. : Luke 1:9
10 : Heb 9:7
13f. : Matt 17:24
35 : Mark 9:49
31:13 : Heb 2:11
13–17 : Mark 2:24
14 : Mark 3:6
18 : Acts 7:38 2 Cor 3:3
32:1 : *Acts 7:40*
4.8 : Acts 7:41
6 : Acts 7:41 *1 Cor 10:7*
15 : 2 Cor 3:3
23 : *Acts 7:41*
32 : Luke 10:20 Rom 9:3
32f. : Rev 3:5
34 : Luke 10:1
33:2 : Matt 15:22 Luke 10:1
3.5 : Acts 7:51
7 : Heb 8:2; 13:13
11 : John 15:15
14 : Matt 11:28

16 : Luke 1:30
18 : John 1:18
19 : *Rom 9:15*
19–23 : Mark 6:48
20 : John 1:18 1 Tim 6:16
20.23 : 1John 3:2
34:2 : Luke 6:12
6 : Mark 6:48 John 1:17 Jas 5:11
6f. : 1John 1:9
7 : Mark 2:7
10 : Luke 13:17 Rev 15:3
21 : Mark 2:24 Luke 6:2
28 : Matt 4:2 Luke 4:2
29f. : Matt 17:2 Luke 9:29
    2 Cor 3:10
30 : 2 Cor 3:7
33.35 : 2 Cor 3:13
34 : 2 Cor 3:16
35 : Luke 9:29 2 Cor 3:10
40:5 : Rev 9:13
9 : Heb 9:21
23 : Matt 12:4 Mark 2:26
34 : Mark 9:7 Rev 15:5.8
35 : Rev 15:8

Leviticus
2:13 : Mark 9:49
7:6.15 : 1 Cor 10:18
12 : Heb 13:15
8:15.19 : Heb 9:21
9:7 : Heb 5:3
22 : Luke 24:50
10:9 : *Luke 1:15*
Ch. 11 : Acts 10:12
2 : Heb 9:10
4 : Matt 23:24
7f. : Luke 8:32
21f. : Matt 3:4 Mark 1:6
41 : Matt 23:24
44f. : *1 Pet 1:16*
12:3 : Luke 1:59 John 7:22
6 : Luke 2:22
8 : *Luke 2:24*
13:19 : Luke 5:14
45f. : Luke 17:12

14:2–32 : Matt 8:4 Mark 1:44
  Luke 5:14
4 : Heb 9:19; 9:7
15:18 : Heb 9:10
25 : Matt 9:20 Mark 5:25
Ch. 16 : Rom 8:3
2 : Heb 6:19; 9:7
4 : Heb 10:22
6 : Heb 5:3
12 : Heb 6:19 Rev 8:5
13–15 : Rom 3:25
14f. : Heb 9:7
15 : Heb 6:19
17 : Heb 5:3
18f. : Heb 9:7
20 : Heb 8:2
27 : Heb 13:11
29 : Acts 27:9
17:7 : 1 Cor 10:20
10–14 : John 6:53 Acts 15:20
11 : Heb 9:22
18:5 : Matt 19:17 Luke 10:28 Rom
  2:26; 7:10; *10:5 Gal 3:12*
6–18 : Acts 15:20
8 : 1 Cor 5:1
16 : Matt 14:4 Mark 6:18
22 : Rom 1:27
26 : Acts 15:20
19:2 : Matt 5:48 Luke 6:36 *1 Pet 1:16*
12 : Matt 5:33
13 : Matt 20:8 Jas 5:4
15 : Acts 23:3 Jas 2:9 Jude 16
16 : Luke 10:29
17 : Matt 18:15 Luke 17:3
18 : *Matt 5:43; 19:19; 22:39 Mark*
  12:31.33; Luke 10:27 Rom 12:19;
  13:9 Gal 5:14 Jas 2:8
32 : 1 Tim 5:1
33f. : Luke 10:29
34 : *Matt 22:39*
20:7 : 1 Pet 1:16
9 : *Matt 15:4 Mark 7:10*
10 : John 8:5
13 : Rom 1:27
21 : Matt 14:4 Mark 6:18
26 : 1 Pet 1:16

21:9 : Rev 17:16
22:10 : Matt 7:6
23:15–21 : Acts 20:16
29 : *Acts 3:23*
34 : John 7:2
36 : John 7:37
40 : John 12:13
40.43 : Rev 7:9
24:5–8 : Mark 2:26
5–9 : Matt 12:4 Luke 6:4
7 : 1 Cor 11:24
9 : Mark 2:26
14 : Mark 15:20b Acts 7:58 Heb
  13:13
16 : Matt 26:66 Mark 14:64 John
  10:33; 19:7 2 Tim2:19
17 : Matt 5:21
20 : *Matt 5:38*
25:10 : Luke 4:19
35f. : Luke 6:35
26:4 : Acts 14:17
11f. : *2 Cor 6:16*
12 : Rev 21:3.7
21 : Rev 15:1.6
41 : Acts 7:51
42 : Luke 1:72
46 : Gal 3:19
27:30 : Matt 23:23 Luke 11:42

Numeri
𝔊
5:2f. : Luke 17:12
6f. : Luke 19:8
12–28 : John 8:3
15 : Heb 10:3
17 : Heb 10:22
6:2–21 : Acts 18:18
3 : *Luke 1:15*
5.13 : Acts 21:26
9.18 : Acts 21:24
9:12 : John 19:36
10:35 : Luke 1:51
11:4 : 1 Cor 10:6
16 : Luke 10:1
21f. : Luke 9:13
25 : Acts 2:3

26–29 : Mark 9:38 1 Thess 5:19
28 : Luke 9:49
29 : Acts 2:18 1 Cor 14:5
34 : 1 Cor 10:6
12:2 : John 9:29
3 : Matt 11:29
7 : Heb 3:2.5 Rev 15:3
8 : John 9:29 1 Cor 13:12 2John 12
14 : Matt 26:67
14:2 : 1 Cor 10:10
3 : Acts 7:39
6 : Matt 26:65 Mark 14:63
16 : 1 Cor 10:5
21–23 : Heb 3:11
22f. : Heb 3:18
23 : John 6:49
27 : Matt 17:17 Mark 9:19 Luke 9:41
29–37 : Jude 5
29.32 : Heb 3:17
33 : Mark 1:13
33f. : Acts 7:36; 13:18
36 : 1 Cor 1:10
15:19–21 : Rom 11:16
30 : Matt 26:66 Mark 14:64
35 : Heb 13:13
35f. : Mark 15:20b Acts 7:58
38f. : Matt 9:20 Mark 6:56 Luke 8:44
Ch. 16 : Jude 11
5 : *2 Tim2:19*
11–35 : 1 Cor 10:10
22 : Heb 12:9
28 : John 7:17
30.32 : Rev 12:16
33 : Rev 19:20
17:23.25 : Heb 9:4
18:3f. : Heb 9:6
8 : 1 Cor 9:13
21 : Heb 7:5
31 : 1 Cor 9:13
19:2 : Mark 11:2 Luke 19:30
6 : Heb 9:19
9 : Heb 9:13
13 : Heb 9:10
16 : Luke 11:44
17 : Heb 9:13
20:2 : Heb 3:8
7–11 : 1 Cor 10:4

21:5f. : 1 Cor 10:9
8f. : John 3:14
22:7.17f. : 2 Pet 2:15
16 : Acts 9:38
22.32 : Mark 8:33
28–30 : 2 Pet 2:16
23:19 : Rom 11:29 Heb 6:18
22 : Matt 2:15
24:8 : Matt 2:15
17 : Matt 2:2 Rev 22:16
25 : Luke 24:12
25:1.9 : 1 Cor 10:8
1f. : Rev 2:14
26:62 : 1 Cor 10:8
27:14 : Acts 7:51
16 : Heb 12:9 Rev 22:6
17 : *Matt 9:36 Mark 6:34* John 10:9
18.23 : Acts 6:6
28:3 : Heb 7:27
9f. : Matt 12:5
30:3 : Matt 5:33
31:16 : 2 Pet 2:15 Rev 2:14
22f. : Mark 9:49
33:55 : 2 Cor 12:7
35:30 : Heb 10:28

Deuteronomium

1:7 : Rev 9:14
8.21 : Matt 5:5
13 : Heb 13:7 Jas 3:13
16f. : John 7:51
31 : Acts 13:18
35 : John 6:49
2:5 : Acts 7:5
14 : John 5:5
3:11 : Rev 21:17
26 : Luke 22:38
27 : Matt 4:8
4:1 : Luke 10:28
2 : Rev 22:18
6 : Jas 3:13
7f. : Rom 3:2
10 : Acts 7:38
11 : Heb 12:18
12 : John 5:37 Acts 9:7 Heb 12:19
15–18 : Rom 1:23

24 : *Heb 12:29*
28 : Acts 17:29
29 : Acts 17:27
34 : Acts 13:17
35 : *Mark 12:32*
37 : Acts 13:17
40 : Luke 1:6
5:4f. : Gal 3:19
8 : Rev 5:3
9 : Matt 4:10
12–14 : Luke 23:56
13f. : Luke 13:14
14 : Matt 12:2 Mark 2:27
15 : Acts 13:17
16 : *Matt 15:4; 19:19 Mark 7:10*
  Eph 6:2
16–20 : *Mark 10:19 Luke 18:20*
17 : *Matt 5:21*
17f. : *Jas 2:11*
17–20 : Matt 15:19; 19:18
17–21 : *Rom 13:9*
18 : *Matt 5:27*
19 : Eph 4:28
21 : Matt 5:28 *Rom 7:7*
22f. : Heb 12:18
6:4 : Mark 2:7; *12:29.32* Luke 18:19
  1 Cor 8:4 Jas 2:19
4f. : John 5:42
5 : *Matt 22:37 Mark 12:30.33 Luke*
  10:27
8 : Matt 23:5
13 : *Matt 4:10 Luke 4:8*
16 : *Matt 4:7 Luke 4:12* Heb 3:9
7:1 : Acts 13:19
1–5 : Matt 5:43
6 : Titus 2:14
8 : John 14:23
9 : 1 Cor 10:13
15 : Matt 4:23
8:1 : Luke 10:28
2 : Matt 4:1 Luke 4:1
3 : *Matt 4:4 Luke 4:4, 22* 1 Cor 10:3
5 : Heb 12:5
15 : Luke 10:19
9:3 : *Heb 12:29*
4 : *Rom 10:6*

5 : Titus 3:5
9 : Matt 4:2 Luke 4:2 Heb 9:4
10f. : 2 Cor 3:3
16 : Acts 1:25
19 : *Heb 12:21*
26.29 : Acts 13:17
27 : Rom 2:5
10:8 : Heb 10:11
12 : Luke 10:27
15 : Acts 13:17
16 : Mark 10:5 Rom 2:29
17 : Acts 10:34 Gal 2:6 Rev 17:14;
  19:16
18 : Luke 18:3
19 : Luke 10:29
20 : *Matt 4:10 Luke 4:8* 1 Cor 6:17
21 : Luke 1:49
11:6 : Rev 12:16
11 : Heb 6:7
14 : Jas 5:7
18 : Matt 23:5
29 : John 4:20
12:5 : John 4:20
9 : Matt 11:29
12 : Acts 8:21
14 : Matt 28:20
13:1 : John 11:47 Rev 22:18
2 : Mark 13:22
2–4 : Matt 24:24
3 : John 11:47
6 : Matt 24:24 Mark 13:22
14:1 : Rom 9:4
2 : Titus 2:14
8 : Luke 8:32
22 : Luke 11:42
22f. : Matt 23:23
27 : Acts 8:21
29 : Luke 14:13 Acts 8:21
15:4 : Acts 4:34
7f. : Matt 5:42 1John 3:17
9 : Matt 6:23
10 : 2 Cor 9:7
11 : Matt 26:11 Mark 14:7 John 12:8
16:1–8 : Mark 14:1.12 Luke 2:41
3 : Luke 22:19
16 : Luke 2:41 John 7:2

20 : Rom 9:31

17:6 : Mark 14:56 John 8:17 *Heb 10:28*

7 : John 8:7 Acts 7:58 *1 Cor 5:13*

20 : Acts 1:25

18:1–3 : 1 Cor 9:13

7 : Heb 10:11

10–14 : Acts 19:19

13 : Matt 5:48

15 : Matt 17:5 Mark 9:7 Luke 9:35 John 1:21; 5:46 *Acts 7:37*

15s.18f. : *Acts 3:22*

19:15 : *Matt 18:16* Mark 14:56 Luke 7:18 John 8:17 *2 Cor 13:1 1 Tim 5:19* 1John 5:7

21 : *Matt 5:38*

20:6 : 1 Cor 9:7

17 : Matt 15:22

21:6–8 : Matt 27:24

20 : Matt 11:19 Luke 7:34

22 : Acts 5:30

22f. : Matt 27:58 Mark 15:42 Luke 23:53

23 : John 19:31 *Gal 3:13*

22:4 : Luke 14:5

10 : 2 Cor 6:14

12 : Matt 9:20 Mark 6:56

22–24 : John 8:5

23:2 : Gal 5:12

5 : 2 Pet 2:15

19 : Matt 27:6

22 : Matt 5:33

22–24 : Acts 5:4

25f. : Matt 12:1 Mark 2:23

26 : Luke 6:1

24:1 : Luke 16:18

1–3 : Matt 5:31

1.3 : Matt 19:7 Mark 10:4

5 : Luke 14:20

14 : Mark 10:19

14f. : Matt 20:8 Jas 5:4

15 : Eph 4:26

16 : John 8:21

25:3 : 2 Cor 11:24

4 : *1 Cor 9:9 1 Tim 5:18*

5f. : Matt 22:24 Mark 12:19 Luke 20:28

9 : Matt 26:67

26:5 : Acts 7:15

27:12 : John 4:20

25 : Matt 27:4

26 : John 7:49 *Gal 3:10.13* Heb 8:9

28:4 : Luke 1:42

10 : Jas 2:7

22 : Acts 23:3

28f. : Acts 22:11 2 Pet 1:9

35 : Rev 16:2

53 : Rom 2:9

58 : Gal 3:10

64 : Luke 21:24

29:3 : *Rom 11:8*

17 : Acts 8:23 *Heb 12:15*

19 : Rev 22:18

30:4 : Matt 24:31 Mark 13:27

6 : Rom 2:29

10 : Gal 3:10

11 : 1John 5:3

12 : *Rom 10:6*

13 : Rom 10:7

14 : *Rom 10:8*

15f. : Matt 7:14

16 : Rom 2:26

16–20 : John 5:39

31:1 : Matt 26:1

6.8 : *Heb 13:5*

26 : John 5:46

32:4 : Rom 9:14 1John 1:9 *Rev 15:3.4.5*

5 : Matt 17:17 Luke 9:41 Acts 2:40

6 : Matt 6:9

8 : Acts 17:26 Heb 2:5

11 : Matt 23:37 Luke 13:34

15 : Eph 1:6

17 : 1 Cor 10:20 Rev 9:20

20 : Matt 17:17 Mark 9:19 Luke 9:41

21 : *Rom 10:19* 1 Cor 10:22

28f. : Luke 19:42

35 : Luke 21:22 *Rom 12:19 Heb 10:30*

36 : *Heb 10:30*

39 : John 5:21

40 : Rev 1:18; 10:5
43 : *Rom 15:10 Heb 1:6* Rev 6:10;
   12:12; 19:2
47 : Acts 7:38
49 : Acts 7:5
33:2 : Matt 25:31 Acts 7:53 Jude 14
3f. : Acts 20:32

5 : Eph 1:6
9 : Matt 10:37 Luke 14:26
12 : 2 Thess 2:13
16 : Acts 7:35
29 : Eph 1:6
34:1–4 : Matt 4:8
5 : Rev 15:3

Appendix 2
Review of *Adam and the Genome*

Dennis R. Venema and Scot McKnight, *Adam and the Genome* (Grand Rapids: Brazos, 2017).

> Author's Note: Because of the extreme importance for conservative Protestant, Catholic, and Orthodox Christians of the issues that Genesis 1–3 raises about the origins of humanity, the original sin, the fall, and related matters, and especially because of the questions raised about *the historical substance of these stories in light of modern evolutionary theory*, this detailed review of a recent book that deals with all these subjects is offered here as a possible guide for the perplexed and for further discussion.

On first blush the title of this book suggests an Indie rock band. But seriously, this is a very well-researched book on genetics, and biblical interpretation vis à vis the origins of human life and whether or not Adam (and Eve) were historical persons. The genetics part of the book by Dennis R. Venema is a difficult read for those not familiar with genetics, even at the layperson's level, whereas Scot McKnight's half of the book (beginning at p. 93) is quite clear, but in some ways more problematic, from my point of view. Nonetheless, it is written with the sort of style and grace and honesty that we have come to expect in McKnight's books.

If we ask what prompted the book, all is made clear by statements late in the study on pp. 172–73. The concern is about people losing their faith due to an encounter with science, particularly evolutionary theory, especially perhaps those who have come from more fundamentalist Protestant backgrounds. McKnight deals regularly with such students and frames the matter this way:

Here is what is vital for this book: [a] person's faith was challenged by his realization about evolution and he was forced to make a choice about whether the Bible or evolution was the truest description and understanding of the world. *He chose science because the understanding of the Bible was in his view demonstrably wrong.* Dennis and I are proposing another alternative: accepting the reality of genetic evidence supporting a theory of evolution along with an understanding of Adam and Eve that is more in tune with the historical context of Genesis.

In other words, the interpretation of the Word should be adjusted on the basis of the assumed fait accompli of science to demonstrate it has the facts on its side. Neither side of these assumptions, the science or the biblical interpretation assumptions is without its problems. But I absolutely agree that we need to have a good discussion about this because science is one thing and pseudoscience that denies the geological and genetic evidence for an old earth and ancient human race needs to be countered. The great shortcoming in this book is there really is no discussion or dialogue between the two authors about their respective disciplines and conclusions in the text itself. Instead, we simply have two presentations, one from the scientific side of things and one from the theological side of things.

Perhaps it will be well if I first state a few personal disclaimers. I have no problem with (1) the idea that different areas of knowledge require different methodologies to arrive at theories that explain the facts; (2) the usual observation that the Bible is not a scientific textbook, it does not teach cosmology, biology, anthropology, geology, and so on; (3) the observation that a proper critique of modern science cannot rest solely on pointing out gaps in the fossil record, or the lack of positive evidence for missing-link creatures to connect critter A to critter B through evolutionary processes; (4) the notion that a species can adapt and change as its environment changes over time, indeed being affected by the environment (in other words, with microevolution within a species); and finally (5) the notion of a very old earth and a long prehistory before humankind created in God's image shows up on planet earth. Genesis 1 is a piece of Hebrew poetry that demonstrates the divine origins and design of it all. It does not tell us how long it took to accomplish the process, nor does it fill in all the blanks along the way. In a broad sense, in any case, it comports with evolutionary ideas about human beings being the apex and most complex of all living things.

On the other hand, what *is a problem* with science is an assumption that one can globalize a scientific theory to be all-encompassing, even impinging on areas clearly outside the discipline of genetics, areas such as history and theology. What I mean by that is that the pre-suppositions of modern science are purely naturalistic or, better said, materialistic. All things can be explained if we just figure out the nat-ural processes that produced these facts, and then connect the dots. The problem with this is of course it *assumes* that God (if God is allowed into the conversation at all), at least in these spheres, only works by natural processes. It rules out miracles a priori. For example, it takes for granted that when you find common physical features in a whale and in a tetrapod that is a purely land-based creature, that there *must be* a link and a transition between A and B.

This leads to the quite proper question: If God is the CEO and director of all creation (not merely the one who fired the starter gun, having provided the raw materials for the human race and other crea-tures) why in the world *could God not simply use some of the same fea-tures in two different species of creatures?* No reason is given. Why, for example, is it not possible that God decided fish would have vertebrae and at least front limbs, and so would humans without any necessary connection between these species? These differing types of creatures could have each developed along their own natural lines, but shared some features in common with other species. Genetic similarities do not *necessarily* lead to the conclusion of genetic connections.

The real problem here is however when science impinges on human history, not animal history. The Bible may not teach science, but it certainly teaches some specific things about human history, as we shall see in this review.

THE SCIENCE CHAPTERS

The heart of the genomics and genetic case *against a historical Adam and Eve* seems to be that human beings today descend from an origi-nal group of about ten thousand hominids. But this is hardly a prob-lem for those who realize that the Bible is not the story of the whole human race, it is the story of God's chosen people who began some-where in the Middle East, apparently in Mesopotamia, between the Tigris and the Euphrates. The Bible only mentions other races of people insofar as they come in contact with God's chosen people, for instance, already near the outset of Genesis, when we hear about

Cain and Abel having wives, and Cain having to go off to the land of Nod, but with a protective sign so other humans don't kill him. Is Acts 17:26 a possible objection to this reading of Genesis? I would say not. The text of Acts 17:26 involves variants, with some manuscripts simply reading "one" and some manuscripts reading "one blood." No manuscripts say that all human beings came from one initial human being, and the reading "one blood" is in any case more likely as the more difficult reading, not least because it contrasts with the description in Genesis that Adam was made from the dust of the earth, not from blood.[1] This reading should be compared to the phrase "not from blood" in John 1:13 that means not from physical descent or kinship. The idea in Acts 17 is that all human beings are the same sort of beings, sharing kinship, regardless of nationality, ethnicity, and so on.

Furthermore, most Evangelical Bible interpreters also do not think that Genesis 6–9 is recounting a worldwide flood that wiped out everyone. It was a massive regional flood that wiped out many of Noah's contemporaries in the ANE, as also recorded in the Babylonian Genesis and elsewhere. In other words, modern genetic theory and genomes need have no bearing at all on what the Bible says about Adam and Eve unless one *falsely* assumes that the story is about the first two human beings from whom *all* the rest descended (on which see below on Y chromosome Adam). But this is not what the story claims. Nor is it what, for example, Paul is talking about in Romans 5:12–21. He is saying that the first and the last Adams were heads of a whole group of people, such that their actions affected all those who were under the influence of Adam, and all those who were "in Christ." Adam was the representative head of all hominids and his actions affected them all. Similarly, Christ is the representative head of all those who are in Christ.

Chapter 2 provides us with a useful analogy drawing from the incremental development over time of a language (e.g. the word *treuth* becomes *truthe* and then *truth*) compared with the development of a human genetic code. While languages can change rather quickly, biological speciation and change takes place over thousands of years and herein lies another problem: (1) No one is around that long to observe the oh-so-gradual change, indeed whole civilizations rise and fall in the time it takes for even an incremental change of that sort. (2) No one was around when this process began. In fact Venema is

---

1. See Metzger, *Textual Commentary*, 456.

clear enough that even the fossil record only goes back 200,000 years maximum, but evolutionary theory requires a much, much longer timeline to account for all the genetic permutation and combinations. Thus, we are talking about extrapolation back in time based on modern science, *when the actual empirical observation of the change has not taken place over the time period required.* (3) The assumption is that things are operating now as they always have done according to the modern theories of evolution and natural development. But alas, we have no time machine to go back and check the math and the genetics from long, long ago. Again, no room is allowed for God to tinker with the process along the way, at most he simply set it in motion and is observing.

But what about that language analogy Venema uses?

Evolutionary theory could be guilty of the etymological fallacy, assuming notable similarities between things *must be caused* by a shared common ancestry. Since Venema uses the analogy with language, I shall do the same at this point. Let's take the English word *bare*, which in Old English was *baer*, very close, and having exactly the same letters as *bear*. Ah ha, you say, these two words must share a common ancestor! Not a bit of it. *Bare* seems to come from the Dutch *baar*, and ultimately from the proto-Germanic *bazaz*. By contrast *bear* comes from the old word for *brown* or the "brown one," *beron* in proto-Germanic or in old Norse *bjorn*, like the current Scandanavian name. Genetics has done a wonderful job of showing lots of similarities in the "letters" of the genetic code. It's when they try to *explain* the similarities that the train comes off the tracks, or at least gets sidetracked. There are other possible, legitimate explanations for similarities other than "they must share a common ancestor."

Imagine a builder who intend to build two different buildings, serving different purposes. But the construction materials are exactly the same, cinder blocks, boards, shingles, electrical wires, plumbing and so on. One building is an exercise gym, the other building is an apartment complex. One building is single story, the other is a high rise. Would anyone actually want to say that building B came from or is an evolved form of building A, just because they shared lots of common materials or building blocks and the same builder? No. Similarity of makeup is no proof of derivation.

DNA, genes, genomes, tell us a lot about the building blocks that go into the making of all sorts of creatures on earth. Detailed genetic study can show *possible* connections based on similar genetic patterns and codes. But we all know the problem of coming up with a very good hypothesis, or even a theory (a hypothesis that provides the "best" explanation of a particular sort for the known facts on the ground), that *does not take into account all the evidence.* You can argue consistently and coherently with and within a certain circle of evidence, and be incorrect, because you have not taken into account (or in some cases even deliberately eliminated) some of the evidence.

Modern evolutionary science, including the science of genetics, is based on the hypothesis that most, if not all, things can be explained in a natural way through empirical research. A theistic evolutionist will simply say that evolution is the way God works things. Suppose however that God is not like a watchmaker who creates a watch, winds it up, and leaves it to the empirical parts to do their jobs thereafter? Suppose God is constantly involved not merely in human history but in all things great and small. Suppose the designer constantly has his hand on the design, and makes changes and modifications? Suppose he designed human beings to be like other higher order creatures so that humans would feel some *kinship* with them, and take care of them, and be good governors of God's creation? Evolution is a theory that leaves God constantly out of the equation, or alternately simply says, "this is the natural mechanism God chose to accomplish things." There are other viable possibilities.

The same problems arise in applying this sort of information to the historical figures of Adam and Eve as arises in the neuro-scientific discussions about the mind and the brain, where the assumption is that human beings are psychosomatic wholes, and as such, when the body goes the whole person dies. There is no human spirit, human personality that survives death. Of course, no scientist has gone to the other side of death and done an empirical study of whether there might be spirits of the departed in heaven or elsewhere. The assumption again is that this world, this life, these natural processes, like evolution, are all there is, and so a theory that explains some things is globalized to explain everything, including ruling out ongoing divine action in the natural and human worlds—never mind ruling out the afterlife. My point by drawing attention to these two differing attempts at discussing science and the Bible together is that science often has to extrapolate or theorize from the known to the unknown to come up with a purely materialistic and empirical explanation for things.

I have no problems with scientists like Venema pursuing a theory as far as one can go with it; no problem with pushing the envelope to the limits of a theory to see if it still holds up. This is good and logical. What I do have a problem with is the globalizing of a theory to explain most everything when in fact it only explains *some things*. What I especially object to is the notion that "science deals with the facts as they are" and "religious opinions" do not. The notion that science somehow is more in touch with the reality of the material world than say, theology is, is not helpful, or for that matter true. So, for example, when Venema (p. 40) suggests that the very few biologists who do not accept evolutionary theory, do not accept it because of purely *prior religious commitments*, rather than for scientific reasons, one is setting up categories and dichotomies in such a way that the conclusion must be "religious commitments are *apriori* and not grounded in the facts." But wait a minute—*science also has apriori commitments*.

For example, science assumes there is an objective world outside the human mind that can be known with reasonably high degrees of certainty through the five human senses. *These frankly are faith assumptions*, both in terms of the reality of a world outside the human mind, and the reliability of the human sense, as anyone who has studied Pascal and Descartes knows. In other words, epistemology, how we know what we know, involves faith assumptions. Frankly, there are many faith assumptions behind modern science. So let's drop the pejorative language about a priori faith commitments as if science had none of those, and find a better way to have a conversation that does not intimate that somehow theology, once called the queen of the sciences, provides merely religious opinions about the material world.

All academic disciplines are based on certain presuppositions and faith assumptions about reality. All of them. If you are a scientist of Christian faith, you are convinced that there is such a thing as non-material reality which no material analysis could ever explain; I'm referring to God who is spirit, as Jesus says in John 4. One could also talk about angels and demons as well. Part of the problem goes all the way back to the Enlightenment, where material reality and empirical facts were lumped into one category, and theological statements and faith were lumped into another category, which led to the latter being eventually seen as a mere matter of religious opinion, and not grounded in factual reality. The problem with these sorts of pigeon-holes is they do a disservice to both science and religion. Both science and Christianity have faith assumptions and presuppositions and both deal with facts. In the case of Christianity, we are talking about historical facts, rather than, say, chemical or genetic facts; and the historian has exactly the same problem as the geneticist does when it comes to such things, because there are no time machines so that one can travel back to the real origins of things. Just as the geneticist relies on fossil records, so too do historians, and on other sorts of archaeological data as well. So enough with the "Christianity needs to conform itself to modern science or vice versa" sort of not so subtle forms of discourse. We need to listen hard, understand, and appreciate what truths and facts and faith assumptions have been discovered whether through studying the book of nature, or studying the book of God that he revealed to his people.

Perhaps for starters we could begin with Venema's observation on p. 64: "These children descend uniquely from one man (for the Y chromosome DNA) and one woman (for their mitochondrial DNA), but from at least four ancestors for their regular chromosomal DNA." Let's have a conversation about Mitochondrial Eve and Y chromosome Adam and the ten thousand other ancestors who supply our regular DNA. I don't see anything in Genesis 1–5 or elsewhere in the Bible which rules out such observations. Again, what the Bible is about, after the description of the initial creation, is the history of God's people. Where did God's people come from, Abraham, Isaac, Jacob, and the rest? The answer is Shem, and Noah, and before that Adam (see the genealogy in Luke 3). The Bible is simply not the story of every race of human beings. Other non-Hebrew peoples only come into the story in so far as they intersect with or interact with God's people. Full stop. This is not different than the observation that in the Gospels, persons other than Jesus only come in for discussion in so far as they interact with or have some bearing on the Jesus story.

One of the odd things about Venema's discussion is that at times he talks about evolution as if it had a mind of its own (see, e.g., on p. 86, he talks about evolution solving problems, overcoming defects, etc.). Now processes, even something as big as the process of evolution are not brains, not minds, they do not have willful intentions and plans and purposes. They just don't. Why not discuss the fact that these processes suggest not merely a mind behind it at the start, but a mind involved with it right along, helping it to adapt? Why talk about an object or process that can "self" assemble (p. 89), when in fact we could talk about the providential guidance of God in such matters? My point is, it's not enough to talk about a "powerful mind behind it all," some assembly required thereafter (good luck). God is not merely the creator, he is the sustainer of it all. He works all things together for good for those who love him. He's not just the designer, he's the weaver of the tapestry, and the maintenance person as well. The fact that you cannot see his fingerprints literally, is neither here nor there. You cannot see his Spirit either, but you can certainly see the effects of the Spirit's work on humans and other things. Indeed, many of the most important realities in this world are not tangible, nor can they be studied under the microscope, for instance the love of God. For that matter, history as well cannot be subjected to empirical lab tests where one can replicate things until you figure out its nature because no two historical events are alike—and that leads us to the second half of the book, which we must attend to more closely.

THE THEOLOGY CHAPTERS

McKnight's first chapter deals with four principles with which to read the Bible. As McKnight says at the outset: "Theology which is designed to investigate *that* nonempirical reality in some ways, can provide a map onto which we can locate science and which can challenge science" (p. 95). Exactly my point. The empirically observable and testable world is not all there is to reality. McKnight's concern is "we will all gain clarity if Christians learn how to speak about Adam and Eve in a context that both affirms conclusions about the genome and challenges some conclusions drawn from the Human Genome Project" (p. 97). Fair enough thus far.

The first of the four principles by which to study the Bible and talk with others about it is respect and respectful discourse for other disciplines than biblical studies, and in this case science, and particularly genetics. I agree with McKnight's statement on p. 99 that it is disrespectful to Scripture itself to expect the authors of Genesis 1–11 to be scientists in advance of the scientific era, scientists that already understand DNA, and the rest. There is no evidence that they did. If one takes the related field of cosmology, what we have in the Bible is the use of phenomenological, not scientific, language about the relationship of our sun to earth. They talk about the sun rising and setting, which is true from an earthbound observational point of view. That's how it looks to us. It's not the reality of the situation however. Such observations are not intended to teach us cosmology, merely how things appeared to these ancient people, and indeed, how it appears still today to us. McKnight spends considerable time situating Genesis 1–11 in its ANE context in some helpful ways, as we shall see. He even recites my favorite dictum: a text without a context is just a pretext for whatever you want it to mean.

The second valuable principle is honesty, and again I fully agree. Fundamentalists react to science as if it were a contagious disease, and come up with fear-based theories about both the Bible and science, neither of which are helpful. It results in bad history and Bible interpretation, and bad science too, the worst of both worlds. I will certainly never forget the time I hitchhiked back from the mountains of North Carolina in 1969 with two flat-earthers, who insisted that the moon walk by Neal Armstrong and all those pictures of a beautiful round and revolving earth were a Hollywood stunt. When my friend Doug asked why they thought it was fake the answer was, "it says in the book of Revelations that the angels will stand on the four corners of the earth." Can't be round if it has four corners. Beware of anyone who starts a sentence, "it says in the Book of Revelations." That isn't even the name of that book. Bless their hearts; those folks did not know that apocalyptic literature isn't teaching cosmology, its teaching eschatology, and the whole point was the angels would round up people from all points on the compass, not that the earth was flat! Sometimes invincible ignorance is hard to dialogue with. I must admit, I am less willing to critique all the intelligent design folks the way Venema does at the end of his last chapter. I think there is far more to some of their arguments than some would allow. Some of these folks are actual scientists who are also people of faith and are struggling to make sense of both the Bible and evolution. Good for them.

The third principle McKnight mentions is sensitivity to students of science, and again, I totally agree. I do not know if McKnight's claim on p. 104 that the *number one* reason kids leave the faith is because of questions about science, is true, but certainly some do. And the fourth principle is also a useful one: McKnight says *prima Scriptura* is better than *sola Scriptura*, and I agree if we are talking about knowledge or truth in general. If we are talking salvation, *sola Scriptura* is closer to the truth.

For me, where the problem really arises in McKnight's presentation is on pp. 107–8 where McKnight says that when the adjective "historical" is attached to Adam and Eve it means *all* of the following things: (1) two actual persons named Adam and Eve existed suddenly as a result of God's creation; (2) those two persons have a biological relationship with all subsequent human beings; (3) their DNA is our DNA; (4) those two died and brought death into the world; (5) those two passed on their sin natures to their descendants; (6) without (5) happening and involving all humans, then not all human beings would be in need of salvation; and (7) therefore if one denies the historical Adam one denies the Gospel of salvation.

Now as a historian myself I must say, to use a British metaphor *this is way over-egging the pudding.* I agree with McKnight that too often we have read the Bible through the lens of Augustine and subsequent interpreters of the Bible, to the detriment of getting at the truth of what the Bible actually says. My own view would be yes to (1) with a caveat, that we don't fully know *how exactly* God created Adam and Eve "in his image" and this last clause is the crucial one. The account we have in Genesis 2 is poetic, but it is also some sort of historical account, more like a primeval saga clothed in ANE garb, than a modern newspaper report. I do not think (2) above is a necessary conclusion from any of the statements about Adam in the Bible; (3) may or may not be true, (4) is true in regard to the death of Adam and Eve, and certainly Paul thinks this affected the rest of our kind. The issue is, are we talking about physical death or spiritual death or both? I incline to the view that we are talking about spiritual death here, which leads in fact to premature physical death in various cases. Or one could argue that Adam and Eve were created vulnerable to death but not "inherently mortal." (5) I agree with McKnight that I don't think the later Christian notion of seminal transmission of a sin nature from Adam is a necessary conclusion from what the Bible says. It is the curse that affects the whole human tribe, not Adam's sin nature. (6) Since all have sinned and lack God's glory now, it is not necessarily the case that without the historical Adam we don't need the gospel of salvation, but I would say that Adam's sin is the *presenting cause* that led to the curse that in turn led to fallen human beings. It is hard for me to doubt that the sorry history of the human race, full of wickedness, bloodshed, hatred, wars, and so on is not a profound testimony to sin and fallenness. Besides, the psalmist say in Psalm 51:5, "surely I was sinful from the time my mother conceived me." That is hardly a statement about volitional sin after birth. I suspect as well that Paul's language about "flesh" and his discussion in

Romans 7:14–25 that people can know better, but apart from Christ cannot do the law, should have some bearing on whether we've all "fallen and can't get up" without redemption.

By historical Adam and Eve, I simply mean real people in space and time, the progenitors of God's people who were the sinners in question that set in motion the train of murder and death and iniquity that followed, no sooner than they stepped outside the garden (see the story of Cain and Abel). I do not think it is adequate to suggest that the writers of the NT or for that matter of the intertestamental period were simply referring to Adam and Eve as archetypal or literary figures in a story. No, they believed these folks actually existed on planet earth long, long, ago.[2] Indeed, so much did they take that for granted, that they argued from that basis to be able to say other things about Adam and Eve. I find weird the argument of John Walton cited on p. 109 that says because Christ is called the last Adam, since he was not the last biological specimen, one cannot conclude that when Paul refers to the first Adam he means the first biological specimen. Paul is talking about two founders of the race of God's people—the first one, who is the progenitor of God's people and the last one who will ever be the progenitor of God's redeemed people. Biology is neither implied nor denied by this rhetorical comparison, for either Adam.

The chapter about the twelve major theses, which begins on p. 111, makes up the bulk of McKnight's main argument. It begins with a very ironic quote from Walter Brueggemann on p. 112. Speaking about the theologians who wrote Genesis 1–11 he says of them "they resist a scientific view of creation which assumes the world contains its own mysteries and can be understood in terms of itself without any transcendent referent." Indeed— it's a pity that the first half of this book on Adam and the genome did not approach the matter more like the writers of Genesis 1–11. Brueggemann's quote accurately describes what we find in this book in the discussion on genetics.

On p. 113 McKnight suggests that the authors of Genesis 1–11 were familiar, at least at the level of ideas with some of the concepts found in other ANE creation and flood stories. In an age before there were many texts, and mostly oral traditions, one wonders how the authors of Genesis would have come across such traditions in the holy land. Might it not be better to suggest that various of these cultures knew of events in the past, for example, a large regional flood

2. See the discussion about Noah and Lot above, pp. 76–93.

that wiped away existing civilizations in the then known world, and that they then all wrote about them using their own ideologies and theologies? As for the similarities in the creation stories, honestly there isn't much to say, except on a few rather minor points. There are actually mainly dramatic differences: (1) Apart from the Genesis account we are dealing with a polytheistic description of the origins of the universe. (2) Creation takes place due to war in heaven, or at least a struggle in these other accounts. (3) While there is similarity in the assumption that some deity created human beings *de novo* (no evolution in any of these accounts) the purpose of creating humans in the non–Genesis accounts is so that the gods can stop working, and pass off their workload onto human beings. As the Atrahasis account says, "let them carry the toil of the gods" (p. 116). (4) Both accounts do speak of the humans being fruitful and multiplying for the sake of the prosperity of the land, but note the reason why in the other accounts: so the gods can be served (with sacrifice, etc.). Yahweh, however needs no such service, and the working of human beings is so they can fulfill the divine mandate of being cocreators and cogovernors of the earth with God. (5) As McKnight mentions in thesis 1 (p. 119), the biblical God is not part of the cosmos, he is outside it, unlike the gods of the ANE, and the cosmos is created not from pre-existing parts (even parts of deities in some ANE accounts), but simply by God speaking.

My colleague Bill Arnold sums up things nicely: "In a word, ancient religion was polytheistic, mythological, and anthropomorphic, describing gods in human forms and functions while Genesis is monotheistic, scornful of mythology, and engages in anthropomorphism only as figures of speech" (quoted on p. 119). Just so, and this brings up an important point. The authors of Genesis 1–11 are *not* simply reflecting ANE culture in their account. They are not bound to such conventions and accounts, indeed if anything *they are critiquing such accounts, and substituting a monotheistic one.*

This being the case, I don't much see the point in saying that the Genesis account borrows in any significant way from these other accounts, or in saying it reflects the ancient science of such accounts. It really doesn't. It has very different basic assumptions about God and about how creation happened and why it happened. This certainly *doesn't* make Genesis 1–11 a modern scientific account of things. It's not an attempt at any kind of science, ancient or modern. It's a poetic description of what God did long, long, ago. On the plus side, I agree with McKnight's take on the role of Wisdom as God's agent of creation as seen in Proverbs and NT literature later, such as Colossians 1:15–20. Genesis 1–2 however don't really mention Wisdom personified, never mind Jesus as God's Wisdom. In regard to thesis 2, there is a tad of evidence for the use of conflict motif found in the ANE accounts in Psalm 74:13–16, and in fact much more in Revelation 12, for example. Michael Heiser in his book *The Unseen Realm* I think demonstrates beyond reasonable doubt that it is one thing to say of pagan deities that they are not genuine gods, it's another thing to say those beings that some people call gods *don't exist*. The biblical authors, including Isaiah, are misread if one thinks the latter is what they are saying. As Paul suggests in 1 Corinthians 8–10, these other entities are not nothing, they are lesser beings he calls demons that can bother, bewitch, and bewilder God's people, and so one must be wary of them.

As for thesis 3 discussed beginning on p. 124, namely that God orders creation into a temple, I have a hard time finding this theme in Genesis 1–3. God rests or ceases from his work and admires it. This is all about God's activity. There is nothing said at all about human beings worshiping God, nothing about sacrifices either. None of the language of biblical worship shows up in these chapters.

Instead, we hear about what Adam and Eve are supposed to do as jobs, as their work. Nothing is said about how they should relate to, adore, worship, sing praises of God, unless very indirectly in the sense that doing your job right glorifies God (see my book on work).[3] Here again I think we have a case of over-reading ANE accounts into the Genesis account. Adam and Eve are not presented as priests here, kings maybe, but not priests. And since there is as yet no sin, there is as yet no need for a sacrifice in a temple. I do however take the point that earth is the footstool of God, and that one can say that the heavenly sanctuary can extend down to and include the earthly one (which is what Isaiah 6 is about). Isaiah 6 is a proper worship scene, rather like Revelation 4 and 5. Genesis 1–2 is not. The place where Adam and Eve dwell is called a park or a garden, not a palace or a temple, and notice that in Revelation while there is a garden and Eden motif, John sees no need for a temple in the new creation. It is unwise to read later Israelite literature from the monarchy when there was a temple, texts such as Psalm 132:7–8, back into Genesis 1–3, written probably during a time when there wasn't such a Jew-

---

3. Ben Witherington III, *Work: A Kingdom Perspective* (Grand Rapids: Eerdmans, 2011).

ish temple. Even less convincing is an appeal to Ezekiel 43:7 from the exilic period!

I also have to disagree with the statement on p. 127 that all of creation was designed "not for humans but for God." Wrong, it is quite specifically designed for human and animal life; God doesn't need it! Or better said, it is designed for human life so that we can both have a relationship with God, being in his image, and with the rest of creation, and of course worship the creator of it all.

Under thesis 4 we have some helpful discussion of male and female made in God's image. Following J. R. Middleton, McKnight suggests on p. 129 by quoting Middleton that the "imago Dei designates the royal office or calling of human beings as God representatives and agents in the world, granted authorized power to share God's rule or administration of God's resources and creatures." I would say this is the *task* we are given as a result of our being God's representatives on earth, but it is not the meaning of the concept itself. The concept has to do with our being in some way like God in who we are, which distinguishes us from all other creatures on earth, some of whom also have ruling functions.

While it is helpful to note that unlike in the ANE where only the king was said to be the "son of God" and share in God's rule, but here it is all of us, this does not define the image itself. More helpful is the discussion by Sandra Richter in *The Epic of Eden* that the reason we are not to make graven images, is because humans *are uniquely God's image*, God's idol on earth. But behind and undergirding all of this is what the *image is*—we are to manifest the character of God on earth, his holiness, his love, and so on. What being in the image enables in the first place is our having a unique and personal relationship with God that none of the lower order of creatures can have. We are created in God's image for relationship with God. The functions come out of the relationship, being in the image enables both the relationship and the functions.

McKnight is right, on p. 131, that since only humans image God, it is no surprise it is said that Jesus incarnate, perfect human, perfectly images God on earth. Indeed, salvation and sanctification is all about our being conformed to the image of Christ himself. More interesting is the assertion of McKnight that humans are to rule over other creatures, but *not* over other human beings. The human desire to dominate or rule over other human beings is not God's intent for creation. Having a king rather than a theocracy represents a fall away from the original design. So McKnight says tyranny is the strongest form of idolatry. As he says on p. 132, humans are most human when, like God, they are artisans, enabling the rest of creation to flourish.

Thesis 6 is about the fact that humans are bigendered for the sake of procreation, so humans can multiply and flourish themselves. They are gendered not just for multiplication but also for mutuality, for relationship, a one-flesh relationship that only a male and female can share. McKnight discussion of *ezer kenegdo* is right on target (pp. 134–35). It means a suitable helper, and since God himself can be called the helper of Israel (Ps 121:1–2), the term implies no subordination of one party to the other (p. 138). Adam found no such helper among the animals, only in Eve, his equal in the image of God.

There is a helpful discussion on the importance of naming, and how that is an exercise of authority over other creatures on pp. 136–38: "To name is to know and understand by observation and then to assign oneself a relationship to and a responsibility for that which is named. In fact, the absence of a name is virtual nonexistence in the ANE, and hence naming in a sense gives something of an existence in the knowable and known world." It is also true that names usually connote something about the nature or character of the person named.

One of the best insights comes with Thesis 9 (pp. 139–40), namely the sharing of responsibility with God to govern the creation necessarily implies freedom; "you are free to eat from any tree except" implies both permission and prohibition, and more importantly it implies that humans have the power to freely choose one or the other. Where I would disagree with McKnight is that it does seem to me that he has underestimated what the Bible actually says about human fallenness as a result of the curse. It is clear enough from the curse on Eve that it affects intrahuman relationships, to love and to cherish becomes to desire and to dominate. It is clear enough that it affects their children too, see the story of Cain and Abel.

While McKnight is right that each individual must bear and own responsibility for their own sin, and Genesis says nothing about a seminal transmission of sin, it is simply not true that the OT does not bear witness to and discuss human fallenness in ways similar to later Christian ideas. Human beings don't just all randomly choose to imitate Adam's sin again and again. Their very natures are bent by the warped relational situation they find themselves in—both a distorted relationship with God and with others. The Hebrew concept is *yetser hara'* the inherent inclination to do evil. Yes, this is paired with a *yetser tov*, the still extant inclination to do good. The point is that humans are not merely good any more after Adam and Eve, unlike God's original intent and their original condition. All humans bear the effects of the curse, not only in their tasks, but in who they are. So while the term "the fall" is not very accurate, what happened to Adam and Eve happened by their bad choices, not by accident, and would be better called "the jump" rather than "the fall," it is not true that the notion is completely inaccurate.

I like the line on p. 140 from Durham's own Venerable Bede— "Adam had the burden of embarrassment, but not the humility of confession." McKnight's next comment is near the mark on the same page: "Every conceivable relationship is affected by their choice, and this infection begins to spread until in [Genesis] 8:21 God can say this of humans 'every inclination of the human heart is evil from childhood.'" I agree with the view that the banishment from the garden is to prevent Adam and Eve from eating from the tree of life and becoming everlasting fallen creatures on earth. In other words, I think Adam and Eve were created vulnerable, just as Jesus himself. Physical vulnerability is a natural trait of all creatures before the fall. Were death simply a product of sin, including the original sins, it would be rather difficult to explain how "death on a cross" didn't entail Jesus being a sinner. No, the natural limitations of all humans are limitations of time, space, knowledge, power, and fragility, none of which are inherently a result of sin. Jesus was like us in all respects, including vulnerability, save without sin. He had no fallen human nature, and yet he could be killed. Again, this is a different point from saying Adam and Eve were created with an inherent expiration date.

On pp. 143–44 we run into more problems. Adam and Eve are not Israel, they are the progenitors of the people who became Israel. Yes, Israel's later experience mimics the experience of Adam and Eve right down to the exiling part, but the two should not be equated, any more than Christ is Israel. Christ is the last Adam, that's clear from Paul, but it is equally clear in Paul that Israel means non-Christian Jews in Romans 9–11, who are distinguished from their messiah in Romans 9:1–5. So, it is a mistake to mush together either Adam and Eve with Israel or Christ with Israel; and it is especially unnecessary to suggest that the story in Genesis is more about Adam and Eve being Israel than about historical and genealogical Adam and Eve. It's pretty hard to deny the author of Genesis intends to speak about people he thinks really existed when he proceeds to give their genealogy and write their obituaries! This genealogical Adam is not first conjured up by Luke in Luke 3. Adam and Eve are not depicted as "everyone" any more than Christ is depicted as "everyone." The concept of federal headship is in play with both the first and the last Adams. Their actions affect all those who are "in them," so to speak. They represent and act for the group. The whole principle of a rhetorical comparison like that in Romans 5:12–21 is that one is comparing apples to apples, one historical person to another, and then drawing some contrasts.

Tom Wright's suggestion (cited on p. 145) that maybe Adam and Eve were picked out of the ten thousand hominids and endowed with representative power as in the image of God, is certainly possible, but not necessary. As McKnight says, the Genesis story leaves the *impression* that Adam and Eve are the only persons around. One could argue they are the only progenitors of God's people, who are the only people about whom the story is told. Adam and Eve may not be Israel, but the story is suggesting they are the origins of the chosen people of God, *not* necessarily of everyone, as the wives of Cain and Abel show. Again, the point is that the Bible is not the story of the whole human race, but about the beginnings, middle, and ends of God's people. Other peoples come into the story only when they come into contact with Israel. Perhaps the story is suggesting that God's people were uniquely created by God to bear his image. Perhaps Wright is correct, if evolutionary genetics is right about human origins. Either way, Adam and Eve are clearly viewed as real people who are the ancestors of Noah, and Shem, Abraham, and the rest. It is true, but insufficient to call Adam and Eve merely literary figures in a story. The writers of Genesis 1–11 would be surprised to hear it.

Again, the flood as depicted in Genesis 9–11 is not a problem if it is a description of a flooding of the then-known ANE world, in other words a massive regional flood devastating that population. In fact, there are mud layers and other geological evidence in that region that something cataclysmic did happen thousands of years before Christ in that locale. The ANE writers are not making up a fairy tale in their various tales about a Noah figure, a boat, a survival of a massive flood. There is also no reason to think that the genealogical Adam is a later byproduct of thinking about the Adam in the story in Genesis 2–5. All of that is part of the original story. First Chronicles 1:1–3 and Luke 3:38 are just following Genesis 5:3–5's lead.

Chapter 7, which begins on p. 147, is a helpful review of the mentions of Adam (and sometimes Eve) in intertestamental Jewish literature. McKnight is right that they are depicted in various ways, and the story is developed and analyzed in various ways. This is correct. The point I want to make is that in each case, so far as we can tell, the assumption that there was a historical Adam and Eve is the basis of the further development of the tradition depicting Adam at least as an archetype, a progenitor, a bad example, and so on. It is worth adding that a prototype, or representative of a people is not the same thing as calling the prototype "everyman."

So I will simply pause to point out the evidence that these Jewish writers clearly assume Adam was a real person: (1) In Sirach he is called the glorious ancestor of Israel, not Israel itself but her ancestor (Sir 49:16). Adam foreshadows the behavior of Israel. Sirach is not suggesting Adam is just a literary cipher for Israel, so that where you see the term Adam, read Israel, he's talking about the beginning of the race with Adam. (2) Sirach also blames human sin on a particular human ancestor—in this case Eve (see 25:15–26)—"from a woman [Eve] sin had its beginning and because of her we die." It is true, but inadequate to say that Sirach's Adam and Eve is not viewed entirely like later Christian views of the matter. The point is, no one so far as I can see in this literature is viewing Adam and Eve as merely literary figures, or nonhistorical figures, or ciphers for a whole people. (3) Wisdom of Solomon, written just before or early in the NT era, depicts Wisdom personified as having a relationship with Adam and Eve, and protecting them. Wisdom of Solomon 10:1–2 says, "Wisdom protected the first-formed father of the world, when he alone had been created; she delivered him from his transgression and gave him strength to rule all things." Wisdom of Solomon 7:1 is even clearer—every human being is a descendant of the first formed person. It is not that the author merely knows of a literary figure in a story. He *assumes* the story is historically correct about who the first parents were and reasons on the basis of that assumption. (4) Philo (*Creation* 151), like Sirach, blames the woman Eve (not just any woman) for the fall of Adam. He is viewed as happy and virtuous before the femme fatale shows up. Of this sort of misogynism the author of Genesis knows nothing, so of course there are interpretations and misinterpretations of Adam and Eve in early Judaism, but none of them involve the notion "these are merely literary figures, not real people." Philo asserts Adam is the first father of the human race, the ancestor of the race (*Creation* 79, 136). (5) Jubilees provides us with some more fanciful elaborations of the story, for instance in its insistence that Eve was shown to Adam in the second week of existence, but he only enters the garden forty days later, and she enters it eighty days later in order for her to be pure enough (Jubilees 3:1–12). (6) Pseudo-Philo in *Biblical Antiquities* 13.8 complains that Adam was persuaded by his wife, who in turn was deceived by the serpent, and so death was ordained for the generations of human beings. The presupposition here is that the historical cause of death ever since is Adam and Eve. (7) Josephus simply retells the Genesis story with some Platonic sprinkles, referring to God fashioning Adam from dust and inserting into him spirit and soul (*Ant.* 1.34). Eve is formed from Adam's rib, but as McKnight says (p. 163) is not seen as his equal. (8) One of the characters in 4 Ezra wants to put blame mostly on Adam and on the fallenness of humans for sin. The sin of Adam has implications for all humans (see 4 Ezra 3:4–7; 7:127–28). Adam is clearly said at 3:7 to have physical descendants. At 7:18 we have the famous line "the fall was not yours [Adam's] alone, but ours also who are your descendants." Now I would say that this both/and kind of approach is also what we find in Romans 5:12–21. In the second century CE document 2 Baruch we finally hear the notion each of us has become our own Adam. But in none of this literature is Adam "everyman," any more than Eve is "every woman," though there are some hints in the latter direction in Sirach. What is in any case assumed in all these intertestamental reflections is that Genesis is telling a historical story about real people who affected not only themselves but their descendants in various ways. They are not merely literary figures that set bad examples for those who read their stories. It is thus not helpful to say, "no author cared about giving Adam a historical reading" (p. 168). None of these authors defended the historicity of Adam because it was not a question or an issue, nor did any of them view the historical Adam in light of later Christian tradition. This is however very different from saying none of them thought Adam was a historical (= real) person in space and time. In fact, none of them would have spoken of Adam as they do in regard to genealogies and effects on descendants if they did not take it for granted that he and Eve were real persons. Finally, at Qumran the story is the same; CD 10.8; 4Q504; 4Q167; 1QS 3–4 depict an Adam who is the first breaker of faith with God, the first breaker of the covenant, the first formed in, and the first to deform the image of God, and so on. Yes, the later full form of the Christian analysis of

Adam by Augustine and subsequent interpreters is not found in these texts, and doubtless some of those interpreters went not just beyond but against what the Bible says and need correction. This however doesn't mean that anyone in the biblical and intertestamental tradition thought Adam and Eve were mere literary figures, or ciphers for everyone, but not real ancestors of God's people.

In the last main chapter of the book (pp. 171–87) McKnight addresses the issue of what Paul says about Adam and Eve. He is correct that Paul does not say in Romans 5:12–21 that all have sinned "in Adam." He says all are condemned because all have sinned like Adam. But one has to ask: Why would that be universally true if there was not a universal bent to sinning? If there is such an inclination, where did it comes from, if God didn't make us that way? One of the things I think is least helpful about the ongoing argument of McKnight's is the idea that Paul and the gang are using the literary Adam and Eve to make an argument, and the literary Adam and Eve is all they know, say, for example, in Romans 5:12–21; 1 Corinthians 15; 1 Timothy 2:13; and so on. It is not merely the literary Adam and Eve that Paul is using for theological reasons. He is drawing historical and theological conclusions for historical and theological reasons based on the clear assumption that there really was an Adam and Eve that affected their descendants. The theses in this chapter are all true enough as far as they go: Adam is a prototype, Adam is a progenitor, Adam is a bad moral example, but they do not really grasp the nettle when it comes to the historical bases of these assertions. More helpful is thesis 4 (p. 183) that involves the proposition that we do not have original sin understood as original guilt and damnation for the whole race on the basis of Adam's sin in Paul. Perhaps that *is* deducing too much from Paul. But it is not a helpful either/or to say

> The issue however is not whether the historical Adam is important to soteriology but what kind of Adam Paul has in mind in Romans 5:12–21. Does Paul reveal an Adam who is a real person, who is biologically connected to all humans, a genetic or DNA Adam? Or does Paul have in mind the standard Jewish Adam—that is the literary, genealogical Adam who becomes an adjustable figure [he uses the term wax in some places] who can be used in theology for a variety of presentations and ideas?

This is a false dichotomy. A discussion of genealogy, of "begats," is necessarily a discussion of biology.

Whether or not one says there is a transmission of a sin nature from Adam to all us, or that Adam's sin led to a curse on all of us that distorts our relationships and leads to sin and spiritual death, either way the outcome is the same, and it is not just because we have all sinned and lack the glory of God at this point. There is a history to our sinning, and Paul says the rot started at the outset, as do various other early Jewish interpreters. Death spread to all, not just because of Adam's sin, but also because of our own sin, but Paul mentions both in the same breath, in the same argument, as causes.

I'm fine with the cited quote from Wright on p. 187: "Paul's meaning must in any case be both that an entail of sinfulness has spread throughout the human race from its first beginnings and that each individual has contributed their own share to it. Paul offers no further clue as to how the first of these actually works or how the two interrelate." Fair enough, but it is clear Paul wants to say *both* from the beginning of the race, and yes we contributed to the problem.

Finally, it is not adequate to follow Joseph Fitzmyer's suggestion that in Genesis Adam is a mere cipher for or symbolic figure for the whole of humanity. Clearly not, since we have human mates showing up from somewhere else for Cain and Abel! It is not true that Paul should be charged with historicizing Adam. This is demeaning to Paul, and indeed the whole Jewish tradition before him that assumes Adam was a real person in space and time. So, the conclusion on p. 191 is incorrect—the historical Adam doesn't show up first after Paul was dead. This involves an overloaded concept of what the term historical must mean. In fact, he shows up in the very beginning chapters of the Bible. We should not be beguiled by the poetic form and the saga-like qualities of the Genesis account. This is no myth of origins, it is rather a historical narrative that deconstructs the myths of origins of other ANE accounts.

The afterword does not need to be reviewed as it offers nothing to the argument, it simply cavalierly says "don't worry, be happy," it doesn't matter if there was a historical Adam and a historical origin to human fallenness. Yes it does matter, it matters if the biblical authors think and say it matters. It even mattered to Jesus who said that marriage is an idea that God came up with "from the beginning" and involved the first couple, Adam and Eve (Matthew 19; Mark 10). The biblical religion is irreducibly a historical one, grounded in history from start to finish. The theology of Christianity grows out of the historical situations, circumstances, events. It is not a building of theological castles with no historical foundations, whether we are talking about the creation of the human race, its fallenness, or its redemption.

As a final comment, I do honor McKnight and Venema's attempt to have a meaningful engagement between science and biblical theology. This book does an excellent job of having a respectful presentation and of teasing the mind into active thought. I think their aim is noble, to rescue various Christians students from a fundamentalist approach to either of these subjects. But sometimes one's urgencies leads one to argue in a way that goes beyond the evidence and indeed even against the biblical evidence in particular. I'm afraid this has happened in this book on several counts.

"Let the reader understand" that these things are complex, and equally devout Christians can come to very different conclusions on such matters. But as for me and mine, we will continue to insist on a real, historical Adam, a proper doctrine of creation, on humans being uniquely in the image of God, on universal human fallenness whatever the mechanism by which it happened, and on all of that as the precursor to our redemption in Christ. I'm not prepared to say *felix culpa*, but I am prepared to say Adam and human fallenness matter to Christian faith. The rule of parsimony, that all other things being equal, the least elaborate theory that seems to best explain the facts is most likely to be true, is a good one. The least elaborate theory is that science is true up to a point in regard to all things empirical and the Bible is also true in what it asserts about history, theology, and ethics. It does not teach science. How we get those truths together, or to talk with one another is a conversation for another day, but this book is a good prompt to such a conversation. I would hope that next time we would have less urgency to try and minimize the historical character of the Bible and more urgency to ask hard questions about the globalizing of materialistic scientific theories.

Appendix 3
Ascending Enoch, or Jesus and Falling Spirits

Author's note: One of the greatest cruxes of all the passages in the NT is the material found in 1 Peter 3 about the spirits in prison. One of the keys to unraveling this text's meaning is recognizing its intertextual echoes not only of Genesis 6:1–4 but also of the later interpretations of Genesis 6 in 1 Enoch. This appendix shows the problems that arise when intertextual echoes are not recognized or ignored, especially when it is not just the OT that is being used or alluded to, but rather the OT as filtered through later Jewish use of the text, something I would called "layered intertextuality." This material appeared in a different form in my earlier commentary on 1 Peter in *Letters and Homilies for Hellenized Christians, Vol. 2.*

Commentators have long known that there is some connection between 1 Enoch and what is said in 1 Peter 3:18–22, but the exact connections have been vigorously debated. Indeed, so vigorous has the debate been that some have dubbed this passage in 1 Peter the most difficult one in the whole NT to understand. Certainly, clarity is not to be had if one fails to read this material in the light of its Jewish and apocalyptic contexts; and one must say that this passage especially presumes a lot of the audience. Indeed, it presumes too much if the audience is largely composed of converted pagans not privy to the vagaries of early Jewish apocalyptic speculations. It will be useful at this juncture to consider the relevant material from 1 Enoch in a closer way to see if we cannot unravel some of the mysteries of our text.

First a little background. 1 Enoch is a book composed and edited over several centuries before the turn of the era. In other words, it is a composite document, but the important point for our consideration at this point is that it was all extant long before the time when 1 Peter was written. George Nickelsburg, one of the few real experts on 1 Enoch, tells us that 1 Enoch was

> composed and edited over the three and half centuries before the turn of the era, the earliest [parts] of them were composed within a century after the time of Ezra. Running through these texts is the belief in an imminent great judgment that will terminate the present age dominated by the evil spirits generated by the rebel angels, and that will usher in a new creation and new age marked by God's final and universal sovereignty.[1]

It should be immediately apparent why Peter would find this text of use and interest for what he wants to claim in 1 Peter. Nickelsburg rightly characterized what we find in 1 Enoch as apocalyptic eschatology. The same could be said about the eschatology in 1 Peter, especially 3:18–22. What is of note however is that it is not just one verse here or there that Peter seems to be familiar with and possibly indebted to; there seems to be a wider range of familiarity with the 1 Enoch literature by our author. But let us start with the most obvious echo.

First Enoch tells the tale of the fallen angels of Genesis 6:1–4 and their fate. Enoch, who ascended into heaven without first dying on earth, is sent on a mission to speak a word of judgment to these fallen angels. He is commissioned by the "watchers of the Great Holy One" (i.e., the unfallen angels still serving God in heaven) as follows:

> Enoch, righteous scribe, go say to the watchers of heaven, who forsook the highest heaven, the sanctuary of their eternal station, and defiled themselves with women. As the sons of the earth do, so they did and took wives for themselves. And they wrought great desolation on the earth. [Say to them] "You will have no peace or forgiveness" and concerning their sons in whom they rejoice "The slaughter of their beloved ones they will seek; and over the destruction of their sons they will lament and make petition forever, and they will have no mercy or peace." And Enoch go and say to Asael "You will have no peace. A great sentence has gone forth against you, to bind you. You will have no relief or petition, because of the unrighteous deeds that you revealed" (1 Enoch 12:4–6)

---

1. George W. E. Nickelsburg, *Ancient Judaism and Christian Origins: Diversity, Continuity, and Transformation* (Minneapolis: Fortress, 2003), 123.

What is to be noted and stressed about this passage is that the content of the message to the fallen spirits is clearly negative and condemnatory. If, as seems likely, the story of Jesus in 1 Peter 3 is being patterned after this, then we are meant to assume that his message to these spirits was one of judgment, or perhaps even triumph over the spirits. Notice as well that in 1 Enoch 10:4–6 (cf. 1 Enoch 67) these fallen spirits are said to be imprisoned in the burning valley of Gehenna or Dudael. It is worth noting that 1 Enoch 21:10 and 2 Enoch 7:1–3 and 18:3 tell us quite specifically that we should call the dwelling place of these fallen spirits a prison. First Enoch 18:14 speaks of the prison house for the stars and the powers. The location of this place is assumed to be below or within the earth, not above it, just as Tartarus is assumed to be in the lower regions of Hades.[2] This comports with the reference in Isaiah to a pit in the ground, or the pit that Satan is thrown into in Revelation 20.

Nickelsburg has been able to show considerable parallels between 1 Enoch 108, the very end of the Enoch corpus, and 1 Peter in general, including 1 Peter 3:18–22 in particular. For example, 1 Enoch 108 speaks of the spirits punished (vv. 3–6) and this follows hard on the announcement in 1 Enoch 106:16–18 that Noah and his sons were saved.[3] He notes the reference to perishable seed both in 1 Peter 1:23 and 1 Enoch 108:3b. The reference to disdain for silver and gold in 1 Peter 1:7, 18 is like that found in 1 Enoch 108:8; the discussion of blessing and reproach in 1 Peter 3:9, 16; 4:4, 16 is like that in 1 Enoch 108:7–10; the discussion of exaltation in 1 Peter 5:4, 6 is similar to 1 Enoch 108:12; and the similarities in the discussion of righteous judgment in 1 Peter 1:17 and 2:23 should be compared to 1 Enoch 108:13. There is in addition the common use of Psalm 34 (see 1 Enoch 108:7–10 and compare 1 Peter 3:10–12).[4] None of this is a surprise when we recognize that 1 Enoch is influential in various of these Jewish Christian eschatological works, for instance Jude not merely refers to the text of 1 Enoch in vv. 4, 6, and 13, he even cites it in vv. 14–15 of his discourse. 2 Peter as well is directly dependent on 1 Enoch at 2 Peter 2:4 and 3:13. It is important for our purposes here that we note that it is the Book of Noah, part of 1 Enoch, which

2. See now the discussion in Heiser, *Unseen Realm*, 335–38.

3. Willem C. Van Unnik, "Le role de Noé dans les Épîtres de Pierre," in *Noé, L'homme universel, Colloque de Louvain 1978*, Publications de l'Institutum Iudaicum 3 (Brussels: Institutum Judaicum, 1979), 207–39.

4. See Nickelsburg, *1 Enoch 1*, 560.

includes 1 Enoch 6–11, 64–69, and 106–108, that is almost exclusively being drawn on in 1 Peter.[5]

I must stress that the story of the "sons of God" coming down and mating with the daughters of humanity immediately precedes the story of Noah and the flood (see Gen 6:1–4). Especially important are 1 Enoch 106:13 and 2 Enoch 7:3 that connects the story of Noah with the punishing of the fallen angels. As Jude v. 6 says, these fallen angels are bound in chains in everlasting darkness, or as 1 Peter puts it, they are in prison.[6] Just as Enoch went and spoke to them according to the tradition in 1 Enoch, so too does Jesus, Jesus being depicted here as the new and true Enoch. It is worth adding that Sheol, or the land of the dead itself, is never called a prison in the Bible. We are talking about the confinement of some angels here, that is all. We are told that Jesus went and proclaimed to them—but proclaimed what? If we see Peter as continuing to draw on the Enoch material then we must remember that Enoch proclaimed their punishment to these fallen angels (cf. 1 Enoch 12:4 to 1 Pet 3:19). Further, we are told in 1 Peter 3:22 of the angels being put in subjection to Christ. The context mentions nothing about how they responded to the preaching. This is understandable if Christ simply went to proclaim their punishment, not try to convert them. We certainly do not find here any sort of second chance beyond death theology, not least because the text is about angels not humans and we are not told Jesus went and preached any good news to anyone. Lest we find it hard to imagine that Jesus preached to these fallen angels in Hades or in heaven somewhere on his way to the throne, consider 2 Enoch 7:1–3 where Enoch is taken to the second heaven and shown "a darkness greater than earthly darkness" and "prisoners under guard, hanging up, waiting for the measureless judgment." This last text raises the possibility that the author of 1 Peter views the locale of these lost angels not somewhere in the land of the dead, but in a holding tank in the heavens.

In any case, it is very difficult for me to doubt, after the extensive work of Nickelsburg, William J. Dalton, and others that we are talking about a considerable influence of the Enochian material in 1 Peter, and especially in 1 Peter 3:18–22. The import of this is hard to

5. The definitive and detailed study of William J. Dalton, *Christ's Proclamation to the Spirits: A Study of 1 Peter 3:18–4:6*, AnBib 23 (Rome: Pontifical Biblical Institute, 1989), see esp. 164–71 makes so very clear the connections between 1 Pet 3:18–22 and various materials in 1 Enoch that it is hard to understand why some scholars are so insistent on denying these parallels.

6. See the detailed discussion in Witherington, *Jesus the Seer*, introduction.

underestimate. It means, among other things, that this text has nothing to do with proclaiming the gospel to the human dead. It certainly also has nothing to do with the coming of the preexistent Christ to earth either during the time of Noah or in the incarnation. Here we have a story about the proclamation of judgment on the principalities and powers, and the triumph beyond death of Christ in glory. Its relevance to the Jewish Christian audience is quite apparent.

They are being told that they are following the same trajectory as Christ, and indeed before him of Noah. Though they may be being reviled and slandered and abused during their earthly life, nevertheless despite their current suffering, they will one day triumph over their foes whose "doom is sure." It is interesting that Peter does not specifically connect the "spirits" with the powers behind the pagan government, but rather the association is made more broadly with the fallen world in general that the audience is being abused by. Truly 1 Peter 3:18–22 is one text about which it is most accurate to claim that without knowledge of the context of this material, in particular the Jewish apocalyptic context, all sorts of misinterpretations are likely to follow, including even the generation of doctrines of purgatory, second-chance theology, and the like.[7]

---

7. See the helpful summary in Richard J. Bauckham, "Spirits in Prison," *ABD* 6:177–78.

Select Bibliography

COMMENTARIES

Achtemeier, Peter J. *1 Peter: A Commentary on First Peter*. Hermeneia. Minneapolis: Fortress, 1996.

Arnold, Bill. *Genesis*. NCBiC. Cambridge: Cambridge University Press, 2009.

Attridge, Harold W. *The Epistle to the Hebrews*. Hermeneia. Philadelphia: Fortress, 1989.

Barrett, C. K. *A Commentary on the Epistle to the Romans*. BNTC. Peabody, MA: Hendrickson, 1987.

Beale, G. K., and D. A. Carson. *Commentary on the New Testament use of the Old Testament*. Grand Rapids: Baker Academic, 2007.

Bellinger, W. H., Jr. *Leviticus, Numbers*. Grand Rapids: Baker, 2001.

Best, Ernest. *1 Peter*. NCB. London: Oliphants, 1977.

Bock, Darrell L. *Luke 9:51–24:53*. BECNT 3B. Grand Rapids: Baker Academic, 1996.

———. *Luke: The NIV Application Commentary from Biblical Text to Contemporary Life*. NIVAC. Grand Rapids: Zondervan, 1996.

Brosend, William F. *James and Jude*. NCBiC. Cambridge: Cambridge University Press, 2004.

Bruce, F. F. *The Epistle to the Hebrews*. NICNT. Grand Rapids: Eerdmans, 1990.

Buchanan, George W. *To the Hebrews*. AB 36. New York: Doubleday, 1972.

Byrne, Brendan. *Romans*. SP 6. Collegeville, MN: Liturgical Press, 1996.

Cassuto, Umberto. *Commentary on the Book of Exodus*. Jerusalem: Magnes, 1967.

Childs, Brevard. *The Book of Exodus: A Critical, Theological Commentary.* OTL. Philadelphia: Westminster, 1974.

Christensen, Duane L. *Deuteronomy 1–11.* WBC. Waco, TX: Word, 1991.

Craddock, Fred. "The Letter to the Hebrews." *NIB* 12:1–173.

Cole, Dennis R. *Numbers.* NAC 3B. Nashville: Broadman & Holman, 2000.

Cole, R. Alan. *Exodus: An Introduction and Commentary.* TOTC 2. Downers Grove, IL: InterVarsity, 2008.

Craigie, Peter C. *The Book of Deuteronomy.* NICOT. Grand Rapids: Eerdmans, 1976.

Cranfield, C. E. B. *A Critical and Exegetical Commentary on the Epistle to the Romans.* ICC. 2 vols. Edinburgh: T&T Clark, 1975.

Culy, Martin M., Mikeal Parsons, and Joshua J. Stigall. *Luke: A Handbook on the Greek Text.* BHGNT. Waco, TX: Baylor University Press, 2010.

Davids, Peter H. *The Epistle to James.* NIGTC. Grand Rapids: Eerdmans, 1982.

DeSilva, David A. *Perseverance in Gratitude: A Socio-Rhetorical Commentary on the Epistle to the Hebrews.* Grand Rapids: Eerdmans, 2000.

Dogniez, Cécile and Marguerite Harl. *Le Deuteronome.* BA. Paris: Cerf, 1992.

Dozeman, Thomas B. *Exodus.* ECC. Grand Rapids: Eerdmans, 2009.

Elliott, John H. *1 Peter: A New Translation with Introduction and Commentary.* AB 37B. New Haven: Yale University Press, 2011.

Elliott, Neil. *The Rhetoric of Romans: Argumentative Constraint and Strategy and Paul's Dialogue with Judaism.* JSNTSup 45. Sheffield: Sheffield Academic, 1990.

Evans, Craig A. *Luke.* NIBCNT. Peabody, MA: Hendrickson, 1990.

Fitzmyer, Joseph A. *Romans: A New Translation with Introduction and Commentary.* AB 33. New York: Doubleday, 1992.

Furnish, Victor P. *2 Corinthians: Translated with Introduction, Notes, and Commentary.* AB 32A. Garden City, NY: Doubleday, 1984.

Hagner, Donald A. *Encountering the Book of Hebrews: An Exposition.* Grand Rapids: Baker Academic, 2002.

Hartley, John. *Leviticus.* WBC. Dallas: Word, 1992.

Johnson, Luke Timothy. *The Letter of James: A New Translation with Introduction and Commentary.* AB 37A. New York: Doubleday, 1995.

Käsemann, Ernst. *Commentary on Romans.* Translated by G. W. Bromiley. Grand Rapids: Eerdmans, 1994.

Kidner, Derek. *Genesis: An Introduction and Commentary.* TOTC. Downers Grove, IL: InterVarsity, 2008.

Koester, Craig R. *Hebrews: A New Translation with Introduction and Commentary*. AB 36. New York: Doubleday, 2001.

Levine, Amy Jill, and Ben Witherington III. *The Gospel of Luke*. NCBiC. Cambridge: Cambridge University Press, forthcoming.

Long, Thomas G. *Hebrews*. IBC. Louisville: Westminster John Knox, 1997.

Luz, Ulrich. *Matthew 1–7: A Commentary*. Hermeneia. Minneapolis: Augsburg, 1989.

Marshall, I. Howard. *1 Peter*. IVPNTC. Downers Grove, IL: InterVarsity, 1991.

Martin, Ralph P. *James*. WBC. Waco, TX: Word, 1988.

McKnight, Scot. *1 Peter*. NIVAC. Grand Rapids: Zondervan, 1996.

Metzger, Bruce M. *A Textual Commentary on the Greek New Testament: A Companion Volume to the United Bible Societies' Greek New Testament (Third Edition)*. 2nd ed. New York: United Bible Societies, 1971.

Michaels, J. Ramsey. *1 Peter*. WBC 49. Grand Rapids: Zondervan, 2015.

Milgrom, Jacob. *Leviticus 1–16: A New Translation with Introduction and Commentary*. AB 3A. New York: Doubleday, 1991.

Miller, Patrick. *Deuteronomy*. IBC. Louisville: John Knox, 1990.

Moo, Douglas. *2 Peter and Jude*. NIVAC. Grand Rapids: Zondervan, 1996.

———. *The Letter of James*. PNTC. Grand Rapids: Eerdmans, 2000.

———. *The Epistle to the Romans*. NICNT. Grand Rapids: Eerdmans, 1996.

Nelson, Richard D. *Deuteronomy*. IBC. Louisville: Westminster John Knox, 2002.

Nickelsburg, G. W. E. *1 Enoch: A Commentary on the Book of 1 Enoch, Chapters 1–36, 81–108*. Hermeneia. Minneapolis: Fortress, 2001.

Perkins, Pheme. *First and Second Peter, James and Jude*. IBC. Louisville: Westminister John Knox, 2012.

Rad, Gerhard von. *Genesis: A Commentary*. Translated by John H. Marks. OTL. Philadelphia: Westminster, 1961.

Schreiner, Thomas. *1 and 2 Peter, Jude*. NAC 37. Nashville: Broadman & Holman, 2003.

Stowers, Stanley K. *A Rereading of Romans: Justice, Jews, and Gentiles*. New Haven: Yale University Press, 1997.

Tannehill, Robert C. *Luke*. ANTC. Nashville: Abingdon, 1996.

Van Seters, John. *The Pentateuch: A Social-Science Commentary*. London: T&T Clark, 2015.

Wenham, Gordon J. *Genesis 1–15*. WBC. Grand Rapids: Zondervan, 2015.

———. *Genesis 16–50*. WBC. Grand Rapids: Zondervan, 2015.

———. *The Book of Leviticus.* NICOT. Grand Rapids: Eerdmans, 1979.

Westermann, Claus. *Genesis 1–11.* Minneapolis: Augsburg, 1984.

Witherington, Ben, III. *Acts of the Apostle: A Socio-Rhetorical Commentary.* Grand Rapids: Eerdmans, 1996.

———. *A Commentary on Revelation.* NCBiC. Cambridge: Cambridge University Press, 2003.

———. *Conflict and Community in Corinth: A Socio-Rhetorical Commentary on 1 and 2 Corinthians.* Grand Rapids: Eerdmans, 1996.

———. *The Gospel of Mark: A Socio-Rhetorical Commentary.* Grand Rapids: Eerdmans, 2001.

———. *Grace in Galatia: A Commentary on St. Paul's Letter to the Galatians.* Grand Rapids: Eerdmans, 1998.

———. *John's Wisdom: A Commentary on the Fourth Gospel.* Louisville: Westminster John Knox, 1995.

———. *Letters and Homilies for Hellenized Christians Volume One: A Socio-Rhetorical Commentary on Titus, 1–2 Timothy, and 1–3 John.* Downers Grove, IL: InterVarsity, 2014.

———. *Letters and Homilies for Hellenized Christians Volume Two: A Socio-Rhetorical Commentary on 1–2 Peter.* Downers Grove, IL: InterVarsity, 2014.

———. *Letters and Homilies for Jewish Christians: A Socio-Rhetorical Commentary on Hebrews, James and Jude.* Downers Grove, IL: InterVarsity, 2016.

———. *The Letters to Philemon, Colossians, and Ephesians: A Socio-Rhetorical Commentary on the Captivity Epistles.* Grand Rapids: Eerdmans, 2007.

———. *Matthew.* SHBC. Macon, GA: Smyth & Helwys, 2006.

Witherington, Ben, III, and Darlene Hyatt. *Paul's Letter to the Romans: A Socio-Rhetorical Commentary.* Grand Rapids: Eerdmans, 2004.

Wright, N. T. "Romans." NIB 10:395–770.

MONOGRAPHS

Allison, Dale. *The New Moses: A Matthean Typology.* Minneapolis: Fortress, 1993.

Bailey, Lloyd R. *Noah, The Person and Story in History and Tradition.* Columbia: University of South Carolina Press, 1989.

Barrett, C. K. *From First Adam to Last: A Study in Pauline Theology.* New York: Scribner, 1962.

Carr, David. *The Formation of the Hebrew Bible*. Oxford: Oxford University Press, 2011.

Carson, D. A., Peter T. O'Brien, and Mark A. Seifrid, eds. *Justification and Variegated Nomism*. 2 vols. Grand Rapids: Baker Academic, 2001–2004.

Charles, J. Daryl. *Literary Strategy in the Epistle of Jude*. Scranton, PA: University of Scranton Press, 2005.

Clements, Ronald. *God's Chosen People. A Theological Interpretation of the Book of Deuteronomy*. Valley Forge, PA: Judson, 1969.

Crawford, Sidnie White. *Rewriting Scripture in Second Temple Times*. Grand Rapids: Eerdmans, 2008.

———. *The Temple Scroll and Related Texts*. Sheffield: Sheffield Academic, 2000.

Cullmann, Oscar. *The Christology of the New Testament*. Rev. ed. Philadelphia: Westminster, 1989.

Dalton, William J. *Christ's Proclamation to the Spirits: A Study of 1 Peter 3:18–4:6*. AnBib 23. Rome: Pontifical Biblical Institute, 1989.

Davidman, Joy. *Smoke on the Mountain: An Interpretation of the Ten Commandments*. Philadelphia: Westminster, 1985.

Dozeman, Thomas B. *God on the Mountain. A Study of Redaction, Theology, and Canon in Exodus 19–24*. SBLMS 37. Atlanta: Scholars Press, 1989.

Eisenbaum, Pamela. *The Jewish Heroes of Christian History: Hebrews 11 in Literary Context*. SBLDS 156. Atlanta: Scholars Press, 1997.

Evans, Craig A., Joel N. Lohr, and David L. Petersen. *The Book of Genesis: Composition, Reception, and Interpretation*. VTSup 152. Leiden: Brill, 2012.

Falk, D. K. *The Parabiblical Texts: Strategies for Extending Scripture among the Dead Sea Scrolls*. LSTS 63. London: T&T Clark, 2007.

Fisch, Harold. *Poetry with a Purpose: Biblical Poetics and Interpretation*. ISBL. Bloomington: Indiana University Press, 1988.

Fishbane, Michael. *Biblical Interpretation in Ancient Israel*. Oxford: Clarendon, 1988.

Furnish, Victor P. *The Love Command in the New Testament*. Nashville: Abingdon, 1972.

Gaventa, Beverly R. *Our Mother St. Paul*. Louisville: Westminster John Knox, 2007.

Glueck, Nelson, and Alfred Gottschalk. *Hesed in the Bible*. Eugene, OR: Wipf & Stock, 2011.

Grant, Robert M. *Second Century Christianity: A Collection of Fragments.* 2nd ed. Louisville: Westminster John Knox, 2003.

Harris, Murray J. *Raised Immortal: Resurrection and Immortality in the New Testament.* Grand Rapids: Eerdmans, 1985.

Hays, Richard B. *Echoes of Scripture in the Gospels.* Waco, TX: Baylor University Press, 2016.

———. *Echoes of Scripture in the Letters of Paul.* New Haven: Yale University Press, 1989.

Heiser, Michael. *The Unseen Realm: Recovering the Supernatural Worldview of the Bible.* Bellingham, WA: Lexham, 2016.

Heschel, Abraham Joshua. *The Prophets.* New York: Perennial, 2001.

Hill, Craig C. *Hebrews and Hellenists: Reappraising Division within the Earliest Church.* Minneapolis: Fortress, 1992.

Horsley, Greg H. R., and Stephen Llewelyn, eds. *New Documents that Illustrate Early Christianity Vol. 2.* North Ryde, NSW: The Ancient History Documentary Research Centre, Macquarie University, 1982.

Horton, Fred L. *The Melchizedek Tradition: A Critical Examination of the Sources to the Fifth Century A.D. and in the Epistle to the Hebrews.* SNTSMS 30. Cambridge: Cambridge University Press, 1976.

Jeremias, Joachim. *The Eucharistic Words of Jesus.* Philadelphia: Fortress, 1966.

Koch, Dietrich-Alex. *Die Schrift als Zeuge des Evangeliums: Untersuchungen zur Verwendung und zum Verstandnis der Schrift bei Paulus.* BHT 69. Tubingen: Mohr, 1986.

Kümmel, Werner G. *Romer 7 und das Bild des Menschen im Neuen Testament zwei Studien.* TB 53. Munich: Kaiser, 1974.

Lambrecht, Jan. *The Wretched 'I' and its Liberation.* LThPM 14. Louvain: Peeters, 1992.

Lange, Tineke de. *Abraham in John 8:31–59: His Significance in the Conflict between Johannine Christianity and Its Jewish Environment.* Amsterdam: Amphora, 2008.

Longenecker, Bruce W. *Rhetoric at the Boundaries: The Art and Theology of the New Testament Chain-link Transitions.* Waco, TX: Baylor University Press, 2005.

MacMullen, Ramsey. *The Second Church, Popular Christianity A.D. 200–400.* WGRWSup 1. Atlanta: Society of Biblical Literature, 2009.

Martin, Dale B. *The Corinthian Body.* New Haven: Yale University Press, 1999.

Meier, John P. *A Marginal Jew: Rethinking the Historical Jesus, Vol. 4; Law and Love*. AYBRL. New Haven: Yale University Press, 2009.

Menken, Maarten J. J. and Steven Moyise, eds. *Deuteronomy in the New Testament*. LNTS 358. London: Bloomsbury, 2008.

———, eds. *Genesis in the New Testament*. LNTS 466. London: T&T Clark, 2012.

Middleton, J. Richard. *The Liberating Image: The Imago Dei in Genesis 1*. Grand Rapids: Brazos, 2005.

Mitchell, Margaret M. *The Heavenly Trumpet: John Chrysostom and the Art of Pauline Interpretation*. Louisville: Westminster John Knox, 2002.

———. *Paul, the Corinthians, and the Birth of Christian Hermeneutics*. Cambridge: Cambridge University Press, 2012.

Moberley, R. W. L. *The Bible, Theology and Faith: A Study of Abraham and Jesus*. Cambridge: Cambridge University Press, 2000.

———. *The Old Testament of the Old Testament: Patriarchal Narratives and Mosaic Yahwism*. OBT. Minneapolis: Fortress, 1992.

Motyer, J. Alec. *The Message of Exodus: The Days of Our Pilgrimage*. BST. Downers Grove, IL: InterVarsity, 2005.

Moyise, Steven. *Jesus and Scripture. Studying the New Testament Use of the Old Testament*. Grand Rapids: Baker Academic, 2011.

———. *The Old Testament in the New: An Introduction*. 2nd ed. London: Bloomsbury, 2015.

Nickelsburg, George W. E. *Ancient Judaism and Christian Origins: Diversity, Continuity, and Transformation*. Minneapolis: Fortress, 2003.

Patrick, Dale. *Old Testament Law*. Atlanta: John Knox, 1985.

Richter, Sandra L. *The Epic of Eden: A Christian Entry into the Old Testament*. Downers Grove, IL: InterVarsity, 2008.

Ringe, Sharon H. *Jesus, Liberation, and the Biblical Jubilee: Images for Ethics and Christology*. Eugene, OR: Wipf & Stock, 2004.

Rusam, Dietrich. *Das Alte Testament bei Lukas*. BZAW 112. Berlin: de Gruyter, 2003.

Sanders, E. P. *Judaism Practice and Belief, 63 BCE–66CE*. Philadelphia: Trinity Press International, 1992.

———. *Paul and Palestinian Judaism: A Comparison of Patterns of Religion*. Philadelphia: Fortress, 1977.

———. *Paul the Apostle: Life, Letters, and Thought*. Minneapolis: Fortress, 2015.

Schüssler Fiorenza, Elisabeth. *In Memory of Her: A Feminist Theological Reconstruction of Christian Origins.* New York: Crossroad, 1985.

Stanley, Christopher D. *Arguing with Scripture: The Rhetoric of Quotations in the Letters of Paul.* London: T&T Clark, 2004.

Steck, Odil H. *Israel und das gewaltsame Geschick der Propheten: Untersuchungen zur Überlieferung des deuteronomistischen Geschichtsbildes im Alten Testament, Spätjudentum und Urchristentum.* WMANT 23. Neukirchen-Vluyn: Neukirchener Verlag, 1967.

Stockhausen, Carol Kern. *Moses' Veil and the Glory of the New Covenant.* AnBib 116. Rome: Pontifical Biblical Institute, 1989.

Swetnam, James. *Jesus and Isaac: A Study of the Epistle to the Hebrews in the Light of the Aqedah.* AnBib 94. Rome: Pontifical Biblical Institute, 1981.

Teeple, Howard M. *The Mosaic Eschatological Prophet.* Journal of Biblical Literature Monograph 10. Philadelphia: Society of Biblical Literature, 1957.

Theissen, Gerd. *Psychological Aspects of Pauline Theology.* Philadelphia: Fortress, 1987.

Toorn, Karel van der. *Scribal Culture and the Making of the Hebrew Bible.* Cambridge: Harvard University Press, 2009.

Venema, Dennis R., and Scot McKnight. *Adam and the Genome.* Grand Rapids: Brazos, 2017.

Wagner, J. Ross. *Heralds of the Good News: Isaiah and Paul in Concert in the Letter to the Romans.* Leiden: Brill, 2002.

Wall, Robert W. *Community of the Wise: The Letter of James.* Valley Forge, PA: Trinity Press International, 1997.

Watson, Francis. *Paul and the Hermeneutics of Faith.* London: T&T Clark, 2004.

Wevers, John W. *Notes on the Greek Text of Deuteronomy.* SCS 39. Atlanta: Scholars Press, 1995.

———. *Text History of the Greek Deuteronomy.* MSU 13. Göttingen: Vandehoeck & Ruprecht, 1978.

———. *Text History of the Greek Genesis.* MSU 11. Göttingen: Vandenhoeck & Ruprecht, 1974.

Witherington, Ben, III. *The Christology of Jesus.* Minneapolis: Fortress, 1990.

———. *Isaiah Old and New: Exegesis, Intertextuality, and Hermeneutics.* Minneapolis: Fortress, 2017.

———. *Jesus the Sage: The Pilgrimage of Wisdom.* Minneapolis: Fortress, 2000.

———. *Jesus the Seer: The Progress of Prophecy.* Minneapolis: Fortress, 2014.

———. *Making a Meal of It: Rethinking the Theology of the Lord's Supper.* Waco, TX: Baylor University Press, 2007.

———. *New Testament Theology and Ethics.* 2 vols. Downers Grove, IL: Inter-Varsity, 2009–2016.

———. *Paul's Narrative Thought World: The Tapestry of Tragedy and Triumph.* Louisville: Westminster John Knox, 1994.

———. *The Problem with Evangelical Theology: Testing The Exegetical Foundations of Calvinism, Dispensationalism, Wesleyanism, and Pentecostalism.* 2nd Edition. Waco, TX: Baylor University Press, 2015.

———. *Psalms Old and New: Exegesis, Intertextuality, Hermeneutics.* Minneapolis: Fortress, 2017.

———. *Reading and Understanding the Bible.* Oxford: Oxford University Press, 2015.

———. *What's in the Word? Rethinking the Socio-Rhetorical Character of the New Testament.* Waco, TX: Baylor University Press, 2009.

———. *Women and the Genesis of Christianity.* Cambridge: Cambridge University Press, 1990.

———. *Women in the Ministry of Jesus: A Study of Jesus' Attitudes to Women and Their Roles As Reflected in His Earthly Life.* SNTSMS 51. Cambridge: Cambridge University Press, 1984.

Zimmerli, Walther. *Old Testament Theology in Outline.* Translated by David E. Green. Edinburgh: T&T Clark, 1978.

ARTICLES

Ahearne-Kroll, Stephen P. "Genesis in Mark's Gospel." In *Genesis in the New Testament*, edited by Maarten J. J. Menken and Steve Moyise, 27–41. LNTS 466. London: T&T Clark, 2012.

Aletti, Jean-Nöel. "Rm 7.7–25 encore une fois: enjeux et propositions." *NTS* 48 (2002): 358–76.

Andersen, F. I. "2 (Slavonic Apocalypse of) Enoch." *OTP* 1:91–221.

Barstand, H. M. "The Understanding of the Prophets in Deuteronomy." *SJOT* 8 (1994): 236–51.

Bauckham, Richard. *Jesus and the God of Israel: God Crucified and Other Studies on the New Testament's Christology of Divine Identity.* Grand Rapids: Eerdmans, 2008.

Brown, Jeannine K. "Genesis in Matthew's Gospel." In *Genesis in the New*

Testament, edited by Maarten J. J. Menken and Steve Moyise, 42–59. LNTS 466. London: T&T Clark, 2012.

Byron, John. "Cain and Abel in Second Temple Literature and Beyond." In *The Book of Genesis: Composition, Reception, and Interpretation*, edited by Craig A. Evans, Joel N. Lohr, and David L. Petersen, 331–51. VTSup 152. Leiden: Brill, 2012.

Collins, John J. "Sibylline Oracles." *OTP* 1:317–472.

Culpepper, R. H. "The High Priesthood and Sacrifice of Christ in the Epistle to the Hebrews." *TTE* 32 (1985): 46–62.

Daly, R. J. "The Soteriological Significance of the Sacrifice of Isaac." *CBQ* 39 (1977): 45–75.

Docherty, Susan. "Genesis in Hebrews." In *Genesis in the New Testament*, edited by Maarten J. J. Menken and Steve Moyise, 130–46. LNTS 466. London: T&T Clark, 2012.

Dumbrell, W. J. "The Spirits of Just Men Made Perfect." *EvQ* 48 (1976): 154–59.

Duncan, Julie A. "Deuteronomy, Book of." In *The Encyclopedia of the Dead Sea Scrolls*, edited by Lawrence H. Schiffman and James C. Vanderkam, 1:198–202. Oxford: Oxford University Press, 2000.

Dunn, James D. G. "2 Corinthians 3:17: The Lord is the Spirit." *JTS* 21 (1970): 309–20.

Evans, Craig A. "Genesis in the New Testament." In *The Book of Genesis: Composition, Reception, and Interpretation*, edited by Craig A. Evans, Joel N. Lohr, and David L. Petersen, 469–94. VTSup 152. Leiden: Brill, 2012.

Feuillet, André. "Le péché évoqué aux chapitres 3 et 6,4 de la Genèse: Le péché des anges de l'épître de Jude et de la Second épître de Pierre." *Divinitas* 35 (1991): 207–29.

Flint, Peter W. "The Book of Leviticus in the Dead Sea Scrolls." In *The Book of Leviticus: Composition and Reception*, edited by Rolf Rendtorff and Robert A. Kugler, 323–41. VTSup 93. Leiden: Brill, 2003.

Flynn, E. L. "Moses in the Visual Arts." *Int* 44 (1990): 265–76

Geertz, Jan C. "The Formation of the Primeval History." In *The Book of Genesis: Composition, Reception, and Interpretation*, edited by Craig A. Evans, Joel N. Lohr, and David L. Petersen, 107–35. VTSup 152. Leiden: Brill, 2012.

Godsey, John D. "The Interpretation of Romans in the History of the Christian Faith." *Int* 34 (1980): 3–16.

Greenlee, J. Harold. "Hebrews 11:11: Sarah's Faith or Abraham's?" *Notes* 4 (1990): 37–42.

Grelot, Pierre. "Note sur 2 Corinthiens 3.14." *NTS* 33 (1987): 135–44.

Häfner, Gerd. "Deuteronomy in the Pastoral Epistles." In *Deuteronomy in the New Testament*, edited by Maarten J. J. Menken and Steve Moyise, 136–51. LNTS 358. London: T&T Clark, 2007.

Hamerton-Kelly, Robert. "Sacred Violence and Sinful Desire: Paul's Interpretation of Adam's Sin in the Letter to the Romans." In *The Conversation Continues: Studies in John and Paul in Honor of J. Louis Martyn*, edited by Robert T. Fortna and Beverly Roberts Gaventa, 35–54. Nashville: Abingdon, 1990.

Hanson, A. T. "Rahab the Harlot in Early Christian Tradition." *JSNT* 1 (1978): 53–60.

Hiebert, R. J. V. "Textual and Translation Issues in Greek Genesis." In *The Book of Genesis: Composition, Reception, and Interpretation*, edited by Craig A. Evans, Joel N. Lohr, and David L. Petersen, 405–26. VTSup 152. Leiden: Brill, 2012.

Himbaza, Innocent. "Le Decalogue de Papyrus Nash, Philon, 4QPhyl G, 48QPhyl 3 et 4QMez A." *RevQ* 79/20 (2002): 411–28.

Instone-Brewer, David. "Jesus' Old Testament Basis for Monogamy." In *The Old Testament in the New Testament: Essays in Honour of J. L. North*, edited by Steven Moyise, 75–104. JSOTSup 189. Sheffield: Sheffield Academic, 2000.

Jeppesen, Knud. "Is Deuteronomy Hostile towards the Prophets?" *SJOT* 8 (1994): 252–56.

Jeremias, Joachim. "Paul and James." *ExpTim* 66 (1955): 368–71.

Kaminsky, Joel S. "The Theology of Genesis." In *The Book of Genesis: Composition, Reception, and Interpretation*, edited by Craig A. Evans, Joel N. Lohr, and David L. Petersen, 635–56. VTSup 152. Leiden: Brill, 2012.

Kraus, Deborah. "The One Who Comes Unbinding the Blessing of Judah: Mark 11:1–10 as a Midrash on Genesis 49:11, Zechariah 9:9, and Psalm 118:25–26." In *Early Christian Interpretation of the Scriptures of Israel: Investigation and Proposals*, edited by Craig A. Evans and James A. Sanders, 141–53. Sheffield: Sheffield Academic, 1997.

Labahn, Michael. "Deuteronomy in John's Gospel." In *Deuteronomy in the New Testament*, edited by Maarten J. J. Menken and Steve Moyise, 82–98. LNTS 358. London: T&T Clark.

Lim, Timothy. "Deuteronomy in the Judaism of the Second Temple Period."

In *Deuteronomy in the New Testament*, edited by Maarten J. J. Menken and Steve Moyise, 6–26. LNTS 358. London: T&T Clark.

Lincicum, David. "Genesis in Paul." In *Genesis in the New Testament*, edited by Maarten J. J. Menken and Steve Moyise, 99–116. LNTS 466. London: T&T Clark, 2012.

Longenecker, Richard N. "The 'Faith of Abraham' Theme in Paul, James and Hebrews." *JETS* 20 (1977): 203–12.

Lyonnet, Stanislas. "L'histoire du salut selon le ch. 7 de l'Épître aux Romains." *Bib* 43 (1962): 117–51.

Mallen, Peter. "Genesis in Luke-Acts." In *Genesis in the New Testament*, edited by Maarten J. J. Menken and Steve Moyise, 60–82. LNTS 466. London: T&T Clark, 2012.

Menken, Maarten J. J. "Genesis in John's Gospel and 1 John." In *Genesis in the New Testament*, edited by Maarten J. J. Menken and Steve Moyise, 91–95. LNTS 466. London: T&T Clark, 2012.

Metso, Sarianna, and Eugene Ulrich. "The Old Greek Translation of Leviticus." In *The Book of Leviticus: Composition and Reception*, edited by Rolf Rendtorff and Robert A. Kugler, 247–68. VTSup 93. Leiden: Brill, 2003.

Meyer, Paul W. "The Worm at the Core of the Apple: Exegetical Reflections on Romans 7." In *The Conversation Continues: Studies in John and Paul in Honor of J. Louis Martyn*, edited by Robert T. Fortna and Beverly Roberts Gaventa, 62–84. Nashville: Abingdon, 1990.

Moberly, R. Walter L. "Exemplars of Faith: Abel." In *The Epistle to the Hebrews and Christian Theology*, edited by Richard Bauckham, Daniel R. Driver, Trevor A. Hart, and Nathan MacDonald, 353–63. Grand Rapids: Eerdmans, 2009.

Moran, William L. "The Ancient Near Eastern Background of the Love of God in Deuteronomy." *CBQ* 25 (1963): 77–87.

Moyise, Steven. "Genesis in Revelation." In *Genesis in the New Testament*, edited by Maarten J. J. Menken and Steve Moyise, 166–79. LNTS 466. London: T&T Clark, 2012.

Neyrey, Jerome H. "Jacob Traditions and the Interpretation of John 4:10–26." *CBQ* 41 (1979): 419–37.

———. "'Without Beginning of Days or End of Life' (Hebrews 7.3): Topos for a True Deity." *CBQ* 53 (1991): 439–55.

Pearson, Birger. "A Reminiscence of Classical Myth at II Peter 2.4." *GRBS* 10 (1969): 71–80.

Römer, Thomas. "Abraham Traditions in the Hebrew Bible outside the Book of Genesis." In *The Book of Genesis: Composition, Reception, and Interpre-*

tation, edited by Craig A. Evans, Joel N. Lohr, and David L. Petersen, 159–80. VTSup 152. Leiden: Brill, 2012.

Rooke, Deborah W. "Jesus as Royal Priest: Reflections on the Interpretation of the Melchizedek Tradition in Heb 7." *Bib* 81 (2000): 81–94.

Rosner, Brian S. "Deuteronomy in 1 and 2 Corinthians." In *Deuteronomy in the New Testament*, edited by Maarten J. J. Menken and Steve Moyise, 118–135. LNTS 358. London: T&T Clark.

Ruiten, Jacques T. A. G. M. van. "Genesis in Early Jewish Literature." In *Genesis in the New Testament*, edited by Maarten J. J. Menken and Steve Moyise, 7–26. LNTS 466. London: T&T Clark, 2012.

Rusam, Dietrich. "Deuteronomy in Luke-Acts." In *Deuteronomy in the New Testament*, edited by Maarten J. J. Menken and Steve Moyise, 63–81. LNTS 358. London: T&T Clark.

Schmid, Konrad. "Genesis in the Pentateuch." In *The Book of Genesis: Composition, Reception, and Interpretation*, edited by Craig A. Evans, Joel N. Lohr, and David L. Petersen, 27–50. VTSup 152. Leiden: Brill, 2012.

Steyn, Gert J. "Deuteronomy in Hebrews." In *Deuteronomy in the New Testament*, edited by Maarten J. J. Menken and Steve Moyise, 152–68. LNTS 358. London: T&T Clark.

Tilly, Michael. "Deuteronomy in Revelation." In *Deuteronomy in the New Testament*, edited by Maarten J. J. Menken and Steve Moyise, 169–88. LNTS 358. London: T&T Clark.

Toorn, Karel van der. "The Significance of the Veil in the Ancient Near East." In *Pomegranates and Golden Bells: Studies in Biblical, Jewish, and Near Eastern Ritual, Law, and Literature in Honor of Jacob Milgrom*, edited by David P. Wright, David Noel Freedman, and Avi Hurvitz, 327–39. Winona Lake, IN: Eisenbrauns, 1995.

Unnik, W. C. van. "Le role de Noé dans les Épîtres de Pierre." In *Noe, L'homme universel, Colloque de Louvain 1978*, 207–39. Publications de l'Institutum Iudaicum 3. Brussels: Institutum Judaicum, 1979.

Witherington III, Ben. "The Anti-Feminist Tendencies in the 'Western' Text in Acts." *JBL* 103 (1984): 82–84.

———. "The Influence of Galatians on Hebrews." *NTS* 37 (1991): 146–52.